The Global Corporation

This text brings together case studies focusing on specific instances of corporate best practices. All too often, we highlight cases based on questionable or unethical corporate behavior. Instead, the editors bring together in this book examples of how some firms *got it right*. Certainly, there is no claim that the companies in these cases are perfect; some of them may have histories that include questionable practices. But, these are companies that work to foster trust, both internally and in their relationships with customers, suppliers, shareholders, and the communities in which they operate.

The book is not, however, merely a descriptive iteration of effective corporate conduct. The editors conclude with an analysis of frameworks for corporate and managerial ethical decision-making-frameworks that help to establish *models for best practices*. These frameworks then can be generalized and applied to other corporate situations, and replicated by other companies in their search for excellence and the resulting avoidance of misconduct.

Laura P. Hartman is a Professor of Business Ethics and Legal Studies in the Management Department at DePaul University's College of Commerce and also serves as Research Director of DePaul's Institute for Business and Professional Ethics. She has served as the Gourlay Professor at the Melbourne Business School/Trinity College at the University of Melbourne (2007–2008), as an invited professor at INSEAD (France), HEC (France), the Université Paul Cézanne Aix Marseille III, and at the Grenoble Graduate School of Business, among other European universities.

Patricia H. Werhane is the Peter and Adeline Ruffin Chair of Business Ethics and Senior Fellow at the Olsson Center for Applied Ethics in the Darden Graduate School of Business Administration at the University of Virginia, and also holds a joint appointment as the Callista Wicklander Chair of Business Ethics and Director, Institute for Business and Professional Ethics, at DePaul University. She has been a Rockefeller Fellow at Dartmouth College, an Arthur Andersen Fellow at the Judge Institute, Cambridge University, and Erskine Visiting Fellow at the University of Canterbury in New Zealand. She is the founding editor of *Business Ethics Quarterly*.

The Global Corporation

Sustainable, Effective and Ethical Practices:
A Case Book

Edited by Laura P. Hartman and
Patricia H. Werhane

 Routledge
Taylor & Francis Group

NEW YORK AND LONDON

First published 2009
by Routledge
270 Madison Ave, New York, NY 10016

Simultaneously published in the UK
by Routledge
2 Park Square, Milton Park, Abingdon, Oxon OX14 4RN

*Routledge is an imprint of the Taylor & Francis Group,
an informa business*

© 2009 Taylor & Francis

Typeset in Galliard by
RefineCatch Limited, Bungay, Suffolk
Printed and bound in the United States of America
on acid-free paper by
Sheridan Books, Inc.

Library of Congress Cataloging in Publication Data
The global corporation : sustainable, effective and ethical practices,
a case book / edited by Laura P. Hartman and Patricia H. Werhane.
    p. cm.
  1. Social responsibility of business—Case studies.
2. International business enterprises—Management—Case
studies.   3. International business enterprises—Environmental
aspects—Case studies.   4. Business ethics—Case studies.
I. Hartman, Laura Pincus.   II. Werhane, Patricia Hogue.
  HD60.G558 2009
  658.4'08—dc22   2009006000

ISBN10: 0–415–80161–3 (hbk)
ISBN10: 0–415–80160–5 (pbk)

ISBN13: 978–0–415–80161–4 (hbk)
ISBN13: 978–0–415–80160–7 (pbk)

Contents

Preface

There are many case books in business ethics, and most textbooks include case examples, as well. But, most of the cases cited explore either ethical dilemmas that companies face or the questionable behavior of their decision-makers. This case book takes a different approach. While we would never claim that there are perfect companies, our collection of case examples drawn from companies operating across the planet demonstrates that there are a number of sustainable, effective and ethical practices that could and should be models for other corporate practices. For skeptics of the future of free enterprise and global capitalism, these cases should help to dissuade the naysayers who contend that those methods cannot succeed without doing grave harm. In fact, many multinational companies have thrived, and many more than we have been able to include in this book are currently engaged in good practices that are exemplars for how a free enterprise system can create value added over the long term, not just for shareholders, but for employees, suppliers, customers, and communities as well.

This book would not have been possible without the assistance of Darden Publishing, where many of the cases originated. Steve Momper and his staff have been invaluable in helping us with cases, permissions and publication. We especially thank our chief case writer, Emily Mead at the Darden School, who was responsible for many of the cases in this volume. Other case writers included Gerry Yemen at Darden and Justin Sheehan at DePaul University.

We also want to thank Ramakrishna Velamuri and IESE Publishing at the IESE School of Management in Barcelona for permission to reprint three of their cases. We are grateful, too, to Klaus Leisinger and Karin Schmitt for their work on the Novartis cases, Charles Brock and his staff at Abbott Laboratories for the Abbott cases, Chris Herbst at Ashoka for the Cemex case, and Holly Lindsay at BHP Billiton, who was instrumental in the development of that case.

The book could not have been completed without the support of Summer Brown at DePaul University, Karen Musselman at the Darden School, Senior Editorial Assistant Felisa Salvago-Keyes and the enthusiastic encouragement of John Szilagyi, Publisher at Routledge/ Taylor & Francis Group.

Chapter 1

Introduction

Over the past several years, a great deal of media attention and popular literature has detailed corporate misdeeds; and much of the reporting has been accurate. At the same time, there are hundreds, even thousands, of companies that behave well and not only survive, but flourish. These companies are the backbone of the industrialized nations and of global economic growth; but this good behavior and its contributions are only found on the back pages of journals and is seldom reported in books or on the Internet. While we certainly do not advocate a casual dismissal of the scandals that have shaken our confidence in free enterprise, it is equally important to consider positive models for commerce, models that have generated value both domestically and on a global scale. We are then able to extract lessons (or patterns, exemplars) for corporate ethical decision-making and behavior that can be emulated by other companies that are just starting up or emerging, as well as those that are revamping their ethics and compliance focus in light of a problem.

This text consists of a series of case studies focusing on specific instances of effective corporate practices. We do not claim that the companies in this study are perfect ones. Indeed, there is no perfect company. Several of these companies may have past practices that have been called into question. But, these are companies that work to foster trust both inside the company and in their relationships with customers, suppliers, shareholders and the communities in which they operate in ways that are surprising as well as profitable, often creating value-added for most of their stakeholders, not merely shareholders. These examples are exemplars of what a company *can* do within its profit-making parameters.

We begin the book with two classic cases: Johnson & Johnson's famous Tylenol capsule case and Merck's involvement with river blindness. After several random poisoning incidents of Tylenol capsules, none of which could be traced to any company employee or practice, the CEO of J&J, James Burke, pulled these best-selling capsules off the market despite protests from J&J's marketing staff and even the FBI. Burke appealed to J&J's Credo, which places customers/patients as its first priority. He further stated that J&J would never again make the capsule form of the pain reliever. Since that famous case, cited widely by J&J, academics and the media, J&J has had other ethical challenges. But, the case remains in J&J lore, and the Credo stands as the moral ideological guide post for all corporate practice. Thus, the case illustrates how a corporate mission or ideology can drive exemplary behavior if it is integrated throughout the company and adhered to in actual practice, even when short-term challenges seem to act as barriers. Tylenol, by the way, is the largest selling pain reliever today without ever reverting to a capsule form.

The second exemplar case involves the pharmaceutical company Merck's challenge to develop a drug for river blindness, a disease that strikes 30 to 100 million people in the poorest countries of the world. Should Merck invest in research to develop a drug for which there are no paying customers? Again, Merck's mission, to cure disease, drove its decision despite little promise of market growth in the foreseeable future; and it has promised to give the drug away "forever."

Many other cases in the collection illustrate companies engaging in activities that are both "good practices" and able to be duplicated by other global companies. These activities are not always driven by a core ideology; rather, they crop up as strategic responses to public pressure or difficult situations. For example, ExxonMobil is hardly a name that comes to mind as an exemplary company to some people, particularly after the *Exxon Valdez* disaster and Mobil's alleged involvement with bribery in Kazakhstan. But, since 2000, ExxonMobil has engaged in a complex drilling project in Chad and Cameroon, two countries often found at the bottom of the Transparency International corruption list. Ignoring past practices where many oil companies simply went in to a country with expatriate employees, drilled and piped the oil out with little concern for the local communities or the environment (Newburry and Gladwin, 2002), ExxonMobil has taken a systems approach to this project (see Figure 1.1). It has partnered with the World Bank to develop an environmentally least damaging approach to drilling; it has also partnered with NGOs to work through social issues that develop as a result of laying pipeline through traditional Pygmy and Bantu territories and rain forests in Cameroon. It has also partnered with the World Bank and local communities to improve the infrastructures in those communities; and ExxonMobil has tried to deal, albeit rather unsuccessfully, with the corrupt government of Chad which has pledged to use the oil royalties for community development. While this is not an entirely successful project (the president of Chad, Mr. Déby, is a notoriously recalcitrant "bad guy" and uses much of the oil royalties for arms), its systemic thinking about most of those who are affected and affect the operation sets up a model that can be emulated in other global projects, both by oil companies and by others.

A similar approach was adopted by the Female Health Company (FHC, an over-the-counter traded company) as it tried to assess marketing strategies for its patented female condom. With the spread of HIV/AIDS and the habits of nonprotection by men in many communities in the poorest countries of Africa, the demand for a product to protect women

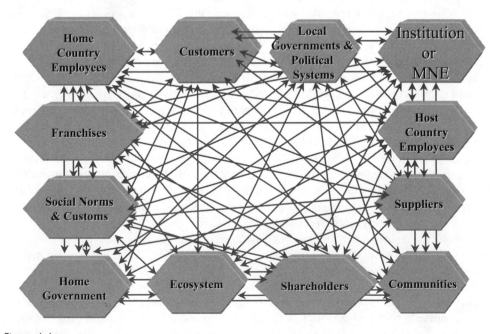

Figure 1.1

against disease worldwide is becoming enormous. Yet, how does one market to customers who have no funds to buy the product? Mary Ann Leeper, the COO of the FHC, came up with a systems-based solution, engaging the company in alliance partnerships with NGOs, international funding organizations, community-based leaders, and social marketing experts. Today, they market the female condom in over 100 mostly less developed countries and, in 2006, for the first time, the Female Health Company was profitable.

A number of the companies in this study have acceded to C. K. Prahalad's thesis that there is a "fortune at the bottom of the pyramid" (Prahalad, 2005). That is, that there are huge markets in poor, heavily populated countries that can and should be explored. For some centuries, probably initiated by the East India Company, companies and colonizing nations have been extracting resources, goods, and services from less developed countries without always addressing the needs or interests of those communities. Yet, the companies in our volume have explored without exploiting. They have developed needed products that also provide jobs and improved standards of living. Cemex, a large Mexican cement manufacturer has helped low-income Mexicans finance low-income, decent housing coupled with technical assistance and educational programs on construction materials. This set of initiatives has also created new housing markets and thus new outlets for cement. Manila Water, a privatized utility in the Philippines, has partnered with communities to provide access to clean water at low rates through collective billing water cooperatives. The result is an enormous expansion of pure water in Manila and a ROI of 19%. Hindustan Lever, a division of Unilever, has created and marketed inexpensive soap products for the poorest of the poor in India while providing sales jobs to local women who market and sell these products. These are examples of creative enterprises that prioritize local communities, even the very poor, as being in need of products, services, and jobs. Such initiatives market products suited for particular environments and, by job creation, enable market development in these communities. These are often outcome-driven projects aimed at finding new customers. At the same time these companies are models of how innovation and creativity can contribute to new markets at the base of the pyramid and contribute value both to communities globally as well as to the company.

What we have all learned from the Grameen Bank of Bangladesh is that a simple credit model with low interest rates can enable poor people to become self-supporting. The challenge is how to develop such mechanisms in traditional Muslim countries. The religion of Islam has existed for 1,400 years; but Islamic economic theory and its financial institutions emerged as an industry only in the 1970s. Islamic financial institutions (IFIs) are designed to help Muslims conduct business internationally while simultaneously upholding traditional Islamic values related to trade finance and currency movement. The basis for their existence is the Islamic moral prohibition on charging interest—interest is a central component of capitalist banking—yet IFIs conduct billions of dollars of business annually in the world economy and the *de facto* Islamic banking transaction is, in most cases, virtually identical to a capitalist banking transaction. Business practices in the industry of Islamic banking and finance have evolved to reinforce some of the major tenets of a moral belief system based on Islamic principles. The Islamic Banking case discusses specific practices put into place by the Islamic banking community that are designed to embody tenets of a belief system based on Islam while at the same time generating profits for the institution and its customers. This case contributes to the discussion of effective corporate practices by introducing some of those practices and exploring how to balance and integrate moral beliefs in an effective economic structure.

In another case illustrating the challenges of working in less developed countries, BHP Billiton, the world's largest diversified resource company at the start of the 21st century, began a feasibility study in 1995 for building an aluminum smelter project in the Maputo province in southern Mozambique. Mozambique was one of the world's poorest countries, emerging from 17 years of civil war and making the difficult transition to a market-oriented economy. The country was hampered by fragile legal, financial and HSEC institutional structures and capacity. Public services were bureaucratic, poorly equipped and with limited capacity. How should BHP Billiton approach this multilayered project, or should it consider investing in smelters in other countries more hospitable to development?

One of the reasons for endemic poverty in less developed countries is the lack of basic infrastructures: potable water, energy, roads, public transportation, access to medicine and health, and other institutionally provided services that we in developed nations take for granted. The lack of potable water, in particular, creates debilitating and fatal water-transmitted diseases such as chronic diarrhea, cholera, and malaria that affect millions of people globally. A single division of Procter & Gamble, one of the largest marketers of household products, developed a simple home-based water purification system. Working through an NGO, it distributes water-purifying packets through local distributors at low cost to over 20 villages in some of the poorest countries in Africa and Southeast Asia. While this began as a philanthropic project it has the potential to become a high-volume low-margin business for local distributors while reducing the loss of the over 2 million children who die each year of diarrheal diseases.

Energy development is another necessity, usually lacking, particularly in poor rural communities. Eskom, South African's national utility, was allowed to privatize after apartheid. It immediately saw a huge potential energy market in the rural communities in South Africa. But, it was faced with the challenges of creating affordable energy for all of rural South Africa and with a tradition of nonpayment developed in protest to apartheid. The simplest and cheapest option was merely to give away electricity, but Eskom found that option to enable a culture of dependency. The means by which they are attacking this problem illustrates how creative imaginative thinking can result in win-win solutions to what seem to be intractable problems.

Outsourcing is a consistent media theme; and the existence of sweatshops, that is, factories that pay less than local minimum wages or subsistence, long working hours, and almost no days off, are always "darlings" of the news. Such factories, like their colonial predecessors, are extractive industries since they produce low-cost goods for the developed world under virtually slave labor conditions. Yet, there are counter-examples to these inappropriate employment practices. In this volume, we highlight Nike, which works with its supplier factories (usually foreign-owned, though not by the brand, and locally managed), to improve working conditions, including the payment of a living wage. In addition, they are impacting further down their supply chain in order to improve working conditions in those factories, as well. Like ExxonMobil and the Female Health Company, these companies take a systems approach to their mission and outlook rather than concentrating inwardly merely on their shareholders, managers, or local employees. Instead, they consider these factories, suppliers and employees as partners in an alliance where the equal focus is on each of the stakeholders, not merely on the company (see Figure 1.2). Nike, like J&J and Merck, has developed a strong code of conduct that it expects all its suppliers to adopt. Again, they do not experience a 100% success rate. There are suppliers who lie and cheat to avoid the perceived costs of compliance; but the operationalized ideal is there and, for the most part, they have been more successful than one could imagine. Taking a strong moral stance towards the improvement of working conditions has improved productivity and morale, thereby improving profits, while avoiding the degradation of basic human rights.

We have included three other examples of effective, replicable labor practices. McDonald's, known for its fast food, should also become known for its labor practices. McDonald's labor

Figure 1.2

force is one of the most diverse, all the way from the first hire in the restaurants to the executive levels. This may be the result of its promotion practices since it promotes its managers and executives primarily from within the organization, and at least 40% of the top executives in the company began as "crew," working in franchise restaurants, many of them beginning as part-time employees.

The Marriott Corporation, one of the largest hotel chains in the nation, had an alternative challenge; it found itself in a lose-lose situation because the turnover for low-paid hotel staff was up to 400% a year. Rethinking that problem, they have engaged in new employment training practices to emphasize to employees the importance of their work. They also provide family counseling and other side benefits ordinarily absent in this industry. As a result, Marriott has significantly reduced turnover and developed a loyal low-wage workforce.

Training and self-esteem go a long way to improving productivity and morale. Included in this section of this volume is the story of a small company, First Impressions. This company began with an investment of $60 in an advertisement promising to provide waiting staff out of the apartment of Judy Wiles, then a waitress at T.G.I. Fridays. Wiles recognized that one of the continual problems in restaurants and catering was that waiting staff did not show up; so she put an advertisement in a Detroit newspaper offering to staff restaurants and parties. She began her own company of part-time waiting staff, training primarily unemployed minority men and women in her community, people many employers may not be likely to hire, with skills and discipline so that they would have jobs. Today, her company is the largest part-time employer of waiting staff in the Detroit area and many of her former employees now manage other restaurants and catering operations.

Often, global companies are cautious about doing business in countries that have a reputation for corruption. But, as discussed above, ExxonMobil moved into such a situation in

Chad, although they are not free from its corrupt practices. In a series of three cases, we present companies that operate without paying bribes or engaging in extortion in countries near the bottom of the Transparency International Corruption Index. Econet, the largest (and virtually only functioning) telecommunication company in Zimbabwe, has managed to operate without paying off government officials for several years. In India, InfoSys, an IT service provider, and Alacrity Housing, which builds low and middle-class housing, have both survived and are profitable notwithstanding their refusal to bribe and pay off officials, common practices in India, and notwithstanding their relatively small size. Often critics charge that refusal to pay bribes is a luxury limited to only those enormous multinationals with the global leverage to do so; but these cases are instructive. These companies all set models for how business can be done even under trying circumstances; they set the bar high, and should encourage more global companies to engage in such exemplary practices.

Environmental sustainability is on the forefront of public interest and corporate thinking, despite its skeptics. We present a series of cases showcasing companies working at the frontiers of this thinking. Unilever, the multibillion global company, has developed a triple-bottom-line initiative instigated by a middle manager in its Netherlands company. The ideal is to measure social impact, environmental sustainability, and economic value-added equally and quantitatively throughout Unilever. Although the project is not complete, triple-bottom-line initiatives are spreading, particularly in Europe and Africa, as models for evaluating corporate responsibility in economic terms.

Other cases illustrate environmentally sustainable programs that defy standard operating protocols. DesignTex, a division of Steelcase, the world's largest manufacturer of office equipment, in partnership with the Swiss clothing manufacturer, Rohner Textil, have produced a completely compostable high-quality fabric for office furniture and wheelchairs in a factory that recycles its water and most of its energy. These companies take the lead from Ecover, a Belgian company that has been making edible, biodegradable soap products in its fully self-sustaining factory for over 15 years. All of these are exemplars of what can be done environmentally, without sacrificing profitability for "green" objectives.

Not all the cases in this collection are descriptions of for-profit ventures, although funded by global corporations. But, these not-for-profit organizations have engaged in funding models that are replicable in the for-profit sector. The Novartis Foundation and the Abbott Fund, both foundations created by their companies, focus their funding on projects that are closely related to that in which the company engages: health. Although each of these foundations is not-for-profit they are each intimately tied to their corporate mission. Their giving is truly "strategically focused philanthropy." Each carefully measures every possible project in terms of its value-added to various communities, the possibility of the project becoming self-sustaining, and the ability of those communities to maintain the project over time. Indeed, as an outcome of its Tanzanian initiative to fund clinics for HIV-infected pregnant women, Abbott has developed a five-point strategy for dealing with global issues such as disease. The Novartis Foundation, the non-profit arm of the large pharmaceutical, Novartis, does not have an HIV/AIDS drug. Despite that, however, because of their mission to focus on health, they have established a program to address the psycho-social needs of children orphaned because of their parents' HIV/AIDS and to help these children become self-sufficient in their communities.

Some projects are small in scale and scope, yet make a big difference. For example, the Abbott Fund's involvement in HealthReach, a small free clinic located near Abbott headquarters, is such an example. By providing $50,000 as seed money, the Abbott Fund enabled HealthReach to provide its medical staff with Spanish lessons so that they could communicate with its overwhelming number of Hispanic patients. This is not without benefits to Abbott,

the company, as well, since those patients will remember that contribution long after they have forgotten which drugs they take are from Abbott Laboratories.

The PricewaterhouseCoopers Ulysses Project demonstrates effective and ethical practices in connection with leadership development. PwC, the largest global professional services firm, worried about how its over 120,000 employees worked in diverse settings globally and yet also as one company. PwC opined, how do their managers mobilize others to think creatively about issues that cannot be anticipated in advance through standard professional training? After a great deal of thinking, PwC came up with the Ulysses Project, aimed at developing global leaders within the company. The unusual feature of this project is that it extracts potential leaders from the positions for a three-month program. In this program, PwC managers are sent to foreign cultural settings beset by structural challenges where their expertise could make a difference. By changing the traditional professional or management scenario, PwC aims to develop morally imaginative managers who can tackle challenges of leading in diverse settings in a global economy.

Stepping back from this set of cases, we find overlapping themes that will help in developing a framework with which to model these cases as exemplars for other effective corporate ventures that, at least, avoid moral morasses and, at best, create positive long-term value-added. Let us begin with the most obvious: the existence of framing or cognitive lenses through which companies and their managers view their mission, their activities, and their goals. The idea of a cognitive lens is what Peter Senge calls "mental models," the "deeply held internal images of how the world works" (Senge, 1990: 174) that frame, focus and even bias, limit, or distort our experiences. According to Hamel and Prahalad,

> [e]very manager carries around in his or her head a set of biases, assumptions, and presuppositions about the structure of the relevant industry, about who the competition is and isn't, . . . about what customers want and don't want, about which technologies are viable and which aren't, and so on. This [network of mental models or cognitive frames] encompasses beliefs, values, and norms about how best to motivate people; the right balance of international cooperation and competition; the relative ranking of shareholder, customer, and employee interests; and what behaviors encourage and discourage. . . . Managerial frames . . . limit management's perception to a particular slice of reality. Managers live inside their frames, and, to a very great extent, don't know what lies outside.
>
> (Hamel and Prahalad, 1994: 53–54)

The companies in our collection, all of them, have used a stakeholder frame in thinking though their decisions. That is, they do not focus solely on bottom-line returns for shareholders but think, instead, of value-added, although not always economic value-added for a number of primary stakeholders, those that affect and are affected by their decisions and actions (Freeman et al., 2007). This does *not* imply that shareholders are neglected; indeed, shareholders are one of the most important set of stakeholders, but they are not the only ones (Figure 1.3). For example, companies like J&J with its strong and enduring Credo, prioritize their healthcare professionals and patients; but, as a result, their shareholders prosper as well. Marriott's preoccupation with low-wage employee satisfaction illustrates such a prioritization, as well. First Impressions started in order to create employer satisfaction with waiting staff, second as a conduit for the unemployed, and only third to make money for its founder.

Some of the companies in our study are mission-driven. Some years ago, Collins and Porras studied companies who had existed for a long period of time, which had been very profitable,

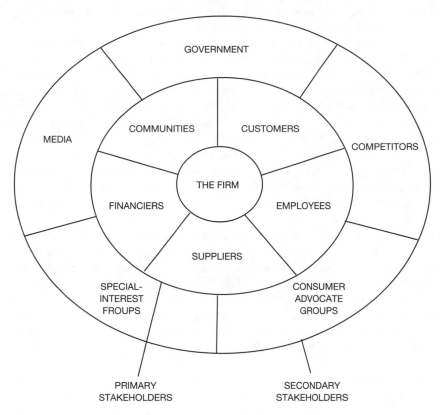

Figure 1.3

and were companies admired by other CEOs. These companies, referred to as "visionary companies," were quite different from each other in almost every respect; and many of them had changed product lines and direction during a 50-year span. What was strikingly the same in each company was a "core ideology that transcended purely economic considerations" (Collins and Porras, 1994; 2004, 55), an ideology or core mission that stayed the same throughout their histories. What we learn from their study is that a well-stated mission or credo, as evident in J&J, Merck and Nike, reiterated and reinforced over time, can become the guiding ideology of a company despite its fluctuations, market share, product choices, etc. This helps any manager by delimiting decision-making within the parameters of the corporate mission, often precluding some choices that may be detrimental in the long term. Collins and Porras's study revealed a second finding. They wrote, "[c]ontrary to business school doctrine, *we did not find 'maximizing shareholder wealth' or 'profit maximization' as the dominant driving force or primary objective through the history of most of the visionary companies*" (Collins and Porras, 1994; 2004, 55). Yet, these companies greatly surpassed their sister companies in profitability and return on investment.

Other companies in our study are outcomes-driven, and no company in business can afford not to think about outcomes. But, these desired results include more than mere profitability, although that can never be far from an executive's mind. Rather, companies like ExxonMobil, surely one of the most profitable in the world, at least as exhibited by the practices we have documented, are thinking about their long-term prospects in the developing energy world, and that point of view must take into consideration a wide range of stakeholders. It is the

long-range outcome orientation that is a key component for avoiding questionable practices even when they may produce short-term profits.

One of the challenges for global companies, particularly in less developed countries, are institutional barriers to entry and operation, such as a paucity of a rule of law, a culture of corruption or violence, and/or a lack of a well-developed infrastructure. These institutional barriers make entry into those markets difficult, at best. Indeed it has been argued that whether an organization engages in market ventures, much less socially responsible activities, depends on the institutional environment it faces. It is contended that companies are unlikely to engage in some countries under certain competitive conditions and/or unless the institutional environment is favorable. For example, in an unfavorable institutional environment characterized by little competition, small profit margins, poorly-conceived and ineffective state regulations, rampant corruption and no ongoing system of dialogue with the local communities, companies often eschew entry or partner with local producers who often take undue advantage of local stakeholders, even if such harm is brought to their attention (Campbell, 2007). Nevertheless, as counterexamples to this conclusion, some practices of the companies in this study, while not flaunting their financial largesse, have successfully pushed back against institutional barriers. InfoSys, Econet, and Alacrity are obvious examples of companies who are successful in corrupt environments without succumbing to corruption. Others simply operate as if these barriers were either nonexistent or not insurmountable. P&G markets PUR in some of the most institutionally challenging markets, but the value of their product overcomes barriers to entry and operation.

One of the ways to get around or to circumvent institutional barriers is to take a systems approach, and a number of companies in our study are engaged in what is called "systems thinking." A systems approach presupposes that most of our practices and institutions are interrelated and interconnected. Almost everything is in a network of interrelationships such that each element of a particular set of interrelationships affects some other components. Corporations are mezzo-systems embedded in larger political, economic, legal, and cultural systems. Global corporations are embedded in many such systems, that are open and interactive, thus able to change themselves and affect change in their interactions with other systems (Plsek, 2001). Particularly in less developed countries, every activity in which a transnational corporation is engaged, particularly if it is a large international company, has a domino effect on that culture, that economy, the environment, political stability, and so on. Thus, the most effective company practices try to take as many of these interrelationships as possible into account as best they can (Figure 1.1). A systems approach may also decenter attention on the company and consider the company as existing in and relating to a vast network of players with whom it interacts (see Figure 1.2). ExxonMobil's operations in Chad and Cameroon illustrate that decentering.

As the Female Health Company found out, in many settings, standard Western financing, marketing, and operating procedures (what is taught in traditional MBA programs in the West) just do not work and a company will fail in those non-Western markets. As both the P&G and FHC cases demonstrate, some culturally ingrained habits that truly are harmful, such as drinking clear, but not clean water or failing to use protection against sexually transmitted diseases, are difficult to overcome, despite the worthwhile nature of the product. At the same time, acceding to cultural mores such as these can be equally harmful for obvious reasons. There is, then, a fine line between cultural intervention and creating value-added. A systems approach alerts companies to these shoals. To attack that shoal, one approach, that taken by FHC and Nike, was to create alliances between various international and local stakeholders that develop partnership relationships rather than paternalistic intervention, where each participant is an important player. Mary Ann Leeper, the COO of FHC, describes

the model this way. She said that she entered the female condom market with a product. But, in the 100 or so less developed countries in which the condom is marketed, she now has a program in which the product is only one element.

Many of these cases showcase companies that take moral risks and exhibit moral courage. The moral risk is evident because in many of these operative environments a company is not sure whether its operations will be successful, nor whether they will cause additional harms rather than improvements. The courage of First Impressions CEO, Judy Wiles, to hire and train unemployed convicted felons is also a risky proposition that most of us will not dare to take on. In corrupt cultures, trying to operate without paying bribes in a corrupt environment is not only courageous but, some might say, foolhardy, since it is a good way to anger governmental officials or to lose business. Yet, as the founder of Econet demonstrates, this can be done, and done successfully. And, as the InfoSys and Alacrity cases illustrate, a company needs to be creative in working around ethical challenges such as bribery and extortion.

Moral risk occurs, too, when a company is operating in an alien environment, not ever sure that the possible positive outcomes net out against negative ones. Is Nike creating cultural challenges by trying to enforce its ethics code all the way through to its subcontractors? Are ExxonMobil's royalty payments abetting the questionable activities of the Chad and Cameroon governments or actually improving the country and its citizens? There are no quantitatively simple measurable answers to these challenges, but not to engage in these business practices, too, has its risks of missing opportunities in new markets.

Companies that take a stakeholder approach without sacrificing profitability, that engage in systems thinking in multi-cultural settings, create stakeholder alliances, and/or exhibit courage in morally risky ventures are all engaged in what we will call morally imaginative practices. Such practices have enabled them to think "out of the box" and to create truly creative and beneficial initiatives. Moral imagination is "an ability to imaginatively discern various possibilities for acting within a given situation and envision the potential help and harm that are likely to result from a given action" (Johnson, 1993: 202). Developing moral imagination involves disengaging from, and becoming aware of, one's situation and the ways in which we frame that situation, one's mental model. It includes envisioning new possibilities that may have not been possible given the original cognitive frame, and the ability to evaluate both the context-dependent choices of one's original cognitive frames and outcomes of the new possibilities (Werhane, 1999). Eskom, the South African utility, for example, began its operations as an all-white apartheid-dominated company. But, seeing that there was going to be a sea change in South Africa, it began early on to train people of color for management positions and to imagine what a fully-electrified South Africa would entail. Thus, it was prepared for the end of apartheid and for taking up the difficulties of rural electrification in cultures where nonpayment was the morally right thing to do as a protest against apartheid. As a result, Eskom is one of the world's largest utilities and most profitable, as well. But, without moral imagination, the company would have been mired in an apartheid mental model that would have precluded its success in a new integrated environment. Only by thinking about energy from another perspective in a constantly evolving process was Eskom able to develop sustainable practice models. Similarly, Manila Water could simply have foregone trying to serve the poor and concentrated on its thousands of paying customers. Instead, it changed the way it framed the concept of "paying customer." It created a cooperative system that enables the company to provide clean water at low cost to very poor Manilans without giving it away.

Finally, there is the question of choice. Every company in our study has chosen to engage in these effective practices that at first glance seemingly are not necessary for their survival, growth, or profitability. They could do otherwise and be successful, at least in the short term. Cemex is a successful housing manufacturer with a growing middle-class clientele. P&G could

continue to sell "Tide" and other standard household products to make enormous returns for its shareholders. Nike could have continued to subcontract to sweatshop factories. After all, they do not own them; why is it their responsibility? Unilever was a highly successful company before delving into triple-bottom-line accounting. Hindustan Lever could have simply continued to market to the growing middle class in India. Steelcase is the largest office furniture manufacturer in the world. Why worry about compostable fabrics? Judy Wiles at First Impressions had a perfectly good job as an exemplary waitress. McDonald's could have hired MBAs rather than promoting its part-time crew. Novartis and Abbott both create and manufacture life-saving drugs; is that not enough? Apparently not.

What is evident is that what we are documenting are not merely effective and ethical, but also visionary practices. It is in these instances that strong moral leadership paves the way to decision processes that find new markets, create value-added for more human beings, and explore new possibilities for a richer, larger, more meaningful and prosperous global economy.

References

Campbell, J. L. 2007. Why Would Corporations Behave in Socially Responsible Ways? An Institutional Theory of Corporate Social Responsibility. *Academy of Management Review*, 32: 946–967.

Collins, Jim and Porras, Jerry I. 1994; 2004. *Built to Last*. New York: Harper Business.

Freeman, R. E., Wicks, A. C. and Harrison, J. S. 2007. *Managing for Stakeholders*. New Haven: Yale University Press.

Hamel and Prahalad. 1994. *Competing for the Future*. Boston: Harvard Business School Press.

Johnson, Mark. 1993. *Moral Imagination*. Chicago: University of Chicago Press.

Newburry, W. E. and Gladwin, T. N. 2002. "Shell and Nigerian Oil," in Donaldson, T., Werhane, P. H. and Cording, M. (Eds.). *Ethical Issues in Business, 7th edition*. Upper Saddle River, NJ: Prentice-Hall, 522–540.

Plsek, P. 2001. "Redesigning Health Care with Insights from the Science of Complex Adaptive Systems." In *Crossing the Quality Chasm: A New Health System for the 21st Century*, edited by: Committee on Quality of Health Care in America, Institute of Medicine, Washington D.C.: National Academy Press, 309–323.

Prahalad, C. K. 2005. *The Fortune at the Bottom of the Pyramid: Eradicating Poverty Through Profits*. New Jersey: Wharton School Publishing.

Senge, Peter. 1990. *The Fifth Discipline*. New York: Doubleday.

Werhane, Patricia H. 1999. *Moral Imagination and Management Decision-Making*. New York: Oxford University Press.

2.1 Johnson & Johnson's Tylenol Controversies[*]

> We should encourage physicians to talk with their patients about all the risk factors, while at the same time, finding more ways to educate the public about this avoidable risk.
>
> Robert Fontana, Asst. Prof., University of Michigan Health System, talking about Acetaminophen-related liver and kidney problems

Tylenol Deaths

In September 1982, a 12-year-old girl, Mary Kellerman of Chicago, US died after taking extra strength Tylenol for headache. Three more people, Adam Janus, his brother and sister-in-law died on the same day after taking extra strength Tylenol. Three more deaths were reported on the next day due to Tylenol. The news of the incident spread quickly causing a nationwide panic. Responding to the crisis, Johnson and Johnson (J&J)[1] recalled 31 million bottles of extra strength Tylenol worth over $100 million from all retail stores in the US. In addition, the company offered to exchange tablets for capsules at no extra cost for all customers.

According to an analyst, J&J suffered a loss of $1.24 billion due to the depreciation of the company's brand value. Tylenol's share fell from 37% of the US analgesics market in early 1982 to just 7% by late 1982. According to media reports, the sudden deaths occurred because the Tylenol capsules had been laced[2] with cyanide. The capsules had been opened and filled with 65 mg of cyanide.[3] Inspite of the deaths, J&J was praised for its quick action and sincere efforts in recalling Tylenol and giving consumer safety as top priority.

In 1986, J&J faced a similar crisis when yet another incident of product tampering was reported. A woman in New York died after taking a cyanide laced extra strength Tylenol capsule. J&J had to once again recall all the capsules. The company promised to offer Tylenol only in the tablets or caplets[4] form.

In 1989, J&J faced another problem when deaths were reported due to overdoses of Tylenol. Following this, there were hundreds of deaths and severe liver damage all attributed to Tylenol's main ingredient—acetaminophen. Many analysts felt that J&J's label should have been more explicit in warning customers.

According to media reports, at least 100 suits had been filed against J&J over acetaminophen poisonings between 1990 and 1997. However, despite the bad publicity and the costly legal settlements, J&J did not seem keen on warning its customers. Analysts wondered about the company which had been a role model in prioritizing consumer safety during the 1982 crisis.

Background Note

Inspired by the discoveries[5] of Sir Joseph Lister (Lister),[6] Robert Wood Johnson (Robert) and his two brothers[7] formed a partnership firm to nurture the idea of a practical application of Lister's discoveries. Robert planned to enter the surgical dressings industry with a new type of readymade, sterile, wrapped and sealed surgical dressing in individual packages and suitable for instant use without the risk of contamination. In 1887, the trio converted the partnership into a company and the company was incorporated as Johnson & Johnson.

Over the years, J&J established itself as a leading player in the healthcare industry. The company introduced revolutionary surgical dressings, acquired established companies,[8] and expanded internationally.

In 1956, Tylenol became a part of J&J, when the company acquired McNeil Laboratories.[9] Tylenol was sold as an over-the-counter (OTC)[10] drug. During the 1960s, J&J aggressively promoted Tylenol among doctors and pharmacists as an alternative pain reliever. Soon, the product became very popular among consumers, as it was less irritating to the stomach as compared to other OTC analgesics[11] like Aspirin or Ibuprofen (see Exhibit 2.1.1).

In 1974, J&J acquired StimTech, a healthcare company selling a unique product—Transcutaneous Electronic Nerve Stimulator (TENS). The product reduced pain by electronic means and was claimed to be effective against headaches, backaches and arthritis. Industry observers expected TENS to become a substitute for analgesics including Tylenol. However, while J&J's marketing made Tylenol the leader of the US analgesics market, TENS failed. StimTech's founders filed a suit against J&J saying that the latter bought the company to suppress TENS' growth as it was seen as a potential competitor to Tylenol. StimTech's founders won the suit and J&J had to pay them US$170 million.

In early 1975, Tylenol faced heavy competition from a similar low-priced product called Datril, manufactured by Bristol-Myers. In late 1975, J&J reduced Tylenol's price by one-third and also advertised it aggressively. This increased the revenues of Tylenol's line of products (see Exhibit 2.1.2) from $50 million to $400 million by 1981 (see Table 2.1.1). According to the figures for financial year ended 1981–82, Tylenol was the leader with 37% share of the US $1.3 billion[12] analgesics market (see Table 2.1.2). Tylenol accounted for about 17–18% of J&J's net earnings and 7.4% of the worldwide revenues for the same period.

By mid-1980s, J&J had further expanded its presence in a broad range of products in healthcare and other fields. The company's products were grouped under four segments namely consumer, professional, pharmaceuticals, and industrial (see Exhibit 2.1.3).

The Fall and Rise of Tylenol

Tylenol received a major setback in late 1982 when it was found that many bottles of Tylenol extra strength capsules were laced with cyanide. The publicity about the poisoned capsules caused a nationwide panic. A hospital in Chicago received 700 telephone calls about Tylenol in just one day. People in cities across the US were admitted to hospitals on suspicion of cyanide poisoning. Within the first 10 days of the crisis, J&J received 1,411 telephone calls.

J&J acted immediately after the first reports of deaths came in. The company immediately alerted consumers across the US, via the media, not to consume any type of Tylenol product. The police drove through Chicago where the incidents were first reported, announcing the warning over loudspeakers, while all the three national television networks reported the deaths on their evening news broadcasts. The company told consumers not to use the product until the extent of the tampering could be determined. It recalled all Tylenol bottles and publicized the recall with full-page newspaper ads. Consumers were asked to return the

Chapter 2

Seminal/Paradigm Cases

Exhibit 2.1.1 Comparative Study: Aspirin, Acetaminophen and Ibuprofen

Aspirin

Aspirin is widely used for relieving pain and reducing fever in adults. Aspirin also relieves mild itching and reduces swelling and inflammation. As it is effective against pain, swelling and inflammation, aspirin is often specifically recommended for treating arthritis, as well as many other conditions and injuries. However, people who have the following problems are cautioned against taking aspirin:

- People who get stomach irritation after taking aspirin,
- People who are allergic to aspirin,
- People who take blood thinners, and
- People who have a hangover.

In addition, a person should not take aspirin if he or she has ulcers or gout. Also, people with asthma or hearing loss may have problems taking aspirin. Children and teenagers should not take aspirin as its use in these age groups is associated with a rare and serious brain and liver disorder called Reye's syndrome.

Acetaminophen

Acetaminophen relieves mild pain and reduces fever as effectively as aspirin, but does not reduce inflammation, making it ineffective for treating arthritis. However, acetaminophen can be used by people who can't take aspirin because of aspirin-related allergic reactions, stomach irritation or ringing in the ears. In addition, acetaminophen is safe for infants, children and teens. Common brands of acetaminophen include Tylenol and Panadol.

While acetaminophen is recommended over aspirin for some people, it does have some side effects. High doses or regular, long-term use can cause liver damage, especially if used with alcohol. Acetaminophen should not be used on a regular basis by people who suffer from anemia or liver or kidney diseases. In addition, it should not be used without a doctor's recommendation to treat:

- A fever over 103.1 degrees for more than three days, or
- Recurring fever.

Ibuprofen

Ibuprofen is effective for relief of pain, fever and inflammation, and for many people, is an effective alternative to aspirin for the treatment of arthritis. It is also less irritating to the stomach than aspirin and does not cause ringing in the ears. It does not cause severe liver problems like acetaminophen. There is less information on the effects of ibuprofen on children and so many doctors still consider acetaminophen as the safest drug for children and teenagers. Ibuprofen is not safe for use if a person has:

- Asthma and nasal polyps
- A stomach or intestinal disorder
- A skin condition called angioedema
- An allergic reaction to other anti-inflammatory medications, including aspirin
- Liver or kidney disease
- A blood clotting disorder, or
- Heart failure.

Source: www.yourhealth.com

bottles to the stores and exchange them for Tylenol capsules that were not subjected to cyanide tampering. The company shut down the production, distribution and advertising of the medicine temporarily. A day later, the Food and Drug Administration advised consumers to avoid taking Tylenol capsules.

From the beginning, J&J worked with federal investigators. After eight million recalled capsules were tested, it was determined that the bottles had been tampered with on store shelves. The poisoned capsules were placed on the shelves of six different stores in Chicago, IL, US. Only 75 capsules from eight different bottles had actually been laced with cyanide.

Exhibit 2.1.2 Tylenol's Product Line

Product Line	Product Name
For Adults	
For Pain	Tylenol Regular Strength
	Tylenol Extra Strength
For Arthritis	Tylenol Arthritis Pain Extended Relief
For Pain with sleeplessness	Tylenol PM
For Sleeplessness	Simply Sleep
For Menstrual Pain	Women's Tylenol
For Joint Health	Aflexa Glucosamine
For Sore Throat	Tylenol Sore Throat
For Colds	Tylenol Cold Complete Formula
	Tylenol Cold Non-Drowsy
	Tylenol Cold Severe Congestion
For Flu	Tylenol Flu Non-Drowsy
	Tylenol Flu Night Time
For Sinus	Tylenol Sinus Non-Drowsy
	Tylenol Sinus Night Time
For Allergy	Tylenol Allergy Sinus
	Tylenol Allergy Sinus Night Time
	Tylenol Severe Allergy
For Children	
For Pain/Fever	Infant's Tylenol
	Children's Tylenol
	Junior Strength Tylenol
For Flu	Children's Tylenol Flu
For Sinus	Children's Tylenol Sinus
For Cold	Infant's Tylenol Cold
	Infant's Tylenol Cold Plus Cough
	Children's Tylenol Cold
	Children's Tylenol Cold Plus Cough
For Allergy	Children's Tylenol Allergy-D

Source: www.tylenol.com

Table 2.1.1 Sales of Tylenol: 1975–83
(in $ million)

Year	Sales
1975	50
1976	80
1977	110
1978	150
1979	200
1980	280
1981	400
1982	210
1983	70

Source: Strategic Management, John A
Pearce and Richard B Robinson

Exhibit 2.1.3 J&J's Product Segments

Segment	Products
Consumer	Products that are marketed to the general public and distributed both through wholesalers and independent and chain retail outlets. It includes toiletries and hygienic products, baby care items, first aid products and non prescriptive drugs.
Professional	Ligatures and sutures, mechanical wound closure products, dental products, medical equipment and devices, surgical dressings, surgical instruments and related items used by hospitals, physicians, dentists, diagnostic laboratories, and clinics.
Pharmaceutical	Prescription drugs, including contraceptives and therapeutics, and veterinary products.
Industrial	Textile products, collagen sausage casings, and fine chemicals.

Source: Strategic Management by John A Pearce II and Richard B Robinson Jr.

Table 2.1.2 US Analgesics Market—March 1982

Product	Market Share (%)
Tylenol	37
Anacin	13
Bayer	11
Excedrin	10
Bufferin	9
Anacin 3	3
Others	17

Source: Strategic Management, John A Pearce and Richard B Robinson

Analysts opined that recalling all Tylenol products was not an easy decision for J&J. There was a great deal of discussion on recalling Tylenol at the national level. Some executives were worried about the panic that could result in the industry over such a widescale recall.

A month after the crisis, J&J launched an aggressive campaign to re-build (see Exhibit 2.1.4) Tylenol's image. The then Chairman and CEO of J&J, James E. Burke said, "It will take time, it will take money, and it will be very difficult; but we consider it a moral imperative, as well as good business, to restore Tylenol to its preeminent position." The company decided to re-launch the product in a new triple-tamper-resistant package by the end of 1982. Its efforts paid off and the company was able to recapture 32 of its original 37 percent market share just six months after the cyanide poisoning.

According to analysts, the way J&J handled the crisis became the model for crisis management. They said that the company's response to the crisis demonstrated its commitment to customer safety and the quality of its product. Also, J&J's openness and communication with the public helped the company maintain a high level of credibility and customer trust. Burke repeatedly assured the public of J&J's commitment to customer safety. Rather than thinking about the financial implications, Burke followed the company's Credo[13] (see Exhibit 2.1.5). He immediately sent a team of scientists to find the source of tampering. R. David Pittle, former commissioner for the US Consumer Product Safety Commission, commented, "They did the right thing and they did it promptly. Putting consumer safety above all else can help develop a loyalty from the consumer." Though J&J's stock declined in the initial weeks of the crisis, it soon rebounded because of the company's positive communications.

An article published in *The Washington Post (Post)* on October 11, 1982, said, "Johnson &

Exhibit 2.1.4 J&J's Tylenol Comeback Campaign (1982)

Step 1
Their first order of business was designing a tamper-resistant container.

Step 2
J&J strongly favoured federal legislation making tampering a felony. They also urged legislators to require tamper-proof packaging for a wide range of over-the-counter drugs.

Step 3
The company held a 30-city video teleconference from New York just six weeks after the cyanide deaths. J&J's CEO, at that time, and other company officials spoke during the 90-minute teleconference. They showed their new packaging and gave every reporter a sample of the new product.

Step 4
To overcome the public's fear of its product, the company made an offer. Former users were invited to call a toll-free number to request a free bottle in the new packaging. There was no need to prove that one had purchased a bottle previously. J&J was more keen on getting back its old customers and gaining new ones. Cost didn't matter.

Step 5
The company placed ads in Sunday newspapers with a circulation of 40 million people. The ad read, "Thank You, America." One could clip the ad to receive a $2.50 discount on the purchase of any Tylenol product.

Step 6
J&J sent about 50 million capsules to physicians for free distribution. Patients who received the samples from doctors felt assured that Tylenol was safe. This also reinstated the medical confidence in the product.

Step 7
The company thanked the media. Very often, companies treat the media as the enemy which leads to more probing by reporters and editors. They try to uncover the true story as they suspect a cover-up. Thus, when a company acts suspicious more questions arise in a journalist's mind.

Source: www.advertising.about.com

Johnson has effectively demonstrated how a major business ought to handle a disaster. What Johnson & Johnson executives have done is communicate the message that the company is candid, contrite, and compassionate, committed to solving the murders and protecting the public." *Post* applauded J&J for being honest with the public. It stressed that it must have been difficult for the company to withstand the temptation to disclaim any possible link between Tylenol and the deaths. It added that the company never attempted to do anything, other than try to get to the bottom of the deaths. It also mentioned that J&J almost immediately put up a reward of $100,000 for the killer.

In 1986, while the public fear about Tylenol was subsiding, J&J was again in the news due to product tampering. A woman in New York died after taking Tylenol. J&J had to once again recall all capsule products. The company decided to permanently discontinue capsule products. It replaced the product with new solid caplets that were relatively less susceptible to tampering.

The 1986 incident, however, attracted negative criticism from analysts. They said that after the 1982 incidents, J&J should have been more proactive and vigilant about product safety. A section of industry observers remarked that the media had played an important role in J&J's public relations campaign in 1982. They said that if J&J had not been cooperative with the media, it would have received less positive media coverage which in turn would have affected Tylenol's reputation permanently.

Exhibit 2.1.5 J&J's "Our Credo"

We believe our first responsibility is to the doctors, nurses and patients, to mothers and fathers and all others who use our products and services. In meeting their needs everything we do must be of high quality. We must constantly strive to reduce our costs in order to maintain reasonable prices. Customers' orders must be serviced promptly and accurately. Our suppliers and distributors must have an opportunity to make a fair profit.

We are responsible to our employees, the men and women who work with us throughout the world. Everyone must be considered as an individual. We must respect their dignity and recognize their merit. They must have a sense of security in their jobs. Compensation must be fair and adequate, and working conditions clean, orderly and safe. We must be mindful of ways to help our employees fulfill their family responsibilities. Employees must feel free to make suggestions and complaints. There must be equal opportunity for employment, development and advancement for those qualified. We must provide competent management, and their actions must be just and ethical.

We are responsible to the communities in which we live and work and to the world community as well. We must be good citizens—support good works and charities and bear our fair share of taxes. We must encourage civic improvements and better health and education. We must maintain in good order the property we are privileged to use, protecting the environment and natural resources.

Our final responsibility is to our stockholders. Business must make a sound profit. We must experiment with new ideas. Research must be carried on, innovative programs developed and mistakes paid for. New equipment must be purchased, new facilities provided and new products launched. Reserves must be created to provide for adverse times. When we operate according to these principles, the stockholders should realize a fair return.

Source: www.jnj.com

The Tylenol Overdose Controversy

In 1989, J&J faced yet another problem when deaths occurred due to Tylenol overdoses. In 1989, five-year-old Lacy Keele died after being given four extra strength Tylenol tablets in one day, twice what she should have taken. In early 1990s, fourteen-month-old Sophie Regosin-Hodges was given an overdose of Tylenol, which severely damaged her liver. As per the pediatrician's advice, Sophie was given infant Tylenol drops. The infant drops were three and half times stronger than the children's medicine. Though Sophie survived with a transplant of liver tissue from her father she was put on immunosuppressant[14] drugs for the rest of her life. In another incident reported in 1993, Antonio Benedi, an alcoholic, took ten extra strength Tylenol in four days. He survived only after a liver transplant.

In the following years, there were hundreds of deaths and severe liver damage that were all attributed to Tylenol's main ingredient—acetaminophen. Acetaminophen was used to treat mild to moderate pain and fever including simple headaches, muscle aches and mild forms of arthritis. The drug was more useful for patients who could not use Aspirin or Ibuprofen, because of gastrointestinal ulcers or bleeding disorders. It was the main ingredient of Tylenol and other pain relieving drugs (see Exhibit 2.1.6) and damaged the liver severely, if the medications were taken in large doses (see Exhibit 2.1.7).

Slowly, people became aware that though safe in proper doses, Tylenol could be dangerous even in a little overdose. Even twice the prescribed dose could damage the liver. Unfortunately, overdoses could happen due to many reasons. For children, Tylenol came in kid-pleasing flavors and was marked as a "SAFE" alternative to Aspirin. As children liked the flavor, they could just take another dose. It was also found that in many cases, one parent was not aware that the other had given the dose, and accidentally gave a second dose. Also, parents were not aware about the strengths and doses of the Tylenol line of products. Acetaminophen

Exhibit 2.1.6 Brands of Pain Killers
Containing Acetaminophen

Aceta	Genebs
Acetamin	Liquiprin
Anacin 3	Neopap
Apacet	Oraphen-PD
Aspirin free Anacin	Panadol
Atasol	Phenaphen
Banesin	Redutemp
Dapa	Snaplets-FR
Datril Extra Strength	Suppap
Feverall	Tapanol
Genapap	Valorin

Source: www.wholehealthmd.com

Exhibit 2.1.7 Harmful Effects of Overdose of Acetaminophen and Other Analgesics

The reaction as a result of excessive intake of acetaminophen is called acetaminophen poisoning. In adults, a dose more than 10–15 gms causes liver failure and more than 25 gms causes deaths. Common symptoms of acetaminophen poisoning include nausea and vomiting, profuse sweating and oliguria (scanty amounts of urine). As the drug toxicity increases, other symptoms like jaundice, pain in the upper abdomen, abnormality in the brain tissue and kidney failure become apparent.

Apart from liver damage, acetaminophen also causes permanent kidney damage when used for a long period. The damage could be severe for those who already have problems. Studies have also revealed that people using acetaminophen in combination with other painkillers were 3–8 times more prone to kidney cancer, which is very difficult to treat. Excessive dose of acetaminophen also results in high heart rate and blood pressure in some patients.

Analgesics also caused an "analgesic rebound"—headaches caused by the rebound effect of stopping large doses of analgesics. The problem begins when people take an analgesic for a few recurring headaches. They continuously increase the dose and later find that they are addicted to the drug. However, the medicine fails to relieve the pain and headaches recur due to the rebound effect of cessation of the large doses of medications. The only treatment for such headaches is to stop all analgesic medications.

Source: www.lef.org

was also harmful to people with liver problems, if taken along with alcohol and certain other medicines or on an empty stomach. However, Tylenol was marketed with the ad line "Nothing's Safer." The required warning labels as per the US Food and Drug Administration rules only stated alcohol-related risks. Some health practitioners felt that stronger warnings against overdoses were very important.

According to analysts, inspite of the bad publicity and legal settlements, which cost the company millions of dollars, J&J refused to put explicit warnings on its Tylenol labels. The company had only made just cosmetic changes on the warning label. After the Keele case, J&J added to the extra strength package: "Not for use for children." In 1994, after Benedi's case, it added a warning about using any pain reliever after a drink. Analysts said that J&J resisted writing the kind of label that would really alert people about the dangers of taking overdoses. For example, according to J&J it resisted warning customers about possible liver failure because the company felt that "organ specific" warnings would confuse people. Similarly, the company resisted warning about the risk of death to avoid suicides: If people knew that acetaminophen was potentially deadly, they might use it for suicide. In response to the studies revealing Tylenol-related liver damage, J&J advised its sales representatives not to discuss the issue with the doctors. Rather than taking some concrete measures to prevent patients from taking overdoses, J&J recommended that the patients should keep a log for doses taken. The recommendation was made in a patient education brochure given to the doctors.

According to media reports, at least 100 suits had been filed against J&J over acetamino-phen poisonings between 1990 and 1997. In four cases, the company reportedly made out-of-court settlements under agreements that required the plaintiffs to maintain silence about the terms. Analysts felt that the huge profits were the main reason behind J&J's reluctance to make people aware of Tylenol's side effects. Wall Street analysts estimated J&J's revenue for Tylenol at $1.3 billion a year in 1996. The fact that acetaminophen was available at about half the price suggested that J&J's profit margin was very high. J&J spent a major part of this profit to strengthen Tylenol's image. According to *Advertising Age*, the company's domestic ad budget for Tylenol was $250 million in 1997, more than Coca-Cola spent on Coke.

Analysts remarked that J&J's response to the overdose issue was in steep contrast to its quick and sincere efforts in 1982. Burke had taken personal responsibility for the public's safety. The American Association of Poison Control Centers reported about 100 deaths a year from acetaminophen. This figure seemed to be understated since hospitals were not required to report such cases.

An article[15] published in 1997 commented on the alternatives available to Ralph Larsen,[16] J&J's new CEO, "He can rewrite the label, putting on it the verbal equivalent of a skull and crossbones. Or he can go on paying off victims, and hope for the best. Which is the moral choice? Which, in the long run, is the best business decision?"

Making the Public Aware of Risks

In September 1997, the FDA's OTC drug advisory committee recommended additional changes in the labeling for acetaminophen used in painkillers. The FDA wanted manufactur-ers to explain the correct dosages for children under two years, instead of simply directing parents to consult a doctor before using the medication.

In October 1997, J&J announced that it would inform parents about Tylenol's side effects on children through labels and advertisements (see Table 2.1.3). The new labels cautioned consumers against overdose. From November 1997, J&J also released magazine and TV ads informing parents about correct dosages.

Table 2.1.3 Changes in the Label of Tylenol as per New FDA Rules

* Added the warning "Read the instructions carefully" to the front panel of all Children's Tylenol dosage forms.
* Changed the language to emphasize the importance of using the specific dosing device—for example, dropper or cup—that came with the product.
* Added the statement "Taking more than the recommended dose (overdose) will not provide more relief and could cause serious health risks." to ensure that parents and other caregivers understand that there is no advantage to exceeding recommended doses.
* Changed the front panel of Infants' Tylenol drops to read "Concentrated Drops" instead of "Suspension Drops."

Source: www.fda.gov

Notes

* This case was written by D. Sirisha, under the direction of Viveck Gupta, ICFAI Center for Management Research. © 2002, ICFAI Center for Management Research. All rights reserved.

1 McNeil Laboratories, the manufacturer of Tylenol, was acquired by J&J in 1956.
2 The capsules were emptied and refilled with cyanide.
3 About 10,000 times more poisonous than a human body can resist.
4 Single compartment sealed capsules.
5 Identified airborne germs as a source of infection in the operating room.
6 A noted English surgeon.
7 James Wood and Edware Mead Johnson.
8 Some of the major acquisitions of J&J included McNeil Consumers Products Ltd., Frontier Contact Lenses, Janssen Pharmaceutica, RoC S.A. and Neutrogena Corp. (manufacturers of skin and hair care products), Clinical Diagnostics, Biopsys Medical (produced products for minimally invasive breast biopsies), DePuy, Inc. and Cordis Corp.
9 A manufacturer of pharmaceutical products including Tylenol.
10 Drugs that can be purchased without a doctor's prescription.
11 Pain relieving medications.
12 According to "Tylenol's capsule crisis—I", Strategic Management, John A Pearce and Richard B Robinson.
13 J&J's corporate business philosophy written by Robert Wood Johnson in 1943.
14 Immunosuppressant drugs are medicines that reduce the body's natural defenses against foreign bodies or materials. In transplant patients, these drugs help prevent their bodies from rejecting transplanted organs.
15 "J&J's Dirty Little Secret," www.torahview.com
16 Ralph Larsen took over as the Chairman and CEO in 1989. He joined J&J in 1962 as a manufacturing trainee.

2.2 Merck Co., Inc. (A) *

In 1978, Dr. P. Roy Vagelos, then head of the Merck research labs, received a provocative memorandum from a senior researcher in parasitology, Dr. William C. Campbell. Dr. Campbell had made an intriguing observation while working with ivermectin, a new antiparasitic compound under investigation for use in animals.

Campbell thought that ivermectin might be the answer to a disease called river blindness that plagued millions in the Third World. But to find out if Campbell's hypothesis had merit, Merck would have to spend millions of dollars to develop the right formulation for human use and to conduct the field trials in the most remote parts of the world. Even if these efforts produced an effective and safe drug, virtually all of those afflicted with river blindness could not afford to buy it. Vagelos, originally a university researcher but by then a Merck executive, had to decide whether to invest in research for a drug that, even if successful, might never pay for itself.

River Blindness

River blindness, formally known as *onchocerciasis*, was a disease labeled by the World Health Organization (WHO) as a public health and socioeconomic problem of considerable magnitude in over 35 developing countries throughout the Third World. Some 85 million people in thousands of tiny settlements throughout Africa and parts of the Middle East and Latin America were thought to be at risk. The cause: a parasitic worm carried by a tiny black fly which bred along fast-moving rivers. When the flies bit humans—a single person could be bitten thousands of times a day—the larvae of a parasitic worm, *Onchocerca volvulus* entered the body.

These worms grew to more than two feet in length, causing grotesque but relatively innocuous nodules in the skin. The real harm began when the adult worms reproduced, releasing millions of microscopic offspring, known as microfilariae, which swarmed through body tissue. A terrible itching resulted, so bad that some victims committed suicide. After several years, the microfilariae caused lesions and depigmentation of the skin. Eventually they invaded the eyes, often causing blindness.

The World Health Organization estimated in 1978 that some 340,000 people were blind because of onchocerciasis, and that a million more suffered from varying degrees of visual impairment. At that time, 18 million or more people were infected with the parasite, though half did not yet have serious symptoms. In some villages close to breeding sites, nearly all residents were infected and a majority of those over age 45 were blind. In such places, it was said, children believed that severe itching, skin infections and blindness were simply part of growing up.

In desperate efforts to escape the flies, entire villages abandoned fertile areas near rivers, and moved to poorer land. As a result, food shortages were frequent. Community life disintegrated as new burdens arose for already impoverished families.

The disease was first identified in 1893 by scientists and in 1926 was found to be related to the black flies. But by the 1970s, there was still no cure that could safely be used for community-wide treatment. Two drugs, diethylcarbamazine (DEC) and Suramin, were useful in killing the parasite, but both had severe side effects in infected individuals, needed close monitoring, and had even caused deaths. In 1974, the Onchocerciasis Control Program was created to be administered by the World Health Organization, in the hope that the flies could be killed through spraying of larvacides at breeding sites, but success was slow and uncertain. The flies in many areas developed resistance to the treatment, and were also known to disappear and then reinfest areas.

Merck & Co., Inc.

Merck & Co., Inc. was, in 1978, one of the largest producers of prescription drugs in the world. Headquartered in Rahway, New Jersey, Merck traced its origins to Germany in 1668 when Friedrich Jacob Merck purchased an apothecary in the city of Darmstadt. Over three hundred years later, Merck, having become an American firm, employed over 28,000 people and had operations all over the world.

In the late 1970s, Merck was coming off a 10 year drought in terms of new products. For nearly a decade, the company had relied on two prescription drugs for a significant percentage of its approximately $2 billion in annual sales: Indocin, a treatment for rheumatoid arthritis, and Aldomet, a treatment for high blood pressure. Henry W. Gadsden, Merck's chief executive from 1965 to 1976, along with his successor, John J. Horan, were concerned that the 17-year patent protection on Merck's two big moneymakers would soon expire, and began investing an enormous amount in research.

Merck management spent a great deal of money on research because it knew that its success ten and twenty years in the future critically depended upon present investments. The company deliberately fashioned a corporate culture to nurture the most creative, fruitful research. Merck scientists were among the best-paid in the industry, and were given great latitude to pursue intriguing leads. Moreover, they were inspired to think of their work as a quest to alleviate human disease and suffering world-wide. Within certain proprietary constraints, researchers were encouraged to publish in academic journals and to share ideas with their scientific peers. Nearly a billion dollars was spent between 1975 and 1978, and the investment paid off. In that period, under the direction of head of research, Dr. P. Roy Vagelos, Merck introduced Clinoril, a painkiller for arthritis; a general antibiotic called Mefoxin; a drug for glaucoma named Timoptic; and Ivomec (ivermectin, MSD), an antiparasitic for cattle.

In 1978, Merck had sales of $1.98 billion and net income of $307 million. Sales had risen steadily between 1969 and 1978 from $691 million to almost $2 billion. Income during the same period rose from $106 million to over $300 million. (See Exhibit 2.2.1 for a 10 year summary of performance.)

At that time, Merck employed 28,700 people, up from 22,200 ten years earlier. Human and animal health products constituted 84% of the company's sales, with environmental health products and services representing an additional 14% of sales. Merck's foreign sales had grown more rapidly during the 1970's than had domestic sales, and in 1978 represented 47% of total sales. Much of the company's research operations were organized separately as the Merck Sharp & Dohme Research Laboratories, headed by Vagelos. Other Merck operations included the Merck Sharp & Dohme Division, the Merck Sharp & Dohme International

Exhibit 2.2.1 10 Year Summary of Financial Performance

Merck & Co., Inc. and Subsidiaries
(Dollar amounts in thousands except per-share figures)

Results for Year:	1978	1977	1976	1975	1974	1973	1972	1971	1970	1969
Sales	$1,981,440	$1,724,410	$1,561,117	$1,401,979	$1,260,416	$1,104,035	$942,631	$832,416	$761,109	$691,453
Materials and production costs	744,249	662,703	586,963	525,853	458,837	383,879	314,804	286,646	258,340	232,878
Marketing/administrative expenses	542,186	437,579	396,975	354,525	330,292	304,807	268,856	219,005	201,543	178,593
Research/development expenses	161,350	144,898	133,826	121,933	100,952	89,155	79,692	71,619	69,707	61,100
Interest expense	25,743	25,743	26,914	21,319	8,445	6,703	4,533	3,085	2,964	1,598
Income before taxes	507,912	453,487	416,439	378,349	361,890	319,491	274,746	252,061	228,555	217,284
Taxes on income	198,100	173,300	159,100	147,700	149,300	134,048	121,044	118,703	108,827	109,269
Net income**	307,534	277,525	255,482	228,778	210,492	182,681	151,180	131,381	117,878	106,645
Per common share**	$4.07	$3.67	$3.38	$3.03	$2.79	$2.43	$2.01	$1.75	$1.57	$1.43
Dividends declared on common stock	132,257	117,101	107,584	105,564	106,341	93,852	84,103	82,206	76,458	75,528
Per common share	$1.75	$1.55	$1.42½	$1.40	$1.40	$1.23½	$1.12	$1.10	$1.02½	$1.02½
Gross plant additions	155,853	177,167	153,894	249,015	159,148	90,194	69,477	67,343	71,540	48,715
Depreciation	75,477	66,785	58,198	52,091	46,057	40,617	36,283	32,104	27,819	23,973
Year-End Position:										
Working capital	666,817	629,515	549,840	502,262	359,591	342,434	296,378	260,350	226,084	228,296
Property, plant, and equipment (net)	924,179	846,784	747,107	652,804	459,245	352,145	305,416	274,240	239,638	197,220
Total assets	2,251,358	1,993,389	1,759,371	1,538,999	1,243,287	988,985	834,847	736,503	664,294	601,484
Stockholders' equity	1,455,135	1,277,753	1,102,154	949,991	822,782	709,614	621,792	542,978	493,214	451,030
Year-End Statistics:										
Average number of common shares outstanding (in thousands)	75,573	75,546	75,493	75,420	75,300	75,193	75,011	74,850	74,850	74,547
Number of stockholders	62,900	63,900	63,500	63,500	61,400	60,000	58,000	54,300	54,600	53,100
Number of employees	28,700	28,100	26,800	26,300	26,500	25,100	24,100	23,200	23,000	22,200

* The above data are as previously reported, restated for poolings-of-interests and stock splits.

** Net income for 1977 and related per-share amounts exclude gain on disposal of businesses of $13,225 and 18¢, respectively.

Division, Kelco Division, Merck Chemical Manufacturing Division, Merck Animal Health Division, Calgon Corporation, Baltimore Aircoil Company, and Hubbard Farms.

The company had 24 plants in the United States, including one in Puerto Rico, and 44 in other countries. Six research laboratories were located in the United States and four abroad.

While Merck executives sometimes squirmed when they quoted the "unbusinesslike" language of George W. Merck, son of the company's founder and its former chairman, there could be no doubt that Merck employees found the words inspirational. "We try never to forget that medicine is for the people," Merck said. "It is not for the profits. The profits follow, and if we have remembered that, they have never failed to appear. The better we have remembered it, the larger they have been." These words formed the basis of Merck's overall corporate philosophy.

The Drug Investment Decision

Merck invested hundreds of millions of dollars each year in research. Allocating those funds amongst various projects, however, was a rather involved and inexact process. At a company as large as Merck, there was never a single method by which projects were approved or money distributed.

Studies showed that, on the average, it took 12 years and $200 million to bring a new drug to market. Thousands of scientists were continually working on new ideas and following new leads. Drug development was always a matter of trial and error; with each new iteration, scientists would close some doors and open others. When a Merck researcher came across an apparent breakthrough—either in an unexpected direction, or as a derivative of the original lead—he or she would conduct preliminary research. If the idea proved promising, it was brought to the attention of the department heads.

Every year, Merck's research division held a large review meeting at which all research programs were examined. Projects were coordinated and consolidated, established programs were reviewed and new possibilities were considered. Final approval on research was not made, however, until the head of research met later with a committee of scientific advisors. Each potential program was extensively reviewed, analyzed on the basis of the likelihood of success, the existing market, competition, potential safety problems, manufacturing feasibility and patent status before the decision was made whether to allocate funds for continued experimentation.

The Problem of Rare Diseases and Poor Customers

Many potential drugs offered little chance of financial return. Some diseases were so rare that treatments developed could never be priced high enough to recoup the investment in research, while other diseases afflicted only the poor in rural and remote areas of the Third World. These victims had limited ability to pay even a small amount for drugs or treatment.

In the United States, Congress sought to encourage drug companies to conduct research on rare diseases. In 1978 legislation had been proposed which would grant drug companies tax benefits and seven-year exclusive marketing rights if they would manufacture drugs for diseases afflicting fewer than 200,000 Americans. It was expected that this "orphan drug" program would eventually be passed into law.

There was, however, no U.S. or international program that would create incentives for companies to develop drugs for diseases like river blindness which afflicted millions of the poor in the Third World. The only hope was that some Third World government, foundation, or international aid organization might step in and partially fund the distribution of a drug that had already been developed.

The Discovery of Ivermectin

The process of investigating promising drug compounds was always long, laborious and fraught with failure. For every pharmaceutical compound that became a "product candidate," thousands of others failed to meet the most rudimentary pre-clinical tests for safety and efficacy. With so much room for failure, it became especially important for drug companies to have sophisticated research managers who could identify the most productive research strategies.

Merck had long been a pioneer in developing major new antibiotic compounds, beginning with penicillin and streptomycin in the 1940s. In the 1970s, Merck Sharp & Dohme Research Laboratories were continuing this tradition. To help investigate for new microbial agents of potential therapeutic value, Merck researchers obtained 54 soil samples from the Kitasato Institute of Japan in 1974. These samples seemed novel and the researchers hoped they might disclose some naturally occurring antibiotics.

As Merck researchers methodically put the soil through hundreds of tests, Merck scientists were pleasantly surprised to detect strong antiparasitic activity in Sample No. OS3153, a scoop of soil dug up at a golf course near Ito, Japan. The Merck labs quickly brought together an interdisciplinary team to try to isolate a pure active ingredient from the microbial culture. The compound eventually isolated—avermectin—proved to have an astonishing potency and effectiveness against a wide range of parasites in cattle, swine, horses and other animals. Within a year, the Merck team also began to suspect that a group of related compounds discovered in the same soil sample could be effective against many other intestinal worms, mites, ticks and insects.

After toxicological tests suggested that ivermectin would be safer than related compounds, Merck decided to develop the substance for the animal health market. In 1978 the first ivermectin-based animal drug, Ivomec, was nearing approval by the U.S. Department of Agriculture and foreign regulatory bodies. Many variations would likely follow: drugs for sheep and pigs, horses, dogs, and others. Ivomec had the potential to become a major advance in animal health treatment.

As clinical testing of ivermectin progressed in the late 1970s, Dr. William Campbell's ongoing research brought him face-to-face with an intriguing hypothesis. Ivermectin, when tested in horses, was effective against the microfilariae of an exotic, fairly unimportant gastro-intestinal parasite, *Onchocerca cervicalis*. This particular worm, while harmless in horses, had characteristics similar to the insidious human parasite that causes river blindness, *Onchocerca volvulus*.

Dr. Campbell wondered: Could ivermectin be formulated to work against the human parasite? Could a safe, effective drug suitable for community-wide treatment of river blindness be developed? Both Campbell and Vagelos knew that it was very much a gamble that it would succeed. Furthermore, both knew that even if success were attained, the economic viability of such a project would be nil. On the other hand, because such a significant amount of money had already been invested in the development of the animal drug, the cost of developing a human formulation would be much less than that for developing a new compound. It was also widely believed at this point that ivermectin, though still in its final development stages, was likely to be very successful.

A decision to proceed would not be without risks. If a new derivative proved to have any adverse health effects when used on humans, its reputation as a veterinary drug could be tainted and sales negatively affected, no matter how irrelevant the experience with humans. In early tests, ivermectin had had some negative side effects on some specific species of mammals. Dr. Brian Duke of the Armed Forces Institute of Pathology in Washington, D.C. said the cross-species effectiveness of antiparasitic drugs is unpredictable, and there is "always a worry that some race or sub-section of the human population" might be adversely affected.

Isolated instances of harm to humans or improper use in Third World settings might also raise some unsettling questions: Could drug residues turn up in meat eaten by humans? Would any human version of ivermectin distributed to the Third World be diverted into the blackmarket, undercutting sales of the veterinary drug? Could the drug harm certain animals in unknown ways?

Despite these risks, Vagelos wondered what the impact might be of turning down Campbell's proposal. Merck had built a research team dedicated to alleviating human suffering. What would a refusal to pursue a possible treatment for river blindness do to morale?

Ultimately, it was Dr. Vagelos who had to make the decision whether or not to fund research toward a treatment for river blindness.

Note

*   This case was researched and written by *David Bollier* and adapted by *Stephanie Weiss*, under the supervision of *Kirk O. Hanson*, senior lecturer at the Graduate School of Business. Copyright 1991 by The Business Enterprise Trust. The Business Enterprise Trust is a national non-profit organization that honors exemplary acts of courage, integrity and social vision in business.

Chapter 3

Pharmaceutical

3.1 Abbott and the AIDS Crisis[*]

In January 1999, Miles White became the new CEO of Abbott Laboratories, and in June, was made chairman of the board. White had plans to transform Abbott into a major player on the international stage, leveraging its core competencies in pharmaceutical development to focus on its primary area of expertise and commitment: HIV/AIDS.[1] Over the next decade, White would increase the global presence of Abbott through both internal innovation and intelligent acquisitions. And he would transform the company's foundation, Abbott Fund, into a significant global contributor in the fight against AIDS in the developing world.

During this same period, a number of factors had put Abbott at a crossroads in the worldwide HIV/AIDS pandemic. As Rick Moser, who worked in Abbott's Corporate Public Affairs Department at the time, recalled, there was a growing sense of awareness of how large the AIDS crisis was becoming in developing countries. Abbott, which had offered the first HIV diagnostic test in the 1980s and had developed one of the first protease inhibitors, Norvir,[2] was taking notice, as were other businesses and organizations. Bristol-Myers Squibb had set an important example earlier in 1999 with its Secure the Future program, "a $100 million commitment to advance HIV/AIDS research and community outreach programs in five southern African countries: South Africa, Botswana, Namibia, Lesotho, and Swaziland."[3] This was the first time a pharmaceutical company had launched an aggressive program to combat the pandemic in the developing world. And *Newsweek* was about to publish a big article on the AIDS crisis and its horrific impact on children in the developing world—"it exploded the issue, gave it broad prominence."[4]

In addition, there was the upcoming AIDS Conference in Durban, South Africa, in July 2000. Holding the International AIDS Conference in South Africa was significant, Moser said, not only because it was the first time it was hosted in a developing country, but also because the province in which it was being held, Kwa Zulu Natal, had the highest rates of HIV prevalence in the world. Choosing South Africa, the country with the highest number of AIDS infections in the world, highlighted the fact that sub-Saharan Africa was the world's epicenter of HIV/AIDS.

Introduced in the mid-1990s, protease inhibitors played a significant role in changing the Western view of the AIDS crisis. These drugs were more successful than earlier therapies, such as AZT and DDI, which offered initial hope, but had limited effect. People quickly became resistant to the drugs and consequently became ill and died. Moser said:

> Until that point, there had been no effective drug therapies. In the United States and throughout the developed world, the focus had been inward—what do we do about this crisis that *we* are facing *here*? With the widespread availability of protease inhibitors, HIV infection went from being a death sentence to a chronic, treatable disease. It was then that the world would see the bigger crisis that had been under the radar.[5]

Up to that point, there was little worldwide recognition of the extraordinary infection rates and prevalence rates of countries in the developing world.

"And Abbott," said Moser, who had been with the company since the development of the first AIDS test in 1985 and then Norvir in 1996,[6] "[had] a new CEO and a vision to expand its presence globally. It was an opportunity to build something that would truly change the lives of those who needed it most. It was an exciting moment and tremendous challenge.

What can we reasonably do?"[7]

The Advent of the HIV/AIDS Crisis

In the early 1980s, newspapers began reporting on a smattering of strange or rare diseases in gay men; for example:

- There had been five cases of *Pneumocystis carinii* pneumonia in Los Angeles, according to a June 1981 Centers for Disease Control and Prevention (CDC) *Morbidity and Mortality Weekly Report*.
- There had been an increase in cases of Kaposi's sarcoma, a rare skin cancer formerly found almost exclusively in older men of Eastern European descent.

Initially termed GRD (Gay Related Disease) because it appeared to affect only gay men, this syndrome was renamed AIDS in 1982. By then, however, a quarter of a million men and women were already infected with HIV, a virus that severely weakened a person's immune system and left him or her susceptible to a variety of normally benign illnesses. HIV/AIDS quickly penetrated society and began a devastating assault on people throughout the world. In the early 1980s, no one could have predicted the enormity of the pandemic that would develop, the difficulty of fighting HIV/AIDS, and the human and social toll this disease would take over the next several decades. HIV/AIDS transformed personal lives as well as the world of medicine, pharmaceuticals, nonprofits, and nongovernmental organizations, among many others.

The first drug that treated AIDS was zidovudine (AZT), which was initially developed as a potential cancer treatment. Called a wonder drug, it was approved by the U.S. Food and Drug Administration (FDA) in 1987. AZT (produced by Glaxo Wellcome) was in the first group of drugs developed to fight HIV; others included Epivir, Videx, and Hivid. But although these drugs lowered the amount of the virus in the blood, they did not eradicate it completely, and they also began to lose their effectiveness over time as the virus developed resistance.[8]

Between the early 1980s and 1998, more than 47 million people were infected with HIV, and almost 14 million people died (leaving about 33.4 million people living with HIV/AIDS).[9] During 1998, there were 2.5 million AIDS-related deaths, and HIV/AIDS had become the leading infectious cause of death in the world, replacing tuberculosis and outstripping malaria by almost threefold.

The Global Epicenter

At the close of the 20th century, the 20-year-old AIDS crisis had ravaged many developing countries and, in particular, the continent of Africa. Whereas access to drugs, a modern health care system, and greater financial resources had helped the United States and Europe battle

Exhibit 3.1.1 Worldwide AIDS Statistics—1998

Region	Adults & Children Living with HIV/AIDS	Adults & Children Newly Infected with HIV	Adult Prevalence Rate
Sub-Saharan Africa	22.5 million	4.0 million	8.0%
North Africa & Middle East	210,000	19,000	0.13%
North America	890,000	44,000	0.56%
Latin America	1.4 million	160,000	0.57%
South & Southeast Asia	6.7 million	1.2 million	0.69%
East Asia & Pacific	560,000	200,000	0.068%
Australia & New Zealand	12,000	600	0.1%
Western Europe	500,000	30,000	0.25%
Caribbean	330,000	45,000	1.96%

Source: UNAIDS Joint United Nations Programme on HIV/AIDS, "AIDS Epidemic Update: December 1998," 5, http://www.aegis.com/files/unaids/WADDec1998_epidemic_report.pdf (accessed 20 February 2008).

the epidemic, less developed countries were suffering from lack of information, health care infrastructure, financial means, and readily available medicines. Of the estimated 33.4 million people living with HIV/AIDS worldwide in 1998, almost two-thirds (22 million) were in sub-Saharan Africa, considered the "global epicenter" of the disease. Already 12 million had died, and life expectancy in the region plummeted from 62 years to 47. Experts predicted that, left unchecked, the AIDS crisis would, over the next two decades, wreak economic havoc and create profound political instability. As the 20th century drew to a close, "[t]he effect of AIDS in many African countries superseded that of war, drought, famine, or any other prior emergencies in magnitude, duration, and challenge for programme response."[10] (Exhibit 3.1.1 presents 1998 worldwide HIV/AIDS statistics and comparisons.)

Abbott Laboratories

As the 21st century began, Abbott Laboratories, a midsize, midtier health care company, had been involved with products that helped diagnose or treat HIV/AIDS since the disease began to spread. The company had its origins in 1888, when Wallace C. Abbott, a Vermont physician, purchased a pharmacy in Chicago. At its inception, Abbott focused on alkaloidal medicine, but in the early 20th century it shifted its attention to synthetic (chemical) medicines and, in 1915, changed its name from Abbott Alkaloidal Company to Abbott Laboratories. During World War I, the company's importance in the medical community increased when, in the absence of German medicines, Abbott produced substitutes, including procaine, an anesthetic, and cinchophen, a remedy for a number of ailments. Until his death in 1921, Wallace Abbott worked tirelessly at producing and promoting his medicines, building an enthusiastic work force, and hiring top-notch scientists and physicians. Over the years, the company changed its emphasis and focus in several different areas and, as the 20th century drew to a close, Abbott was a broad-based health care company with a portfolio of leading pharmaceutical, nutritional, and medical device products. (Exhibit 3.1.2 presents a brief timeline of Abbott's history.)

In 1999, Abbott employed almost 60,000 people worldwide and operated in 130 countries. The company was smaller than many of the other well-known pharmaceutical companies such as Pfizer and Merck. Its leading brands included Similac, Ensure, and Pedialyte. The company has paid dividends without interruption since 1924.[11]

Exhibit 3.1.2 Selected History of Abbott Laboratories—Timeline

Pre-1920s

1888: Abbott Alkaloidal Company founded by Wallace C. Abbott, MD.

1906: Establishes first sales force.

1910: Establishes its first European agency in London; also opens branches in New York, San Francisco, Seattle, Toronto, and India.

1915: Changes its name to Abbott Laboratories.

1916: Acquires Chlorazene, an antiseptic and synthetic agent used to clean wounds. Chlorazene was used extensively in World War I.

1920s

1920: Begins construction of headquarters in North Chicago.

1923: Officially enters the anesthesia market with its development of the antiseptic Butyn, a synthetic drug. Butyl alcohol, the basis of the drug, becomes a major component of the company's research on sleep-inducing agents.

1929: With an offering of 20,000 shares priced at $32 each, Abbott stock makes its appearance on the Chicago Stock Exchange.

1930s

1930: Introduces Nembutal, a sedative, which becomes one of the company's best-known and most enduring products.

1931: Establishes its first international affiliate, in Montreal, after merging its newly acquired Swan Meyer Co. and an existing sales office.

1936: Introduces what will be the most widely used induction anesthetic for the next 50 years, Pentothal (thiopental sodium), and begins supplying hospitals with bulk intravenous solutions.

1938: Abbott's 50th anniversary. Dedicates its North Chicago Research Center.

1940s

1941: Agrees to help Britain mass produce penicillin (discovered in 1928 in Great Britain), and begins commercial production of the medicine.

1942: During World War II, steps up antibiotic research, and produces the water purification tablet Halazone, which is then shipped to the millions of troops fighting in the war.

1943: Opens its first facility in Puerto Rico. Over the years, this was to become one of the company's largest manufacturing operations.

1945: Introduces epilepsy treatment, Tridione; high-potency vitamin Surbex; and the first fully disposable intravenous administration set, Venopac.

1946: First pharmaceutical to have laboratory for "radiopharmaceuticals," setting the stage for becoming the world's leading immunodiagnostics business.

1949: Introduces 74 new products in one year.

1950s

1950: Introduces its first truly consumer product Sucaryl.

1951: Introduces dandruff-control shampoo Selsun Suspension. Employee contributory stock purchase plan established.

1952: Introduces antibiotic Erythrocin, eventually one of the company's most successful drugs.

1960s

1962: Enters joint venture with Japan's Dainippon Pharmaceuticals to manufacture radiopharmaceuticals. Then becomes Dainabot, then Abbott Japan, the company's largest operation outside the United States.

1963: Introduces Triosorb diagnostic kit; patients no longer have to swallow a radioactive substance; instead, a blood sample is used.

1964: Acquires Similac infant formula makers M&R Dietetic Laboratories (eventually becomes Ross Products Division).

1965: Enormous growth leads to expansion of its headquarters locations; some operations move from North Chicago to Abbott Park.

1970s

1973: Forms diagnostics division; introduces Ensure, the first adult medical nutritional.

1977: Forms TAP Pharmaceuticals, a joint venture with the Japanese Takeda Chemical Industries.

1980s

1985:   Wins U.S. approval to market the first AIDS diagnostic test, which enables widespread screening of the world's blood supply and of individuals; launches intravenous drug delivery system ADD-Vantage; TAP receives approval for the cancer drug Lupron.

1990s

1990:   Launches Clarithromycin, known as Biaxin in the United States.

1991:   Launches several major products worldwide, including a prostate-specific antigen (PSA) test to screen and monitor therapy for prostate cancer.

1992:   First company to win FDA approval for a simultaneous HIV-1 and HIV-2 antibody diagnosis system; ABT-538 synthesized to become Abbott's landmark protease inhibitor ritonavir, or Norvir.

1995:   2,000 patients worldwide receive Norvir, the neediest at no cost, through Abbott's Norvir Expanded Access Program.

1996:   Norvir receives accelerated FDA approval, making it available to patients with early and advanced HIV.

1997:   Norvir is one of the first protease inhibitors to received FDA approval for use in children; launches Similac Advance, an improved version of Similac.

1998:   Introduces diabetes-specific nutritional products Glucerna shakes and snack bars.

1999:   Norvir receives full FDA approval; Kaletra Early Access Program reaches its first patients outside the United States.

Source: Reprinted with permission from the Abbott Web site: http://www.abbott.com; slightly modified to conform to house style.

Abbott and AIDS: The Early Stages

Abbott was one of the first companies on the scene when the AIDS crisis erupted in the early 1980s. By 1985, almost 8,500 cases of AIDS had been diagnosed in the United States, with 4,000 deaths since the virus had emerged. Approximately 113 of the deaths had been attributed to blood contaminated with the virus.[12] In 1985, Abbott became the first company to be licensed by the government to produce and sell a test that would detect the AIDS virus. Given FDA approval, in March of 1985, Abbott embarked on an intense production effort and "compress[ed] six weeks of work into two days,"[13] distributing the test to more than 100 U.S. blood banks. Soon after, four other companies joined Abbott in the commercialization of an HIV screening test. The American Red Cross, which collected six million units of blood, approximately half of the total annual amount, used the Abbott HIV screening test.[14] Abbott was soon the market leader, with 60% of the HIV screening test market. Despite some bumps in the road (e.g., Abbott's AIDS test was not 100% accurate; there was a patent dispute between France and the United States in 1986), the company introduced an improved and more effective test in 1987, which was used by the American Red Cross and 75% of U.S. blood banks over the next decade.

From the early stages of the AIDS crisis, Abbott embarked on intense research. Robert A. Schoellhorn, who was serving as the company's chairman and CEO, at the time, commented on Abbott's efforts:

> AIDS research was made one of our highest corporate priorities, even before the virus was identified. We have applied the resources to this project that we believe will make effective and economical tests available as soon as humanly possible . . . the spirit of cooperation between industry, government, and the medical community remains strong.[15]

By 1988, Abbott's AIDS test was "an increasingly significant portion of the company's diagnostics operations, expected to post revenues in the range of $1.3 billion."[16]

By mid-1990, Abbott had developed an experimental protease inhibitor, called A-74704, which blocked replication of the AIDS virus. HIV protease inhibitors, which lowered the viral load carried by AIDS patients, were considered the first breakthrough in a decade of AIDS research.

In 1996, the FDA approved Abbott's protease inhibitor,[17] Norvir (ritonavir), in a record-breaking 72 days. The drug was lauded for its effectiveness in treating AIDS (and later in boosting the potency of other protease inhibitors) and for its safety and effectiveness. The following year, nine Abbott scientists won National Inventor of the Year awards for their research and development of the protease inhibitor. Norvir contributed to the changing landscape of the AIDS crisis; no longer was the presence of HIV an immediate death sentence.

Kaletra was Abbott's blockbuster follow-on drug to Norvir. It was a combination of the new chemical lopinavir and Norvir (ritonavir) and enabled higher HIV-fighting levels of the drugs to circulate in the blood to block the enzymes needed for replication of the AIDS virus. Kaletra received FDA approval in September 2000, and studies showed that the drug suppressed the virus for longer than other drugs with minimal side effects. The development of Kaletra provided a much-needed boost to Abbott, which for years had lacked a promising blockbuster drug in its pipeline.[18] The drug was soon considered the gold standard in the HIV/AIDS community.

Reeta Roy, Abbott's divisional vice president for global citizenship and policy, reiterated the intensity of the company's efforts to target the disease. "For a long time," Roy said, "diagnostics tests were the only tools that doctors had in the fight against HIV/AIDS. But Abbott had scientists who cared a great deal about this issue and were very committed to stopping this virus."[19] There was a "strong association" between Abbott and the fight against HIV, said Roy. "We did a lot of outreach to the patient community to understand its needs. The relationship between the company and the community that has been most impacted by the disease . . . runs deep."

At the beginning of the HIV/AIDS crisis, said Roy, there was a "huge focus on prevention." But once epidemiologists started to better understand the virus, "larger questions were being posed not only to pharmaceutical companies but also to top agencies and minds around the world, such as UNAIDS [the Joint United Nations Programme on HIV/AIDS] and WHO [the World Health Organization]: What do we do to arrest this disease?" Treatment for those afflicted throughout the world was discussed, she said, but in the context of "How do we administer a fairly potent therapy in conditions and situations where there are limited resources, limited trained personnel, and in some cases, limited health care infrastructure? And, given the fact that it was a chronic disease, how are we able to deliver care over a period of time consistently?"[20]

The Abbott Fund

In 1951, the company established the Abbott Fund, a nonprofit philanthropic organization that would support programs in health and welfare, education, culture, art, and civic and public policy. Initially, the Abbott Fund focused on the communities where it had a site and where its employees worked. Cindy Schwab, director of global citizenship and policy and vice president of the Abbott Fund, said that the fund's activities and support evolved through the years, but that there was always a strategy for how the dollars were allocated. In the 1950s, the focus was on higher education; in the 1960s, that expanded to include hospitals, and Abbott incorporated an employee matching grant program in which the corporation matched employee gifts to nonprofit organizations. In the 1970s, the charitable efforts included community health and welfare organizations. Cultural and arts activities followed, along with civic activities in the 1990s. In 2000 and beyond, the Abbott Fund's focus would expand again, with a focus on expanding access to health care, fighting HIV/AIDS, promoting science and innovation, and strengthening communities.

Abbott: How to Address the AIDS Crisis

The enormity of the HIV/AIDS crisis made addressing it seem insurmountable. HIV and AIDS presented no easy or short-term solution. Miles White, in his new role as CEO, was committed to using the substantial scientific and financial resources of Abbott to change the course of HIV/AIDS. He charged Vice President of Public Affairs Cathy Babington and one of her senior deputies, Rick Moser, to develop a global philanthropic strategy for the Abbott Fund. Moser and the others at Abbott considered the various options, and what Abbott's long-term involvement would or should be. Whatever decision was made would necessitate a sustainable strategic model that would provide a platform for Abbott and the Abbott Fund to support patients for the foreseeable future.

In August 1999, Rick Moser, divisional vice president of corporate communications, telephoned his friend and colleague Jeff Richardson. Richardson had been the executive director of Gay Men's Health Crisis in New York City; it was the nation's largest AIDS service organization. He started doing AIDS work in 1983 as a volunteer, and was a natural choice to help Abbott set up a philanthropic program to address the HIV/AIDS crisis. He was familiar with Abbott's commitment to tackling the HIV/AIDS crisis, he was well respected and "he'd been around AIDS from the beginning."[21] Richardson knew the territory well and he was "very passionate about the fight against AIDS."

A year later, Richardson was hired as the Abbott Fund's first executive director for its HIV/AIDS philanthropic programs.

Drugs: "Only Part of the Response"

Abbott announced a new program called "Abbott Access," through which it would sell its two AIDS drugs, Norvir and Kaletra, and its rapid HIV test at a loss in the 69 least developed countries, including all of Africa. But it was clear that simply supplying HIV-related drugs and tests would have little value if a country's health care infrastructure were incapable of delivering care to the masses. The reality on the ground was that many of the countries in sub-Saharan Africa did not have enough health care workers to treat the escalating number of HIV/AIDS patients and prescribe the life-saving drugs.

Treatment issues were compounded by the fact that much of the HIV-infected population lived in remote areas with no electricity, contaminated water, poor roads, no health facilities within walking distance, and little food to provide nourishment and help with the absorption of these high-powered HIV drugs. The constraints were real, but the stakes were high.

Although some AIDS activist organizations pushed Abbott and other pharmaceutical companies to donate medicines to developing nations, Miles White said, "As critical as it is, providing drugs is only one part of a much larger response that is needed. Fighting AIDS in a sustainable manner means putting partnerships and community engagement at the center of all of our initiatives."[22]

Defining the Philanthropic Options

Richardson and Moser considered a number of philanthropic options that could make a difference and define the focus for Abbott and the Abbott Fund's charitable programs. Although the cause was humanitarian, it was considered important that the programs align strategically with Abbott's leadership in the HIV/AIDS arena. Discussions were far-reaching and included input from many AIDS advocates and thought leaders. How much could Abbott reasonably do, where did it start, what should it do, and what competencies could Abbott and the Abbott Fund bring to bear on the issue? The strategy needed to be thought through completely because it would guide future Abbott Fund investments.

Orphans and Vulnerable Children

In 2000, the United Nations described Africa as "a continent of orphans." More than 12 million children had been orphaned by HIV/AIDS in sub-Saharan Africa. UNAIDS (Joint United Nations Programme on HIV/AIDS) predicted that by 2010, between 25 million and 50 million African children, from newborns to age 15, would be orphans. In a dozen African countries, up to one-quarter of the nation's children would be orphans.

The statistics on the orphaned and vulnerable children were startling. Who was going to care for and raise 12 million children and ensure that they were healthy, educated, and protected from lives of servitude or prostitution? How would these parentless children look after their siblings or their own children? The HIV/AIDS pandemic had marginalized and made vulnerable an entire generation of children in sub-Saharan Africa. This was an area of overwhelming unmet need. The social and economic implications of huge numbers of orphans without help and without hope were unfathomable.

Richardson and Moser believed this was an area where the Abbott Fund could make a significant and sustainable contribution.

Defining the Abbott Fund's HIV/AIDS Programs

Moser and Richardson met with many of the involved parties, including Abbott's marketing, research and development, and various regulatory and medical departments to define a program and build a coalition.[23]

It was, however, not as easy a sell as had been expected. Moser gave all members of the group credit for good ideas:

> The majority of the people in the room saw it very differently. Most wanted to work around funding the development of consensus HIV/AIDS treatment guidelines for the developing world, which they thought was more in line with Abbott's strengths. There were a lot of people in the room who thought that it was a more substantive thing in the long term to run a program that would guide the treatment of people.

It was a worthy idea, Moser said, but "not what [Richardson] and I felt the company was trying to accomplish with this program. So we had a lot of negotiation and coalition-building to do with the group."[24]

Convincing senior management of the value of this focus was easier.

> We'd been chartered by senior management to create a program, and we convinced them that we were thinking about it the right way and that this was the right thing for the

company to do. Management asked some tough questions about how the program was going to work and so forth, but they were extremely supportive and in the end, committed to a multiyear philanthropic program.[25]

The Chosen Path

The Abbott Fund officially launched the Program for Orphans and Vulnerable Children in June of 2000. The program assisted orphans and vulnerable children infected and affected by HIV/AIDS as well as the communities that cared for them. There would be model programs in Burkina Faso, India, Tanzania, and Romania that would address four interrelated areas: health care services and infrastructure; voluntary HIV counseling and testing; education; and basic community needs, such as the provision of clean water.

In early 2000, the Abbott Fund brought in an Irish private consultancy group, Axios, which had expertise in setting up and implementing HIV programs in the developing world, to help refine the programs in select countries.

Choosing Locations for the Pilot Program

The fund wanted both geographical and programmatic diversity. Richardson said that, in choosing the countries in which to launch the program, the Abbott Fund looked for the criteria of political stability; government commitment to and ability to host the program; a history of functioning and thriving nongovernmental organizations (NGOs) and grass-roots organizations; and the country's HIV/AIDS incidence level. The first two criteria eliminated many of the countries. Tanzania, however, became an immediately apparent good choice because it was politically stable; the country had never had a civil war. In addition, under the leadership of President Benjamin Mkapa, the Tanzanian government was already investigating health care reform and strategies to address HIV and AIDS among its population; each year, 7% to 8% of the Tanzanian population was diagnosed with new infections. Few donors and organizations were focusing on Tanzania; the focus up to then had been on South Africa and its immediate neighbors. (See Exhibit 3.1.3 for detailed information about Tanzania.)

Taking Steps Forward

In June 2000, Moser, Richardson, and other Abbott executives made their first visit to Tanzania, where Abbott officially announced the program locally. Information about the new program was also available at the International AIDS Conference in Durban, South Africa, that July. Richardson said the introduction of the program was deliberately very low key. "We had a few photos in the Abbott booth, and we spoke to people as they came to the exhibit. We let them know that we were just embarking upon this program." Modest publicity and a low profile were deliberate. "We've been very concerned from day one that we wanted to report on our program *after* we had some concrete results. That principle continues to guide our efforts."[26]

Abbott decided to work with three partners at the outset: Baylor College of Medicine, which had already distinguished itself in pediatric AIDS; the U.K.-based International HIV/AIDS Alliance, which had a young but established program in India and Burkina Faso; and Ireland-based Axios, which employed existing strategic counselors. The partner organizations, Richardson said, had various levels of experience and expertise. For example, Baylor was focused on HIV-infected children who needed care and treatment. The Abbott Fund started

Exhibit 3.1.3 Tanzania

One of the poorest countries in the world, the Eastern African country of Tanzania (formed when the two countries of Tanganyika and Zanzibar merged in 1964) achieved independence from Britain in the early 1960s. With few natural resources or minerals, there was not the marked contrast between rich and poor that characterized many other developing countries. Starting in 1985, its leaders worked, with some success and by liberalizing the economy, to attract foreign investment and loans from the World Bank and the International Monetary Fund. Despite painful fiscal reforms, the economy nonetheless grew. Despite topography that limited cultivated crops to only 4% of the land, Tanzania's economy depended heavily on agriculture. Tourism was also a major industry in Tanzania; attractions included Kilimanjaro (Africa's highest mountain) and the famed Serengeti National Park. AIDS cases in Tanzania were first reported in 1983, and the disease spread quickly through the country. By 1999, there were an estimated 1.3 million AIDS cases and that year saw approximately 140,000 AIDS-related deaths. Tanzania's AIDS prevalence rate was 8.8%, higher than the average prevalence rate of the whole sub-Saharan region (7.5%) as well as the global rate (1.1%). The Abbott Fund, Axios, and International Alliance worked closely with the Tanzanian government in an attempt to set up programs to treat and eradicate the disease.

Source: UNAIDS/Economic Commission for Africa, "AIDS in Africa," Africa Development Forum 2000, Geneva, December 2000, 221.

Tanzania's response to the AIDS crisis would become even more serious in 2001, when it created the Tanzanian Commission for AIDS (TACAIDS). TACAIDS was responsible for guiding policy, acting as a clearinghouse for AIDS activities nationwide, and for mobilizing additional funds to fight the epidemic. Tanzania would receive kudos from the Joint United Nations Program on HIV/AIDS (UNAIDS) in 2001 for moving quickly to address AIDS. "Not only has it mainstreamed HIV/AIDS issues into development strategies, but the government has also placed AIDS high on its expenditure agenda by giving it high priority for resource mobilization and allocation. This is a clear indication of how seriously it takes the epidemic."

Source: UNAIDS Press Release, 9 February 2001, http://www.aegis.com/news/usis/2001/US010203.html (accessed 15 November 2006).

with Baylor in Romania by helping build their first outpatient pediatric AIDS clinic, which later became a model for several other Baylor clinics in the developing world.

By the end of 2000, the Abbott Fund grants were distributed and the money started to flow. The program, said Richardson, "was getting its sea legs and starting to take off."[27]

Implementing the Tanzania Program

In Tanzania, the first step was meeting with Minister of Social Welfare Anna Abdallah, and signing a memorandum of understanding. "There was excitement and enthusiasm about the program in the ministry,"[28] according to Reeta Roy, divisional vice president of global citizenship and policy, who oversaw the Abbott Fund. Rather than starting in the capital of Dar es Salaam, the government suggested the Abbott Fund start in the Mbeya province in southwestern Tanzania because that was the area with the greatest need. In Mbeya, the Abbott Fund program representatives met with local officials who could provide insight into the needs of the health, education, and social welfare systems.

The first intervention was in health care, but the Abbott Fund took a broader perspective. "Just because it's a health issue," Roy said, "you can't just look narrowly at the health care system. With children, you need to start in school and link the school system to the health system."[29] To do so, they trained teachers and used simple interventions including the provision of first aid kits and helping teachers and the community to identify which children were susceptible to problems. "When you lift up one school," said Roy, "you lift up everybody, including those children"[30] who are HIV-positive.

In Tukuyu, a small village in southwest Tanzania, the Abbott Fund looked at how it could help the Kipande Elementary School, which was the center of the community because it provided educational, nutritional, and other support for the children. The Abbott Fund supported newly renovated classrooms and teachers' quarters, new latrines, school supplies, a community garden, a school kitchen and dining hall, and a new water-harvesting system to provide clean drinking water. Within a year, attendance increased from 50% to 94%, and the school's academic ranking soared to the top in its district.

"The payback, if you want to call it that, is enormous," Roy said. "When kids go to school and graduate to the next level, it has an impact on the community, the children, the parents, and the local leaders. District officials are able to share what works." In short, she said, investing in schools "pays dividends for the entire community."[31]

"I Learned More in 10 Minutes . . ."

In April 2002, Miles White visited Tanzania to see the program's progress firsthand. It was, he wrote, "One of the most informative, productive, humbling, and uplifting trips I have ever made."[32] White traveled to several different small villages. In talking to doctors in these villages, White said, "I learned more in 10 minutes there than I had in reading all the newspapers and reports."[33] In addition, he toured the Muhimbili National Hospital, the country's teaching hospital, in the capital of Dar es Salaam. There, he saw the serious issues preventing effective health care: poor infrastructure, overcrowding, no place to counsel patients in private, the laboratory in disrepair, inexperienced or ineffective management, and little to no funding and support, not just for HIV/AIDS care and treatment but for basic care as well.

White returned from this trip committed to expanding the Abbott Fund's efforts in Tanzania and, more specifically, to help modernize the country's health care infrastructure. He announced plans to partner with Tanzania's Ministry of Health over the next five years in order to restore the laboratory in Muhimbili, build an HIV center (an outpatient clinic and counseling/support facilities), create a national HIV teaching center, and introduce pharmacy, health information, and management systems. While acknowledging the enormity of the task of addressing HIV/AIDS in developing countries, White said in an interview that he believed in small steps. "I saw the [AIDS] problem as something you can do something about, but only a hospital at a time, a clinic at a time, a village at a time."[34]

Indeed, Reeta Roy said that it was Miles White's visit to Tanzania that helped crystallize the thinking around what the company would do next. White not only wanted to elevate Muhimbili's level of care, but also to look at how the Abbott Fund could help expand HIV/AIDS counseling and testing across the country and implement a program to help prevent mother-to-child transmission, an important part of the company's overall philanthropic approach to HIV/AIDS. Upon his return, White announced that he would invest $100 million over the next five years to combat the HIV/AIDS pandemic. Richardson explained that this commitment underscored White's promise to be a leader in AIDS research and the provision of top quality AIDS drugs and also to be a leader in the AIDS philanthropic world.

Tanzania Care and "Back Office Work"

In 2003, the Abbott Fund began its Tanzania program to help modernize the country's health infrastructure and systems. Roy said that the Abbott Fund did extensive research on how it could help. "We went to Muhimbili, sat down with the CEO, and did a needs assessment."[35] The needs seemed endless and there were many fundamental management questions about how to run a complex organization efficiently and cost-effectively. What initially was perceived as simply building an HIV/AIDS clinic, said Roy, became much more complicated after the needs assessment.

Abbott donated consultants' time to Muhimbili in the form of employee volunteers who had expertise in hospital administration to work with the hospital CEO to identify a number of issues, including management and accountability problems. Other recommendations included revamping the finance department, introducing IT systems into day-to-day operations, instituting a building maintenance program, and making the kitchen and laundry more efficient. "There were enormous logistics operations . . . a lot of work needed to be done on the core back-office hospital functions," Roy said.[36] The Abbott consultants analyzed these logistical issues, and then presented the options to the hospital administration. The results were remarkable. Once the roles and responsibilities were defined and select personnel changes made, said Roy, hospital administration immediately ran more smoothly.

Limited data-sharing in the hospital's operations had affected the finances of the hospital and prevented transparency of operations. For example, nobody could determine how many patients were admitted and were being treated. This had implications for revenue collection, pharmacy operations, and basic but vital information needs, such as the correct correlation between patient diagnosis and prescribed medication. Abbott employee volunteers put together a Request for Proposal for an IT system and helped assess the proposals that were returned. The hospital selected the vendor and the Abbott Fund financed the hospital's new $2 million IT system.

Having visited the Muhimbili Hospital early on, Roy knew firsthand the dismal conditions. In the patient information storage room, for example, "literally from the floor to the ceiling, there were reams and reams and reams of paper and patient files. I don't know how anyone could find anything in there."[37] When the IT system was finally installed and staff were trained, the increased efficiency was dramatic. Admission personnel knew exactly how many beds were available, and once a patient was admitted, information (e.g., diagnosis, prescribed medication) was accurately and instantly available. Almost every operation in the hospital was positively affected, and staff could identify and address different patterns: drug consumption in the hospital or disease incidence, for example.

With financial grants and support from highly skilled Abbott employee volunteers, the Abbott Fund built an outpatient clinic at the hospital for all patients including those with HIV/AIDS. The AIDS clinic, which had been a mere shed at the corner of the hospital, was small and depressing, with people lying throughout the narrow corridors. Many people would not come for treatment for fear of being seen, because it was clear that anyone entering was an HIV/AIDS patient, and the stigma was still significant. When the new outpatient center was built, it served everybody, not just HIV/AIDS patients, which helped alleviate the embarrassment patients felt when entering. For the first time, HIV/AIDS patients were fully integrated into the hospital's outpatient center. The new facility was three stories, 40,000 square feet, and served hundreds of patients daily. In addition, the center included more than 30 patient examination rooms, a pharmacy, and training facilities for medical students and health care professionals.

The Abbott Fund also renovated Muhimbili Hospital's laboratory facilities, converting the dilapidated space into a 54,000-square-foot state-of-the-art laboratory with the most modern diagnostic equipment.

As part of the Muhimbili initiative, more than 4,300 health care workers were trained in effective HIV/AIDS patient care, including testing, counseling, and treatment. Two hundred physicians eventually served as trainers for other professional health staff. The Abbott Fund supported the training of 1,800 staff members to use the new computer system. In addition, more than 150 staff members were trained in laboratory equipment operations, 200 senior doctors and hospital directors received management training, and key personnel were sponsored to receive MBAs.

Dramatic Growth and Global Focus

The dramatic growth of the Abbott Fund HIV/AIDS programs suggested a strategic turning point for the Abbott Fund, transforming it from a domestic philanthropic program to one with a global focus, now aligned with Abbott's international business focus. By 2003, nearly $20 million from the Abbott Fund was being invested in its developing-world AIDS programs.

What Lies Ahead?

In 2005, U.S. Secretary of Health and Human Services Tommy G. Thompson visited Muhimbili National Hospital and saw firsthand the impact of Abbott and the Abbott Fund programs. Thompson likened Abbott's efforts to "paving the road that would allow the metaphorical trucks bringing financial support from the United States and other development partners to deliver and expedite the care and treatment so desperately needed."

"That was a profound statement," said Reeta Roy, Abbott's divisional vice president for global citizenship and policy. "When I look at where Tanzania is today in terms of their national plan, the number of people that have enrolled in treatment plans . . . it's not that our work is done, but I think our work has really accelerated assistance from other countries and organizations."

The partnership between Abbott and the government of Tanzania that had begun with President Mkapa's administration continued to flourish under the leadership of the new government of President Kikwete. As a demonstration of Abbott's long-term commitment to Tanzania, in 2007, the Abbott Fund opened its first office outside Abbott headquarters in Illinois. The new office in Dar es Salaam, led by Divisional Vice President Christy Wistar, oversaw the expanding number of philanthropic projects in Tanzania. Wistar summed up the rationale for the new office: "When you live and work here in Tanzania, you are confronted by the daily challenges and struggles of HIV/AIDS. As part of the community, you see opportunities to help in ways you could never see or contemplate from your desk at headquarters."

In June 2007, Abbott CEO Miles White returned to Tanzania for the third time and joined high-level Tanzanian government officials to dedicate the Abbott Fund's latest project, the newly modernized Mt. Meru Regional Laboratory in Arusha. The dedication gave White the opportunity to announce the Abbott Fund's future plans to modernize the 23 regional laboratories across Tanzania. By the end of 2007, the Abbott Fund had invested more than $50 million in Tanzania alone, strengthening and modernizing the health care infrastructure and systems countrywide. Also in 2007, one out of three patients on HIV therapy in Tanzania received care from one of the 90 facilities across Tanzania that benefited from Abbott Fund support. Tanzania, because of the work of Abbott and the Abbott Fund, now had a much higher profile, and the U.S. government, through the President's Emergency Plan for AIDS Relief (PEPFAR), had promised to deliver more than $300 million in assistance to Tanzania in 2008.

The Abbott Fund continued to deepen its investment in Muhimbili National Hospital. Two new projects were planned for 2008: a water project to ensure the hospital had sufficient quantities of high-quality water, and an extensive renovation of the hospital's emergency

Exhibit 3.1.4 Projects of the Public-Private Partnership

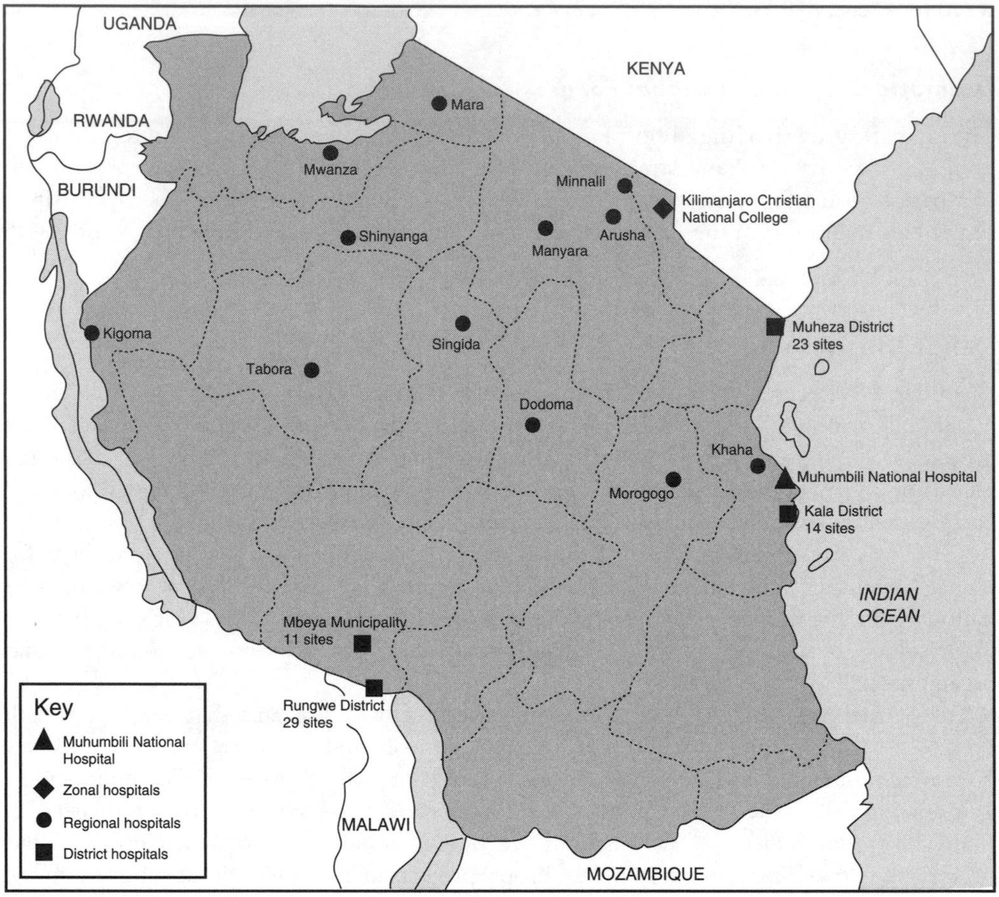

Source: Abbott Web site http://www.abbottglobalcare.org/sections/Strengthening/improvements.html.

department. The Abbott Fund planned to continue its support of numerous programs and organizations that were working to prevent mother-to-child transmission of HIV/AIDS and deliver effective care and treatment to HIV-infected patients. The Abbott Fund also supported programs that provided the basic needs of orphans and vulnerable children in Tanzania and elsewhere in Africa and India. See Exhibit 3.1.4 for projects and improvements throughout Tanzania that were part of the public-private partnership between the government of Tanzania and the Abbott Fund.

Reeta Roy said that the payoff of these programs for Abbott was huge: "I've really come to respect the impact it has on the culture of our organization." Abbott Fund employees on the ground and the Abbott employee volunteers, Roy said, had been profoundly affected by the experience to give back. "It illustrates what our mission is really all about. It's not just our products, but we realize that we can leverage the expertise of our people and the financial support of our organization to make a real difference."[38]

Philanthropy may have been what had opened the door, Roy explained, but "what's come back through the other side of the door is much richer for the organization. There have been some big bumps in the road as well, but the journey's been very exciting."[39]

Notes

* This case was prepared by Senior Ethics Research Associate Jenny Mead under the supervision of Patricia H. Werhane, Ruffin Professor of Business Ethics. It was written as a basis for class discussion rather than to illustrate effective or ineffective handling of an administrative situation. Copyright © 2008 by the University of Virginia Darden School Foundation, Charlottesville, VA. All rights reserved.

1 Human immunodeficiency virus (HIV) causes acquired immune deficiency syndrome (AIDS); the illness compromises the body's ability to combat infection, making it prone to opportunistic infections that can be deadly.

2 The name Norvir is derived from "no viruses."

3 "A Brief History of Bristol-Myers Squibb," http://www.bms.com/aboutbms/content/data/ourhis.html (accessed 18 September 2007).

4 Richard Moser, telephone interview conducted by author, 11 May 2007.

5 Moser interview.

6 Moser interview.

7 Moser interview.

8 Anne Christiansen Bullers, "Living With AIDS—20 Years Later," *FDA Consumer* 35, no. 6 (November–December 2001).

9 UNAIDS Joint United Nations Programme on HIV/AIDS, "AIDS Epidemic Update: December 1998," 1, http://www.aegis.com/files/unaids/WADDec1998_epidemic_report.pdf (accessed 21 February 2008).

10 Eyitope O. Ogunbodede, "HIV/AIDS Situation in Africa," *International Dental Journal*, 54 (2004): 352.

11 "Miles White of Abbott Laboratories: On the Mend," Euromoney Institutional Investor PLC, *Institutional Investor* (March 2005): 1.

12 Robert Pear, "AIDS Test to Be Available in 2 to 6 Weeks," *New York Times*, 3 March 1985, 23.

13 PR Newswire, "Abbott Laboratories Has Provided More Than 100 Major Blood Banks with AIDS Test Kids," 7 March 1985.

14 Marilyn Chase and Joe Davidson, "Abbott Labs Receives First U.S. License for AIDS Test to Screen Blood Donors," *Wall Street Journal*, 5 March 1985.

15 PR Newswire, "Abbott Labs Reports Promising Research Underway on Diagnostic Tests for AIDS," 31 July 1985.

16 Barbara Marsh, "Abbott Eyes Doubled Market with its New AIDS Virus Test," *Crains Chicago Business* 11, no. 17 (25 April 1988): section 1.

17 Protease inhibitors block enzymes in HIV, and their use in combination with other drugs resulted in a sharp decline in AIDS-related deaths in the 1990s.

18 Bruce Japsen, "New AIDS Drug to Boost Illinois-Based Abbott Laboratories, Analysts Say," *Chicago Tribune*, 19 September 2000.

19 Reeta Roy, telephone interview conducted by Jenny Mead and Patricia H. Werhane, 23 March 2007.

20 Roy interview.

21 Rick Moser, interview conducted by author, 11 May 2007.

22 Miles D. White, "Fighting AIDS in Africa," *In All Things*, Fall/Winter 2002, Office of Social and International Ministries at the United States Jesuit Conference. Available at http://www.globalhealth.org/reports/text.php3?id=82 (accessed 30 October 2007).

23 Jeff Richardson, telephone interview conducted by author, 23 April 2007.

24 Moser interview.

25 Moser interview.

26 Richardson interview.

27 Richardson interview.

28 Reeta Roy, telephone interview conducted by author, 23 March 2007.

29 Roy interview.

30 Roy interview.

31 Roy interview

32 Miles D. White, "Fighting AIDS in Africa."

33 Michael Waldholz, "Abbott Labs Improves Its Efforts to Combat AIDS in Africa," *Wall Street Journal*, 27 June 2002, D4.

34 Waldholz.

35 Roy interview.

36 Roy interview
37 Roy interview
38 Reeta Roy, telephone interview conducted by author, 23 March 2007.
39 Roy interview.

3.2 HealthReach and HABLA[*]

When Jim Zimmerman became the executive director of HealthReach clinic in 2004, he was faced with revamping the tight budget and choosing which of the free clinic's programs to expand. HealthReach was the only free clinic serving the uninsured poor in the Lake County, Illinois, area. The clinic offered traditional primary and preventive health care and was developing several other programs, including a primary care clinic for women and an eye care clinic for diabetic patients. One of several promising programs was Healthcare Access by Language Advocacy (HABLA), a medical interpretation program developed in 2001 to bridge the frustrating language gap between the volunteer medical staff and their Hispanic patients, many of whom spoke little or no English.

Barriers to Healthcare

In 2004, there were 50 million non-English speakers in the United States and an additional 22 million who had marginal English proficiency. These two groups intersected broadly with the 45.8 million people living in the country who had little to no medical insurance.[1] Although there were no precise national figures, the population of medically uninsured, non-English-speaking individuals was significant.

Nationally, this language gap led medical experts to estimate that injuries and serious illnesses as a result of medical miscommunication and delayed treatment numbered in the thousands every year. In a case reported by the Medical College of Wisconsin, miscommunication between the health care professional and the patient led to a delay of treatment resulting in a ruptured aneurysm and quadriplegia.[2] In another instance, a 17-year-old girl was faced with informing her aging grandfather that he was in the final stages of liver cancer because the patient was unable to understand his physician.[3]

In the early 21st century, national health care costs rose steeply as a result of numerous legislative and economic factors, and the cost to the uninsured was increasing faster than the average cost to those who were insured. Although the seriously ill were rarely refused medical aid, the bills that resulted from such care could financially devastate a family. Additionally, the cost of emergency care necessitated by delayed treatment usually greatly exceeded the cost of preventative care. The high cost of emergency care for the uninsured contributed heavily to the rising cost of health care nationwide.

Whereas insured patients had the benefit of the collective bargaining power of massive companies such as Aetna, the uninsured had little leverage and often had to choose between medical care and food and shelter. Although it would seem that employers and unions were the primary advocates for medically insured patients, they were only one link in a larger bargaining chain that made medical care more affordable for the average insured family. After employee advocate groups negotiated a premium, the insurance giants then used the collective power of all of their clients to lower the price of health care in hospitals and doctor's offices. Massive medical insurance companies represented the purchasing power of thousands or even millions of patients, and sometimes paid less than 10% of what an uninsured patient might pay.

The Free Clinic Model

In the last several decades of the 20th century, communities across the country responded to the growing health care crisis in America by establishing private free clinics to provide low- or no-cost health care to the uninsured.[4] Free clinics were rarely equipped to offer emergency care, but focused on primary and preventive medicine, specifically targeting chronic conditions such as diabetes, which often required a long-term, expensive regimen of medicine and examinations. These clinics sometimes were able to fund small dispensaries or licensed pharmacies, but expansion for free clinics was often piecemeal and standardization between organizations was nonexistent and virtually impossible.

Free clinic funding generally came from private and corporate donations, extremely limited federal grants, and the United Way. Sometimes, clinics were attached to hospitals or universities as a part of the organization or as the result of an endowment. The clinics constantly had to focus on fundraising, as few, if any, were self-sustaining. Some clinics established endowments that provided a partially self-sustaining stream of income, but still required extensive donations to fund operations, pharmacies, and expansion as the rapidly increasing number of uninsured Americans strained the free clinics' resources.

Lake County Health Care

As of 2000, 76,000 Lake County, Illinois, residents spoke Spanish in the home. More than half of those residents had limited English-language proficiency and had little to no access to primary medical care.[5] Before HealthReach opened in 1992, these residents, as well as other medically uninsured Lake County residents, relied largely on local hospital emergency rooms for emergency care, and were regularly unable to obtain care that would have prevented emergency room visits altogether.

The HealthReach Clinic

Founded in 1992, the HealthReach clinic had a mission to provide primary and preventative medical care as well as referral services to patients who needed surgical or otherwise specialized attention not offered at the clinic. It offered primary and preventative medical care to the medically underserved of Lake County, Illinois, operating two clinics, in Waukegan and Mundelein. The primary HealthReach clinic catered to a patient population that was 75% Hispanic. At the nearby Mundelein clinic, Hispanics accounted for more than 95% of patients. The majority of patients at both clinics had limited to no proficiency in English.

HealthReach distinguished itself from traditional free clinics by offering additional care to patients in the form of programs specifically targeted at diabetics, pregnant women, and non-English speakers. By offering these programs, HealthReach was able to serve patients who might otherwise be left untreated until their conditions worsened or even became life-threatening. The development and maintenance of these programs were costly and drew heavily on the clinic's tight budget.

The HABLA Program

In 2001, HealthReach's Dr. Richard Keller, with the assistance of Coordinator Mariela Hernandez, founded the HABLA initiative to address the language gap between medical professionals and patients in the organization's two free clinics. From its inception, the HABLA program trained Spanish- and English-speaking personnel to facilitate patient-doctor communication at the clinic. Initial funding for the project came from the Catholic Campaign for Human Development as and from federal grant funding. In writing a proposal for the grant, which was specifically intended for job training and development programs, Keller partnered with "SER – Jobs for Progress National, Inc.," a national nonprofit employment resource organization that catered largely to unemployed or underemployed Hispanics. The grant requested funds to establish a job training program at HealthReach. At its inception, the goal for the nascent program, which eventually would become HABLA, was to teach local Spanish speakers the skills necessary to enter the rapidly expanding medical interpretation field.

Before the advent of HABLA at HealthReach, Spanish-speaking patients, who made up three-quarters of HealthReach's patient population, were often unable to communicate with staff members directly. Medical staff members attempting to communicate serious illness or complex pharmaceutical regimens were often forced to use patients' children or relatives to interpret what they said, without assurance the information was being communicated accurately. The goal for the program that eventually became HABLA was to train and certify personnel to serve as a liaison between health care professional and patient, ensuring accurate information was delivered by personnel trained both to explain the specifics of a patient's health care program and to consider the delicacy of the information they had to communicate.

The initial funding supported three years of operating expenses for the HABLA program. With that funding, the center began developing a series of educational modules that would facilitate training new interpreters in both English and Spanish medical terminology, and preparing them for patient interaction. The first years of the program's operations produced several dozen certified medical interpreters, but as funding dwindled, self-sustainability seemed a long way off.

As 2004 drew to a close, Zimmerman had several choices. He could divert funds from another of the clinic's initiatives to the HABLA program; seek funding from a private source; or let HABLA's funding run out, leaving its future in question. If HABLA were not funded, the Spanish-speaking poor of Lake County would continue to suffer from the language gap that existed between them and their health care professionals. If HABLA were funded, Zimmerman faced an interesting challenge: If HealthReach could operate HABLA and other programs while maintaining its free clinic business model, it could become a nationwide model for free clinics. It would also meet the needs of the tens of thousands of uninsured Spanish speakers in the Lake County area and possibly expand the HABLA program to other regions. But if HealthReach failed to meet the budget demands of traditional and specialty operations, the clinic could disappear altogether, leaving their poor and uninsured patients without access to affordable health care.

In late 2004, the HealthReach's HABLA program was one of several initiatives facing extinction due to budget constraints. The program had produced a number of successes and presented interesting expansion possibilities, such as the development of more precise training materials in order to produce larger classes of HABLA certified interpreters from the local community. But the funding generated during HABLA's development was drying up, and executive director Jim Zimmerman was forced to consider suspending the program. He decided to approach the Abbott Fund, one of the organizations that helped fund HABLA in 1992 and had served as an invaluable strategic partner in its growth and development.

As Zimmerman discussed program opportunities with two members of the Abbott Fund team, he outlined several possible initiatives for funding. The first was a much-needed care center for pregnant women in the Lake County area. Second was an eye care center focused on treating patients with diabetes. Finally, Zimmerman discussed the promising and invaluable HABLA program. As he outlined the program, both Abbott representatives expressed considerable enthusiasm for it. As the meeting drew to a close, Zimmerman was hopeful that the HABLA program would be a primary candidate for sponsorship. Indeed, the Abbott Fund became a sponsor of HABLA, pledging $100,000, to be split over two years, which would keep the program afloat and support its expansion.

Abbott and the Abbott Fund

The Abbott Fund was a nonprofit philanthropic arm of Abbott Laboratories, a global leader in health care with a decades-long history of corporate social responsibility (CSR). Founded in 1951, the fund initially was active primarily in the communities in which its employees lived and worked; it invested in community vitality initiatives (such as HABLA), innovative medical research, and other programs that would expand access to and promote the science of health care.[6] The fund also had an Executive Service Corps composed of volunteers, many of them retired executives, who gave their services to programs in need of leadership and consulting. Over the years, the Abbott Fund's reach grew global and contributed to the fight against the spread of AIDS in Africa and malnutrition in Vietnam[7] and to disaster relief of an international scope.

Expanding HABLA

Using the funds, Zimmerman and the program's coordinator, Mariela Hernandez, developed a series of training tools to facilitate training and prepare for the growth of training classes. The initial training course, a self-guided study of 10 modules culminating in a series of real-life tests, proved valuable and practical for students. For a low fee, candidates for the medical interpretation program could purchase the textbook and medical terminology dictionary and study at their own pace. They would then take a written exam and, finally, be tested in a real-life interpretation situation.

Although the course material for the first HABLA trainees was successful in producing a number of HABLA-certified medical interpreters, the program was unwieldy and difficult to scale for larger numbers of students. Using the funds provided by Abbott, the HealthReach staff devised a series of advanced materials. Working locally, HealthReach found bilingual actors and used transcripts of actual doctor-patient interactions to film a DVD exam that could be administered to more candidates. The combination written and oral exam streamlined the certification process. With Abbott's funding and under the direction of Zimmerman and Hernandez, the HABLA program continued to expand.

Media Attention

In March 2006, the HealthReach clinic and the HABLA program caught the attention of the Telemundo news network, which aired a two-part human-interest piece. In the following days, the clinic was inundated with phone calls from several hundred candidates seeking entry into the program. Realizing the potential of the program for commercial success, Zimmerman and HealthReach staff began to draw plans to promote the HABLA program as a regional model for professional interpretation programs and fuel the expansion of the clinic and program.

Legislative Initiative

In concert with the expansion of the HABLA program, Zimmerman and Hernandez collaborated with lifetime Lake County resident and Illinois Senator Terry Link to create statewide legislation that would standardize requirements for certification in medical interpretation. The proposed legislation would boost considerably the value of the certification materials HealthReach had developed within the state of Illinois, and could possibly bring additional media recognition to the small clinic.

Achieving Sustainability

The HABLA program brought funding and media attention to HealthReach, but creating an environment in which the clinic's operations were sustainable had been a major concern for Zimmerman and the HABLA staff. To that end, Zimmerman began to draft a new series of materials that would support a much larger training program. HealthReach planned to market the materials nationwide as a certification tool for medical interpreters in multiple languages. Zimmerman hoped proceeds from sales of the HABLA program could sustain the program indefinitely.

In the meantime, the Abbott Fund's support of HealthReach operations continued to grow. In early 2007, the Abbott Fund pledged $1 million to support the clinic in a number of projects, including a renovation of the clinic's Mundelein location that would double its capacity; engineering support from Abbott employees during the renovation; a donation of $125,000 in Abbott products for dissemination to clinic patients; and a challenge grant that would give HealthReach an incentive to reach out to other strategic partners for support.

Notes

*   This case was prepared by Justin Sheehan under the supervision of Patricia H. Werhane, Ruffin Professor of Business Ethics, and Jenny Mead, Senior Ethics Research Associate. It was written as a basis for class discussion rather than to illustrate effective or ineffective handling of an administrative situation. Copyright © 2008 by the University of Virginia Darden School Foundation, Charlottesville, VA. All rights reserved.

1   U.S. Census Bureau, Current Population Survey, 2004 and 2005 Annual Social and Economic Supplements.

2   Medical College of Wisconsin, "Language barriers compromise health care for 50 million Americans who do not speak English," http://www.mcw.edu/display/router.asp?docid=17695 (accessed 21 October 2006).

3   MSNBC.com, "Doctors, patients struggle with language barrier." http://www.msnbc.msn.com/id/13924005/page/2/ (accessed 23 October 2006).

4   The first official American "free clinic" was the Haight Ashbury Free Medical Clinic in San Francisco, founded in 1967 when tens of thousands of youths came for the "Summer of Love" and brought with them a myriad of medical problems, most prominently the effects of drug abuse. For more information, see "A General Survey of Free Clinics as Alternatives to Existing Health Care Institutions," Office of Youth Development, http://www.eric.ed.gov/ERICDocs/data/ericdocs2sql/content_storage_01/0000019b/80/39/62/3d.pdf (accessed 22 January 2008).

5   U.S. Census Bureau, American Community Survey, Profile of Selected Social Characteristics 2000, Lake County, IL.
6   Case writer interview with Cindy Schwab, Divisional Vice President, The Abbott Fund, Abbott Park, Illinois, 1 June 2007.
7   Abbott Fund Web site, Global Citizenship – Community Vitality. http://www.abbott.com/global/ url/content/en_US/0.80.30:30/general_content/General_Content_00073.htm   (accessed 7 November 2006).

3.3 The Novartis Foundation for Sustainable Development

Tackling HIV/AIDS and Poverty in South Africa*

In 1998, sociologist Kurt Madörin from the Swiss-based NGO *terre des hommes schweiz*[1] approached Klaus Leisinger and Karin Schmitt of the Novartis Foundation for Sustainable Development in Basel, Switzerland. There was an acute problem with orphans in sub-Saharan Africa, he told Leisinger, Novartis president and executive director, and Schmitt, director of foundation affairs and special projects. With one or both parents dying from AIDS, many African children were left vulnerable to homelessness, exploitation, abuse, violence, starvation, and other dangers. There were more than 8 million AIDS orphans in Africa, a number expected to reach 42 million by 2008.[2] Being an orphan often meant being a social outcast, and orphaned children were more likely to fall into greater poverty. At the time, there was no effective solution for dealing with the crisis; these parentless children were either put into orphanages, if available; lived on the streets; or were taken care of by an NGO, which gave them food, shelter, and clothing. The result often was deep psychosocial trauma for the orphans, which no group was equipped to handle. Madörin wanted to develop a program that would help the orphaned children of Africa deal with this psychosocial trauma. He wanted to start in Tanzania, where the number of orphans who had lost both parents had risen from 71,100 in 1992 to 174,400 in 1998.[3] A pilot program in Tanzania would help him assess the feasibility and effectiveness of such a program. But he needed financial and other assistance. Madörin asked Leisinger and Schmitt if the Novartis Foundation could help. They agreed to consider the proposal, although Novartis, one of the largest pharmaceutical companies in the world, did not manufacture or sell any HIV/AIDS-related products.

The HIV/AIDS Crisis

As the close of the 20th century approached, the 20-year-old AIDS crisis had ravaged many developing countries. Particularly hard-hit was sub-Saharan Africa, called by some the "global epicenter"[4] of the crisis. Of the estimated 33.4 million people living with HIV/AIDS worldwide in 1998, 22 million of them were in sub-Saharan Africa. Already, in this area, 12 million had died and life expectancy had plummeted from 62 years to 47. See Exhibit 3.1.1 (page 35) for 1998 worldwide HIV/AIDS statistics and comparisons. Although the AIDS crisis was obviously a worldwide issue, the scale of the epidemic in Africa made "its repercussions qualitatively different from those in other parts of the world."[5] Because HIV transmission in African countries occurred primarily through heterosexual contact, AIDS was considered a family disease.

Of particular concern, and cited in a sobering 1997 U.S. Agency for International Development (USAID) report called "Children on the Brink," was the number of orphans (or "children affected by AIDS," as the specialists preferred) the pandemic created. The statistics for Africa were deeply disturbing: AIDS had accounted for 16% of the deaths that orphaned African children in 1990, but estimates were that the proportion would be 68% by 2010.[6] The USAID report forecast that by the year 2010, 40 million to 42 million children worldwide, primarily in Africa, would be without one or both parents because of HIV/AIDS. The results of being orphaned, the report continued, would include severe emotional distress, malnutrition, no health care, and a lack of identity. These orphans also would face a variety of painful futures including child labor, no education, loss of inheritance, destitution, forced migration, and a vastly increased exposure to HIV infection. Historically, the worldwide percentage of orphans was around 2%, but predictions for 2010 were as high as 17% to 25%. In addition to the devastating physical effects (e.g., starvation and abuse), of great concern also was the psychosocial trauma these orphans were experiencing.

Previously, the "orphan" problem in African countries was mitigated by the fact that children who lost their parents were taken in by other family members: The extended family was the "safety net."[7] But AIDS had overburdened and weakened this informal social structure by increasing the number of orphans, reducing the number of caregivers, and damaging the overall safety net. Paradoxically, "the effectiveness of the traditional African social system in absorbing millions of vulnerable children has contributed to the complacency of governments and agencies in addressing the orphan crisis."[8]

Novartis

Novartis was the product of a record-breaking 1996 merger between "two Swiss giants of the pharmaceutical world"[9] and long-time competitors, Ciba-Geigy and Sandoz. The histories of the companies that formed Novartis in 1998 dated back to the 18th and 19th centuries. In addition to pharmaceutical products, Ciba-Geigy produced, among other things, pesticides, photographic products, eye care items, and synthetic plastics and resins. Sandoz specialized in pharmaceutical products, various industrial-use chemicals, infant and diet foods, and distribution of agricultural raw materials. Both companies had also acquired a number of U.S. biotech and genomics companies (Sandoz had a large stake in both Genetic Therapy and Systemix; Ciba-Geigy in Viagene and Chiron), although profits from these were not expected until at least 2006.[10] The merger, announced in early 1996 and officially sanctioned by the U.S. Federal Trade Commission in December of that year, was a seismic transaction, worth more than USD30 billion.[11] It took many people by surprise because the two companies had long been competitors, although their physical locations' being just across the Rhine River from each other allowed them to "stare into each other's labs from buildings on opposite banks of the river that flows through Basel."[12]

The merger made Novartis the second-largest drug company after Glaxo Wellcome. At the time, in the mid-1990s, mergers of large pharmaceuticals were understandable due to the difficult times for drug companies in general. Not only were the new drug pipelines "lackluster," but "[i]mportant drugs lose their profitability with age. Prices drop as similar, me-too drugs are approved."[13] And perhaps most importantly, "Patent protection for the original groundbreakers eventually runs out, and prices decline even further."[14] The patent on Voltaren, Ciba-Geigy's enormously popular and profitable antiarthritis drug, was on the verge of expiring.

The name Novartis was derived from *novae artes*, Latin for "new skills" and, according to the Novartis web site, "reflects our commitment to bringing new health care products to patients and physicians worldwide."[15] In 1997, its first full year as a new company, Novartis did well: Total sales were up by 9% to (Swiss francs) CHF31.2 billion. Net income had grown by 43% to CHF5.2 billion, and operating cash flow saw a 31% increase to CHF4.7 billion.[16] To reduce costs, the company had trimmed 9,100 employees, primarily through "natural fluctuation and early retirement" and, in the case of job redundancy, "offered severance packages that reflect our commitment to social responsibility."[17] The company had spun off some of its divisions, including Ciba-Geigy's specialty chemical unit (textile dyes, pigments, and polymers), choosing instead to focus on its Gerber products (Sandoz bought the baby-product business in 1994), pharmaceuticals, agricultural chemicals, and its over-the-counter medications such as Tavist, Ex-Lax, Gas-X, and Maalox. By the end of 1997, Novartis was competing "head-to-head" with Glaxo Wellcome, and had introduced five new products: Migranal, a migraine preventative nasal spray; Foradil, for asthma; Femara, a treatment for hormone-dependent cancer (e.g., breast cancer); Apligraf, a human skin regenerative bio-technology product; and Diovan, a hypertension drug.[18] Novartis was not involved in research and development of HIV/AIDS medicines, but its health care effort included fighting leprosy, malaria, and tuberculosis. See Exhibit 3.3.1 for company financial information and Exhibit 3.3.2 for the 1995 percentage of pharmaceutical world market share.

Origins of the Novartis Foundation for Sustainable Development

Development aid and humanitarian assistance had been a tradition of several Basel-based companies and started in a small Tanzanian location in 1949. At the request of the local bishop in Ifakara, zoologist Rudolf Geigy, an expert in pathogens and tropical diseases, visited Tanzania to see if he could devise a solution for the malaria, sleeping sickness, river blindness, and other diseases that ravaged the community. Using an improvised laboratory, Geigy studied ticks, fleas, and other regional insects. Eventually, the Rural Aid Centre was established in 1961, with financing by the Basel Foundation for Assistance to Developing Countries. This foundation was the creation of the former Ciba, Geigy, Sandoz, and companies based in Basel, which Geigy recruited for continued support. Geigy's firm belief was that "aid should have a sustainable impact and . . . be more than the distribution of charity,"[19] which became the credo of the Novartis Foundation.

In the early 1970s, the chairman of Ciba-Geigy, just recently formed from the merger of J. R. Geigy AG and Ciba, asked a young graduate student, Klaus Leisinger, to outline a working set of guidelines for an international company doing business in Africa. What Leisinger came up with, said Novartis's Karin Schmitt, was legendary for that time. "He had some very funny and courageous ideas," said Schmitt. "He felt you should Africanize the companies, that the local CEOs should be African."[20] In addition, Leisinger's paper emphasized selling solutions, not just products. The result was an "unequivocal" set of guidelines and obligations for doing business in a poor country. From Leisinger's paper emerged an Africa Policy, which then became a Corporate Policy for the Third World. At the same time, Novartis established a Third World Staff Unit, followed by a Third World Committee, which then, in 1979, became the Ciba-Geigy Foundation for Cooperation with Developing Countries on the basis that "the company did not content itself with declarations, but actually put its principles into practice."[21]

The purpose of the organization, according to its founding document, was to promote development of the poorest countries in the Third World, primarily by collaborating in agriculture, health care, and education, with the ultimate purpose of fostering self-help and providing aid in the event of a disaster. In 1990, this purpose was amended and "scientifically based analyses" and "consultations and information on development policy issues" were added to the list of resources to be made available. The objective of the foundation thus became three-pronged: consulting on development policy inside and outside the company, engaging in dialogue about development policy and human rights, and using its knowledge and insights in development projects.[22]

Exhibit 3.3.1 Novartis AG 1997 Financial Information (all figures in CHF millions)

Summarized Consolidated Income Statements

For the years ended 31 December 1997 and 1996	1996*	Pro forma 1997
Sales	31,180	26,144
Cost of goods sold	−9,847	−8,414
Operating expenses	−14,550	−12,803
Operating income	6,783	4,927
Financial income/expense, net	120	−83
Taxes and minority interests	−1,692	−1,207
NET INCOME	5,211	3,637

Summarized Consolidated Balance Sheets

	31 Dec. 1997	1 Jan. 1997
ASSETS		
Long-term assets		
Tangible fixed assets	11,589	11,534
Other long-term assets	6,069	4,912
Total long-term assets	17,658	16,446
Current Assets		
Inventories, trade accounts, receivables, and other current assets	15,684	15,273
Marketable securities, cash, and cash equivalents	18,486	18,527
Total current assets	34,170	33,800
TOTAL ASSETS	51,828	50,246
EQUITY AND LIABILITIES		
Equity		
Share capital, net	1,370	1,377
Reserves	25,431	22,187
Total equity	26,801	23,564
Liabilities		
Long-term liabilities		
Financial debts	3,611	5,254
Deferred taxes, other long-term liabilities, and minority interests	4,360	3,892
Total long-term liabilities and minority interests	7,971	9,146
Short-term liabilities		
Financial debts	7,465	6,722
Trade accounts payable and other short-term liabilities	9,591	10,814
Total short-term liabilities	17,056	17,536
Total liabilities and minority interests	25,027	26,682
TOTAL EQUITY AND LIABILITIES	51,828	50,246

Source: Novartis Operational Review, 1997, 29.

Schmitt emphasized that although the then Ciba-Geigy had a tradition of philanthropic work, the emphasis really was on achieving sustainable results. "You can give just money away," Schmitt said, "but that was never the purpose." Although Ciba-Geigy did give charitable donations, the company took development assistance very seriously. "You don't just throw money into things, make a nice publication, make photos, and make public relations

Exhibit 3.3.2 Percentage of Pharmaceutical World Market Share in 1995

Top 33%	
Glaxo Wellcome	4.7%
Novartis (Ciba and Geigy)	4.4%
Merck	3.5%
Hoechst Marion Roussel	3.5%
Bristol-Myers Squibb	3.1%
American Home Products	3.0%
Pfizer	2.9%
Johnson & Johnson	2.9%
Roche Pharmaceuticals	2.8%
SB	2.5%
Balance: 66.7%	

Source: Reuter, "Sandoz-Ciba Merger Hailed as World's Biggest," *The Financial Post* (Toronto), 8 March 1996, 5.

with it, but you really build up something." The Novartis Foundation's charitable efforts were never designed to build markets where there are none because, as Schmitt said, that might lead to a conflict of interest between the company's commercial efforts and its interests in Third World country development. Its Leprosy Fund worked closely with governments, the World Health Organization (WHO), and nongovernmental leprosy organizations to address the sociocultural problems as well as medical needs of those suffering from leprosy in countries such as India, Sri Lanka, Madagascar, and Brazil.

The foundation staff was small, but its activities were wide and varied. There was, according to Schmitt, think tank and publication work.

> We work very much academically on issues like corporate citizenship and business ethics; but we were also greatly interested in green biotechnology, population policy "with a human face," and other broader issues of social and political relevance. We also take a scientific approach to our assistance programs, so that we really can disseminate knowledge in a form that is acceptable to the most different circles of stakeholders—to academia but also to lay people, to people who are working in development and also to those working in governments.

Experimenting in Tanzania

What Madörin proposed doing in Tanzania had in a similar fashion already been tried out independently in Zimbabwe, where the HIV/AIDS orphan crisis was also severe. Stefan Germann, a Swiss aid worker who was at the time with the Swiss Salvation Army, had just founded the Massiye Camp, primarily to help develop the coping capacity of children affected by HIV/AIDS, and to focus on psychosocial support and life-skills development for orphans and other vulnerable children. Madörin wanted to do his work in a very remote rural area of Tanzania, where NGOs rarely go, because he thought if his concept could work there, it would work everywhere.

This type of project inevitably would have a modicum of controversy, with some questioning why an organization would focus on the psychosocial issues of children rather than their material needs. The answer, according to Madörin, was that giving children food and clothing was no longer enough. There was a "causal relationship between death, poverty, and alienation, resulting in grief, anger, and antisocial behavior."[23] If left unaddressed, Madörin contended, this "failure to support children to overcome this trauma will have very negative impact on society and might cause dysfunctional societies, jeopardizing years of investment in national development."[24] Nonetheless, Madörin's proposal was unusual and did not fit the normal profile of suggested programs to combat the effects of AIDS in Africa. Novartis also did not manufacture any HIV/AIDS medical products, leading some to question why the company would even consider addressing this particular problem. Novartis and its foundation did have the choice of many worthwhile opportunities to address crises in developing countries, whether or not related directly to its products. In addition to AIDS, there was leprosy, malaria, and tuberculosis, and although Novartis had addressed these health crises with various programs, in this case, the company decided to support a project that tried to approach, in an innovative way, a real socioeconomic need of vulnerable children. The idea was to develop "good practices," proof of the concept, and a sustainable program. Novartis also wanted to make all lessons learned in this process and implementation available to interested donors worldwide.

Developing a Pilot Program

The increasing problems of millions of HIV/AIDS orphans and the perceived necessity of an innovative and creative solution to tackle the psychological, social, and economic needs of vulnerable children tipped the scales in favor of accepting Kurt Madörin's proposal: Klaus Leisinger and Karin Schmitt of the Novartis Foundation for Sustainable Development gave Madörin the go-ahead for setting up a pilot program in Tanzania to address the psychosocial needs of children who had lost parents to AIDS. With the financial help of the foundation as well as the Swiss Agency for Development and Cooperation (SDC), Madörin traveled to Kagera, Tanzania, where approximately one-third of children had lost one or both parents to AIDS. His pilot program was called "Humuliza" (a Kihaya word meaning "consolation"). The two stated goals of Humuliza were to (1) develop practical instruments to enable teachers and caregivers to support orphans psychologically, and create a supportive environment for children affected by HIV/AIDS; and (2) develop children's capacity to cope with the loss of their caregivers in an effort to enhance their resilience.[25]

Madörin discovered that the orphaned children in Tanzania faced daunting challenges: surviving on their own, caring for younger siblings and sometimes grandparents, and no money for food, clothing, or school fees. Many were forced to leave school and work in the fields to survive. Many fell prey to drug traffickers and prostitution. In addition to the physical challenges, many of these children experienced "a loss of emotional security and confidence as the world around them collapsed."[26]

Accomplishing this was teaching the orphans to cope with their grief and loss. Children were also taught to "cultivate life skills, develop goals, build self-esteem, learn through play, provide peer care, and manage the stigma associated with HIV/AIDS."[27] In Madörin's models, children could describe their feelings and their emotions, and act out these feelings in many ways, including by crying. Through talking, the children were better able to work out their trauma. Madörin's therapeutic approaches included many different exercises. In one, for example, children collected stones and put them in a bag, which symbolized how heavy their emotional burden was.

A key component of the program was creating groups of children and teenagers in which they would help each other to cope and survive on their own and not end up in orphanages.

The emphasis was on helping them get back to community life. The children eventually would help the elders around them; in turn, the elders would care for the youth. These children learned survival mechanisms such as how to grow food and how to take care of themselves physically. At the same time, they were able to stay in school; the Novartis Foundation paid the school fees. A nine-person professional local team provided support. There were agricultural courses, English classes, and self-defense classes for girls. A mobile farm school was established and there was a bank offering microcredit loans, and financial assistance for those in dire need. Over several years, older children began leading the organization and supporting the younger ones. The program grew; manuals for adult caregivers and teachers were prepared, children were taught to help each other cope, and teachers and other adults associated with the program were trained in counseling distressed children. At the same time, awareness of the problems of AIDS orphans was raised through radio programs. And "self-managed youth organizations were created, so that orphans could experience friendship and mutual help."[28]

Creation of REPSSI

After several years of successfully working with children in Tanzania, Madörin and Stefan Germann of the Salvation Army Zimbabwean camp wanted to expand and broaden the program and export it to other African countries. They believed that a collective approach to dealing with AIDS orphans—such as creating a knowledge bank—would be extremely useful in transferring their knowledge and experience to new countries where help was also desperately needed. Using their experience in Tanzania and Zimbabwe, Madörin and Germann wrote up a model psychosocial program; it was translated into other languages and made available on the Web. Humuliza soon caught the interest of larger organizations, including UNICEF and UNAIDS.

In October 2000, Madörin presented his program in a workshop at Massiye Camp. The creation of a Regional Psychosocial Support Initiative (REPSSI) occurred in 2001 at a psychosocial support (PSS) "Think Tank" meeting whose attendees included providers of support to AIDS orphans, various aid organization representatives, scientists and doctors, and also children and young people. The goal was to combine the different approaches of various relief agencies in the area, and to increase awareness among these agencies of concepts of PSS. Initially, REPPSI was just a "loose" initiative, but two organizations, the International HIV/AIDS Alliance and the Southern Africa AIDS Training Program (SAT) were brought in. These two NGOs, in collaboration, became the governing umbrella for REPSSI. The organization as a whole also committed to the goals outlined in a June 2001 U.N. General Assembly Special Session on HIV/AIDS, with particular emphasis on the articles relating to children both orphaned and made vulnerable by the pandemic. See Exhibit 3.3.3 for Novartis Foundation financial information. The costs of the Humuliza and REPSSI programs were projected to be approximately USD500,000 per year, about 7% of the foundation's overall budget.[29] See Exhibit 3.3.4 for UNGASS AIDS commitments involving children and AIDS.

But a stable donor community was necessary. In March 2002, the Novartis Foundation along with SDC and the Swedish International Development Cooperation Agency banded together to provide this support. The organization recruited staff members and "then grew at breathtaking pace," until it became clear that it was unable to keep up with the constantly increasing demands. The management team had to learn to set priorities, while the donors had to appreciate that the managers needed additional professional support.[30] Also, in May 2002, the REPSSI initiative became a regional technical psychosocial support

Exhibit 3.3.3 Budget 2007 of the Novartis Foundation for Sustainable Development (in CHF)

Think Tank Activities and Networking	1,000,000
Health projects	6,200,000
• The Fight against Leprosy	890,000
• Preventive and Basic Health	3,710,000
• Access to Treatment	1,600,000
Human Rights and Knowledge Management	700,000
Administration	1,858,000
Total Budget 2007	9,758,000

Plus Product Donations for Leprosy, Tuberculosis, and Malaria in the order of magnitude of CHF10 million

Exhibit 3.3.4 United Nations General Assembly Special Session on HIV/AIDS: AIDS Commitments, Articles 65–67

Children orphaned and made vulnerable by HIV/AIDS

Children orphaned and affected by HIV/AIDS need special assistance

65. By 2003, develop and by 2005 implement national policies and strategies to: build and strengthen governmental, family and community capacities to provide a supportive environment for orphans and girls and boys infected and affected by HIV/AIDS including by providing appropriate counselling and psycho-social support; ensuring their enrolment in school and access to shelter, good nutrition, health and social services on an equal basis with other children; to protect orphans and vulnerable children from all forms of abuse, violence, exploitation, discrimination, trafficking and loss of inheritance;

66. Ensure non-discrimination and full and equal enjoyment of all human rights through the promotion of an active and visible policy of de-stigmatization of children orphaned and made vulnerable by HIV/AIDS;

67. Urge the international community, particularly donor countries, civil society, as well as the private sector to complement effectively national programmes to support programmes for children orphaned or made vulnerable by HIV/AIDS in affected regions, in countries at high risk and to direct special assistance to sub-Saharan Africa.

For a complete list of articles from the Declaration of Commitment on HIV/AIDS published by the U.N. General Assembly Special Session on HIV/AIDS (June 25–27, 2001) see http://www.un.org/ga/aids/coverage/FinalDeclarationHIVAIDS.html.

capacity-building program. The aim of the program was "to improve and scale up psycho-social assistance for CABA [children affected by AIDS] in East and Southern Africa through partner organizations."[31]

Those working on the initiative, however, needed an organizational structure, defined logistics, and contracts and legal protection. In short, the initiative needed an organizational developer. In addition, REPSSI needed to be based in a safe and stable location, allowing the program to grow, endure, and flourish. Because of political problems in Zimbabwe, the initiative, which was then based there, had to move elsewhere. The Novartis Foundation and the other organizations involved had to assess different countries and determine which one would be the best headquarters for REPSSI, and they had to focus on creating a strong and effective organizational operation.

REPSSI: Growth and Evolution[32]

The donors jointly commissioned Ernst & Young to conduct a risk assessment of how REPSSI could be brought to other African countries both legally and effectively. The original initiative had to be transformed into an organization, and a host country had to be chosen to implement the program. South Africa, where the HIV/AIDS problem and its effects on children seemed the most severe, was chosen. Johannesburg became the headquarters of REPSSI, with branches in 13 countries. Schmitt recalled that serendipitously, at that juncture, she was approached by the head of the Novartis international human resources division, who offered to help with human resource and organizational development and finance management for the new venture.

Representatives from Novartis human resources traveled to South Africa to assess all the gaps and weaknesses in the organization. To strengthen the program, Schmitt said, "They drew together not only our resources, but specialist organizations like coaches, organization builders, finance management people." At the same time, they worked with universities, including Harvard, to build and strengthen REPSSI.

First Annual Review

In 2003, REPSSI had its first annual review in which it emerged that there was a need for stronger planning and reporting processes, and for REPSSI to operate in a results-based management framework. In the early months of 2004, REPSSI team members underwent intense training, and the ensuing "Results Chain" was developed to enable the organization "to work toward achieving long-term positive impact in the lives of children affected by AIDS in East and Southern Africa."[33]

Novartis Foundation Philosophy

An organization's ability to make progress in development in other countries, as several decades of experience had proved, hinged on the domestic political and economic conditions in partner countries. This justified the increasing international demands on the governments of developing countries for better governance. For the same reasons, many people and organizations were acknowledging the need for a trade policy favoring poor countries through a genuinely free world market (at least theoretically).

Sustainable development could only take place, the Novartis Foundation believed, by overcoming obstacles to this development. The need for changes aimed at overcoming such obstacles might have seemed obvious, given the widespread destitution in developing countries. But the foundation believed that a pragmatic development policy could not afford to wait for these changes to occur and obstacles be diminished before implementing strategies designed to alleviate poverty. The Novartis Foundation, Schmitt said, sought "to promote practical development measures that take account of existing conditions, and to take immediate action wherever we see the best potential for implementing our concept of sustainable development."

The less room there was for maneuvering with regard to poverty-oriented development strategies at the higher level of political action, Schmitt explained, the greater the intrinsic value of poverty alleviation projects at the local level. She said the foundation was aware that its development work could not have any direct impact on the conditions shaping the national or international framework. "Questions of this type require discussions well beyond the project level—between policymakers for the donors and recipients in the public sector, in the context of bilateral governmental consultations and multilateral coordinating committees such as the World Bank Consultative Group." Ideally, such discussions would result in the formulation by the donors of explicit allocation conditions, with the aim of intentionally changing the existing framework. For these reasons, Schmitt said, the Novartis Foundation normally restricted itself to measures that focused on the grass-roots level. The foundation did not regard development assistance as an alternative to political solution nor as a purely charitable form of philanthropy. Schmitt said:

> We make a continual effort to ensure that our decision-making processes reflect a developmental perspective by focusing on criteria that allow us to expect the maximum effectiveness and sustainability from the collaborative work we undertake. The criteria relate to the conditions that can have a substantial influence on the success and effectiveness of a project or program.

Schmitt enumerated the elements that projects and programs supported by the Novartis Foundation should have:[34]

- Maintain a direct relation to poverty—focusing on developing neglected productive resources in disadvantaged population groups (rather than focusing, for example, on expanding existing potential without clearly linking such expansion to the target population);
- Take account of the core problems in the developing country concerned (rather than focusing on problems of little relevance). Core problems were those that posed the greatest obstacles to economic and social development.
- Take account of a partner country's potential for development (rather than initiating work when the potential for development is low).
- Take account of the partner country's experience (rather than making commitments in areas where previous experience had been rather problematic, or the foundation had little expertise);
- Take account of the partner country's priorities (rather than pursuing priorities in which the partner country had no interest);
- Take account of the conditions for achieving a goal, and for the effectiveness and sustainability of an intervention (rather than making an effort where the pressure of problems was great but the conditions unfavorable);
- Take account of the need for external assistance (rather than choosing areas of development in which the country concerned was capable of self-help);
- Take account of other donors' commitments. (In negative terms: Avoid duplicating the efforts of other donors; in positive terms: Determine whether other donors' commitments could be effectively complemented to achieve synergistic effects);
- Take account of the amount of resources available to the foundation (because this determined the extent and the focus of the contribution the foundation could make in solving a significant problem).

Despite all attempts to be objective and to reason from a developmental perspective during the selection process, in the final analysis, determination of priorities always required evaluations (of core problems, development potential, conditions, willingness of the partner to pursue development, etc.) by Novartis's project managers. These priorities often varied greatly in terms of the resources they required. But a specific level of funding, Schmitt emphasized, was never the starting point for a development priority. Complementary situations, however, were often created. For example, support for a psychosocial counseling program or project for African children orphaned by AIDS might have been a priority when it contributed to solving a locally significant development problem, even if the program's activities required a minimal budget and involved primarily information and educational efforts.

Novartis was guided by the overriding aim that the effectiveness and impact of the resources it committed to problem-solving could be improved by concentrating on the priorities in each case. All the development activities underwent independent evaluations to assess their degrees of effectiveness, which facilitated a continual learning process and allowed Novartis to replicate successful approaches.

Schmitt emphasized the incremental approach that the Novartis Foundation took. Whether it's "leprosy, malaria, or AIDS, one actor can hardly do anything. So the foundation comes in, starts with a small initiative like Humuliza in Tanzania, and finds ways to make the impact bigger." The Swiss and Swedish governments supported the program. They provided funds, while the Novartis Foundation, in addition to the funding, provided organizational development assistance. For the biggest influence the foundation focused on building the capacity of the organization and consequently advancing the whole field of psychosocial care for AIDS orphans.

The philosophy behind helping children, whether in South Africa or in countries such as Sri Lanka with its civil war, or in Gaza, Schmitt said, was to reach them at a very early age:

> I believe in supporting early childhood development and youth development. This is the most important thing if you want to have sustainable development. You have to break the vicious circle because children who grow up in violence, who grow up with abuse, are incapacitated for their whole life. They simply repeat the circle.

Medical and physical care is vitally important, she said, but so was looking at what's happening inside children. "It's like a volcano, and this volcano breaks out sooner or later," she said. "The number of those children growing up in these circumstances is simply enormous and it's growing."

Schmitt emphasized taking an almost scientific approach to complex problems to imbue the programs with credibility. At the same time, even the most complex problems, she said, had to be presented in a simple way. "As a single actor, you're just one little mosaic stone in the huge picture of mosaics," Schmitt said. "But other actors bring in the other mosaic stones." REPSSI was an organization that shared this philosophy and worked hard to realize mutual principles in their program work.

Types of Cooperation

The foundation's development assistance took two main forms: supporting projects and programs and contributing to small projects and shared initiatives.

Project and Program Assistance

More and more of the resources devoted to development were allocated to programs. Whereas projects consisted of individual health development measures and were limited in terms of duration and funding, program assistance involved several coordinated measures. For example, programs focused on a region or a particular population group (such as AIDS orphans). The programs and projects concentrated on activities that directly addressed the basic needs of the poor and disadvantaged. Ecological aspects and approaches enhancing the position of women in society received special attention.

Technical Cooperation

Wherever it was necessary to strengthen a local project partner by improving its functional capacities—as was particularly the case for REPSSI—financial and technical cooperation were required. In the area of technical cooperation, Novartis provided advisors, trainers, specialists, consultants, and other experts; it also offered training and further education of local specialists and managers in developing countries.

Cofinancing with Other Donors

Novartis considered cofinancing along with other bilateral and multilateral donors to be an appropriate instrument for supporting complex projects and programs (again, such as REPSSI). The advantages of cofinancing included joint pursuit of common development aims, combined experience and financial resources, and division of labor. But the foundation was careful to observe its own criteria for development cooperation in all such cases. By doing so, the foundation would be free to initiate additional program activities if and when necessary or desirable even if other donors might choose not to participate in these programs. The foundation looked specifically for activities and project elements that would continue after its own involvement ended; to achieve this goal, the foundation introduced a project module with performance-based funding.

Small-Scale Projects

In addition to projects and programs, in exceptional cases, Novartis also supported small-scale projects that required rapid, effective assistance to promote self-help. The measures that seemed the most worthy of support in this regard were those which would be successful only if they were rapidly implemented, and which could not be financed by local agents qualified to execute them (such as churches). These small-scale projects were not meant to have any direct connection with other projects being supported by the foundation, and they had to consist of self-contained measures that did not result in continuing obligations.

REPSSI in 2006

By 2006, REPSSI, through its various organizations and institutions throughout sub-Saharan Africa, had touched the lives of more than 300,000 orphans. It had worked at various times with more than 140 aid organizations. The collaboration had, in particular, been extremely successful in "transferring best practices in labor management, leadership, and financial skills."[35] Many of the services provided for the NGO by businesses and universities were pro bono. REPSSI continued to grow as 2006 came to a close and, with management stretched thin, those involved with REPSSI looked once again to Novartis's corporate human resources as well as the foundation itself to guide them to greater growth.[36]

REPSSI goals were also, according to Novartis, in line with the eight Millennium Development Goals (MDGs), established by the United Nations in 2000 and to be achieved by 2015. The MDGs were a summary of the actions and targets outlined in the Millennium Declaration, adopted by 189 nations and signed by 147 heads of state and governments during the September 2000 U.N. Millennium Summit. These goals were to

1   eradicate extreme poverty and hunger
2   achieve universal primary education
3   promote gender equality and empower women

4   reduce child mortality
5   improve maternal health
6   combat HIV/AIDS, malaria, and other diseases
7   ensure environmental sustainability
8   develop a Global Partnership for Development.[37]

Building Leadership Skills

In 2006, as the growth of REPSSI outpaced some of the team's own management capabilities, Novartis's corporate human resources offered to provide leadership and management training. The knowledge and skills Novartis could transfer to the REPSSI staff would build the organization's long-term effectiveness as the leading authority in psychosocial support in southern and eastern Africa. The leadership of Novartis South Africa also became active in coaching, training, and providing consultative support.[38]

The Novartis Foundation, REPSSI, and Novartis corporate learning identified specific areas for leadership development and agreed on a midterm strategy:

- Reviewing REPSSI HR policies and procedures
- Providing training in basic leadership skills for the REPSSI team
- Establishing project management skills to support the planned growth of REPSSI
- Developing business acumen for the REPSSI leadership team to manage growth and build increasing independence from the group's funding partners
- Improving REPSSI's communications strategy

Motivation and Creative Partnerships

Internally, Schmitt said, the corporate citizenship efforts helped motivate employees and brought particular satisfaction as well as a new dimension to the work of those who participated directly (such as Novartis's corporate HR department's and Novartis South Africa's involvement with REPSSI). Employees had an opportunity to address a significant social need as individuals and as part of a larger team. Because of the REPSSI case, Novartis employees in 2007 set up an "expert pool" intended to offer specific skills needed in development programs. They would not only focus on the foundation, but also would work with other NGOs and organizations involved in development assistance. Schmitt said a direct benefit of this employee involvement was better retention and recruitment for the company. Employees and others were aware that the foundation, by involving itself early in the AIDS orphan problem, not only demonstrated a clear sense of corporate social responsibility, but also enhanced its role beyond merely providing funds. The foundation gained a reputation as a leader in developing pioneering programs and initiatives particularly with U.N. organizations and other NGOs. The foundation's work, said Schmitt, simply "exemplifies how social problems can be tackled through creative partnerships."

By 2007, the project was financially secured for another three years by the Swedish Development Agency (SIDA), the Swiss Development Cooperation (SDC), the Novartis Foundation for Sustainable Development and other donors. The Novartis Foundation's goal was to make REPSSI the "implementing agency of choice" for such programs and securing long-term financing through expanding the donor base.

Notes

* This case was prepared by Senior Ethics Research Associate Jenny Mead under the supervision of Patricia H. Werhane, Ruffin Professor of Business Ethics. It was written as a basis for class discussion rather than to illustrate effective or ineffective handling of an administrative situation. Copyright © 2008 University of Virginia Darden School Foundation, Charlottesville, VA. All rights reserved.

1 *terres des hommes schweiz* focused on the health, social care, and rights of children worldwide.

2 Benjamin F. Nelson, "Global Health: The U.S. and U.N. Response to the AIDS Crisis in Africa," *U.S. General Accounting Office Testimony* (February 2000): 2. http://www.gao.gov/archive/2000/ns00099t.pdf (accessed 12 September 2007).

3 "Number of AIDS Orphans Rapidly Increasing in Sub-Saharan Africa," *Reproductive Health Matters* 11, no. 22 (2003): 193.

4 http://www.thebody.com/content/world/art33120.html (accessed 25 April 2007).

5 Geoff Foster, "Supporting Community Efforts to Assist Orphans in Africa," *New England Journal of Medicine* 346, no. 24 (13 June 2002): 1907.

6 Foster, 1907.

7 Foster, 1907.

8 Foster, 1907.

9 Milt Freudenheim, "Merger of Drug Giants: A New Image for Corporate Switzerland," *New York Times*, 8 March 1996, D1.

10 Stephen D. Moore, "Novartis Leaps last Regulatory Hurdle," *The Wall Street Journal*, 18 December 1996, B11.

11 According to Freudenheim, this was the third-largest deal at that time, following Mitsubishi Bank's acquisition of the Bank of Tokyo for USD33.8 billion and Kohlberg Kravis Roberts's deal for RJR Nabisco for USD30.6 billion.

12 Stephen D. Moore and Philip Revzin, "Challenge for Novartis Lies in the Lab," *Wall Street Journal*, 30 July 1996, B8.

13 Freudenheim.

14 Freudenheim.

15 http://www.novartis.com/about-novartis/company-history/index.shtml (accessed 04 November 2007).

16 Novartis Operational Review 1997, 4.

17 Novartis Operational Review 1997, 4.

18 Bale Communications Inc., "Novartis Looking To Be the Biggest," *Adnews Online*, 18 December 1997.

19 "Success Through Perseverance and Patience: The History of the Novartis Foundation is One of Continuity Over 25 Years," 19, http://www.novartisfoundation.org/platform/apps/Publication/getfmfile.asp?id=652&el=543&se=634215889&doc=14&dse=1 (accessed 17 July 2007).

20 Karin Schmitt (Novartis), interviewed by Jenny Mead, April 4, 2007, Darden Graduate School of Business Administration, Charlottesville, Virginia.

21 "Success Through Perseverance and Patience," 20.

22 "Success Through Perseverance and Patience," 21.

23 Stefan Germann, Kurt Madörin, and Ncazelo Ncube, "Psychosocial Support for Children Affected by AIDS: Tanzania, and Zimbabwe," *SAFAIDS* 9, no. 2 (June 2001): 11.

24 Germann et al., 11.

25 http://www.humuliza.org/index.php?option=com_content&task=view&id=1&Itemid=1 (accessed 20 August 2007).

26 Novartis, "Regional Psychosocial Support Initiative: Bringing Hope to AIDS Orphans," 4.

27 http://www.humuliza.org/.

28 http://www.humuliza.org/.

29 For more detailed information about the Humuliza Project, see http://www.humuliza.org/index.php?option=com_content&task=view&id=1&Itemid=1 (accessed 04 November 2007).

30 http://www.novartisfoundation.org/page/content/index.asp?Menu=3&MenuID=237&ID=526&Item=44.6 (accessed 27 August 2007).

31 "History of REPSSI," www.repssi.org/home.asp?pid=31 (accessed 20 August 2007).

32 Karin Schmitt (Novartis), interview by Jenny Mead, April 4, 2007, Darden Graduate School of Business Administration, Charlottesville, Virginia. (Unless otherwise noted, all Schmitt quotations in the case are from that interview.)

33 "History and Background of REPSSI," http://www.repssi.org/home.asp?pid=31 (accessed 1 September 2007).

34 Schmitt emphasized that this list of criteria was not complete; the degree of specification in Novartis's criteria for development work was too extensive to catalogue in this case.

35 Novartis, "Regional Psychosocial Support Initiative: Bringing Hope to AIDS Orphans in Africa," 2, http://www.novartisfoundation.org/platform/content/element/1172/Bringing_Hope.pdf (accessed 24 August 2007).

36 In addition, by 2006, the Novartis Foundation had been involved in a number of other projects including: improving access to leprosy services in Sri Lanka (1989–2006); integrated health care project in Mali (2001–05); community development program in Sri Lanka (2000–05); organization and community development in Brazil (1993–2004); support for youth training centers in Tanzania (1998–2002); rural women's project in Bangladesh (1992–96); and empowerment of women in Gaza (1992–96).

37 For more information about the Millennium Goals, see http://www.un.org/millenniumgoals (accessed 17 January 2008).

38 The cost of this particular venture was not readily determined because the Novartis corporate human resources department put it together and paid for it. By 2007, approximately 500 man-hours and 10 airfares from Switzerland to South Africa had been attributed to this program.

Chapter 4

Energy

4.1 Eskom and the South African Electrification Program[*]

(A) The Beginning of the Electrification Program

The year was 1994 and Tienz[1] sat at his desk contemplating the enormous scope of the job that was in front of him. Eskom and the provision of electricity had always been an integral part of the economic and social evolution of the South African nation. Because of its important role in helping to shape the formation of South Africa, Eskom now saw itself as a necessary participant in the reconstruction process that the new ANC government was outlining in an effort to rebuild the country in the post-apartheid era.[2,3] The company even participated in the creation of upliftment programs under apartheid.[4] For example, in the late 1980s the company had implemented an affirmative action policy to recruit black South Africans into management positions; they had also created programs to improve the school systems within black South African communities.

However, the present situation was somewhat more complicated than Eskom's past initiatives: in 1994 the new government had specifically stated that electrical access to all citizens was essential to the Reconstruction and Development Program (RDP), which laid out initiatives to help the country rebuild itself.[5] Management informed Tienz that the company had decided to aid the new government in its reconstruction process and implement a nation wide electrification program—a far cry from simply extending the grid a few kilometers from urban centers.

The scope and scale of the proposed electrification program seemed overwhelming to Tienz. How was he going to develop a system to provide electrical connections to approximately 1.75 million homes (approximately 9 million people) by the year 2000 in a cost-effective manner? Not only would new transmission lines have to be constructed, but safe and reliable distribution meters had to be designed to meet the unique conditions that existed in black South African townships, squatter camps, and villages.[6] The project would be demanding technologically—at one look the possibility of recapturing the capital costs involved seemed impossible. The consumer market—i.e., the black South Africans—to whom Eskom was going to be providing electricity not only had grown accustomed to using coal, wood, and paraffin for all of their energy purposes but they also had dramatically low and inconsistent monthly incomes. So how was Tienz supposed to develop a pricing structure for these new connections, given the depressed economic situation that existed in those areas?

On his drive into work each morning, it was easy for Tienz to see the economic differences that apartheid had created between white and black South Africans. The highway was lined with hundreds of shacks that people had built out of spare wood, tin, and even cardboard in order to have a home closer to the city and the economic activity close to its borders, bizarre for a country that had a standard of living comparable to that of the highest-rated countries in the world. The average monthly income for a black South African was R294,[7] small when contrasted with the fact that average monthly expenditures for food and housing were R28 and R251 respectively. Half of all black South Africans lived below the poverty line; moreover, approximately 41 percent of the black South African population was unemployed, and those who were employed had jobs either seasonal in nature or inequitable in salary structure.[8] For example, black South Africans made up 75 percent of South Africa's population, but they earned only 28 percent of the country's total income, whereas white South Africans were only 13 percent of the population but earned 61 percent of the country's income.

The electrification program was seen as a "basic need" by the ANC government because only 20 percent of black South Africans had access to electricity in 1994. Housing and water were identified as the two other basic needs: one-fourth of all blacks either had no housing or lived in shacks, and 40 percent did not have access to clean water. These basic needs were identified because of the wide discrepancies between white and black South Africans, which were not only economic. For example, a typical black South African's life expectancy was 57 years compared to 73 years for a white South African, and infant mortality was 57 per 1,000 live births for blacks compared to 13 per 1,000 live births for whites.

An electricity program was further seen as a viable option because the country already had an electrical grid in place to supply both residential areas and industry with electricity. In fact, there were approximately 240,000 km of lines currently employed in the country to transmit and distribute electricity. However, extensions to the existing electrical grid would undoubtedly be capital-intensive; for example, a one km extension of low-, medium-, and high-voltage lines would cost Eskom R40,000, R100,000, and R1,000,000 respectively. Although the line extensions in the electrification process would use mostly low-voltage line extensions, some medium- and high-voltage extensions would be necessary to carry the needed electrical capacity to the areas being electrified. Although Eskom was operating at about 10 megawatts in excess capacity, the new customers would demand more electricity from the system, wiping out the excess capacity. The company could possibly find itself in the position of having to build more generation facilities and incur the associated capital expenditures in order to meet the new demand that they were in essence creating.[9]

The cost of the program had been estimated at R1.2 billion annually. However, Eskom's revenues were R15,417 million, with operating expenditures at R11,864 million, which left the company with a total operating income of R3,553 million at its disposal.[10] The latter meant that Eskom needed to fund the program with approximately 35 percent of its operating income annually, which would be an enormous expenditure for the company to make on a project that had an uncertain future. But three factors made the RDP's goals achievable by Eskom:

1   Eskom's policies were determined by the Electricity Council, which was linked closely to the government executive and the finance ministry;
2   Eskom had much experience with generating revenue by issuing bonds on financial markets;
3   Eskom had reserve generation capacity, which meant that capital expenditures for electrification excluded generation equipment, significantly reducing total expenditures.

Given the size of the capital expenditures that Eskom would undertake in the electrification program, the company needed to develop a program that would be affordable, add value to the lives of the people to whom they were providing electricity, and contribute to South Africa's reconstruction.

How to Deliver Service

Because of the possibility of not receiving a sufficient return on their investment, Eskom considered several options for the delivery of electricity. Of these options, two surfaced as being the most viable alternatives: (1) a prepayment metering system or (2) fixed-cost connections. In the former case, people pay for electricity before they actually use it, and, in the latter, people pay a monthly fixed fee for unlimited use at a fixed current level. Option (1) would allow Eskom the opportunity to offset the risk of people defaulting on their bills and the costs associated with recovering money owed, and option (2) would allow people to use as much electricity as they needed for growth at a low, fixed monthly fee.

The option of providing fixed-rate connections had already been used in other countries for similar electrification projects because of the lowered capital expenditures associated with being able to distribute electricity with low-voltage lines and not having to supply meters with each connection, which also offsets additional maintenance costs. However, would it be possible for Eskom to set an affordable, fixed monthly fee that these consumers, who had variable monthly incomes at best, would be willing to pay each month? Again, the people being connected were struggling with high unemployment and sporadic monthly incomes. Since employment was variable at best, would the average person be able to afford the service that was being provided? If Eskom could develop an affordable monthly fee that people would agree to pay, would these people be willing to switch to a usage-based fee in the future if their electrical demands surpassed the amount of electricity available under a fixed-rate option? On the other hand, prepaid meters would cost more than fixed-rate connections and even more than traditional meters, thereby raising the capital costs associated with the electrification program. However, the advantage of the prepaid metering system was that consumers could stop using electricity and not pay whenever they did not have sufficient income or even a job.

Tienz now needed to decide which option would be better for the electrification program and why. He had to figure out how to finance a capital-intensive program that was projected to cost approximately R20 billion to complete. So how was Eskom to raise the capital that was necessary for a program that would take R1.2 billion annually? How was Eskom to develop sustainable communities to use the electricity that was being supplied to them?

Appendix A: Early South African Beginnings

In 1652 an expedition by the Dutch East India Company landed at what is now South Africa to establish a garrison to supply East India ships with fresh water and food. Soon the garrison grew into a colony, and in 1657 the first settlers built their homes on the grazing land of the local indigenous people, which inevitably sparked conflict between these two groups of people in southern Africa.[11] In 1660, after winning a number of conflicts with tribes, the Dutch settlers planted a thorn hedge across 6,000 acres of the Cape in order to separate the colony from the tribe.[12] This hedge, used to separate the races, serves as an early symbolic representation of the apartheid doctrine that would come later.

Although these periods of clashes between the white and black South Africans were frequent, there was a fair degree of trading and social interaction between the two groups.[13] Soon, however, further measures were placed into effect in order to regulate black and white interaction. For example, in 1829 a pass system was implemented to monitor and control the flow of black South Africans into white areas.

Then, as more Europeans settled in the country, stern competition arose between the two races for the limited amount of land and water in the country; this led to more frequent and serious conflicts. The fight for land started in the mid-1850s when 70 percent of the white population was forced into black-controlled lands because of the limited land available in white-controlled areas.[14] The white population eventually learned to survive in these areas by dominating and controlling the black populations. The white population felt superior to the blacks, on both the battleground and in farming, and a master-servant relationship came into being with black indigenous people doing manual work for the white population in southern Africa.

The agricultural economy of southern Africa soon turned into one centered upon mining when, in 1867, diamonds were discovered. The master-servant relationship between the black and white populations deepened when the white-owned mines recruited cheap black labor, leading to a huge influx of blacks into white-controlled lands. The whites, to control race interaction, enacted the Native Land Act, granting blacks temporary status to live and work within South Africa. A portion of land was even set aside far from white areas for the incoming black population to inhabit. However, white control went even farther than controlling black populations in the white areas of South Africa. In the early 1900s, the white government went further in their control over the black populations in their midst by placing restrictions on black mobility, education, and housing.

Appendix B: Beginning of Electricity Supply

It's hard to imagine that one of the far corners of the world was where electricity was first utilized, but given that "necessity is the mother of invention," South Africa's mining industry inevitably called for the use of electricity in the mid-1880s.[15] Mining companies installed their own electrical reticulation systems in order to supply electricity to the mines for illumination and power for equipment. These systems soon grew to the point of supplying the nearby cities with electricity, and it was soon recognized that large centralized power stations would supply more reliable and cheaper power than smaller dedicated mining power stations. This eventually led to the formation of the Rand Central Electric Works[16] and the Victoria Falls Power Company in 1906.

Eventually, the Electric Supply Commission (Escom) was established in 1923 in order to supply electricity more cheaply and efficiently to industry and local authorities.[17] In 1937, Eskom's headquarters was the tallest building in South Africa (21 stories tall), indicating the growth that Escom underwent to meet the growing needs of the mining industry. During the boom years after WWII, electrical demand was soaring and Eskom had met these demands effectively. However, although South Africa was blessed with a wealth of natural resources,[18] the country did not have an adequate water supply, so Eskom recognized that they had to turn to the huge coal reserves to produce electricity. In fact, the coal seams in the country were abundant, thick, shallow, and unfaulted, which meant that extraction costs would be minimal and that these lowered costs could be passed on in the form of cheaper electricity prices.

During the 1960s more coal-fired generation facilities were constructed and Eskom successfully designed dry cooling towers for burning the lower-quality coal that was abundant in South Africa. In the 1970s, future electrical demand and load growth were expected to increase even more, so new facilities (one nuclear plant and several pumped storage plants) were built. However, load growth did not increase as planned and Eskom was left with a surplus of generation capability at their disposal, which would ultimately lead to Eskom being able to supply even cheaper electricity in the 1990s.

At the end of 1997, Eskom was one of the five largest utilities in the world with total assets equaling R96,894 million, total revenue equaling R20,448, and approximately 40,000 employees.[19] The company supplied more than 98 percent of the electricity used in South Africa, which constituted approximately 60 percent of the electricity used on the entire continent of Africa. The electricity was generated by 20 power stations with a 39,154 total megawatt capacity. The power was distributed by way of more than 26,065 km of high voltage power lines within South Africa. Because of the overanticipated electrical demand in the 1980s and the additional generation sites that were constructed as a result, Eskom was operating at a surplus capacity of approximately 10,000 megawatts. Moreover, estimates showed that Eskom's surplus capacity would not be exceeded until the year 2007, even with the electrification project and growth in demand for industrial power.[20]

Appendix C: The "New" South Africa

After winning the seat of government in the first open elections in South Africa[21] by receiving 62.5 percent of the vote and obtaining 252 of 400 seats in the legislature, the African National Congress (ANC) then sought to implement a plan to make a better life for all.[22] Recognizing the need for infrastructure development, they created the Reconstruction and Development Program (RDP) to guide the post-Apartheid state in South Africa. RDP was a socio-economic policy that sought to mobilize all of South Africa's people and resources to eradicate the lingerings of apartheid and build a non-racially based, democratic government and nation. The program consisted of six basic principles and five key programs.

The six principles were:

1   Maintain an integrated and sustainable program.
2   Center on a people-driven process.
3   Ensure peace and security for all.
4   Embark on nation-building.
5   Link reconstruction and development.
6   Democratize the nation.

The principles were set to be achieved by the five programs:

1   Meet basic needs.
2   Develop human resources.
3   Build the economy.
4   Democratize the state and society.
5   Implement the RDP.[23]

However, as the statistics in Tables 4.1.1 and 4.1.2 illustrate, the task would not be easy.

Table 4.1.1 Income Statistics for Different Ethnic Groups[24]

	Asians	Colored	Whites	Blacks
% of Population (out of 42 million)	3	8	16	73
% Unemployment	17.1	23.3	6.4	41.1
Avg. monthly personal income	R1,304	R711	R2,875	R294
Avg. spent monthly on food/housing	R871/R640	R521/R275	R1,072/R827	R251/R28

Table 4.1.2 South African Statistical Indicators[25]

GDP	R433 billion
GDP/capita	$3,004
Unemployment	32.6%
Inflation	12.5%
Interest Rate	18.4%

Appendix D: Early Social Investment by Eskom

During the apartheid era, before the electrification program, an estimated 98 percent of all white households had electricity; 80 percent of black households lacked it.[26] In addition, the power that was sold to blacks was subjected to highly arbitrary rates. Eskom acted as a wholesaler of electricity to approximately 450 municipalities, which were typically white-controlled under the apartheid system. Because of the number of municipalities involved, over 2,000 different rate structures were constructed. In some areas, like Soweto, on the border of Johannesburg, black residents were paying double the rates of nearby whites within Johannesburg proper. Moreover, it could be argued that the electrical service for black areas was of much lower quality than for white customers: "If the power went out, you could wait a week, a month or even longer for a crew to show up."[27] Thus, Eskom's history of corporate social investment (CSI), not surprisingly, was racially-directed.

In 1985, anticipating the likely changes in the apartheid regime,[28] Eskom committed to cultural change. It initiated an affirmative action program to create contact between the races and by the 1990s began to recruit talented black personnel into executive positions. In 1988 it launched its "New South African" program, a corporate social investment (CSI) program initially funded with R4 million. About two thirds of this budget was initially spent on electrifying 10 schools per year in Soweto. The rest of the budget was largely spent on funding education-oriented, non-government organizations which sought to improve the educational conditions in poor, black regions.[29]

Moving to alleviate further some of the problems associated with the apartheid system, Eskom accelerated its investments in electrification and expanded beyond schools to an "Electricity for All" program. At the end of 1990 it launched this program with the philosophy that economic development within South Africa's black communities would not occur until they had access to electricity. However, there were no accurate statistics on the proportion of the South African population that lacked electricity, and there was no accurate database of housing in South Africa. Accordingly, Eskom's first task was to compile housing statistics to determine the extent of electrification in South Africa's urban and rural areas. Results showed that out of 7.2 million homes in South Africa, only 3 million had access to electricity: i.e., approximately 23 million people—just over half of the population of South Africa at the time—were without electricity.[30, 31] Almost all of these homes were in black impoverished urban, township, and rural regions.

Eskom piloted the first electrification program, and by the end of 1991 Eskom succeeded in connecting 31,000 residences to the electrical grid. Eskom worked with local government councils and offered incentives to regions if they could electrify homes in their areas. Viewed as a success, the program continued, connecting an additional 159,000 homes in 1992 at an average cost per connection of R2,600. At the end of 1992, approximately 1 million black South Africans had been connected to the grid and over 260 electrification projects were underway. Eskom recognized that mere connections were not all that the poorer people in

South Africa needed in order to have access to electricity. The company made it their goal to reduce the "real price"[32] of electricity in order to stimulate economic growth and provide an affordable service to their new customers. Eskom had achieved substantial momentum in electrification just at the time when political power was changing hands in South Africa.

Appendix E: Eskom's Commitment to the RDP

John Maree[33] wrote in Eskom's 1992 Annual Report:

> As the new South Africa becomes a reality, large organizations will need to have relevance to our society and demonstrate that, through the conduct of their business, they bring value, not only to their own stakeholders, but also to the wider society. Their products and services will have to meet the emerging consumer needs and contribute to the well-being and progress of the community and particularly the disadvantaged.

Access to electricity was identified as one of the top two needs of the citizens of the country. Eskom's early electrification efforts had been embraced by the new government, and the electrification of homes was identified as one of the most important aspects of the "meeting basic needs" program. An accelerated and sustainable electrification program was planned to provide access to electricity for an additional 2.5 million households by the year 2000, thereby increasing the level of access to electricity to about 72 percent of all South African households, double the 1992 number of households with access to electricity. Eskom would play a major role in meeting the goals set out by the RDP, and these goals became central to Eskom's electrification goals. Eskom's 1995 stated goals based on the RDP were:

1   Further reduce the real price of electricity by 15 percent, to become the world's lowest-cost supplier of electricity.
2   Electrify an additional 1,750,000 homes, improving the lives of 11 million South Africans.
3   Change the staffing profile so that 50 percent of management, professional, and supervisory staff are black South Africans.
4   Educate, train, and upgrade sufficient numbers of people to meet Eskom's future managerial, technical, and other professional staff needs, by employing 370 black trainees and bursars per year and enabling all Eskom employees to become literate.
5   Maintain transparency and worker consultation in decision-making.
6   Contribute R50 million per year to electrification of schools and clinics, and other community development activities, particularly in rural areas.
7   Enable all Eskom employees to own a home.
8   Encourage small and medium enterprise development, through Eskom's buying policies and give managerial support.
9   Protect the environment.
10   Finance the above from Eskom's own resources and from overseas development funding.

Because the company believed that electricity was a vital part of modern life and that it would encourage economic growth within the newly electrified areas, Eskom committed to the RDP goals of electrifying approximately 2.5 million of the 4.2 million homes (60 percent of the people without electricity) through both grid and non-grid (solar) connections. The remaining number "would be difficult to electrify due to either structure of the dwelling, the distance from the existing grid, access to alternative energy sources, or simply as a matter of affordability." Other reasons why Eskom proclaimed commitment were: (1) the standard of living improved through access to hot water, stoves, and TV; (2) gender-specific roles could be revamped (e.g., time previously spent on collecting firewood could be used for other goals); (3) educational standards improved by access to lighting; and (4) health standards improved through access to refrigeration, since food and medicines could be kept handy and since smoke from cooking fires could be eliminated.[34] The company cited Japan, Taiwan, and Korea as "winning nations," and stated "economic growth could not reach impressive figures before the overwhelming number of homes in the country had electricity."[35] In addition to electrifying 300,000 homes per year until the year 2000, Eskom also made a pledge to reduce the price of electricity in real terms by 15 percent by the year 2000 in order to provide the newly connected homes with an affordable service. The latter is in keeping with Eskom's overall vision of offering the lowest electricity rates in the world.[36] All such goals stem from Eskom's belief that little economic growth can occur without the widespread use of electricity.

In 1994 it was estimated that the electrification program would cost around R12 billion (approx. U.S. $3.5 billion), with annual investments peaking at around R2 billion.[37] How would it be possible to implement such a large social investment project in a viable manner? Although Eskom was producing the lowest-priced electricity in the world at the time and was operating at an excess capacity, the capital expenditures that would be incurred would be astronomical. Moreover, given the history of apartheid, the people that they were going to provide electricity to had become dependent on other sources of energy[38] for their daily needs. Was there a guarantee that these people would use the electricity when it was supplied to them? The unemployment rate in South Africa also lingered at approximately 45 percent and there was a history of "nonpayment" among the black population,[39] so how was Eskom going to implement a system which would lower the risk on return for their investment?

(B) A Culture of Nonpayment

During the apartheid years there was a great deal of conflict between the black South Africans opposing the established government and the military and police of South Africa. The conflicts ranged from public demonstrations to covert ANC bombings. One of the most commonly used forms of protest against the apartheid state was the consumer boycott, when blacks used nonpayment as a form of protest against the government. The idea behind nonpayment was to withdraw support of the infrastructure that the apartheid government had forced upon the black South Africans. Black South Africans boycotted rent, electricity, and consumables.

Boycotts started during apartheid as a method supported by the ANC to undermine the South African government and spread widely through the poor population that was eager to avoid paying for anything out of their scarce incomes. Boycotting went further, when local authorities would typically respond by cutting off services to the areas boycotting payment. The residents of these areas naturally adapted by pirating the services (tampering with the electrical grid and water system) that were being denied to them.[40] Many of the problems that the new South African government faced were a result of the past boycotts that they helped to support.

In fact, ANC members of government, who had anticipated the use of nonpayment to stop as soon as power was democratically held in the country, openly called for an end to the boycotts when the nonpayments were threatening the supply of services on a national scale. However, a culture of nonpayment had permeated the country. It threatened the development of the new South African government and the RDP campaigns, and it also inhibited foreign investment when companies from abroad recognized a risk of negative returns on investments.[41] The government implemented extensive educational reforms in order to help the citizens recognize the need of payment for services.

van Rooyen was assigned the task of determining what to do about the fact that Eskom was owed a total of R1.5 billion by black municipalities that had not paid for service during apartheid, and the fact that further nonpayment would hinder the electrification program.[42] Although van Rooyen remembered that the company had historically approached the problem of nonpayment with the threat of cutting off the power to municipalities, he soon decided that this policy was not viable for a number of reasons. First, there was a question of equity and fair treatment of the people living within those communities who were paying their bills. Would it be fair to remove access to a service for which these people had in fact paid? Second, the effects of the apartheid regime were now more noticeable and the company was committed to helping these people improve their living standards. Third, past action by municipal authorities against non-payment had led to riots and violence. van Rooyen had the difficult dual goals of both realizing a return on the company's investments and contributing to the quality of life of the citizens of South Africa.

(C) Residential Tampering

Muenda,[43] one of Eskom's top managers, looked at the figures and couldn't believe what he was seeing. On average, as much as 40 percent of Eskom's pre-paid connections had been tampered with and this led to a loss in revenue amounting to R300 million annually.[44] This wasn't surprising to him considering that even children in the sixth grade had the knowledge of how to pull electricity illegally off the electrical grid. In fact, they could even demonstrate how the recoil would knock a person down if a mistake happened while tampering with the grid (many were electrocuted to death while tampering).[45] During apartheid, people in these communities had learned that, in addition to not paying for services, they could further undermine the local white authority by tapping into the electrical grid and drawing service for free.[46]

Muenda looked more closely at the numbers and determined that it would be cheaper for the company to connect people to electricity and not charge for usage.[47] The cost per connection averaged R3,000 and Eskom performed 1,000 connections on a daily basis, which amounted to approximately R1.095 billion annually. However, Muenda decided to calculate the present value of this venture and determine the payback period, which would be a bit more complicated than simply looking at the overall costs and revenues associated with the program. In order to offset illegal draws from the grid, Eskom would have to go through the additional expenditures of monitoring the grid. Not only would Eskom have to pay for the man-hours and expenses associated with inspection, but many times these employees were attacked or had their cars hijacked when in the areas that they were inspecting, which was by itself a valid argument for supplying fixed-rate connections because of the concern over employee safety. Upon examining the figures, Muenda discovered that, although the total annual sales per customer receiving electricity were R96, the total annual operating costs per customer were R104. Therefore, the excess costs of collection, maintenance, and inspection due to nonpayment and tampering reduced Eskom's return to a negative R8 per customer. In other words, Eskom would not only absorb the initial capital expenditure of R3,000 per customer to connect people to electricity, it would also incur a R8 fee annually for each customer connected to the electrical grid under the electrification program.

What was Muenda to do? According to his figures the program was providing the company with a return on its investment, even several years after the project began. In fact, Muenda determined that it would simply be more cost-effective for the company to give electricity away for free and thereby lower the costs associated with billing, maintenance, and metering equipment. But the company had not only committed to the RDP goal of electrifying 1.75 million households by the year 2000, but was also attempting to foster a responsible culture of payment within the consumer base.[48] Should he recommend that the company stop the electrification program until his group could plan a way to generate adequate revenue from the consumer base? Although the costs of the program were increasing because some of the residents were tampering with their connections, there were people who were managing their connections responsibly within the communities and had been paying their bills. Would it be fair to the latter type of consumer to stop the electrification program because of the people who were being irresponsible? Should these people be denied access because of what others were doing in the community? From a theoretical perspective, it was easy to determine that it would not be fair to deny electrical connections to future responsible consumers because of past irresponsible behavior customers. But what was Muenda to do when he found hundreds of illegal connections coming off the grid in a community? The question of who was responsible, the individual or the community at large, became very difficult to answer in such a situation. Should Eskom disconnect the entire community in such a case?

(D) Training to Tamper

Mr. Withers[49] was reading the paper and he noticed the headline that said that the unemployment rate for black South Africans currently hovered at 41.1 percent of the total population in South Africa.[50] He remembered the issue of poverty being addressed by the African National Congress in the following way:

Poverty is the single greatest burden of South Africa's people, and is the direct result of the apartheid system and the grossly skewed nature of business and industrial development which accompanied it. Poverty affects millions of people, the majority of whom live in the rural areas and are women. It is estimated that there are at least 17 million people surviving below the Minimum Living Level in South Africa, and of these at least 11 million live in the rural areas. For those intent on fomenting violence, these conditions provide fertile ground.[51]

In order to improve the quality of life for all South Africans, the RDP stressed that poorer citizens must be empowered to take control over their own lives.[52] Part of the government's strategy to promote empowerment was to improve living conditions, boost production, and household income through job creation, and create opportunities for all citizens to sustain themselves. In fact, job creation was specifically linked with public works projects and projects aimed at meeting people's basic needs in the RDP.[53] In these ways, job creation was a primary focus of the ANC government, and Mr. Withers, a manager at Eskom, recognized the role that Eskom could play in the RDP.

Therefore, Mr. Withers recommended that Eskom use local labor as part of the electrification process. By providing people with basic electrician's skills, he was attempting to meet the problem of unemployment in South Africa. The plan was that the people trained in basic electrical wiring and repair would be paid for assisting in the electrification process of the surrounding areas. Although they would not be full-time employees with Eskom, because others would be trained to assist with the electrification process in their respective areas, these people would have a marketable skill to use when attempting to procure jobs. Electrician's skills would be marketable to industry and these skills would also provide a means for people to start small businesses within their communities. As load growth and electrical demand increased in newly electrified areas, people would start to use more electrical appliances.

Therefore, a market would arise for the repair and resale of these appliances, which would fall into the hands of the people being trained by Eskom.

Mr. Withers was astonished to learn that, although illegal connections had been discouraged, electricity was being consumed in areas in which people were not purchasing tokens for their prepaid meters. In order to examine what was going on, Mr. Withers chose pilot sites and placed meters on the connections going into the communities to determine how much electricity was going into the community for a given time period. He then looked at electricity sales for that community for the same time period and compared the amount of electricity going in to the sales of electricity. It was determined that tampering was prevalent in almost all of the communities that had been electrified—even as high as 80 percent in some areas.[54] After investigating the matter, Mr. Withers noticed that the people who had been trained and paid to assist in the electrification process had actually been stealing electricity from Eskom. In other words, he had inadvertently trained people to steal from the company. These people would approach their neighbors and bypass prepaid meters for small fees, thereby providing free electricity to the people who would pay for illegal connections.

This situation only compounded the problem that Mr. Withers had encountered with residential tampering. If the company decided to continue with the electrification program, what type of message would the company be sending the residents when Eskom employees themselves were aiding in illegal tamperings? The purpose of training local laborers in the electrification process was an attempt to help curb the high unemployment rate for black South Africans. So what should he recommend the company do? Should they continue to train, pay, and use local labor in the electrification process, even though the company already had approximately 40,000 employees operating in a country that was only a little more than twice the size of Texas,[55] which meant that they had the existing infrastructure to perform the electrification process on their own, without training and employing local labor? In fact, it even cost Eskom an additional amount on top of the electrification process to train these people at all. But now they were helping to steal from the company. Obviously, this type of employee behavior was driving the costs of operation even higher. But what was more important, providing people with a marketable skill and curbing the unemployment rate or lowering the costs involved? How could Mr. Withers's group achieve both?

(E) Electrical Development vs. the Environment

Ndlovu, a new hire at Eskom,[56] read Eskom's corporate slogan which was "To provide the lowest priced electricity in the world in order to promote growth and development," and he knew that the utility was, in fact, in yearly competition with other countries for producing the lowest priced electricity in the world.[57] One factor influencing the low price of Eskom's electricity is the lowering finance charge that the company has experienced. The finance charge has mainly decreased as a result of the enormous capital expenditures, which the company incurred in the 1970s and '80s[58] in building excess generation facilities, finally reaching a break-even point and because of a temporary moratorium placed upon Eskom from acquiring new debt in 1985.[59] As a result, the finance charge has decreased by 62 percent since 1987, which has led to the reduction of the total price of electricity by 61 percent.[60] Moreover, because of the reduction of investment programs, the company has been able to finance many of its expenditures from its own treasury[61] and lower its debt to 40 percent of its 1985 level.[62]

Ndlovu also knew that Eskom's low price was also influenced by the improvement of internal management practices and the gain in operational performance that resulted from such practices. For example, although typical coal generation facilities are considered efficient for remaining on-line 31 percent to 33 percent of the time, Eskom was able to achieve a 96 percent measure of availability in 1997. In other words, Eskom was able to meet unanticipated peak demand with plants already on-line providing electricity to the grid, instead of having to keep excess plants in reserve in order to meet the risk of peak load demand. Accordingly, this improvement of availability, and the offset costs of keeping excess plants in reserve, was transferred to the customer in the form of lower electricity prices. When these cost saving practices are added to the fact that electrical sales have increased by as much as 50 percent or more from the 1985 levels,[63] it becomes easier to understand how Eskom is able to provide some of the lowest electricity prices in the world. Other factors influencing the lowered cost of Eskom's electricity were the lowering of labor costs due to the downsizing of Eskom from 66,000 in 1985 to 40,000 in 1998 and the depreciation of coal costs by as much as 30 percent since the mid-1980s. All in all, Ndlovu knew that the electrification program, and its increasing costs, was possible because of Eskom's over-investment in the 1970s and '80s. For the excess generation capability that was built into Eskom's infrastructure during that period of time has allowed the company to meet new demands and growth with marginal capital expenditure.

However, Ndlovu couldn't ignore the fact that the price of South Africa's coal was an eighth the price of other countries and 46 percent the price of U.S. coal. He also realized that South Africa relies upon coal for 72 percent of its energy needs, and although the country accounts for 0.8 percent of the world's population, it contributes 1.6 percent of the world's greenhouse gas emissions.[64] In fact, the coal fired facilities require approximately 90 million tons of coal[65] annually to produce electricity, which means that the environment is being adversely effected from the mining that is necessary to extract such large amounts of coal. Moreover, Ndlovu had just discovered that the burning of this coal in generating electricity produces approximately 1300 kilotons of Sulfur Dioxide, 600 kilotons of Nitrogen Oxide, 170 kilotons of Carbon Dioxide, and 10 kg/Mwh of fine particulate emissions[66] annually.[67] Therefore, Eskom was averaging a daily contribution of 40ppb[68] of Sulfur Dioxide and Nitrogen Oxide, both greenhouse gases, to the atmosphere. But the company was within South African operating guidelines because the Department of Environmental Affairs and Tourism had placed the allowable limit of Sulfur Dioxide and Nitrogen Oxide to be 100ppb and 400ppb respectively, which meant that Eskom was currently emitting approximately 40 percent (~40ppb) of the allowable Sulfur Dioxide limit and 10 percent (~40pbb) of the allowable Nitrogen Oxide limit.[69] However, these South African standards may not be as strict as the standards imposed in more developed countries. For example, the World Bank's guideline for Sulfur Dioxide emissions is no more than 500 tons of emission per day regardless of generation capacity, which meant that the company was emitting 1117.5 kilotons of excess Sulfur Dioxide than allowed.

Ndlovu's dilemma derived from the fact that the low price of Eskom's electricity was not only related to the price of coal but also to the fact that the company has not retrofitted the generation facilities with SOx or NOx emission controls. The company did not place these environmental measures on their facilities. The costs associated with the retrofits are not justified because they are already operating well below the set environmental guidelines.[70] In fact, recent studies had also shown that the current levels of SO2 and NO2 would have only negligible effect on the vegetation of South Africa.[71] Moreover, the money that would be used to retrofit the plants with emission controls could be used to provide the people of South Africa with access to electricity instead.[72] Also the retrofitting of the plants with filters would raise the price of electricity by 30–50 percent, which would impede Eskom from providing the lowest priced electricity in the world to its customers. Whereas, the costs associated with electrifying the people of the country would be cheaper, wealth generating, and also improve the environmental impact by supplying electricity to people who would otherwise be burning coal for residential energy needs. In 1990, Andre van Heerden said:

> Our dilemma lies in where we should be spending our money. For the price of R6 billion (R2 billion less than fitting desulphurisation filters on the eight largest plants), the townships can be electrified. At present much of the atmospheric pollution is caused by the townships with coal fires. (The pollution levels are 2/6 times more higher than where the power stations are based.) The coal that the household stoves burn is low-grade heavy pollutant. Eskom burns the coal more efficiently than an individual ever could.[73]

However, the problem was not as simply stated. For when Ndlovu decided to look into the situation he discovered that wood is the primary domestic energy source[74] for half of all South Africans, which translates to 11 million tons annually. In fact, eight million tons of wood are cut from natural woodlands annually, which is roughly equivalent to the natural production rate.[75] The latter is obviously an unsustainable situation and would soon lead to the deforestation of South African woodlands. Moreover, the burning of this wood in homes accounts for the majority of carbon monoxide and methane emissions in South Africa, which is higher than that released by Eskom's generation facilities. As a result of this discovery, Ndlovu commissioned a study in order to determine where emissions were originating. The study[76] found that although coal-fired stations were contributing more greenhouse gases to the atmosphere than residential burning of biomass, the facilities were only accounting for 11 percent of particulate emissions; whereas approximately 41 percent of the particulate emissions were coming from residential use. Although this finding did not initially seem significant when compared with such things as greenhouse gases and global warming, Ndlovu soon discovered that people were being exposed to 65 times the U.S. Environmental Protection Agency's guideline[77] for particulate emissions and double the WHO's guidelines for carbon monoxide. These levels were shocking for Ndlovu because similar levels of exposure had been linked to illnesses and deaths from respiratory disease, cardiac arrest, and lung cancer.[78] This air pollution from residential use seemed to be the obvious cause of the fact that respiratory infections were the second highest cause of infant mortality in the country, which was 270 times higher than the Western rate.

Ndlovu couldn't help but to think that these types of situations could be avoided by providing people with electricity, for they would then have a safer source of energy for cooking and heating and not have to rely upon wood or coal. Although Ndlovu did not like the fact that the generation facilities were contributing to a global greenhouse gas situation, they were currently operating well below the set South African guidelines and also producing the lowest priced electricity in the world, which is exactly what the people in these communities needed given the high rate of unemployment and variable incomes. Therefore, Ndlovu was struggling with the question of what was presently more important: the environment or development? What should he do? Should he recommend that the company incur the capital expenditures to make the retrofits and operate at lower emission levels, but offset the costs associated with retrofits by either raising the price of electricity or slowing the electrification program?

Notes

* This case was prepared by Brian D. Cunningham under the supervision of Michael E. Gorman, School of Engineering and Applied Science at the University of Virginia, and Patricia H. Werhane, Ruffin Professor of Business Ethics at the Darden Graduate School of Business Administration, University of Virginia. Partial support for this project was supplied by grants from the Ethics and

Values in Science Program of the National Science Foundation and the Darden School. This case was written as a basis for class discussion rather than to illustrate effective or ineffective handling of an administrative situation. Copyright © 1999 by the University of Virginia Darden School Foundation, Charlottesville, VA. All rights reserved.

1 Fictitious Afrikaans name for the decision-maker in this case.
2 The African National Congress which took control in 1994 during the first racially open elections in South Africa.
3 For a brief historical perspective of South Africa, see Appendix A; a historical description of Eskom's background, Appendix B; a description of the 1994 elections and the Reconstruction process that was outlined, Appendix C; a description of Eskom's corporate initiatives and policies under Apartheid, Appendix D; and for a description of Eskom's stated commitment to the South African reconstruction process, Appendix E.
4 Programs that were used to narrow the discriminatory gap between the white and black South Africans.
5 African National Congress, *The Reconstruction and Development Programme* (Johannesburg, South Africa, 1994).
6 People could settle on municipal lands under new South African law, which meant that thousands of people were constructing make-shift structures for houses in areas that were not designed for residential development (e.g., areas beside freeways and even airport runways).
7 The South African Rand fluctuated against the U.S. Dollar in the range of 3:1 in 1994 to 6:1 in 1998.
8 Reconstructed from *SA to Z: The Decision Maker's Encyclopedia of the South Africa Market* (Johannesburg: Eskom, 1996).
9 One generation facility would cost approximately R16 billion and take several years to build.
10 Eskom, 1994 Annual Report (Johannesburg).
11 The Khoikhoi (aka the Hottentots).
12 L. Louw and F. Kendall, *South Africa: The Solution* (Ciskei, South Africa: Amagi Publications, 1986).
13 Ibid.
14 Orpen, Christopher (1976) *Productivity and black workers in South Africa* (Cape Town: Juta).
15 The mining shafts were going deeper into the ground and needed to be ventilated.
16 The first commercially supplied electricity in South Africa.
17 Escom was renamed Eskom in 1987.
18 South Africa has 91 percent of the world's manganese reserves, 82 percent of its platinum group metals, 58 percent of its chrome, 53 percent of its gold. As a result, South African mines are deeper than any other country in the world, at depths of almost 4 kilometers in places (e.g., Western Deep Levels Mine).
19 Eskom, 1997 Annual Report, Johannesburg.
20 Jon OffeiAnsah, "South Africa: Large Energy Economy Enjoyed by Few," *African Economic Digest* (July 31, 1995). Although this fact is not emphasized in Eskom's literature, it is likely that this excess capacity may be one of the main reasons why Eskom began electrifying schools and homes as early as 1988 and the early electrification programs in 1990.
21 April 26–28, 1994.
22 "South Africa," *Hilfe Country Report* (July 1996).
23 The Conference Board, 4.
24 Table constructed from data from *SA to Z: The Decision Maker's Encyclopedia of the South African Consumer Market* (Johannesburg: Eskom, 1996).
25 Ibid.
26 "South Africa: Large Energy Economy Enjoyed by Few," *African Economic Digest* (July 31, 1995).
27 Peter Adams, Eskom spokesman, in Bob Drogin, "South Africa Bringing Power to the People," *Los Angeles Times*, January 31, 1996, A1.
28 For details on the political changes of this period, see Elling Njal Tjonneland, *Pax Pretoriana: The Fall of Apartheid and the Politics of Regional Destabilization* (Uppsala, Sweden: Scandinavian Institute of African Studies, 1989).
29 Myra Alperson, *Foundations for a New Democracy: Corporate Social Investment in South Africa* (Johannesburg: Ravan Press, 1995) 70.
30 Eskom, "Bringing Power to the People," video prepared for the Edison Electric Institute, 1996.
31 Drogin, "South Africa Bringing Power to the People."
32 Eskom's goal was to produce and distribute the cheapest electricity in the world.

33 Chairman of the Electricity Council.
34 Eskom, Eskom Corporate Profile, 1995.
35 Ibid.
36 Rob Stephan, "Challenges and Innovations Facing Eskom," *Transmission & Distribution World* (January 1996), 30.
37 African National Congress, *The Reconstruction and Development Programme: A Policy Framework* (Johannesburg: ANC, 1994) 31.
38 Paraffin, coal, candles, dung, and wood.
39 Used as a protest against the apartheid government. See Eskom Case B.
40 R. W. Johnson, "Riots and Bulldozers Return to Townships," *The Times*, Overseas News, August 9, 1997.
41 "Africa and Latin America," Weekly Economic Report, Part 5, The British Broadcasting Corporation. March 21, 1995.
42 Kevin Morgan, legal adviser to the South African National Electricity Regulator, in an interview with Africa News, August 9, 1996.
43 Fictitious Zulu name used for case example.
44 Robyn Chalmers, "Meter Tampering Costs Eskom R300m," *Africa News*, May 21, 1998, http://www.africanews.com.
45 Bill Keller, "Township Gets Electricity (and It's Free, Too)," *The New York Times*, September 1, 1993.
46 Boycotting payment for service as a protest of the Apartheid government.
47 Interview with Paul Maree (current Eskom manager for the Electrification Program).
48 See Eskom, Case A.
49 Fictitious name used for case example.
50 *SA to Z: The Decision Maker's Encyclopedia of the South African Consumer Market* (Johannesburg: Eskom, 1996).
51 Section 2.1.1 of *The Reconstruction and Development Programme*, African National Congress, 1994.
52 Ibid. Section 2.2.3.
53 Ibid. Section 2.3.2.
54 Soweto, South Africa.
55 Total area of 471,000 square miles as compared to 270,000 square miles.
56 Fictitious Zulu name used for case example.
57 Eskom's price per kWh in 1997 was 1/2 the U.S. price.
58 See Appendix B of Case A for Eskom's history.
59 De Villiers Commission of 1985.
60 Davis, M. (1997) *Household electrification. How and why in South Africa*. EDRC, UCT. Cape Town, South Africa.
61 In 1994 Eskom's treasury was given a credit rating equal to the South African government by the international community.
62 Van Horen, C. Eskom, its finances and the national electrification programme. Development Southern Africa. 189–204.
63 Due to the electrification program.
64 Wells, R.B. *Air Pollution and its Impacts on the South African Highveld: Global Issues*. Environmental Scientific Association. Cleveland, South Africa. 1996.
65 Eskom's 1997 Environmental Report.
66 Coal ash in the atmosphere.
67 Eskom's 1997 Environmental Report.
68 Parts per billion.
69 Eskom's 1997 Environmental Report.
70 The result of the coal having a low Sulfur content.
71 Walmsley, R. *Air Pollution and its Impacts on the South African Highveld: Impacts*. Environmental Scientific Association. Cleveland, South Africa. 1996.
72 The Electrification Program.
73 Euromoney Supplement. September 12, 1990. Page 7.
74 Cooking and space/water heating.
75 Helas, G. and Pienaar, J. *Air Pollution and its Impacts on the South African Highveld: Biomass Burning Emissions*. Environmental Scientific Association. Cleveland, South Africa. 1996.

76 Ammegarn, H. et al. *Air Pollution and its Impacts on the South African Highveld: Residential Air Pollution*. Environmental Scientific Association. Cleveland, South Africa. 1996.

77 The EPA's *Revised Particulate Matter Standard* sets the health limit at 65 micrograms per cubic meter in a 24 hour period; however, the South African example is being exposed to 2367 micrograms per cubic meter in a 24 hour period.

78 van Horen, C. *Energy and Environment Policy in South Africa: Assessing the Priorities After Apartheid*. EDRC. Cape Town, South Africa. 1995.

4.2 ExxonMobil and the Chad/Cameroon Pipeline *

In November 1999, ExxonMobil CEO Lee Raymond faced the potential collapse of the Chad/Cameroon Oil and Pipeline Project on which the company was about to embark. Both Royal Dutch/Shell and France's TotalFinaElf, ExxonMobil's partners in the Pipeline Consortium, had just withdrawn, citing environmental concerns among other things and leaving its future temporarily in doubt. This withdrawal delighted many environmental groups long opposed to the pipeline. A spokesperson for the Rainforest Action Network (RAN), a grassroots environmental organization and longtime pipeline opponent, said in a press release:

> Based on its experience in Nigeria, Royal Dutch/Shell recognizes a bad situation when it sees one, and Elf Aquitaine will avoid becoming part of the tragedy. The human and environmental costs of proceeding with an oil pipeline that cuts through the heart of Africa's rainforest are simply too great.[1]

In 1996, after years of economic and environmental feasibility studies of accessing oil reserves in the Central African country of Chad, a consortium of oil companies that included ExxonMobil, Shell, and Elf signed a memorandum of understanding (MOU) with the governments of Chad and neighboring Cameroon. The Chad Development Project involved, over the span of 25 to 30 years, developing oil fields in southern Chad, drilling approximately 300 wells in the Doba Basin, and building a 650-mile underground pipeline through landlocked Chad and the adjacent Cameroon to transport crude oil to the coast for shipping to world markets. Cost of the project was $3.5 billion; expected production was one billion barrels of oil; according to World Bank estimates, the project would generate $2 billion in revenues for Chad, $500 million for Cameroon, and $5.7 billion for ExxonMobil and its project partners.[2]

Shell's and Elf's pullout threatened to sideline the whole operation and seemed to give credence to those critics who thought that environmental and human risks of oil exploration and extraction in the extremely poor countries of Chad and Cameroon were too great. The project's many issues burned in CEO Lee Raymond's mind as he considered whether ExxonMobil should follow suit or proceed with the pipeline project.

ExxonMobil

At the time of their December 1998 merger, which some oil industry analysts called "seismic," Exxon and Mobil, each a multi-billion dollar operation, were the world's two largest oil companies. In 1997, Exxon had a net income of $8.5 billion; a "AAA" debt rating; revenues of $137.2 billion; and it sold 5.4 million barrels of petroleum products daily. Mobil had a net income of $3.3 billion; revenues of $65.9 billion; and total petroleum product sales of 3.3 million barrels a day.[3] Many analysts attributed the merger to tough times for oil companies, which in the 1990s faced lower prices, decreased demand, fierce competition, oversupply, and a general global economic weakness.[4] Indeed, just three months before this merger, Mobil had attempted, unsuccessfully, to merge with Amoco, which then merged with BP. (Ironically, the Exxon Mobil merger reassembled the legendary Standard Oil, John Rockefeller's company. In 1911, antitrust authorities forced Standard Oil to break into two companies: Standard Oil of New Jersey, which later became Exxon, and Standard Oil of New York, which later became Mobil.) Nonetheless, the two companies had very different images in the oil industry. Mobil was seen as having a "combative feistiness," whereas Exxon had a "relentlessly efficient stuffiness."[5] Because of the size of the companies, the merger was scrutinized by antitrust regulators and, in order to complete the merger, both companies had to get rid of certain operations, including almost 2,500 service stations in the United States and Europe.

By the mere fact that a growing population of environmentally concerned people worldwide was skeptical of large oil companies and their promotion of fossil fuel use, both Exxon and Mobil struggled with their public image. Exxon had the most damage to contain, however, because of the 1989 Exxon Valdez oil spill in Alaska's Prince William Sound, when the single-hulled oil tanker, while dodging icebergs, hit a reef outside the shipping lane. The tanker then spilled 53,094,510 gallons (equal to 1,264,155 barrels) of oil. The spill covered 460 miles; took four years to clean up (although some Alaskan shores were still covered with oil at the start of the 21st century); and killed an estimated 250,000 seabirds, 2,800 sea otters, 300 harbor seals, 250 bald eagles, approximately 22 killer whales, and billions of salmon and herring eggs.[6] Worldwide public outcry was fiercely negative, and Exxon's reputation was severely tarnished.[7] After the accident, Exxon Shipping, owner of the Valdez, was renamed Sea River Shipping Company, and the repaired Valdez was renamed the Sea River Mediterranean. Prohibited from ever returning to Prince William Sound, the tanker began carrying oil back and forth across the Atlantic. Nonetheless, Exxon's handling of the Valdez episode and its subsequent appeal of a $5 billion jury award to spill victims "was derided as an example of how not to handle a public-relations disaster."[8] Exacerbating the situation was an Exxon representative's claim at a 1993 Atlanta symposium that some of the oil attributed to the Valdez spill actually came from other sources such as natural underwater fields.[9]

After the Valdez incident, Exxon tried to establish an environmentally friendly image[10] and began using more tugboats and increasingly sophisticated navigational equipment, such as global positioning systems, to guide its tankers through the waters.[11] Many of ExxonMobil's web site pages dealt with the issues of environment and sustainability and several acknowledged the damage done in the Valdez incident and confirmed that the company had developed an "Oil Spill Response Preparedness" program. ExxonMobil stated that its concerns now lay not only with responding to spills but in preventing them: "ExxonMobil is committed to achieving and maintaining excellence in environmental care throughout our operations. Our aim is to continuously improve our performance with the goal of driving operational incidents with environmental impact to zero."[12] The site also included a link to the company's "Environmental Performance Indicators," which provided: statistics on the company's marine spills, regulatory compliance (number of penalty assessments), cogeneration capacity, greenhouse gas emissions, and the reduction of nitrous oxide (NOx), volatile organic compounds (VOCs), and sulfur dioxide ($SO2$).

In part because it had no Valdez incident, Mobil's public image—on the surface at least—was different; the company, with a focus on support of the arts, sponsored *Masterpiece Theatre* and ran full-page "advertorials" featuring discussions of timely issues. Aside from *Masterpiece Theatre* and PBS programming, the company had funded community projects focusing on minorities, the handicapped, the elderly, and critical human needs.[13] Perhaps foreshadowing its eventual participation in the Chad/Cameroon pipeline, Mobil had sponsored "The Art of

Cameroon," a traveling exhibition, in 1984. Mobil had also initiated some environmentally friendly programs, which included planting half a million trees around the United States in the mid-1990s and proposing the same for Peru and Indonesia (Exxon was a tree proponent too, with its "Esso Living Tree Campaign," a reforestation project in both the United States and England). In smaller, more specific ways, Mobil had a softer image; in its service stations, the oil company had reinstated the practice of having employees clean car windows and offer coffee to drivers.[14] But the bottom line remained for Mobil, which in the early 1990s had exited the more environmentally friendly solar power business "because it was not economically attractive."[15]

Less visible to the public than Exxon's Valdez crisis was Mobil's involvement with some allegedly corrupt regimes. In an early 1990s attempt to enter the oil-rich Central Asian country of Kazakhstan, run by the brutal dictator Nursultan Nazarbayev, Mobil was involved with James Giffen, a corrupt American "consultant" or go-between for countries wishing to deal with Kazakhstan. (In April 2003, Giffen was indicted by a New York grand jury on charges of bribing foreign officials.)[16] Mobil had also dealt with the poverty-stricken Equatorial Guinea's oppressive ruler, Teodoro Obiang Nguema Mbasogo, in exploring and drilling the Zafiro Oil Field in 1995.

Exploration Areas

By 1999, ExxonMobil, with almost 60 exploration projects worldwide, was considered one of the strongest oil companies in Upstream Operations.[17] Its exploration and production efforts were scattered throughout the world, with 58 major projects under way in various countries. Some of the emerging exploration areas were West Africa, South America, the Middle East, the Caspian region, and Eastern Canada.

The major areas of exploration included:

North America:	Gulf of Mexico
Eastern Canada:	Nova Scotia, Newfoundland
Western Canada:	Cold Lake Field
South America:	Argentina, Venezuela, Brazil, Trinidad, Guyana
Europe:	North Sea, Netherlands, Germany, Norway, United Kingdom
Africa:	Nigeria, Equatorial Guinea
West Africa:	Angola, Chad, Cameroon
North Africa:	Egypt
Asia-Pacific:	Malaysia, Australia, Indonesia (North Sumatra)
Caspian:	Azerbaijan, Kazakhstan
Middle East:	Abu Dhabi, Yemen, Qatar, Kuwait
Russia:	Sakhalin Island

Source: ExxonMobil 1999 Annual Report.

Alternative Energy

Despite public pressure from environmental groups favoring alternative fuel sources, ExxonMobil remained firmly committed to fossil fuels. Other fuel sources such as solar, biomass, water and wind power, and electricity were simply impractical, the company claimed, and were "economical only in niche markets."[18] To illustrate the impracticality of other energy sources, ExxonMobil utilized a Manhattan Institute senior fellow's estimate that to power New York City on solar power alone would take four times the area of the city to hold the required solar panels, even on a sunny day.[19] Ethanol alcohol, another fuel source identified by environmentalists as more earth-friendly, was not as harmless as claimed, according to ExxonMobil, because of all the agricultural effort (and byproducts such as wastewater) that grain production required.[20] Future efforts looked dim; in a 2000 corporate report publication, ExxonMobil claimed that despite significant efforts to develop alternative energy sources such as solar or wind, those sources comprised less than 0.25% of the world's energy supply and would not, in the foreseeable future, be economical without significant governmental subsidies.[21]

Chad and Cameroon

In the late 20th century, Chad and Cameroon were two of the poorest countries in the world. Although Cameroon was more developed than its neighbor and had a higher literacy rate, many of the same problems assailed both countries. Both nations had rampant disease, poor nutrition, extreme poverty, and very little safe drinking water. Although three times the size of France, Chad could claim only 166 miles of paved roads, no rail system, a substandard telecommunications system (only two phones per thousand people), and overall insubstantial infrastructure and erratic access to electricity (see Table 4.2.1 and Exhibit 4.2.1 for maps of both countries).

Chad

Chad gained its independence from the French in 1960 (although the French stepped in four times over the next two decades to help the Chad government fend off coups). Almost immediately, the country was thrown into civil war, primarily between the Muslim northern rebel groups, called by one journalist "an explosive ethnic mix," vulnerable to outside manipulation (from Libya and Sudan, among others), and the government in the south. Politically, culturally, and geographically, the northern and southern regions of Chad were immensely different. The north was arid, desertlike, primarily Muslim; the south tropical and animistic. Internal turmoil continued through the next three decades, resulting in more than 20,000 deaths. As one analyst put it, "Undoubtedly Chad can pride itself as the African country with the largest number of rebellious groups since independence from France."[22]

In 1990, French-trained 38-year-old General Idriss Deby staged a coup, ousting President Hissene Habre. Deby, the fifth Chad head of state in the country's 30 years of independence, promised human rights, a multiparty system, and democracy; under his leadership; however, corruption and human rights abuses ran rampant. According to Transparency International, a

Table 4.2.1 A socioeconomic comparison of Cameroon, Chad, and the United States

	Cameroon	*Chad*	*United States*
Per capita GNP	$610	$230	$29,240
Life expectancy	54 years	48 years	77 years
Infant mortality	77 per 1,000 births	99 per 1,000 births	7 per 1,000 births
Literacy Rate	80% men	49% men	97% (both sexes)
	67% women	31% women	
Country GNP	$ 8.7 billion	$ 1.7 billion	$9,400.2 billion
Annual Exports	$ 2.3 billion	$ 328 million	

Source: Chad/Cameroon Development Project Fact Sheet 2001, Esso Exploration & Production Chad, Inc., p. 2.

global organization monitoring corruption levels globally, Chad and Cameroon repeatedly had two of the world's worst records for corruption.[23]

Skepticism about Exxon's dealings in Chad were exacerbated by a 1994 incident in Doba, where a local peasant, having taken his family to watch an airplane land at the Exxon exploration field, was shot to death by the security forces guarding the Exxon staff. Miscommunication was the cause: Security forces claimed that the peasant was a rebel, while villagers claimed he was just a man who wanted to watch the "miracle" of a plane landing. Ultimately, the cause of the incident was assigned to "language problems." That incident was indicative of potential problems in the ExxonMobil project. "Language differences may indeed exacerbate tensions in the Doba region. The Chadian security forces, which protect the oil consortium, are mainly recruited from the ethnic group of Chad's president, Idriss Deby. Most of these recruits are Arabic speakers from the North who do not know the local languages of the South."[24]

Other tragic incidents occurred, most notably in 1998 when Chadian security forces allegedly killed 200 civilians in the Dobara and Lara villages in the Doba region, a massacre that was never investigated. According to Amnesty International, "The Chadian government also utilized extrajudicial killings and disappearances, illegal searches and wiretaps, home demolition, threat of death or grave bodily harm, rape, and arbitrary arrest and detentions against its political opponents and their neighbors and family members."[25]

Cameroon

Cameroon achieved independence in 1960, after years of foreign domination by the Portuguese, Germans, British, and French. In World War I, the country was divided into French- and British-mandated regions. The French mandate was eliminated in 1960, giving the country independence, although part of the British mandate remained. The next 20 years saw a repressive government under President Ahmadou Ahidjou, which was nonetheless accompanied by investment in agriculture, education, health care, and transport. Prime Minister Paul Biya succeeded him in 1982 and, with pressure from Cameroonians, instituted a multi-party system. Although the country's literacy rate was one of the highest on the African continent, its development was slow because of widespread corruption and huge military and security expenditures.[26] In 1972, the country was the United Republic of Cameroon; it became the Republic of Cameroon in 1984. This West African country was 475,400 square kilometers, roughly the size of California, with 402 kilometers of coastline. In the late 1990s, the population was approximately 16 million.

In the 1980s, Cameroon had severe economic problems because of the worldwide drop in prices for its staple products, coffee, rubber, and cotton, and because the country was dependent on French companies, which controlled almost half of the export market. There was also internal friction between ethnic groups and regions as each fought for oil revenues.[27] Government repression increased in the 1990s, and while political parties were allowed to emerge, rampant fraud permeated the elections, and the government arrested opposition leaders. In 1997, Biya was re-elected president, although half of the country's population was excluded from voting for various reasons.

The Pipeline

Working with oil companies from various other countries, the Republic of Chad began exploring its own oil resources in the late 1960s. By 1975, after many exploration wells had been drilled, it was clear that oil was abundant. Further exploration was halted by Chad's 1979 civil war and did not resume until the late 1980s. In 1988, an Exxon consortium signed an

Exhibit 4.2.1 Maps of Chad and Cameroon

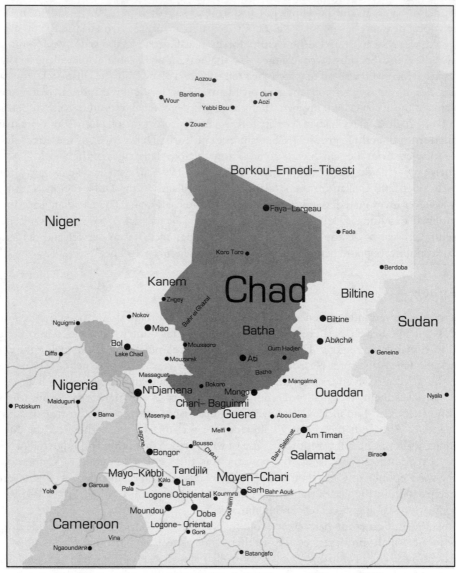

Source: http://www.cia.gov/cia/publications/factbook/geos/cd.html (accessed 24 January 2007).

agreement with Chad that set the framework for the eventual pipeline project; Exxon had 30 years to develop the oil fields at Doba in southern Chad and produce and transport the oil to market. Because Chad was landlocked, the Exxon Consortium signed an agreement with neighboring Cameroon to build a 1,070-km (approximately 600-mile) underground pipeline to carry the crude oil to a shipping terminal just offshore from Kribi, on the Gulf of Guinea. In January 1995, Exxon, through its affiliates, Esso Exploration and Production Chad Inc., signed an agreement with Chad and Cameroon outlining the principal terms for the pipeline. In 1997, the Chad government enacted an amendment to the 1988 Exxon Consortium convention, outlining the relationship between the Consortium and Chad,

Exhibit 4.2.1 *Continued*

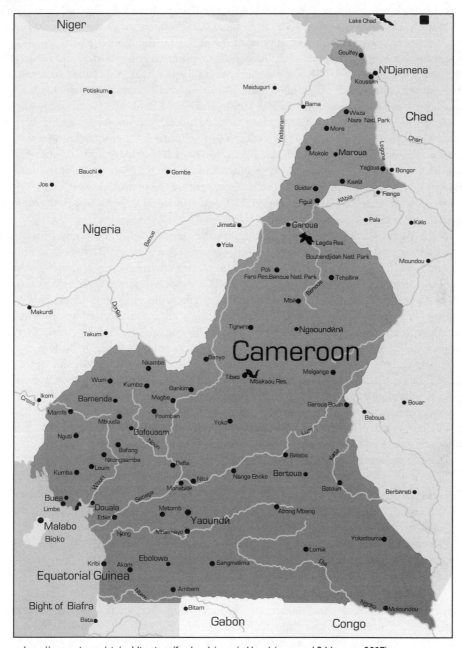

Source: http://www.cia.gov/cia/publications/factbook/geos/cd.html (accessed 24 January 2007).

"including the processes for environmental protection, land acquisition, and compensation, as well as royalty and tax payments that could approximately double the size of Chad's annual budget."[28]

World Bank Involvement[29]

The World Bank was conceived and founded in 1944, initially to help rebuild Europe after World War II. The bank's first loan was to France: $250 million for postwar reconstruction. Though reconstruction remained an important mission, over the years the bank expanded to lending money for relief from "natural disasters, humanitarian emergencies, and postconflict rehabilitation needs." The 1980s was a critical period for the bank, which had suffered from "macroeconomic and debt rescheduling issues," and faced criticism from many regarding its environmental and social positions. By the 1990s, the World Bank was focusing on stimulating economic development throughout the world, particularly in poorer countries. In 1999, the bank lent approximately $15 billion to developing countries.[30] Before becoming involved in the Chad/Cameroon Oil and Pipeline Project, the bank had helped fund 10 other pipeline projects around the world. Its return on earnings had averaged 22% over the years, although the returns on investments in Africa and oil and gas ventures were much lower.[31] By 1999, the bank's worldwide staff of 10,000 included 250 environmental experts and 800 employees working on sustainable development issues.[32]

Although World Bank involvement in the pipeline project did not become official until 1997 (a date for final project financing approval was not slated until 1999), the bank originally took an interest in 1993. In 1995, to ascertain the various environmental and social risks, the bank commissioned the governments of Chad and Cameroon, scientists, various nongovernmental organizations (NGOs), and environmental engineers to analyze the pipeline's impact on the areas through which it would run and produce an environmental assessment plan. Many of the villagers in the path of the pipeline were consulted, primarily through village meetings. The Environmental Assessment Plan covered a variety of topics including environmental management, compensation and resettlement, regional development, and waste management. The report, which was submitted to the World Bank in mid-1999, took five years to compile; at completion, it was a 19-volume, 3,000-page study.

The Environmental Assessment Report identified key problems and their potential solutions. The report acknowledged that the pipeline would cross over and thus affect "a number of ecological zones and a variety of socioeconomic groups."[33] The report also identified the potential environmental and social costs to both Chad and Cameroon:

- oil spill costs
- health costs
- agriculture production losses
- livestock fodder losses
- forest and bush product losses
- small emission of greenhouse gases.[34]

The report acknowledged the "uncertainty in estimating incremental environmental and social costs," but it claimed that "most of these potential costs will be mitigated and/or compensated for by the private sponsors, and any remaining impacts are expected to be negligible in comparison to the large benefits that both Chad and Cameroon stand to gain from the project."[35] A result of the report and the research was the Environmental Management Plan, country-specific documentation on construction and operations.[36]

On its web site, the World Bank explained its participation:

> This project could transform the economy of Chad. The country is so poor at present that it cannot afford the minimum public services necessary for a decent life. By 2004, the

pipeline would increase government revenues by 45% to 50% per year and allow it to use those resources for important investments in health, education, environment, infrastructure, and rural development, necessary to reduce poverty.[37]

Pipeline foes derided the World Bank's investment in the project, however. A Rainforest Action Network spokesperson was cynical, claiming that if the bank were truly committed to the environment and ending poverty, it would fund non-oil-related projects with direct benefits to local communities rather than large corporations and "corrupt governments."[38] One World Bank official conceded the occasional collision between the bank's goals and environmental responsibility: "The bank can't run away from a project that might harm the environment when it is being put forward by 'a country which may not have many development options.' . . . Poverty alleviation and the environment often are at odds. There are some real tradeoffs you have to make."[39]

Environmental/Social Issues

Beginning in 1993, during the pipeline initial planning phase, ExxonMobil began an evaluation of the project's potential environmental and social issues. Company representatives met with Chad and Cameroon government officials at all levels and with residents in the pipeline area. By 1998, ExxonMobil had held many village meetings and met with approximately 20,000 people in 65 affected villages. ExxonMobil also consulted with NGOs, including Africare, Care, and the Worldwide Fund for Nature. The company set up informational reading rooms in Cameroon, distributed a survey questionnaire, and set up consultations with the Bakola Pygmies, many of whom lived along the pipeline route.

Cameroon's Indigenous People

In central African countries, there were an estimated 250,000 Pygmies;[40] Cameroon's Pygmies were primarily the Bagyeli (or Bakola) people, with a population of approximately 4,000; there were also the Baka and the Medzan in the southeastern section of the country. Although the history of the Pygmies in Cameroon was somewhat unclear: Were they the original inhabitants of the forest, or did they move there with farmers and fishermen from elsewhere?—their connection with the forest was strong and clear: "They see the forest as a personal god, fruitful and kind, and enact their relationship with it and with the spirits of the forest in ritual and song."[41]

"What they do have in abundance is an intimate knowledge of the forest: the ability to read animal tracks, to know the flowering and fruiting cycles of plants, to locate a bee's nest from the flight of a bee. They know the individual properties of thousands of plants for food or medicine."[42]

Known for their short stature, Pygmies' average height was 4 foot 8 inches. Each group had its own language, with some common words indicating that once there was a shared language. Because they were hunters and not farmers, Pygmies had few possessions and were transient, moving around in groups of 15 to 60 people. As the 20th century came to a close, however, the Pygmy lifestyle was becoming more sedentary, with more or less permanent villages springing up.

The Chad Export Project's Indigenous People's Plan (commissioned by the Cameroon Oil Transportation Company, the pipeline project's management) outlined the primary characteristics of the Bagyeli Pygmies. They were sensitive to the ecological environment and dependent on the forest resources; they had limited interaction with Cameroon's mainstream population, in large part because of "pre-existing socioeconomic prejudice based on their way of life and physical appearance." The Bagyeli were also highly susceptible to disease, a condition exacerbated by their poor access to health care and health facilities. The Bagyeli had little to no access to formal schooling, and little motivation to acquire an education anyway. Because of their hunting lifestyle and their lack of agricultural training, the Bagyeli were unable to farm for subsistence or a living. In addition, the Bagyeli's habitat had already been severely damaged by industrial logging, which had started in the 1950s.[43]

Other reports, focusing more on the Pygmies' social situation, warned of the Bagyelis' fragile place in Cameroonian society as a whole:

> The Bagyeli are indeed a highly marginalized and vulnerable group. They are not recognized as Cameroonian citizens, have no identity papers, never participate in local elections, have no recognized collective land and property rights under law. They are thus marginalized in all local decision-making.[44]

Cameroon's Environment

By the mid-1990s, Cameroon was one of the world's top five exporters of tropical logs; however, the logging that had taken place for more than 40 years had decimated much of the country's forests. Between 1959 and the late 1990s, 81% of the country's unprotected forests had been logged. Although legislation to protect the forests was established in 1994, compliance with the legislation was problematic, with more than half of the licensees ignoring the regulations.[45] Cameroon's forests were some of the most diverse in the Congo Basin, but they faced the worst depletion. Experts agreed, "If managed properly, Cameroon's forests could offer long-term revenues without compromising the ecosystems' natural function"[46] but that this safeguarding would require careful monitoring. The pipeline was slated to go through the pristine M'bere Rift Valley and Deng Deng Forest, home to rare plant life, endangered species, and several thousand Pygmies, with their hunting grounds, settlements, and sacred sites. In the words of one of the Bagyeli people:

> Today, we don't recognize the forest anymore, we don't understand it. The logging companies destroy the forest. . . . Our children have no future. Where will they find the animals to hunt? The bark and the leaves and the fruits for food and medicine? We ask the government not to forget us, to do something so that our life today and tomorrow will not be as black as a night without stars. Protect us, protect the forest.[47]

The Rainforest Action Network (RAN), a major pipeline foe, claimed in a November 1999 press release:

> . . . [T]he African Rainforest Pipeline project will slice through the heart of pristine rainforests, and will put hundreds of millions of dollars into the pockets of Exxon and two corrupt governments. Southern Chad is so dangerous and politically unstable that neither Amnesty International nor the U.S. State Department was able to visit and confirm the massacre of hundreds of people. A 1999 U.S. State Department report on Chad shows a government engaged in indiscriminate human rights abuses.[48]

The African Forest Action Network (AFAN), a network of 60 West and Central African nongovernmental organizations, concurred with RAN's fears that the pipeline threatened biodiversity, forests, and the watersheds. An AFAN representative pointed out that, in its 670-mile route, the pipeline would cross 17 rivers used extensively by local communities for bathing, drinking, and washing, as well as five habitat zones. As it approached the Cameroon coast, the pipeline would run extremely close to a coastal national reserve with endangered marine life, as well as the Lob Waterfalls, one of the world's few falls which flowed directly into the ocean.[49]

According to RAN and AFAN, the pipeline posed threats to "forests, mangroves, and coral reefs," all of which played a vital role "in sustaining local communities, particularly for thousands of indigenous cultures around the globe that depend on them for their economic survival, cultural grounding and spiritual relations."[50] A combination of logging, air pollution, and climate change had led to extreme deforestation by the late 20th century. Deforestation then led to loss of biodiversity and the environmental benefits such as watershed protection, nutrient recycling, and climate regulation that forests provided.[51] Petroleum exploration only exacerbated the situation, because every stage of this exploration involved cutting down trees. In order to ascertain the path of petroleum, oil companies used explosive devices in the ground; these explosions added to the damage caused by deforestation, particularly in chasing away wildlife. The drilling process itself had enormous environmental fallout, producing drilling wastes (water, fluid, mud, and rock cuttings, all often toxic). Waste management processes to lessen the toxic waste generated were expensive and thus often ignored by the oil companies. There was also the infrastructure that needed to be built to support the drilling and pipeline communities; construction of these roads affected both the surrounding environment and communities. Indeed, in the extreme poverty both of rural Chad and Cameroon, the simple loss of a piece of land or a fruit-bearing tree could severely affect a family's ability to survive.[52]

Mangroves trees are an important part of the ecosystem, serving as a spawning and nursery area for many species such as fish, waterbirds, crustaceans, and aquatic mammals. Groves of mangrove trees help prevent erosion, mitigate climate change, and buffer land against storm-generated sea-level rises. Because they are coastal trees, mangroves could suffer greatly from any marine oil spills or pollution generated by offshore rigs.[53] Studies showed that it could take more than a century for mangrove trees (as well as coral reefs) to recover from damage caused by an oil spill, primarily because once their shallow roots were covered with oil, the trees could not breathe and consequently would die off. Cameroon had large expanses of mangrove trees along the Rio del Rey and Cross Rivers estuary; those trees were important for the country's large fishing industry.

Although ExxonMobil had commissioned an "Environmental Impact Assessment" for the pipeline project in the mid-1990s, many critics, such as the Dutch Commission on Environmental Impact Assessment, claimed that the report lacked key information, particularly about the effect on the two countries' ecosystems and inhabitants (especially the Pygmies) and also lacked emergency response and compensation plans in the case of an oil spill.[54] Critics even derided Exxon's decision to place the pipeline three feet under ground to avoid tampering and its leak-monitoring system.

> Even with the latest state-of-the-art technology, oil leaks in pipelines can go undetected until a huge amount of damage has been done. The most sophisticated technology has a detection capacity of a leakage of 0.002% of the oil passing through. [T]his means that under the best of circumstances 2,000 gallons could leak a day without being noticed.[55]

Other critics pointed out the dangers to Cameroon's Atlantic Littoral Forest, one of the world's most undisturbed classified rainforests, home to a myriad of plant and animal species, such as chimpanzees, elephants, gorillas, black rhinos, as well as the Bakola Pygmies.[56] As this forest was opened up to pipeline construction, critics argued that it would be more susceptible to logging and poaching, thus putting the forest's health and survival at risk.[57] Still other opponents argued that the consortium's stationary offloading vessel off the coast of Cameroon was only a single-hulled tanker, which was not as protective as a double-hulled tanker.

History of Oil Drilling in Less-Developed Countries (LDCs)

ExxonMobil faced another challenge: the history of oil company exploration in less developed countries. The most publicized case was Shell's operations in Nigeria. Shell had drilled for oil in Nigeria since 1937 and until the mid-1990s was the largest oil operation in that country. In the early 1990s, its joint venture with Elf and Agip produced more than 900,000 barrels of oil a day, mostly from a region inhabited primarily by the Ogoni people, one of Nigeria's 240 minority tribes. At the same time, between 1982 and 1992 approximately 1.6 million gallons of oil were spilled in the Nigerian oil fields, some precipitated by dissident Ogoni unhappy with the oil ventures, the environmental degradation, and the lack of improved social impact the drilling had on the local villages and communities. Although Shell claimed to have invested more than $100 million in environmental projects in Nigeria, there was little to show for this investment. Even the *Wall Street Journal* described Ogoniland as "a ravaged environment."[58] Finally, when Shell did not try to intervene or protest the government's assassination of a number of prominent dissidents, including Ken Saro-Wiwa, the worldwide media attacked Shell for what was perceived to be complicity in these deaths.[59] Despite $300 billion earned from oil since 1975, Nigeria's per capita income dropped 23% in that time period.

A similar controversy assailed Canadian Talisman Energy, Inc., which came under fire in 1999 for drilling oil in Sudan, Africa's biggest country and a place notorious for its human rights abuses. One journalist wrote that Sudan was "a place of epic misery. . . . In this largely arid and badly eroded land, rogue militias routinely enslave women and children. . . . At the centre of this conflict stands a fundamentalist Muslim government that has bombed hospitals, torn down Christian churches, and denied famine relief to its people."[60] To accommodate oil drilling, the government had displaced approximately 4.5 million of its 33 million inhabitants.

The Oil Industry in the Late 20th Century

In a report, "Changing Oil: Emerging Environmental Risks and Shareholder Value in the Oil and Gas Industry," the World Resources Institute (WRI) examined and evaluated the state of worldwide oil exploration in the late 20th century. In this 39-page assessment of the state of the oil industry, WRI presented some conclusions about the financial implications of restricted access to oil reserves:

- As traditional oil-producing regions mature and yield progressively less oil, the industry is increasingly choosing to explore and produce in new areas where environmental and social controversies may be significant.
- New information technologies and emerging networks between NGOs ensure that companies' activities become more transparent to their principal markets and shareholders.
- In environmentally and socially sensitive areas, access to reserves can be denied, restricted, or kept in limbo. Where access is permitted, opposition from local communities can constrain production operations, making them more costly. One prominent example is the case of Shell in Nigeria, where production has at times been cut to 40% of capacity and lower due to opposition and sabotage from local communities.[61]

The WRI report also touched on other issues facing the oil industry. Aside from increasingly limited access to reserves, companies must deal with the issues of climate change and environmental and social effects and how those would affect sales, operating costs, asset values, and shareholder values. In the late 20th century, environmental issues had already had an impact on oil companies and would hold even greater sway in how these companies conducted business and how profitable they ultimately would be. Investors were (and would be) increasingly eager to gauge the environmental "conscience" of a company, and any lack of transparency would affect investor relations.

Conclusion

If ExxonMobil did not proceed with the pipeline project, undoubtedly another country or company would take its place. Two possibilities were neighboring Sudan, which had financed its own pipeline, and Libya, whose president Muammar Qaddafi had encouraged Chad to ignore the western oil companies and let Libya ship the oil. ExxonMobil certainly could look elsewhere for oil reserves both in Africa and other continents. As a World Bank press release pointed out, "Chad is not the only country with untapped petroleum reserves. Exploration is underway right across the continent to find new oil sources—which could prove cheaper and more accessible. If Chad does not seize this opportunity, it may well pass the country by."[62]

All these issues went through Lee Raymond's mind as he considered the course of action that ExxonMobil should take.[63]

Notes

* This case was prepared by Research Assistant Jenny Mead under the supervision of Patricia H. Werhane, Ruffin Professor of Business Ethics, R. Edward Freeman, Elis & Signe Olsson Professor of Business Administration, and Andrew C. Wicks, Associate Professor of Business Administration, Darden Graduate School of Business, University of Virginia. It was written as a basis for class discussion rather than to illustrate effective or ineffective handling of an administrative situation. Copyright © 2003 by the University of Virginia Darden School Foundation, Charlottesville, VA. All rights reserved.

1 "On Anniversary of Nigerian Executions, Shell, Elf Pull out of African Oil Project," *Rainforest Action Network* Press Release, 10 November 1999; http://www.ran.org/news/newsitem.php?i-d=139&area=newsroom (accessed .6 March 2003).

2 For maps of the project, see http://www.esso.com/Chad-English/PA/Operations/TD_ProjectMaps.asp (accessed 09 January 2007).

3 "Exxon and Mobil Sign Merger Agreement," *Business Wire*, 1 December 1998.

4 Tim Smart, "Increasingly, Size Counts; Falling Prices in a World of Plenty Drive Mergers Such as Exxon-Mobil," *Washington Post*, 4 December 1998, D-01.

5 "From Mobil to Exx-Mobil: Pegasus Gets His Wings Clipped," *Petroleum Review* (1 January 1999): 38.

6 http://www.oilspill.state.ak.us (accessed 6 March 2003).

7 If there was a silver lining to the Valdez incident, it was that the spill prompted passage of the long-debated (14 years) Oil Pollution Act of 1990, 17 months after the spill.

8 "Merger Mixes Oil, Water: Aggressive Mobil Joins Stiff Exxon," *New Orleans Times-Picayune*, 3 December 1998, C-3.

9 Paul Leavitt, "Pa., Wis. Residents Boiling Tainted Water," *USA Today*, 27 April 1993: 3-A.

10 http://exxonmobil.com/corporate/Citizenship/Corp_citizenship_enviro_policy.asp for Exxon-Mobil's Environment Policy (accessed 09 January 2007)

11 "10 Years after Valdez Oil Spill, Such Disasters are Less Likely, But Dangers Are Still There," *Houston Chronicle*, 21 March 1999, 1.

12 http://www.exxonmobil.com/Australia-English/PA/Citizen/AU_Citizenship_Environment.asp (accessed 09 January 2007).

13 "American Business and the Arts," *Forbes* (Special Advertising Section), 28 October 1985.

14 "Merger of Exxon and Mobil: Opposites Attracted; Must Mesh Different Cultures," *Record*, Northern New Jersey, 3 December 1998, B01.

15 "Tree Lover," International Petroleum Finance (Energy Intelligence Group), 31 October 1999.

16 Daniel Fisher, "Dangerous Liaisons; Selling Oil Means Cutting Deals with Dictators," *Forbes*, Vol. 171, Issue 9, 28 April 2003, 84.

17 Oil companies in general had four major divisions: Upstream operations, for exploration and production of crude oil and natural gases; downstream operations, for transportation and sale; chemicals, for the manufacture and marketing of petrochemicals; and coal, minerals and power, for mining exploration and the generation of power.

18 "An Anniversary to Celebrate," ExxonMobil press release, http://www.exxon.mobil.com (accessed 1 June 2000).

19 "An Anniversary to Celebrate."

20 "An Anniversary to Celebrate."

21 http://www.exxonmobil.com/Corporate/Newsroom/Publications/shareholder_publications/c_fo_00/c_corporate_06.html (accessed 6 March 2003).

22 Janet Matthews, Information Services, "Chad Review," *Africa Review* (Sidcup, Kent, United Kingdom: World of Information, August 23, 2001), 1.

23 See http://www.trans.de/index.html.

24 Korinna Horta, "Fueling Strife in Chad and Cameroon: the Exxon-Shell-Elf-World Bank Plans for Central Africa," *Multinational Monitor* Vol. 18, No. 5 (1 May 1997): 10.

25 "Chad & Cameroon: Oil Pipeline Project Threatens Local Communities and Fragile Ecosystems," Amnesty International, www.amnestyusa.org/justearth/chad-cameroon.html (accessed 6 March 2003).

26 Country Profile: Cameroon, *BBC News*, http://news.bbc.co.uk/2/hi/africa/country_profiles/1042937.stm (accessed 24 June 2002).

27 http://gbgm-umc.org/country_profiles/country_history.cfm?Id=227 (accessed 6 March 2003).

28 http://www.essochad.com/Chad/Project/Development/Chad_Development.asp (accessed 6 March 2003).

29 Much of the information in this material is taken from the World Bank Web site: http://web.worldbank.org.

30 Benjamin C. Esty, "The Chad-Cameroon Petroleum Development and Pipeline Project (A)," Harvard Business School Publishing, Case # 9–202–010, January 17, 2002 (Rev.), 6.

31 http://www.environmentaldefense.org/documents/465_Letter%20to%20World%20Bank%2C%20July%201998%2Ehtm (accessed 6 March 2003).

32 Abid Aslam, "Environment: Taking the World Bank's Measure," Inter Press Service, September 26, 1999.

33 "Project Appraisal Document-Chad/Cameroon Petroleum Development and Pipeline Project," Washington, D.C., The World Bank, Report #19627-CM, Annex 14, March 30, 2000, 139.

34 "Project Appraisal Document-Chad/Cameroon Petroleum Development and Pipeline Project," 74.

35 "Project Appraisal Document-Chad/Cameroon Petroleum Development and Pipeline Project," 76.

36 See http://www.esso.com/Chad-English/PA/Newsroom/TD_Documentation.asp for environmental assessment documents (accessed 09 January 2007).

37 http://www.worldbank.org/afr/ccproj/project/pro_overview.htm (accessed 6 March 2003).

38 "World Bank Approves 'Nightmare' African Oil and Pipeline Project," RAN Newsroom, http://www.ran.org/news/newsitem.php?id=118&area=newsroom (accessed 6 March 2003).

39 Aslam.

40 Many of Africa's indigenous people over time had grown to dislike the word "pygmy" because of its often derisive use.

41 "Peoples of the Forest: Pygmies in Central Africa," Background Sheet (London: Survival for Tribal Peoples Organization, 1998).

42 "Peoples of the Forest."

43 Information taken from the Indigenous Peoples Plan, Environmental Management Plan, Cameroon Portion, Vol. 4, the Chad Export Project, May 1999.

44 Thomas Griffith and Marcus Colchester, "Indigenous Peoples, Forests, and the World Bank: Policies and Practice," World Rainforest Movement, August 2000 http://www.wrm.org.uy/actors/WB/IPreport2.html#box11 (accessed 6 March 2003).

45 For statistics and information on world forest depletion, see the World Resources Institute publica-

tion, "The Last Frontier Forests," at http://pdf.wri.org/last_frontier_forests.pdf (accessed 09 January 2007).

46 "An Overview of Logging in Cameroon," Global Forest Watch & World Resources Institute, 2000, 5.

47 "Peoples of the Forest."

48 "On Anniversary of Nigerian Executions, Shell, Elf Pull out of African Oil Project," Rainforest Action Network Press Release, 10 November 1999 http://www.ran.org/news/newsitem.php?id=139&area=newsroom (accessed 6 March 2003).

49 Horta, 10.

50 "Drilling to the Ends of the Earth: The Case against New Fossil Fuel Exploration," http://www.ran.org/oilreport/ecosystems.html, 1998 (accessed 6 March 2003).

51 "Drilling to the Ends of the Earth."

52 Horta, 10.

53 Horta, 10.

54 "Drilling to the Ends of the Earth: The Case against New Fossil Fuel Exploration, Offshore Boom, Onshore Impact: Central Africa," Rainforest Action Network, http://www.ran.org/oilreport/africa.html, 1998 (accessed 6 March 2003).

55 K. Walsh, "World Bank Funding of Chad/Cameroon Oil Project," Environmental Defense Fund, March 17, 1997, www.hartford-hwp.com/archives/32/031.html (accessed 6 March 2003).

56 There were an estimated 1,000 Bakola Pygmies in the entire pipeline project area.

57 Rachel Naba, "Oil Exploited, Nature Disturbed," http://theearthcenter.com/chad.html (accessed 6 March 2003).

58 Brooks, 1994, rpt. in Newburry and Gladwin, 2002, 526.

59 William E. Newburry and Thomas N. Gladwin, "Shell and Nigerian Oil," (1997 report) eds. Thomas Donaldson, Patricia H. Werhane, and Margaret Cording, *Ethical Issues in Business: Philosophical Approach*, 7th Edition (Upper Saddle River, NJ: Prentice Hall, 2002), 522–40. In 1993, Shell shut down its operations in Ogoniland but continued to drill for oil and gas in other parts of Nigeria. Shell then dramatically revised its code of ethics, invested at least $100 million in cleaning up Ogoniland, and pledged more than half a billion dollars in exploring alternate energy sources. (http://www.shell.com; accessed 6 March 2003).

60 Andrew Nikiforuk, "Oil Patch Pariah," *Canadian Business Magazine* (10 December 1999).

61 "Changing Oil: Emerging Environmental Risks and Shareholder Value in the Oil and Gas Industry," (Washington, D.C.: World Resources Institute, July 2002), 25.

62 "World Bank Group Approves Support for the Chad-Cameroon Petroleum Development and Pipeline Project," Washington, D.C., World Bank, News Release No. 2000/AFR, 6 June 6 2000, 2.

63 When the news of Shell and TotalFinaElf's withdrawal became public on November 11, more than 10,000 Chadians took to the streets of capital city N'Djamena to protest the withdrawal.

Chapter 5

Global Poverty

5.1 Hindustan Lever Limited (HLL) and Project Sting*

At 9:30 a.m. on a Monday morning in June 1987, the top managers of Hindustan Lever Limited (HLL), the Indian subsidiary of the giant multinational Unilever PLC, were gathered at HLL headquarters in Bombay to discuss the launch of Project STING or the "Strategy to Inhibit Nirma Growth." In its over forty years in the Indian market, HLL had maintained a largely unbeatable reputation and performance history, so it was fairly strange that top management would spend time discussing strategies to inhibit the growth of a small company like Nirma. Over the past decade, however, Nirma had seemingly emerged from nowhere to overtake HLL in the detergent sector. So far HLL had ignored rural India as a potential market, but Nirma's recent success in this area had sent HLL straight to the drawing board.

At this particular meeting, HLL's top executives planned to discuss how best to regain the country's dominance in India's detergent market. The first goal of Project STING was to understand the Nirma business model and determine how this upstart company had become so successful. Following this, HLL would have to evaluate its performance and rethink the HLL strategy in order to compete effectively with Nirma and overtake them. HLL also had to decide whether it should enter the rural Indian market and, if it did so, what products, strategies, and tactics would be the most effective.

Hindustan Lever Limited

Hindustan Lever Limited (HLL) was the Indian subsidiary of Unilever PLC, one of the world's largest multinational corporations. Founded in 1930 and based jointly in the Netherlands and the United Kingdom, Unilever sold its products in approximately 150 countries. Before the founding of Unilever, Lever Products arrived in India at the end of 19th century when India was part of the British Empire. The first Lever product to be introduced in India was Sunlight soap in 1888, followed by Lifebuoy in 1895, and Pears, Lux, and Vim over the next several years. Only the British citizens in India and a small section of the Indian population could afford these soaps, thus establishing early on an upscale profile typical of HLL's customers in India.

In 1931, Unilever had established the Hindustan Vanaspati Manufacturing Company, its first Indian subsidiary, which produced vanaspati, granular edible oil. Two years later, Unilever created Lever Brothers India Limited specifically to manufacture soaps and, in 1935, United Traders Limited to market personal products. These three companies merged as Hindustan Lever Limited in 1956. Along with Lipton, Brooke Bond, Pond's, Quest, and Assam and South India tea estates, HLL was one of Unilever's seven India-based companies. Unilever was a popular and respected company in India, in no small part because the company's "think globally, act locally" principle led it to train and appoint Indian managers instead of Europeans. Unilever realized the importance of employing managers who understood both the "Indian way" and the "Unilever way." After a series of exclusively non-Indian managers, Prakash Tandon became the first Indian director of the company in 1951. By 1955, 65 percent of all managers were Indian. As in all other countries where it had a presence, Unilever brought the local managers to train at the Unilever head offices in London.

HLL was among the first foreign subsidiaries to offer Indian equity at that point and had 10 percent Indian participation. By the late 1970s, HLL had gained the reputation of being a role model for companies looking to succeed in India and was one of the most sought after places to work at in the country. With products ranging from food and beverages to home and personal care products, HLL was considered India's largest household packaged mass consumption goods (PMCG) company. Unilever gradually divested its stake in HLL and, by 1982, held only 52 percent equity in the company.

HLL was also the undisputed leader in the Indian detergent market. Traditionally, Indians had used bars or tablets of soap to wash their clothes, a process which had involved scrubbing a wet garment with soap and then beating it with a club (similar to a baseball bat) or against a stone. By introducing the revolutionary Surf washing powder, bright blue and packaged in a large, colorful carton in 1959, HLL effected an enormous change as people switched from the club to the bucket. HLL's marketing strategy involved giving demonstrations of washing clothes in buckets with washing powder. Surf was an immediate success and occupied the top spot in the national detergent market.

While switching from a bar of soap to washing powder promised to revolutionize the way that Indian women washed clothes, only a fraction of them could afford Surf, so most of the rural poor continued to use soap bars and clubs. Expensive to begin with, Surf doubled in price in the early 1970s because of a rise in the price of crude oil and a massive increase in the cost of raw materials, putting the detergent even more out of the reach of rural people. Nonetheless, even though more new medium-sized competitors appeared in the Indian market, HLL maintained dominance until Karsanbhai Khodidas Patel, a chemist in the western state of Gujarat, and his product Nirma arrived on the clothes-washing scene.

The Rise of Nirma

In 1969, Karsanbhai Patel's life typified that of millions of other Indians. A chemist with the Gujarat Minerals Development Corporation in a dingy Ahmedabad factory in Gujarat, he struggled to make ends meet on a meager salary. "The work was dull," Patel would say later, "and my salary of Rs.400/- was grossly insufficient to take care of all my expenses."[1] Patel recognized, however, that there was a vacuum in the rural Indian market for affordable detergent. Either there were low-quality soap bars that did not wash well so were very time-intensive, or there were upscale detergent brands that were effective but too expensive. Recognizing the need for an affordable detergent and concluding that a good product would create its own market, Patel used his background as a chemist to conduct detergent-making experiments in his kitchen. His efforts finally yielded a pale whitish-yellow powder that he named "Nirma" after his then one-year-old daughter Niranjana.

Soon Patel was producing small quantities of his washing powder and selling it to his neighbors in small stapled and nondescript pouches. Even though Nirma's quality was inferior to Surf's, Patel's powder was far more effective for washing clothes than the traditional slab of soap had been. Every morning Patel rode his bicycle door-to-door selling his washing powder at an average of 200 kgs a day. His efforts were so successful that Nirma began appearing in neighborhoods, towns, and cities all over the state of Gujarat. Then wholesalers and distributors from farther afield began arriving at Patel's doorstep asking to buy and redistribute

Nirma. In 1972, Patel registered his company as Nirma Chemical Works and opened two more production facilities over the next couple of years. Soon afterwards, his product was available all over India, and the rural poor finally had an easier option for washing their clothes.

A New Business Model: The Nirma Way[2]

Although he hired additional employees as Nirma expanded, Patel stuck to his simple means of production for the next 10 years. He kept his company lean by outsourcing all the administrative functions and contracting out the sales, accounting, and technical production capabilities and distribution. By keeping his internal costs minimal, Patel had the flexibility to negotiate price during slow periods. Until 1985, the Nirma ingredients were simply mixed by hand and so did not require machinery or capital investment. Due to the scale of the product and the simple nonmechanized production process, Nirma was granted a number of tax exemptions and benefits for not using electricity and did not have to pay excise duties that were levied on multinationals.

As a cottage industry Nirma was not compelled to abide by minimum-wage rules and saved millions in labor costs. Patel used contract workers who were paid 85 rupees per ton (in 1985, US$1 = Indian rupee 12.368)[3] for mixing raw materials and then bagging them into bags weighing one kg each. Because payment was by the bag and no worker was permanent, Patel did not have to pay any worker benefits. By the mid-80s, when Nirma started to mechanize the production process, the company was well established.

Patel also kept an eye on costs when setting up a distribution system. Once the demand for Nirma had outgrown his ability to make deliveries by bicycle, he moved on to using vans and then later to trucks. Nirma employed neither a field sales force nor owned a distribution network. Patel negotiated prices with truck and van suppliers on a daily basis. As sales grew, Patel eventually hired stockists, who stocked additional quantities of the goods, as commission agents, a move that helped him avoid a central sales tax. He made the stockists responsible for all transportation, octroi,[4] handling and delivery costs. Initially, these stockists were friends or family members, but as the operation grew others were brought into the fold. To minimize risk for Nirma, there was also a strict system of protocol, and distribution depended on prepayment for stocks. Despite small trade margins, these stockists remained intensely loyal to Patel because of the high volume, the quick turnover, and the business opportunity (and increased income) that he and Nirma had provided.

At first, Patel did not advertise, but as television slowly spread throughout rural India in the late 1970s, he put Nirma ads—with simple messages and catchy jingles—on television. By the early 1980s, Nirma became synonymous with good quality and low price. The stockists were also responsible for promotions, and they funded 50 percent of the promotional expenditure for their goods. Nirma's sales reached a rate of growth that was two to three times that of the industry in general. As a result of all these measures, Nirma survived and flourished on what looked like a minuscule margin per unit. Patel even created a new word "nirmagenic," in the late 1990s, to describe a product's successful production and ongoing strength in the marketplace.[5]

Nirma's extremely simple distribution system stood in sharp contrast with HLL's multi-layered system. Put into place in the late 1940s, this system had four tiers: the factories, carrying and forwarding agents, redistribution stockists, and retailers. While this system provided an extensive network for the sale of HLL products, it also contributed to the higher cost of these products.

Marketing, Packaging, and Other Innovative Nirma Ploys

At first, packets of Nirma featured a generic picture of a woman washing clothes. In 1973, Patel put a picture of his daughter, for whom the soap was named, on the package, giving it a distinctive and personal aspect that helped Nirma stand out from the other detergents. Patel then embarked on some innovative marketing strategies. To gain trade acceptance, he hired women to go into retail shops and ask for the product. The company then began holding drawing contests, with large sums of money as reward. The Nirma calendar along with plastic shop boards were introduced in 1982, and Nirma was the only Indian company to advertise at the 1980 Moscow Olympics. To spread its name recognition even farther, the company plastered Nirma advertisements in stores, village shops, newspapers, and vans. Television and radio ads featured a constant stream of Nirma ads accompanied by the catchy jingle "Nirma washes clothes white as milk." By 1986, Nirma had the highest "top-of-mind" recall and an overall awareness level of 90 percent.

Nirma had first caught HLL's eye and piqued its curiosity in 1977 when, S. Sen, a former HLL marketing director, had noticed during an official tour of North India that Nirma was ubiquitous, whether in shops, on posters, or in advertisements plastered throughout remote villages and in newspapers. Sen's mental calculator had been at work, and he soon began to realize that this small upstart detergent was taking away business that could have belonged to HLL. Curious to meet the reclusive Karsanbhai Patel, Sen nonetheless was turned away before he could gain an audience with him. Thinking quickly, Sen asked for a cup of water, a request that could not be refused in this polite society and a tactic that brought him into the Nirma offices. Once there and face-to-face with his eventual competitor, Patel told Sen:

> You are selling detergents. I am selling detergents. We are competing. I don't want to talk. Soon, you see, I will be bigger than Surf. I will be number one in India. After that, I will be number one in the world.[6]

Despite Patel's strong words and Sen's genuine concern that this competitor was probably right, it still took many years for HLL to take Nirma seriously.

Product Differences

The key difference between Surf and Nirma was the price, but the ingredients also set the two products apart. Aware that soda ash, the main raw material for his product, was abundant in Gujarat, Patel set up shop in the vicinity. In designing his product, Patel kept things simple, and essentially violated all of HLL's detergent-design rules. Nirma contained no "active detergent," whitener, perfume, or softener. Indeed, tests performed on Nirma confirmed that it was hard on the skin and could cause blisters. Despite these differences, Nirma soap was a success.

Understanding the Rural Market

HLL's dismissal of the huge market segment of India's rural poor was based in part on traditional business theories. C. K. Prahalad and Allen Hammond, however, have likened the worldwide market to a four-tiered pyramid.[7] (See Exhibit 5.1.1 for the World Pyramid.) The top tier consists of the 75 to 100 million people earning more than $20,000 a year. These people are considered to belong to the elite and middle- and upper-income segments of society, with most of them living in the developed world. The second and third tiers

Exhibit 5.1.1 The World Pyramid

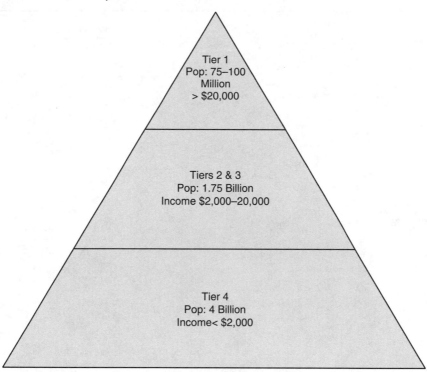

Source: C. K. Prahalad & Stuart L. Hart, "The Fortune at the Bottom of the Pyramid," *strategy+business*, Issue 26, First quarter 2002, Booz Allen Hamilton, Inc., and http://www.digitaldividend.org/pdf/bottompyramid.pdf (accessed on May 24, 2004).

(estimated at approximately 1.75 billion people) consist of the rising middle classes that live mostly in developing countries and earn between $2,000 and $20,000 a year. At the bottom of the pyramid, in tier 4, approximately 4 billion people live mostly in developing countries, earning less than $2,000 a year.

Typically, multinational companies (MNCs) have focused on the first tier since it provided for the highest margin of returns. In many cases, people in the second and third tiers of the pyramid receive attention, but the people at the bottom of the pyramid usually have been ignored. It is interesting to note, however, that the top three tiers represent only 34 percent of the world's population. MNCs have made the assumption that people in tier 4 do not have any disposable income and so cannot afford most products. Nirma's success in rural India, however, dispelled this myth. However, MNCs also ignored tier 4 markets because they were considered a "disorganized sector" where a lack of infrastructure and development made effective marketing and distribution of products almost impossible. MNC's high overhead costs also made it hard to be price competitive with local companies and thus serve as an additional barrier to entering this market.

The Case of Rural India

With an estimated annual growth rate of 1.7 percent in the early 1980s, India was the second most-populous country in the world. The country's total population was around 750 million,

Exhibit 5.1.2

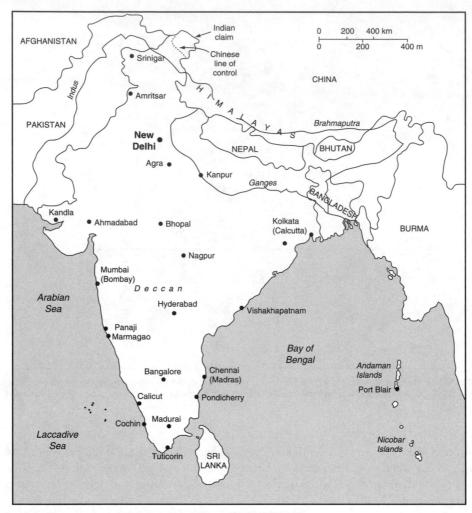

Source: http://www.countrywatch.com/cw_country.asp?vCOUNTRY=78.

with 70 percent living in rural areas. (See Exhibit 5.1.2 for a map of India.) This 70 percent—or 525 million people—was almost twice the population of the United States of America and constituted 12 percent of the world's population. By the year 2010, its population was expected to reach 1.15 billion.[8]

Despite the sheer size and potential volume of business in India's rural areas, HLL avoided this potential market for the simple reason that it was physically very difficult to penetrate. Rural Indians lived in approximately 570,000 villages spread across the Indian countryside. Approximately 90 percent of these villages were small (populations of less than 2000) and extremely remote. Most villages lacked electricity and running water as well as telephones and Internet access. Because of a lack of infrastructure, only 45 percent of the villages were accessible by road, and many of these roads were impassable in bad weather.

HLL had been deterred from entering these markets not only because of the physical challenges, but also because of "social and cultural" climates in these villages and the ineffectiveness of conventional marketing and advertising tactics. This rural "client group" had never been approached by the multinationals. Creating product awareness through banners and leaflets was ineffective because only 43 percent of the rural population could read; television and radio were almost equally ineffective as only 57 percent of the population was reachable by mass media. A media campaign was complicated by the 15 recognized languages and the over several hundred dialects. If HLL was going to make any dent in this market, it would have to be extremely innovative in its approach.

HLL Slumbers, While Nirma Overtakes Surf: The War of the Bubbles

Even though Nirma was the second-largest volume seller in the country by 1977, other companies did not take the product seriously, believing that it was a regional product that would only have temporary success. HLL marketing executives predicted that at such a low sale price, the margins Patel was making per unit would not sustain his business for long. HLL believed itself a superior company with a superior brand and that the only clients worth pursuing were the Indian middle class and elite. HLL continued to avoid the rural and low-income market, believing that it was too disorganized, a poor market, and that its high overhead costs would restrict it from producing a low-cost detergent. Besides, HLL did not consider Nirma a true threat and decided to wait and watch.

Despite its somewhat inferior quality, Nirma was in high demand by rural housewives because it sold at a third of the regular price. By 1977, with a 12 percent market share, Nirma was the second-largest volume seller of detergent in India; Surf was the leader with 33 percent. Still, HLL did not consider Nirma a threat, laughed at the minuscule per unit margins they were making, and simply waited for its bubble to burst. But by 1984, Nirma was the number one brand in Asia.[9] Patel explained the phenomenal growth: "I found a massive market segment that was hungry for a good-quality product at an affordable price . . . so I decided to keep my margins very low, and was happy if I could net between three and five percent . . . profits really came from the huge volumes we generated."[10]

With its leap from no market share in 1976 to 61.6 percent of the market share in 1987, Nirma had pushed HLL from the top spot. Despite being ousted from the top by the little detergent upstart, HLL still did not reduce the price of Surf, which remained between 2.5 to 3.6 times as expensive as Nirma. According to HLL—and proven by laboratory tests—Nirma did not contain any whitening ingredient, had insufficient active detergent, had no perfume, and was rough on the skin. In short, "Nirma was inferior to Surf and other premium powders on every single characteristic normally measured."[11] Yet despite all these factors, Nirma had outperformed Surf in the market. (See Exhibit 5.1.3.)

HLL Reacts

By 1985, Nirma was outselling Surf three to one. While Nirma had a market share of 58 percent, Surf's had dropped to 8.4 percent. From nowhere, Nirma had risen to become one of the largest-selling detergent brands in the world, not only increasing its share of the pie but increasing the size of the pie itself. Moving into a thus far untapped market, Patel was responsible for expanding the detergent market 10 times. To HLL's surprise, consumers were starting to compare HLL's high-quality Surf powder with Nirma. HLL researchers reported that persistent use of Nirma caused blisters on the skin and damaged clothes by weakening fabric in the long run. According to HLL's research and development team, these side effects were due to the high soda ash content in Nirma. Despite these criticisms, Nirma was being perceived as a much cheaper and fairly comparable alternative to Surf.

Exhibit 5.1.3

Surf: Nirma Market Share			Surf: Nirma Price Ratio			
Year	Market Share Volume		Year	Price per kg (Rs)		
	Surf	Nirma		Surf	Nirma	Price Ratio
1975	40.8	–	1975	10.65	–	
1976	38.2	–	1976	10.15	–	
1977	30.6	11.9	1977	12.80	4.35	2.94
1978	26.3	11.7	1978	12.25	4.75	2.58
1979	24.7	21.3	1979	11.95	4.45	2.69
1980	21.8	31.00	1980	18.50	6.00	3.08
1981	19.4	33.2	1981	20.20	6.25	3.23
1982	15.2	43.2	1982	21.05	6.00	3.51
1983	11.5	51.5	1983	20.90	6.25	3.34
1984	9.4	57.3	1984	22.20	6.80	3.26
1985	8.4	58.1	1985	23.15	7.20	3.22
1986	8.4	59.1	1986	23.70	8.00	2.96
1987	7.4	61.6	1987	27.10	8.50	3.19

Source: Butler, Charlotte and Ghosal, Sumantra, Hindustan Lever Limited: Levers For Change, Insead Euro-Asia Center, 302-199-1, Fontainebleau, France, 2002.

This jolt in consumer confidence and massive decrease in sales forced HLL to finally "get it," recognizing that Nirma was here to stay and that its competitor was successfully toppling the giant from the bottom of the pyramid. Finally, in 1986, Nirma started testing a new detergent bar that would be directly marketed as a challenge to Rin, HLL's leading and most profitable detergent bar at the time. At this point, HLL was aware that Nirma was systematically undermining its dominance in the industry and, for the first time, HLL got a glimpse of what could be the "beginning of the end" of their detergent business. It was time for HLL to react. The company had taken the first step with the creation of Project STING; now it had to put its plan into action.

Hindustan Lever Limited's New Strategy

The success story of Karsanbhai Patel's Nirma detergent had shown that many people in rural India did in fact have the money to buy packaged goods—if only the products could be delivered to them cheaply enough. Because Nirma threatened the very existence of Hindustan Lever Limited's (HLL) detergent business, HLL had formed Project STING in 1987 to develop a strategy to inhibit its growth. Project STING's participants had decided that HLL should enter the rural market, and now HLL needed to decide how best to compete with Nirma and its efficient and lean low-cost business model. This was a big step for HLL, and everyone was watching: Unilever, the parent company, Nirma, the competition, and all the critics. Under tremendous pressure to succeed, HLL faced some daunting questions.

Could the company even produce a product that was competitive to Nirma in price? There were several options to consider. Should they repackage Surf for rural consumption? Should they give the uneducated rural consumer a cheaper version of the urban counterpart or should they design a new product for the rural market? What would be the research and development costs involved in developing a new product? Additionally, HLL had to strategize distribution;

unless the company could ensure the availability of its products at all centers and to all vendors on a continuous basis, entering rural India was not a worthwhile endeavor.

As had been evident from Nirma's success, the bottom of the pyramid could be very profitable as long as a company understood that low costs combined with high unit sales were essential. In rural India, the game was about volume and capital efficiency. HLL had to ensure that every aspect of the process, be it product design, marketing, or distribution, was as innovative as possible. As C. K. Prahalad and Stuart Hart state in their analysis of the world's market, which they divided into a four-tiered pyramid, "The bottom of the pyramid poses a fundamentally new question: How do we marry low cost, good quality, sustainability, and profitability at the same time?"[12] HLL needed to think of all these issues during the product design stage.

If HLL could understand the everyday needs of this new client group, the company could develop a product for the poor. Unlike Patel's kitchen, HLL had its own R&D facilities, as well as those of Unilever's subsidiaries in other countries. In addition, if their product became a success, they would not only profit in India but also would have the choice of exporting it and related technologies to other Unilever markets.

Entering rural India would be a costly experiment for HLL if the new product failed; however, if it were a success, Unilever would be the MNC that led the way into the tier 4-market. This would give the company an additional advantage in the other developing markets where it did business. At the same time, the Indian government was opening its doors to more companies, and, with liberalization around the corner, HLL was well aware that it would soon be faced with even more competition. The positive side of these deregulation policies was that HLL would now face far fewer constraints on output volume and taxes and could be more competitive in terms of price.

Analyzing the Market

Fraught with difficulties, rural India, with its 525 million people spread across a country the size of continental Western Europe, was both a challenging and attractive market. As part of their background work, HLL conducted research on rural income levels. Contrary to the popular belief that rural people were poor, the company's research showed that a typical rural family earned approximately 4,800 rupees ($103) a year from crops and odd jobs in the city.[13] In most cases, unlike city dwellers, rural Indians did not pay for either food or housing. While they had less total income, rural Indians had a higher percentage of disposable income than their urban counterparts who paid for both food and rent. India's rural market was comprised of 525 million people, approximately 12 percent of the world's population.[14] Once HLL had established the fact that rural Indians had the ability to buy goods, the company decided to go the extra distance to bring its goods to this new, unusual but sizeable, client group.

HLL did not define this market in the traditional fashion of calculating the number of times rural Indians used detergent, but instead looked at the number of times these potential customers washed their clothes. Rural clients did not use detergent every time they washed their clothes; unlike their urban counterparts, detergent was a luxury for rural Indians, so they would only use a detergent "x percent" of the time. HLL's goal was not to get 50 percent of the existing detergent market, but to get customers to increase the number of times they washed in a year and then to ensure that 50 percent of all these "washes" were done with the HLL product. An increased percentage of washes done with washing powder meant an increase in demand for that detergent.

While HLL seemed to be on the right track, the problem was how to increase the number of washes per year in rural areas where most villagers did not even have running water. If people often washed their clothes and bathed in the same river water, would multiplying the number of times they washed their clothes result in a more polluted river? Higher pollution levels would not help HLL in the long run because people would stop buying the company's products, and the number of washes would decrease. In addition, how would HLL convince rural consumers to buy more detergent when they had a limited amount of disposable income? Stimulating demand by launching a convincing and appealing ad campaign would have to be part of the process.

Designing a Product to Fit the Needs of a Market

Many questions and issues confronted HLL in its design of an appropriate product for the rural Indian market. The company could just re-price and re-package a mediocre version of the urban variant of the product and sell it in rural India. This would not build brand loyalty but it would keep costs down for HLL, and the poor might not even know the difference. While there were different opinions within the company about whether the rural consumer was savvy enough to tell the difference between a low-end and high-end detergent, HLL decided to go with the latter. To create brand loyalty and win customers away from Nirma, HLL reasoned that its product would have to be both high quality and good value for the money. Peddling low-quality products at cheap prices would not motivate clients to buy their products in the future. HLL decided that building brand loyalty was essential because the hope was that some day the residents of each rural village would join India's ever-growing middle class and trade up to more expensive HLL products. In a market where people gravitated towards the cheapest product, building brand loyalty was a challenge, and product quality was the essential first step.

Understanding the consumer was important in product design. Rural Indian consumers were very different from any of HLL's previous clients. Because rural consumers bathed and washed their clothes in the same river water, low toxicity and pollution levels were a vital element in the product design. Additionally, consumers lived in remote places, difficult to access by traditional means of transport, so the product had to be durable. Poor storage facilities in rural areas necessitated a product able to withstand heat and dust exposure. Unlike their urban counterparts who bought in bulk at the Sam's Clubs and Cosco's of India, the rural consumer would never have the spare income to follow suit. Consequently, HLL would have to package the product into small packets so that per unit costs could be kept low. HLL was hoping to make a profit not on margin per unit but on total volume.

For the top managers at HLL, project design meant coming up with a product that would fulfill the following criteria:[15]

- high quality (superior to Nirma)
- non-toxic and minimal pollution levels
- durable for rough transportation conditions
- tolerance for heat, dust, and long shelf life
- high value for the money
- low unit price and high functionality
- self-visibility and display
- easily disposable and dispensable
- available in small packages
- strong but cost efficient marketing campaign
- wide distribution through rural India (available at every corner of rural India).

A New Definition of Product Design

In its attempt to create brand equity and develop long-term relationships with rural consumers, HLL had to keep in mind how the product would be used (in rivers) and focus on defining the benefits of its product to rural consumers. In determining the pricing strategy, HLL had to understand that the rural Indian had little money to spare. Finally, because HLL thought its product was superior to Nirma, part of its marketing strategy had to be convincing the consumer of that superiority; as it stood, consumers had started to perceive Nirma as a cheaper substitute for Surf. The perception of a new product would not be based solely on product performance and quality but on a combination of factors, and HLL had defined and articulated these factors. The list of demands for product design and marketing was long and unusual, and the top managers on the Project STING team needed to determine how HLL could fulfill these demands and then move forward.

Taking the Plunge

In the spirit of its corporate purpose,[16] which aimed to "meet the everyday needs of people everywhere—to anticipate the aspirations of our consumers and customers and to respond creatively and competitively with branded products and services which raise the quality of life," Hindustan Lever Limited (HLL) had examined all the logistical hurdles and decided to enter the rural Indian market. Now the company had to determine the exact marketing and distribution approach. Meeting the demands of poor consumers was not just about lowering prices but also about being creative with the product to ensure that it fulfilled the needs of this target group. HLL's success also depended on large sales volumes of low-priced products.

The Product: Wheel

To contest Nirma's dominance of the detergent market, HLL produced Wheel detergent. (See Exhibit 5.1.4.) The HLL Research and Development team's mandate had been to produce "a low-cost product that gives a better performance in terms of whiteness, but without the side effects of wear and tear and itching caused by Nirma's high soda ash content."[17] Since 1984, HLL had been working on a new NSD (nonsoap detergent)[18] powder

Exhibit 5.1.4 HLL's Wheel Detergent

Source: http://www.hll.com/HLL_Flash/ArchiveContent/PhotoGallery/wheel1.jpg.

and, in the next few years, conducted sample consumer research on it. By 1986 (a year before Project STING had begun), the new NSD detergent mix was ready. Looking for a good brand name for the detergent, HLL decided to use the name of a detergent bar that had been partially launched a decade earlier—Wheel.[19] The detergent was packaged in smaller, 30-gram plastic sachets instead of the one-kg bags used for urban consumption. The sachets were hardy and able to bear most of the adverse conditions typical of rural India.

In creating Wheel detergent, HLL also had kept in mind that rural consumers bathed in rivers, and so the product needed to be as environmentally benign as possible. As a result, the company experimented with the levels of oil and water in the soap and ended up substantially reducing the amount of oil that Wheel contained.

A History of Research and Development

"We need to apply top-class science to solve simple problems at a reduced cost for the consumer," said Dr. V. M. Naik, deputy head of HLL's research laboratory in Bangalore, India. Naik spent about 70 percent of his time in the lab developing HLL's mass-market products. The Hindustan Lever Research Centre, created in 1958 and staffed by scientists and technologists, focused on developing "new products and processes, improving benefits and quality of existing products" and "optimal use of resources, energy conservation and pollution control"[20] and, by 2003, had 184 patents for different technologies.

The Hindustan Lever Limited Website, in 2003, detailed the history of its technological breakthroughs and claimed a number of innovations in the manufacture of detergents:

> . . . a proprietary technology which reduces water consumption and time taken for rinsing by 50%. It is a significant benefit, given the acute water scarcity in most of India. Given that laundry consumes up to 20% of household water, this technology will have a big impact. New technology has helped manufacture concentrated powders without going through the high-energy route of spray drying. These powders being of high bulk density also need less packaging material for a given weight compared to low bulk density powders. All the money saved in energy conservation and processing has been reinvested in better formulations and performance of products. Fundamental research in the area of particulate soil-fabric wash liquor interactions has led to filing of several patents that deal with avenues to improve detergency.[21]

HLL research also helped the scientists improve the properties (lather, appearance, size) of soap and increased their understanding of "network-forming structurants." This knowledge helped them create a milder, less abrasive soap. Research efforts were not confined to soap and detergent, however. Recognizing that children needed iodine (through salt) in their diets and that shipping, storage, and cooking often depleted the mineral, HLL scientists also developed an iodine-stabilizing technology for salt. They formulated a technology to manufacture powder for instant tea, and "one of the most significant breakthroughs of HLL's research initiative has been the development of a technology to use non-conventional forest seed oils for soap-making, which, since the 1970s, has helped save around $1.2 billion in foreign exchange."[22]

HLL scientists were also strides ahead in manufacturing technology, with "the capability to design and manufacture machines in-house or have them assembled by third parties as per given specifications," enabling HLL:

> . . . to set up plants at half the cost of others. Such technological developments have also led to significant improvement in productivity. The capacity of a toilet soap line has gone

up from 6,000 tonnes per annum in the early nineties to 20,000 tonnes per annum now, while that of a detergent bar line has gone up from 7,000 tonnes per annum to 40,000 tonnes per annum now, thus substantially increasing capital productivity.[23]

Distribution Dilemmas

Over the years HLL had developed a highly sophisticated and efficient distribution system in urban areas to ensure that wherever there was a demand for goods there was never a shortage of them. This system involved setting up redistribution stockists (those who stocked HLL goods and then redistributed them) who were responsible for warehousing and distribution as well as demand stimulation activities on behalf of the company. The redistribution stockist dealt directly with wholesalers and large retailers. In time this system was further modified to ensure that the stockist was continuously restocked. This led to the establishment of the company depot system that helped transshipment (movement from one wholesale buyer to the next), bulk breaking, and minimized stock-outs at the redistribution stockist level. The system was constantly being improved upon to maximize efficiency and reach.

HLL could not replicate this system in rural India for the simple reason that rural areas did not have the same infrastructure as urban areas. Whatever system HLL invented for rural distribution would also have to be extremely cost efficient in order to allow HLL to keep the unit cost of its products competitive.[24] The sheer vastness of the task of distributing goods in a region without basic infrastructure had deterred many other multinational corporations (MNCs) from entering these rural areas.

In addition, HLL needed to determine how to get its message across to consumers in an area with minimal media infrastructure and low levels of literacy. How could the company best position its product? In 1985, HLL successfully launched a new advertising campaign in urban India. In this campaign, Surf was portrayed as being good value for money. The protagonist, "Lalitaji," was a responsible and discerning housewife who compared buying cheap (therefore unhealthy) tomatoes for her family to the more expensive (therefore healthier) tomatoes that would make her children strong. The advertisement clearly stated that while Surf was three times more expensive than any "ordinary" washing powder, on a cost-per-wash basis it was only one and a half times more expensive. Could HLL use this pre-existing urban advertising campaign in rural India or should it develop a new one? Developing a new campaign targeting the specific needs of the rural market would be more effective but much more costly. In a market where the margins per unit were so low, could HLL afford such high advertising costs? How could the company get its message across effectively and at a low cost in this environment?

The Advertising Campaign: Ogilvy Outreach [25]

HLL needed to assess whether its advertising agency, Ogilvy & Mather (O&M) was capable of executing a campaign that meant diverging from the norms of corporate advertising. This campaign would involve a totally new (and untested) client group, and the conventional marketing and advertising tools would be absent. The ad campaign would have to go to the villages where it could utilize events such as markets, cattle fairs, and festivals as forums for communication. How would HLL and O&M get their message across in such an environment?

O&M belonged to O&M Worldwide, which was owned by WPP,[26] one of the largest communications groups in the world. While O&M had a number of operations and divisions in India, the most appropriate division for handling the Wheel campaign was Ogilvy

Outreach, the nonprofit arm of Ogilvy & Mather. Outreach had been established in 1994 with the objective of reaching the "unreachable" or those people living in the "media-dark" corners of rural India where HLL was trying to sell Wheel. Outreach specialized in advertising to low-income consumers, specifically to those in the rural areas. By recognizing and addressing the limitations of this unusual client group, HLL and Outreach had to create a campaign that attempted to understand and address the needs of the rural consumer and, in preparation, considered a number of questions: How did a villager think? What was his or her mindset and needs? How did villagers evaluate brands? How different was the rural environment? What forms of "folk" advertising would succeed here?

Launching Wheel

Together, HLL and Ogilvy Outreach took the Wheel advertising campaign throughout rural India, presenting their message through colorful flyers, posters on shop fronts, street performances with entertaining jingles, traveling cinema vans, and at any local gathering place where consumers were present. They created short video ads that were shown in the back of cinema vans throughout the rural countryside. While a HLL television ad for the urban consumer lasted no longer than thirty seconds, these video van ads ran anywhere from two to seventeen minutes. This was not just advertising; this was entertainment.

HLL organized performances with magicians, singers, dancers, and the local news update at cattle and trade fairs. HLL and Ogilvy Outreach recruited local magicians, dancers, and actors who knew each market and village that the company wanted to target. In total, 50 teams of 30 performers were recruited to serve as connections between the brands and the residents. Scripts were changed to accommodate the different dialects, education levels, and religions. In all, Ogilvy coordinated two hour-long performances at 2,005 haats (bazaars) in over six months.

Dalveer Singh, the vice president of Ogilvy Outreach explained:

> For both washing and for taking a bath . . . one requires water. Now for rural markets there are three sources of water: wells, hand pumps and ponds. For the first time in the history of advertising . . . these were branded. Special stickers were put on hand pumps, the walls of the wells were lined with advertising tiles, and tinplates were put on all the trees surrounding the ponds. The idea was to advertise not only at the point of purchase but also at the time of consumption.[27]

The aim was to ensure that whenever the consumer purchased and then used the product, they were reminded of it and its popularity. By seeing Wheel advertised while simultaneously washing their clothes, consumers would feel a sense of satisfaction that would help create brand loyalty. At the same time, the advertising campaign was designed to create the sense of "missing out on something good" for those not using the advertised brand. Technology was used to push the product. Using ultraviolet light sensors, HLL marketing representatives scanned the villagers' hands to show that, even when skin looks clean, dirt and germs can be present.[28] See Exhibit 5.1.5 for the Wheel advertisement.

Creating a Rural Distribution Network

HLL faced two major challenges in setting up a rural distribution system: the lack of infrastructure in rural India and the problem of transporting products to remote villages. The company also needed to identify who within the local populations could represent its

Exhibit 5.1.5 Advertisement for Wheel Detergent

Source: http://www.hll.com/HLL_Flash/ArchiveContent/PhotoGallery/wheeldancingkids.jpg.

products and serve as distributors. Drawing on its experience in urban areas, HLL set up a rural distribution system based on population size and accessibility. As a first step, HLL outlets were set up in villages that had both all-weather roads and a population of more than 2,000. In the early 1990s, 60,000 of India's 570,000 villages qualified under these criteria, and, by 1994, HLL had outlets in 34,000 of them. At a later point, HLL set up regional distribution warehouses in these villages.

For villages with fewer than 2,000 people, HLL developed a new approach called Project Streamline, which aimed to gain further control of the rural supply chain by developing a network of rural sub-stockists[29] based in the remote villages. A rural distributor in the area would supply about 15–20 rural sub-stockists. The sub-stockists were responsible for transporting the goods deeper into the countryside for resale. Transportation involved using whatever was available, which could be anything from a bullock cart to a tractor. In 1998, HLL rolled out Project Streamline in select states where a lack of good roads or the poor stage of market development made ordinary distribution systems unviable. Project Streamline extended direct HLL reach from 25 percent in 1995 to 37 percent by 1998. By 2003, HLL hoped to expand coverage to 50 percent of the rural population.[30] In time the system became fine-tuned, so that goods were distributed from carrying and forwarding agents to redistributors who then passed the goods on to distributors identified as "star sellers." Having the star sellers was beneficial in that they eventually took on a cross-functional role and sold everything from detergents to personal products, thereby bringing all HLL products closer to the consumer.[31]

Creating New Consumers

After a successful test market in 1987, HLL launched Wheel in 1988. Initially Wheel sold at Rs. 5.50, only 0.25 paise higher than Nirma. One year later Wheel was the second-largest brand in India, and, by 1990, it had gained leadership in value, although not in volume. By that point, Wheel was larger than any other Unilever brand in the world.[32] HLL, stimulated by its emergent rival and its changed business model, registered a 20 percent growth in revenues per year and a 25 percent growth in profits between 1995 and 2000. Over the same period, HLL's market capitalization grew to $12 billion—a growth rate of 40 percent per year. By 2002, Nirma and HLL had become close competitors in the detergent market with approximately 38 percent market share each.

In addition to its financial success with Wheel, HLL began using this network of advertising and distribution for all its products in rural India. By 2000, HLL began expanding into smaller villages. Because disposable income levels were lower in the smaller villages, HLL decided to link distribution with income generation. In November 2000, HLL organized a meeting of 150 women residents of villages with fewer than 2,000 people in the state of Andhra Pradesh. Many were illiterate, agrarian workers wanting to start a business. They belonged to self-help groups that ran micro-credit operations. The women had saved money from their daily wages and wanted to find ways of making those savings grow. Through Project Shakti (Strength), HLL offered to sell them company products at cost and teach them how to re-sell these products at a profit. Amway and Avon had pioneered a similar strategy in urban areas, but HLL was the first to use the direct-sales model in rural areas.[33]

HLL had reached the point where it viewed the lack of infrastructure in rural India as a challenge rather than a deterrent. By the early 1990s, HLL's database of knowledge on the geography of rural India allowed it to locate every village, with dots reflecting the presence of HLL product distributors and blank spaces indicating potential areas of growth. By the mid-1990s, HLL had gained the reputation of being better informed about the geography of rural India than the Indian government. As S. M. Datta (chairman of HLL in 1990) said, "We have government officials telling us that there is no road here, or this village is there, but from our maps we know there *is* a road, and that village is not where they think it is."[34]

HLL's Success

With its foray into the rural Indian market, HLL regained its much-respected position as a trendsetter. Unilever also greatly benefited from HLL's experiment and, over the years, replicated what it learned in rural India in many of its other international markets. For example, during the Asian economic crisis in the late 1990s, Unilever moved to making smaller quantity products to encourage people to continue purchasing and claimed to have come out of the crisis stronger. The company used many of these lessons in other emerging markets including Brazil, Indonesia, the Philippines, and the Congo. Most importantly, through the example of HLL and Project STING, Unilever adopted the bottom of the pyramid as a strategic priority at the corporate level.

Notes

* This case was written by Research Assistants Pia Sabharwal Ahmad and Jenny Mead under the supervision of Patricia H. Werhane, Ruffin Professor of Business Ethics, Darden School of Business, University of Virginia, and Michael E. Gorman, Professor of Technology, Culture & Communications and Systems Engineering at the School of Engineering and Applied Science, at the University of Virginia. It was written as a basis for class discussion rather than to illustrate effective or ineffective handling of an administrative situation. Copyright © 2004 by the University of Virginia Darden School Foundation, Charlottesville, VA. All rights reserved.

1 "Karsanbhai Patel, "A Clean Sweep," <http://www.indiaprofile.com/people/karsanbhaipatel. htm> (accessed on May 20, 2004).

2 Charlotte Butler and Sumantra Ghosal, "Hindustan Lever Limited: Levers for Change," Insead Euro-Asia Center, 302-199-1 (Fontainebleau, France, 2002). Much information in this section is attributed to the Butler and Ghosal case.

3 Seen at <http://pacific.commerce.ubc.ca/xr/CADpages.pdf>.

4 "Octroi is a tax levied on the entry of goods into a municipality or any other specified jurisdiction for use, consumption, or sale. Octroi is levied at the time when the goods enter the municipal limits where the goods are to be ultimately sold, used, or consumed." Source: http://www.ahmedabad. com/business/taxation/indirecttax.htm#octr.

5 "We Don't Feel the Need to Adopt Any Hardsell," *Economic Times* (Times of India Group), July 23, 1999.

6 Butler and Ghosal, 11.

7 C. K. Prahalad & Allen Hammond, "Serving the World's Poor, Profitably," *Harvard Business Review*, September 2002, pgs 48–57 and http://www.digitaldividend.org/pdf/bottompyramid. pdf.

8 Population statistics taken from the following sites: http://www.undp.org.in/report/IDF97/ idftab.htm, http://mohfw.nic.in/popindi.htm, http://www.library.uu.nl/wesp/populstat/Asia/ indiac.htm, http://www.eia.doe.gov/emeu/cabs/india/indiach1.htm, http://www.cs.colostate. edu/~malaiya/india.html#Populations%20in%20the%20Subcontinent.

9 "One Man Show Rivals Multi Nationals," *Responsive Database Services, Inc., Business and Industry* 37, 2 (Rodman Publishing Corp., Happi-Household & Personal Products Industry, 2000): 26.

10 "Karsanbhai Patel, "A Clean Sweep.""

11 Butler and Ghosal, 8.

12 C. K. Prahalad and S. Hart, "Strategies for the Bottom of the Pyramid," 1999. http://www.wri.org/ meb/wrisummit/pdfs/hart.pdf (accessed May 20, 2004).

13 Rekha Balu, "Strategic Innovation: Hindustan Level Ltd.," *Fast Company* 47 (June 2001): 120.

14 Population statistics taken from the following sites http://www.undp.org.in/report/IDF97/idftab. htm, http://mohfw.nic.in/popindi.htm, http://www.library.uu.nl/wesp/populstat/Asia/indiac. htm, http://www.eia.doe.gov/emeu/cabs/india/indiach1.htm, http://www.cs.colostate.edu/ ~malaiya/india.html#Populations%20in%20the%20Subcontinent.

15 Hart, Prahalad, and S. Ramachander, "The Concept of Marketing Insight: Linking Innovation to Business Goals." Presented at the International Conference on Corporate Marketing Communications at the University of Strathclyde in 1998.

16 <www.hll.com> (accessed on May 20, 2004).

17 Charlotte Butler and Sumantra Ghosal, "Hindustan Lever Limited: Levers For Change," Insead Euro-Asia Center, 302-199-1, (Fontainebleau, France, 2002): 15.

18 In the past edible oil was used in the manufacture of soap, which made them less effective. With the introduction of NSD, the oil ratio in detergent decreased, making it more effective.

19 Butler and Ghosal, 15.

20 "Hindustan Lever Limited Website, Hindustan Lever Limited: Meeting Everyday Needs of People Everywhere," *Profile* (Jan. 2003): 5; <http://www.hll.com/HLL/knowus/companyprofiles/ Company_Profile.pdf>.

21 *Profile*, 6.

22 *Profile*, 7.

23 *Profile*, 6.

24 <www.hll.com> (accessed on May 20, 2004).

25 Background information about O&M in this section was taken from Venkatesh Raghavan, *O&M: The Big Surge* at http://www.business-leaders.com/2002april/feat02.htm.

26 The acronym stands for Wire & Plastic Products, the original name of the company acquired by its founder, Martin Sorrell, in 1985.

27 Taken from an interview with Dalveer Singh, vice president of Ogilvy Outreach. http://www.indiainfoline.com/bisc/mdms01.html (accessed on May 20, 2004).

28 Rekha Balu, "Strategic Innovation: Hindustan Lever Ltd.," *Fast Company* 47 (June 2001): 120.

29 Sub-stockists may be explained as smaller warehouses that supply to the outlying rural regions where transportation is problematic.

30 Seen at www.hll.com.

31 Seen at www.hll.com/hll/knowus/ourheritage.html.

32 Charlotte Butler and Sumantra Ghosal, "Hindustan Lever Limited: Levers For Change," Insead Euro-Asia Center, 302-199-1, (Fontainebleau, France, 2002), 16.

33 Balu, 123.

34 Hamish McDonald, "Cleaning Up," *Far Eastern Economic Review* 157 (December 30, 1993– January 6, 1994).

5.2 Enabling the Poor to Build Housing
Pursuing Profit and Social Development Together – Cemex and Patrimonio Hoy *

The Cemex Corporation of Mexico has launched an innovative experiment that enables very poor people to purchase building materials and upgrade their homes. It blends the pursuit of profit with significant social gain.

Kris Herbst

GUADALAJARA, Mexico—The poorest people here live in small houses constructed from raw cinder blocks or more flimsy materials like cardboard and corrugated sheet metal.

"Most of the houses aren't finished and have only one or two rooms per family," says Consuelo Silva, a resident of the Mesa Colorada settlement on the northern outskirts of Guadalajara. "Most families have at least six to ten members, and these rooms are occupied by the bedrooms and a kitchen."

Such crowding aggravates tensions that accompany life amidst poverty. "The quality of the relations between family members will determine a family's future," says Israel Moreno, director and founder of Patrimonio Hoy, an initiative of Cemex that enables poor families to finance expansion of their homes. "Imagine one room with ten persons living together, yelling and fighting all day long. So the children are propelled out into the streets at a young age. What do they learn in the streets? Vicious delinquency, theft and prostitution. If the first thing in your life is contact with the street, your future will be the street, with its related risks."

Families in these neighborhoods tend to be resigned to making little progress on their home expansion efforts and thus to suffering the ill effects of crowding. But since it was founded four years ago, Patrimonio Hoy has given 20,000 families in Mexico a way to finance and build better housing in a timely manner.

Patrimonio Hoy is one of Guadalajara's most dynamic and successful programs, which addresses the problems of housing in these settlements—indeed it is one of the only such programs. But what truly sets it apart is that it is neither operated nor subsidized by the government or a non-governmental organization.

Rather it is a for-profit initiative of Cemex, Mexico's largest multinational corporation. Within five years, one million Mexican families will benefit from this new way of doing business if the program continues to grow as planned.

Cemex manufactures cement, the principal ingredient for construction in developing countries. Cemex, along with some of the world's most savvy multinational corporations, is discovering that the poorest of the poor represent the next major frontier for companies struggling to maintain rapid growth.

Cemex: Pursuing Innovation and Global Expansion

Mexico is not the obvious place to find an innovative multinational corporation, much less one that is conducting a groundbreaking experiment in combining corporate social responsibility with the pursuit of profits in low-income communities. Cemex was founded in 1906 in the northern state of Nuevo Leon as Mexico's first cement company.

For nearly 90 years Cemex operated like a typical Mexican corporation in Mexico's highly-protected markets. Until the mid-1990s, it could afford to be relatively passive and slow-moving because competition between the handful of domestic cement companies was rather slack, and they competed primarily on price rather than service.

An economic crisis and opening of Mexican markets in the mid-1990s was a social, political and economic upheaval that changed the rules for businesses in Mexico. Suddenly, Cemex was operating in an open, globalized market.

"It was a breakthrough," Moreno said. "For me, it was an explosion—a moment to create a new business model based on how employees can develop solutions that make more satisfied customers. Before, our focus was on operations—and Cemex has the highest production standards in the world—but there is another side to the business: the customer. When you are the customer's only option, you are making good sales—but oftentimes you forget the customer or the market. On the other hand, when you are just one of the options, customers have a choice, and they have memories. If we are not able to maintain or develop a long-term relationship with our customers, we are lost—we are out of business. That is why companies now emphasize their social responsibilities—to build long-term relations with the customer."

Cemex's CEO Lorenzo Zambrano led the charge to modernize Cemex by surrounding himself with executives who pursued the latest management and technology innovations in order to empower employees and streamline operations. Since the mid-1990s, "we have been acting with a new attitude of listening, awareness, innovation, and continuous improvement," Moreno said. "We need to keep very alert and awake, thinking about how to do things better, reading the markets, and listening to the customers."

Recognizing this, Wired Magazine added Cemex to its Wired Index mutual fund in July 2002. For the first time, it added a manufacturer of a heavy, old-fashioned commodity like cement to its list of 40 companies that power the global economy by mastering innovation, intelligent use of new tools, strategic vision, global reach and networked communication.

Since 1995, Cemex has spent nearly $5 billion acquiring cement companies that now operate as subsidiaries in 25 countries. They have provided further access to capital markets in Europe and America, helping fuel Cemex's expansion.

Cemex has vaulted from the world's 28th-largest cement company to the third largest in the world. It produces 80 million metric tons of cement annually—enough cement to fill 1,000 football stadiums to the brim—and recorded sales of $6.9 billion in 2001.

Cemex operates 524 cement plants worldwide, and is the world's largest producer of white cement. It is also the world's leading exporter of cement and related services, using a fleet of freight ships and 54 strategically located marine terminals to sell and ship 13.2 million metric tons of cement to more than 60 countries.

Cemex acquired the U.S.-based Southdown Inc. cement company in 2000 for $2.8 billion, the largest-ever acquisition of a U.S. company by a Mexican firm. This has made Cemex the largest seller of cement in the United States, a dominant position it also enjoys in Spain, Venezuela, Panama, and the Dominican Republic.

As it has expanded, Cemex has gained a reputation for acquiring and then converting troubled cement plants into profitable operations—most of them located in developing countries—by imposing uniform strict standards of modernization and efficiency. In the process, it has become by far the world's most profitable cement company, achieving the highest cash flow, pretax margins of 37 percent, and a market capitalization that reached $9.3 billion in April 2002. Earnings before interest, taxes, depreciation and amortization have been growing at an average annual compounded rate of 20 percent for the past 10 years.

By focusing on international markets, Cemex has become Mexico's top multinational corporation: nearly two-thirds of its revenues come from outside Mexico. Only two Mexican companies are larger: Pemex, the national oil and gas monopoly, and Telmex, a telecommunications monopoly that was privatized in 1990. It is the only Mexican corporation generating more profits than Cemex. These accomplishments have made Cemex's CEO Zambrano worth an estimated $2.8 billion, making him Mexico's third-wealthiest individual after the owners of Telmex and a booming joint Wal-Mart venture, according to Forbes magazine.

Discovering Opportunity in Low-Income Markets

Cemex has achieved extraordinary profitability through a shrewd strategy of targeting developing countries (Bangladesh, Egypt, Indonesia, Thailand, Philippines and countries in the Caribbean and Central and South America). Its forecasts show the world demand for cement through 2010 will grow by 4 percent annually in developing countries, compared to only 1 percent annually in developed countries.

The poorest residents of these developing countries represent a special opportunity for businesses. During Mexico's economic crisis in 1994, when the value of the peso crashed, Cemex noticed that the revenues from its big-ticket sales to traditional large-scale customers, and to middle- and upper-income individuals, dropped by 50 percent, but sales to its low-income, do-it-yourself homebuilder customers dropped only 10 to 20 percent.

Although the average value of a sale to a low-income customer is minuscule, their numbers are enormous compared to Cemex's better-heeled customers. This makes low-income communities a more stable market that is less affected by the cyclical fluctuations of the economy.

Cemex saw opportunities here: sales to the low-income market could offset its losses during economic downturns. And the low-income market offers the possibility of sustained growth that could offset erosion of Cemex's overall market share by international competitors.

Cemex embarked on a strategy of learning how to tap the enormous markets of low-income customers in developing countries by studying how to do business with the poor in Mexico, where 60 percent of the population survives on less than $5 per day.

To help cope with the 1994 economic meltdown, a Cemex management team headed by Francisco Garza Zambrano, president of Cemex's North America Region and Trading, turned to Business Design Associates (BDA), a consulting firm founded by Fernando Flores— a philosopher, business consultant and former finance minister to Chilean President Salvador Allende. BDA led the first stage of social research in the low-income communities. Later, the Cemex team began developing the idea for Patrimonio Hoy by identifying the low-income do-it-yourself homebuilders as a neglected "last consumer segment."

Above this segment on the ladder of individual consumers are wealthy homeowners at the top, middle-class homeowners, and then low-income consumers who are part of the formal economy by virtue of having a regular job. These low-income consumers have the option of allocating deductions from their paychecks, matched by government subsidies, to help pay for their housing.

But do-it-yourself homebuilders who are at the bottom of the ladder and outside the formal economy, living in burgeoning informal settlements, are left to fend for themselves. Significantly, they account for about 40 percent of cement consumption in Mexico and have potential to be a market worth $500–600 million annually—a conservative estimate according to Cemex.

Before it could successfully enter this market, Cemex needed to figure how to help do-it-yourself homebuilders overcome their resignation about not being able to improve their housing in a timely manner. Patrimony Hoy managers began by carefully studying the methods of the Grameen Bank, the organization that invented the concept of microlending: providing tiny loans to the very poor so they can launch their own businesses and become micro-entrepreneurs.

Grameen started in Bangladesh in 1979 and has disbursed roughly $3 billion to 2.4 million borrowers. Although they lack collateral, Grameen's borrowers have an excellent repayment record: at least 90 percent according to Grameen Bank figures.

Grameen discovered that women, who comprise 94 percent of its customers, are highly reliable borrowers. Cemex has adopted strategies it learned from Grameen, such as doing most of its business with women and shaping business procedures to fit traditional values such as a reliance on community solidarity.

Obstacles to Progress

The average low-income homebuilder takes four years to complete just one room, and 13 years to finish a small four-room house that typically consists of a kitchen, bathroom, bedroom and a second bedroom that doubles as a family's common space. This discouraging rate of progress reflects the many obstacles that low-income homebuilders face. Banks and other businesses will not engage with poor residents of informal settlements where the legal status of their property ownership is murky, and residents cannot document assets, collateral, references or regular sources of income.

So poor people here, as elsewhere in the world, use a traditional method for saving money: they form a savings club or *tanda*. Typically women form groups of ten persons who each make a small, weekly contribution of about 100 pesos (US$10) to a pool for a period of ten weeks. Each week, one member of the *tanda* is selected by lottery to receive the entire pool until every member has taken the pool once.

While studying low-income communities in Mexico, Moreno found that 70 percent of women who participate in *tandas* are saving money to construct improvements on their homes. But just 10 percent actually spend the money on building materials.

Often the money is spent before a family even receives it. What little can be saved in poor communities typically gets claimed for unanticipated emergencies, loans to friends and family, school fees, and clothes, etc.

Further, a person's social status in low-income Mexican communities is measured not so much by wealth or assets, but by "social capital"—a person's reputation and participation in the life of the community.

"Much of their money goes to these festivities: weddings, music and parties," Moreno said. "There is a party for everything: my favorite soccer team won, my political party won, my neighbor's daughter just turned 15, I just put a new floor in my house. That is a very important reason why people don't have a better house, education or clothing—their money goes to non-primary necessities."

The challenges of putting aside enough money to buy a bag of cement—up to two times the average daily earnings—are great. In the past, homeowners attempted to hoard materials as a hedge against runaway price inflation, but because they lacked adequate storage they lost materials to theft and spoilage. A bag of cement left lying on the ground in front of a house will soon be rendered useless by rain, hardening before it can be put to use.

It is common in low-income communities for building materials to be purchased in small lots and to be of poor quality—dealers give customers leftovers from their larger orders, prices charged by middlemen are high, and deliveries are delayed. Because most do-it-yourself homebuilders lack construction skills, they often waste materials by failing to specify the exact quantities they require. Home design and construction tends to be haphazard and suffers from substandard circulation patterns, structural integrity, ventilation and lighting.

Cemex discovered that successfully entering the low-income market will require "cultural innovation" on both sides—the values and culture of low-income communities must be shifted, but Cemex also must change the way it treats its customers. To succeed in low-income communities, companies must build bridges between a community's familiar traditional practices and a new set of more modern values. This will provide the seeds for a new way of life.

As the Patrimonio Hoy program began taking shape in October, 1999, its structure reflected this bridging approach.

Replacing Resignation with Ambition

Translated to English, Patrimonio Hoy means "Patrimony Today." Patrimony refers to the tradition of creating something of value that can be passed down to future generations.

In this sense, patrimony is seen as a statement of solidarity with the traditional community. It may be something intangible like education, personal values or a sense of personal empowerment, or it may be something material, the most substantial instance of which is a family's house.

At the same time, low-income communities are pervaded by a sense of resignation that extends to the station of life to which a person is born, fate, and an inability to reconcile traditional values—such as making expenditures for communal celebrations—with modern aspirations such as financial planning and asset accumulation. "Their mental model is 'We cannot do it, we cannot have a better life. This is my life, this has been my parents' life, and this will be my children's life'," Moreno said. "They are resigned. We are convinced that this is a very big lie. But we are certain this will not be the model for the future because otherwise the world will be lost."

As a slogan on posters and publications, "Patrimony Today" replaces this resignation with the assertion that it provides an opportunity to achieve a better way of living, more quickly, beginning today. "Our philosophy is that if we make a promise, we will make it reality," Moreno said. "This is the Patrimonio Hoy way of relating, of making transactions and doing business—no more false promises."

Banking on Social Capital

No paperwork is required to join Patrimonio Hoy: prospective members need not provide identification, proof of address, co-signers, documentation of assets, collateral or paycheck stubs. Instead, like traditional organizations such as *tandas*, applicants are asked to provide the one thing they do possess: social capital: their word, honor and reputation. All they need to enroll is to promise to be consistent about making weekly savings payments.

"The less economic capital you have, the more you depend on your social capital," Moreno said. "The only thing they have is social capital. Their most precious treasure is their identity, because if you don't have money you depend on your name. You must honor your commitments."

Members are invited to form savings clubs, like *tandas*, in which each member contributes a minimum of 120 pesos per week. Each Patrimonio Hoy savings group consists of three persons. After members join a savings group, Patrimonio Hoy calls its members "partners" rather than customers.

"We learned that the solidarity is stronger for a group with three partners than with ten because of the relationships between the partners," Moreno said. "A group of three is tightly bonded—people pick their closest relations, while a group of ten has weaker links. This system is based on trust. My leverage is that the group of three consists of the most trusted persons in each other's lives."

The structure of the saving club expands the idea of the *tanda* to a 70- to 86-week commitment with a well-defined plan. The rules of the group, such as the penalties for missing payments, are formalized and specified in advance to help prevent fraud and abuse. The lack of hidden consequences helps members trust the system.

A group's members take turns collecting payments and playing the role of contract enforcer for one month at time. By separating this function from Patrimonio Hoy staff, members gain a better understanding and commitment to the process.

This structure, and the use of simple, transparent rules, avoids a more familiar arrangement in low-income communities: the hierarchical relationship between patron and supplicant where care is exchanged for loyalty and the patron may be expected to forgive transgressions of the rules. Instead, Patrimonio Hoy works to develop reciprocal responsibility: it delivers quality materials and services; the customer gets the possibility of getting a better house by paying on time and doing the building.

A New and Rewarding Experience

The savings group differs from the *tandas* model in one all-important respect. To ensure that their savings actually get spent for housing, group members receive raw materials for building—cement, iron, etc.—rather than cash. After two weeks, Cemex makes a first delivery of building materials to each member of the group. Because this occurs before sufficient savings have accumulated to fully pay the bill, Cemex is, in effect, advancing credit.

Additional deliveries of materials are made to each member every 10 weeks. The structure is more fair than the *tanda's* system of awarding pool pay-offs by lottery because *tandas* give an advantage to those who receive the pool first.

Participation in the savings clubs is a breakthrough for community members because, for the first time, they are being offered a chance to do business with a legitimate corporation and to join a secure savings and credit plan. For most, it's a new and rewarding experience to be transactional equals, free to bind themselves in serious commitments to each other and to a company.

They have become accustomed to living in a culture permeated with distrust due to generations of dealings with people who have cheated and swindled them. This unhappy situation is the product of their marginal political and legal status as poor, uneducated residents of informal settlements.

This has created a risky political environment that helps explain the paucity of NGOs and other community development programs that would otherwise address the problems of these communities, such as inadequate housing. "There aren't many social entrepreneurs in the area of home construction because of difficulties over 'gray property titles'," said Charles Spinosa, leader of marketing practices for VISION Consulting USA, a New York-based consultancy. "They also must compete with government agencies that, for many years, have been focused on ending the disorder of these communities rather than simply giving people wealth. The government's ambition and funding, although noble, gets in the way of the simple, more pragmatic wealth-building ambitions of social entrepreneurs."

High-Touch Outreach Builds Community and Trust

Patrimonio Hoy tackles these problems by employing a "high touch" method of community outreach to build community in a variety of ways. It is especially important to manage the spread of information because low-income communities are highly networked by word-of-mouth, and rumors, paranoia and jealousies spread rapidly.

Patrimonio Hoy begins operating in a city by opening an office staffed by four employees in one of the outlying areas with the greatest concentration of low-income people. Patrimonio Hoy calls these areas "cells." Typically a cell has a population of 100,000, or 20,000 families. Patrimonio Hoy is operating eight cells in Guadalajara.

The program has just come through an explosive period of expansion. It grew by 250 percent last year, ballooning from 9 cells in 3 cities to 30 cells in 19 cities that are located in 15 states throughout southern and central Mexico. This rate of growth is being allowed to level off temporarily so that the program's systems and software can be upgraded and consolidated to support a large number of customers, Moreno said.

Since it was founded four years ago, Patrimonio Hoy has enrolled more than 20,000 families, directly affecting some 100,000 people. Even with the current pause in growth, it is adding new families at the rate of 2,000 per month, and sales are growing by 15 percent monthly. "Our goal is to reach 1 million families in Mexico in five years," Moreno said.

Patrimonio Hoy targets about one-fourth of the population of a cell (5,000 families) for its services because they can afford to save 120 pesos per week and will need assistance with their housing. Rather than using advertising to reach them, Patrimonio Hoy's staff identifies and recruits informal leaders in the community, 98 percent of who are women, to serve as "promoters" who will engage in a highly-personalized form of selling.

Promoters tend to be housewives who love to meet and spend time with people, and to contribute to their community. They often are already earning money by selling multilevel marketing products for companies like Avon, Tupperware and Amway.

Promoters first form a savings group with neighbors, family or friends, and then begin enrolling others to form their own savings groups. When they sign up new members, they get points, which they can exchange for cash or building materials.

Promoters are given ID badges and bright blue t-shirts emblazoned with Patrimonio Hoy logos to distinguish them from the parade of scam artists who pass through the community claiming to solicit for charities. "It's very important that people trust us," Moreno said. "We are dealing with some of the most distrustful people in the world because for many years people have been robbing them."

Women are the Key

Patrimonio Hoy's managers have been surprised to discover how much they rely on women as their primary clients in low-income communities. They have found that women assume the responsibility for maintaining household unity and a family's progress.

"In the low-income market, the man is the provider and his only worry is what to bring to the house the next day," Moreno said. "But women see daily that the children are growing up in the streets. We discovered that women ensure the future—they are worried about what kind of life they can expect for their children, and about their education. When you deal with a woman, you can be more secure that she will respect agreements, on average, than if you sign with a man. It's very difficult to gain her confidence, but when we do, it's a guarantee of her loyalty."

Consuelo Silva lives with her husband and four children in the Mesa Colorada district on the northern outskirts of Guadalajara. She has been a Patrimonio Hoy promoter for three years. "We are accustomed to having men be the ones who lead in Mexico," she said. "Now I know that the women also have an important role in the society, and I feel useful. I can do many more things than just being in the house. On average, there are 200 active partners that I have enrolled. That means a lot to me—it's a big achievement. I feel a lot more confident, like I can conquer the world."

Safety in Numbers

Community members are introduced to Patrimonio Hoy in a group session at the local Patrimonio Hoy office rather than as individuals. This helps make their first encounter a sanctioned, communal activity. It also helps prevent new members from being socially isolated when they begin pursuing new habits that aren't a part of the traditional culture. Otherwise, envy, suspicion and misunderstanding can spread as others notice that Patrimony Hoy members are beginning to accumulate savings and improve their homes. And this can cause Patrimonio Hoy members to try to avoid notice by taking a low profile rather than proudly promoting the program to their friends and neighbors.

Introducing Patrimonio Hoy in a group setting encourages participants to talk about the problems and obstacles they face and to identify and acknowledge their resulting feelings of resignation. At this point, they are offered Cemex's guarantee of a firm and relatively quick timetable, along with technical support. In this way members are able to build the much-desired family patrimony, room-by-room.

The average do-it-yourself homebuilder in Mexico spends US$1,527 and takes four years to build an average size room of 100-square-feet. But participants in Patrimonio Hoy can build the same size room, with better quality, in less time—1.5 years—and at two-thirds the cost (US$1,038, which includes the cost of materials, technical assistance from an engineer or an architect, and Patrimonio Hoy club fees).

Hearing this offer in a group increases the general level of trust in Cemex's commitment. Community members are reassured that the program is backed by Cemex, a large, credible, and well-managed company (familiar to them, if for no other reason, by its sponsorship of Mexico's most popular soccer team, Guadalajara's Chivas) that will not evaporate and leave them holding the bag.

Partner #1

"I didn't believe this plan would help me build my house in this faster and easier way—I thought maybe they will cheat me," said Rosa Magaña, the first person to join Patrimonio Hoy in 1998. Prior to joining, she and her husband had spent eight years building a 270-square-foot, one-room house for their family of four in the Mirador Escondido settlement on the northeast edge of Guadalajara.

They had attached a kitchen area to their single-room dwelling. It was covered by a sheet of corrugated metal and would flood when it rained so that Magaña had to move her gas stove to keep it from getting wet. Family members went to a neighbor's house to use the bathroom. "Everybody ate and everybody slept together in the same room," Magaña said. "It was very uncomfortable."

After joining Patrimonio Hoy, Magaña became the program's first promoter and she and her husband spent two years expanding their house into a neat, 475-square-foot, two-bedroom house complete with a kitchen and bathroom. "Now I have a house in which my family lives a much better and more dignified life," Magaña said. "My children sleep in the other room. It was a big opportunity to be able to give 100 pesos a week to Patrimonio Hoy. I realize I have something that I couldn't have done if I hadn't known Patrimonio Hoy. My dream is to finish building my house because this is the only asset we have to pass on to our children. My plan is to start building a second floor this year."

Integrating Old and New Values

Patrimonio Hoy integrates the tradition of communal celebrations by publishing its customers' achievements in local newspapers, sponsoring block parties and open houses, and holding a twice-annual event to honor its top savers, builders, and program promoters. "We organize parties—festivals—with every delivery of materials we make," said Teresa Martinez, Patrimonio Hoy Operations Manager. "This attracts the attention of neighbors so they see that the partners are actually meeting their commitment—that they are for real."

When a family finishes a room, they become a living testimonial to the program and are issued a diploma. They also are delivered "a box with family-size soft drinks and a bowl with tacos for the party they will throw for their neighbors," Moreno said. "We call it the celebration kit."

These activities help bridge the gap between the traditional value of maintaining social status by contributing to communal celebrations, and the desire to get ahead in life. Traditionally, the latter attitude has been viewed with suspicion and envy, and seen as weakening the community fabric.

Savings group members are invited to participate in biweekly support groups to help reinforce their new values and behavior, celebrate their accomplishments and acknowledge their setbacks. "Everything is focused on these solidarity groups," Martinez said. "I have seen cases where one of the partners broke his leg and couldn't work. The other partners helped him make his payments while he recovered. In another case, a partner was going through a divorce and he received psychological, emotional and economic support from the group."

Services are Crucial to Low-Income Customers

Not all of a partner's 120-peso weekly payment buys building materials. Patrimonio Hoy collects 15 pesos out of each payment as a "club membership" fee.

Their payments cover the cost of cement and other materials. The fee pays for services given to Patrimonio Hoy members in addition to their building supplies. Their payment for services helps reinforce the commercial nature of the transaction, as opposed to the more traditional patron–client relationship.

Patrimonio Hoy quickly discovered these extra services are crucial because simply supplying "cement by itself doesn't solve anything," Moreno said. Low-income homebuilders need a new way of doing things that includes help with financing, technical assistance and social development. "We had to retire our brain chips as a Cemex sales force and think about how to resolve these problems," Moreno said.

Patrimonio Hoy services include:

- Technical assistance from architects and engineers.
- Support for education by financing upgrades to school buildings.
- A school for beginning do-it-yourself homebuilders for those who want to cut costs by doing their own construction, freeing up more money for materials. Here they learn basic skills such as how to dig foundations, mix cement and make level walls with square corners. Some 450 homebuilders are attending the school and 1,000 have graduated.

- A more advanced school that provides professional certification for masons.
- Guaranteed quality of building materials and timely delivery. Cemex collects feedback forms from customers who evaluate the quality of the materials and delivery service they receive from Cemex's authorized dealers.
- A guaranteed freeze on the price of construction materials for 70 weeks, beginning the day a customer enrolls in the program, regardless of price fluctuations in the economy. Locking-in prices protects customers from inflation.
- Free storage of all building materials for up to two years to protect against spoilage and theft. A family may want to wait to claim its materials if it lacks its own storage space, or if it needs to save money to pay for the help of a mason, or if a husband has gone to work in the United States for six months.
- An interest charge of about 12 percent for the loan of building materials is incorporated into the membership fee.

Doing Well While Doing Good

Cemex is determined to make a profit in low-income markets. It will not compete on price—its 110-pound bag of cement costs slightly more (about 3.5 pesos) than competing brands.

Instead, it offers a competitive package of services that it hopes will allow low-income customers to purchase a premium-quality "first world" product, and to work toward attaining a higher quality of life. "I prefer to invest in helping our partners discover ways to live a better life," Moreno said. "I think that is a more responsible and intelligent way of doing business."

So far, Patrimonio Hoy has helped the Cemex bottom line by tripling the rate of cement consumed by its low-income, do-it-yourself homebuilders. This amount has increased from 2,300 pounds consumed once every four years, on average, to the same amount being consumed in 15 months.

Already, Cemex brands are growing stronger in low-income communities, Moreno said. "Some people say, 'Thanks to Tolteca (Cemex's premium cement brand) I have my house'," Moreno said. " 'For 20 years I couldn't build my home, but now we have two more rooms, thanks to Tolteca.' When I hear testimonies like that, I know we are doing well and that our brand is well positioned."

The Patrimonio Hoy program itself is not required to generate a profit. Cemex wants the program to break even so that it covers its costs. "This program has cost the company a lot of money—millions of dollars since we started four years ago," Moreno said. He predicts Patrimonio Hoy will reach the break-even point by October or November 2002.

"This is not a charity organization," Moreno said. "We have to meet two objectives: we have to collaborate in providing a better life for these people and the next generations of their families, and we have to do business. If we achieve both these two objectives we will be OK. But you cannot manage this as only a business or a charity organization. This is my main concern: that we take both parallel courses. If you do only one of these, you will be out of business in less than six months. This is what wakes me up in the middle of the night."

Calle Digna: Financing City Infrastructure

After Patrimonio Hoy partners complete a home improvement project, they begin looking for ways to upgrade their neighborhood, Moreno said. "They say, 'Please extend the program to the streets. Let me pave my sidewalk and street with the same system'."

But residents of Mexico's informal settlements often wait years or even decades for street and utility improvements because they lack the legitimate legal status and political clout to demand such services. Nevertheless, city governments have been taking notice when Patrimonio Hoy members' home improvements cause the level of investment in their neighborhood to rise, and this makes the city more likely to upgrade the public infrastructure.

"The municipal governments came to us and said we have seen what you are doing for the people and their houses," Moreno said. "Most important, we have seen the change in attitude—you have a way of getting these people to be self-sufficient and we need that. But we don't have enough money to pave streets and create drainage."

So Patrimonio Hoy developed a program called Calle Digna ("Worthy Street") that allows partners to make weekly payments for public improvements to their neighborhood streets. Their payments cover the cost of cement and other materials.

The city government pays a matching amount that includes the cost of labor and engineering. The overall cost of the improvements is split 50:50 between the city and neighborhood residents.

The city installs street paving, drainage improvements and water mains. Cemex loans the building materials so that construction can begin 18 weeks after members begin making weekly payments. Patrimonio Hoy has launched the program with the paving of ten streets in the Tonala municipality in a suburban area of Guadalajara.

"Before Patrimonio Hoy was here, the people were very isolated from each other," said Gloria Noemí Cárdenas, a Patrimonio Hoy project supervisor. "But when they started working together they learned they could get more from the government."

Magaña said the government is now installing water lines in her neighborhood. "When Patrimonio Hoy got started, we started seeing construction sites everywhere and the government paid more attention," she said. "When people get organized, they start looking for other things for their own neighborhood like schools, water pipes, police officers, and buses for public transportation. So there have been some changes here."

Patrimonio Hoy Services

Technical Assistance from Architects and Engineers

Patrimonio Hoy has discovered that 50 percent of homebuilders in low-income communities do their own construction rather than hire a mason to help them. This has elevated the importance of providing technical assistance to do-it-yourself homebuilders.

When a person joins Patrimonio Hoy, two things happen immediately: they make their first weekly payment and they schedule an appointment with an engineer or architect to get help with the design of their construction project. "This is one of the most—if not the most—appreciated service," Moreno said.

"Never before could these people have accessed a professional to design the construction of their house. They think they don't deserve these kinds of solutions because they are living in the poorest neighborhoods, and in any case they think they can't afford to pay an architect or engineer. Now, with the money they are saving each week, they can access such benefits."

Patrimonio Hoy's architects and engineers employ a software program they call "the calculator" to provide various scenarios for the exact quantity of materials required, the costs involved, and delivery and construction schedules given available laborers. This tool helps them produce high-quality designs that optimize the use of land, interior space and materials, and to account for possible future growth. They also help homeowners set priorities regarding which improvements to make first.

Rosa Magaña's first house, a single room that now serves as her kitchen, was built before she was involved in Patrimonio Hoy by bricklayers who did not guarantee their work. "My husband spent a lot of money, but it is not well built," she said. "I haven't been able to put a window there because of the way it was constructed, and the room is really dark."

She expanded the house with the assistance of a Patrimonio Hoy architect. "He really helped us," she said. "He drew a sketch and advised us how to design it. He told us the measurement of the iron beams and the exact quantity of materials we'd need, so we didn't waste any material."

Magaña, who now has three children, plans to add a second-floor that includes three bedrooms. But adding a second floor above the original one-room structure will require adding columns to support the weight "because the room has no structural support—it has a concrete beam and could collapse," she said. "Without the advice from the architect, we'd have same structural problems with our new addition."

Support for Education: Patrimonio Hoy Escolar

Recognizing that housing and education are the two key components of patrimony, Patrimonio Hoy links support for education to its services through a program called Patrimonio Hoy Escolar. It donates building materials worth about four percent of a member's weekly club fees to the elementary school of the member's choice.

"If you ask partners about their main worries for the future, two topics will emerge: housing and education," Moreno said. "The conditions in school are very poor. When a school is not attractive and a family needs money for food, they will say, 'Sorry son, quit the school and get a job to get some money to feed this household.' So there are a lot of school drop outs. Giving parents a way to contribute to better conditions in the schools means that their sons and daughters will get a better education."

School principals meet with their local parents' representative to decide how to use the funds that accumulate in a school's Patrimonio Hoy account. Typically, Patrimonio Hoy donates about US$1,500 worth of building materials to a school each year, which is equivalent to the amount of support a school receives from the government for improvements each year.

Some 400 public preschools, kindergartens and elementary schools are receiving this support from Patrimonio Hoy. It is another way to help build community, and it motivates school principals to promote Patrimonio Hoy to students' parents.

Professional School for Masons

Those who have some building experience can professionalize their skills, or learn more advanced techniques like roof construction, by attending Patrimonio Hoy's school for masonry (Escuela Para Albaniles) and get certified to work as a mason. "In many cases their knowledge comes from traditions handed down from their father and grandfathers," Moreno said. "Many of them are still using non-functional materials like dirt or mixtures that are not well proportioned. This is the cause of much poor construction, failures, and high costs for the client."

Some 500 members have completed the school. "Now we have a database of masons, so that when the people come to us to register as partners and they say 'I don't have a mason,' we can offer them referrals to partners who have graduated from the school," Moreno said. "This generates work for our partners, another benefit of being in Patrimonio Hoy. Now they have a new competency—a new way to make more money."

The school opens up new possibilities for women. "There are cases where a woman is doing the construction and her husband is the helper during weekends and holidays," Moreno said.

"It's surprising when you see a woman buying bricks, and impressive when you see that she is a mason's assistant."

Guaranteeing Quality Materials and Delivery

Patrimonio Hoy pays dealers of building materials from the savings it has collected from its members. "If a customer isn't satisfied, Patrimonio Hoy can penalize the dealer with a discount, or reduce or stop orders to that dealer," Moreno said.

In the past, low-income consumers who wanted to buy half a truckload of sand or 55 bricks from a dealer were told they must buy the minimum full truckload, or 500 bricks—making for an expensive waste of the excess materials. "Now, if you need 55 bricks, you will get 55 bricks," Moreno said. "Patrimonio Hoy has the information and the money, and that's changing the rules of the game in favor of the customer. We are concentrating consumer power. Now the customers have the power, not the suppliers. Before, the entire industry was involved in price-based competition. Now, some competitors don't know how to react to this because it has nothing to do with prices. It is value offered to the customer."

Alicia Guerrero is a dealer who began selling Cemex cement products eight years ago. She owns the Perez hardware store in Guadalajara's Mesa Colorada settlement, a business she founded with her husband 11 years ago.

Each week Patrimonio Hoy gives Guerrero delivery orders for its members. This gives her a more consistent, reliable stream of sales and has increased her business, she said. Cemex cement products comprise about 50 percent of her sales, and this percentage is growing.

"If I deliver on time to these Patrimonio Hoy customers, then I'll gain a good reputation with them and they will become my clients," she said. "I think the way Patrimonio Hoy is working is fine. I think that they should work more on their sales department—promote more—so they can keep growing."

Lessons and Innovations from Low-Income Markets

While working to create cultural innovation in low-income communities, Cemex has been forced to adjust its own business culture to meet the requirements of low-income customers. Past attempts by Cemex and other Mexican cement companies to serve this market failed when the fundamental relationship between companies and their customers did not change.

Some of the lessons learned: introduction of easy-to-carry small bags of cement designed to reduce spoilage failed because customers wanted to have large bags of cement sitting in front of their house as a status symbol. Early educational programs took on the aura of the patron–client relationship, and this weakened customers' incentive to honor payment commitments.

Opening retail outlets near low-income communities stimulated bargain-hunting behavior in customers, which suppressed the potential for profit, or discouraged customers who felt the products must be for more wealthy customers. These stores, and the technical advice they offered, sometimes made customers feel pressured to undertake home improvement projects that were too daunting for them. And stores would not extend credit to poor people who lacked formal documents.

Cemex is learning that developing a market in low-income communities is a slow process. Extra time is required to earn the trust of residents and to enable low-income customers to see themselves as producers who can afford aspirations of owning quality, mainstream products.

When introducing the program, time must be allowed for intense exploratory conversations and testimonials from community members who have already joined the program. Patrimonio Hoy encourages members to consider expanding their homes one room at a time to avoid overwhelming them with the expense and effort required for a more comprehensive expansion. Loan sizes are kept small so they are not fearful sums that paralyze borrowers.

To be viable, Patrimonio Hoy must find ways to compensate for the added cost of recruiting low-income customers. It can do so by maintaining high levels of customer retention, encouraging repeat business, and getting customers to move up to more valuable and profitable products.

It helps that its customers tend to stay engaged after completing their first 70 weeks of payments because usually they have saved enough to build walls for a 100-square-foot room, but not for the roof. By continuing to save with Patrimonio Hoy they can complete the room and are likely to want to continue adding more rooms later. As they do this, they begin to identify themselves as successful producers who can afford higher aspirations.

Members who achieve a good payment record during their first 70-week savings period get the opportunity to "ladder up" to preferred customer status, for which they get added benefits. This includes free delivery, including to relatives or friends in other states, the opportunity to belong to a smaller savings group, receive more credit, receive all building materials in three weeks, and to accelerate payments by paying more frequently than weekly or by making larger payments. Earning these privileges helps to make establishing a good credit record an attainable and meaningful achievement for customers without a credit record.

Through its experience with Patrimonio Hoy, Cemex is learning to develop new kinds of services that go beyond simply manufacturing and selling cement. Cemex's Construmex service is an example of such an innovation. Through a toll-free 800 number in Houston, Cemex relays calls from customers in the United States to an account center in Guadalajara.

Construmex targets Mexicans who work in the United States and want to send money back to relatives in Mexico to help them construct a house. "Statistics show that at least 40 percent of the money coming to Mexico from the U.S. goes to building materials," Moreno said. "For Mexicans who go to the U.S. to make a better life, it's a very strong dream to build a house for their wife or parents."

Construmex charges a flat fee of $1 to transfer funds regardless of the amount. It's a much better deal than funds transfer services that charge commissions of 8 to 12 percent.

Money repatriated to Mexico for home construction often gets spent for other purposes as unanticipated emergencies and other various pressing needs arise. Construmex guarantees its customers that 100 percent of funds will be spent for building materials because it delivers the materials—not cash—to the recipients.

Construmex offers Cemex's guarantees of quality for materials and delivery. Over the phone, it can offer the same type of technical assistance that Patrimonio Hoy members enjoy and it can facilitate the same type of expedited, reliable construction timetable.

The Patrimonio Hoy program is an important source of lessons for how to operate in more affluent markets. Through it, Cemex is learning to listen to its customers, who are becoming more intelligent and demanding at all income levels, Moreno said. "In selling to poor people, you have to treat them like producers and not consumers," said Market Expansion Partners' Spinoza. "I believe that's a shift that's coming in our culture in general. Twenty years from now, this is a cultural innovation that we will say is true for all consumers. More and more, the kinds of products that sell will be things that help you make changes in your life. One of the models for doing this is working with poor people. It's a cutting edge way to work with how we are going to innovate in the future."

Conclusion

"Our focus is not just on material things," Moreno said. "Doing business and finding solutions for these people are of equal importance.

"Yes, it's important to have your car and bank account, but if you're not able to empower your children with an ambition, vision and mission for the future, these material things will be lost for the next generation. Our philosophy is to give them the means—a bridge to possibilities—not just the things.

"We are making promises to them about having a better future, education, housing, public infrastructure, schools, quality of life and status. But people are tired of decades of so many false promises. That's why people in this low-income market are very distrustful. That's why Mexico has had some severe social conflicts in the past five years.

"We are trying to change that situation and mentality with these people. Cemex is committed to social responsibility and to collaborate in the making of a different Mexico."

Note

*   © Ashoka's Changemakers.com. Used with permission.

5.3 Manila Water Company*

Fernando Zobel de Ayala, chairman of the board, and Antonino Aquino, president of the Manila Water company looked back with considerable satisfaction on what their management and staff had been able to accomplish in a short nine years. Manila Water Company was not only hitting all the growth milestones, it was also quite profitable (see Exhibit 5.3.1 for Manila Water's income statement over the years). For 2006, Manila Water posted gross revenues of P6.8 billion (US $125 million) and a net income of more than P2.4 billion ($45 million).[1]

Manila Water Company, Inc. (Manila Water) was a water and wastewater concessionaire operating in the east service zone of Metro Manila. It was the exclusive provider of water and wastewater services to approximately 5.3 million[2] people in the east service zone of Metro Manila. The service area included 23 cities and municipalities and spanned approximately 1400 square kilometers. (See Exhibit 5.3.2 for a map of the east zone concession area.)

Manila Water's concession was awarded by the Government of Philippines in 1997 as part of the privatization of the government-owned water supply and sewerage system in Metro Manila—the Metropolitan Waterworks and Sewerage System (MWSS).

Looking forward, Zobel de Ayala and Aquino relished the challenge of addressing all the goals they had undertaken at the time of acquiring the concession, without, of course, losing sight of the company's profitability. But there was an interesting opportunity that had come up recently, which drew their attention for now. After years of financial struggles and legal

Exhibit 5.3.1 Financial Highlights (in million pesos[1] except per-share data)

	2001	2002	2003	2004	2005	2006
Operating Results						
Revenues	1,664	2,683	3,778	4,291	5,763	6,785
EBITDA[2]	304	930	1,814	2,023	2,955	3,507
Net Income	161	558	1,151	1,332	2,011	2,394
Resources at Year End						
Total Assets	5,967	7,846	9,683	12,743	17,929	24,263
Net Debt	1,218	2,080	2,714	4,021	1,513	1,425
Stockholders' Equity	2,486	2,738	3,387	5,121	10,123	11,874
Stockholders' Data						
Earnings per Share	0.06	0.28	0.60	0.85	0.94	1.05
Cash Dividends Paid	–	–	110	230	333	507
Cash Dividends per Share[3]	–	–	0.06	0.10	0.14	0.21

Source: Manila Water 2005 Annual report

1 The average exchange rate during the 2001–2006 timeframe was $1 = 55 pesos.
2 Earnings before interest, tax, depreciation and amortization
3 Adjusted for the effect of IPO shares Source: Manila Water 2005 Annual Report

Exhibit 5.3.2 East Zone Concession Area

Source: Manila Water Sustainability Report 2004

proceedings, the majority owner of Maynilad Water Services, the West Zone concessionaire (with 7.9 million people), finally pulled out of their Concession Agreement in January 2006. Meanwhile in the East Zone, Manila Water continued to meet performance targets and maintain profitability. The Regulatory Office (RO) was satisfied enough with Manila Water's performance to change the terms of the Concession Agreement and remove the clause requiring different Concessionaires to operate the two service zones (east and west), opening up the opportunity for Manila Water to bid for the West Zone concession contract.

The burning question facing Manila Water's top management and owners was whether to bid on the West concession, and if so, how to structure the bid. Much would depend upon their reading of the differences between the two regions, and Manila Water's capabilities in addressing them.

Unlike the 1997 bidding situation, which was based on who could give the lowest water rates and promote coverage and efficiency, the set-up for the Maynilad bidding would be based on who could provide the largest investment to get the concession functioning again.

Water and Sanitation in Metro Manila before Privatization

The privatization of Manila Water and Sanitation Systems (MWSS) was the largest scale water utility privatization ever completed. It was undertaken to address chronic problems in the Metro Manila water system and the abject state of sewerage and sanitation services.

See Exhibit 5.3.3 for a brief overview of the water system serving metro Manila.

Metro Manila had one of the oldest water systems in Asia, with some sections dating back to 1878. Before privatization, Metro Manila's water system was losing almost two-thirds of the water it was producing (so called non-revenue water) to leaks and illegal connections. MWSS had the highest rate of non-revenue water among major cities in Asia.[3] Piped water reached only about 60 percent of Manila households with the poor—at least 40 percent of the population—disproportionately underserved. Water that did reach households was often only intermittently available and under low pressure. Less than 5 percent of the population was connected to sewerage services.

The average national per capita income in the Philippines in 2006 was about $1,156 (P63,556) while the average for Metro Manila was about $3,360 (P184,758). Metro-Manila housed about 3 million families and nearly 13 million of the country's nearly 80 million residents, but accounted for 30% of the country's gross national product. According to the Philippine government's statistics, about 16 % of the people in metro-Manila were considered below the poverty level.

MWSS was heavily indebted, owing US $380 million[4] to various creditors. Servicing the MWSS debt load prohibited government spending on critical public goods and services, including improvements to the water and sewerage system. With 8,000 employees, MWSS was also known to be overstaffed and inefficient.

Various studies indicated that Metro Manila would soon face serious water supply shortages if nothing was done to correct operational inefficiencies and years of under-investment in the infrastructure.

Having achieved some level of recent success with the privatization of the Philippine power utility, President Ramos created the MWSS Privatization Committee in July 1994. The Philippines Congress passed the "Water Crisis Act" to allow privatization of the water utility under President Ramos in June 1995 with very little controversy or opposition.

Through the privatization, the Philippine government sought private investors to achieve three main objectives: renew and expand water and wastewater service coverage; improve delivery of services; and increase the operating efficiency.

The Concession Agreement

The privatization divided MWSS's operations into east and west service zones. The division was designed to balance the power and obligations of the two concessionaires and the regulatory authorities, ensure greater competition during bidding and allow benchmarking of performance throughout operation. Under the terms of privatization, MWSS, even while retaining title, turned over operational use of its existing facilities (headworks facilities, treatment plants, pumping stations and primary lines) to Manila Water. For new facilities and improvements made by Manila Water after the takeover, Manila Water retained the title during the 25-year concession period. However, these facilities were to be turned over to the government at the end of the concession.

Four companies bid for the right to operate and invest in the two (east and west) 25-year water concessions. The concessions were won on the basis of the largest reduction in tariffs.

Manila Water was a consortium led by Ayala Corporation, one of the oldest and largest business conglomerates in the Philippines, operating since 1834. The corporation is a holding company with assets in real estate, financial services, automotive, telecommunications, electronics and information technology, water infrastructure development and management (Manila Water), and international operations. At the time of gaining the concession, the Ayala

Exhibit 5.3.3 The Water System

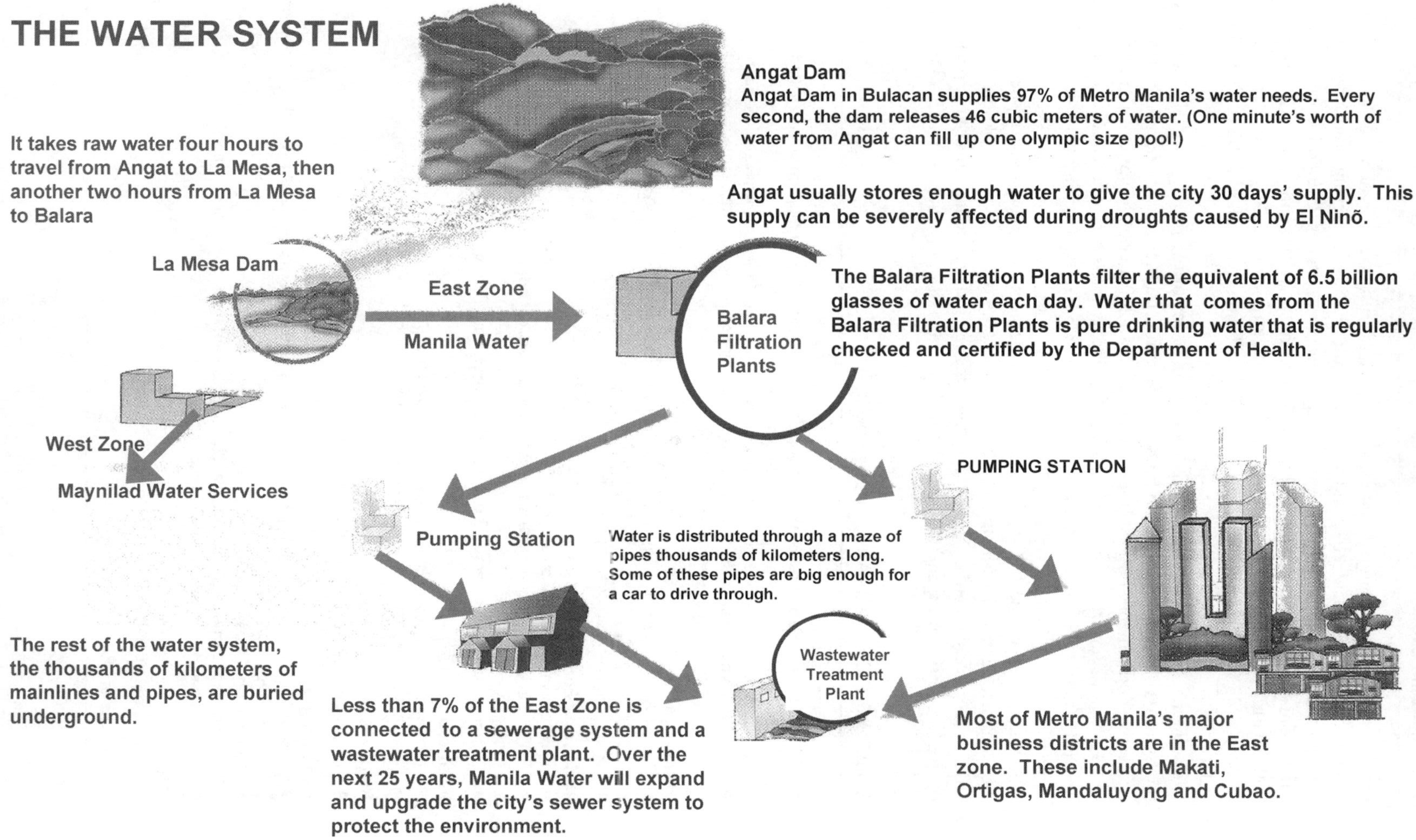

THE WATER SYSTEM

It takes raw water four hours to travel from Angat to La Mesa, then another two hours from La Mesa to Balara

Angat Dam
Angat Dam in Bulacan supplies 97% of Metro Manila's water needs. Every second, the dam releases 46 cubic meters of water. (One minute's worth of water from Angat can fill up one olympic size pool!)

Angat usually stores enough water to give the city 30 days' supply. This supply can be severely affected during droughts caused by El Niño.

The Balara Filtration Plants filter the equivalent of 6.5 billlion glasses of water each day. Water that comes from the Balara Filtration Plants is pure drinking water that is regularly checked and certified by the Department of Health.

La Mesa Dam

East Zone
Manila Water

West Zone
Maynilad Water Services

The rest of the water system, the thousands of kilometers of mainlines and pipes, are buried underground.

Balara Filtration Plants

Pumping Station

Water is distributed through a maze of pipes thousands of kilometers long. Some of these pipes are big enough for a car to drive through.

Less than 7% of the East Zone is connected to a sewerage system and a wastewater treatment plant. Over the next 25 years, Manila Water will expand and upgrade the city's sewer system to protect the environment.

PUMPING STATION

Wastewater Treatment Plant

Most of Metro Manila's major business districts are in the East zone. These include Makati, Ortigas, Mandaluyong and Cubao.

Source: Manila Water Sustainability Report 2004

group owned 60%, United Utilities, the largest private operator of water and wastewater systems in the U.K., had 20%, and Bechtel, a large U.S. engineering contractor, had 20%. After an IPO in March 2005, the Ayala group, held 30.4% shares, United Utilities had 11.4%, Mitsubishi Corporation (Japan), 7.9%, the IFC, a private investment arm of The World Bank, 7.4%, Bank of the Philippine Islands Capital, 4.6%, and the company's employees 2.7%. The rest of the 35.2 % was held by the public, the IPO offering in March of 2005 having raised $75 million.

The Concession Agreement clearly laid out all terms of the privatization. In exchange for the right to collect revenues throughout the 25-year term, the concessionaires needed to meet aggressive performance targets. In the east zone, Manila Water had to offer water connections to 94.6%[5] and sewer connections to 55% of residents in its service area. Non-performance would be met with financial penalties. (See Exhibit 5.3.4 for Highlights of the Concession Agreement.)

A Regulatory Office (RO) was created to implement the provisions of the Concession Agreements. Among its functions, the RO was required to review, determine and enforce rates and service standards; arrange and report regular independent audits of the performance of the Concessionaires; and monitor the maintenance of infrastructure assets. Manila Water

---

Exhibit 5.3.4 Concession Agreement Highlights

Expansion mandate
- Targets expressed as a percentage of population, detailed for each municipality, specified for each five-year period of the term of the agreements.
- Sewerage targets not as high as for water; new infrastructure will gradually replace septic tanks.
- Service from alternative legal sources may contribute to achievement of targets for water.
- In low-income areas, coverage targets may be met using individual connections or standpipes.

Standards
- Water quality must conform to the National Standards for Drinking Water.
- Water availability must be at 24 hours/day by mid-2000.
- Specific standards of water pressure and flow.

Tariffs and connection fees
- Progressive block tariff structure.
- Tariffs can be renegotiated every five years; more frequent adjustments for inflation and exceptional events.
- Maximum connection fees of 3,000 pesos (adjusted for inflation); instalment plans permitted.

Financial
- 60 percent of equity must remain in Filipino ownership.
- Concessionaires assume responsibility for 90 percent of MWSS's debt burden.

Regulatory
- Regulatory Office established to monitor.

Regulation
- The privatization created a third party regulatory body to oversee the terms of the concession, MWSS-Regulatory Office (RO).
- RO responsibilities include monitoring concessionaires' performance, arranging regular independent technical and financial audits and responding to consumer complaints.
- Appeals panel created to settle unresolved disputes.

Other
- Guarantee of raw water availability to the operator.

PPIAF/ADB and Rosenthal (2001)

Source: Company files

was also regulated by the Department of Environment and Natural Resources for wastewater effluent standards and the Department of Health for water quality.

There would be four mechanisms for increasing tariffs over the life of the 25-year concession:

1   Rate Rebasing every five years during which service obligations would be targeted, capital expenditures and operational expendutires projected, and tariffs set
2   Consumer Price Index each year would adjust the Rate Rebasing tariff
3   Foreign currency Differential Adjustment each quarter to cover foreign exchange gains or losses
4   An Extraordinary Price Adjustment on an as-needed basis to cover for unforeseen events such as El Niño

The water concessionaires were allowed a return of 10.4%, which was termed in the Concession Agreement as the Appropriate Discount Rate (ADR). It was defined as the real (i.e. not inflation adjusted) weighted average cost of capital after taxes payable by the concession business. The Regulatory Office determined the 10.4% ADR during the first Rate Rebasing Exercise in year 2002 using estimates of the cost of debt in domestic and international markets, the cost of equity for utility businesses in the Philippines and abroad, and adjusted them to reflect country risk, exchange rate risk and any other project risk. The ADR was used as basis for discounting the "capex" and "opex" to derive the tariff to be charged to customers.

Manila Water submitted the lowest bid for both concession areas; however, the privatization stipulated that each concession must be operated by a different concessionaire. Thus, Manila Water (or MWC) was awarded the east concession, and Maynilad Water Services Inc. (MWSI or Maynilad) was awarded the west concession.

According to a report in *The Manila Times*:[6]

> The deal was expected to generate $7 billion worth of investments over 25 years and improve availability and efficiency of water and sanitation services to most Metro Manila households. It was also a happy arrangement for MWSS, whose debts with the World Bank, Asian Development Bank and other lending institutions were passed on to the new concessionaires—90 percent to Maynilad and 10 percent to Manila Water.
>
> Many could not understand the 90–10 split between the Maynilad and Manila Water. Frankie Arellano, assistant vice president of Maynilad for environmental management, says it's probably because most of those borrowings were for projects in the West Zone.
>
> MWSS sources, however, say it was a way to make investments into the East Zone attractive since the said concession area is less densely populated and has low coverage, thus needing more capital investments. The West side, which lies beside the Manila Bay, has a higher population density and an extensive network, thus requiring less investment.

Figure 5.3.1 shows the projected evolution of average tariff. The rates of the two concessionaires reflect their winning bid rates plus the automatic annual inflationary adjustment and the approved tariff adjustments of the MWSS Regulatory Office. Maynilad (MWSI) rates were higher since the time of the 1997 bid, and retained the higher price difference after the adjustments. For MWSS, the chart shows the projected rates had there been no privatization using their tariff adjustment formula plus annual inflationary adjustments.

At the time of taking over the East, the population of Metro Manila was rapidly expanding, with many people moving in from rural areas. Housing in the city had not kept pace with urban growth and many lived in slums, or squatted in informal settlements, with inadequate

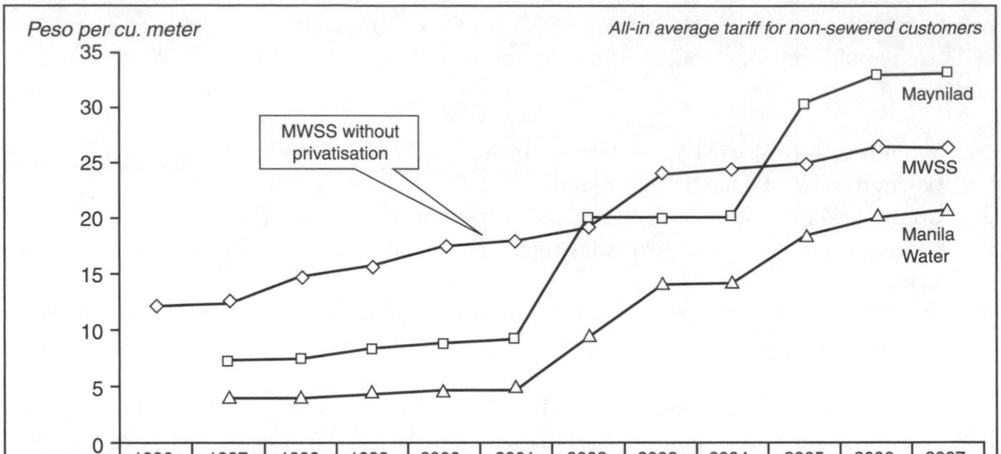

	1996	1997	1998	1999	2000	2001	2002	2003	2004	2005	2006	2007
MWSS	12.14	12.25	14.73	15.64	17.28	17.82	19.11	23.89	24.49	24.97	26.37	26.28
MWSI		7.21	7.21	8.23	8.63	9.18	19.92	19.92	19.92	30.19	32.93	32.99
MWCI		4.02	4.02	4.37	4.55	4.77	9.37	13.88	14.02	18.55	20.09	20.68

Figure 5.3.1 Comparison of Tariff Charges
Source: Company files

or non-existent water and sanitation services. In the impoverished neighborhoods, the poor got water from private vendors selling containers of water from handcarts, from water kiosks, public stand posts, wells, or other methods and at times paid up to seven times more per litre of water than MWSS-connected customers.

Manila Water's customer base was 93% residential and 7% commercial/industrial. Of the residential customers, about 40% belonged to the low-income groups, while 55% were in the middle social class. Only about 5% of Manila Water's residential customers were in the high-income category.

Included in Manila Water's service area were the two biggest business districts in the country as well as several other commercial areas in metro Manila. The company also serviced the two giant broadcasting networks in the Philippines, major colleges and universities, service institutions (i.e. public hospitals, schools, marketplaces, city jails, etc.) and various government agencies.

Given the performance targets set in the Concession Agreement, Manila Water saw the poor and under-serviced areas as potential growth opportunities for expansion. The MWSS Concession Agreement was designed with expansion into poor communities in mind. The concession granted exclusive rights to serve customers in their area but allowed for third party provision as long as the activity was properly licensed and the concessionaire agreed, allowing for partnerships with community based organizations or smaller scale water vendors. Unlike other privatization terms, MWSS allowed for flexibility on requirements for obtaining a service connection by not requiring land title (which obviously the thousands of informal settlers did not have), and allowing installment plans for obtaining a service connection.

Manila Water Performance in the East Zone

The state of both the water and wastewater infrastructure and customer service levels in the East zone had dramatically improved since Manila Water took over operations for the Eastern concession. By 2006, Manila Water had installed 1,877 km of new pipe, representing one-third of Manila Water's entire water network. The company had spent P23 billion ($475 million) on capital investments over the past nine years for projects focused on extending the water network, reducing system losses and improving water quality.

In the same period, the customer base more than doubled, from 325,000 households in 1997 to 909,000 households in 2006 representing more than 5 million people, and the volume of billed water had more than doubled to 992 million liters per day (MLD).[7]

The percentage of areas that had 24-hour access to water had increased from 26% to 98%. System losses, or non-revenue water, decreased from 63% in 1997 to 30% in 2006. Manila Water continued to exceed the 95% target for compliance with the water quality standards set by the Philippine National Standards for Drinking Water; 100% compliance was achieved in 2005.

In terms of wastewater services, sewerage connections more than doubled from 21,769 (or 5 percent coverage[8]) in 1997 to 66,579 (or about 10% coverage) in 2006. Sewerage treatment capacity had more than doubled, from 40 MLD in 1997 to 85 MLD[9] in 2006, primarily from building "package" treatment plants for communal septic tanks.

Septic tanks require desludging (removal of settled solids) every 5–7 years. Manila Water offered free septic tank desludging to all of its customers, transporting the sludge to a septage treatment plant. Manila Water started with just one desludging truck in 1997, and owned 53 trucks for desludging septic tanks by 2006. Since 1997, Manila Water had provided septic tank desludging service to 162,069 households.[10]

Under the terms of the Concession Agreement, Manila Water was authorized to dump the septage at sea. But after considering the views of various community groups, Manila Water decided to forego the practice in 2001. To help manage this waste, the company planned to erect three septage treatment facilities by 2007, designed to accept and treat septage so that the resulting water could be released to surface waters. The sludge that resulted from the treatment of the septage would be used as soil conditioner in volcano hit areas.

Simultaneously, Manila Water successfully completed a loan for the Manila Third Sewerage Project, the biggest wastewater project in the country. This project when completed would serve an estimated 3.3 million people living in the East Zone of Metro Manila by year 2010. The $64 million loan was financed by the World Bank, through the Land Bank of the Philippines. The project, which costs a total of P5 billion, was expected to enhance sewer coverage in the Manila Water concession area from the current 10% to 30%.

Together with the rest of the region, Manila Water weathered the droughts and water shortages of El Nino in 1997 as well as the Asian financial crisis and resultant peso devaluation[11] from 1997 through 2001, yet the company produced solid financial returns. See Exhibit 5.3.5 for a summary of the company's performance since taking over the concession in 1997.

Key Success Factors

According to Tony Aquino, "The success of our company is brought about by several unique elements which, when combined, make Manila Water far greater than the sum of all its parts. One such unique element is the ability of the organization to align its sustainable development initiatives with its business objectives. There was a conscious effort to find this

Exhibit 5.3.5 Manila Water Performance Indicators, 1997 to 2005

	1997	1998	1999	2000	2001	2002	2003	2004	2005	2006
Non-revenue water	63%	55.2%	53%	51%	52%	54%	50.7%	43.4%	35.5%	30%
Billed volume (mld)	440	594	645	706	758	751	767	825	864	948
Households connected ('000)	325	352	383	413	457	526	595	663	708	909
Continuity of supply for the Central Distribution System	26%			56%	60%	69%	83%	89%	95%	98%
Employees/1000 connections	6.3	5.1	4.8	3.8	3.6	3.2	2.9	2.8	2.6	1.8
Revenues (US$ '000)	10,504	25,289	32,496	28,954	31,065	49,130	66,347	73,908	104,383	132,327
Net Income (US$ '000)	(947)	(1,703)	2,493	2,454	3,117	10,485	20,698	23,634	37,889	48,827
Total assets (US$ '000)	37,781	64,545	82,922	91,247	111,996	147,328	174,192	226,177	337,715	489,007
Long-term debt (US$ '000)	–	–	20,000	36,994	46,257	68,966	82,887	89,511	75,760	146,828

Source: Company files

Exhibit 5.3.6 Manila Water Sustainable Development Framework

Source: Company files

alignment, and in the process, we were able to improve the lives of more people, especially those in the poorer sectors of our society, while we also attain our business goals."

Consistent with this philosophy, Manila Water released a Sustainability Report, the first by a Philippine company, that adheres to guidelines issued by the Global Reporting Initiative (GRI) on Corporate Social Responsibility. Exhibit 5.3.6 captures the essence of the company's sustainable development program. Manila Water's Sustainability Report benchmarked the company's performance against international best practices in environmental and social performance, as well as corporate governance. The report focused on programs adopted by the company including measures taken to protect the watersheds, to harness additional water sources to meet the demands of an increasing population, and wastewater treatment. To provide more focus to its drive to supply the population with water, Manila Water adopted several programs targeting crucial institutions, such as schools, hospitals, market places, and the like. The company aimed to improve water distribution and sanitation systems in these institutions by upgrading facilities and regularly monitoring the quality of their supply.

"Our long-term success is intertwined with the well-being of the communities we serve and the natural environment in which we operate. At the same time, the empowerment of our employees and the attainment of the fiduciary goals of our supporters is what gives us the energy to implement our business model aggressively," summed up Aquino.

Organization Culture

Tony Aquino and his senior management team had worked hard on creating a strong organization culture centered on customer service, operating efficiency and employee empowerment.

Manila Water had long placed a strong emphasis on employee development and credited its success to the performance of its people. Following privatization, about 90 percent of Manila Water's 2,200[12] person workforce comprised former MWSS employees. Every employee and worker group had performance indicators for which they were accountable. Manpower productivity had improved dramatically since privatization; what took 8.5 staff per one thousand connections before privatization, required 2.9 staff per one thousand connections in 2003. Most of the downsizing occurred through voluntary retirement and regular attrition. The number of staff members per 1,000 connections had decreased further, to 1.8 in 2006.

In 1997, United Utilities provided around 30 engineers and managers with a great deal of water and wastewater experience. By 2006 there were only two expatriates remaining on staff, one serving as a Group Director and the other as a Director. The organization had a decentralized structure for managing the water and wastewater, divided into eight semi-autonomous Business Areas.

Since the inception of Manila Water, there was a focus on employee development. The company offered exchange programs for middle managers in United Utilities and Manila Water to share best practices, transfer innovation between the companies and a way to develop promising young talent. They also introduced the "Cadetship Training Program" to develop the skills of junior employees with aspirations to management positions. Manila Water recognized employee performance with awards and ceremonies. It also had a strong health and safety program, based on United Utilities' model.

As part of the company's management decentralization policy, business areas were further subdivided into smaller and more manageable territorial boundaries in order to allow greater focus and faster response time to customer problems.

The company's operations and business groups were partitioned into demand monitoring zones (DMZ). Each DMZ territory manager was roughly responsible for 10,000 water service connections, and each DMZ was further subdivided into district metering areas (DMAs), which serviced between 500 to 1,000 connections a piece. The DMZ was managed by a territory team composed of a territory business manager, DMA officers, meter consumption analysts, site officers, and service providers. Each territory team was empowered to oversee and address the needs of the DMZ relating to water supply and demand, NRW (non-revenue water) monitoring and control, and customer concerns. In the previous organization, all service-related decisions almost always emanated and radiated outward from the main headquarters, but under the reorganized set up, all decisions pertaining to the customer's water and wastewater needs were handled in the field where the company's frontline service team made contact with customers every day.

At a regional meeting that one case writer had a chance to attend, the territory business manager made a presentation of the accomplishments of the last quarter. All her DMA's were present. Tony Aquino occupied the front seat, and every once in a while, in a non-threatening, but probing way inquired about a missed target here and there. Even then there was much light hearted banter, but there was no mistaking that these groups were being judged by performance metrics.

We also had a chance to travel with several such MWC field representatives. Their knowledge of the local terrain and community, as well as the close relationship they had forged with their local leaders, was easily discernible. They blended very well into the environment of the many poor communities we visited, and were much appreciated for their services. In one community, the local MWC representative had worked with the local Mayor's office to expedite the approval process for laying pipes into citizens' homes. In another, a MWC representative followed up on the new connections that were being laid by a local contractor. There was ample evidence of work in many of the mud roads and passages leading into the community. Individual households had to pay P700 to P1,000 to procure an in-home connection, to be repaid in 12 installments through the water bill.

A member of the company's board highlighted the advantages of such a system, "In this way we are able to respond faster to customer needs and better address their complaints. As we focus more closely on the needs of our customers, and improve the water service, we are able to increase our sales (billed volume) and improve collection efficiency."

By having people on the ground who actually interfaced with customers daily, Manila Water was able to address all customer needs such as water supply problems or billing complaints. Territory Business Managers and District officers who manage DMZs and DMAs, respectively, were also in charge of conceptualizing projects, overseeing project implementation as well as monitoring business results (see Figure 5.3.2).

The company's 2006 annual report claimed: "Customer satisfaction remained a top priority of Manila Water and more measures to ensure a superior experience for our clients were put in place. The quality of water that flows out of our customers' taps was closely monitored through 923 sampling points throughout our concession area. The Department of Health, together with the MWSS Regulatory Office, confirmed that our water quality consistently exceeded the Philippine National Standards for Drinking Water. This record is further affirmed by an ISO 17025:2005 certification obtained by Manila Water's laboratory for water quality and testing in October 2006."

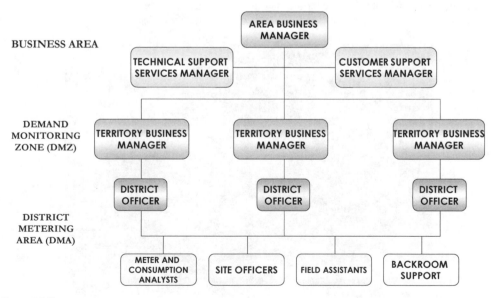

Figure 5.3.2
Source: Manila Water Company

Table 5.3.1 Pricing Structure
Manila Water's Performance for Residential Customers

Monthly Consumption (cubic meters)	% of Total Numbers of Customers	Cost per day (pesos)	% of Average Monthly Income
10	12	2.64	1.2*
30	43	11.16	1.1**
50	24	23.66	
100	16	64.08	
200	3	155.00	
500	1	443.00	

Source: Company files
* Based on minimum wage
** Based on the Family Income and Expenditure Survey, National Statistics Office

Reaching Out to the Poor

Forty percent of Metro Manila's population was poor. These urban poor were an important growth market as well as an important source of cost savings through non-revenue water efficiency improvements.

Manila Water's flagship program, Tubig Para sa Barangay (TPSB), provided low-income communities with quality water service at affordable rates. See Table 5.3.1 above for the tariff structure.

Areas that qualified for the TPSB program had large clusters of urban poor, often in shanty-towns or illegal squatter communities (some on Manila Water's Right-of-Way). In these areas, people typically purchased water in jerry cans from street vendors (at a higher price than they would pay to Manila Water) or relied on illegal connections to the water system (see Figure 5.3.3). The quality of vended water was not subject to control and was expensive at 100 pesos a cubic meter (roughly US $2). Ironically, the poorest residents in Metro Manila paid over seven times what Manila Water charged its regular clients.

Figure 5.3.3 Informal Settlement

The provision of water services in such communities had radically changed the day-to-day lives of residents, particularly the women. Once compelled to stand in line daily for water late at night, they now had the time and resources to devote to other pursuits such as livelihood training.

The TPSB projects relied on Manila Water's ability to identify or help organize local resident cooperatives that collectively took responsibility for a community water connection and metering scheme. With a community organization in place, Manila Water typically installed a "mother meter" to the whole community and individual sub-meters to serve four or five households each. The whole community was accountable for paying the gross water consumption read from the mother meter and each family settled its own bill with the community representative according to the sub-meters. The program reduced illegal connections while lowering maintenance costs and providing clean water at a lower cost than these customers would otherwise pay. Manila Water found that providing clean, safe water to low-income communities reduced illegal connections and built good will (see Figure 5.3.4).

The case writers had a chance to meet several such communities. The leaders (mostly women) were elected by the community and paid by the city government. One such officer, a smart middle aged lady, told us that bill collection was not a problem, and only in rare cases had she had to cut off water supply in order to get the collection. She earned about 7,000 pesos/month (apparently her husband earned as much from his job), making the family lower middle class by Philippine standards. As she took us to visit some of the households in her community, it was noticeable that the homes almost all had electricity and television even though the homes themselves seemed substandard with roofs, partitions and walls all showing signs of wear and tear. Many residents had cell phones. The housing quarters, of course, were cramped and consisted of about three, 120 square feet, rooms for a family of five. The usage of septic tanks was the common method of sanitation, many of which freely leaked effluents into a channel which we were told ultimately led to the Pasig River.

The blue plastic (PVC) pipes of Manila Water were easily sighted as they snaked across in bunches from the mains to the various homes. Sometimes they ran alongside streets, at other times they ran along channels at the back. Just as striking was the cluster of electric wires leading out of a central supply point to people's homes. Electric utility too like water had been privatized in Philippines, and the concession holder happened to be Benpres Holding, the majority owner of the west zone water concession. Like Manila Water, Benpres was held by a local company (Lopez family) that had interests in radio and TV, telephone industry, power generation and real estate.

By providing the poor with access to clean drinking water, incidence of water-borne disease had decreased, health had improved and families no longer devoted large amounts of time and energy to carry drinking water each day. The number of poor households serviced under the TPSB program in the east zone had increased from 1,500 in 1997, to 170,000 in 2006—estimated to represent more than 1 million people.

Community sanitation, or Sanitasyon Para sa Barangay (SPSB) projects, was also being developed for low-income areas, many of which had little or no wastewater services. Each community sanitation strategy was developed in consultation with each community to determine what would be affordable, desirable and acceptable.

Environmental Initiatives

Users of deep wells represented a key challenge to Manila Water. Many of them were owners of larger buildings in the central business district of Makati who had long established their

Figure 5.3.4 TPSB/Metering System

own deep wells. Manila Water attempted to convert them to the distribution network primarily because the quality of its water was more consistent, and also because incessant use of deep wells, where central water was easily available, inhibited supply of groundwater to areas elsewhere where it was needed most.

Hospitals in Metro Manila, for instance, had been typically served by deep wells. Through its "Lingap Ospital" program, Manila Water attempted to convert its hospital users to "central" water. As an incentive for switching to the distribution network, it offered to service and repair selected internal plumbing systems at a discounted rate.

Manila Water's senior leadership, constantly aware of the impact of environmental initiatives on its business, had constructed a number of programs designed to protect the watersheds, for example by planting trees to prevent erosion. Manila Water shipped biosolids (the dried cake from the sewage treatment process) from their wastewater treatment plants to the areas just outside Metro Manila most affected by Mount Pinatubo's volcanic eruption, for application as a soil conditioner for reforestation and non-food producing agriculture.

The wastewater treatment plants also gave away free grey water for irrigating boulevards and other green space, and the company was looking at a waste-to-energy project from biogas at one of the sewage treatment plants. Of course, all improvements to the sewage and sanitation services in Metro Manila had a direct impact on the natural environment, especially the waterways.

Continued Commitment to Sustainable Development

Part of the company's overall sustainable development strategy involved contributing to the local and the national economy. In line with this, Manila Water entered into agreements with two leading banks to provide access to working capital to the company's accredited contractors and suppliers. Through its Kabuhayan Para sa Barangay (KPSB) or Livelihoods Program Manila Water partnered with Bank of the Philippine Islands to offer microfinance loans. KPSB provided more than P1 million [$18,000] in microfinancing and small loans to more than 350 low-income families for start-up consumption-based businesses. Since 2005, the KPSB Program focused on building local capacity in local communities for Manila Water's

Figure 5.3.5 Cooperative

supply chain. The first major partnership was with a pipe rethreading cooperative who supplied meter protectors and other small piping components directly to Manila Water (see Figure 5.3.5).

Through an aggressive capital expenditure program, the company had generated an estimated 12,000 jobs in its nine years of operation. It had helped several small and medium scale entrepreneurs to flourish, by becoming part of Manila Water's list of vendor partners. Almost all the repairs and new connections were outsourced to a list of local contractors as a way of providing employment opportunities and skill development in the community. Moreover, Manila Water found that local contractors were far more responsive to consumer complaints and service calls, because their business interests were located in the same neighborhood as their customers.

Government Relations

An influential board member added yet another reason for Manila Water's success, "I would also attribute our company's success to our ability to manage the regulatory environment. First we were able to address key regulatory issues by building a strong professional and transparent relationship with regulators. Second, we were able to successfully implement our first rebasing in 2003, which provided the framework for future rebasing exercises. Because of these, we were able to prove to our investors and creditors that we have a truly progressive and effective regulatory framework."

An article describing the 2003 rate rebasing captured the essence as follows:[13]

> Every 5 years, rates are rebased to reflect capital expenditure requirements and profit targets . . . Typically such events attract a large number of NGOs and other civil society organizations who appear to resist any proposed rise in rates, whether it is for water, electricity or other utility services. In this case, something extraordinary happened: 90 barangay captains and community leaders showed up to the hearing from all across Metro Manila to express their support for Manila Water's request. Despite the unfamiliarity with such events and formality of the official proceedings, each of these captains spoke to the regulatory commission. They uniformly expressed their appreciation for the powerful and positive impact of Manila Water on their communities, told stories of how their residents used to begin their trek at midnight to get water back to their household by dawn, of new jobs and entrepreneurial activity that had resulted, of support for special

needs and projects. To a person, they supported Manila Water's petition to the commission for a tariff increase.

The chairman of a consumer Price Watch group added this comment: "I have done many reviews of many power and transport companies and Manila Water, I have to say, should be an example for all other regulatory offices, and for all other stakeholders to emulate. We have no difficulty explaining to our consumers whenever there is an increase in Manila Water rates."

The Opportunity to Own the West Concession

The east zone was seen as Manila Water's core business. The company had worked hard to improve and expand service within Metro Manila to reach the unserviced or underserviced customers, estimated to include 2 million people. There was also the need to expand the network to meet demand from the area's growing population. The east zone was estimated to grow from 5.3 million in 2005 to 8.6 million residents by 2022. The east zone of Metro Manila also had opportunities for growth in the expansion of sewerage and sanitation services to unserviced customers.[14]

The west concession had around 7 million customers, or 60 percent of the population of Metro Manila. The area included old Manila and the vast majority of the city's poor. As mentioned earlier in the case, the west concession was structured to inherit 90 percent of MWSS debt because there was a larger existing customer base, with less infrastructure rehabilitation and network expansion required to meet the service obligations outlined in the Concession Agreement.

Maynilad Water Services Inc. (Maynilad) was awarded the west concession in 1997. Benpres Holding Company was the Filipino majority owner (owned by the Lopez family of Manila) and the French multinational Suez Lyonnaise des Eaux (now Ondeo), the minority owner. At the time of receiving the concession, the ownership structure was 60:40.

See Exhibit 5.3.7 for some of the key demographic and geographic differences between the two concessions. Table 5.3.2 below provides the key operating differences.

Debt problems resulted in Benpres' December 2002 announcement that they wanted to pull out of the concession.

Even by 2001, Maynilad's losses had run up to P1.7 billion and debt was at P9.6 billion. The company's non-revenue water had gone up to 69.8% from 65.4% at the time of receiving the concession. According to Maynilad, much of this was because of the antiquated network of 4,000 kilometers of water pipes in its region.

Maynilad also faulted MWSS for its failure to initiate a critical, 300 million litres a day

Table 5.3.2 New Business Development/Opportunities
Key Operating Statistics

	December 2005 Maynilad	December 2005 Manila Water
Ave. Daily Water Production (MLD)	2214	1335
Billed Volume (MLD)	676	864
Non-revenue water	69.4%	35.5%
Average Tariff Rate (April 2006)	33.22 Pesos/Cu. m	19.74 Pesos/Cu.m

Source: Company files

Exhibit 5.3.7 New Business Development Opportunities

	Manila Water New Business Development/Opportunities	
Maynilad (West Zone)		**Manila Water** (East Zone)
971 sq kms	Land Area	1400 sq kms
10	Cities	10
7	Municipalities	13
7.9 Million	Population	5.4 Million
2400 mld	Plant Capacity	1600 mld
604 k	No. of Connections	450 k

Source: Company files

water supply project in Laguna de Bay. To compensate for the delay, MWSS had amended its agreement to allow a tariff increase by P4.21/cu. meter. Furthermore, Maynilad's loans in dollars were inherited at a time when P26 = $1, but after the Asian financial crisis, the peso stood at P50 = $1, which ballooned its debit commitment. To cover this foreign currency differential, the Regulatory authority further allowed a P4.7/cu. meter price increase. Tariff increases did not improve Maynilad's financial position and by November 2003, it had unsecured liabilities of P17.6 billion against recoverable assets of only P2.5 billion. Its stockholders' deficit, at P15.1 billion, was nearly three times its paid-in capital.[15]

From 2003–2006, the government worked with Benpres to retain the concession. In addition to granting Maynilad tariff increases, it forgave the payment of concession fees. But finally in January 2006, its inability to service the $300 million debt burden forced Benpres to hand the concession back to the government. Benpres completely wrote down its equity and Ondeo/Suez, too, adjusted a significant portion of its ownership, leaving MWSS with 85% of the equity and Ondeo/Suez with 15%.

The Bidding Process for Maynilad

MWSS had set a minimum bid price of US$56.4 million for its majority interest in Maynilad. Qualified bidders were asked to submit technical and business qualifications, to be evaluated on a pass or fail basis. Bidders that passed the technical and business criteria would have to post a bid guarantee of US$2.5 million. MWSS would subsequently open the financial bid envelope of qualified bidders to determine the highest offer.

Under the terms of reference approved by the board of directors of Maynilad, the winning bidder would take over and continue operations of the west zone for the remaining years of the 25-year concession (until 2022). The winning bidder would also assume Maynilad's obligations under a "debt and capital restructuring agreement" with the MWSS.

The bidding in 1997 was based on who could give the lowest water rates to promote efficiency gains. The privatization in 1997 attempted to improve service standards, expand service coverage, increase efficiency of the water supply system and eliminate fiscal burden on government while retaining low tariffs.

The set-up in the Maynilad bidding, however, was different. It was based on who could provide the largest investments to get Maynilad out of the rehabilitation program. The tariffs were assumed to be at a fixed rate starting at P30.19 (all-in tariff) to enable Maynilad to complete its rehabilitation program.

The Manila Water Company Board pondered what it should do about the bid.

Notes

* Professor V. Kasturi Rangan, Harvard Business School, Professor David Wheeler, Dean of Management, Dalhousie University, and Jane Comeault, Senior Research Fellow, School of Management, Dalhousie University, prepared this case. HBS cases are developed solely as the basis for class discussion. Cases are not intended to serve as endorsements, sources of primary data, or illustrations of effective or ineffective management. Copyright © 2007 President and Fellows of Harvard College.
1 The average exchange rate during the case timeframe was about $1 = 55 pesos.
2 Source: Company files.
3 In comparison, Asian cities, Singapore, Hong Kong, Seoul and Kuala Lumpur had 100% water coverage, with a 24-hour supply; Bangkok had 82%. Each of those cities had non-revenue water of about 35% (except Singapore at 7%).
4 Esguerra, J. (2003). *New Rules, New Roles: Does PSP Benefit the Poor? The Corporate Muddle of Manila's Water Concessions.* WaterAid and Tearfund.
5 Source: PPIAF/ADB Conference on Infrastructure Development—Private Solutions for the Poor: The Asian Perspective (2002).
6 *The Manila Times*, March 26, 2003.
7 Source: Press release 01 July 2006 http://www.manilawater.com/ir_newspage.cfm?vcatcode= invtr&vnewsdate=2006–0701&vpriority=1.
8 Note—there are conflicting numbers for the 1997 coverage (5% or 7%) within the sewer and sani presentation.
9 Note the difference between the volume of water billed, and volume of sewerage treated.
10 2005 Annual Report.
11 The peso fell significantly, from 26 pesos per US dollar at the start of the crisis in 1997, to 38 pesos in 2000, to 40 pesos by the end of the crisis in 2001. Source: http://en.wikipedia.org/wiki/ Asian_financial_crisis#Philippines.
12 Source: company files.
13 "Developing viable business models to serve low-income consumers: Lessons from the Philippines," by Jaime Ayala, Gerry Ablaza, Antonino Aquino, Christopher Beshouri and Kristine Romano.
14 Note: the concession agreement originally set a targeted increase from 5 percent sewerage coverage to 55 percent by 2022 (the end of the concession). In 2003 Manila Water negotiated with MWSS-RO to change the strategy for wastewater because the cost of installing required infrastructure was prohibitive. In the new strategy, universal sewerage *or* sanitation services will be seen by 2022.
15 Lessons from the Suez-Maynilad Water Venture, by Maitet Diokno-Pascual, Barangay-Tubig.

5.4 Procter & Gamble
Children's Safe Drinking Water[*]

In 1995, Procter & Gamble (P&G) scientists began researching methods of water treatment for use in communities facing water crises. P&G, one of the world's largest consumer products companies, was interested in bringing industrial-quality water treatment to remote areas worldwide, because the lack of clean water, primarily in developing countries, was alarming.[1] In the latter half of the 1990s, approximately 1.1 billion (out of a worldwide population of around 5.6 billion)[2] people lacked access to clean drinking water or sanitation facilities. An estimated 6 million children died annually from diseases, including diarrhea, hookworm, and trachoma, brought about by contaminated water.[3] One report estimated that "about 400 children below age five die per hour in the developing world from waterborne diarrheal diseases"[4] and that, "at any given time, about half the population in the developing world is suffering from one or more of the six main diseases associated with water supply and sanitation."[5]

Procter & Gamble[6]

The Procter & Gamble company dated back to 1837, in Cincinnati, Ohio, when William Procter and James Gamble, married to sisters, started a soap and candle business with $3,596.47 each. By 1859, P&G sales reached $1 million, the company had 80 employees, and it was supplying the Union Army during the Civil War. Gamble's son, a trained chemist, created an inexpensive white soap in 1879 that they named "Ivory" from the Biblical phrase "out of ivory palaces." Ivory soap became one of the first nationally advertised products. In the late 1880s, during a time of labor unrest throughout the country, P&G developed a pioneering profit-sharing program for factory workers, giving them a stake in the company. By 1890, P&G sold more than 30 different types of soap. The company also set up one of the first product research laboratories in the United States. In 1911, P&G developed Crisco, the first all-vegetable shortening, less expensive and considered healthier than butter.

In 1915, P&G built its first manufacturing facility outside the United States, in Canada, and established its chemicals division to formalize research procedures and develop new products. In 1919, Procter revised its articles of incorporation to include the directive that the "interests of the Company and its employees are inseparable." The 1920s saw several marketing innovations: P&G's Crisco was the sponsor of radio cooking shows; the company created a market research department to study consumer preferences and buying habits; and the company developed a brand management system.

As the 20th century progressed, P&G rolled out a number of new and eventually successful products and expanded its product lines through regular acquisitions of well-known and long-standing consumer brands as well as lesser-known products that showed considerable development potential. Products included Camay (1926); Dreft, the first synthetic detergent intended for household use (1933); Drene, the first detergent-based shampoo (1934); Tide detergent and Prell shampoo (1946); Crest, the first toothpaste with fluoride (1955); Charmin toilet paper (a 1957 acquisition); Downy fabric softener (1960); Pampers (1961); Folgers Coffee (a 1963 acquisition); Pringles Potato Crisps, named for a street in Cincinnati (1968); Bounce fabric softener sheets (1972); Always feminine protection (1983); Liquid Tide (1984); Vicks and Oil of Olay (separate 1985 acquisitions); Pert, a combination shampoo/conditioner (1986); Ultra Pampers and Luvs Super Baby Pants, thinner than traditional diapers (1986); Noxell, whose products were CoverGirl, Noxzema, and Clarion (a 1989 acquisition); Febreze, Dryel, and Swiffer, introduced and distributed globally in 18 months (1998); Iams canine products (a 1999 acquisition); and ThermaCare air-activated HeatWraps (2002).

Along the way, P&G celebrated its 100th anniversary in 1937 with sales of $230 million, then its 150th anniversary in 1987 as the second-oldest company among the 50 largest *Fortune* 500 companies. P&G created its first division, drug products, in 1943, and in 1978, introduced its first pharmaceutical product, Didronel (etidronate disodium)—a treatment for Paget's disease. P&G was also a leader in environmental and solid waste prevention practices. In 1988, Germany's retail grocers called P&G's refill packs for liquid products, which reduced packaging by 85%, the invention of the year. In the early 1990s, the company began using recycled plastic for more and more of its products, and in 1992, it received the World Environment Center Gold Medal for International Corporate Environmental Achievement. P&G was also recognized for its affirmative action programs by the U.S. Department of Labor, in 1994, with its Opportunity 2000 Award for commitment to instituting equal employment opportunities and creating a diverse work force. In 1998, P&G began to implement Organization 2005, designed to "push the often slow-moving P&G to innovate, to move fast with product development and marketing and with this, grow revenues, earnings, and shareholder value."[7]

The Global Water Crisis

As the 20th century came to a close, there was general agreement that the characteristics of a developed country included "[i]mproved longevity, reduced infant mortality, health, productivity, and material well-being."[8] But none of these was easily attainable unless the country had a supply of safe, drinkable water and a successful means of disposing of the household and industrial waste that often contaminated the drinking supply in developing countries.

Many of the deaths attributed to contaminated water were preventable, if a product that sanitized water was paired with effective systems of education and distribution. Most of the communities without access to clean water sources lacked the infrastructure to build large municipal water treatment facilities; often, if these facilities existed, they were hard to maintain. Inhabitants of these areas used wells or local surface water for bathing, drinking, and cooking. In addition, animals (both domesticated livestock and those that were wild) frequented the water sources, contaminating them with their feces. Heavily populated areas in some countries were susceptible to natural disaster, which often produced safe-drinking-water crises. Floods, monsoons, and earthquakes often led to the contamination of local water sources when "large runoffs of silt and clay [ran] into the catchment areas of municipal water supplies, which overwhelm[ed] routine sedimentation and filtration methods"[9] and overwhelmed efforts to obtain and then to distribute safe water.

The metal contaminants in water could impair the mental development of children who drank it. The main diseases that resulted from contaminated water included:

- Diarrhea, which occurred when microbial and viral pathogens existed in either food or water. Diarrheal diseases were the big killer and, if they did not result in death, brought about malnutrition and stunted growth in children, because the diseases left the body unable to absorb important nutrients long past the period of the actual diarrhea.
- *Ascaris, Dracunculisis*, Hookworm, and *Schistosomiasis* were caused by infestations of different kinds of worms. Ultimately, people suffering from them experienced disability, morbidity, and occasionally, death.
- Trachoma, which was caused by bacteria and often resulted in blindness.

In addition to the deaths and physical illnesses caused by unsafe drinking water, there were larger economic consequences. These included "economic and health costs of about 10 million person-years of time and effort annually, mostly by women and girls, carrying water from distant, often polluted sources."[10] Entire households suffered financially when the primary breadwinner became ill. Boiling water as a purification technique was time-consuming, often eating up hours each day that could better be spent raising crops as food or, for children, attending school. In short, a shortage of safe drinking water could stunt the growth of a community just as it could stunt the growth of sick and malnourished children.

The Search for a Solution

In the mid-1990s, a number of companies, such as Mioxx Corporation, Innova Pure Water, Pall, CUNO, Millipore, Ionics, and Clorox's Brita, were already in the water-purification business. Their products covered a range of needs, including household, municipal, and military. As the global water access crisis grew, however, there was greater pressure to address the needs of developing countries though new water sanitation products and the alteration of existing technology. Crucial to the success of any water purification program was developing effective models for distribution and combining them with effective education about the use of potential products. A successful program would feature a product that could offer:

- inexpensive, on the spot, or "point-of-use" treatment;
- ease of use, requiring no more than simple educational demonstrations;
- potential to fit into a long-term, sustainable distribution system flexible enough to be utilized in disaster relief efforts.

With a long history of scientific research and innovation in health, hygiene, and nutrition, P&G, with more than 200 scientists, considered ways the company could address the safe drinking-water crisis as the millennium approached. The United Nations was drafting its Millennium Development Goals, which would be presented for resolution by the General Assembly in 2000. Included in the draft document was a 2015 goal to cut by half the world population that currently did not have access to safe drinking water. Although P&G had a vast array of successful products, the company did not offer anything that involved water purification, either domestically or in developing countries where poverty, lack of infrastructure, and inaccessibility of remote communities made the prospect of cleaning up the water more difficult.

In 1999, P&G purchased—through the acquisition of Recovery Engineering in a $265 million deal—PUR Water Filtration System, a point-of-use water filtration system. Harvard graduate and entrepreneur Brian Sullivan had founded Recovery in 1986, and by 1999, the company had 550 employees, annual sales of $77 million (in 1998),[11] and was the number-two water filtration product in the United States behind Clorox Company's Brita.[12] Sullivan said that his company's mission had always been "to solve the world's drinking water problems"[13] and that P&G's marketing clout would help expand sales of the product globally. PUR products had only been distributed domestically, and Sullivan said that "it would take us a long time to have a global impact. . . . The technology . . . is very powerful, with fantastic potential, and it's something that can best be leveraged under the umbrella of a global consumer products firm."[14]

This was a new product category for P&G, said a spokesperson, but—referring to the company's detergent, hair- and skin-care products—"we've been in the water management business for a long time . . . We've learned a lot about water—how to manage it well—so there is some synergy."[15] With this acquisition, P&G took a huge first step toward supplying drinkable water to areas throughout the world.

Development of PUR

The PUR water filtration system used a combination of the flocculant iron sulfate, an agent that caused particles suspended in water to bind and form sediment, and calcium hypochlorite (chlorine), a disinfectant. After acquiring the product, P&G began to develop and expand it. Over the next several years, the PUR product line included home faucet mounts, refrigerator pitchers and dispensers, portable water bottle systems, and eventually, optional flavor packets that created gallons of clean, flavored water through specialized pitchers. P&G also began to experiment with a small point-of-use purifier: small sachets of flocculant-disinfectant. These sachets were approximately the size of a "pack of coffee creamer" and could "suck out dirt, bacteria, and parasites from 10 liters of water."[16] They were simple and easy to demonstrate, as well as inexpensive to produce, affordable to purchase (approximately $0.10 a unit), and easy to distribute. The user would mix a small packet of powder in a container of water. After stirring, the contaminants separated out and fell to the bottom of the container as visible sediment. These contaminants included "dirt, pesticides, toxic heavy metals, such as arsenic and lead, as well as bacteria, viruses and protozoa that [were] resistant to chlorine alone."[17] P&G called this system PUR Purifier of Water.

Strategic Partnerships

In 2001, to combine "a wide range of health-care research into one research institute,"[18] and broaden its philanthropic reach, P&G created the Procter & Gamble Health Sciences Institute (PGHSI), which was "dedicated to identifying, developing, and using leading health care technologies in the development of effective products for both the developing and developed world."[19] PGHSI partnered with the nonprofit International Council of Nurses (ICN) and the U.S. Centers for Disease Control and Prevention (CDC) to improve the technology for use in developing nations. The Switzerland-based ICN, a federation of 124 national nurses' associations that represented millions of nurses globally, had made universal access to clean water a priority, with the following statement:

> ICN believes that the right to water is non-negotiable. Secure access to safe water is a universal need and fundamental human right; an essential resource to meet basic human needs, and to sustain livelihoods and development. . . .
>
> ICN also believes that with commitment and political will by governments and others, clean and safe water can be made accessible to all people at low cost using appropriate technology.[20]

The Atlanta-based CDC was part of the U.S. Department of Health and Human Services. Its Safe Water Systems (SWS) program was "a water quality intervention that employ[ed] simple, robust, and inexpensive technologies appropriate for the developing world."[21] This intervention involved point-of-use treatment of contaminated water, safe water storage in containers, and behavioral techniques to educate the affected populations about the importance of, among other things, hygiene and proper use of water storage vessels.

In April 2001, at the CDC's annual Epidemic Intelligence Service Conference, PGHSI unveiled its small sachets of flocculant-disinfectant, or what it called PUR Purifier of Water. Between 2001 and 2003, the strategic partners conducted part of the PUR development process in parts of Guatemala and Haiti that suffered from a lack of clean drinking water. The studies they carried out tested the utility of PUR in large-scale water relief programs. After several years of testing, an impact study linked the use of four-gram sachets of PUR to a significant decrease in the occurrence of diarrhea. The 20-week study that comprised more than 600 families linked the use of PUR sachets to a 25% decrease in instances of diarrhea among children younger than two.[22] The *American Journal of Tropical Medicine and Hygiene* published an article, based on the studies in Guatemala, about the success of PUR in significantly reducing diarrheal illness in children. In January 2003, the *Journal of Water and Health* published an article called, "Evaluation of a New Water Treatment for Point-of-Use Household Applications to Remove Microorganisms and Arsenic from Drinking Water," also describing the efficacy of the PUR system. PUR not only removed microbial contaminants, but also heavy metal contaminants such as chromium, lead, arsenic, and nickel.

At that point, P&G had spent $20 million developing PUR,[23] although it claimed that the product was "a social marketing breakthrough rather than a commercial initiative."[24] With glowing reports about the water purifier, various nonprofits began purchasing and shipping it all over the globe. The International Rescue Committee in 2003 shipped 350,000 packets to Iraq, where fighting had destroyed or damaged many of the water systems. Relief agency AmeriCares delivered more than a million PUR sachets to Sudanese refuges in Chad. In 2003, the product had been used in Botswana, Malawi, Liberia, and Zimbabwe as well.

Children's Safe Drinking Water

With the success of PUR Water Filtration System, PGHSI and its partners created the Children's Safe Drinking Water (CSDW)[25] campaign in 2003. But there were obstacles to expanding the program effectively in developing countries and to persuading people in target water crisis areas to use it, so PGHSI needed seasoned strategy and expertise. PGHSI found that Population Services International (PSI) and the Aquaya Institute were organizations that were both experienced in the methods of social marketing and disaster relief planning.

Population Services International (PSI)

Founded in 1970 as a nonprofit organization focusing on family planning and reproductive health, PSI expanded to operate programs promoting oral rehydration therapy and HIV awareness in the developing world. PSI utilized social marketing models to promote products that could improve health conditions for the poor. The PSI approach to social marketing "engaged private sector resources and used private sector techniques to encourage healthy behavior and make markets work for the poor" and focused heavily on combining measurable results and private-sector operational efficiency.[26] This often included finding members of target communities to act as contacts for the program and to sell the water treatment systems. These local contacts had access to potential end users, understood local customs, and would be more likely to achieve product acceptance. PSI used performance metrics and review processes to create a level of operational efficiency comparable to a successful for-profit corporation. The organization operated water treatment programs in 23 countries, and used the social marketing model for successful distribution of PUR water treatment sachets in five countries.[27]

Aquaya Institute and PURelief

The Aquaya Institute offered consulting services to organizations planning and implementing safe water programs. It conducted original research on the technology, distribution systems, and impact of safe water programs. Supported by the Procter & Gamble Fund, the institute began developing a geographic information system that would help create sales strategies for communities reliant specifically on surface water. The Aquaya Institute joined the Johns Hopkins University School of Public Health to investigate methods of marketing and distributing PUR in Indonesia in 2004 with funding and support provided by the Procter & Gamble Fund. The program expanded after the December 26, 2004 Asian tsunami, which greatly exacerbated existing water shortages. P&G joined local government organizations, as well as leading NGOs, to provide disaster relief in the form of PUR treatment. Indonesians in disaster areas received a portion of 15 million sachets of PUR, saving thousands of lives. Later, in 2007, the Aquaya Institute joined PSI in a PUR distribution program in Kenya.[28]

With the help of PSI and the Aquaya Institute, P&G expanded the use of PUR to many developing countries. P&G also worked with other organizations and nonprofits, including the Johns Hopkins University School of Public Health, CARE, UNAIDS, WHO, and UNICEF in supplying and distributing the water purification product. See Exhibit 5.4.1 for a description of travels made by PGHSI Executive Director Greg Allgood, to various regions around the world to observe the implementation of and response to the PUR product.

The Economics of PUR

Many of the PUR programs operated either on partial cost recovery, where the user paid only for the product and donor funds subsidized other program costs, or—in the case of emergencies, such as the Asian tsunami, flooding in Haiti, or cholera epidemics in Africa—as fully subsidized free distribution. In general, each PUR sachet was provided to relief or NGOs at a cost of $0.035, but program costs also included "transport, distribution, education, and community motivation."[29] Most often, sachets were sold at product cost recovery for $0.10 each, which translated to $0.01 per liter of treated water.

PUR Expands Globally

In June 2004, P&G's PUR Purifier of Water won the International Chamber of Commerce (ICC) World Business Award in support of the Millennium Development Goals. This was part of the first annual worldwide business awards to "recognize the significant role business can play in the implementation of the UN's targets for reducing poverty around the world by 2015." P&G's Children's Safe Drinking Water program went on to win other awards: the Stockholm Industry Water Award (2005), the Ron Brown Presidential Award for Corporate Leadership (2007), the EPA Children's Health Excellence Award (2007), and the Grainger Challenge Bronze Award (2007). Throughout the Children's Safe Drinking Water program from 2003 to 2007, P&G had sold the sachets at no cost, made no profit on PUR sales, and donated programmatic funding to some of the projects. Between 2003 and 2007, 85 million

Exhibit 5.4.1 Blogging from Borneo [30]

In 2005, industrial toxicologist Dr. Greg Allgood, executive director of Procter and Gamble's Health Sciences Institute (PGHSI), began a blog to tell the story of his travels through the Tsunami-ravaged regions of Southern Asia. The December 26, 2004, tsunami killed hundreds of thousands of people and created water shortages throughout the affected areas, leaving millions without access. As part of PGHSI's Children's Safe Drinking Water Program, Allgood assisted in providing safe, clean drinking water to regions that had lost the ability to maintain the sanitation of water sources in the wake of the disaster. Along the way, Allgood worked to educate the people of each region about the dangers of unsafe drinking water. Over the next three years, Allgood's travels would take him from Sri Lanka to Pakistan, India, parts of Africa, Vietnam and, in late 2007, into Indonesia.

In November 2007, Allgood and representatives from Aquaya Institute, a research and consulting NGO and the Dian Desa Foundation, a well-established Indonesian nonprofit, entered the Indonesian region of Borneo. The trip was organized to promote safe water education in rural parts of the island and to investigate local acceptance of water treatment products. Experiencing the region's torrential downpours, Allgood and his team covered miles of rain-battered roadways, reaching the town of Batulicin and nearby villages. There they offered demonstrations of the PUR Water Filtration System.

Allgood joined a local PUR distributor, Heini, to tour nearby villages and demonstrate the water sanitizing properties of the product. Heini, a local, was chosen by the Dian Desa Foundation to assist Allgood and Aquaya Institute's Jeff Albert in documenting the acceptance of PUR by regional consumers. Using water taken from a river nearby, Heini's demonstrations convinced a number of locals to begin using PUR to sanitize their drinking water. Unfortunately, many potential PUR consumers had difficulty accepting the product, preferring instead to use decades-old purification techniques.

In a community along the route, Allgood watched locals pulling water from irrigation ditches. The water looked clear, but Allgood worried that it was contaminated nonetheless. Surprisingly, villagers preferred the taste of the unpurified water to sanitized water in a blind taste test. When members of his crew paused to join men from the village at a local mosque, they participated in ritual absolution before prayers. "They wash and cleanse their mouths from the irrigation ditch water," Allgood worried, "and I hope they don't get sick from it."

To demonstrate the product, Heini would draw 10 liters of water in one or more vessels from a contaminated local source. After reiterating the threat posed by unsafe water, Heini introduced a single sachet of PUR powder to each vessel, often inviting locals from the audience to participate in the treatment process. After stirring the water for five minutes, they allowed it to sit for another five minutes as the formerly turbid water visibly cleared. When the water was clear, they poured it into another vessel through a piece of cotton fabric, and allowed it to sit for another few minutes before drawing the now purified water into several clear cups. The audience was invited to comment on the clarity and flavor of the water. [31] Reactions varied greatly in each region in which PUR was introduced, as hesitant locals experienced a totally new flavor of water. Reluctance to stray from traditional sanitation methods and familiar flavors would become a major hurdle to acceptance of PUR in some areas.

Local Networks

The final stop in Allgood's tour of Borneo was a village that had only recently been introduced to PUR. The village, located in a swampy region where the well water was saturated with mud, had a tradition of boiling drinking water. Residents had a mixed response to PUR; some preferred to keep old habits of boiling, and others warmed up to the relative ease of cleansing water in this novel way. One villager, a tea and snack merchant named Sutyami, had been using PUR for a week. She was hesitant to use the product at first, but chose to test it to save time and money. Boiling, her habitual method of water sanitation, was expensive and time consuming. She agreed to become a local distributor of PUR, and began selling the sachets alongside her regular wares. Like many other distributors in rural areas, she made a good local contact to provide the sachets to her community, and also generated extra income from selling them. With assistance from programs such as PGHSI's Children's Safe Drinking Water, local distributors like Heini and Sutyami are able to create sustainable water safety outlets for their communities, bringing affordable safe water practices to those most in need.

sachets of PUR, treating 850 million liters of water, had been distributed globally in emergency response or sold through social marketing projects. With the help of its various partners, PGHSI had made the product available in 23 countries.

Notes

* This case was prepared by DePaul University Professor of Business Ethics Laura P. Hartman, DePaul University's, Institute for Business and Professional Ethics Project Developer Justin Shee-han, and the Darden School's Olsson Center Senior Ethics Research Associate Jenny Mead under the supervision of Patricia H. Werhane, Ruffin Professor of Business Ethics. It was written as a basis for class discussion rather than to illustrate effective or ineffective handling of an administrative situation. Copyright © 2008 by the University of Virginia Darden School Foundation, Charlottesville, VA. All rights reserved.

1 "Safe Drinking Water," P&G Health Sciences Institute, http://www.pghsi.com/pghsi/safewater (accessed 15 February 2008).

2 U.S. Census Bureau, International Data Base, "Total Midyear Population for the World: 1950–2050," 16 July 2007, http://www.census.gov/ipc/www/idb/worldpop.html (accessed 28 February 2008).

3 Nigel Hawkes and Nigel Nuttall, "Seeds Offer Hope of Pure Water for the Developing World," *The Times* (London), 15 September 1995.

4 Ashok Gadgil, "Drinking Water in Developing Countries," *Annual Review of Energy and the Environment* 23 (November 1998): 254.

5 Gadgil, 254.

6 "Our History," P&G Web site, http://www.pg.com/company/who_we_are/ourhistory.jhtml (accessed 15 February 2008).

7 Marguerite Nugent, "P&G CEO Sees Transformation in Five Years," Reuters News Service, 12 October 1999.

8 Gadgil, 264.

9 Gadgil, 264.

10 Gadgil, 256.

11 P&G had sales of $38.1 billion and net earnings of $3.76 billion in 1998.

12 In the first quarter of 1999, PUR had 21.2% of the market, compared with Brita's 66.2%, and had gained 49% of the market in the month of July 1999, according to Susan E. Peterson, "Pretty Price for Recovery Engineering," *Minneapolis Star-Tribune*, 27 August 1999, 1-D.

13 Peterson.

14 Peterson.

15 Peterson.

16 Alexander Coolidge, "P&G Water Purifier Aids Third World," *The Cincinnati Post*, 19 June 2003, B6.

17 Procter & Gamble Press Release, "New P&G Technology Improves Drinking Water in Developing Countries," 24 April 2001, http://www.pginvestor.com/phoenix.zhtml?c=104574&p=irol-newsArticle&ID=628966&highlight= (accessed 25 February 2008).

18 "Global Joint Program Partners," Health Communication Partnership, http://www.hcpartnership.org/Partners/gjpp.php (accessed 25 February 2008).

19 "Mission," P&G Health Sciences Institute, http://www.pghsi.com/pghsi/mission/ (accessed 25 February 2008).

20 "Universal Access to Clean Water," ICN Position Statement, 1995, http://www.icn.ch/pswater.htm (accessed 25 February 2008).

21 "Safe Water System," Centers for Disease Control and Prevention, http://www.cdc.gov/safewater/ (accessed 25 February 2008).

22 John A. Crump, Peter O. Otieno, Laurence Slutsker, Bruce H. Keswick, Daniel H. Rosen, R. Michael Hoekstra, John M. Vulule, Stephen P. Luby, "Household Based Treatment of Drinking Water with Flocculant-Disinfectant for Preventing Diarrhoea in Areas with Turbid Source Water in Rural Western Kenya: Cluster Randomised Controlled Trial," *British Medical Journal (BMJ)*, 2005, 331; 478, published online July 26, 2005. http://www.bmj.com/cgi/reprint/331/7515/478 (accessed 19 February 2008).

23 Coolidge, B6.

24 "Financial Express: P&G May Test Waters With PUR," *Financial Express*, 26 May 2004.

25 "Children's Safe Drinking Water," Procter & Gamble, http://www.pg.com/company/our_commitment/drinking_water.jhtml (accessed 25 February 2008).

26 "About PSI," Population Services International, http://www.psi.org/about_us (accessed 21 November 2007).

27 In 2006, PSI estimated that it had treated over 8.6 billion liters of water, averted 4.1 million cases of diarrhea, and prevented 6,000 child deaths that year. "Water/Child Survival: Safe Water and Diarrheal Disease Control," http://www.psi.org/child-survival (accessed 18 December 2007).

28 "Aquaya to Assist PSI in Community Targeting for the Social Marketing of PUR in Kenya," Aquaya Institute press release, http://www.aquaya.org/news.php#010807 (accessed 4 December 2007).

29 "Household Water Treatment Options in Developing Countries," Centers for Disease Control, January 2008, http://www.ehproject.org/PDF/ehkm/cdc-options_pur.pdf (accessed 15 February 2008).

30 Source: Greg Allgood blog at http://childrensafedrinkingwater.typepad.com/pgsafewater/2007/11/boiling-in-born.html (accessed 20 November 2007).

31 A video of a typical PUR product demonstration, produced by members of the nonprofit, Other Paths, may be seen at http://www.youtube.com/watch?v=mij0-3hBKs8&feature=related (accessed 25 February 2008).

5.5 Islamic Banking and Finance

Moral Beliefs and Business Practices at Work[*]

The religion of Islam has existed for 1400 years but Islamic economic theory and its financial institutions emerged as an industry only in the 1970s. Islamic financial institutions (IFIs) are designed to help Muslims conduct business internationally while simultaneously upholding traditional Islamic values related to trade finance and currency movement. The basis for their existence is the Islamic moral prohibition on charging interest—interest is a central component of capitalist banking—yet IFIs conduct billions of dollars of business annually in the world economy and the *de facto* Islamic banking transaction is—in most cases—virtually identical to a capitalist banking transaction. Business practices in the industry of Islamic banking and finance (IBF; Maurer 2005) have evolved to reinforce some of the major tenets of a moral belief system based on Islamic principles. This chapter will discuss specific practices put into place by the IBF community that are designed to embody tenets of a belief system based on Islam while at the same time generating profits for the institution and its customers. This chapter will contribute to the discussion of best corporate practices by introducing some of those practices and discussing how those practices contribute to the success of the industry.

Religion and Business Practices

Religion is deeply concerned with the relationship between individuals and society on earth and the implications of that relationship on salvation: therefore, it is crucial for humans to understand the place of material survival in the cosmological scheme of life. That concern has been intertwined with questions of what it means to be a person and how to identify with a certain kind of community or communities. Opposition between religion and economy has arisen at times when a religious community is trying to carve out an identity for itself vis-à-vis the broader society. Individuals and societies change throughout history; therefore, spiritual and material well being must be constantly renegotiated. As such, it makes sense that human beings struggle to find the appropriate balance between material and spiritual matters. These concerns have carried over into contemporary discussions of religion and economy, and have become visible in the form of social movements based on various conceptions of morality. The basic questions and issues are the same as in the past, but the context of globalization (Appadurai 2000, 1986; Sassen 1998; Jameson & Miyoshi 1998; Hannerz 1996; Scholte 2000) has expanded the scope of the meaning of identity and community, especially in the context of competing moralities (Shweder, Minow and Markus 2002; Gupta and Ferguson 1997; Ong 1999).

In the contemporary world, some types of morally driven economic theories—corporate social responsibility, socially responsible investing and, it will be argued throughout this chapter, Islamic finance—are examples of some approaches to economic behavior that are based on moral discourse. Regardless of whether or not religion is specifically invoked in the moral discourse, it is clear that discussions about religion and economy are as relevant today as ever before. Economic cultures are sensitive to cultural and religious understandings of the implications of moral belief systems on business practices.

Most economic development textbooks do not take into consideration the effects of moral or religious beliefs on economic behavior (Kuran 2004). From the Enlightenment until the publication of Weber's *Protestant Ethic*, scholars took it for granted that religion and economy were unrelated spheres of life. Whereas an emphasis on the compatibility of religion and economy may have waned for more than a century, some groups in contemporary society are very much embroiled in the same kinds of conversations about morality and business that occupied the minds of medieval moralists. These conversations may not be based specifically on *religious* morality, but they do call upon an individual's moral inclinations to curb human greed and to form communities around moral beliefs about economic activity.

Introduction to Islamic Finance

The industry of Islamic banking and finance is growing daily. In 2006, the Islamic Development Bank in Saudi Arabia estimated that Islamic financial institutions manage more than USD$800 billion. There are more than 500 Islamic financial institutions worldwide and the world's potential market for Islamic finance consists of more than one billion Muslims, in addition to non-Muslims, who are welcome to participate in Islamic finance. Islamic finance has been compared to an environmental fund in that its policies are based on a certain philosophy of life yet its participants also expect to make a profit on investments. Practitioners in the industry define Islamic finance by the ways in which it objects to conventional financial practices in addition to the ban on *riba*, which is translated from Arabic as interest or usury. Islamic financiers are not allowed to trade in specific goods forbidden under Islamic law, such as pork and alcohol. Islamic finance prohibits taking unnecessary risks or gambling (El Gamal 2000). Islamic financial institutions should adhere to a code of Islamic business ethics and should maintain a Shari'a Standards Board composed of Islamic scholars to maintain the purity of the institution's products and conduct (Lewis and Algaoud 2001; Beekum 1997). Ultimately, all features of Islamic finance are designed to uphold theological concepts of God-consciousness (*tawhid*) and social justice (*adalah*) in a business environment.

Framework of an Islamic Economic Theory

The framework of Islamic economic theory was developed in pre-Partition India in the early 20th century by Islamic scholar Mawlana Mawdudi (1903–1979) and expounded upon by one of his students, economist Khurshid Ahmad, who later moved to Pakistan. At the time, Indian Muslims as a group were relatively disadvantaged economically compared with the majority population of Hindus. The British Raj had provided some economic protections to Muslims, farmers in particular, but at the time it was unclear how or if a Hindu-led government would provide the same protection (Kuran 2004). Mawdudi believed that economic activity and technology were crucial to success in the modern world, and he was dedicated to providing Muslims in pre-Partition India with economic opportunities that allowed them both to function in the modern world and to retain their Muslim identity. He and Ahmad believed that it was possible and desirable for Muslims to embrace systems and institutions of modernity while at the same time adhering to the teachings and practices of Islam (Mawdudi 1980; Ahmad and Ansari 1979). One goal of Mawdudi was to redefine Islamic practices to conform to economic changes. Mawdudi's ideas were put into practice in the 1970s in the

Arabian Gulf, with the establishment of Dubai Islamic Bank and the Islamic Development Bank in Saudi Arabia.

At first the industry grew slowly. Until very recently Islamic financing was only sporadically available throughout the world, and mostly it was not available at all. Recent developments in the global economic structure due to improved technology and fewer restrictions on capital flows have made world conditions much more amenable to the possibility of IBF making a meaningful contribution to the reformation of business practices to bring them more in line with the Islamic belief system. IBF business practices reflect and reinforce certain key concepts of an Islamic moral economy (Tripp 2006) such as community, partnership and trust. Financial structures and practices provide evidence of adherence to these beliefs.

Business Practices Under Islamic Law

The existence of Islamic finance institutions solves a difficult problem for the Muslim desiring to participate in international finance while adhering to Islamic law, or *Shari'a*. Islamic law does not allow for individuals or institutions who lend or borrow money to charge or pay interest on that money. Yet in the early twenty-first century global economy, trade finance and other crucial banking transactions are dominated by capitalist financial practices in which return on investment is based upon charging interest.

The Islamic finance industry intends to improve upon global financial institutions by maintaining their positive features and cleansing them of negative features (Maurer 2002a, 2002b; Al Saud 2000). Islamic banks strive, in the words of a prominent Islamic bank's vision statement, to uphold "deep-rooted traditions in the new world" (Dubai Islamic Bank brochure). Islamic finance professionals claim that an Islamic bank is a conventional bank without its immorality. The framework used to determine morality is based on Islamic text and tradition, yet the institutional framework is, on the surface at least and to the untrained eye, indistinguishable from the capitalist financial structure.

Islamic law is specific about what constitutes permissible trade behavior. Business practices fall under the set of normative relationships between human beings (*muamalat*) that are ultimately governed by the will of Allah, or God (Waines 1998:65). Therefore, banking, finance and trade are regulated by specific rulings found either in the *Qur'an* or in *hadith*.[10]

Discussions of Islamic finance fall into two categories: moral/ethical and social justice concerns. The first category is the better known and involves the prohibition of specific types of transactions: *riba* and *gharar* (El Gamal 2000) as well as more general trading prohibitions regarding goods forbidden under Islamic law such as pork, alcohol and tobacco. *Riba* broadly refers to any goods or services traded in unequal amounts. Muslims cite a well-known *hadith* to support this concept:

> Gold for gold, silver for silver, salt for salt, dates for dates, barley for barley, and wheat for wheat, hand-to-hand in equal amounts; and any increase is *riba*.
>
> [El Gamal 2000:147]

The concept of usury may be applied to both monetary and material goods and its prohibition serves a major purpose of keeping relations among businesspeople equitable. This conception of *riba* is, of course, a simplification and its technical properties are widely discussed and debated by Islamic economists (see, for example, Ahmad 1976; for an alternative economic view of *riba*, see El Gamal 2000).

In the area of religious thought Judaism and Christianity, in addition to Islam, have struggled internally throughout history with moral challenges posed by "interest" (Weber 1968).

Interest calculation is based on the measurement of time. Foucault (1978) asserts that early Christians viewed time as a gift from God; therefore, it has different value for different people, making the calculation of interest immoral. The original intention of timetables, he asserts, was a religious invention designed to eliminate the dangers of wasting God's gift of time. The move of instituting schedules served to appropriate the use of time in daily human life. In addition, Landes emphasizes the importance of time to the link between Protestantism and the formation of a capitalist subject (Landes 2000). However, Foucault argues that today time is understood as a material possession to be manipulated and shaped at will. The perception of time as a gift has been negated in capitalist society by the "principle of a theoretically ever-growing use of time" (Foucault 1978:154). Islamic thought designates a similar spiritual orientation to the concept of time (Bamyeh 1999; Waines 1998), which some scholars contend has been lost in the modern world (Wilson 1997). Although Islamic practice employs scheduled activities (most notably prayers), Islamic finance intensifies its rejection of the model of interest on the basis of its objectification of time as a material entity (Wilson 1997: see pages 5–7 for a complete discussion). Christianity and Judaism (with similar arguments to those we see in Islamic finance today, see El Gamal 2000) has resolved the moral issue of time in a way that advances capitalist enterprise, where Islam seems to critique capitalism while at the same time advancing it.

Present day IBF institutions avoid the problem of interest by structuring transactions as profit sharing or lease-to-purchase arrangements. Practically speaking, it is challenging for a bank to function without some kind of reference to "interest." This difficulty was made clear when the author decided to open a checking account at an Islamic bank. *Johara* means "jewel" in Arabic. *Johara* is also the name of a bank for women: the stand alone ladies' branch of an Islamic bank in Dubai, United Arab Emirates (UAE) where the author did fieldwork in 2003. The teller was asked to explain exactly how the annual profit sharing payment on the account worked. Immediately, she responded, "Well, it's basically like an interest payment." Although her reference to "interest" may have in part stemmed from the fact that the researcher is American, it was nevertheless hard for her to find the words to explain the payment without reference to the better-known concept of interest, in which she was fully conversant. This is a common tactic employed in Islamic finance, and it is not seen to be at odds with the ban on interest.

Community Financial Transactions

Community discourse permeates discussions about and within the Islamic finance community. From the outset, the industry was meant to address community concerns. The focus on community stands in contrast to a capitalist understanding of economic activity, which is built on the assumption that the individual is the locus of economic activity, as Adam Smith so elegantly noted in *Wealth of Nations* (1976). Islamic economics subverts the neoclassical economic model by asserting that individuals are (or should be) driven to cooperate for the good of society. *This is a very important difference between conventional finance and Islamic finance, and one that is mentioned regularly in conversations with Islamic financiers.* Because the Islamic finance industry defines itself with reference to the conventional finance industry, it is valuable to understand how that difference in meaning is instilled into financial practices.

Classical Financial Structures

One of the first differences one notices between conventional finance and Islamic finance is the structure of financial transactions. This business practice is not visible unless one delves into the minutiae of the financial details. Yet, when Islamic financiers are asked what is the most important difference between conventional and Islamic finance, the most common answer is that the transactions are structured differently. In response to the prohibition against charging or paying *riba*, great attention is paid to how well the cash inflows and outflows are conceptualized. In addition to attention to *riba*, transactional structures are meant to reinforce the idea that the provider *and* recipient of funds share in the risk and return as much as possible. Therefore, the first business practice I will discuss is the practice of structuring the transactions themselves.

There are four classical Islamic financing structures used by the IBF industry intended to avoid *riba* and emphasize the communal nature of business practices. When I began reading about Islamic finance in the early 1990s, these were the *only* transactions available to people who wanted to participate in Islamic finance. Present day Islamic finance transactions are based on these four basic methods; however, there are now countless ways to structure a transaction that adheres to Islamic law but provides competitive returns in the market. They are based on the notion of partnerships, and highlight the importance of business practices that encourage community members to work together as partners. Although each financing structure specifically addresses the concerns of Islamic finance, each is also compatible with conventional banking practices. Knowledge is acquired together with one's fellow community member, rather than autonomously through rote learning. Each kind of transaction will be described below.

The first two structures relate to debt finance. First is a *murabaha*, or trade finance, which accounts for some 80% of Islamic financing (Wilson 1997). This transaction is very formal, and involves a buyer, a seller, goods for trade and a financier. The seller and buyer wish to exchange goods or services and agree upon a price, all according to lawful means. A financier, in turn, provides the money for the goods at their cost plus a predetermined financing fee. The financier then owns the goods (but does not take possession of them) until the buyer pays for the goods in full (Wilson 1997). This method is a short term financing technique, and, except for the predetermined fee, looks and operates like capitalist trade finance.

In other words, say we run a lemonade stand. We need to buy pitchers to serve lemonade to customers and do not have enough cash to purchase those pitchers. We need financing to help us. In order to finance the pitchers on a *murabaha* basis, a financial institution would purchase the pitchers from the supplier and immediately resell them to our business for a marked up price based on administrative costs and a profit margin. Remember that there is no prohibition on profit, just the means by which it is acquired.

A second form of debt financing is a lease finance structure. Short term (*ijara*) and long term lease purchase contracts (*ijara-wa-iqtina*) are functionally equivalent to their capitalist counterparts. Both are normally used to finance machinery or other equipment. As under a *murabaha* arrangement, in an *ijara* the bank purchases the goods and the buyer pays the bank through a periodic (usually monthly) fee. At the end of the lease term the purchaser may either purchase the item or let the bank dispose of it. The major difference between a capitalist lease and an *ijara* is that, under an *ijara*, the lessor assumes responsibility for owning and maintaining the asset, whereas that responsibility falls to the lessee under the capitalist tradition (Wilson 1997). This stipulation is consistent with the requirement of a seller's responsibility to take care of merchandise before the sale.

In our hypothetical lemonade stand, another way we can finance the pitchers is via an *ijara*. The financial institution would purchase the pitchers and then lease them to our business. At the end of the lease period, we would either purchase the pitchers outright or return them to the financial institution.

The first Islamic finance structure the author encountered in her professional life was an *ijara*. The company the author worked for in Dubai financed an oil rig, located in Angola. The financial company actually owned the title to the oil rig and received monthly payments as lease payments on that lease. This situation was brought to the author's attention because the cash flow did not look any different from other loans' cash flows, yet the funds were separate from the company's other funds. It was only after looking at the original financing agreement that the author realized the structure was meant to be "Islamic" and the sharing of risk between financial company and lessee were built into the financial plan.

There are two classical forms of equity finance. The first, a *mudaraba*, is a partnership between a provider of capital and a provider of labor. A capital provider may be a bank, individual, or one of many groups of investors (Wilson 1997). Profit and loss sharing are in proportion to the amount of capital invested, and no one except the partners may receive profit (al-Misri 1994). Most importantly, liabilities are limited to the amount of capital invested by each investor (Wilson 1997). This type of arrangement is virtually the same as a limited liability company in capitalism, and is compatible with equity financing through a stock exchange.

Another type of partnership is a *musharaka*, under which both parties supply capital (in contrast to a *mudaraba*, in which only one party or group supplies capital). Losses are not limited to the amount of investment, so risk is greater for all parties. The capitalist equivalent would be a venture capital firm providing capital for smaller ventures (Wilson 1997).

Contemporary Financial Structures

Some contemporary transactions were designed in response to contemporary conventional transactions, but are based specifically on built-in partnership arrangements in keeping with the focus on community and cooperation. The most noticeable difference between classical and contemporary Islamic transactions is the presence of an institution called an Islamic bank. If we look closely at the *murabaha, mudaraba, musharaka* and *ijara* methods of finance, we notice that not one of them requires the existence of an institution. Each form of financing is a partnership arrangement that can easily take place between any entity with available capital and any entity in need of capital. In fact, in the Middle Ages, merchant families themselves financed trade in the Muslim world, not unlike trade finance in Europe at the same time (Udovitch 1970). For example, a neighbor and you could both contribute some money to make a lemonade stand, agree that you will oversee the daily operations of the lemonade stand, and that each person would get a share of the profits according to the relative amounts each of us invested into the project. In this scenario, the neighbor and you have agreed to open a lemonade stand under a *musharaka* agreement. You did not need an institutional intermediary. The transactions discussed below require an intermediary in their financial structure. That intermediary is an IFI or some kind of special purpose investment vehicle. They are more complicated than the classical financial structures.

Salaam and Istisna

The *salaam* and *istisna* transactions are both sales contracts used when a commodity is not available for delivery at the same moment financing is needed. A *salaam* contract is used for commodity transactions when the financial institution (on behalf of a buyer) advances the purchase price of goods to the commodity owner. The goods are delivered at a later date to the financier, who then delivers them to the buyer. The buyer pays the financier the purchase price upon delivery of the goods.

An *istisna* works in a similar manner, except that it is used principally for manufacturing and construction finance. The financial institution pays the construction company as work is completed (say, on a building project). The construction company delivers the asset when it is complete. The financier delivers the asset to the customer, who then pays the purchase price to the financier.

The difference between *salaam* and *istisna* is based on the nature of the goods in question. A *salaam* is used to finance goods (commodities) that do not yet exist but are almost assured to exist in the future; e.g., agricultural goods (say, soybeans) that need to be grown during the growing season. The "production process" makes no difference to the transaction: the contract cannot specify how the soybeans are grown, merely that soybeans of a certain quality will be produced. The *istisna*, on the other hand, is tied to goods that would not otherwise be produced, like a commercial office building. The *istisna* is usually tied to a specific production process, which is essential to the final product and which is included in the price as part of the risk structure of the contract (Vogel and Hayes 1998; Bahrain Monetary Agency 2002).

At first glance, there does not seem to be anything particularly "modern" about either of these transactions. After all, it has always been necessary to finance commodities trades or to provide a farmer with financing based upon the anticipated production of agricultural products. Udovitch (1970) points out that trade finance was always prevalent in Muslim societies, just that merchants would provide financing instead of financial institutions. Vogel and Hayes (1998) draw attention to the modern nature of the *istisna* contract: until the Industrial Revolution few goods were exchangeable on a commodity basis as most people produced their own necessary goods. There was little need for manufacturing finance. It was only after the transformation of the nature of goods by the industrial production process that it became necessary to provide long term manufacturing finance (see also Appadurai 1986 for an extended analysis of the history of the commodity and its uses). The *istisna* is a response to the changing commercial environment. It must be noted, also, that the *istisna* is only valid under the Hanafi legal tradition (Vogel and Hayes 1998). Hanafi was the first legal school to be recognized by Muslims, and is therefore the oldest *madhhab*. Hanafi is generally considered to be the *madhhab* most amenable to modernization. It is also the school most closely associated with the geographical area of South Asia (India, Pakistan, and Bangladesh) that gave inspiration to Mawdudi.

Sukuk

The two most prevalent financing structures in Islamic finance today are the *sukuk* (bond) and *takaful* (insurance). The author does not have any first hand data on either *sukuks* or *takaful*[1] from fieldwork because they were first issued in 2002, when she was in the field. They have since become one of the most popular financing vehicles: therefore, it will be described briefly.

A *sukuk* is a form of bond usually issued by a government, or by a corporation in partnership with a government. It is based on a conventional government bond, and is used for long term financing. A conventional government bond is a method of financing by which a government (local or state/national) sells paper (bonds) to investors in exchange for 1) periodic (usually annual) payments to the investor and 2) repayment of capital at the end of the term. A bond is essentially an IOU from the government to investors. Profit to the investor is based on an interest rate determined by a measure of the stability of the government issuing the bond. The more stable the government—and therefore the better able to repay the funds—the lower the interest rate. Less stable governments must pay a higher interest rate. For example, if a local government wants to build a bridge across the river, it would sell bonds in order to raise cash to pay the contractors. Upon completion of the project, the government would repay the investors from its own capital account.

The cash flow of a *sukuk* looks similar to the cash flow of a conventional bond. The difference, as with most Islamic financial structures, lies with the underlying assumptions and asset structure. Whereas a conventional bond is backed by the goodwill and stability of the government, a *sukuk* is backed by tangible assets. In the example of the bridge financing, the government might pledge the income stream from some government properties or buildings to the *sukuk*. Investor return would be derived from that income. In the event of a government default, investors could theoretically sue the government for the income from its property.

Sukuks are "hot" at this time in the Islamic finance market. On the global market, issues of *sukuks* increased from $1.9 billion in 2003 to $6.7 billion in 2004 to more than $10 billion in 2005 (www.zawya.com). The largest single *sukuk* issuance on record to date was just issued by Dubai Islamic Bank on December 10, 2006 in the sum of $3.52 billion (www.zawya.com). In July 2007, the government of the United Kingdom agreed to issue the first ever *sukuk* offered by the government of a non-Muslim country.

Takaful

Takaful is Islamic insurance. Insurance is a modern concept and therefore is not found in any of the classical Islamic texts. Insurance means that a person or business (the insured) makes periodic payments (insurance premiums) to an insurance provider so that in the event of loss (of inventory, house, car, etc.) the insurance provider will compensate the insured party for that loss. The concept of insurance is controversial; nevertheless, *Shari'a* scholars have come to recognize the importance of insurance in the international business arena. *Takaful* is one of the fasted growing areas of Islamic finance. I did not interview anyone specifically about *takaful* during my fieldwork because the field is generally considered to be somewhat separate from traditional Islamic finance. It will be described briefly, however, to illustrate how a conventional method of managing risk can have huge implications for the practice of Islamic finance.

What are the problems with insurance? First, the industry is built upon uncertainty about events beyond its control. Insurance deals with an amount of uncertainty (*gharar*) because the outcome of a future event is uncertain in the present. In a sense insurance is gambling (*maysir*), which is forbidden under Islamic law. Because it is highly unlikely that every insured party will incur a loss in the future, insurance companies effectively take a gamble that it will make a profit from insurance premiums even after it pays its insured customers in the event of a loss. This is the second objection to insurance (Lewis and Algaoud 2001). Life insurance presents a particularly difficult challenge to the concept of insurance because of the idea that no one can predict the end of life and that to insure the event shows distrust in God's life plan.[2] A third objection to conventional insurance is that most insurance companies invest their premiums in forbidden *riba* (interest-bearing) investments (Vogel and Hayes 1998). However, this objection can easily be overcome by investing in one of the many Islamic institutions available today.

Conventional insurance operates on a contract basis; i.e., the insured party and the insurance company enter into a contract specifying terms of payment and coverage. The word for Islamic insurance, *takaful*, means "solidarity" and reflects the worldview built into a *takaful* arrangement. In general, a *takaful* agreement is a collective enterprise, in which Muslims pool their resources in order to aid each other in the event of a loss (Vogel and Hayes 1998). Members make periodic payments into the fund and the company invests those funds Islamically. This investment is made on a *mudaraba* basis, with the member acting as the financier and the *takaful* company as the *mudarib* (entrepreneur). This arrangement also helps to mitigate the element of uncertainty about future payments, as the members would expect periodic payments on their capital investment. This arrangement is also consistent with the concept of *tawhid* (unity), because economic actors are pooling their resources to benefit the group.

Partnerships in Business Practice

Just as financial structures reflect an emphasis on partnerships, individuals working in the industry view IBF's business practices as a way to emphasize that same concept. The author interviewed Mohammed, of a government Private Investment Office. He states that what makes an IFI distinct from a conventional bank is that the customer expects to be a partner with the IFI. He emphasizes the situation in which the IFI and the customer have more interaction with each other. In addition, they share the financial risk of the transaction.

MOHAMMED: It's more of a partnership . . . if I am your client, my relationship with you is [based on] taking the same risk. Any opportunity and any investment . . . if, for instance, take a decision of making a real-estate investment. So, in this case, the bank and the client take on [together] sharing the risk. That's the relationship that I expect from the Islamic bank.

INTERVIEWER: Right, so maybe more interaction.

MOHAMMED: More interaction, more involvement, more of knowing the customer and what I have seen from my own experience, once you get into an Islamic bank you almost get to know everybody.

Partnerships link suppliers and consumers of funds and reinforce the idea of community.

Rania, the general manager of a ladies' branch of a major Islamic bank, states that the partnership aspect of Islamic banking is as important as the actual amount of profit made by the bank or the customer. She believes this is because the bank plays a role in the community of a support system:

> And then they also have the flexibility of supporting you, Islamic banking. It supports you through it in terms of partnerships with you, in terms of management, so that gives you another flexibility and choice so that in case the business fails for some reason, you are not completely left on your own, high and dry, in a sense, not knowing what to do. Children aren't driven out of the house because you owe the bank some money or something like that. We try to help you out in all possible ways to prevent that.

From the customer's perspective, an emphasis on partnership is a positive aspect of Islamic finance. The author talked to a customer about the partnership concept: Manoj is a very successful owner of multiple businesses in Dubai, including marble and tile factories. He had been living in Dubai for over thirty years so he had watched the growth of Islamic finance from ground zero. He is Hindu, from India, but strongly emphasizes that anyone can participate in Islamic banking as he does. Part of what has made him so successful is the fact that he finds the best deal in the market, and he says that, often, Islamic finance provides the best financial deal. In addition to that, he feels that Islamic banks look more at the merits of the project and the customer rather than the interest rate, as the international banks do. The Islamic bank's profit is tied more to the project than the world interest rate. He feels very comfortable with this method of financing and stated that he would rather have a partnership relation with his bank.

Hamad was the director of the Islamic Banking division of the Dubai International Financial Center (DIFC) during the time of my fieldwork. He is a UAE national who was educated (undergraduate and graduate) at a prestigious, socially liberal university in the United States. He is very philosophical about the state of Islamic finance in the Gulf region. The discussion had digressed from the formal questions and we were talking about what he sees as strengths and weaknesses of the industry. In addition to what he perceives as a lack of innovation in IBF, he sees the "entanglement of religious behavior" in business to be a weakness of the industry. He sees IBF focus too much on paperwork where it should be taking the principles of Islam and applying them on a more fundamental level.

> HAMAD: I think we have to get rid of this model if we want to have a truly international Islamic finance. We have to separate it. I mean, if you create a truly new industry that does things in a certain way that will be more than just paperwork. So the contractual terms change—this is what you do in Islamic finance—so the contractual term changes and reposition what you are to commercial finance from *lenders to investors to partnership* (italics added). This is what they do. Islam rejected the usury concept, and consider[ing] that most financing is usury, then the contractual terms only change where the *financial institution turns into more of a partner* (italics added).

Hamad's critique of the industry is that it needs more innovation to truly uphold the principles of Islamic finance.

In addition to the emphasis on community building business practices, IBF institutions strive to contribute to the welfare of the Muslim community. For example, Masood of East-West Bank Corporation (EWBC)—an international, conventional bank with an Islamic division—views his involvement in IBF as a way to promote the Muslim community's welfare:

> Well I always as a Muslim had a passion for this Muslim community welfare as such . . . and I always had a realization that you can't have a strong economy unless you have a strong banking system. And when you have a strong, . . . to have a strong banking system you need strong indigenous banks. And I was involved in Islamic banking in supporting Islamic financial institutions in either managing their money or doing transactions for them as a banker.

It appears that the discourse of "IBF as community service provider" is a theme in the offices of EWBC: the idea that banking is providing a needed service for the Muslim community is echoed by Masood's colleague, Peter:

> I mean there are things that you once used to share with the community—for example the building of your house—the whole village comes together. You help me, tomorrow, you want to build your house—I'll help you. Now we are living in a different more specialized society and everybody does its own job so we pool our resources in financial institutions, so instead of me going house to house to ask for help to build my house, [I] borrow money, build my house and then I will repay my share to that society so there is a social function—very important.

Peter also recognizes a very important fact in the world today: that institutions have taken over some community functions. If institutions and aid agencies are now providing assistance to the community, then it follows naturally that those institutions should share some of the core values of the community they intend to help.

The Financial Community and Trust

Being part of a community also means being able to trust other members of that community. The author spoke with Hesham, who was born in Pakistan but left when he was a small child. He has lived in the Middle East and in the United States, and now runs a conventional financial management company in the US that also structures Islamic transactions. At the time of the interview, he was relatively new to the field of Islamic finance and was going through the process of introducing an Islamic hedge fund. He had some observations about the function of the Islamic finance industry as a bridge between cultures.

> It's been interesting to create that particular product actually . . . the world view of Islam has changed in my opinion because Islam is truly global today. American Muslims will be very different from European Muslims will be very different from Asian Muslims or Middle Eastern Muslims and so on and so forth because they're American, European, Middle Eastern, Asian and they have their own perspectives in that sense. I never really thought of it as a—as a truly global (religion)—I never really saw it as that.

Hesham became aware of the diversity within Islam only after beginning to work in an Islamic finance space. In conjunction with that diversity, the unity of being part of a Muslim community allows its members to build trust among themselves. It is important for the purposes of looking at the self, though, to understand that Islamic finance does provide a mediating influence in how Islamic practitioners see the role of the industry in their lives. Many IBF practitioners see themselves as part of a community, a role that transcends participation in a mere profession.

Rania, who was introduced earlier in the chapter, also confirms this feeling of trust, and feels it especially in the Islamic banking environment:

> I feel that it's a very fair system. The only thing is that there are no hidden charges; they are very fair with the customers. I mean I worked in foreign banks and when I compare it I know. And people in general have a feeling of more trust and faith and caring. I've seen the compassion in here which I have not seen in foreign banks.

Just as Mandaville (2004) suggests in his analysis of the history of the Muslim community, many Islamic financiers recall in their imagination the early days of Islam when thinking about Islamic finance. Tony is an accountant who has worked with Islamic finance in the accounting practice run by his father and himself.

TONY: Islamic banking probably has more because that was probably set as a precedent by the prophet himself because a lot of people entrusted assets to him.
INTERVIEWER: Right.
TONY: Because he's honest, honorable and he would look after those assets—so Islamic financial institutions—probably that is the most important principle that they should adopt—that whatever's entrusted to you, you have to look after in the best possible manner.

Association with this golden era of Islam (Maurer 2005) allows Tony to see IBF as being inculcated with a high level of trust.

Yasir, of Ethical Investing Corporation, raises the issue of trust not only from within the

IBF community itself, but as a way to promote interaction with the conventional banking community:

> YASIR: We actually try to tell them [conventional bankers] that "what we do is very, very similar to what you do" but we have a sort of filtering that we have to superimpose over what it is that they do. So we always try and make them feel, especially because there is a little bit of aura and, you know you don't trust what you don't know, we want to avoid confusion. A lot of Islamic institutions that I've come across tend like to create a mystique around the whole you know Islamic industry, to make it inaccessible to their Western counterparts. They feel threatened so they say "no no no there's no way you guys can do it"; "you need the *Shari'a* [Board] and it's impossible to talk to them and it's impossible to reach them and you have understand this and that." It's actually not so, it's an accessible market. We've seen that demonstrated by Western institutions that have already set up shop and we take an opposite view. I mean we tell people literally "I do exactly what you do however I have to do it within these guidelines." You have to do it within your guidelines but amazing similarities.

Yasir sees trust as an important component of the "bridge" function of IBF.

Shari'a Standards Board

Another way of strengthening community through the structuring of transactions is to require *Shari'a* board approval for every transaction, or type of transaction. A *Shari'a* Standards Board (SSB) is composed of Islamic scholars, who are fluent in both Islamic commercial law and international financial principles. The SSB's purpose is to insure that Islamic law is being followed accurately in the business practices and financial arrangements of the IFI. A separate financial standards board evaluates the efficacy of financial transactions, just as it does in a conventional institution, and the two boards often work together.

Islamic scholars must publicly declare that a transaction adheres to Islamic law before a company can go ahead with that transaction. A company's SSB does this by issuing a *fatwa* (religious declaration). A transaction does not adhere to Islamic law if it is not accompanied by a *fatwa*, as Khurram explains: "the *fatwa* is kind of more expected by the retail clients . . . the retail market wants to see a *fatwa*." The issuance of a *fatwa* makes the transaction Islamic in a way that is recognizable to members of the community, and members trust that transaction will meet their moral criteria for business practices.

Conclusion

The industry of Islamic banking and finance structures its business practices and financial transactions according to a belief system that counts community, partnerships and trust as its highest priorities. Islamic financiers reinforce business practices and financial structures that emphasize the mutual benefits of sharing both profits and losses with fellow humans, rather than a system that focuses attention on profit only. IBF practitioners align themselves morally with corporate social responsibility and socially responsible investing movements in the way they expect to receive profit on investments while at the same time improving upon moral imperatives, such as building community and fostering healthy business practices. IFIs take the additional step of monitoring their own activities through a *Shari'a* Standards Board charged with upholding and monitoring the moral efficacy of the company's activities. Through its financial structures, business practices and corporate governance, Islamic finance provides an example of how business practices can be aligned with moral beliefs.

Notes

*   This case was prepared by Karen Hunt Ahmed, Assistant Professor of Finance at DePaul University. Used with permission by author.
1   The first *takaful* (Islamic insurance) company was launched in the UAE in October of 2002 (*Khaleej Times* newspaper article, October 12, 2002).
2   Vogel and Hayes (1998) point out that this should not be a concern because insurance protects the living from "adverse material consequences" (p. 151) of death and does not make any prediction about death itself.

References

Ahmad, Khurshid, editor. 1976. *Studies in Islamic Economics*. Jeddah: International Centre for Research in Islamic Economics, King Abdul Aziz University.

Ahmad, Khurshid and Zafar Ishaq Ansari, editors. 1979. *Islamic Perspectives: Studies in Honour of Mawlana Sayyid Abul A'la Mawdudi*. United Kingdom: The Islamic Foundation.

al-Misri, Ahmad ibn Naqib (1994), "Zakat" in: Reliance of the Traveller (Umdat al-Salik) – A Classical Manual of Islamic Sacred Law, translated by Nu Ha Mim Keller, Beltsville (Maryland, USA: Amana Publications), pp. 244–76.

Al Saud, M.A.F. 2000. "Forum opening address: A review of Islamic finance." In *Proceedings of the Third Harvard University Forum on Islamic Finance*, October 1999, p. xiii. Boston: Harvard University Center for Middle Eastern Studies.

Appadurai, Arjun, editor. 1986. *The Social Life of Things: Commodities in Cultural Perspective*. Cambridge University Press.

Appadurai, Arjun. ed. 2000. *Globalization*. Durham, NC: Duke University Press.

Bahrain Monetary Agency. 2002. *Islamic Banking & Finance in the Kingdom of Bahrain*. Bahrain: Arabian Printing Press.

Bamyeh, Mohammed A. 1999. *The Social Origins of Islam: Mind, Economy, Discourse*. Minneapolis: University of Minnesota Press.

Beekum, Rafik Issa. 1997. *Islamic Business Ethics*. Virginia: International Institution of Islamic Thought.

El Gamal, Mahmoud. 2000. *A Basic Guide to Contemporary Islamic Banking and Finance*. http://www.ruf.rice.edu/~elgamal.

Foucault, Michel. 1978. *Discipline and Punish: The Birth of the Prison*. New York: Random House.

Gupta, Akhil and James Ferguson, eds. 1997. *Culture, Power, Place: Explorations in Critical Anthropology*. Durham: Duke University Press.

Hannerz, Ulf. 1996. *Transnational Connections*. London: Routledge.

Jameson, Frederic and Miyoshi, Masao, editors. 1998. *The Cultures of Globalization*. Durham: Duke University Press.

Kuran, Timur. 2004. *Islam & Mammon: The Economic Predicaments of Islamism*. Princeton: Princeton University Press.

Landes, David. 2000. *Revolution in Time: Clocks and the Making of the Modern World*. Boston: Belknap Press.

Lewis, Mervyn K. and Latifa M. Algaoud. 2001. *Islamic Banking*. Cheltenham, UK: Edward Elgar.

Mandaville, Peter. 2004. *Transnational Muslim Politics: Reimagining the* Umma. London: Routledge.

Maurer, Bill. 2002a. "Anthropological and Accounting Knowledge in Islamic Banking and Finance: Rethinking Critical Accounts." *Journal of the Royal Anthropological Institute* 8:645–667.

Maurer, Bill. 2002b. "Repressed Futures: Financial Derivatives' Theological Unconscious." *Economy and Society* 31(1):15–36.

Maurer, Bill. 2005. *Mutual Life, Limited: Islamic Banking, Alternative Currencies, Lateral Reason*. Princeton: Princeton University Press.

Mawdudi, Abu'l A'la. 1980. *Towards Understanding Islam*. United Kingdom: The Islamic Foundation.

Ong, Aihwa, 1999. *Flexible Citizenship*. Durham: Duke University Press.

Sassen, Saskia. 1998. *Globalization and Its Discontents*. New York: The New Press.

Scholte, J.A. 2000. *Globalization: A Critical Introduction*. Houndsmills: Macmillan.

Shweder, Richard A., Martha Minow and Hazel Rose Markus, eds. 2002. *Engaging Cultural Differences: The Multicultural Challenge in Liberal Democracies*. New York: Russell Sage Foundation.

Smith, Adam. 1976. *An Inquiry Into the Nature and Causes of the Wealth of Nations*, Edwin Cannan editor. Chicago: University of Chicago Press.

Tripp, Charles. 2006. *Islam and the Moral Economy: The Challenge of Capitalism*. Cambridge University Press.

Udovitch, Abraham L. 1970. *Partnership and Profit in Medieval Islam*. Princeton: Princeton University Press.

Vogel, Frank E. and Samuels L. Hayes, III. 1998. *Islamic Law and Finance: Religion, Risk, and Return*. The Hague: Kluwer Law International.

Waines, David. 1998. *An Introduction to Islam*. Cambridge University Press.

Weber, Max. 1968. *Economy and Society: An Outline of Interpretive Sociology*, volume 1. Guenther Roth and Claus Wittich, eds. New York: Bedminster Press.

Wilson, Rodney, 1997. *Islamic Finance*. London: FT Financial Publishing, Pearson Professional Limited.

5.6 BHP Billiton and Mozal

BHP Billiton, the world's largest diversified resource company at the start of the 21st century, did business in the fields of aluminum, energy coal and metallurgical coal, copper, manganese, iron ore, uranium, nickel, silver and titanium minerals, with interests in oil, gas, liquefied natural gas, and diamonds. In 1995, it began a feasibility study for building an aluminum smelter project in the Maputo province in southern Mozambique.

Mozambique was one of the world's poorest countries, emerging from 17 years of civil war in 1994 and making the difficult transition to a market-oriented economy. The country was hampered by fragile legal, financial, and health, safety, environmental, and community HSEC institutional structures and capacity. A limited number of people had the training and skills required for the project's construction and operational phases. Malaria was widespread and debilitating to the communities from which the plant would draw most of its work force; the disease was also a threat to attracting expatriate managers and skilled workers. HIV/AIDS was prevalent in the area, and infection rates were exacerbated by the influx of construction workers from neighboring South Africa.

Public services were bureaucratic, poorly equipped, and had limited capacity. Functions such as customs, immigration, public works, public health, port operations, and police would face challenges in coping with the magnitude of the project. Infrastructure such as roads, water supply, sewerage, and waste disposal was poorly developed and poorly maintained. Access to appropriate, affordable housing was limited. Most suitable development sites were occupied by concentrations of medium to large informally structured communities. High prices and poor quality of goods and services plagued local commerce and industry. In short, the area was limited in its capacity to satisfy the needs of a major project such as the proposed smelter.

BHP Billiton

BHP Billiton was committed to sustainable development and believed that social and environmental performance were critical factors in business success. The company's stated aim was to enhance the societal benefit of its operations and to reduce its environmental impact while creating value for many of its stakeholders. BHP Billiton believed firmly that sustainable development involved engaging and partnering with its community stake-holders to address the challenges associated with establishing resource projects and to share the benefits of success. Was this possible in Mozambique, given the nation's social and political challenges, the prevalence of malaria and HIV, and the weak infrastructure? Acknowledging that stakeholders had a role to play in achieving a successful and sustainable project, BHP Billiton adopted "Together we make a difference" as the slogan for this project.[1] They called the project "Mozal." But would or could they be successful? And at what cost?

Mitigating Financial Risk

An initial step in project development was to involve the International Finance Corporation (IFC), the private sector arm of the World Bank Group,[2] as a partner in phase 1. The IFC, whose mission was to reduce global poverty and improve lives by promoting a sustainable private sector in developing countries, provided a loan of USD120 million, its largest single investment in the nonfinancial sector. This helped mitigate financial risk and also facilitated loan syndication and promoted the project internationally. The IFC had robust environmental and social policies, as well as procedures and guidelines drawn from the World Bank Group. Requirements for strict compliance with the guiding principles gave assurance to other lenders and the host country that the project would achieve minimum standards relating to social and environmental impacts. To contribute to sustainable development, the company also had to put in place health, safety, environment, community, and socioeconomic initiatives, which were to be developed and implemented by the operation.

Even with IFC involvement, this was, at best, a corporate challenge and a very risky venture. How should BHP Billiton approach this multilayered project, or should it consider investing in smelters in other countries more hospitable to development?

The Mozal Aluminum Smelter: Project Profile

Designed as an advanced, cost-efficient plant, phase 1 of the Mozal project officially began in July 1998. At a budgeted cost of USD1.18 billion, it was to be the first major development in Mozambique in 30 years and the country's largest private investment ever. Phase 1 was successfully completed six months ahead of schedule and more than USD120 million under budget. The first aluminum was cast in June 2000, and the first ingots were exported in August of that year. In June 2001, phase 2 of the project—an expansion—was started; its construction budget was USD860 million. The expansion of the smelter would double its capacity. It was completed in August 2003, seven months ahead of schedule and USD195 million under budget.

From its earliest days, the project presented a number of significant challenges for BHP Billiton (BHP Billiton) and its venture partners, Mitsubishi Corporation of Japan and the Industrial Development Corporation (IDC) of South Africa.

During the two construction phases, the project contributed more than USD160 million to the local economy, principally through the employment of Mozambican laborers and the use of local contractors and suppliers. Between 1998 and 2008, local spending grew to more than USD140 million annually. Mozal was one of the largest smelters of its kind in the Western world, producing more than 500,000 tons of aluminum per year. In 2008, the operation employed more than 1,100 people.

Health and Safety Initiatives

In addition to caring for the health and well-being of its employees, BHP Billiton also worked with its host communities to set up programs focused on significant community health matters.

Malaria Prevention Programs

A baseline malaria survey conducted in southern Mozambique in December 1999 found that infection rates in the area surrounding the Beluluane Industrial Park, where Mozal was located, exceeded 85%. The Mozal Community Development Trust MCDT[3] conducted a spraying program within a 10 km radius of the smelter and contributed funds to the Lubombo Spatial Development Initiative, a joint venture between the governments of South Africa, Mozambique, and Swaziland aimed at eradicating malaria in the region. MCDT also sent community members to training courses in manufacturing treated mosquito netting to help keep people from contracting malaria while they slept. The MCDT also provided sewing machines, insecticides, netting material, and consumables, and bought the initial batch of 1,000 bed nets.

After three years of intensive effort, the infection rate in the Beluluane area was reduced from 85% to 18.6%. During phase 1, the company had a peak of more than 9,000 employees; it established a malaria diagnosis and treatment facility at which it provided medical treatment to staff. The large number of expatriate workers with no natural immunity to malaria posed a major challenge. Thousands of cases were diagnosed, treated, and documented during phase 1. Analysis of those records steered the malaria management strategy toward awareness, early diagnosis, and prevention in phase 2, which resulted in significantly reduced malaria incidence.

HIV/AIDS Programs

The control of sexually transmitted diseases and opportunistic infections was an important strategy in the fight against HIV/AIDS. From 2001 to 2003, the MCDT sponsored the Total Control of Epidemic program, in which a group of 100 field officers educated approximately 200,000 people in the local communities of Boane, Matola, and Maputo on the dangers of HIV/AIDS and how to prevent it. Pivotal to the prevention of the disease was a person's knowledge of his or her HIV/AIDS status and management of behavior and health. Beginning in 2001, Mozal provided assistance for a Voluntary Counseling and Testing Center (VCT) in Boane, managed on behalf of the Ministry of Health by a Danish nongovernmental organization (NGO) called Ajuda De Povos Para Povos (ADPP). Eleven satellite units of the VCT were opened in Boane and Matola. Community leaders were trained to manage the facilities and provide counseling services and with the approval of provincial authorities, Mozal supplemented the stock levels of appropriate drugs at local clinics.

The Beluluane Public Health and Maternity Clinic

The local public health clinic, operated by the District/Provincial Health Directorate of the Mozambican Ministry of Health, served a community of about 18,000 people within a 10-km radius of the smelter. The MCDT provided the clinic with doctors' facilities, a laboratory, and three residences for staff, and constructed a maternity center within the facility. Initiatives further afield included the provision of a mother-and-child health care facility within the Matola health clinic, which served more than 300,000 people in the Matola municipality.

Environmental Initiatives

BHP Billiton decided early to focus on an integrated approach to the management of its social and environmental responsibilities. The IFC and the Mozambique Ministry of Environmental

Coordination (MICOA) rigorously reviewed comprehensive social and environmental impact assessments. Subsequent environmental management programs provided the blueprint for the appropriate design of physical environmental aspects of the construction and operation of the plant, in line with BHP Billiton's philosophy of "Zero Harm"[4] to the environment. Regular monitoring and auditing, both internally and by external bodies (IFC and MICOA), provided a basis for correcting deviations and implementing continuous improvement processes. The environmental management programs included frequent public meetings as well as task force meetings; the task force was composed of environmental consultants, the contractors, and representatives from key government ministries, large state-owned enterprises, district administration, community groups, and Mozal.

Community Initiatives

According to BHP Billiton's Company Charter, an indicator of success was that its host communities valued the company's presence. From the outset, the Mozal initiative identified community needs and supported programs put in place to achieve sustainable outcomes for the community.

Relocation of Communities

The original site proposed for the smelter was densely populated, and construction there would have required the relocation of approximately 7,500 people. The social impact assessment led to selection of an alternative site, requiring the resettlement of 80 families and the provision of agricultural land for 910 farmers. The land, allocated to Mozal by the government of Mozambique, formed part of the Beluluane Industrial Park development. In September 1998, ACER Africa, a specialist resettlement consultant appointed by Mozal, drew up a Resettlement Action Plan. The government, with support and financing from Mozal, managed the relocation process in accordance with the World Bank Operational Directive on Involuntary Resettlement. Formal monitoring of the program over the years indicated that the quality of life of most of the affected people improved.

The Mozal Community Development Trust

The MCDT's development initiatives began in January 2001, with an initial annual budget of USD2 million, which increased each year. To achieve its mission, the MCDT defined four key policies:

- Align development initiatives with those of national, provincial, and local governments
- Act as a catalyst and facilitator in establishing pilot projects that could be replicated (e.g., the IFC is funding the local replication of some projects)
- Form partnerships with stakeholders to achieve sustainable results
- Involve relevant stakeholders from all levels of government, nongovernmental organizations (NGOs), communities, and the private sector, as well as Mozal employees.

The MCDT initiated approximately 200 projects and programs, with expenditures exceeding USD10 million.

Educational Projects

To overcome the lack of secondary education facilities in the region, the Nelson Mandela Secondary School was built, the first such school in the Mozal vicinity. The project was a joint initiative: Mozal provided funding, the local communities provided 10 hectares of land, and the government managed the school's construction and operation. In 2008, the school was in its second year of operation; it accommodated 1,800 students, and there were plans to expand the capacity to 2,400 students. The total investment by Mozal would be approximately USD1 million. The MCDT also donated 41 computers to the school.

The primary school closest to Mozal was an abandoned house with no roof. A new school, constructed in two phases, included seven new classrooms, an administration unit, three staff houses, and sports facilities. Twelve other primary schools in the region were significantly upgraded, with improvements that included new classrooms, sports grounds, and water and electricity reticulation.

To build teaching capacity in the region, each year the MCDT supported the training of 40 teachers in new teaching methodologies and national curricula. Through the Look of Hope Project administered by the Ministry of Education, the MCDT donated 52,000 workbooks annually to disadvantaged children. The MCDT also funded new facilities at the Bilibiza Agricultural School in the northern province of Cabo Delgado, which had a population of more than one million. As more than 80% of the population depended on subsistence agriculture, the school played a key role in helping to reduce poverty in the region.

Other initiatives included a community theater, construction of a new police station (as well as the purchase of four police vehicles), a road safety awareness campaign, sports events (e.g., an annual beach volleyball tournament), and cultural development (e.g., funding for theater groups and support of youth activities in art, sculpture, and handicrafts). Another community initiative involved developing and supporting various interaction channels between the community and BHP Billiton.

Socioeconomic Initiatives

The company believed that a stable, healthy, and supportive society facilitated the effective operation of its business. By contributing to the social and economic fabric of its host communities, the company hoped to create an environment in which its business could grow and, in turn, support sustainable development of the region.

Work Force Training and Development

To help ensure that Mozambican workers had the skills to execute their duties in a safe and productive manner, Mozal provided funding to establish local facilities for the training of mechanical and electrical maintenance and construction workers. Training at these centers, located in Maputo and Machava, was conducted in conjunction with the National Institute of Labour and Training (INEPF). The two facilities were able to operate autonomously starting in 2004. The Maputo center conducted courses in electrical and mechanical disciplines, and the Machava center provided training in bricklaying, plumbing, carpentry, painting, and welding. Several Mozambican industries recruited graduate trainees from the courses and sent technical staff to the centers for training. During the two establishment phases of the project, 9,846 Mozambicans received training in various construction disciplines; as a result, more than 70% of the Mozal construction work force was local.

Other initiatives by Mozal to enhance employee competency and promote career opportunities included an Operators Development Program, Supervisory Capacity Building Program, "MY" Development Program (self-driven, competency-based training), Assisted Education Program (degree and postgraduate education), and a Graduate Development Program (GDP). Overseas assignments, to Brazil and South Africa, for example, were arranged for employees to prepare them for promotion.

Housing Project

BHP Billiton believed it was important to develop a residential area within the vicinity of the smelter. Many employees had difficulty buying homes, which affected work force stability and motivation. Under the Beluluane Land Use Management Plan established by Mozal, a site was selected and 96 houses constructed. An additional 96 homes were built in the second stage. Mozal managed the construction process, the procurement of materials, and the training of local enterprises to provide services.

Public Infrastructure

Through the Mozal project, the region was provided with significant public infrastructure, including roads and bridges, potable water, electricity, telephone services, sewage treatment works, housing units, and general amenities buildings. Mozal also funded the construction of a smelter import/export quay, infrastructure at the Matola port, and a modern landfill facility to handle hazardous waste from industries in the region.

Supporting Small and Medium Enterprises in Mozambique

During phase 1 of the Mozal project, the use of local contractors and particularly small and medium-size enterprises (SMEs) was limited. To address this situation and boost local participation, BHP Billiton developed the Small and Medium Enterprise Empowerment and Linkages Program (SMEELP). Following a review of the Mozal 1 experience, it was clear that, if the expansion project was to succeed in involving local SMEs, a new methodology would have to be developed. This imperative was reflected in the broader Mozal Empowerment Policy, which stated that "the management of the Mozal Expansion Project is committed to maximizing sustainable benefits to the local community using a combined strategy of development and use of local goods, services, and personnel, without compromising project objectives."
A commitment was made to:

- maximize the use of local labor (more than 65% Mozambican);
- provide skills training for local labor (train more than 3,800 workers in construction);
- actively encourage the use of local contractors;
- actively encourage the establishment of joint ventures between international and local contractors;
- allocate selected work packages solely for execution by local SMEs;
- promote SME training programs to enable local SMEs to be competitive and successful;
- establish systems for monitoring and reporting the project's empowerment progress.

The target for the total local spending, including SMEELP and all other forms of local expenditures, was set at USD80 million. Specific objectives were then established for the SMEELP, to facilitate the successful delivery of at least 25 SME contracts and the establishment of a sustainable SME training program.

To improve the likelihood of success of the program, the SMEELP was established as a collaborative joint venture between Mozal, the Africa Project Development Facility (APDF) of the International Finance Corporation (IFC), and the Centre for Promotion of Investment (CPI) of the Mozambique Government. After completion of the Mozal expansion project, the CPI planned to take over management of the program to ensure its sustainability. The methodology was designed to be suitable for any company wanting to successfully utilize local SMEs.

The key steps in developing an effective SMEELP were deemed as follows:

1   Creation of SME packages

   ● Packages solely allocated to SMEs
   ● Realistic scope in terms of size and complexity ensured
   ● Sufficient backup time in case of failure provided
   ● Standard packages, whenever possible, include SMEs.

2   Preassessment of SME capabilities

   ● SMEs financial/technical capabilities pre-assessed
   ● Capable SMEs recommended to the project by CPI
   ● SME database established and periodically updated.

3   Training

   ● Tender training (pre-tender): how to tender
   ● Induction training (post-award): how to execute contracts
   ● On-demand training: Quality Assurance (QA)/Quality Control (QC), Business Management, etc.
   ● Training modules written and presented in local language, periodically updated.

4   Mentorship

   ● Custom-made mentorship plan for each SME
   ● Business mentorship: financial/commercial assistance
   ● Technical mentorship: on- and off-site technical assistance, including Safety, QA/QC and Industrial Relations.

To help overcome the challenge of language differences and to facilitate the upgrading of SME infrastructures and technical standards, a dedicated bilingual empowerment coordinator was assigned to the SMEELP. The appointment also helped ensure the project's engineering, procurement and construction management (EPCM) contractor embraced the concept of SME participation. This was a major factor in the success of the SMEELP, with the EPCM contractor's team playing a key role in driving the project.

The program was successful, significantly increasing local participation during the construction of Mozal 2. The program, considered sustainable, was then used successfully in BHP Billiton's Hillside 3 expansion project in Richards Bay, South Africa. As of 2008, the SMEELP results included: creation of 27 SME contract packages; training for 36 SMEs; awarding of 28 contract packages (including one standard package) to 14 SMEs; successful delivery of 12 contract packages; no contract package cancelled; and allocating a total of more than USD5 million to SMEs.

Mozlink

The SMEELP program was extended under the name of Mozlink, which was also supported by the IFC and CPI. Through training and mentorship, Mozlink helped to build local capacity and increase business in Mozambique. Smelter operations relied on more than 200 Mozambican suppliers. Local spending exceeded 30% of goods and services procurement (excluding major raw materials and electricity). An SME Development Centre was established to coach, train, and expose SMEs to best practices in supplying goods and services to the smelter and to measure ongoing performance improvements by registered SMEs in the areas of safety, maintenance, and financial and HR management.

A knowledge-sharing and linkage Internet site was developed to provide information for SMEs about available packages, financing, best practices, tender procedures, and quality standards. The site allowed Mozal and other businesses to more easily locate SMEs. For example, a local supplier of brooms, which were previously imported from South Africa, was identified and used through Mozlink.

Small Business Development

A small and micro enterprise program was established to train women in the region in raising and selling chickens and eggs, carpet-making, and embroidery. Other initiatives included training farmers in cashew nut and other crop production. To provide an outlet for families participating in income-earning activities, the MCDT established the 80-stall Rhulani Market in the Beluluane area.

Capacity-Building in State Functions

Mozal, through provision of facilities, equipment, training, and facilitation, assisted state functions to improve service delivery. For example:

- Customs processes were streamlined at the Mozambique–South African border. Clearing times were reduced from days to hours. A new customs building at Mozal was fully equipped to manage exports from the operation.
- Transportation of abnormal loads was aligned with best practices through training and mentoring by professional load transporters and the donation of three escort vehicles.
- Town planners from the Department of Public Works and Housing received training in modern town-planning methodologies.
- Comprehensive training was provided to staff of the Ministry of Environmental Coordination on the operation of the hazardous waste facility.

Engineering Development in Mozambique

In October 2003, Mozal initiated a project aimed at raising the level of education of the country's engineers and technologists to international standards. International experts, relevant ministries, educational institutions, and other companies collaborated in a three-year pilot project to strengthen the engineering faculty at the University Eduardo Mondlane in Maputo. In addition, a range of professional development courses was introduced and a broad-based computer-aided design training facility established. A registration system for engineers was also developed, based on global best practices. Mozal and BHP Billiton invested approximately USD300,000 in the engineering project.

Agricultural Programs

An Agriculture Development Program (ADP), recommended by the IFC, was implemented over a four-year period, starting in 2000, to benefit farmers relocated from the Mozal site. Prior to the program, annual yields of maize were 300 kg per family. The ADP boosted yields five-fold, with a record average yield of 1,900 kg in 2002. Farmers were also supported in diversifying their crops to include drought-resistant crops using seed supplied by the MCDT. The 2004 harvests indicated that the scheme had the potential to alleviate poverty during drought. After severe floods in 2000 in the Boane district, a program was implemented to rehabilitate irrigation infrastructure, repair equipment, supply seed, improve access to markets, and provide training and mentorship. The program enabled the local farmers' association to again supply produce to markets and catering companies. In partnership with CARE International, the MCDT constructed 10 rural dams in the northern province of Nampula, helping to stabilize water supplies for agricultural development and domestic use and to minimize damage from heavy rainfall.

Mozal: Focusing on Sustainability, for Business and for the Community

Careful planning of the construction and operational phases of Mozal took into account all the challenges posed when investing in Mozambique. Since commencement, the project had complied with the environmental and social requirements of the IFC. Following phase 1, any gaps related to the values embodied in the BHP Billiton Charter and Zero Harm philosophy were addressed in phase 2. The entire project delivered significant achievements:

- Both project implementation phases were completed well under budget and ahead of schedule.
- Following good HSEC performance during phase 1, considerably better performance was recorded during phase 2 and the organization of operations.
- Harmonious industrial relations were exemplified by the phase 2 construction period, totaling 16 million work hours, when no days were lost due to industrial action.
- Operational performance ran at benchmark levels.
- The region and the country benefited from needs-based infrastructure, and social and community development projects.
- Ongoing projects and programs delivered by Mozal and the MCDT reinforced the principles of sustainable project implementation.

The IFC, in its publication *The Environmental and Social Challenges of Private Sector Projects*, stated that "Mozal has set a precedent for future projects in Mozambique. It illustrates the clear advantages of incorporating environmental and social issues early in a project, and reflects the approach and procedures IFC has been refining and putting in place to deal with environmental and social issues."[5] For BHP Billiton, the Mozal experience demonstrated that, when establishing a major resource project, it made good business sense to invest not only in the venture but also in the host community.

Notes

* This case is an authorized adaptation of the BHP Billiton socioeconomic case study, "Mozal: A Model for Integrating Sustainability Into Resource Projects," *BHP Billiton Sustainability Report 2005*,   http://sustainability.bhpbilliton.com/2005/repository/socioEconomic/caseStudies/

caseStudies38.asp (accessed 29 February 2008). The original case was condensed and slightly revised with the permission of BHP Billiton.

1   Mozal web site, "Governance and Ethics," http://www.mozal.com/gae.htm (accessed 22 February 2008).

2   The World Bank Group, often referred to as the World Bank, consisted of five different organizations. In addition to the International Finance Corporation, there was the International Bank for Reconstruction and Development, the International Development Association, the Mulitlateral Investment Guarantee Agency, and the International Centre for the Settlement of Investment Disputes.

3   The Mozal Board created the MCDT in August 2000 with the specific mission of facilitating projects and programs to improve the quality of life of the communities surrounding Mozambique's Beluluane Industrial Park.

4   Mozal web site, "Governance and Ethics," http://www.mozal.com/gae.htm (accessed 22 February 2008).

5   Ramamohan Mahidhara, "The Environmental and Social Challenges of Private Sector Projects: IFC's Experience," *The International Finance Corporation*, Washington, D.C., 2002, 40.

Chapter 6

Employment

6.1 First Impressions, Inc. *

Judy Wiles was president and owner of First Impressions Inc. in Detroit Michigan. By 1999, Wiles had built the company to become the lead sheep of the flock among temporary food service employment agencies in the state. Yet her competitors held most of the market in the private club and party scene predominately located in the suburbs. Wiles was troubled with the realization that having technical superiority did not mean First Impressions would always get the deal. She was aware that social capital like whom you golfed with or what parties you were invited to often influenced who got the business. Most troubling was her own analysis that her face and voice, as a woman of color, were barriers to market entry. She removed her round-rimmed reading glasses as she rubbed her temple.

Judy Wiles: President of First Impressions

Judy Wiles was working as a trainer and waitress for TGI Fridays and found she was constantly training people. It was the nature of the business that, on any shift, one or more employees would not show up. Wiles also knew that once trained, servers would work a week or two and then quit—food industry workers tended to be very transient. Restaurants and caterers persistently had a problem maintaining consistent reliable, competent employees. Wiles remembered telling her boss, "There ought to be some kind of service you can call instead of wasting your money training people who are not going to stay." And as soon as she said it, "This little light went off in my head." Wiles started calling around to restaurants and hotel kitchens to ask whether they would use an on call service that readily provided staff 24 hours a day, seven days a week. The response was overwhelmingly positive with statements like "Of course I would where are they . . . give me the company's number."

So Wiles enrolled in, and graduated from, a community education program at Wayne State University (WSU) that targeted women and minorities and offered marketing, sales, and accounting classes. WSU was located in the heart of Detroit. Wiles developed a five-year business plan with over 200 pages and set her goal to establish First Impressions Inc. as a professional, trustworthy alternative agency that offered temporary employees to the food service industry.

The WSU program offered graduates low-cost office space complete with computers, copy, and fax machines so Wiles had a place to set up shop. Her next step was to look for funding. She didn't have the connections required for equity financing so Wiles started seeking a line of credit or securing a personal loan from banks. After unsuccessfully trying to finance through banks, Wiles finally opened her food service temporary agency in 1988 funded by a $600 cash advance on her VISA card. She sent out flyers advertising her services and was surprised when she got her first phone call two days later from the Pontchartrain hotel wanting six servers, two chefs, and a couple of bar tenders. Chrysler sent Wiles her second order with a request for six servers every day of the week. Wiles, not having secured any employees yet, scrambled over to TGI Fridays and convinced her former colleagues to come work for her when their shifts ended. Shortly thereafter Wiles hired Eric Giles, First Impressions' operations manager, as her first employee and waiter. According to Wiles:

> In the beginning I did everything. I was a fake secretary—I would answer the phone in a different voice, place the person on hold, and then I would put myself on the phone. I completed all the sales. I hired Eric as a waiter one month after I opened. We shared the same desk in my tiny little office upstairs in the Metropolitan Center for Higher Technology at WSU. Luckily for me, nobody came to my office.

First Impressions Inc.

First Impressions was a temporary food service employment agency. The company was based in Detroit, Michigan. First Impressions supplied hotels, businesses, banquet halls, and caterers with temporary restaurant staff personnel. Initially Wiles was highly selective about who she hired. Her criteria for hiring was simple: i) be on time for the interview ii) look me in the eyes when you talk to me iii) speak loud enough for me to hear you but with a soft voice iv) give a strong handshake v) smile. Wiles soon discovered that to get to the level of service she wanted her company to provide, she had to start training future employees.

First Impressions developed new training methods complete with numerous manuals of which the most popular was *Fifty Ways To Empty A Dining Room*. The training programs were customized according to employees' previous experience, with five-day, five-week, or six-month training periods. Wiles' company started training previously unskilled employees to be professional restaurant staff personnel, ranging from chefs and bartenders to dishwashers and waiters. Most years the annual cost of training food-service employees reached nearly $50,000. Once she developed the training component Wiles realized that essentially she could train anyone who wanted to work to be a professional server, chef or bartender. All she needed was a labor force with the desire to work. So she began using a previously untapped labor pool—the "have nots." Wiles opened her door for welfare to work program participants, the homeless, and felons who had paid back their debt to society.

To weed out unreliable employees Wiles implemented a lengthy interview process. She advertised positions in the local newspaper, at high schools, churches, social services agencies, and back to work programs. When potential employees called they were given a specific interview time. They were also instructed to wear a white shirt, black pants, and black shoes. If the interviewee arrived late, Wiles explained why she would not interview them and sent them home with a different day and time to try again. Often potential employees lacked a white shirt or came to Wiles' office with visibly poor hygiene. Instead of sending them home, she would offer clean uniforms and a toothbrush or whatever it was they lacked. The office closet housed make-up, deodorant, hair and toothbrushes, and various other grooming supplies.

Employee training started the moment an individual walked through the door at First Impressions' office. For example one potential employee called and asked if he had the right place to "get a bet" which was street slang for getting work. He was asked what he meant by the word "bet" and was then instructed to call it a "job." During the interview Wiles asked if he had black shoes and he replied that he might have some at his "crib" (jargon for house). Once more Wiles patiently explained why he needed to use the word house or home. Each applicant was asked to read and sign a lengthy document that outlined expected employee behavior while on the job with First Impressions. It was through this mechanism that Wiles was able to discover those applicants who were unable to read. The company started to provide time and transportation for non reading employees to attend literacy classes.

Being on time was key to First Impressions' success in the business world. Wiles was well aware that for a person of color, either as an owner or an employee, existing stereotypes meant being late was doubly a problem. It was critical for her company that her employees were on time. On the other hand, she was also sensitive to the fact that many of her employees were single moms, economically disadvantaged or homeless, so child care, school issues, or other problems in life arose that validated lateness. To deal with the issue, Wiles repeatedly stressed during the interview process, and after individuals were hired, that if they were going to be late they needed to phone First Impressions as soon as possible to let her know. She explained the huge costs to being late or absent. For example the company double docked pay for lateness and required a five hour lead time notification for absence. Yet she also paid employees a minimum of five hours when they were called to staff events—even if the gig lasted only two hours. Wiles was trying to get workers to understand the severity of being unreliable.

As time went on Wiles realized that transportation was a major barrier for many of her workers. Detroit lacked an underground subway and buses often stopped running before her employees finished work. Understanding these challenges, Wiles bought a company van to transport staff.

Wiles' own style of management was profit driven and her mission statement was, "The customer is first and the customer is right. The client wants service and we will work as a team to provide the most efficient, effective, and friendly assistance available." While faced with stiff competition, Wiles and her operational manager, Eric Giles, built the firm's reputation on reliability and professionalism. By 1999, First Impressions Inc. employed over three hundred temporary employees and generated annual sales of over $1 million. The company's major clients included the caterers for the Detroit Grand Prix, the Marriott Hotel, the Pontchartrain Hotel, Blue Cross/Blue Shield, Ford Motor, Chrysler Corporation, Detroit Diesel, Kelly Services, the University of Detroit, Wayne State University, Mercy and Marygrove Colleges, and Oakland University.

Just Judy Wiles

Wiles had expected to encounter obstacles that would require a modification to her business plan. Yet with all her vision and determination, she had not foreseen that potential clients' initial reaction to her would compel Wiles to disguise the ownership of First Impressions Inc.:

> When I first started out, I proudly displayed "President" beside my name on my business card. But it worked against me. I wasn't taken seriously as a black woman and a business owner. This much was clear from the reactions I encountered when I first started meeting prospective clients.
>
> In an effort to establish a client base, I would read the want ads in the local newspapers. I focused on those that advertised for food service staff. I would call these companies and offer the First Impressions alternative. On several occasions I had customers who expressed keen interest, on the telephone, but, when I showed up in person, the most frequent response I received was "Oh that's ok. We're going to do something else." I would respond by saying, "Wait a minute, you are spending three or four hundred dollars a week on advertising for people when you could be paying me to supply your staff, guaranteed and hassle free for your business."

Now I grew up in a neighborhood called Mac and Bewich. Everybody in Detroit knows that means I can handle myself. So I refused to give up. I started to keep track of the names of each company that initially seemed receptive but turned me down when I showed up in person. If they kept advertising for help I just marched right back into these businesses the next week and said, "I read your advertisement in the paper again this week, why aren't you calling?"

At this point I also realized I needed to revise my marketing strategy. I felt there was reluctance out there to hire personnel through a black-run company. Either they automatically assumed that a black company was not going to provide professional, reliable staff or they did not think that I personally was capable of carrying out the commitments I promised on the telephone. But to make a dollar I needed to reassess the barriers to my market entry.

The channel power of my services came from the client. Although I planned a strategy that new competitors could not easily copy—to provide the best-trained, reliable, professional food service personnel in the industry—I had not calculated that showing my face, as the owner of the company, would affect sales. I had counted on my product being superior, but if my product was not even given a chance to reach the consumer I could not make profits! It was the restaurant or catering company that dictated the terms of our business relationship.

So by the second run of her business cards Wiles had "President" removed. Her cards now read, "Judy Wiles, First Impressions Inc."

Expansion Opportunities

As First Impressions developed a solid reputation of service and reliability, Wiles attempted to break into the suburban culture outside the city of Detroit. The billing rates were higher in the suburbs and the volumes of orders were greater (see Exhibit 6.1.1). Her competitors held most of the market but Wiles managed to attract the attention of several well-connected, influential individuals. She thought it was symbolic when her client base expanded through the gateway of Grand Circus Park and headed towards Grosse Pointe.[1] Having clients who lived in Grosse Pointe provided First Impressions with an enviable calling card. But it also presented a brutal reminder that some social hierarchies had not changed much. One of the most compelling instances occurred when a wealthy potential client called First Impressions to book services for a party she was planning. A valuable customer had referred the caller to First Impressions with glowing recommendations. Eric Giles handled the first call and it did not take long for Giles to realize that the caller had no idea First Impressions was a minority-owned company.

The Initial Phone Call

Ayesha Anderson possessed an arresting personality and had been with First Impressions for almost 10 years. She worked as the firm's accountant but also occasionally served as a receptionist. With her razor sharp memory and vast organizational skills, Anderson was a valuable employee. Anderson lived in Detroit most of her life and had, on occasion, been made to feel sick at heart by some person's contemptuous judgment. But this caller stunned her as she recalled:

Exhibit 6.1.1

FIRST IMPRESSIONS,
INCORPORATED

July 26, 2000

Gerry Yemen
Case writer – Diversity Case Bank
Darden Graduate School of Business Administration
University of Virginia
PO Box 6550
Charlottesville, Virginia 22906-6550

Dear Gerry,

How wonderful it was to speak with you earlier today. Please find below a comparative listing of the staff that we currently provide to AVI Foodservice at the General Motors Poletown facility and the staff that we could possibly supply to the Oakland Hills Country Club. I hope this is what you needed. if you need more information please call me. Thank you.

Sincerely,

Eric S. C. Giles
Operations Manager, First impressions

AVI FOODSERVICE AT GENERAL MOTORS POLETOWN FACILITY (ACTUAL)
1 grill cook
1 prep cook

OAKLAND HILLS COUNTRY CLUB (HOPED FOR)
3 dining room servers
4 bussers
4 dish & utility staff
2 prep cooks
1 line cook
(The potential for higher sales in the suburbs is greater not only because of higher volume orders but because of increased billing rates)

1274 Library Street, Suite 203 ❖ Detroit, MI 48226 ❖ (313) 989-2483 ❖ (313) 989-2867 FAX

I answered the telephone the same way I do most days, polite and professional. I had no idea things were about to get so nasty. The woman told me that a reputable caterer, a name I immediately recognized as one of our big and influential accounts, had referred First Impressions to her. I began to describe the type of service we provide when she suddenly interrupted and said, "Well, you sound black, are you?" Although I was quite taken aback, I am proud to be who I am, so I replied, "Yes." Then to my astonishment, she curtly said, "Well, is there anyone else I can talk to?"

It took me a couple seconds before I registered the conversation we just had. I put her on hold and handed the phone to Eric, who had no idea what was going on.

So Giles, unsuspecting of any problems, continued with the client's call. Giles had the perfect radio voice and the wealthy woman from the suburbs assumed he was white. According to Giles:

> She told me she was looking for staff to work a private party at her estate. She indicated that a reputable caterer had recommended us. She mentioned several times that she was hosting 50 of Detroit's most influential couples so she wanted things done just right. I gathered, from her conversation, that she wanted to impress her guests. She did not want to have any glitches in the professional manner of her food service providers. I assured her we were the best in Detroit; we built our clientele base on our reputation.
>
> At the end of our conversation I got a taste of what Ayesha experienced as she told me she did not want any blacks to work for her. The casual manner in which she had easily spoken those words disarmed me for a second as I hung up the phone. But it didn't take long for them to sink in.
>
> I immediately went into Judy's office. I slammed my hand down on her desk and said, "Judy, I know the customer is first and the customer is right but what are we going to do about this one?"

Wiles' office overlooked the tar and gravel roof of the building beside it. The left-hand side of the room was completely blanketed with bookshelves. Stacks of *Business Week* and *The Nation's Restaurant News* filled the space between books as eclectic as *The Ten-Day MBA* and *The Dusk of Dawn*. A stylish black tuxedo hung from an old-fashioned wooden coat rack in the right-hand corner. Wiles sat behind her long blond desk and unconsciously tapped her well-manicured nails as she pondered the conversation Giles had described. Her mind followed the dichotomous path of "if I do and if I don't." Wiles described her reaction:

> I needed to expand into the suburbs and was doing so, but very slowly. It was almost street by street. The referring client was a lucrative account and her recommendation had generated other business for us. I had targeted the suburbs and considered that clientele base necessary to continue to succeed. So I told Eric to go ahead and book the party. Eric cocked his head to the side, raised his eyebrows, pointed his finger at me and said, "I hope you know what you are doing, Judy!"

Giles followed through on Wiles' directive and throughout the planning stage the client told him she did not want any black people to be serving. He tried to calm her fears assuring he would assign only the best, and that color had nothing to do with it. He told her that First Impressions sent out only the most professional, well-trained, staff available in Detroit and that she had his word she would not be disappointed in their performance. Giles recalled:

> I started to agree with Judy that we had an opportunity to educate this woman. If she let our staff do their job we had a chance to break down some of her racial assumptions. I knew we were the best and once she gave us a chance, there would be no other company for her. But we had to get her past that huge first hurdle.

A Dress Rehearsal

The day before the booked party, one of the assigned waitresses decided to take 45 minutes, out of her own personal time, to drive from the city to the new client's house. She did not intend to be late and wanted to make sure that she knew where she was going. Not five minutes after the server left the client's home, the customer called First Impressions to complain. Giles remembered:

> The call came in and I happened to answer the telephone. She said, "Listen, the person that is supposed to be working tomorrow's party was just here. And don't you have any white staff you can send me?" She still had no idea I was not white. As the conversation continued the tones became more and more offensive. I tried to tell her that server was one of our finest employees. It just did not matter to her. She became more belligerent until she blurted out, "I do not want any niggers in my house. I am going to have furs here, silverware, china, and diamonds. You know how those people take all that stuff. My silverware costs more than those people cost. I am not going to allow them in, I want white staff only."

The torrent of her words hit Giles with the force of gale winds. The harsh tone and firmness of her voice made it sound like she was using a public address system.

> It took all the moral courage I had to present a collected and calm voice as I asked her to hold. My entire body filled with heat and humiliation. Her words fell like a scar upon my soul. I can be emotional and I just felt denigrated. I had to talk to Judy. I needed to know if we should really have booked this party.

With the client on hold, Giles went into his boss's office and explained what he had just been told. Wiles finished:

> I had spent my lifetime attempting to educate others to be colorblind and I wanted to be colorblind. But how was I going to profit if I couldn't get past go? I broke into the market, and in a big way, with the Detroit Grand Prix contract. That deal helped me establish credibility and earn a reputation as providing the most professional, reliable staff in the food service industry. Yet I was still faced with clients full of reluctance and apprehension to use my company, particularly as I expanded into the suburbs. It was fine for Eric or me to do the client research, develop the sales strategy, and make the initial telephone contacts, but we could not be the people who went to the clients' office or home to get the deal signed.

Wiles had believed that removing the word "President" from behind her name was the solution. She soon realized, however, that it might have only been the first rung on the ladder.

She absently twisted the ends of her long curly hair. Eric Giles had just barged through both Wiles' office door and her peace of mind. His usual cheerful disposition was obviously shaken. According to Wiles:

> Eric, who was normally even-tempered, was flushed and nervous as he told me what this customer had just said. I asked Ayesha to tell the client we would call her right back. Then we sat down and had a heart-filled talk. Eric told me he thought we should drop this client. Even though we desperately wanted to break into the suburban market, we should

make a stand on principle. We discussed the possible impact our decision could have on the referring account. It looked like a lose-lose situation. We would probably lose the catering account if we took the job and the party did not go over well or if we declined the booking and it offended the woman. So finally, after discussing all our options and perceived costs, I told Eric, "You do this: you call her, you tell her that everything is taken care of and organize this engagement exactly like you would any other one. Mark in the books that all preparations are complete and then *do not* send a solitary soul from this company to that house. Just confirm the order done."

Bartender, Cook and Server

The next afternoon the telephone rang and interrupted Giles as he studied staff assignments for the upcoming Grand Prix race. The voice on the other end sounded painfully familiar to Giles:

It was our favorite client from the suburbs and she said, "Well, why isn't anybody here yet?" I told her they should be there any time. She kept calling and I kept telling her the same thing.

Wiles decided to call the woman back and inform her that First Impressions was a black-owned company. She remembered:

She slammed down the receiver on me. Now she had asked for a bartender, a cook and a server for that party that she told us was for 50 of the best people in Detroit. And when she hung up on me, I said to myself, "Lady, you just became a bartender, a cook and a server!"

Epilogue

In brooding silence, Judy Wiles, president and owner of First Impressions Inc, stared at the application form on her desk. A single image occupied her mind as she read the first line of the employment form—William Ashley. He was a man of 50, clean-cut, salt-and-pepper gray hair, above-average height, well built. His deep blue eyes, covered by glasses, had an intellectual cast to them. While his professional manner and gentle voice impressed Judy, his credentials were unremarkable. He had been employed in the food-service industry for several years and worked his way up from server to trainer to sous-chef. His references served him well but Wiles had numerous candidates with similar experience. Yet there was a feature of this application that consumed Wiles' thoughts. It was the color of William Ashley's skin—he was white. Given her recent experiences, Wiles wrestled with the idea of disguising that First Impressions was a minority-owned business. Wiles wondered whether she should hire William Ashley to present the *face* of First Impressions, Inc.

Looks Can Be Deceiving

Wiles considered hiring Ashley as part of her strategy to disguise First Impressions' minority ownership. She had gone through a series of steps to accomplish the concealment. First, she removed the word "President" from her business card. Then she created a portfolio of working engagements to show on sales calls. In the opening pages of the portfolio two white women stood by the door in bow ties, tuxedo shirts, and black pants. A white male wore a chef's hat and was pictured carving a roast. Page after page showed no indication of color; only her white models were featured. She took the approach that it was about feeling comfortable doing business with someone who looked like you. Wiles' rationale was that she faced stiff competition from other temporary food service providers, so it was not worth the risk of ignoring any prejudice in the market. Her concern was for the bottom line.

Another factor kept Wiles and her management team, Eric Giles and Ayesha Anderson, committed to increasing revenue and ensuring the company succeeded. That was their employee base. Their hiring practices and training program had developed into an avenue of employment to groups normally excluded. First Impressions hired former gang members, high school dropouts, single parents, ex-felons, the homeless, and others who many managers viewed as the "unemployable." First Impressions gave scores of "have nots" the chance to prove themselves—a much needed break to develop and show their capability. The company used their interview process as a strategy to find employees who showed a promise of work ethic. Wiles and her management team did not care about physical appearance believing they could fix poor attire and hygiene. Their training program offered potential employees advantages like learning to be a professional server, gaining confidence so they would not spill, learning to speak with a polite practiced voice, and developing skills that led to full time management positions in the service industry. First Impressions was a temporary employment agency so managers encouraged and recommended their employees for positions with clients that offered benefits and career building opportunities beyond their business.

Not the First and Probably Not the Last

Although Wiles was troubled that she believed perceptions about people of color forced her to make compromises, she wanted to make money and also felt an obligation to her employees. Wiles was not the first person of color to conclude that her race prevented her from certain opportunities. John H. Johnson, entrepreneur and publisher of *Ebony*, experienced difficult choices similar to Wiles. Johnson was unable to secure a $500 bank loan to establish Johnson Publications in the 1940s.[2] So he borrowed cash from a loan company with his mom's household furniture as collateral. After becoming a millionaire, Johnson hired a white front man in the 1950s. His bid to purchase a building had been refused so Johnson pretended to be the janitor for a company that expressed interest in buying the property so he could inspect it. He then had the white front man work the deal for his ownership.[3]

When Reginald Lewis, another successful entrepreneur first tried to buy McCall Patterns, he handled the negotiations but did not introduce himself as a buyer. Instead, Lewis led everyone to believe that a consortium of investors was attempting the leveraged buyout.[4]

Conclusion

Wiles credited disguising the ownership of her company with her ability to break into the market and maintain the status of being the best agency in Michigan. So she contemplated continuing with the same strategy to ensure success by hiring William Ashley. She recalled, "During my interview with William Ashley, I told him I just could not afford to lose a contract because some clients held preconceived notions about blacks. He certainly seemed to grasp the reality of our situation." Ashley explained that he believed minorities often gained only a limited acceptance in the circles of privilege. He also stated he would relish a position in a minority-owned company that offered him the opportunity to help educate others and challenge stereotypes or disparities.

Notes

*   This case was prepared by Gerry Yemen, under the supervision of Patricia Werhane, Ruffin Professor of Business Ethics. It was written as a basis for class discussion rather than to illustrate effective or ineffective handling of an administrative situation. Copyright © 1999 by the University of Virginia Darden School Foundation, Charlottesville, VA. All rights reserved.
1   There is a path which leads through the archway of Grand Circus Park, away from the direction of downtown Detroit, towards the theater district, and heads to the suburbs. Grosse Pointe is an affluent suburb of Detroit.
2   Juliet E.K. Walker, *The History of Black Business in America* (New York: Twayne Publishers, 1998). 337.
3   Ibid. 338.
4   Ibid.

6.2 Nike, Inc. *

Nike was founded in 1964 by Philip H. Knight as "BRS (Blue Ribbon Sports)," and later changed to "Nike" in 1972. Phil Knight remains Nike's Owner, Chairman, and CEO today. Nike, based in Beaverton, Oregon, has more than 22,000 employees and over 800 contracted suppliers in about 52 countries throughout the world, employing more than 550,000 workers on any given day creating sports and fitness footwear, apparel, equipment and accessories for worldwide distribution (over 400 of these suppliers are located in Asia).[1] Approximately 175 million pairs of shoes are manufactured each year for Nike, contributing in part to Nike's annual revenue for 2001, which totaled almost $10 billion.[2] Nike's Code of Conduct, first sent out to manufacturers in 1992 and the second to be developed in the entire industry,[3] binds all Nike contract manufacturers and requires that all "manufacturing partners must post this Code in all major workspaces, translated into the language of the worker, and must endeavor to train workers on their rights and obligations as defined by this Code and applicable labor laws"[4] (Exhibit 6.2.1). In its code, Nike sets a standard for its partnerships by seeking contractors who are committed to best practices and continuous improvement in the following areas:

- Management practices that respect the rights of all employees, including the right to free association and collective bargaining
- Minimizing our impact on the environment
- Providing a safe and healthy work place
- Promoting the health and well-being of all employees.

Specifically, Nike's code binds its partners to core standards of conduct, as set forth below:

1 Forced Labor
2 Child Labor
3 Compensation
4 Benefits
5 Hours of Work/Overtime
6 Environment, Safety and Health: The Nike Corporate Responsibility Compliance Production SHAPE
7 Documentation and Inspection[5]

When Nike chooses to establish a relationship with a new production factory, it requires that the factory agree to, pay for and undergo a pre-sourcing audit conducted by a third party, as well as a Nike internal SHAPE inspection.[6] The goal is that SHAPE inspections will happen at least four times four times a year for footwear factories and twice a year for each apparel or

Exhibit 6.2.1 Nike Inc. Code of Conduct

Nike Inc was founded on a handshake

Implicit in that act was the determination that we would build our business with all of our partners based on trust, teamwork, honesty and mutual respect. We expect all of our business partners to operate on the same principles.

At the core of the NIKE corporate ethic is the belief that we are a company comprised of many different kinds of people, appreciating individual diversity, and dedicated to equal opportunity for each individual.

NIKE designs, manufactures, and markets products for sports and fitness consumers. At every step in that process, we are driven to do not only what is required by law, but what is expected of a leader. We expect our business partners to do the same. NIKE partners with contractors who share our commitment to best practices and continuous improvement in:

- Management practices that respect the rights of all employees, including the right to free association and collective bargaining
- Minimizing our impact on the environment
- Providing a safe and healthy work place
- Promoting the health and well-being of all employees

Contractors must recognize the dignity of each employee, and the right to a work place free of harassment, abuse or corporal punishment. Decisions on hiring, salary, benefits, advancement, termination or retirement must be based solely on the employee's ability to do the job. There shall be no discrimination based on race, creed, gender, marital or maternity status, religious or political beliefs, age or sexual orientation.

Wherever NIKE operates around the globe we are guided by this Code of Conduct and we bind our contractors to these principles. Contractors must post this Code in all major workspaces, translated into the language of the employee, and must train employees on their rights and obligations as defined by this Code and applicable local laws.

While these principles establish the spirit of our partnerships, we also bind our partners to specific standards of conduct. The core standards are set forth below.

Forced Labor

The contractor does not use forced labor in any form – prison, indentured, bonded or otherwise.

Child Labor

The contractor does not employ any person below the age of 18 to produce footwear. The contractor does not employ any person below the age of 16 to produce apparel, accessories or equipment. If at the time Nike production begins, the contractor employs people of the legal working age who are at least 15, that employment may continue, but the contractor will not hire any person going forward who is younger than the Nike or legal age limit, whichever is higher. To further ensure these age standards are complied with, the contractor does not use any form of homework for Nike production.

Compensation

The contractor provides each employee at least the minimum wage, or the prevailing industry wage, whichever is higher; provides each employee a clear, written accounting for every pay period; and does not deduct from employee pay for disciplinary infractions.

Benefits

The contractor provides each employee all legally mandated benefits.

Hours of Work/Overtime

The contractor complies with legally mandated work hours; uses overtime only when each employee is fully compensated according to local law; informs each employee at the time of hiring if mandatory overtime is a condition of employment; and on a regularly scheduled basis provides one day off in seven, and requires no more than 60 hours of work per week on a regularly scheduled basis, or complies with local limits if they are lower.

Environment, Safety and Health (ES&H)
From suppliers to factories to distributors and to retailers, Nike considers every member of our supply chain as partners in our business.

Documentation and Inspection
The contractor maintains on file all documentation needed to demonstrate compliance with this Code of Conduct and required laws; agrees to make these documents available for Nike or its designated monitor; and agrees to submit to inspections with or without prior notice.

Source: http://www.nike.com/nikebiz/nikebiz/jhtml?page=25&cat=compliance&subcat=code (as updated by Paula Valero, Director, Compliance Systems and Services, Nike Inc.) Reprinted with permission of Nike, Inc.

equipment factory. In order to continue with the relationship or to place an order, both of the above inspections must conclude that the factory is in "substantial compliance" with the Nike Code of Conduct. If not, the factory may choose to resubmit at a later date, striving toward compliance at that time. The entire monitoring process strives to achieve the following schedule of events:

- Identification of factory by Nike production/sourcing staff
- SHAPE inspection carried out by production and/or LP manager
- Pre-sourcing monitoring visit conducted by Global Social Compliance/Pricewater-houseCoopers (PwC)
- Factory approved by Vice President of Compliance
- Production begins in the factory
- Quarterly SHAPE inspections carried out for footwear manufacturers and biannually for apparel and equipment manufacturers
- When non-compliance issues identified, recommended action plan compiled for factory by Nike labor practice department working in conjunction with Nike production staff
- Follow-up monitoring visit to measure corrective action taken by factory.

Nike has developed a new management audit designed to quantitatively measure a contract factory's compliance with Nike management standards, which include pay, wage, benefits, forced labor, non-discrimination, age, freedom of association, and the treatment of workers. This new instrument is in-depth; and Nike is focusing on global consistency, striving to find ways to link performance on this audit with sourcing decisions and incentive schemes. The audit evaluates contract factories on the basis of four areas of risk assessment: country location, size of factory, type of operation and factory-specific historical compliance performance record. In conjunction with the development of the audit, Nike's President Mark Parker approved the hiring of 21 new internal labor compliance auditors for the Compliance Department. Based on Nike's assessment of its contract factories, these auditors will categorize them as high, medium, and low risk. Each year, using this tool, Nike plans to audit 100% of high risk factories, 50% of medium risk factories, and 10% of low risk factories.[7]

Evolution of Nike's Approach to Global Labor Issues

Attention to the labor practices of Nike's suppliers began around 1988 when journalists focused several news stories on the situation in Nike's Jakarta, Indonesia suppliers. USAID then funded a large-scale survey in order to document wage law violations that was later supported by a study of the Indonesian shoe industry. Between 1988 and 1996, the minimum wage rate in Indonesia rose more than 300% (from $0.86 to $2.46 per day), in large part due to this attention and efforts by large MNEs such as Nike.[8] The rate of inflation in Indonesia for the same time period was 205%.[9] On May 12, 1998, Nike CEO Phil Knight delivered a speech at the National Press Club that became a turning point in Nike's approach to the issues facing its suppliers (Exhibit 6.2.2).[10] In that speech, Knight accepted responsibility at the corporate level for the labor activities of its suppliers by establishing six initiatives for the firm. Knight explained that, as of that day, Nike committed to:

- Increasing the minimum **age** of new footwear factory workers to 18, and the minimum age for all other new light-manufacturing workers (apparel, accessories, equipment) to 16;
- Adopting the personal exposure limits (PEL) of the U.S. Occupational Safety and Health Administration (OSHA) as the standard for indoor **air quality** for all footwear factories;
- Funding university **research and open forums** to explore issues related to global manufacturing and responsible business practices such as independent monitoring and air quality standards.
- Expanding worker **education programs**, including middle and high school equivalency courses, for workers in all Nike footwear factories;
- Increasing support of its current **micro-enterprise loan program** to 1,000 families each in Vietnam, Indonesia, Pakistan and Thailand; expanding its current independent monitoring programs to include non-governmental organizations (NGOs), foundations and educational institutions and making summaries of the findings public;
- **Involving NGOs** in the process of factory monitoring, with summaries released to the public.[11]

The *New York Times* applauded Knight's commitments, claiming that they "set a standard that other companies should match."[12] To the contrary, however, come critics chastised Knight for not including several other commitments, including the protection of whistle-blowers within the factories, Nike-directed worker rights education programs, guarantee of living wages and reasonable working hours, and protection of workers' right to freedom of association.[13]

Since the time of Knight's pronouncement, Nike has developed a system of comprehensive monitoring and remediation.[14] This includes a health management and safety audit program, and a significant global labor practice team that visits factories on an everyday basis,[15] and conducts training and awareness initiatives. In connection with auditing programs, not only has Nike coordinated these activities from inside, but Nike has also engaged external auditors, as well as nongovernmental organizations, to monitor, audit and report on ongoing activities from an external perspective. Nike is also a founding member of the Fair Labor Association and has committed to external independent monitoring throughout its factory base. Though many have praised these efforts,[16] not all of Nike's critics have been pacified by these efforts, as is specifically evidenced by scholar Dara O'Rourke's critique of the PwC labor monitoring program where he claims not only that PwC failed to catch and assess several violations, but also that it allowed for management bias in the audits and failed to effectively gather information.[17]

In 2001, Nike invited Global Alliance for Workers and Communities ("GA") to evaluate challenges existing in its suppliers' factories in Indonesia, Thailand and Vietnam. Though some have questioned the validity and credibility of GA's work as a result of its relationship with Nike (along with The Gap, St. John's University, Kent State University, the World Bank, and the John D. and Catherine T. MacArthur Foundation, Nike has contributed funds to GA),[18] GA maintains strict standards relating to conflicts of interest and autonomy of its

Exhibit 6.2.2 "New Labor Initiatives," speech by Nike Chairman and CEO Phil Knight (May 12, 1998)

On May 12, 1998, Nike CEO Philip H. Knight announced a series of new initiatives to further improve factory working conditions worldwide and provide increased opportunities for people who manufacture Nike products.

In his remarks at the National Press Club, Knight said, "we are committed to improving working conditions for the 500,000 people who make our products. The initiatives we are announcing today build upon input from factory workers, factory partners, non-governmental organizations, health and safety specialists, academics, religious groups, President Clinton's Apparel Industry Partnership (AIP) and our auditors."

"Effective today, Nike commits to:

- Increasing the minimum age of new footwear factory workers to 18, and the minimum age for all other new light-manufacturing workers (apparel, accessories, equipment) to 16.
- Adopting the personal exposure limits (PEL) of the U.S. Occupational Safety and Health Administration (OSHA) as the standard for indoor air quality for all footwear factories.
- Funding university research and open forums to explore issues related to global manufacturing and responsible business practices such as independent monitoring and air quality standards.
- Expanding education programs, including middle and high school equivalency courses, for workers in all Nike footwear factories.
- Increasing support of its current micro-enterprise loan program to 1,000 families each in Vietnam, Indonesia, Pakistan and Thailand.
- Expanding its current independent monitoring programs to include non-governmental organizations (NGOs), foundations and educational institutions and making summaries of the findings public."

Over the past 13 months, there has been a lot of progress made. What follows is an internal memo to Phil Knight that provides an update on the initiatives he announced:

Age Limits

We have effectively changed our minimum age limits from the ILO standards of 15 in most countries and 14 in developing countries to 18 in all footwear manufacturing and 16 in all other types of manufacturing (apparel, accessories and equipment.). Existing workers legally employed under the former limits were grand-fathered into the new requirements. Our partners indicated they were able to meet the new standards with their newly-hired employees. Our independent auditors certify on an on-going basis that these new standards are being met.

During the past 13 months we have moved to a 100 percent factory audit scheme, where every Nike contract factory will receive an annual check by PricewaterhouseCoopers teams who are specially trained on our Code of Conduct Owner's Manual and audit/monitoring procedures. To date they have performed about 300 such monitoring visits. In a few instances in apparel factories they have found workers under our age standards. Those factories have been required to raise their standards to 17 years of age, to require three documents certifying age, and to redouble their efforts to ensure workers meet those standards through interviews and records checks.

Environmental Health and Safety/Sustainable Design

This initiative has three components: Indoor air quality; sustainable business practices and design; and Management-Environment-Safety-Health (MESH) systems for all footwear factories.

A. Indoor Air

Our goal was to ensure workers around the globe are protected by requiring factories to have no workers exposed to levels above those mandated by the permissible exposure limits (PELs) for chemicals prescribed in the OSHA indoor air quality standards.

The number one priority in this initiative is to eliminate the source of potential health hazards from the workplace, specifically, petroleum-based solutions that are commonly used in the production of athletic shoes. We noted in May 1998 that nine out of ten Nike shoes were manufactured using water-based adhesives. Some shoe types (soccer and baseball, for example) initially did not perform well using water-based adhesives, but we have since had further success. We are closer now to 95 out of 100 shoes (or 95%) made with water-based adhesives. There is still some work to do. In parallel, we have succeeded in reducing the use of the petroleum-based solvents significantly. From 1995 through 1998, solvent usage was reduced 73%. We expect the next quarterly report to indicate the total reduction is

Exhibit 6.2.2 *Continued*

more than 80%. Each succeeding reduction becomes harder and harder to achieve as we work toward the margins of the issue. But the remaining 20% is primarily in the priming area, and today we are already running trials on water-based primers, which are showing encouraging results. In the meantime, any worker using these solvents will be protected to OSHA levels or better using improved ventilation and personal protective equipment (PPE) (worker rotation?).

Our second priority was to assess the actual quality of indoor air in our footwear factories, and then make corrections. Independent certified industrial hygienists and other health professionals from Reliance Insurance, one of the country's largest and most respected commercial risk assessment consultants, has overseen indoor air quality tests in all of our Asian footwear manufacturing factories. We tested the factories in Italy.

The results are encouraging, but the most important aspect of that work is to pinpoint areas in factories where improvements should be made. We shared this information, as well as our water-base work and conversion, with the rest of the athletic footwear industry at an open forum in Bangkok in November 1998.

To provide a better sense of what we are finding and the steps we are taking in all countries of manufacture, here are some top-line results from one country, Vietnam, where we have five footwear manufacturing partners. Here is what the studies found there:

Testing began in December 1997, and continued through 1998, with additional re-testing in 1999. There are a combined 40,000 workers in these five factories. Of that number, testing indicated about 50 people potentially may have been exposed above the OSHA permissible exposure levels (PELs). It is important to note that in those limited areas where chemical exposures still exceed the OSHA PELs, Nike factory workers can still be adequately protected through the mandatory use of appropriate personal protective equipment (PPE). When such equipment is properly used, the over-exposure potential is eliminated.

So long as one worker faces an issue of over-exposure, our work is not complete. As we continue to upgrade our processes, the factories have been directed to take the necessary steps to achieve levels at or below OSHA-prescribed PELs. These steps include ventilation equipment upgrades, mandated PPE use, and changes in work practices to accomplish our compliance objectives.

Throughout the last year, these tests and re-tests, conducted by Reliance Insurance, have verified the findings using laboratories in the United States certified by the American Industrial Hygiene Association (AIHA).

On the administrative front, OSHA administrators encourage or in some cases mandate certain procedures for dealing with over-exposure issues in manufacturing facilities within the United States. We have taken the same steps in Vietnam and other Asian source countries. These steps, which are on-going, include:

- Elimination of toxic source chemicals (e.g. methylene chloride and toluene) which may affect the overall health and safety of workers. Substitution of water-based compounds, which do not give off potentially harmful vapors.
- Implementation of better administrative controls, including rotating workshifts and duties of persons to limit their long-term exposure to certain chemical agents; also, altering the positioning and containment of chemicals at individual work stations.
- Implementation of engineering controls, including materially upgrading the work stations and ventilation systems of factories through new equipment. Plexiglas booths and hooded ventilation systems have been effective in clearing potentially harmful vapors from the workplace.
- Ensured through managerial controls and training that workers receive the proper personal protective equipment (PPE), including safety glasses, goggles, gloves, earplugs and appropriate respiratory protection.

In addition to the installation of new ventilation equipment, the factories have also increased their medical facilities to treat respiratory conditions, regardless of whether they are lung infections and viruses common among the general population of Vietnam, or conditions potentially triggered by factory work. Tae Kwang Vina, for example, has tripled the capacity of its medical facilities and doubled the size of the medical staff during the past year. We are working now with three different NGOs to evaluate the wellness of workers through studies and standards in nutrition, workplace safety, the use of personal protective equipment, and the quality of health care and health education provided by the factory clinics.

Exhibit 6.2.2 *Continued*

B. MESH (Management-Environment-Safety-Health)
A second environmental program we committed to was to require all footwear factories to adopt an Environmental Health and Safety Management System. Using outside consultants Gauntlett Group of San Francisco and Environmental Resource Management (ERM) of Hong Kong, in June and August 1998, we inaugurated the first of the EHSMS workshops for factories in China. In the fall and winter of 1998 and into Spring of 1999 these workshops and follow-up brought the concepts and workshops to factories in Korea, Taiwan, Thailand, Vietnam and Indonesia. This year we decided to expand MESH to encompass all corporate responsibility programs, including labor practices and community affairs (management); environmental programs (environment), and the worker wellness programs (safety and health). Although MESH will be a work in progress for years to come, we believe it will have a marked impact on worker populations, factory impacts and the basic quality of management of these issues across the board.

C. Sustainable Business
The third of the environmental initiatives was adoption of the goal of sustainable business practices. We have engaged McDonough Braungart Design Chemistry on the first element of that concept, sustainable product design. On September 9, 1998 we inaugurated a new Nike Environmental Policy. We have also committed to eliminate polyvinyl chloride (PVC) from all of our business activities.

Forums/Rising Tides
In May 1998 we committed to a policy of open communications on corporate responsibility issues. In the spirit of sharing our knowledge and continued challenges on improving indoor air quality, Nike hosted our first open forum on factory environmental issues on November 26, 1998 in Bangkok, Thailand. On the following day, we invited representatives from the footwear industry, governmental health officials and non-governmental organization (NGOs) representatives to a tour of our Thailand factories.

The objective of the forum and factory tours was to share knowledge and best practices on worker health and safety issues that will primarily benefit the footwear industry and perhaps other global companies seeking to export measurable standards to their contractors abroad.

We published a compendium of results of that forum, including complete results of all air quality testing; and information on water-based compounds. We have also developed from that work a manual for air quality correction.

In addition to Forums, the second of which we are exploring now, we also committed to fund university studies of corporate responsibility issues. To date, the Tuck School of Business at Dartmouth College has undertaken wage and spending surveys of workers in factories in Vietnam and Indonesia, and will continue that work for us. The University of North Carolina's School of Public Health is working with us to develop a long-term study of health impacts and training in footwear factories.

Education
On May 12, 1998, we committed Nike to work with manufacturers who take a leading interest in their worker welfare. A key component of that commitment is that every Nike contract footwear factory must have a supplemental worker education program. To date, such programs are up and operating in about half of the footwear factory base, or 20 factories, in four countries (China, Thailand, Vietnam and Indonesia). Our goal in this fiscal year is to add 10 more factories to that list, and to ensure through the Global Alliance, World Vision and other outside resources that the existing programs are operated to standards of best practice.

Each factory produces its own program guides based on our standard (the Jobs & Education Program guide); local requirements; and advice and counsel from outside resources. In Indonesia, factories who have started education programs have done so in conjunction with the Ministry of Education, using certified teachers and curriculum. Three of those factories have been formally recognized by the Indonesian government for their contributions to literacy.

In China, our partner is the Washington State-based NGO, World Vision, which through its World Vision Hong Kong and World Vision China organizations has conducted worker surveys to see what programs are desired; designed a program concept that encompasses academic as well as life skills components; and then staffed the programs with trainers and managers.

In Vietnam and Thailand the factories have developed programs using local teachers and facilities.

Exhibit 6.2.2 *Continued*

Micro-Loans

In May 1998 we committed to providing small business loans to women in Vietnam and three other Asian countries. In the intervening year the Vietnam program through the Vietnam Women's Union and the Colorado-based NGO Friendship Bridge has been expanded to also include workers who lost jobs. To date, more than 2,300 rural women and former workers have created small businesses in Vietnam, and the success rate has been absolutely amazing. Thus far there have been no defaults on loans, and business borrowers have come back to expand businesses with second and third loans. The typical business involves raising of pigs, ducks or chickens, the production of rice paper for spring rolls, or the production of incense sticks and other basic manufactured goods.

In Indonesia, our NGO partner Opportunity International (OI) has launched a micro-loan program using Nike working capital that is targeted at an area of Jakarta where many people have lost jobs as a result of the economic downturn. OI projects several thousand businesses will be created from this program in the coming 3–5 years.

In Thailand, our partners, the local NGO called Population and Community Development Association (PDA), and Union Footwear, have collaborated with Nike to establish a rural village stitching center around which a number of related programs will be built, including a micro-enterprise cooperative, a vegetable bank, tree bank, school and women empowerment center. The concept is to create a center for enterprise and education that keeps jobs in the countryside, reverses migration to the city, and builds re-forestation and cash crop projects. Although small in scale, we hope the village concept will stimulate similar efforts on the part of other businesses.

We are investigating a micro-loan program in Pakistan, but to date have not come to resolution as to a partner or program.

Independent Monitoring

On May 12, 1998 we committed Nike to involve NGOs in the process of monitoring our factories. In the past year we have expanded our program in Vietnam with the University of Economics, which conducts worker focus groups; we have engaged one NGO in Indonesia to work alongside Nike auditors in factory oversight; and, most importantly, we have joined as a charter member in the Global Alliance, what will eventually be a global system of engaging local NGOs to survey workers in factories, report those results, and help us and our factory partners to devise programs that address issues that are raised and prioritized by the workers themselves.

The Global Alliance for Workers and Communities has been established by the International Youth Foundation (IYF), with participation from the World Bank, the John D. and Catherine T. MacArthur Foundation, Nike and Mattel. Our goal for this fiscal year is to have assessment and feedback from workers in factories in four countries which all together have 100,000 workers, or about 20% of our total contract labor force. Assessment begins in the first factories in July or August.

The White House Apparel Industry Partnership since May 12, 1998 has come to agreement on principles of monitoring, and is working now to establish a Fair Labor Association, which would manage the oversight of each member company's monitoring process. In addition to the seven member companies, the FLA also has the commitment of more than 80 universities that have their logos licensed to apparel manufacturers like Nike. Many of the schools with which we have licensing agreements have joined the FLA. Our hope is that this program will be operating by Fall 1999.

Source: http://www.nike.com/nikebiz/news/pressrelease.jhtml?year=2001&month=05&letter=g, reprinted with permission of Nike, Inc.

research. As a result of Nike's invitation, GA produced a report entitled "Workers' Voices: An Interim Report on Workers' Needs and Aspirations in Nine Nike Contract Factories in Indonesia." The report was based on interviews with more than 4,450 workers at nine Nike supplier factories.[19] Currently, the Global Alliance is engaged with Nike in a tailored training program focused on supervisory skills in Thailand, Indonesia, Vietnam, India and China.

Most recently, in September 2001, Knight and Nike's Board of Directors created a Corporate Responsibility Committee of the Board. The committee's responsibility is to review, report and make recommendations to the full board regarding Nike's alignment with corporate responsibility commitments. Issues to be addressed include labor compliance initiatives, environmental practices, community affairs programs, human resources, diversity issues and philanthropic efforts.

Vietnam Operations

Nike has been manufacturing in Vietnam through factory partners since 1995, currently employing more than 43,000 workers making 22 million shoes annually and exporting apparel totaling over $450 million. Nike production accounts for 8% of Vietnam's manufactured exports and 32% of its footwear exports.[20]

Based in Ho Chi Minh City, Vietnam, American Chris Helzer has served as Nike's Director of Government Affairs for Southeast Asia and Australia for the past two and a half years. Lalit Monteiro is the General Manager of Nike – Vietnam and works on ethics-related issues with Steve Hewitt, the Corporate Responsibility and Compliance Manager. As a modification to its earlier structure, the Vice President for Apparel Sourcing now has the oversight for corporate responsibility and may veto any given source as a result of its failure to comply with corporate responsibility standards.

Leverage toward compliance is much greater in the Vietnam footwear industry than in apparel or other industries since most footwear factories serve Nike 100% and since there is little, if any, slow season. Of Nike's over 850 supplier factories worldwide, 68 are footwear factories (five footwear and seven apparel factories are located in Vietnam). Current turnover in these factories numbers only 1% of its 46,000 workers in Vietnam,[21] and is usually due to lack of desire to return after pregnancy or marriage by female worker. Being the largest employer in Vietnam, Nike's business has a significant impact on the Vietnamese economy. While the above discussion evidences prior challenges, even one of Nike's most harsh critics, Medea Benjamin of Global Exchange, notes that "things are changing for the better"[22] and that the firm has made an "astounding turnaround."[23]

FII. Nike, Inc. – Program Analyses

A. Program 1: After Hours Education Program

1. INSPIRATION AND VISION SETTING: IDEA GENERATION/INCEPTION

The *inspiration* or vision-setting process for the Nike after hours education program began during one of the ongoing meetings with suppliers coordinated by Nike when the owner of a Korean-owned supplier located in Vietnam, Dae Shin, noted that the workers had requested and would benefit from an education program that could be attended after working hours. It was determined by this supplier and others interested that the best program would be one that balanced worker interest, slots available, and the nature of the educational need. In his May 1998, initiatives speech, Knight made the education program a Nike standard, promising that by the end of 2001 Nike would only order footwear from manufacturers that offer a "Jobs + Education" program to workers.

2. INTEGRATION: THE APPROVAL PROCESS

The approval process for this project was informal. A group of individuals involved in supply chain compliance and integrity at Nike, including CEO Phil Knight and President Dave Taylor sat down to explore how Nike might be able to best support this project. During this stage of the project's establishment, the group discussed the parameters of their corporate responsibility as well as the investment that they hoped to make, not only in these suppliers, but also in the workers and the countries in which they lived, highlighting the importance of *top management commitment* to the responsibility vision Nike was establishing. It was determined that the most effective program would be one which was coordinated in partnership with the Ministry of Education to ensure GED compliance where desired by the students. (GED-equivalent is the norm for Vietnam. However, in other countries, workers were more interested in obtaining life and other skills. Thus, education programs in some countries do not necessarily result in granting of GED equivalency.)

3. INTEGRATION, ESTABLISHMENT AND IMPLEMENTATION

The supplier, in partnership with Nike, and the Ministry of Education worked together in the *integration* process and established GED programs by hiring teachers and renting classrooms in local educational facilities near the factories. The program covers the expenses of each student including books and other supplies and a meal allowance. Nike currently participates in the after hours education program by funding 50% of the cost of the program to each supplier. All Nike footwear suppliers in Vietnam currently have active education programs in accordance with this model. One of the factory owners involved in this program identifies the program as a foundation for personal development, "We would like to be able to promote from within and can only do that once these workers have additional educations." In fact, this owner has already promoted several Vietnamese workers to line management positions upon completion of the education program. He explains that he and his firm "want to go beyond compliance, both for the business relationship with Nike as well as for its own impact on the workers and our organization. To achieve our profits, we have to address the employees from an emotional perspective, as well."

As these practices are *integrated* into Nike's training programs, they serve as a foundation for long-term relationships.[24] Dusty Kidd, Nike's Vice President for compliance, explains that the value here is not only as a gesture of Nike's commitment to the work force and supplier's future, but also results in the long-term efficiencies that can be realized by investing in education. By investing matching funds ranging on average from $15,000 to $20,000 per supplier, Nike "can touch 300 people for a lifetime."[25] To date, over 10,000 contract workers have participated in these programs. The education program at one factory, Cheng Shin, is currently the largest program, with 400 students having originally enrolled and an 85% completion rate, which are important *indicators* of success that provide a basis for *improvement and innovation*. In addition, the Chang Shin Vietnam factory also suggested a literacy program for the workers, jointly funded with Nike, Chang Shin Vietnam and the local government, to which Nike agreed. Chang Shin Vietnam also offers "livelihood training" for interested workers, coordinating sessions on hand-knitting, embroidery, and other skills which the worker can then also teach their relatives. It is hoped that this program might offer the workers' families skills that could be used by the families for additional income.

Though the subjects vary depending on worker demand and interest, the programs themselves range from high school equivalency, to vocational, to short-term education programs on specific subjects such as personal health or financial management. After hours education programs now exist in Korea, Vietnam, Taiwan, China, Thailand and Indonesia. Educators are generally hired from the local region in order to best meet the needs of the workers and to comply with education regulations of education ministries in various countries.

4. INDICATORS: CONTINUED PROGRAM ASSESSMENT

For program assessment, Nike considers the following factors as important *indicators* that help measure performance during its bi-annual audit visit:

- Are students remaining in the classes? If not, is it because of lack of interest, lack of time from work, the level or quality of the instruction or other variables? (In one situation, Nike learned that the students did not feel that the quality of instruction was good; so it worked with local programs to find more high quality instructors and a better curriculum.)
- Are the students able to learn from and complete the coursework?
- What is the absentee rate? Why?
- Are the programs offered at appropriate times? Appropriate, accessible locations?
- What does our monitoring program report in connection with these programs? What do we learn from pre-tests and post-tests or GED completion rates?

Since the workers have expressed a great deal of satisfaction with this program and encourage its continuation, Nike has encouraged its and others' suppliers from around Vietnam and throughout Southeast Asia to visit the factory and learn about the program. To date, factory owners and others from adidas, Fujitsu, and Nike itself have visited the program. Nike has institutionalized these types of visits in order to allow its suppliers to share best practices, providing a basis for on-going *improvement* initiatives. Once a month, general managers from each factory come together in a different factory and discuss accomplishments and challenges. Every six months, this same group travels to factories in other countries to learn about their processes (with Nike financial support).

As of June 1999, there were 20 separate education programs in the factories of 37 Asian Nike footwear contractors, including five footwear factories in Vietnam; six footwear factories in Indonesia; six in China; and three in Thailand. In Vietnam, this program has been extended to include two contract apparel factories, and a third will begin participating soon.

5. EXIT STRATEGY

In terms of an exit strategy, Nike expects that it will remain as long as necessary or as long as it has a relationship with that supplier. However, by participating in this program, Nike also hopes that it might impact the general standard of education in that country such that the supplemental programs are no longer necessary, as regional education programs are enhanced.

B. *Program 2: The Nike Jobs and Microenterprise Program*

1. INSPIRATION AND VISION SETTING: IDEA GENERATION/INCEPTION

Conceived in 1997 and beginning in 1998, Nike established a microenterprise loan program to provide some support for women in the communities surrounding its suppliers. The *inspiration* or vision for the program originated in Vietnam and was later expanded to include Thailand and Indonesia. The purpose of the program is to allow women a chance to build small businesses that will ultimately boost their family's economic well-being, as well as contribute to the community's overall development. Though there is no direct financial gain for Nike, "the microloan program helps to create a more healthy community, which then provides other sources of income in the community, better workers, and additional sources of support for the families of current workers, raising the whole village's standard of living," says Helzer.

Microloans respond to another difficult challenge in the Southeast Asian region. Nike has a global prohibition against any at-home work. However, this might have the impact of discriminating against women who, for social and cultural reasons, have either chosen not to work or are not allowed to work outside of the home. Therefore, by prohibiting any at-home outsourcing, these women may not have any financial means to protect their rights in other areas. The microloan program can provide this financial stability without outsourcing Nike manufacturing.

2. INTEGRATION, ESTABLISHMENT AND IMPLEMENTATION

In each country in which the program is located, Nike has teamed with local NGOs in an effort to ensure that ongoing support is available for borrowers and that the programs are well *integrated*. The Vietnam programs were established as a joint effort between Nike, Colorado-based Friendship Bridge (an NGO devoted to creating loan programs for developing economies that was involved in the first three years of the program) and the local Vietnamese Women's Unions (who notify and solicit the borrowers). Currently, there have been approximately 3,200 loans in place with the average loan standing at approximately $65 [maximum loan = 1 million Vietnamese Dong (~ $75 US) and the minimum loan = 500,000 VND (~ $37 US)]. Total Nike investment to date has been approximately 3.5 billion VND ($244,755 US) which includes an administrative fee paid to Friendship Bridge. Usually women will borrow the minimum amount for their first loan and increase the amounts for subsequent loans.

The Vietnam program includes potential borrowers within a 30 mile radius of Nike suppliers. The loan program currently operates in 6 villages in the Dong Nai province and 12 villages in the Cu Chi province. The borrowers must submit a business plan and go through basic business training and health seminars before the plans and loans are approved. The business plan must include a provision for saving a part of the money earned and mini-classes are available to borrowers regarding good saving habits. An additional component of the program requires children of borrowers to remain in school.

Those receiving the loans included groups of women who team together to borrow funding to raise small livestock, to produce incense sticks and other basic manufactured items (garments), or to tend to rice fields in the production of rice paper for spring rolls. More than 2,300 rural women and former workers have received funds to help them in creating small businesses and, in Vietnam specifically, there have been *no defaults* on the loans.[26]

The loans are granted in a "trust bank" format to teams of individuals in order to build in a support structure to the program. The 5–20 team members of each trust bank guarantee each other's loans. The borrowers meet weekly or monthly to make loan repayments, share business tips, address community concerns, and receive training in both business topics such as financial management as well as personal subjects such as nutrition, hygiene, child care and so on. After repaying loans, trust bank members can qualify for larger loans, and their payments are recycled to others in the form of new loans. Trust Bank clients have maintained an average repayment rate of 97% or better (see Table 6.2.1).

In Indonesia, the microenterprise loan program is offered in conjunction with Opportunity International, an NGO that has fighting global poverty as its primary goal. The basis of the program is the belief that a very small loan [such as less than US$100] may allow individuals to expand their inventory or to buy their raw materials in bulk, so that they can increase their profit margin, improve their business, and perhaps begin to accumulate savings.

Table 6.2.1 Steps in the Trust Bank Cycle [27]

1. Feasibility study	to select a community where Trust Banks can make a difference
2. Promotional meeting	to explain the Trust Bank program to interested entrepreneurs
3. Eight to ten weekly meetings	to build group solidarity, strengthen leadership skills, develop business plans, and train clients in managing their own loan repayments
4. Verbal examination	to assess readiness of group to take on a loan commitment and guarantee each other's loans
5. Loan disbursement	
6. Beginning of first loan cycle (usually 16–20 weeks)	with weekly meetings for collecting repayments and savings, trading business tips, and discussing family and community concerns. Trust Bank members elect their own leaders, who plan and conduct the meetings.
7. Final repayment of the loans	
8. Beginning of new loan cycle	

Through a partnership with an NGO called the Population and Community Development Association and Union Footwear, Nike also supports a microenterprise program in northeastern Thailand where it helped to establish a rural village stitching center and surrounding infrastructure such as a vegetable bank, a tree bank, a school and a women empowerment center. Nike invested in order to provide jobs and to support the rural development of the region, reversing migration to the city, and to build cash crop projects. For Nike, this type of assistance represents a small loan that can put thousands of individuals to work. These efforts represent significant local community improvement and innovation efforts associated with the program.

> *Case Example:* In conducting research for this report, one author visited the home of one of the Vietnamese microloan borrowers in the Cu Chi province. This young woman had borrowed money from the program each year for the past four years and used the funds to purchase equipment with which to create rice paper. Prior to her involvement in the program, this woman engaged in a variety of domestic services in neighboring communities but never held a stable job until she began this work for herself. Currently, she produces between 10 and 20 kilograms a day of rice paper (depending on the weather), and is the sole support for her family of four. While her youngest child is still in school, her husband and daughter assist in the production. With proceeds from the sale of her rice paper, this woman was able to rebuild her house using a brick structure and has been able to repay each of the four loans on time. Admittedly, while she earns significantly more money than she would earn in a factory working the same hours, she has no benefits available to her and is joined in her work by other family members.

3. INDICATORS: CONTINUED PROGRAM ASSESSMENT

Until the program reaches self-sufficiency, Nike receives quarterly or biannual reports from the program coordinators as *indicators* of progress.

4. EXIT STRATEGY

The program was developed and structured with the intent of self-sufficiency within several years. Based on interest charged and reinvestment of capital, the program will soon be able to afford its loans with no additional infusion of capital from Nike.

C. *Program 3: Nike Cultural Sensitivity Training Program*

I. INSPIRATION AND VISION SETTING: IDEA GENERATION/INCEPTION

Nike's Office of Labor Practices (now called Corporate Responsibility Compliance) was established in 1996. At that time, one of the more pressing issues revolved around a culture gap apparent in Vietnamese Korean- and Taiwanese-owned factories between the Vietnam nationals and the foreign supervisors. The Korean- and Taiwanese-owned suppliers used local labor in Vietnam and found that they were faced with significant management challenges in connection with cultural issues.

In early 1997, Nike asked Andrew Young to visit the factories in China, Indonesia, and Vietnam for purposes of assessing how well Nike's Code of Conduct was being implemented. Young also reported on the cultural gap between the workers and the managers in these particular factories and identified specific areas of challenge in connection with cultural differences. He suggested that special human relations and cultural sensitivity programs should be designed and organized and that participation should be mandatory for all expatriate management.[28] His report, combined with the earlier identification of the problem, served as the *inspiration* for the vision setting process that was to occur at Nike.

It should be noted that Young's report was not without criticism. Critics contended that Young avoided the main issues and used a flawed research method that did not uncover the facts about conditions facing workers who produce Nike products. He was criticized for relying in part on prior, purportedly imprecise Ernst & Young audit reports; for failing to meet with certain NGOs; spending insufficient time in various factories; and for issuing vague recommendations.[29] However, other investigators reported agreement with Young's findings.[30]

In response to Young's report on cultural challenges, Nike determined that it should assist the factories in bridging the cultural divide by assigning human resource expert Fukumi Hauser as its Global Training Manager. (Hauser is currently Nike Director of global compliance, monitoring and training.) These findings were also later supported by the work of the Center for Economic and Social Applications (CESAIS, now Troung Doan), which visited seven Vietnamese footwear factories in 1999. They found that one of the primary issues facing these Vietnamese workers was better relations between workers and managers.[31] Hauser visited the factories herself and identified several specific hurdles over which she might be able to assist the suppliers.

First, on the most basic level, there were language differences. These differences in language served to exacerbate other differences because of a general inability to communicate.

Second, the Taiwanese and Korean supervisors managed the Vietnamese workers according to their home standards, rather than those in place in Vietnam. However, when the Vietnamese workers were displeased, they did not come forward for fear of losing their jobs or because sharing concerns was not encouraged. Other cultural management differences abounded. A specific example related to Taiwanese culture is the Taiwanese response to illness. If one is sick, a Taiwanese will often look to her or his ancestors, their graves, their ancestral homes, to determine whether something is amiss, perceiving the illness to be a sign that the ancestors are disturbed. The Vietnamese culture does not share this perception and therefore would consider mending the illness itself if a worker were sick. Understanding these distinctions was vital to working together.

Third, the Vietnamese workers were accustomed to a rural, self-paced agricultural work routine and found it hard to adjust to a regimented factory routine with thousands of coworkers.

Fourth, the Vietnamese workers did not have a great deal of education and therefore were not aware of their basic worker rights. This naïveté discouraged them from coming forward to assert their rights, as they did not know the parameters of those rights.

When one merges an expectation gap as a result of different management styles, a language barrier that prevents free-flowing communication, a power differential, and a lack of awareness regarding rights, the result is lower productivity, higher attrition, a possible abridgement of rights, and a consequent low sense of morale in the workplace. These conditions, obviously, make *stakeholder engagement* difficult.

2. INTEGRATION, ESTABLISHMENT AND IMPLEMENTATION: CULTURAL SENSITIVITY TRAINING

Confronted with these significant barriers to healthy working relationships, Hauser considered her options. In lieu of asking the Vietnamese workers to modify their perceptions and to learn new communication skills, Hauser concluded that those in power had the responsibility to learn about those with whom they worked. Hauser developed an awareness campaign and, after training the top management staff from Nike footwear supplier sites in Vietnam, Indonesia and China (and simultaneously creating *top management commitment*), she was asked to go to the home offices of the suppliers in Korea and Taiwan. Currently, the cultural training program has been integrated into Nike's monitoring program called SHAPE ("Safety, Health, Attitude of Management, People Investment, Environment").

The cultural sensitivity campaign encompassed three segments. The training began by exploring the nature of a "culture." What is culture? We all are part of some culture but how do we define those cultures beyond simply food and language distinctions to differences in respect, relationships, communication styles and so on? For example, cultures differ based on whether they are future-oriented or past-oriented. This is critical to understand since a past-oriented culture will place great weight on how one has acted, while a future-oriented culture will place great weight on how one modifies her or his actions. The second segment of the training asked the participants to identify for themselves their own particular culture and its specific components. Finally, Hauser explores with the participants the nature of Vietnamese culture in order to allow them to better understand their subordinates.

She explains the impact of this type of awareness by referring to American culture and its impact on American workers. For instance, in the United States, we often hear about "The American Dream," insinuating that anything is possible; if one just reaches for a goal, s/he can attain it. However, consider the implications of these messages for American workers. Where a supervisor manages workers on the basis of this cultural belief system, any worker's failure must only be her or his own. If one can do anything, the failure to do something is also one's responsibility.

Moreover, if someone has a problem, that person is expected to speak up and voice the problem in an attempt to solve it. In other cultures, speaking up causes conflicts in two areas. First, it may be viewed as dull-witted since silence connotes wisdom and understanding. Second, in certain cultures, the individual with the problem expects the manager to know their problem, even if they have not voiced it. By voicing a problem, one may be implying that the manager did not know enough to be aware of that issue. Therefore, one may be insulting their manager if they raise a problem – not a good result. Also specifically "American" are the concepts of individualism and freedom of choice. As with those above, these values are not necessarily considered to be "positive" values in some other cultures. In a culture that focuses its attention on the past and is slow to forgive, mistakes such as these are not easily forgotten.

Hauser relates this to the Vietnamese situation by sharing the following example. One issue of cultural conflict has to do with the basic sounds of the different languages. Vietnamese is a language that is spoken in a soft, somewhat singsong, tone that has been compared to "birds chirping." Korean, on the other hand, is spoken quite boisterously. There were bound to be instances where, as a result of the language barrier, the Vietnamese workers misinterpreted a Korean manager's statement to be full of anger when it was simply basic speech.

Issues of age and respect also play a role in creating possible workplace conflicts. In Vietnam, no matter one's position, the younger worker owes strong respect to an older worker. Consequently, where a younger foreign supervisor managed an older Vietnamese line worker, the older worker may respond indignantly if the manager does not respect the cultural mores connected with age.

Another example of distinction refers to communication styles, as opposed to the words or sounds that are used. Hauser explains that the Korean and Taiwanese managers expressed concern that the Vietnamese workers were making mistakes but refused to accept responsibility for them. "They would deny it and I would ask them to admit it." They then found that the workers would giggle and laugh at them as they continued to try to get the worker to own up to his or her mistake. The managers explained that all they wanted was for the worker to accept responsibility and things would be all right.

Hauser was able to diffuse this type of conflict by explaining to the managers that, in Vietnamese culture, (1) reproach should be handled in private; (2) public reproach is the source of shame and embarrassment; (3) workers smile or giggle when they are embarrassed or ashamed; and (4) Vietnamese expect to have to pay harshly for their mistakes. Therefore, the managers learned that the more they reproached the individual for not accepting responsibility, the more likely it was that the worker would smile or laugh. As the manager would get more and more angry, the worker would continue to be ashamed and, therefore, smile. It was also very difficult for the Vietnamese workers to *trust* that they would not be fired when a manager expressed anger at a mistake.

As a resolution of this issue, Hauser did not suggest that the managers refrain from pointing out mistakes; instead she suggested through her training program that the reproach take place in a private area and that the trust would grow as workers were able to see that every mistake did not result in a termination. The response: "Aha! We had no idea!" Thus by sharing differences, Hauser was able to allow for greater understanding and compassion, and these *improvements* could be *integrated* into daily management practice.

Finally, cultural differences exist in connection with reporting violations. Predictably, when one feels that she or he is not protected by promises of due process, reporting a supervisor's violation is an extremely risky venture. Moreover, when that retribution may be inordinately more severe than the violation, one is discouraged from bearing that responsibility. In one instance, a journalist reported a violation by a Vietnamese line supervisor but refused to offer the person's name for fear of inappropriate punishment. In that situation, Nike resorted to retraining all management in this particular area.

3. INTEGRATION, ESTABLISHMENT AND IMPLEMENTATION: MANAGEMENT TRAINING

It is critical that these suppliers be able to promote from within to management positions since not only do expatriate managers often choose to return home after a stint overseas, but also because fewer and fewer managers choose to go into this industry and accept foreign postings. Consider today's young Taiwanese and Koreans. As education standards in their own countries have increased, these individuals are less likely to go into footwear manufacturing but instead will gravitate towards other, more attractive and lucrative industries such as those in the hi-tech arena. Therefore, there is a shortage of possible managers and these Korean- and Taiwanese-owned firms must be able to recruit management and supervisors from within their Vietnamese ranks.

As a result, while there was improved communication between expatriate managers and the Vietnamese workers, there was one additional challenge in connection with training that had been left unsolved. During newly implemented exit interviews, the suppliers were finding that Vietnamese workers who were promoted to first level supervisory roles found themselves in those roles with no management training. Therefore, they simply replicated some of the original management styles of the Korean and Taiwanese managers who first supervised them. They were often under the impression that this was what was expected of a manager and, if they failed to resemble the foreign management style, they might be fired.

In order to create a management training program appropriate for the Vietnamese workers, Hauser enlisted the assistance of a Vietnamese-American trainer named Tuan Nguyen, who was experienced in management training through Levi Strauss and other firms in the United States. Together, Hauser and Nguyen created and coordinated a five-day supervisor training program for Vietnamese workers. The training program was designed to improve the management abilities by enhancing self-awareness, improving communication skills, and working with cultural differences. Nike paid fully for a pilot of the weeklong program first with five workers from each factory. After responding to feedback from the pilot effort, Nguyen returned for twenty-two weeks, training 100 supervisors from each of the five participating factories. For this segment of the training, Nike covered two-thirds of the cost with the supplier covering one-third.

The aim of the program was to create a self-sustaining system where trainers were available in each factory, and training materials were tailored for each factory's needs, so that later training could be initiated and be fully paid for by the supplier. This *integration* into factory specific systems allows individual factories to develop the *improvement* process needed for their specific situation.

Currently, managers in many of Nike's suppliers receive support materials regarding some of these issues upon joining the factory. For instance, expatriate managers in one factory received a booklet entitled, "Vietnamese Language for Daily Communication." In this way, though all foreign managers or supervisors are required to learn the local language, they also have additional support tools to help in day-to-day operations. In one factory, Vietnamese line managers and above are chosen to participate in the factory's "Innovation School," where additional business skills are developed.

4. INDICATORS: CONTINUED PROGRAM ASSESSMENT

Currently each footwear factory in Vietnam conducts its own on-going supervisor training using the modified material. Continued regular dialogues with workers, departmental representatives and the trade unions, surveys, suggestion boxes and self-reviews provide *indicators* that allow Nike both to ascertain the efficacy of the programs as well as to identify areas that continue to need to be addressed. (In fact, one firm receives thousands of suggestions each month.) For instance, during one review, a problem was identified about gift-giving. It seems that Vietnamese culture dictates small gifts on certain occasions, holidays, accomplishments, and so on. The factory owner, a Korean, was unfamiliar with this practice so the workers simply believed that he chose not to do so. Once notified of this error, he instituted certain awards or benefits such as calendars, raincoats, or token amounts of money on appropriate occasions. The same challenge proved surmountable when one Korean factory president,

C.T. Park, realized that female workers no longer spoke to him and some even sneered at him from time to time. Later he learned that this "snub" treatment was the result of his failure to attend or even respond to their wedding invitations – a major cultural faux pas and one that could be easily ameliorated.[32]

One unexpected consequence of the training, however, is that workers are confused by the modified behavior. Hauser reports that workers have asked their supervisors, "Why are you like this now? Why are you treating me differently?" When asked to create additional training materials to help them to "integrate" into the workplace, Hauser responded that what was needed was not more training, but more problem-solving sessions that would empower the workers and the supervisors to jointly explore challenges and resolve issues on their own.

Notes

* Reprinted from *Rising Above Sweatshops*, Ed. Laura P. Hartman, Denis G. Arnold, and Richard E. Wokutch. Westport, Ct: Praeger Publishers, 2003, pp. 145–190. Used with permission.

1 Nike, Inc., "Corporate Responsibility Report, 2001," p. 1; *see also* Amanda Tucker, Nike Director of Compliance for the Americas, during presentation transcribed in Richard Wokutch, "Nike and Its Critics," *Organization & Environment*, v. 14, n. 2 (June 2001), pp. 207–237, 212.

2 Nike Annual Report 2001, http://www.nike.com/nikebiz/invest/reports/ar_01/pdfs/financials. pdf (accessed July 15, 2002).

3 Nike's code was second behind Levi Strauss, which disseminated its code in December, 1991.

4 Nike, "Code of Conduct," http://www.nike.com/nikebiz/nikebiz.jhtml?page=25&cat=compliance &subcat=code (accessed July 15, 2002).

5 Nike, "Code of Conduct," *supra* n. 4.

6 For Nike's explanation of this and other processes, as well as a Nike-produced visual tour inside one Nike contract supplier, see Nike, Inc., "An Online Look: Inside Nike's Contract Factories," http:// www.nike.com/nikebiz/nikebiz.jhtml?page=25&cat=overview&subcat=factorytour.

7 Discussion with Amanda Tucker, Director of Compliance, Nike, Inc., and Fukumi Hauser, Director of global compliance, monitoring and training (November 4, 2002) and email from Amanda Tucker (July 26, 2002).

8 Jeff Balinger, "Once again, Nike's voice looms larger than that of its workers," www. BehindTheLabel.org, http://www.behindthelabel.org/oped.php?story_id=22 (accessed July 15, 2002).

9 The World Bank International Economics Department, Development Data Group, *World Development Indicators* (1999).

10 http://www.nike.com/nikebiz/news/pressrelease.jhtml?year=2001&month=05&letter=g (accessed July 15, 2002) (link to speech at bottom of page). See also, http://cbae.nmsu.edu/ ~dboje/NIKphilspeech.html (accessed July 15, 2002).

11 http://cbae.nmsu.edu/~dboje/NIKphilspeech.html (accessed July 15, 2002); *see also* http:// www.nikebiz.com/labor/time.shtml.

12 Tim Connor, *Still Waiting for Nike to do it* (San Francisco, CA: Global Exhange 2001), http:// www.globalexchange.org/economy/corporations/nike/stillwaiting.html (accessed July 15, 2002), p. 1.

13 Tim Connor, *supra* n. 12 at p. 5.

14 For Nike's overview of the challenges and successes of these initiatives to date, see http:// www.nike.com/nikebiz/news/pr/2001/p_challenges.jhtml (accessed July 28, 2002).

15 Currently, there are over 100 individuals in Nike's Compliance Department, including more than 20 people permanently housed overseas.

16 Daniel Akst, "Nike in Indonesia, Through a Different Lens," *New York Times* (March 4, 2001), sec. 3 p. 4; Editorial, "Smelly Sneakers," *The Asian Wall Street Journal* (March 2, 2001), p. 6; "Knight Speaks Out on Improving Globalization," *Financial Times* (August 1, 2000), p. 15; Holger Jensen, "A Tale of Two Swooshes in Indonesia," Rockymountainnews.com, 7/2/2000 [related article in the *San Jose Mercury News* (July 5, 2000), p. B6]; David Lamb, "Economic Program Revitalizing Thailand's Countryside," *Los Angeles Times* (February 27, 2000), p. A34; Business Brief, "Indonesian Workers to Get Boost in Entry-Level Wages," *Wall Street Journal* (March 24, 1999), p. B2; Editorial, "For Citizens of Vietnam, Nike is the Place to Work," *Oregonian* (March 6, 1999), p. C7.

17 Dara O'Rourke, "Monitoring the Monitors: A Critique of PricewaterhouseCoopers Labor Monitoring" (Sept. 2000), http://web.mit.edu/dorourke/www/PDF/pwc.pdf (accessed July 15, 2002).

18 Jeff Balinger, "Once again, Nike's voice looms larger than that of its workers," *supra* n. 8.

19 Results of the report can be found at http://www.theglobalalliance.org/section.cfm/6/30 (accessed July 15, 2002).

20 "Envoy Defends Nike's Practices in Vietnam," *Financial Times* (April 12, 1999), p. 4.

21 Interview with Steve Hewitt, Nike-Vietnam, Corporate Responsibility Manager, 7/6/01.

22 Id.

23 "Nike Critic Praises Gains in Air Quality at Vietnam Factory," *New York Times* (March 12, 1999), p. C3.

24 Nike has done business with many of the same Vietnamese suppliers for over twenty-five years.

25 Conversation with Dusty Kidd, April 27, 2001.

26 Phil Knight, "New Labor Initiatives," (May 12, 1998), text at http://cbae.nmsu.edu/~dboje/NIKphilspeech.html (accessed July 15, 2002), also reported in "PBS Newshour," http://www.pbs.org/newshour/forum/may98/nike.html (accessed July 15, 2002) (confirmed in discussions with Dusty Kidd). For additional information on the loan program, see http://www.nike.com/nikebiz/nikebiz.jhtml?page=26&item=asia (accessed July 15, 2002) and http://www.nike.com/nikebiz/nikebiz.jhtml?page=25&cat=communityprograms&subcat=smbizloans (accessed July 15, 2002).

27 Women's Opportunity Fund, http://www.womensopportunityfund.org/Pages/main_what.html, reprinted with permission of the Women's Opportunity Fund.

28 GoodWorks International, LLC, "Report: The Nike Code of Conduct" (1997), pp. 33, 47–8.

29 Tim Connor, "A Response to Andrew Young's report into Nike's Code of Conduct," The Nike-Watch Campaign at Oxfam Community Aid Abroad, http://www.caa.org.au/campaigns/nike/young.html (accessed July 15, 2002); Campaign for Labor Rights, "The Andrew Young/Good Works Report on Nike," *Labor Alerts* (June 28, 1997), http://www.hartford-hwp.com/archives/26/004.html (accessed July 15, 2002); Eric Lourmand, "Nike drops the Ball: The Andrew Young Report," http://www-personal.umich.edu/~lormand/poli/nike/nike101-5.htm (accessed July 15, 2002).

30 Lynn Kahle, et al., "Good Morning, Vietnam: An Ethical Analysis of Nike Activities in Southeast Asia," *Sport Marketing Quarterly*, vol. 9, no. 1 (2000), pp. 43–52.

31 Nike, Inc., "Corporate Responsibility Report, 2001," p. 35.

32 Samantha Marchall, "Executive Action: Cultural Sensitivity on the Assembly Line," *Asian Wall Street Journal* (Feb. 25, 2000).

6.3 Started as Crew
McDonald's Strategy for Corporate Success and Poverty Reduction[*]

The following case contains background on the development of poverty as a strategic concern of multinational corporations, as well as a historical perspective on McDonald's Corporation. The main case then explores in detail McDonald's corporate culture and its emphasis on promotion from within. It then provides a relatively brief overview of two particular experiences in this culture: Darlene Calhoun's rise to responsibility and success from her position as a night shift cashier, and Jan Fields' choice to take a part-time position at McDonald's, which was the first step en route to her role as Chief Operations Officer for McDonald's USA. Appendices A and B include far more detailed case studies on both Calhoun and Fields for those who seek additional information or who prefer to read and/or teach these cases on a stand-alone basis.

From the early 1970s to the beginning of the 21st century, multinational corporations (MNCs) had increasingly participated in the reduction of poverty as part of their business strategies. Such participation reflected an increasing awareness of the widening gap between rich and poor across the globe. It also revealed a growing understanding of the commercial potential of responding to the needs of those who lived at the bottom of the economic pyramid.[1] As Stuart Hart pointed out, there was significant "potential for a new private sector-based approach to development that creates profitable businesses that simultaneously raise the quality of life for the world's poor, respect cultural diversity, and conserve ecological integrity of the planet for future generations."[2]

Understanding Poverty[3]

On the surface, poverty was a simple concept. MSN Encarta on-line Dictionary defined it as the "state of being poor: the state of not having enough money to take care of basic needs such as food, clothing, and housing." Questions and debates arose almost immediately about the causes and appropriate measurements of poverty. Although not a comprehensive list, it was generally accepted that poverty resulted from some combination of the following: hunger, famine, and malnutrition; lack of education and illiteracy; gender; lack of land ownership; lack of access to clean water; and war and political instability.

Measurements of poverty focused on absolute poverty and relative poverty. Absolute poverty measurements were concerned with identifying a minimum standard of living below which an individual was deemed to be poor. Relative poverty attempted to identify income disparity and focused on the gap between rich and poor within economies or economic regions as well as across economies, in an effort to understand global poverty. The standard or threshold for absolute poverty was translated into a dollar amount and raised questions about the methods used to gather data and the adequacy of the threshold itself. In the United States, poverty thresholds were expressed in terms of household income. In 2008, the thresholds were $10,210 annually for an individual and $20,650 annually for a family of four.[4]

Measures for global poverty were based on purchasing power parity (PPP). Though PPP was widely accepted as the standard measurement, efforts were ongoing to ensure that data obtained were seen as more accurate and reliable.[5] In 2007, research conducted by Shaohua Chen and Martin Ravallion of the World Bank Development Research Group[6] indicated that the number of people with a PPP of $1 a day or less "fell below 1 billion for the first time in 2004. However, progress has been slower for the $2 line. The number of people living below the $2 line actually rose over most of the period, only falling briefly in the mid-1990s and since the end of the 1990s."[7] More than 2.5 billion people—approximately 48% of the world's population—had a PPP of $2 or less per day. Approximately 18% of the world's population—969 million people—had a PPP of $1 or less per day.[8] See Exhibit 6.3.1 for the geographical distribution of people living on PPP $2 or less a day in 2004.

MNCs and Poverty Reduction

Though some progress had been made in reducing global poverty, many argued that it was too slow. Critics questioned whether traditional development efforts alone could make significant and timely inroads in poverty reduction. As noted above, many people were convinced that bringing the power of the market to bear on the issue of poverty was a more effective strategy in the fight against global poverty. In particular, they argued that MNCs were well suited for this task, given their economic power and transnational reach.

Exhibit 6.3.1

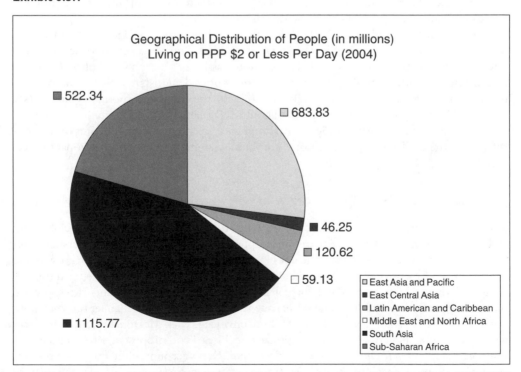

Source: Shaohua Chen and Martin Ravallion, "Absolute Poverty Measures for the Developing World, 1981–2004." *Proceedings of the National Academy of Sciences* 104, no. 43 (23 October 2007).

MNCs were, however, often perceived as suspicious partners in poverty-reduction efforts. Those traditionally involved in such efforts were often skeptical because of previously well-publicized patterns of exploitation by some business interests. Others considered poverty reduction to be tangential to core business interests and dismissed claims about the potential of the market to respond to these fundamental human needs.

In the face of this skepticism, it might have seemed counterintuitive that fast food giant McDonald's Corporation was an unintentional but active participant in poverty reduction. After all, conventional wisdom seemed to dictate that, although most fast food industry jobs might provide some supplemental household income or pocket money, they offered few, if any, prospects for upward mobility. It was this belief that led to the coining of the term "McJob," which *Merriam-Webster's Collegiate Dictionary* defined as "a low-paying job that requires little skill and provides little opportunity for advancement." Though McDonald's strongly objected to this term as inaccurate and denigrating to its work force, the fact remained that an unwelcome consequence of being a "Quintessential American Brand" was the negative connotation given to words prefaced with "Mc," such as "McMansion."[9] This same iconic status was "exactly what ma[de] the corporation a daunting target for human rights activists," according to Michael Moore in a report on efforts by the Student/Farm-worker Alliance (SFA) to raise awareness of the "near-slavery conditions" Florida farm workers were subjected to while picking tomatoes for the fast food restaurant.[10]

Given these and other negative perceptions, how could a company in an industry historically known for low-paying, dead-end jobs make any contribution to alleviating poverty, especially as part of its business plan? Was it possible that conventional wisdom was wrong?[11] Could a crew job at McDonald's lead to career advancement for more than a select few? Was it possible for McDonald's to have a business strategy that was successful by Wall Street standards and that also contributed to significant wealth creation, not just for shareholders, but also for employees and other stakeholders as well?

Groomed in the tradition of McDonald's founder Ray Kroc, Jan Fields, executive vice president and chief operations officer of McDonald's USA, Peter Breckenridge, development director of Southern Australia, and Darlene Calhoun, assistant supervisor of Lofton & Lofton Management, were among many employees whose stories demonstrated that it was possible to begin as crew and progress through the ranks to the highest corporate positions (see Appendix A and Appendix B). What was it about McDonald's business strategy that enabled the company to be successful in the industry and to contribute to the reduction of poverty? What were the challenges to the company's business strategy, and how did McDonald's meet them?

Ray Kroc: Mr. McDonald's

Ray Kroc lived the classic American rags-to-riches story. In 1954, the high school dropout and Multimixer milkshake-machine salesman approached the McDonald brothers and presented his plan to put Multimixer machines in their restaurants as a strategy for growth and expansion. To Kroc's surprise, the brothers were uninterested in expansion, preferring simply to live off their single location and current limited franchising arrangements. Kroc pressed them, suggesting they find someone to manage their franchises rather than let the enormous potential of the restaurants go to waste. Still unconvinced, Dick McDonald wanted to know who they might find to open the additional franchises Kroc proposed. Kroc recalled his response in *Grinding it Out: The Making of McDonald's*, his account of the rise of the restaurant chain: "I sat there feeling a sense of certitude begin to envelop me. Then I leaned forward and said, 'Well, what about me?' "[12]

Seven years and more than 238 stores later, Kroc bought the rights to the McDonald's name from the brothers and accelerated the expansion of the booming chain. In the same year, Kroc and Fred Turner, a former grill man who had risen through the ranks to become the vice president of operations, began sending store manager candidates to training courses in the basement of an Elk Grove Village, Illinois, restaurant. The training center, named Hamburger University, was one of the nation's first "corporate universities." In the years that followed, it continued to play an important role in fostering and enhancing the esprit de corps and passion for the business that explained both the success of so many people who started as crew and the success of the company. By 2006, McDonald's corporate-owned and franchised locations had expanded to more than 31,000 restaurants in 119 countries and catered to more than 54 million customers each day.

It was not just veteran employees of McDonald's Corporation who recognized the impact that Ray Kroc had and continued to have on corporate culture. From the first day on the job, employees learned about McDonald's hardworking culture—a culture that started with Kroc. "If you know anything about Ray Kroc," Steve Russell, senior vice president for human resources, observed:

> You know he was a work-hard kind of person. When he went to a restaurant, he'd roll up his sleeves and he'd work. He literally would get the hose out and spray the parking lot, if the parking lot was not clean, and this was when he was the head of a big organization. It just wasn't in the beginning.[13]

This work-hard attitude was coupled with an emphasis on performance and promotion based on merit. Fields was clear that it was "not relationships or who you are or your educational background or pedigree or anything like that" that determined your advancement in the company.[14] It was merit. Russell confirmed this sentiment: "Individuals who work hard are the ones that advance within the restaurant, and advance beyond the restaurant." That this merit-based attitude permeated McDonald's culture was not surprising given Ray Kroc's iconic imprint on the company. It was an imprint that went beyond the attention to detail and the systems and structures he put into place. "The four pillars on which Kroc built the McDonald's empire were quality, service, cleanliness, and value,"[15] but it went beyond that. It had to do with the man himself, with his energy and commitment, with his integrity, with his philosophy of life.

" 'If you work just for money, you'll never make it,' Kroc was known for saying. 'But if you love what you're doing and you always put the customer first, success will be yours.' "[16] "Krocisms," as they were fondly called, abounded: "Free enterprise will work if you will"; "If you act like a leader and feel like a leader, you are a leader"; "It's not what you do but the way you do it."[17] The "McDonald's Mystique" and the pervasiveness of Kroc's influence, which was detailed in a 1988 *Fortune* magazine article, lived on. Employees who did not know Kroc personally still felt connected to him.[18] Steve Eng, who joined McDonald's after Kroc's 1984 death, said he was "able to comprehend Kroc's passion and spirit by word-of-mouth inspiration from other McDonald's owner-operators."[19]

Elements of Success

Although there were many factors that contributed to the success of McDonald's, three were particularly vital: the company's strong corporate culture, McDonald's renowned training program, and its tradition of promoting from within. These same factors also played a role in the company's ability to contribute to the reduction of poverty, not simply through its many philanthropic activities, but as a direct result of its business strategy.

Ray Kroc was without doubt *the* iconic figure within McDonald's culture, but he was not the only person whose story shaped the culture of the company. Past and current CEOs Fred Turner, Charlie Bell, and Jim Skinner were legendary figures who each contributed to shaping that environment. Though they were the most well known, there were also other people and factors that continued to contribute to McDonald's hardworking, service-oriented, people-centered culture. Darlene Calhoun was among them.[20]

When Calhoun began working at McDonald's in 1977, she was not looking for a career. The main attraction was flexible hours. She and her family were living in Portland, Oregon, where her husband, who was in the military, was stationed. Neither of them was comfortable leaving their child in day care. Her husband worked during the day, so she took a job as a cashier on the night shift, which ensured that one of them would always be home with their daughter. It was at a time when the family was relocated every six to eight months, and Calhoun soon realized that McDonald's offered more than flexible hours. It offered mobility as well. Despite the fact that she continued to work at McDonald's, she did not have any career aspirations. As she saw it at the time, her job simply provided a good opportunity for her to supplement the household income and meet the needs of her family. (For stand-alone case on Darlene Calhoun and additional details, please see Appendix 6.3A.)

Jan Fields, who after three decades at McDonald's was well on her way to becoming another legend, told a similar story. Married right out of high school, she had decided not to attend college. With her husband in the armed forces, she needed to get a job to earn money for college tuition and to help support the family. It was 1977, and Fields was on her way to a job interview when she walked into a McDonald's restaurant to get a Coke. While she sat in the restaurant killing time before her interview, she noticed a sign on the milkshake machine. "Now hiring, flexible hours," it promised. She asked the manager what flexible hours meant. As she recalled, he answered, "Whatever you want them to mean. We need people at lunch-time, we need people at night." She filled out the application and started work the next day. In 2006, with almost 30 years of service, she became executive vice president and chief operations officer of McDonald's USA.

For someone who was not an immediate fit with the McDonald's environment, it was quite an accomplishment. Her first day as a "crewmember" left her doubting her potential at McDonald's. "I literally cried when I got home," she remembered. Afraid she would be unable to keep up with the rigorous pace of the shift and the strict rules governing the preparation of the company's famous french fries, she told her husband she would not make it at McDonald's. Then she got a call asking her to work the next evening. She agreed and found herself operating the cash register. At the end of the evening, she was asked to help close. "I didn't know what that meant, so I asked and they said, 'Do dishes.' I'm a clean freak, even to this day, so I thought, 'Yeah, okay,' and the rest is history."

Eventually Fields mastered each crew position, including the infamous french fries. She quickly learned the benefits of teamwork, particularly when she was helping to close and wanted to get home to her family. Her hard work and team spirit did not go unnoticed. Within months of starting at the restaurant, she was offered a management position.

At the time, Fields helped her husband support the family on a meager budget, but she did not consider herself poor. "You don't know that you are . . . you just live on what you have." Her husband, then an officer in the U.S. Air Force, made an annual salary of $5,600. As the primary shopper, Fields fed her young family on a $50 monthly grocery budget. The income from her job at McDonald's helped with expenses, including her college tuition. She had decided to finish college and was promoted several times when, as she puts it, "it got to a point, after almost 10 years, where I finally ended up saying, I guess I'm making a career out of this. I'm here." (For stand-alone case on Jan Fields and additional details, please see Appendix 6.3B.)

Components of Value

As satisfying as it was on a personal level to have completed her degree, it was not the degree that led to Jan Fields's success; rather, it was her willingness to work hard and her passion for the business. As Jack Daly, senior vice president of corporate relations, pointed out, "Some people think it's just tedious burger-flipping and some people catch the whole act. And if you catch the whole act, you'll rise very quickly. There aren't a lot of barriers; there aren't a lot of educational barriers."[21]

Darlene Calhoun eventually caught the act. She had been a McDonald's cashier for two years when her husband was transferred to San Diego, California. As she had in the past, she found a position with a local McDonald's restaurant. This time it was not a franchisee restaurant; it was a "McOpCo," the McDonald's term for a company-owned restaurant (a McDonald's-Operated Company). As a crew member in the San Diego store, Calhoun had the opportunity to participate in on-site training programs, which involved studying the management development books and working one on one with a restaurant manager to learn the skills needed to work the various positions. As Calhoun recalled, "You had to be a self-starter, you had to train yourself." Her efforts did not go unnoticed. Within three months of starting in the San Diego store, she moved from cashier to shift manager. "I didn't aspire to do that, but they saw something in me, and they sort of pushed me along," she said.

When her husband left the service, the family moved back to Chicago. Once again, Calhoun found a neighborhood McDonald's that was hiring. This time, it was back to an owner-operator store. The owner was a first-time operator, who had been advised by the field person that "this lady has some experience; maybe she can help you run the store." Indeed, Calhoun did just that. Being in Chicago provided Calhoun the opportunity to participate in formal training programs and to attend Hamburger University. Eventually, she finished her classes and earned a promotion to store manager. She learned that the classes were accredited and remembered thinking, "Fine, I can use that toward something else." She had been back in Chicago for five years and was a store manager, but still "hadn't decided to make it a career."

McDonald's was serious about and valued education. But formal education per se was not an automatic passport to success. Richard Floersch, vice president and chief human resources officer, explained that despite regular interaction on a professional level, most of the top executives never discussed their educations. "Nobody ever talks about where they went to school," he said, "even here in corporate. It's not even talked about. It just isn't part of our culture."[22]

In fact, it became evident that overemphasizing formal education had a detrimental effect on the corporate culture. In the late 1990s, companies placed a great deal of importance on MBAs. McDonald's was no exception and the company hired a number of MBAs for high-level positions. Whether intentional or not, this conveyed the message that hard work and passion for the business were no longer enough; what was required was an MBA. "It was so countercultural," according to legend-in-the-making Jan Fields, "I felt like I wasn't going to go anywhere because of all these MBAs. I felt outclassed by them." Many people who had risen through the ranks stopped mentioning this aspect of their McDonald's career, which reinforced the perception that without an MBA, upward mobility was no longer possible. This undermined the strong focus on diversity.

At McDonald's, Fields said, diversity was not simply about nationality, race, ethnicity, or gender. It was also about respect for and inclusion of people with different educational backgrounds, both formal and informal. Formal education was valued—after all, McDonald's had made the effort to have many of the Hamburger University courses approved for college credit by the American Council on Education (ACE)[23]—but education based on experience and training was equally valued, as Darlene Calhoun's success attested. The emphasis on and pride in having "started as crew" permeated McDonald's culture and reinforced realistic hopes that upward mobility was available to all.

Hamburger University

McDonald's centralized training program, founded in 1961, grew to become one of the most globally recognized corporate training programs. The company invested $1.2 billion per year in training programs, which were an essential component of the corporation's business model. The emphasis on and quality of training made it possible for McDonald's to maintain consistently high standards of service and quality across the globe. Uniformly high standards were a hallmark of the company's success. Wherever they found themselves across the globe, customers came to expect the same McDonald's quality of service and food. The fact that customers were rarely disappointed was, in large measure, due to the systemized, continuous training that employees at all levels received.

Quality control was not the only benefit that came from emphasis on training. There were other benefits as well, though sometimes they were less obvious. The programs reinforced the McDonald's culture and the team approach that was central to smooth restaurant operations. In addition, they left no room to doubt the diversity that was present throughout the company. The legal department with its staff of 140 attorneys was a good example. Of those, 50% were women. The figure was higher in the United States where 60% of attorneys were women and 20% were minorities.[24] Diversity was, arguably, most visible in the Hamburger University classroom.

Class sizes of 10 to 12 students in the 1960s boomed to 200 or more in 2008, as the value of corporate training was recognized as a means of personal and professional growth and more employees took advantage of the program and the upward mobility it offered. With campuses in cities across the world, including Sydney, Munich, London, Hong Kong, Tokyo, and Rio de Janeiro, Hamburger University saw its enrollment grow from 14 in 1961 to approximately 5,000 in 2007. As of January 2008, approximately 80,000 McDonald's employees from around the globe had graduated from the program.

Richard Ellis, vice president, U.S. communications, who hailed from Canada, stressed that the potential for growth and advancement was borderless. Visitors to Hamburger University's Oak Brook, Illinois, campus saw, according to Ellis, "the people that we circle in and out of class every day, and the number of languages that are spoken. It's crazy what we do. It's so amazing, what we do. That's a lot of the reason why people who hit their stride and understand what McDonald's offers stay with the company."[25]

Part of that understanding was recognizing the need to take personal initiative. Regardless of a person's position in the company or his or her background, it was clear that personal initiative and responsibility for growth and development was essential. Jan Fields was adamant: "You have an obligation, at every level, to do personal development. And it's your personal responsibility. It's not mine to teach you. It's mine to provide opportunities for you, to pay for them, but the fact of the matter is that you've got to be the one. I can't make you learn." Ray Frawley, president of McDonald's Korea, echoed this view, "You join McDonald's in a part-time role or full time in the stores, but where it leads, who knows. What we need to do is to make sure we give people the opportunity. Once given the opportunity, the people really rise to the occasion to become really great long-term employees."[26] Calhoun agreed. "The only thing that would hold somebody back is themselves, because the opportunity is there," she said. "If you want it, regardless of whether you're in a McOpCo or a licensee [restaurant], the opportunity is there."

The seriousness with which McDonald's Corporation took this obligation to provide opportunities for employees was widely recognized. In 2005, McDonald's UK received a profile award from Investors in People, a nondepartmental public body, sponsored by the U.K. Department for Education and Skills. The Work Foundation, a London-based nonprofit research and advocacy group, also recognized the company for recruiting "young people for their qualities rather than qualifications and providing them with valuable skills to boost their position in the labour market."[27] That same year, the Queensland Training Awards presented McDonald's Australia the Large Employer of the Year Award at the regional finals.[28] On the other side of the globe, "McDonald's was ranked as a Best Employer in Latin America in both Mexico and Venezuela by *AméricaEconomía* business magazine and Hewitt Associates, and the Latin-American organization overall was cited by the Great Place to Work® Institute."[29]

There was no doubt that training and education was an integral component of McDonald's overall business strategy, and individual employees appreciated the personal growth and development that it encouraged. Shelly Hicks, human resources manager for the Ohio region McOpCo, never felt like a college degree was a requirement for success. But when she realized that the classes she had completed at Hamburger University tallied up to a full year of college credits, she enrolled in University of Phoenix's online program and earned a bachelor's degree. Hicks went on to enroll in Penn State's MBA program and was named Adult Learner of the Year for 2005 by ACE.[30]

Although he had the same training as Hicks—completion of both the Hamburger University program and a traditional degree program—the path taken by Peter Breckenridge, development director of Southern Australia, had a different twist. Breckenridge, who was from Nunawading, Australia, was 16 when he began working at McDonald's to fund his college tuition. The flexibility of a position at McDonald's enabled him to keep pace with his studies in electrical engineering. Before he knew it, he found himself rising through the ranks and using his college breaks to attend classes at McDonald's Sydney campus. By the time he finished his traditional degree in electrical engineering, he also held a diploma in management from Hamburger University. He put both disciplines to use in identifying locations for new store construction and worked to expand McDonald's presence in his region. Asked about his long-term goals, Breckenridge, who attributed his success at McDonald's to his Hamburger University training, was forward-thinking. "I hope one day to head up McDonald's Australia," he replied.[31]

The stories of Hicks, Breckenridge, Calhoun, and other employees highlighted their awareness of and appreciation for the personal and professional benefit they gained from the company's emphasis on training and education. But the strategic importance of this training could not be overlooked. These programs were responsible for the quality and uniformity of service at McDonald's restaurants around the world. They strengthened the camaraderie and commitment to the corporate culture. They also provided a steady stream of skilled people who could and did advance to leadership positions in the company.

Promotion from Within

One might argue that the degree to which McDonald's promoted from within was the company's best-kept secret, given the perceptions that jobs at McDonald's were dead-ends.

In the United States, 70% of store managers began their careers as crew, as did 50% of corporate staff. In the United Kingdom, the rate was even higher, with 80% of store managers having started as crew.[32] Even in India, 40% of the middle management team started as crew.[33] The personal pride that came from having risen through the ranks was part of the McDonald's culture. At executive meetings, the 40% of executive officers who began as crewmembers wore bright red "Started as Crew!" pins, denoting the achievement they had made in climbing the organization's career ladder. When defining the values that had created this atmosphere at McDonald's, executives were often at a loss for words. Though they regularly invoked the images of Ray Kroc, Charlie Bell, Fred Turner, and other former crewmembers, for the most part, they pointed to the stories of hundreds of owner-operators who began working at McDonald's and became business owners themselves after learning the discipline and dedication required to run a restaurant through their careers at McDonald's.

The tradition of rising through the ranks was obviously part of the corporate culture. It was, at the same time, an important component of the company's success. Firsthand experience with the day-to-day operations of the restaurant was a valuable tool for management. It provided an understanding of how the basic product that brought the public through the doors was delivered. It raised an awareness of the workload and the level of skill required for each of the various functions, including dealing with the public. It also led to a better understanding of and appreciation for the values of the corporation and the people who were the backbone of the business.

Hands-on experience was so valued that when people who did not have that experience were brought into the company, one of the essential pieces of their orientation was working in a restaurant for a period of time. This was true at all levels of management. Cesar Martinez, human resources officer for McDonald's Latin America, remembered how impressed he was. "When you're working shoulder to shoulder with the crew at the grill, you realize who the true heroes of this company are—the managers and employees in the restaurant."[34] All new corporate hires were assigned to a local restaurant. "They spend 30 to 90 days as crew persons, learning each of the restaurant's stations and developing a respect for the difficulty of the position," according to Russell. He sees this as crucial: "The process of placing new members of the McDonald's team in stores ensures a dramatic enculturation that leaves little room for misunderstanding. An employee who cannot fit into the McDonald's culture was very likely to crash." Executives so valued the experience that many periodically went back to the stores where they trained. Indeed, as Russell reported, "some even take periodic breaks to work in the store again."

Another strategic advantage of promotion from within was in the area of recruitment and retention of employees. Skilled, dependable, and enthusiastic workers were at the heart of the business. Many factors played a role in successfully recruiting and retaining them. One of these factors was providing possibilities for personal and professional growth and development. The "Started as Crew!" pins were a visible sign to potential and existing employees that at McDonald's, those opportunities were real. Even more effective "signs" were successful employees like Darlene Calhoun.

Calhoun had been at the Chicago store for about seven years when it was sold. When word spread, she was offered positions by other operators in the area, but she decided to stick it out with the new owner, Ron Lofton. It was a tough transition year. Unlike her previous boss who only owned the one store, Lofton had a number of stores, which meant adjusting to new people and a new environment. It also meant new challenges, opportunities, and more responsibility. After a year or so, she said to herself, "Okay, I can do this." It was only at that point that she recognized that she had a career at McDonald's.

Challenges

Rankings and ratings made it clear that McDonald's Corporation was a successful company. As with any successful company, there were challenges. These included among other things facing MNCs' negative perceptions about the business; recruitment and retention of employees; and career opportunity differentials. Arguably, the most challenging of these was responding to the widely held negative perceptions of the company. The criticisms tended to be focused on resistance to the fast food industry in general and the nature of the work, in particular, which had come to be known pejoratively as the "McJob."

At one level it was a mark of the company's success that it became a lightning rod for criticisms of the fast food industry, though that was little comfort for employees and executives who were the target of such criticisms. The term "McJob" was coined by Douglas Copland in his 1991 best seller *Generation X: Tales for an Accelerated Culture*. Copland defined a McJob as "a low-paying, low-prestige, low-dignity, low-benefit, no-future job in the service sector."[35]

By 2003, the term "McJob" had become so accepted that it appeared in the new edition of Merriam-Webster's collegiate dictionary. The reaction from McDonald's was strong and immediate. Jim Cantalupo, then CEO of McDonald's International, criticized the publisher for the entry, which defined the word as slang for "a low-paying job that requires little skill and provides little opportunity for advancement." In an open letter to Merriam-Webster, Cantalupo said that the "the term is 'an inaccurate description of restaurant employment' and 'a slap in the face to the 12 million men and women' who work in the restaurant industry."[36]

As if including the term "McJob" in the dictionary was not enough of a challenge, its use in the media and elsewhere continued to vex employees and executives alike. On "The X-Factor," a popular reality television show in the United Kingdom, judges used the phrase "You're worth nothing more than a job in a McDonald's" when insulting contestants.[37] David Fairhurst, a McDonald's UK vice president, claimed that there was "a huge gap [that] exists between the external perception and the internal reality of working for McDonald's. The simple fact is our employer reputation isn't justified."[38] Noting that Copland referenced the service sector in general, not McDonald's in particular, Fairhurst, however, realistically acknowledged, "we have to accept that this association exists, and correct it."[39]

Chris Nichols, owner of two Colorado restaurants, asked, "How many teachers have you heard say, 'you better study or you'll be flipping burgers for the rest of your life'?" His response was, "I flip burgers for a living and I'll match my salary against anybody's."[40] There was no denying that the stereotypical image that the term "McJob" evoked was a difficult one to overcome. Ignoring the issue, however, was not an option, given the effects that such negative stereotypes could have. Riding the greater wave of anti-fast-food sentiment and the upward-sloping trend of obesity in the United States and across Western Europe, the public contempt for a crew position at McDonald's reached a critical mass in the late 1990s, with annual turnover for crew positions were between 300% and 400%.[41]

The industry as a whole faced challenges in recruitment and retention. Some were directly related to negative perceptions of the industry, but they were not the only concern. In the United States for example, "teen participation in the job market fell 4.1% to 44.1% compared with 48.2% a year ago [August 2004]. In July [2005], the level fell to an all-time low of 43.8% on a seasonally adjusted basis."[42] This presented a challenge given U.S. Department of Labor reports that one-fourth of the 6.5 million food-and-beverage workers were between the ages of 16 and 19 and that job openings would continue to increase through 2012.[43]

Another challenge for McDonald's, at least in the United States, was the potential differential in compensation and other benefits as well as in career opportunities between company-owned and operator-owned stores. For example, McDonald's USA had four different health plans. Employees in McOpCo restaurants could choose from all four of them. In operator-owned stores, the operators determined which benefits were offered; and some of them limited the plans they offered. But the vast majority of operator-owners were like Calhoun's boss: "Ron doesn't have to do these things, you know," she reminded people. "But he provides for us well, with benefits, vacations, whatever."

A related challenge, one that Russell viewed as a "real world" one, was addressing the needs of employees who chose to forego participation in the available health plans. "Although we've done a tremendous job leveraging our size and our scale to really deliver quality benefits at as low a cost as we can," he said, "these individuals are in such an awful situation that they're choosing between food and health insurance. Well we all know what somebody in that position would choose. I know what I would choose; I would choose food." Russell and others wanted to move forward aggressively to tackle this situation.

Addressing the Challenges

As a corporation, McDonald's had been strategic in its response to these challenges. This was most obvious in the media campaigns launched to debunk the "McJob" stereotypes. McDonald's UK created a series of advertisements that highlighted the benefits of a "McJob." Each ended with the tagline, "Not bad for a McJob." There were 18 posters in the series, each with a counterclaim. Examples included:

- "McProspects—over half our Executive Team started in our restaurants. Not bad for a McJob;"
- "McOpportunity—two pay reviews in your first year. Not bad for a McJob;"
- "McFlexible—we've enough shift patterns to suit almost every lifestyle. Not bad for a McJob."[44]

In late 2005, following on the success of the "I'm lovin' it" campaign, which increased sales and employee retention rates, the company kicked off its "My First" campaign, created by the Chicago-based ad agency Leo Burnett, to further respond to the negative perceptions about working at McDonald's. Used in markets around the world, ads featured the likes of Olympic gold medalist Carl Lewis, Japanese artist Suguru Otake, late-night television talk-show host Jay Leno, Amazon.com CEO Jeff Bezos, and Grammy-award-winning singer Shania Twain. According to Larry Light, the executive vice president and global chief marketing officer who oversaw the "My First" ads, the "campaign is intended to inspire our employees, attract new ones, and show our customers that if you begin your career at McDonald's, the sky is the limit."[45]

Although the media campaigns were helpful, strategies for meeting the recruitment and retention challenge went well beyond advertisements. The perception was that McDonald's was a minimum-wage employer, but Ellis insisted, "That's not true. We are not a minimum-wage employer. Does that mean we don't sometimes pay minimum wage? Of course it doesn't." In any given region, wages were often better than average. Nichols, who employed slightly more than 100 people, says "midlevel managers can take home $35,000 a year and top managers in Craig and Steamboat [Colorado] make in excess of $70,000 a year including benefits."[46] "More than 80% of the chain's U.K. staff received above the minimum hourly wage while half of restaurant managers earn [British pounds] GBP40,000 a year or more."[47] In 2003, McDonald's employees earned approximately 29% more than the average wage paid by the Brazilian food industry.[48] In addition, McDonald's corporate-owned restaurants, as well as many franchised locations, took advantage of a large package of employee benefits aimed at training and retaining valuable employees. Many of the programs started regionally and, after some testing within the company, spread throughout the 119 countries in which McDonald's had operations.

In the United States, McDonald's bolstered the incentive to participate in traditional employee programs such as health insurance and 401(k) programs. To ensure a slower increase in health care premiums for in-store employees, top executives in the company had, from the mid-1990s to 2008, accepted 25% to 30% increases in their own insurance premiums. This enabled the company to keep increases in premiums for store managers to 1% to 5% during the same time period.

When a study revealed a surprisingly low enrollment in 401(k) plans, the company began offering better incentives for participation. Realizing that the 1% salary commitment was keeping many employees from enrolling, McDonald's gave all eligible employees a one-time raise of 1% of salary; it then offered a 3% match to that 1% contribution. Employees could commit as much as 4% of their salaries to the investment program, which was met by McDonald's at 7%, an unheard of contribution in the foodservice industry. As employees become eligible, they were automatically enrolled in the program, although they were free to opt out. As a result of the changes, store managers' enrollment in the program increased from 41% to 93%.

Other benefits offered included some that targeted "real-world" issues, which concerned Russell and other senior executives. Among these were the Gold Card and the McResource Line. The Gold Card, which could be used at more than 60 different retail stores, provided employees with discounts on products that ranged from footwear to prescription drugs. Russell saw this as a "real-life benefit" for the 365,000 McOpCo employees who participated in the program, which was free. The McResource Line, another free benefit for McOpCo employees, was "a resource that provides real-time telephone help to an individual—crew person or whomever—who needs help," for example, finding babysitters, obtaining financial counseling, and locating housing.

Beyond traditional employee incentive programs, McDonald's instituted several options for employees working with difficult schedules. In the United Kingdom, McDonald's introduced the Family Contract. The program made it possible for family members who worked at the same location to switch shifts without having to give supervisors prior notice. Rita Cross and her two teenage daughters, who were from Cardiff, Wales, were the first to take advantage of the program. According to Cross, the entire family benefited from "a better work and life balance."[49] The program led to less absenteeism and stress for employees, who appreciated the greater ability to juggle work and other commitments.

Students employed in some franchise locations in the United States were paid to do their schoolwork on the job. Whether in high school or college, students working at either of the two Michigan stores owned by Kathy and Jerry Olinik could "stay on the clock for an extra hour before or after their shifts."[50] The only condition was that they spend the time studying. As Jerry Olinik noted, "Kids are our future. Anything we can do to support that is the responsible thing to do."[51] The Oliniks were not alone. In Wisconsin, one owner "lets students stay on the clock to participate in a study group. Owners in North Carolina and Virginia allow employees to take English language classes as part of their shifts." Ellen Galinsky, who was the president of the Families and Work Institute, pointed out the obvious: They not only benefited students, they assisted with recruitment and retention.[52]

Another recruitment and retention strategy focused on identifying applicants who were the right fit for the job and for the company. Given the focus on youth in entry-level positions, strategies were developed that recognized their cyberspace lifestyles. In Australia, McDonald's was the largest employer of youth. In 2006, the company "launched 'metime,' a fully integrated online recruitment, induction, and training system for its 730 restaurants across Australia."[53] Frank McManus said, " 'metime' allows a candidate to find out what McDonald's has to offer from an employment perspective, if the restaurant of their choice was currently hiring and even allows them to apply to a number of restaurants in one hit thereby saving time."[54] The United States had a similar program called, Hiring to Win. "It's built on selecting people that will succeed in our culture," according to Russell. The response to both programs was positive.

For Russell, these and other benefits reflected the fact that

> McDonald's is a company with true character. Whether it is a community disaster or whether it is a personal situation, McDonald's is a company that continually, time after time, steps up to do the right thing for the individual. And I think that when you work in the company for a long time, or even a short time, you start seeing that, and it ends up really binding you to the company and the culture.

Local Economies Benefit

The most obvious impact of McDonald's business activities was the direct employment of 1.6 million people around the world. Each was offered the possibility to grow and develop personally. The minimal educational requirements for entry-level positions provided opportunities to a wide range of people from diverse backgrounds. All of them had the potential to rise through the ranks as Ray Kroc Award recipient Darlene Calhoun had done.

Almost 30 years after she took the job in Portland, Oregon, Calhoun, who now was responsible for a McDonald's on Chicago's west side, found herself among the top 1% of all managers in the United States. The Ray Kroc Award "was really a surprise," she said, "because you don't focus on trying to win awards." She acknowledged that it took a great deal of work to rise to that level; to be among the top 1%, a store could not have any failures in any area, including food preparation and safety, cleanliness, and customer service. Site visits were often unannounced. And whether it was a scheduled two-day inspection or a shorter unannounced one, "they grade you from the roof to the basement," she said. Calhoun said that even though her McDonald's was in a "tough, tough area," her goal was to make sure that the customers would get the same quality service as people who ate at a restaurant "downtown or Westmont or wherever." She had a bit of advice for those who might want to take advantage of the opportunities McDonald's offered: "They believe in integrity. They believe in high standards. If you want to work for them, you have to follow those high standards. You have to be able to have that commitment and be able to uphold the standards that they set forth and live it and walk it and breathe it every day."

The education and training coupled with the wages and benefits that McDonald's provided for its employees made it possible for countless individuals to rise through the ranks. As Ellis pointed out, "McDonald's has produced more millionaire businesspeople within the African-American community than any other organization in the United States." Those who took advantage of the career opportunities were able to provide for themselves and their families, as Vielka McCollum, manager of an Elk Grove Village, California, McDonald's restaurant did. A Panamanian immigrant raising three children, McCollum, who started as crew in 1996, knew that opportunities abounded: "If it wasn't for McDonald's, I wouldn't have everything I have."[55] She was passionate about her work and the company; "people say I have ketchup in my blood," she said.[56]

Although the economic contribution that resulted from McDonald's ability to assist individual employees move into stable financial situations was considerable, Bob Langert, vice president, corporate social responsibility, argued that the total economic impact was much greater. "We have 1.6 million people that work for McDonald's," he said, "but if you add up our supply chain it's more than that."[57] In Brazil, alone, McDonald's activities generated more than 65,000 jobs. McDonald's Brazil relied on more than 200 local suppliers for products as diverse as chicken, vegetable oil, flour, paper napkins, uniforms, and electricity. The company's "supply chain added [Brazilian real] BRL$1.5 billion [USD772 million] to the economy in 2003."[58]

The wealth creation in markets in which McDonald's operated provided opportunities for advancement to those who were directly employed by the company. Those same activities also provided opportunities for economic betterment to countless other stakeholders across the globe.

Conclusion

The call for MNCs to assist in the reduction of poverty as part of their business plans was based in part on the recognition of the enormous resources that such companies commanded. Prahalad, Hart, and others went beyond simply acknowledging the economic power and resources that these companies had. They made the claim that the companies could, and indeed did, play a vital role in addressing issues of poverty across the globe and that this could be done primarily through a company's day-to-day business operations. As noted in the introduction, Prahalad, Hart, and the others were interested in "a new private sector-based approach" to addressing poverty-related issues.[59] Though it was possible to point to companies that were making inroads and having success in this regard, skeptics remained. Some were doubtful because of a general distrust of MNCs.[60] Some remained unconvinced because they did not believe that focusing on poverty reduction was an appropriate role for business. Others simply had not considered the possibility that there could be a relationship between their businesses and poverty reduction. Langert admitted that McDonald's did not intentionally consider poverty reduction when it developed its business plans and implementation strategies. What was intentional, he said, was "that we work with people that are just starting. We don't say that they're poor or impoverished."

In the face of the claims made by Hart and others, did McDonald's have a responsibility to be more intentional about poverty reduction? Should it have rethought its business model so that poverty reduction became one of the filters in its strategic decision-making process? Did it have an obligation to raise other companies' awareness of their ability to affect development and poverty-related issues? Could and should it have done more to raise public awareness of the impact of its policies and practices on employee growth and development, so that employees were viewed and treated with respect? Or was it acceptable to maintain the status quo, and expect employees to accept the derogatory comments and attitudes toward their work the way that Calhoun came to do? "Raised two kids, bought a couple cars, a home. I think I do pretty good," she said. She was aware that many "still look at it as a mediocre-type job" and attributes that to the fact that people "don't understand what goes on behind the scenes—the training that we get. All they see is flippin' burgers and 'Here's your fries'; they don't see that other side. So it doesn't bother me."

Appendix A: Started as Crew: Darlene Calhoun and McDonald's

As explained at the beginning of the main case 6.3, the following mini-case is intended to represent the perspective of one individual's experience at McDonald's. It incorporates some of the information from the main case in order to allow it to be read as a stand-alone case.

Darlene Calhoun began working at a Portland-area McDonald's in 1977. Her husband was pursuing a military career, and the family relocated every six to eight months when he was reassigned. Calhoun was interested in finding a position to supplement her husband's income, but their young child needed care during the day. New to the city, the Calhouns had decided not to hire a babysitter. But then Calhoun saw a McDonald's ad on television, "and they were talking about flexible hours and, you know, that was something that we needed," she recalled.[61] She soon began working at a local McDonald's as a cashier.

The McDonald's Work Experience

Promotion from Within

In the "quick service" food industry, infamous for high turnover and poor training, McDonald's Corporation defied norms. The international fast food giant used a combination of promotion-from-within strategy and employee training programs to develop an abundant pool of human capital. The success of this strategy, built on the modest, hard-working ethic of company founders such as Ray Kroc and McDonald's Hamburger University creator Fred Turner, had an unexpected impact on the lives of crew members: The wages, benefits, and opportunity for promotion available to every employee of McDonald's gave thousands of workers the opportunity to lift themselves out of poverty.

Human Capital

"It was pretty much hands on . . . and you learned as you went." Calhoun's training at her first McDonald's included cashiering and other aspects of day-to-day business at the restaurant. In 1979, she relocated to San Diego with her husband, and stayed with McDonald's. After three months in San Diego, she was promoted to manager. "That was wow to me . . . because I didn't aspire to do that, but they saw something in me, and they sort of pushed me along." As a new manager, Calhoun completed the training programs that would teach her some of the skills she needed to manage effectively, complemented by hands-on experience.

When her husband's military service ended, the family returned to Chicago. At that point, Calhoun was an experienced restaurant manager. A McDonald's field agent familiar with Calhoun recommended her to Jim Martin, an owner-operator running his first McDonald's restaurant. Over time, Martin sent Calhoun through management training classes at Hamburger U—accredited coursework that could be applied to a degree program. Seven years later, Martin's store was sold to another McDonald's franchisee, and Calhoun stayed with the store.

In 2006, Calhoun was promoted to supervisor, overseeing five Chicago-area restaurants. She was in charge of training new employees and potential managers and overseeing the day-to-day operations of her restaurants. She considered the training to be one of the most positive aspects of a position at McDonald's, particularly for the young crew members who came from low-income neighborhoods in which some of the stores she oversaw were located.

The struggle of inner-city life was often difficult, but Calhoun held her employees to the same high standards she did employees at her other stores, and she found joy in seeing them succeed as they moved on after working at McDonald's. "Circumstances that they have to deal with are tough," Calhoun said, "so to make a difference for one is really, really, really heartwarming to me. I'm proud of it." Calhoun identified, in particular, the work ethic that young crew members learned—"that structure that you get at McDonald's will help take you wherever because of the training that we give . . . and it makes us feel good, that we were able to instill something."

From Cashier to Award-Winner

In 2005, Calhoun was honored with the prestigious Ray Kroc Award. The award recognized the top performing 1% of McDonald's managers nationwide, and was "given to managers who deliver superior results in achieving operational excellence, reinforcing McDonald's commitment to people, and building the business."[62] Owner-operators and supervisors presented her the award during store hours, with balloons, flowers, and a prize check.

The award came as a shock to Calhoun, who had never aspired to win it. "You don't focus on trying to win awards," she explained, "you're trying to focus on that this restaurant is run the way it should run every day." The restaurant's location, on the west side of Chicago, was in a tough inner-city neighborhood. Nonetheless, Calhoun held her crew to the high standards of any other McDonald's restaurant:

> Because you're in the inner city it doesn't mean that because these folks come and spend their dollar it doesn't mean that they're not supposed to get what they get downtown . . . So that was my goal. To make sure that even though I'm in a tough, tough area, these folks deserve the same kind of treatment.

As for the public criticism of McDonald's, and the image of the McJob, Calhoun said, "We see it and hear it every day and it does not bother me at all, because I know what we do." She saw the employee benefits and training and community service done by McDonald's, and, as a company insider, felt that she could see the real McDonald's. "It doesn't bother me at all," she reiterated, "because I'm proud of who I work for and I don't think I would have it any other way."

Appendix B: Started as Crew: Jan Fields and McDonald's

As explained at the beginning of the main case 6.3, the following mini-case is intended to represent the perspective of one individual's experience at McDonald's. It incorporates some of the information from the main case in order to allow it to be read as a stand-alone case.

When Jan Fields stopped by for a soft drink at a McDonald's restaurant in 1977, she was on her way to a job interview elsewhere. She had never considered becoming a part of the company's crew. A wife and mother, Fields was reentering the work force after several years at home as her child's primary caretaker. While she sat in the restaurant killing time before her interview, she noticed a sign on the milkshake machine. "Now hiring, flexible hours," it promised, compelling her to ask for an application. She began work there the next day.

Fields was not an immediate fit with the McDonald's environment. Her first day as a "crewmember" left her doubting her potential at McDonald's. "I literally cried when I got home," she said.[63] Afraid she would be unable to keep up with the rigorous pace of the shift and the strict rules governing the preparation of the company's famous french fries, she told her husband she would not make it at McDonald's. She arrived the following evening and began learning to operate the cash register. After a successful shift, the manager on duty asked if she would help them close. "I didn't know what that meant," she said, "and they said, 'do dishes.' I'm a clean freak, even to this day, so I thought, 'yeah, okay' . . . that sealed the deal that night."

Although Fields supported her family on a meager budget, she did not consider herself to be poor. "You don't know that you are . . . you just live on what you have," she said. Her husband, then an enlisted airman in the U.S. Air Force, made an annual salary of $5,600. As the primary shopper, Fields fed her young family on a $50 monthly grocery budget. She wanted to add to their household income. But could she do this job? And what was her future at McDonald's as a good dishwasher?

The Origin of McCulture

When Ray Kroc, then 52, approached brothers Dick and Maurice (Mac) McDonald about the success of their unusual fast food concept in 1954, he had no idea what kind of journey he had begun. This Multimixer milkshake machine salesman and lifetime entrepreneur would flirt briefly with the edge of ruin and then, over a short period of time, reach the heights of achievement that epitomized the classic American rags-to-riches success story. The image of a fastidiously groomed Kroc, sleeves rolled up, cleaning the parking lot of his first Des Plaines, Illinois, location was an icon for the enculturated employees of the McDonald's Corporation, who looked to Kroc as the first and foremost example of the dedication, discipline, and initiative that had become hallmarks of the McDonald's training program.

Kroc met with the San Bernardino, California-based McDonald brothers over lunch to discuss the potential of their restaurants and his plan to put his Multimixer machines in each new location. To his surprise, the brothers were uninterested in expansion, preferring to live simply off their single location and current limited franchising arrangements. Kroc pressed them, suggesting they find someone to manage their franchises rather than let the enormous potential of the restaurants go to waste. Still unconvinced, Dick asked who the brothers could find to open the franchises. Kroc recalled his response in his account of the rise of the chain, *Grinding it Out: The Making of McDonald's*: "I sat there feeling a sense of certitude began to envelop me. Then I leaned forward and said, 'Well, what about me?' "[64]

Seven years and more than 238 stores later, Kroc bought the rights to the McDonald's name from the brothers and accelerated the expansion of the booming chain. In the same year, Kroc and Fred Turner, a former grill man who had risen through the ranks to become the vice president of operations, began sending store manager candidates to training courses in the basement of an Elk Grove, Illinois, restaurant. The training center, named Hamburger University, was one of the nation's first "corporate universities." By 2006, McDonald's corporate-owned and franchised locations had expanded to more than 31,000 restaurants in 119 countries and catered to more than 54 million customers each day.

Public Criticism of McDonald's

Officially coined by Douglas Copland in his 1991 bestseller *Generation X: Tales for an Accelerated Culture*, the term McJob would come to represent one of the most saturated criticisms of the McDonald's empire. The image of the company suffered as the public began to perceive its jobs as dead-end, unskilled, and unstimulating. Riding the greater wave of anti-fast-food sentiment and the upward-sloping trend of obesity in the United States and across Western Europe, the public contempt for a crew position at McDonald's reached a critical mass in the late 1990s, with annual turnover for crew positions exceeding 400% in some locations.

When Merriam-Webster published a new version of its collegiate dictionary in 2003, "McJob" was included in a list of thousands of new terms and was defined as slang for "a low-paying job that requires little skill and provides little opportunity for advancement." Jim Cantalupo, then CEO of McDonald's International, quickly responded, condemning the publisher for defining the position in a negative light. In a letter to Merriam-Webster, Cantalupo decried the depiction of the crew-level position as unskilled and unrewarding, citing the entry as a "slap in the face to the 12 million men and women of the American food service industry."[65]

The image of the often maligned "McJob," the entry-level customer service position at one of the food service giant's corporate- or franchise-owned restaurants, had been the subject of billions of dollars of internal and external marketing by McDonald's for decades. The company's image as a provider of unskilled, dead-end jobs was a difficult one to erase, even as McDonald's internal marketing continuously promoted the better-than-industry benefits and career potential available to its employees.

The campaign to revitalize the public perspective on the McJob was particularly difficult in the United Kingdom, where it struggled for decades. In a mid-2000s reality television show similar to the U.S. hit talent search *American Idol*, a judge scorned an untalented performer by quipping, "you're worth nothing more than a job in McDonald's."[66] The comment drew hundreds of responses from McDonald's employees, who felt slighted. David Fairhurst, vice president of People for McDonald's UK, responded by promoting morale-boosting programs in Britain, including a series of "my first job" commercials featuring famous McDonald's veterans such as singer Macy Gray and gold medalist Carl Lewis.

In the "quick service" food industry, infamous for high turnover and poor training, McDonald's Corporation defied norms. The international fast food giant used a combination of promotion-from-within strategy and benchmark employee training programs to develop an abundant pool of human capital. Beyond internal marketing, however, McDonald's also found the answer to the development and retention problem in the legacy of founders such as entrepreneur Ray Kroc and Hamburger University founder Fred Turner, and the unusual corporate culture they created.

The Benefits of Being "Crew"

In addition to wages that were often better than average in a given region, McDonald's corporate-owned restaurants, and many franchised locations, could take advantage of a large package of employee benefits aimed at training and retaining valuable employees. Many of these programs started regionally and, after some testing within the company, spread throughout the 119 countries in which McDonald's operated.

In the United States, McDonald's had bolstered the incentive to participate in traditional employee programs such as health insurance and 401(k) programs by appealing to employees with direct benefits. Top officers in the company accepted greater increases in insurance premiums at the end of the 1990s and first years of the 21st century to ensure a slower increase for in-store employees. The resulting 25% to 30% increase in premiums for officers allowed for an increase of 1% to 5% for store managers.[67]

After a study revealed a surprisingly low employee enrollment in 401(k) plans, the company began offering better incentives to assistant and store managers, most of whom were eligible for the program. Fearing that the 1% salary commitment was keeping many employees from enrolling, McDonald's gave all eligible employees a onetime raise of 1% of salary, then offered to match that contribution with 3%. Employees could commit as much as 4% of their salaries to the investment program, which was met by McDonald's at 7%, an unheard of contribution in the food service industry. As employees became eligible, they were automatically enrolled in the program, though they were free to opt out. As a result of the changes, enrollment in the program nationwide increased from 41% of store managers to 93%.

Beyond traditional employee incentive programs, McDonald's instituted several options for employees working with difficult schedules, specifically employees enrolled in school and taking care of young children. The restaurant advertised "McFlexibility," offering adaptable schedules to employees who were unable to work a traditional full-time week. Adding to that flexibility, some stores began to offer additional benefits to families and student employees. In the United Kingdom, McDonald's restaurants began offering the "family contract" program in select regions. Under the program, family members who worked at the same location could switch shifts without prior notice. The program led to less absenteeism and stress for employees, who appreciated the greater ability to juggle work and other commitments. In select franchise locations within the United States, employees who were also students were given the chance to take an extra hour to study, complete homework, or meet with a study group while on the clock.[68]

Employee Education—Hamburger University

Peter Breckenridge of Nunawading, Australia, began working at McDonald's when he was 16. He needed the job to fund his college tuition, and took advantage of the flexibility of a position at McDonald's to keep pace with his studies. He used his college breaks to attend the regional branch of McDonald's corporate training center, Hamburger University. By the time he finished his traditional degree in electrical engineering, he also held a diploma in management from Hamburger U, and was able to use both disciplines as a McDonald's employee on a site-development and -construction team. Promoted to development director of Southern Australia at the age of 27, Breckenridge hoped one day to become a key leader in McDonald's Australian operations. He attributed his success at McDonald's to the training he received at Hamburger U, which translated into college credit at thousands of universities worldwide.[69]

McDonald's centralized training program, an anomaly when it was founded in 1961, grew to become one of the most globally recognized corporate training programs. Founded by McDonald's icon Fred Turner in the basement of an Elk Grove, Illinois, restaurant, the program offered multiple training paths to employees seeking promotion to store management positions as well as to new franchisees and others entering one of the diverse career tracks within the corporation. Many employees who received training through Hamburger U finished the program and continued with further coursework at higher learning institutions to complete two- or four-year degree programs. The benefit of McDonald's training included employability industrywide, because other major food service corporations sought individuals with the Hamburger U skill set.

The program grew considerably in its first five decades. Class sizes of 10 to 12 in the 1960s boomed to 200 or more in 2007 as the value of the corporate training made it a sought-after program for ambitious personnel in the company. The program graduated more than 80,000 McDonald's employees by 2007, and increased from 14 students in 1961 to an annual matriculation of 5,000. Hamburger U operated campuses across the world, including in Sydney, Munich, London, Hong Kong, Tokyo, and Brazil.

Beyond Crew

As Jan Fields continued to train at McDonald's she eventually mastered each crew position, including the french fry station. During her training, senior managers noticed her dedication and willingness to become a part of the team atmosphere. To finish shifts quickly, she would assist managers in closing operations and, within months of being hired, regularly assisted in managerial duties. Eventually, she was offered a management position at the store. Over the next decade, she finished college and was promoted several times. "And then it got to a point," she recalled, "after almost 10 years, where I finally ended up saying, 'I guess I'm making a career out of this. I'm here.'" In 1988, she received the prestigious McDonald's President's Award, the highest award McDonald's bestows on employees, which recognizes the top 1% of "employees who achieve considerable results in strategic initiatives."[70]

Promotion from Within

McDonald's created an environment in which a humble beginning was viewed as a badge of honor, a "work-hard" ethic was part of the corporate culture, and enculturation was key to a successful career. At executive meetings, the 40% of executive officers who began as crewmembers regularly invoked images of Ray Kroc, Charlie Bell, Fred Turner, and in later years, Jan Fields and other former crewmembers. They point to the stories of hundreds of owner-operators who began working at McDonald's and became business owners themselves after learning the discipline and dedication required to run a restaurant through their careers at McDonald's.

At the core of the corporate value system was a reserved humility that many executives strived to cultivate. Richard Floersch, executive vice president and chief human resources officer, explained that, despite regular interaction on a professional level, most of the top executives had never discussed their educations. "Nobody ever talks about where they went to school," he said, "even here in corporate. It's not even talked about. It just isn't part of our culture."

Bob Langert, vice president of corporate social responsibility, agreed. "That's our culture." After one of his promotions within the company, he suggested mentioning his MBA from the prestigious Kellogg School of Management in the company newsletter. The general counsel, responsible for his report, suggested that he not include it. To most McDonald's employees, his degree was a very small part of his value as a coworker.

Steve Russell, senior vice president for human resources and "Chief People Officer," McDonald's USA, recalled that there were times when incoming employees could be slow to enculturate, and the atmosphere of unity in the company would begin to disappear. The cultural distance between new hires and "started-as-crew" personnel became a focal point for hiring managers. "If you don't hire the right person . . . it can upset an organization pretty quickly . . . We had a pretty significant crash rate at one point."[71]

To combat this perception, special care was given to the enculturation of new employees who had come directly into the corporate offices. As part of the training process, all new hires were placed in local restaurants immediately. They spent 30 to 90 days as crewmembers, learning each of the restaurant's stations and developing a respect for the difficulty of each position. Many executives revisited restaurants in which they trained, and some even took periodic breaks to work in the store again. The process of placing new members of the McDonald's team in stores ensured a dramatic enculturation that left little room for misunderstanding. An employee who could not fit into the McDonald's culture was very likely to crash.

"She Started as Crew"

In 2006, after 28 years of service with McDonald's, Jan Fields was named executive vice president and chief operating officer of McDonald's USA, overseeing nearly 14,000 McDonald's locations. "I don't think there's a class that I can go through to get an MBA, which I don't have, to learn how to treat people and how to motivate a team in the kind of environment that we work in." She considered development to be an important part of McDonald's success, however, and participated in internal development programs such as the Career Development program and the McDonald's Diversity Network.

Fields continued to receive awards, including those recognizing her active role in women's leadership and, in 2001, the McDonald's Women Operators Network Recognition Award. She served on the boards of nonprofit organizations such as the Chicago Urban League and United Cerebral Palsy, and chaired the advisory board of the women's organization Catalyst. In 2007, she was named to *Fortune*'s 50 Most Powerful Women in Business list.[72] A testament to her success, her "Started as Crew!" pin was displayed prominently on the desk of her Oakbrook, Illinois, office. "It really is a badge of honor," she said, "it really is."

Notes

* This case was prepared by DePaul University Professor of Business Ethics Laura P. Hartman; DePaul University's Institute for Business and Professional Ethics Project Developer Justin Sheehan, and the Darden School's Olsson Center Senior Ethics Research Associate Jenny Mead under the supervision of Patricia H. Werhane, Ruffin Professor of Business Ethics. It was written as a basis for class discussion rather than to illustrate effective or ineffective handling of an administrative situation. Copyright © 2008 by the University of Virginia Darden School Foundation, Charlottesville, VA. All rights reserved.

1 The major proponents of this view are C. K. Prahalad and Stuart L. Hart. See their seminal article, "The Fortune at the Bottom of the Pyramid," *strategy + business*, Issue 26, First Quarter 2002. See also C. K. Prahalad, *The Fortune at the Bottom of the Pyramid: Eradicating Poverty Through Profits* (Upper Saddle River, NJ: Wharton School Publishing, 2006).

2 Stuart L. Hart, *Capitalism at the Crossroads: Aligning Business, Earth, and Humanity*, 2nd ed. (Upper Saddle River, NJ: Pearson Education, 2007), xl.

3 For more detailed discussions on poverty see: "Total GDP 2006," World Development Indicators database, *World Bank*, 1 July 2007, http://www.siteresources.worldbank.org/DATA-STATISTICS/Resources/GDP.pdf (accessed 28 October 2007); Nanak Kakwani, "Issues in Setting Absolute Poverty Lines," Asian Development Bank, 2003, http://www.adb.org/Documents/Papers/Issues_Setting_Absolute_poverty_lines/default.asp (accessed 28 October 2007); and Raphael Kaplinsky, *Globalization, Poverty and Inequality* (Malden, MA: Polity Press, 2005).

4 U.S. Department of Health and Human Services, "Computations for the 2007 Annual Update of the HHS Poverty Guidelines for the 48 Contiguous States and the District of Columbia," Washington, DC, 24 January 2007. http://aspe.hhs.gov/poverty/07computations.shtml#fd (accessed 28 October 2007).

5 For a discussion of efforts to enhance the quality of PPP data, see Kimberly Zieschang, "Enhancing the Quality of Global Economic Statistics," *ICP News* (World Bank) 3, no. 1 (February 2006): 3, http://siteresources.worldbank.org/ICPINT/Resources/ICPe-Newsletter_Feb2006.pdf (accessed 28 October 2007).

6 Shaohua Chen and Martin Ravallion, "Absolute poverty measures for the developing world, 1981–2004," *Proceedings of the National Academy of Sciences*, 104, no. 43 (23 October 2007). 16757–62, http://www.pnas.org/ (accessed 28 October 2007).

7 Chen and Ravallion, 16759.

8 Chen and Ravallion, 16759.

9 Larry Dobrow, "McBrand: It's not Easy Being Pop Culture Icon," *Advertising Age* 76, no. 30 (25 July 2005): S14.

10 Michael Moore, "Students Take Tomato Pickers' Fight to the Golden Arches," *St. Paul Union Advocate*, 15 November 2006.

11 Recognizing the importance of presenting the voices of those who claimed that employment at McDonald's as exploitative and/or lacked potential for advancement, the authors of this case made an attempt to find credible sources that represented this view. Only a few were found, and for the most part, they focused on specific concerns, such as the Florida farm workers' pay noted above. McDonald's responded to and resolved the issues brought to its attention. In addition to traditional periodical databases, the following web sites were consulted: Center for Media and Democracy (www.prwatch.org); Cragg Law Center (www.cragg.org); Keep Antibiotics Working (www.keepantibioticsworking.com); Center for Science in the Public Interest (www.cspinet.org); Greenpeace (www.greenpeace.org); The Corporate Social Responsibility Newswire (www.csrwire.com); The McInformation Network (www.mcspotlight.org).

12 Ray A. Kroc with Robert Anderson, *Grinding it Out: The Making of McDonald's* (Chicago: H. Regnery, 1977).

13 The source of this and all subsequent Steve Russell quotations is an author interview with Steve Russell, senior vice president for human resources, McDonald's USA, Oak Brook, Illinois, 17 January 2007.

14 The source of this and all subsequent Janice L. Fields quotations is an author interview with Janice L. Fields, executive vice president and chief operations officer, McDonald's USA, Oak Brook, Illinois, 17 January 2007.

15 "Business Heroes: Ray Kroc," *Business Strategy Review* (Winter 2005): 48.

16 "Ray Kroc: Founder's philosophies remain at the heart of McDonald's success," *Nation's Restaurant News: The Golden Anniversary of the Golden Arches* (January 2005): 21.

17 "Ray Kroc: Founder's philosophies," 23.

18 Penny Moser, "The McDonald's Mystique," *Fortune* 118, no. 1 (July 1988): 112.

19 Moser, 21.

20 The source of this and all subsequent Darlene Calhoun quotations is an author interview with Darlene Calhoun, assistant supervisor of Lofton & Lofton Management, DePaul University, Chicago, 27 April 2007.

21 Author interview with Jack Daly, senior vice president of corporate relations, McDonald's USA, Oak Brook, Illinois, 17 January 2007.

22 The source of this and all subsequent Richard Floersch quotations is an author interview with Richard Floersch, vice president and chief human resources officer, McDonald's USA, Oak Brook, Illinois, 17 January 2007.

23 Dina Berta, "Companies Encourage Employees to Pursue Degrees," *Nation's Restaurant News* (7 November 2005): 18.

24 Jaclyn Jaeger, "Finding Work/Life Balance at the Top," *Lawyers Weekly USA*, 24 April 2006.

25 The source of this and all subsequent Richard Ellis quotations is an author interview with Richard Ellis, vice president, U.S. communications, McDonald's USA, Oak Brook, Illinois, 17 January 2007.

26 Kim Ji-hyun, "McDonald's wants to please tastes of young, old in Korea," *The Korea Herald*, 30 November 2005.

27 Andrew Taylor, "McDonald's chips away at image as poor employer," *Financial Times*, 20 April 2006, 5.

28 "Future has fries with that," *The Courier-Mail*, 1 April 2006, E-66.

29 "Putting the Front Line First: McDonald's Commitment to Employees Bolsters the Bottom Line," *Hewitt Magazine Online*, 9:1. http://www.hewittassociates.com/Intl/NA/en-US/Knowledge Center/Magazine/vol9_iss1/departments-upclose.html (accessed 27 October 2007).

30 "McDonald's Hamburger University and University of Phoenix Graduate Named 2005 Adult Learner of the Year," ACE press release, 29 September 2005. http://www.acenet.edu/AM/ Template.cfm?Section=Home&Template=/CM/HTMLDisplay.cfm&ContentID24055 (accessed 14 February 2008).

31 Reta Smart, "Where McDonald's Got their Man," *The Age* (18 February 2006).

32 Taylor, 5.

33 Anjali Prayag, "McDonald's India Believes in Grooming Talent from Within," *The Hindu Businessline*, Internet Edition, 31 August 2005, http://www.thehindubusinessline.com/2005/09/01/ stories/2005090101720800.htm (accessed 26 February 2008).

34 "Putting the Front Line First," 6.

35 Taylor, 5.

36 "McDonald's not lovin' 'McJob' dictionary definition," CNN Entertainment, 10 November 2003, http://www.cnn.com/2003/SHOWBIZ/books/11/08/mcjob.dictionary.ap/index.html (accessed 27 October 2007).

37 Daniel Thomas, "HR challenges . . . I'm lovin' it," *Personnel Today*, 6 September 2005.

38 Taylor, 5.

39 Taylor, 5.

40 Amy Hamilton, "Fast food jobs better than advertised," *The Craig Daily Press* (Colorado), 6 September 2005.

41 Gerald L. White, "Employee turnover: The hidden drain on profits." *HR Focus* (1 January 1995): 15. Eric Schlosser, "The True Cost Of America's Diet," *Rolling Stone Magazine* 794 (3 September 1998).

42 Jennifer Waters, "McDonald's Ads Tout Mcjobs," *MarketWatch from Dow Jones*, 21 September 2005, http://www.marketwatch.com/search/?value=jennifer%20Waters%20touts%20mcjobs (accessed 27 October 2007).

43 Hamilton, "Fast food jobs."

44 Louise Barnett, "Fast Food Giant Bids to Improve 'McJob' Image," *Press Association*, 20 April 2006; Mark Sweney, "Fast food giant says no to 'McJobs'," *Guardian Unlimited*, 20 April 2006; and Clinton Manning, "YOUR money: McFightback," *Daily Mirror*, 20 April 2006.

45 Julia Pearlman, "McD's celebrate McWorkers in Career-Boosting TV Ad Drive," *BrandRepublic* (23 September 2005).

46 Hamilton, "Fast Food Jobs."

47 Taylor, 5.

48 Fernando Garcia & Ana Maria Castelo, "McOnomics 2005: An Incredible Voyage Through the BigMac™ Supply Chain," GV Consult, São Paulo, Brazil, 2005, 3. http://www.mcdonalds.com/ corp/values/report/otherreports.RowPar.0003.ContentPar.0001.ColumnPar.0012.File.tmp/ McOnomics%202005.pdf (accessed 26 February 2008).

49 John Arlidge, "McJobs that all the family can share," *The Daily Telegraph* (London), 26 January 2006, 1.

50 JoAnne Viviano, "Fast-Food Franchisers Show Doing Homework Does Pay," *Chicago Tribune*, 5 August 2005.

51 Viviano.

52 Viviano.

53 "Future Has Fries."

54 "Future Has Fries."

55 Rachel Osterman, "Flipping an image: McDonald's battles the stigma that fast food work is a dead-end job," *Sacramento Bee*, 14 October 2005, D1.

56 Osterman.

57 The source of this and all subsequent Robert Langert quotations is an author interview with Robert Langert, vice president, corporate social responsibility, McDonald's USA, Oak Brook, Illinois, 17 January 2007.

58 GVConsult, *McOnomics 2005*, 3.

59 Hart, *Capitalism*, xl.

60 See for example: William Easterly, *The White Man's Burden: Why the West's Efforts to Aid the Rest Have Done So Much Ill and So Little Good* (New York: Penguin Press, 2006).

61 The source of this and all subsequent Darlene Calhoun quotations is an author interview with Darlene Calhoun, assistant supervisor of Lofton & Lofton Management, DePaul University, Chicago, 27 April 2007.

62 "The Ray Kroc Award," The McDonald's Electric Press Kit, http://www.mcdepk.com/raykrocaward2005/index.html (accessed 15 October 2007).

63 The source of this and all subsequent Janice L. Fields quotations is an author interview with Janice L. Fields, executive vice president and chief operations officer, McDonald's USA, Oak Brook, Illinois, 17 January 2007.

64 Ray A. Kroc with Robert Anderson, *Grinding it Out: The Making of McDonald's* (Chicago, IL: H. Regnerey, 1977), 12.

65 Jim Cantalupo, "Supersize Insult to Industry Workers," *Nation's Restaurant News* 37, no. 44 (3 November 2003): 18.

66 Daniel Thomas, "HR challenges . . . I'm lovin' it," *Personnel Today* (6 September 2005): 11.

67 The source of this and all subsequent Richard Floersch quotations is an author interview with Richard Floersch, executive vice president and chief human resources officer, McDonald's USA, Oak Brook, Illinois, 17 January 2007.

68 JoAnne Viviano, "Fast-food Franchisers Show Doing Homework Does Pay," *Boston Globe,* 7 August 2005.

69 Reta Smart, "Where McDonald's Got Their Man," *The Age* (Melbourne) (18 February 2006): 4.

70 "Janice L. Fields, Executive Vice President and Chief Operations Officer – McDonald's USA." McDonald's Corporation Executive Biographies. http://www.mcdonalds.com/corp/about/bios/janice_l__fields.html (accessed 25 September 2007).

71 The source of this and all subsequent Steve Russell quotations is an author interview with Steve Russell, senior vice president for human resources and chief people officer, McDonald's USA, Oak Brook, Illinois, 17 January 2007.

72 Janice L. Fields biography.

6.4 The Marriott Corporation Human Resources Department

Managing a Low-Wage Workforce[*]

In 1989, Marriott was at the top of the food and lodging business. Few companies, let alone family-operated ones, had achieved Marriott's stature and maintained a deeply felt sense of history and security. In its 62-year history, Marriott had earned a level of shareholder trust that no other hospitality company had even approached. Yet as a premier services company, Marriott's success depended on the people who actually delivered the service—the maids, janitors, kitchen workers, porters, waiters, delivery people, telemarketing representatives, and front desk clerks—the fastest growing and least appreciated segment of the U.S. labor force. Under pressure to please value-driven customers, Marriott was forced to scramble to hire, train, and retain average people capable of performing extraordinary service with a smile. To fill most of these low-level service jobs, Marriott did not need workers with high levels of education, experience, or technical expertise. Instead, in an era of flattening hierarchies and heightened expectations, Marriott needed low-wage-earning people who were also resilient and resourceful—skills previously demanded only of managers. In the 1990s, Marriott faced the challenge of not only finding, but also retaining people willing to work for low wages with few benefits.

The major task facing Marriott's senior vice president for Human Resources, Clifford Ehrlich, was to help his people-dependent company ensure itself an abundant supply of well-trained, loyal, and content workers, dedicated to the overall success of their employer. This would not be an easy task because his job as a human resources manager had undergone a transformation in the 1980s. Ehrlich stated:

> Ten years ago, there was still a large part of human resources that had a compliance (EEO compliance) cast to it, wage and hour compliance, compliance with the National Labor Relations Act . . . Then the world started to change . . . While you still had to have this compliance feature, you had to ask what are the things we can do to help create an environment in which people do get excited about coming to work? . . . As business strategies changed, you had to be sure that the human resource efforts were geared to the change.[1]

The son of a New York Telephone Company union organizer, Ehrlich was the first member of his family to go away to college (attending Boston College Law School at night). Ehrlich's personal values of hard work, personal accountability, self-reliance, and family values mirrored the Marriott corporate culture inspired by the Mormon roots of founder J.W. Marriott, Sr. These values played an important role in shaping Marriott's human resource policies for the 1990s. Ehrlich was faced with the dilemma of developing appropriate human resource policies for Marriott that would not only attract and maintain a large supply of relatively low-paid service employees, but would also fit the Marriott corporate culture without tarnishing the company's long-held reputation as a highly principled family-run concern.

Marriott History

As a recent transplant from Utah, John Willard (Bill) Marriott, Sr. founded what would become the Marriott Corporation in May of 1927, as a nine-seat A&W Root Beer stand in Washington, D.C. The Marriott root-beer stand evolved into a family restaurant chain called Hot Shoppes, which in turn expanded into in-flight airline catering in 1937. In 1957, Marriott went public and at the same time opened its first hotel in Arlington, Virginia. Over the next few years, the company opened a string of hotels and Hot Shoppe Restaurants. In 1964, with 45 Hot Shoppes, 4 hotels, and other successful businesses, Bill Marriott, Sr. handed the presidency of the company to his son, Bill Marriott, Jr. while retaining the office of CEO for himself.

Bill Marriott, Jr. accelerated the pace of the company's growth by focusing on the lodging segment of the business. Through acquisitions and new business start-ups, Marriott quadrupled in size between 1946 and 1970, surpassing its competitors Howard Johnson and Hilton Hotels in both revenues and profits. Marriott became international in 1966 by acquiring an airline-catering kitchen in Caracas, Venezuela. In 1967, Marriott acquired the Big Boy restaurant chain, and in 1968, the company started the Roy Rogers fast-food chain.

Succeeding his father as CEO in 1972, Bill Marriott, Jr. introduced new management techniques, dividing the company into three semi-autonomous groups: food operations, in-flight service to airlines, and hotels and specialty restaurants. Presidents who reported directly to Marriott headed the groups, which were further divided into 16 divisions. Through this strategy, the company never depended on one segment for profits.

Between 1975 and 1984, Marriott increased its room capacity from 14,000 units to more than 60,000 units. This increase was the result of another of Bill Jr.'s innovative strategies—constructing hotels and selling them while maintaining control over the properties through management contracts. This system created rapid profit growth, limited risk, and ensured the uniformity of Marriott service standards that would have been difficult to achieve in traditional franchising arrangements. In the 1980s, Marriott further expanded through the acquisition of Gino's Pizza, Host International (an airport food and merchandizing service), American Resorts Group (a time-share operator), the Howard Johnson Company, Cladieux Corporation, Service Systems, Inc., and the Saga Corporation. Anticipating the glut in luxury-end hotel rooms, in the late 1980s Marriott expanded into the middle-priced hotel market by creating the Courtyard Marriott chain and, with the creation of Marriott Suites, the all-suite hotel market.

The collapse of real-estate prices and the slowdown in the hotel industry in the early 1990s presented Marriott with new challenges. Much of Marriott's growth in the 1980s was debt financed. Marriott's debt-equity ratio increased from 1:1 in 1979 to 4.5:1 in 1989, with a negative surplus cash flow of $7.84 per share, excluding asset sales. Bill Jr.'s strategy was to downsize and restructure, thus slowing the pace of new hotel construction and decreasing capital expenditures from $1.5 billion in 1990 to $1 billion in 1991.[2] To isolate the debt load, the corporation split into two companies: the properties that Marriott owned were grouped within the Host Marriott Corporation, and its contract services were centralized in Marriott International, Inc.

Corporate Culture

Despite their wealth, the Marriott family (which owned slightly less than 30 percent of the company stock) always prided itself on a strong work ethic. Bill Marriott, Jr. stated: "I do what my father did, which is to teach my kids how to work." Bill Sr. and his wife expected their children to do housework when they were young and to work summers when they were older. Bill Marriott's younger brother, Steve, Marriott's director of sales, had started working in the family business at age 16, when he was hired to flip hamburgers at a Roy Rogers restaurant. Not only did he tithe his pre-tax income to the Church of Jesus Christ of Latter Day Saints, he also saved enough money to help with living expenses after his marriage. He did not believe that he should become president of the company "unless he earns it—and doing so will earn him self respect." In a 1987 *Forbes* interview, Bill Marriott, Jr. said that he ran the company with a very strong work ethic.[3]

On occasion, the Marriott family's Mormon beliefs conflicted with business decisions. In the name of business practicality and after much deliberation, the family decided to sell alcohol in its lodging facilities in the 1960s. A desire not to be associated with gambling, however, led to the family's decision not to have its company enter into the booming gaming business in the 1970s.

Labor Unions

Along with tight family and cost control, Bill Marriott, Jr. agreed with his father's philosophy that labor unions helped neither the worker nor the company. Marriott developed a tradition of working hard to keep unions out of all phases of the corporation. Its executives believed that the company could remain more flexible without union rules, and the reduced labor costs would enable them to offer better benefits to their employees. According to Bill Marriott, Jr.:

> Those who work for us must like us. If they like you and have respect for you then they will do almost anything for you. They will look after your customers properly, and a spirit of friendliness will pervade your whole organization.

As an expression of this corporate philosophy, Marriott instituted a profit-sharing plan and a system of bonus incentives. In place of union grievance committees and collective action, Marriott instituted a Guarantee of Fair Treatment policy, which promoted constructive engagement between employees and managers. Under this program, managers were expected to communicate regularly with employees, know about their ambitions, home lives, and work motivations, and involve employees in decisions that affected them. In 1990, only two of Marriott's 500 hotels were unionized. Marriott believed the fact that its employees had never formed a union was a testament to their fair treatment.

At Marriott, the antiunion culture was strong. So strong in fact that in 1992, labor union organizers found and made public a Marriott Human Resources antiunion manual that outlined interviewing techniques for human resources managers designed to weed out potential union sympathizers from among prospective employees. The manual instructed managers to look out for "an applicant who wears an article of clothing or jewelry with union insignias. Be observant, you'll be surprised at what you see."[4]

In the late 1980s, when Marriott expanded into the northern industrialized union strongholds of New York, Chicago, and Boston, it met opposition from broad coalitions of community and labor leaders. This coalition sued Marriott over its practice of giving hiring preference to new employees from suburban areas outside the limits of cities that granted Marriott job-creation tax incentives. In 1989, in Boston a coalition consisting of the Community Task Force on Construction, Women in the Building Trades, and the Black Legislative Caucus protested Marriott's refusal to grant contracting work to minorities and women and its proclivity for hiring contractors from non-union southern states.

Structural Change in the American Labor Force

According to a 1994 Bureau of Labor Statistics Report, occupations with the largest growth projections were low-skilled: food service, retail sales clerks, truck drivers, child-care workers, nursing aids, and janitors. Service occupations accounted for 79 percent of all employment in the United States and 74 percent of U.S. GDP. This category was further projected to account for all net job growth in the coming decade. In 1994, the travel and hospitality industry alone employed 10.5 million people or 8 percent of the total U.S. labor force.

In the late 1980s, however, as the demand for service workers was increasing, the employable unskilled labor pool was shrinking. As the baby boomers aged, the number of people entering the job market to replace them was diminishing because of the decline in the birth rate during the 1960s and 1970s. In addition, many of these new entrants had such limited educational opportunities or work experience that they were ill equipped to enter the labor force. An estimated 25 percent of American high school graduates could not read or write at an eighth grade level, and the high-school dropout rates in major cities ranged from 35 percent in New York City to 50 percent in Washington, D.C. Finally, more than 44 percent of the labor force were women, the majority of whom were of childbearing age; this percentage was projected to rise to 64 by the year 2000. Women with children under the age of six years were the fastest growing segment of the American workforce.

Until the late 1980s, Marriott had a convenient means of augmenting its demands on the shrinking unskilled labor pool. In Los Angeles and Miami, Marriott Corporation vans regularly stopped at designated street corners to pick up day workers to staff the banquet tables, dishwashers, and towel carts at local hotels. Peggy Pfeil, director of Human Resources for Marriott Corporation in 1987, stated: "It's a wonderful resource. These people need the work." Many of these day laborers picked up by the Marriott vans, however, were illegal aliens. Unfortunately for Marriott, the Immigration Reform and Control Act of 1987 enforced criminal penalties against companies with four or more employees who were illegal aliens. The law also required companies to verify the work permits for new employees. Marriott's short-term response to the new legislation was to attempt to shift its low-skilled employment burden in places like Los Angeles, Miami, and New York to private temporary contractors, as a means of transferring the liability for hiring illegal aliens to a third party.[5]

As American labor became increasingly deskilled and the traditional high-paying blue-collar jobs of the post-war era evaporated, the ranks of the low-wage labor pool began to swell. Because wages were so flat, however, these new workers had little allegiance to any particular job or employer. The tendency was for these workers to bounce from one minimum-wage job to another with few if any consequences, as the minimum-wage service sector jobs were plentiful.

Marriott faced the 1990s with the problem of not only hiring people willing to work for low wages, but also keeping them. Annual turnover rates of 100 percent or more were common in the hotel and restaurant industry. Until 1990, the tendency was to think of front-line service workers as a disposable commodity rather than as an economic resource. It cost Marriott as much as $1,100 to recruit and train each replacement—the total bill ran into millions of dollars each year. Ehrlich had to figure out how to recruit and maintain an effective workforce from a traditionally undependable low-skilled labor pool without dramatic wage increases.

Cliff Ehrlich took particular pride in the announcement that the *Personnel Journal* had awarded his company its 1993 Rebuild America Challenge Grant for the Chicago Marriott's innovative approaches to what the Hudson Institute called the problems associated with "Work Force 2000."[6] Under Ehrlich's leadership, Marriott created programs designed to break down the traditional barriers that had kept the "problem categories" of workers—former welfare recipients, single parents, teenagers, recent college graduates, high school dropouts, people with disabilities—out of the American workforce. Marriott's human resource programs focused on instilling a strong work ethic in its problem category employees, emphasizing job training, career development, reward incentives, and family services to not only attract new employees, but also to retain existing workers.

Under Ehrlich's leadership, Marriott developed a marketing approach to human resources based on the premise that Marriott should sell itself to prospective workers rather than the traditional reverse. Ehrlich adapted many of the same techniques used by marketers to build business—surveys, focus groups, and programs to enhance the company's reputation among customers—and applied them to current and future employees. "We're approaching it by saying we have jobs we're trying to sell, and the prospective workforce out there are the buyers." He also reasoned that instead of spending all of Marriott's money and attention going after new employees, an equal amount should be spent retaining old employees. Ehrlich believed that a large part of his job was to help employees feel good about working for Marriott: "That way they'll stay. And that way they'll spread the word . . . If all employees started their day with a little extra oomph, they would be willing to give their employer more than just what was written in their job description." He further stated that it was up to the employer to tap into what he calls "discretionary effort." The trick in management is to create a "work environment in which people do want to spend that discretionary effort . . . in which people contribute to the success of the business."[7] Ehrlich sought to challenge the traditional corporate paternalism of "we take care of our employees" and replace it with "we provide opportunities for our employees to take care of themselves." Ehrlich stated:

> Not only is it relieving the company of obligations that are not necessarily appropriate . . . It is also empowering the employee and recognizing that person as an adult responsible for managing his or her own life and job.[8]

He acknowledged that Marriott provided a lot less security to workers than in previous years due to the changing labor environment. Despite this fact, Ehrlich stated, "We still want loyalty. I believe that people come to work wanting to be loyal. They will exchange their loyalty not for security but for involvement." He saw his job as helping Marriott make the shift in employee management philosophy from the old paternalism to the new focus on individual self-help.

The Marriott human resource programs received a great deal of praise and publicity in the mid-1990s. The Marriott initiatives coincided with nationwide objectives to "eliminate welfare as we know it" and move the traditionally unemployable categories of workers into the workforce. As such, Marriott human resources became not only the industry leader, but also a model for other industries that depended on unskilled labor. Although Marriott managed to increase its retention rates, the rates never climbed above 60 percent. Despite the initial publicity blitz that surrounded new Marriott program announcements, several of the programs were never fully implemented. In addition, the Hotel and Restaurant Workers of the AFL-CIO began to take direct aim at the means through which Marriott maintained its nonunion tradition, resulting in numerous lawsuits. Although Ehrlich received accolades for his innovative programs in 1996, he wondered how long this strategy could be sustained.

Pathways to Independence

In 1990, Marriott instituted the Pathways to Independence program, a six-week welfare-to-work course that included self-esteem training and basic communication and hospitality skills. Initially started in New Orleans, Pathways had expanded to 11 cities including Atlanta, Tampa, and Washington, D.C., by 1996. Six-hundred workers, formerly on welfare, had been through the program. The result was higher retention rates and lower turnover for Marriott. The program was not without controversy, however, particularly because the training was government subsidized. See Appendix A for a 1997 interview with John A. Boardman, executive secretary-treasurer of the Hotel and Restaurant Employees Union, Local 25 of the AFL-CIO, Washington, D.C. Boardman was highly critical of Marriott's anti-union stance and its Pathways to Independence program.

Marriott's Workforce 2000 Programs

New Employee Orientation

Selecting employees who would stay beyond their first three months of employment was one of Marriott's biggest challenges. Until 1993, more than 40 percent of the new employees who left Marriott departed during the first three months on the job. Marriott decided to focus on one of the most neglected areas of employment experience—orientation. Instead of hiring people and putting them immediately to work on a three-month "probationary" period, all fresh recruits attended an eight-hour initial training session, the highlight of which was an elegant lunch, served by hotel veterans. To guide them through the next 90 days, associates were assigned mentors (known as "buddies"). Every member of the entering class attended refresher courses after the second month. When these members reached their ninetieth day of employment, the hotel hosted them at a banquet. This program was based on the rationale that "You cannot expect your employees to delight your customers unless you as an employer delight your employees."[9]

"Partners in Career Management" Program

In 1994, Marriott instituted a workshop called "Partners in Career Management," a program designed to train its managers as "career coaches" capable of helping employees examine and manage their career options. All 6,000 management-level employees were slated to attend the course. The workshop would provide Marriott managers and supervisors with a four-step model to assist them in managing their own careers and prepare them to hold more effective career discussions with their employees. After attending the course, Marriott managers would be able to do the following:

1   Help employees identify skills, values, and interests, as well as answer the question, "Who am I?"
2   Offer ongoing feedback and help employees answer the question, "How am I seen?"
3   Help employees create a set of realistic career goals and answer the question, "What are my career alternatives?"
4   Help associates develop action plans and answer the question, "How can I achieve my goal?"

In addition, managers were expected to learn about career resources available within the organization, hold career discussions with employees on an ongoing basis, and identify developmental activities and experiences to help employees build their knowledge and skills and improve performance.

Marriott saw the creation of the workshop as a means of shifting the responsibility for career management away from the company and toward the employee. In accordance with this logic, at Marriott employees are officially responsible for the following:

- Assessing their own skills, values, interests, and developmental needs.
- Determining long- and short-term career goals.
- Creating, with their manager, a career-development plan to reach their goals.
- Following through with their plan.
- Learning about and taking advantage of other career-management resources offered by Marriott, such as on-line job postings.
- Meeting their managers on a regular basis for career-development discussions.
- Recognizing that career discussions imply no promises or guarantees.
- Recognizing that their career development will depend directly on Marriott's needs and opportunities as well as their own performance and abilities.

The J. Willard Marriott Award of Excellence

As a means of getting the best possible performance from each employee without excessive expenditure, Marriott established the J. Willard Marriott Award of Excellence, an engraved medallion bearing the likeness of the founder and the words expressing the basic values of the company: *dedication, achievement, character, ideals, effort, and perseverance*. Selection for this non-monetary award was based on remarks made by a nominator and the individual's length of service. The recipients represented a cross-section of the Marriott workforce: dishwashers, chefs, housekeepers, and merchandise managers. The Marriott Award was presented at a lavish awards banquet in Washington, D.C., attended by honorees, spouses, nominators, and top executives.

The Department of Work and Family Life

In 1989, to address the issue of employees' needs to balance the demands of home and work, Marriott created the Department of Work and Family Life. A 1989 *Harvard Business Review* article found that the labor force included more than 70 percent of all women with children between the ages of six and 17 and more than half the women with children less than one year old. With the two-income family becoming a norm and an economic necessity, Marriott began to realize the relationship between productivity and "family-friendly" policies. In 1996, *Business Week* announced:

> Work-family strategies haven't just hit the corporate mainstream—they've become a competitive advantage. The exclusive province of working mothers a decade ago, such benefits now extend to elder-care assistance, flexible scheduling, job-sharing, adoption benefits, on-site summer camp, employee help-lines, even—no joke—pet-care and lawn-service referrals.

Marriott additionally noted a direct correlation between family conflicts, particularly child-care issues, and retention levels and absenteeism. It also noted that even when work and family programs existed, they often exclusively focused on the needs of management-level employees.

Marriott sought to tailor these family related services to its low-wage workforce. A Marriott survey determined that 19 percent of Marriott hourly employees had considered leaving Marriott within the previous year because of work and family conflicts. Hourly employees also estimated they had missed an average of four days of work and been tardy seven days within the previous year, because of childcare demands.

Based on these findings, Marriott's Department of Work and Family Life developed a comprehensive plan of financial, research, and educational services for families. Among these initiatives was a nationwide referral service, Child Care Choices, which helped parents with children under age 13 to locate licensed providers in their communities. As of mid 1990, 80 percent of Marriott employees had used the service to find adequate childcare. The department also developed Family Care Spending Accounts to ease the economic strain on employees who were caring for dependents. These accounts allowed participants to take pretax deductions from their wages to pay for child and elder care.

Marriott's Participation in IAM CARES

Since 1985, Marriott participated in IAM CARES (International Association of Machinists Center for Administering Rehabilitation and Employment Services), an international non-profit organization based in Maryland that teamed up with employers to train and help to secure employment for people with disabilities. The premier IAM CARES project was at the Chicago Marriott, which between 1987 and 1994 trained more than 131 individuals with disabilities.

As the Chicago program evolved, other special-interest organizations also became active partners: the Chicago Mayor's Office for People with Disabilities, the Illinois Department for Rehabilitation Services, and the Chicago Public Schools. The Chicago Marriott usually trained 30 people at the hotel each year. The bulk of IAM CARES funding came from the Department of Rehabilitation Services through Title I and Title II funds. The organization also received Job Training Partnership Act funding through the Chicago Mayor's Office on Employment Training. Participants received an on-the-job training wage of $4.25 per hour, paid by IAM CARES's funds.[10]

Marriott's Participation in the Private Industry Council

Located in every area of the United States, Private Industry Councils were the legal arm of the U.S. Department of Labor responsible for linking private industry with certain members of the local unemployed population. Private Industry Councils not only referred individuals for employment, but they also provided training funds under the Job Training Partnership Act (JTPA). Created in 1982, to replace the Comprehensive Employment and Training Act (CETA), in 1996, the JTPA was the federal government's largest job-skills training program. It had a $4-billion annual budget and had aided thousands of employers like Marriott in finding local disadvantaged and disabled individuals who needed job training assistance and who were likely to be qualified for jobs once they had been trained. Its primary goal was to move the jobless into permanent, sustaining employment.[11]

The program targeted educationally disadvantaged and displaced youths and adults, especially women, minorities, and the disabled. Once a candidate was referred, employers like Marriott signed a mandatory contract with the Private Industry Council that stipulated how long the company-specific training would last, what the training would entail, and how much the company would receive in reimbursement. Typically, an employer could not submit an invoice for wage reimbursement until the employee had been on the job for at least 30 days and more often 90 days.

Contracts could cover training for an individual or an entire group. A group's contract was called a customized-training contract and offered a slightly higher reimbursement because the employer also covered some initial costs, such as trainer's salaries, in addition to providing direct training.

Marriott's Participation in the Targeted Jobs Tax Credit (TJTC) Program

The TJTC provided an incentive for companies like Marriott to hire and train former welfare recipients. Marriott estimated that it cost approximately $1,000 to train an entry-level worker. The cost was even higher when training an individual with a poor educational background and sporadic job experience. According to Marriott, the TJTC subsidy enabled them to level the playing field for applications from these targeted populations. Through the TJTC, Marriott established relationships with various community-based organizations as a means of assuring a strong applicant flow.

The federal government discontinued this program because of criticism that some employers were receiving a windfall because eligibility standards were too subjective (i.e., the employer could categorize a prospective employee as "high risk" and receive the "wage subsidy"). The TJTC was replaced by the Work Opportunities Tax Credit Program, which more specifically limited eligibility to welfare recipients, ex-felons, economically disadvantaged veterans, youths in families receiving food stamps, and people with disabilities.[12] Marriott was a major participant in the Work Opportunities Tax Credit Program, which subsidized the salaries of low-wage, difficult-to-employ categories of workers. These programs enabled Marriott to continue to use and keep a low-wage workforce.

Appendix A   Case Note: Organized Labor

Interview with John A. Boardman, Executive Secretary—Treasurer of the Hotel and Restaurant Employees Union, Local 25 of the AFL-CIO, Washington, D.C.

The Union

In 1997, Local 25 of the Hotel and Restaurant Employees had over 6,000 members working in hotels, restaurants, private clubs, and caterers in the Washington, D.C., area. For over 50 years, Local 25 has advocated for "fair treatment, dignity, respect, and improved working conditions" for hotel and restaurant workers. Toward this end, in addition to its unionizing activities, Local 25 has also been politically active in the city of Washington, D.C., lobbying legislators and promoting a civil rights agenda.

Collective Bargaining

The unionization process involves employees in a given workplace electing Local 25 to "collectively bargain" on their behalf. Once elected, the union negotiates a contract between Local 25 and the employer, which guarantees wage rates, benefits, and working conditions. Contracts are usually for three years. Before negotiations begin with a given employer, members are asked to set the bargaining agenda, with the full understanding that not all labor demands will be met. Labor negotiation is a give-and-take process. Once Local 25 and the employer have come to an agreement, the contract only goes into effect after it is presented to the members for their balloted approval. If a contract is not approved, workers may vote to go on strike. The only way a strike can occur is if a majority of workers at a contract meeting vote for it.

Union members pay dues, which go toward maintaining the union. Dues are used to pay the salaries of union representatives who negotiate on behalf of members, lawyers and arbitrators; to educate and train members and shop stewards; and to pay for lobbying efforts to influence legislation that affects members and the communities in which they work.

In a unionized workplace, at least one employee is a designated "shop steward"—the on-the-job union representative. The shop steward is the first person to which a member can turn with grievances or job-related problems.

Benefits

Through their collective bargaining agreements, members are eligible for union-negotiated benefits generally after three months on the job. All benefits are provided by funds paid by the employers with some benefits administered by a joint union-management committee of trustees, and others purchase directly through various benefit providers. Benefits include:

- Dental Care
- Eye Care
- Personal Legal Services
- Pensions
- Credit Union Benefits
- Health Care
- Short- and Long-Term Disability Insurance
- Life Insurance
- 401k Plan

Local 25 and the Marriott Corporation

As a company that prides itself on its "union free environment," the Marriott Corporation and various locals of the Hotel and Restaurant Employees Union across the United States have had a long and turbulent past. In numerous instances, particularly in traditional unionized cities, Marriott has signed "neutrality agreements" (in which Marriott pledges not to interfere with employee attempts to unionize) with municipalities in the interest of getting tax breaks for hotel construction and management and then completely ignoring them once the contract has been awarded.

John Boardman, executive secretary and treasurer of Local 25, described the Marriott Corporation as "Masters of Public Relations." Marriott has always defended its antiunion stance as being in the best interest of its employees. For Marriott, unionization represents increased costs to the employees and the corporation. By keeping unions out, Marriott claims that it can pass the savings on the employee in the form of increased hourly wages. While Boardman acknowledges that Marriott wage rates are comparable to union wage rates in markets where the union has contracts, the similarity ends there.

As opposed to union benefits paid by the employer, Marriott benefits are for the most part completely employee funded.[13] At Marriott, the collectively bargained grievance process has been replaced by a "peer review" grievance system, embodied in the Partners in Management Program. According to Boardman, however, the major shortcoming of this internal review system is the fact that all decisions are reversible by Marriott management staff, particularly in firing decisions. Finally, despite the favorable publicity surrounding the institution of Marriott's Workforce 2000 programs, Local 25 asserts that low-wage employee turnover remains extremely high, especially when compared to the turnover rates at unionized shops.

What disturbs Boardman most is the Marriott "Pathways" program, which specifically targets welfare recipients and the chronically unemployed. Boardman and others at Local 25 see this program, for which Marriott receives federal government subsidies for hiring and training "problem categories" of workers, as an attempt to create a "docile" workforce. Although this program does seek to get the "unemployable" back to work, the federal government ultimately is subsidizing Marriott for hiring from a labor pool that it would have been hiring from anyway (i.e., low-skilled, poorly educated). In addition, the program subsidizes a minimum wage, which, without government interference (according to supply and demand in free market conditions), might have resulted in a natural increase in the wages of the unskilled. The situation has been exacerbated by the passage of the Welfare Reform Act, which essentially creates a labor pool composed of "conscripts."

John Boardman interprets the Marriott approach to its low-wage labor workforce as extremely paternalistic and anti-democratic. Marriott's "caring" approach treats its low-skilled labor as if they were children, and only bad, ungrateful children would attempt to unionize.

Industry Standards

Boardman also acknowledges that the Marriott approach using worker intimidation and reneging on municipal agreements has been extremely successful at confounding workers' unionization attempts. To his dismay, Marriott has been so successful that other hotel chains have been attempting to copy the Marriott model of violating the law. Boardman claims that over the past 20 years, a cadre of "Labor Consultants" have emerged; these consultants are brought into workplaces at the time of union elections. He charges these "Labor Consultants" with utilizing unfair practices and worker intimidation. In addition, even when a workplace has voted in the union, employers have been able to use the judicial system to slow down the implementation process by tying up the union under the National Labor Relations Act in court for a number of years. In some instances, by the time the union ultimately wins a protracted legal battle, the hotel has been sold, and they are forced to repeat the process with a new owner.

In response, labor organizers like Boardman increasingly take a new approach: going outside the National Labor Relations Board process and utilizing other tactics such as protests at the homes of corporate board members, distributing leaflets to hotel guests, or proxy battles, all in the spirit of "If organizing is not war, I don't know what is."[14]

Notes

* This case was written by Orson W. Watson and Research Associate Jenny Mead under the supervision of Patricia H. Werhane, Ruffin Professor of Ethics. It was written as a basis for class discussion rather than to illustrate effective or ineffective handling of an administrative situation. Support for the this project was supplied by funding from the Batten Center for Entrepreneurial Leadership at the Darden School, University of Virginia. Copyright © 2001 by the University of Virginia Darden School Foundation, Charlottesville, VA. All rights reserved.
1 Martha I. Finney, "Fair Game: 'At Marriott, Clifford Ehrlich Bases Decisions on What's Fair,' " *Personnel Administrator* (February 1989): 46.

2 Ralph Raffio, "Company at the Crossroads: Marriott Corp.," *Restaurant Business* (June 10, 1991): 84.

3 Robert McGough, "My son, I brought him up like an Immigrant," *Forbes 400* (October 26, 1987): 74.

4 "Labor's Love Lost," *Washington Post*, 17 February 1992, F3.

5 Sharon Warren Walsh, "Firms Brace for New Law," *Washington Post*, 30 April 1987, 1.

6 Shannon Peters, "Personnel Journal Announces Grant Recipients," *Personnel Journal* (October 1993): 34.

7 Martha I. Finney, "Fair Game: at Marriott, Clifford Ehrlich Bases Decisions on 'What's Fair,' " *Personnel Administrator* (February 1989): 46.

8 Finney, 46.

9 Ronald Henkoff, "Finding, Training, and Keeping the Best Service Workers," *Fortune* (October 3, 1994): 116.

10 Jennifer Laabs, "Individuals with Disabilities Augment Marriott's Workforce," *Personnel Journal* (September 1994): 46.

11 Jennifer Laabs, "How Federally Funded Training Helps Business," *Personnel Journal* (March 1992): 35.

12 Prepared statement of Janet Tull, Marriott International, before the House Government Reform and Oversight Committee and Subcommittee on Human Resources and Intergovernmental Affairs on Work Opportunities Tax Credit as related to job training, April 18, 1996.

13 In Washington, union workers enjoy a 40–45% wage and fringe package advantage over their non-union counterparts. This is almost exclusively the result of the benefits provided in the collectively bargained agreements.

14 Peter Perl, "Workplace Democracy American Style," *Washington Post Magazine* (April 6, 1997).

Chapter 7

Operating in Corrupt Environments

7.1 Econet Wireless Zimbabwe*

Introduction

In July 1998 Econet Wireless had just received the license to operate a second mobile tele-communications network in Zimbabwe. The grueling battle with the government for the license had spanned five long years, and had been fought as much in the tribunals of public opinion as in the courts of law. Even though the company officially had the approval to operate a network, significant challenges lay ahead for Econet's founder Strive Masiyiwa and his team. First, the Zimbabwe Posts and Telecommunications Corporation (PTC), which had enjoyed a monopoly on all telecommunications services in the country, had a two year lead in the mobile telephony business and had cornered much of the corporate market. Second, the Zimbabwean government had recently announced the award of a third mobile telecommunications license, in a country with only 11.5 million inhabitants. Third, significant sums of money would have to be raised to fund the huge up-front investments that the business needed. Finally, telecommunications was a sector with a very high level of governmental intervention, and Masiyiwa was unsure of how the long and bitter five year battle with the government would affect the company's ability to compete.

Strive Masiyiwa

Strive Masiyiwa was born in 1961 in Zimbabwe and attended school in Zambia and Scotland. When he returned to Africa to fight for the liberation of his country from white rule, a Zimbabwean freedom fighter gave him encouraging words: "Look, we're about to win any-way, and what we really need is people like you to help rebuild the country."[1] He then went back to Britain and obtained a Bachelor's degree in Electrical and Electronic Engineering from the University of Wales. After a short stint in the computer industry in Cambridge, UK, Masiyiwa returned to Zimbabwe in 1984 and joined the PTC as Senior Engineer. Masiyiwa was part of the second wave of black managers to join the PTC, whose management at that time was predominantly white. The first wave of black recruits into management was made up of political appointees whereas the second wave was recruited on merit, rather than on political considerations. Masiyiwa commented:

> "It was very interesting because it was a time of tremendous change. There were senior white management around the whole PTC, and then there were these black appointees in senior positions, that didn't do very much except politics. Below you had an organization that was 80% white, that was over the next two or three years to become 80% black. So it was an interesting time from that point of view to be a young engineer in almost a political cauldron."

Masiyiwa was excited at the prospect of making a contribution towards changing a network from one that had been designed for a privileged few into one that had to cater to the needs of the masses. On the other hand, he was frustrated at the highly political nature of the decision making process.

Retrofit: Masiyiwa's First Entrepreneurial Venture

Masiyiwa had at that time no intention of starting his own business. His entry into an entrepreneurial career happened by accident, when he decided to build himself a house. After finding out that the estimates were almost twice the amount of the loan he had been sanctioned, he thought of building the house himself at a lower cost. However, as his employer informed him, the loan could be given only if an experienced builder constructed the house. Even though he was still employed at PTC, he set up a building company called Retrofit Engineering in 1987, looking for work in order to acquire the experience to build his own house. At this time, Zimbabwe, and particularly the capital city of Harare, was experiencing a construction boom. Before long he had a building team of 100 people. He then decided to concentrate on electrical installation, because he understood it better than building. After a year or two of balancing his full time job at PTC and running his new business, he decided that the latter was profitable enough for him to give up his job.

The Difficulty with Business Success

By the late eighties Masiyiwa had acquired national prominence as a business leader, and thus was being watched by the government, to the point where he was abducted at gun-point from his office by the Central Intelligence Organization (CIO). Although he was told that he was being arrested and taken to the CIO headquarters, he was taken to a detention center, which had admitted one person who was never seen again.[2] Masiyiwa talked about this traumatic experience, "I thought I was a dead man. I prayed in the car. In fact, I had been praying all day while in the cell. People say that I am a religious man; it started on that day."[3]

Masiyiwa expounded, ". . . it was the nature of my interrogation which made me realise that the Mugabe government was determined to destroy any successful business. I was the most high profile black businessman at the time because I had just been named by the Chamber of Commerce the Businessman of the Year." Following his abduction, the subject of harassment of black businessmen was raised to Zimbabwe's president, Mugabe. Mugabe denied the harassment charge and agreed to meet with black business leaders. The result was the formation of the IBDC, an organisation aimed at promoting black business in which Masiyiwa played a key leadership role. Masiyiwa commented, "In getting the government to understand that business was a good thing I succeeded beyond my wildest imagination but the result was that suddenly every senior government official and minister wanted to be in business and it led to a lot of corruption and patronage. This was not my intended objective."

One of the biggest problems black Zimbabwean entrepreneurs faced was access to capital, since they had no assets that they could offer as collateral to banks. The IBDC was set up aiming to facilitate the development of small and medium businesses by overcoming this problem.

Masiyiwa's business benefited from his association with the IBDC. At its peak, Retrofit was the biggest electrical engineering company in the country boasting revenues of approximately Zim\$100 million[4] with its main business coming from the armed forces. Retrofit thus had high-level security clearance—it was even given the contract for President Mugabe's rural home.

Masiyiwa's Interest in Mobile Telecommunications

In spite of heading a very successful electrical engineering company, Masiyiwa maintained his interest in telecommunications, particularly mobile telephony.

> "I had tracked it even in my PTC days. We knew what we could do with radio and what was beginning to happen. I felt that from a technical rather than from an entrepreneurial point of view, because the fixed networks that we'd been building, things like networks like the PTC, they relied on—the whole structure was because it required Government intervention. You needed to be a Government in Africa to dig up the streets. Once you got on to radio I knew that the private sector would come in, so I think by the early 90s, I probably, whilst I was busy doing Retrofit stuff, probably 90% of what I read was to do with mobiles. You know, I read everything, I studied everything, I covered every ground. So it became a burning passion for me . . ."

Initially, he was interested in satellite mobile technology, in particular Motorola's Iridium project, which he believed offered an ideal solution to Africa's telecommunications problems. However, he was discouraged by the large capital outlays involved, and therefore turned his attention to terrestrial mobile technology. In 1993, he started discussing his plans with his friend Dr. Nkosana Moyo, who was the Managing Director of the Standard Chartered Bank in Zimbabwe. Moyo was very excited about Masiyiwa's plan for setting up a mobile telecommunications network and its impact on Zimbabwe's economy and society. Based largely on Masiyiwa's enthusiasm and his knowledge of the telecommunications industry, he proceeded to sanction the largest loan his bank had ever sanctioned—Zim$120 million (approximately US$40 million)—to Retrofit to launch the cellular telephone business. Moyo explained his rationale for sanctioning the loan: "it was a self-evident technology."

Laying the Ground Work for Econet

Beyond providing solutions to Africa's telecommunication challenges, Masiyiwa felt that it could become a profitable business. He added:

> "I saw the opportunity to provide a service in a way that had never been provided before. At that time, although cellular was very much a prestige thing, the average African country that had even introduced cellular had an average of five thousand, two thousand subscribers, and I believed that that was a misuse of the technology, where it was just for the rich. And I wrote furiously about this and said: Look, there's no reason why this technology should not open up. At that time things like prepaid had not been developed, which would see millions of people become subscribers. And we were one of the first people to introduce it in Africa. So I was very, very clear in my mind which way I wanted to go."

First Rejection

PTC officials rejected Retrofit's proposal for a joint venture to operate a cellular network, claiming that no demand existed. Masiyiwa then reached an agreement with CellTel International, a company that was involved in the cellular telecommunications business in six African countries. In July 1993, Retrofit indicated its desire to set up a private cellular phone network in Zimbabwe and requested a license from the PTC. This request angered PTC officials, who claimed they had a monopoly on telecommunications services, and that licensing a private firm was out of the question. Masiyiwa was advised by his lawyer that PTC's position was wrong, and that there was a clause concerning radio transmission that negated PTC's monopoly. He was warned that a judicial fight would be costly and difficult, as judges rarely decided against governments.

The Legal Challenge

Masiyiwa used highly technical arguments to appeal to the High Court that PTC's monopoly did not extend to cellular telephony. After six weeks, the judge ruled in Retrofit's favor in January 1994. This decision was quickly reversed on appeal by the Supreme Court, however, favouring PTC's monopoly. Masiyiwa was shaken by this setback. He looked to Biblical principles and his religious faith, which he had discovered during his abduction, to help him through this difficult time. Commenting on this turning point in his life, he said:

> "You know, I'm a born-again Christian, and that was a decision I took . . . every day I must persuade myself that I am practicing my convictions. And, as a businessman in that environment, there was nothing more obvious than to succeed, to do anything it was all about patronage and corruption. I didn't see that we would have a future in African business as long as it was totally associated with corruption. If you go to the average man on the street and you ask them what they think of business people, they talk of kick-backs, corruption. We didn't have an image to present to the next generation. And so I decided that I wanted to make that stand."

The Constitutional Challenge

Masiyiwa then decided to mount a constitutional challenge to PTC's monopoly. Section 20 of the Zimbabwean Constitution said—"Every Zimbabwean has a right to receive and impart information without hindrance." Even though Masiyiwa was advised against the constitutional appeal (because it would be interpreted as questioning the President's leadership), he filed it. He stated that Zimbabwe had only 145,000 telephones, which translated to 1.3 telephones per 100 people; over 95,000 applicants were on the waiting list; and it took an average of five tries to complete a call. As expected, the government reacted badly to the constitutional appeal. Masiyiwa recalled:

> "[T]he Government was just absolutely livid. I mean, people told me that they had—people come and tell me the things that the President had said, and that the generals had said—I mean, the whole system turned on me, the Secret Service, everything. Retrofit lost all its Government work. We didn't just lose the Government work, we were never paid even to this day for any work we had been doing. We were just ordered to leave Government sites, work, everything."

Masiyiwa, his family, friends, and his associates started receiving physical threats and even death threats. One tactic, frequently employed to break a person's spirit was arresting him on a Friday afternoon, so that they could hold him in prison until the next Monday, when the courts opened. However, Masiyiwa would always slip away before the police arrested him (he even hid in the trunk of a friend's car to elude the police), and would spend the weekend in hiding. He was followed, and his telephones were tapped. Plainclothes agents would follow him to his prayer meetings. On one occasion, as he was walking through a park in which people were demonstrating against the government, a secret agent told him, "I'm a great admirer of yours, so please, please, my dear brother get out of the park now. I don't want to file a report that you were here, because there are people who are desperate to show that you are doing this for political reasons, and I know you're not."

By this time, Masiyiwa had also become disenchanted with the government's attempts to take over white owned businesses.

"Although the Mugabe government embraced the idea of the development of black entrepreneurship in the country, it soon became clear that Mugabe now wanted to see only black owned businesses and wanted the blacks to take over the white owned businesses. This naturally found a lot of resonance amongst some of my colleagues in the leadership of the organisation (IBDC). I did not want to have anything to do with this approach so I resigned."

When Masiyiwa realized that he could not save Retrofit, he approached the CEO of its biggest supplier, and asked him to buy the company, insisting that the telecommunications arm would not be included. The CEO readily agreed, because he saw the telecommunications activity as a political liability. Masiyiwa gave birth to his new venture: Enhanced Telecommunications Network (Econet).

Econet Wireless—The Early Days

By the time that Econet Wireless became a business, the PTC had finally woken up to the opportunities in cellular telephony. At that time, there was room for only two operators within the 890–960 Mhz range. The PTC took over one slot.[5] The ruling party announced that it was setting up its own mobile service, took over the other slot, and set up a committee made up of top military and government officials. Masiyiwa saw this as an attempt by the ruling party to kill Econet's battle for a license. The ruling party ordered equipment from Swedish giant Ericsson, but as soon as the equipment arrived, Masiyiwa took out a court injunction against its use. Ericsson, fearing that the equipment might be impounded by the court, shipped it to Durban, South Africa, where it was stored in a warehouse.

The Supreme Court ruled against the PTC in August 1995, stating that the monopoly violated Zimbabwe's constitution. The court also concluded that at the current rate it would take the PTC 14 years to clear the backlog of 95,000 applicants who were waiting for a fixed line. In his ruling, the Chief Justice gave the Minister of Information, Post, and Telecommunications until the end of 1995 to show cause why the monopoly should not be scrapped. The Minister filed a counter-appeal in November 1995 seeking time for the PTC to put in place a regulatory framework and to conduct a major study of the restructuring of the PTC.

Raising Capital

Masiyiwa then appointed a Finance Director with several years experience in international banking to raise funding for Econet. The Finance Director had not anticipated how tough his task would be. He said:

"It was almost impossible, because every bank looked at us as anti-establishment, and therefore up until then there hadn't been any move or party or forum that seriously challenged the establishment, and Econet appeared to be that. So the entire banking community, myself—I started banking as early as 1979, so I knew everybody in the industry. . . . So all the Chief Executives of financial institutions were people I knew personally, and I went to them to say: Can you please help us fund and they all said: We can't have Econet in our books. Because we were viewed as anti-establishment, except for one South African bank that stood with us. They had a totally different view, and subsequently a Government bank helped us with the funding for the operations. That was the Commercial Bank of Zimbabwe. The then Chief Executive took a totally different view and said: I want to support this vision. I believe in what you people are trying to do."

Building the Team

Masiyiwa placed great importance on the character of a person in building his team, believing that professional competence was a necessary but not sufficient condition for recruitment.

Marion Moore, a white Zimbabwean, joined Econet as Chief Financial Officer in November 1995. She had professional accounting qualifications and had worked for several years in the IT industry and later for an American multinational firm. Upon interviewing with Masiyiwa she was surprised by the number of personal questions about her family. She recollected the atmosphere in the firm:

> "It was the most amazing company to work in. I learnt about resilience of willpower and leadership. And in those years Strive—and I think that was one of the things, he's on a huge pedestal for me, he's sort of one of my heroes—and in that time his own dedication and his own—he did it selflessly because when—I mean, we ran on no money, that was another revelation to me is that you can operate with very, very little money, and with the will anything can be achieved."

Due to the capital intensive nature of the cellular telephone business, fundraising was considered a key competence. Moore was responsible for the financial management, whereas the Finance Director settled into a fundraising role. Considerable funding came from Nigel Chanakira, the head of one of Zimbabwe's largest banks, Kingdom Financial Holdings, and a member of Masiyiwa's church. When he was asked why he had offered support to Masiyiwa, he replied—"The Lord spoke to me that I had to help him."

Getting the Equipment and Building the Network

The Supreme Court ruled that PTC could not prevent other players from entering the telecommunications field, and gave Econet permission to proceed to build a network. Masiyiwa met with Ericsson and agreed that Econet would pay US$1 million as deposit and receive the equipment that was originally meant for the ruling party of Zimbabwe, lying in the Durban warehouse. In return, Ericsson would become the sole equipment provider to Econet. He then offered CellTel International[6] a 40% stake in the company. CellTel accepted and agreed to put up US$1 million to fund the purchase of the equipment.

As the equipment was being loaded in Durban for shipment to Zimbabwe, Masiyiwa received information from his friends in government that Mugabe was considering issuing a Presidential Decree,[7] which would overturn the Supreme Court verdict. His lawyer suggested that if Econet could install some equipment and commence transmission before the decree was issued, it could claim grandfather rights[8] to the radio frequency. As soon as the equipment from Ericsson arrived, Masiyiwa's team hurriedly installed a couple of base stations and managed to conclude some transmissions. Econet took out an advertisement in national newspapers announcing that it had acquired the cellular equipment and claimed the right of use of one of the two available slots in the frequency. The public responded—approximately 5,000 subscribers applied for service.

The Reigns Tighten: The Presidential Decree

On February 5, 1996, President Mugabe issued the presidential decree requiring private parties to obtain a license from the PTC before setting up a cellular network, thus restoring PTC's monopoly until the lengthy process of issuing a license could be completed. Mugabe told Newsweek magazine that he was not out to get Masiyiwa, but to ensure other interested parties an equal chance of getting a cell phone license. When asked to explain the reason behind the presidential decree, Masiyiwa simply said—"I don't pay bribes."[9]

Members of the government also pressured CellTel International (which had agreed to take a 40% stake in Econet and had advanced the US$1 million for the equipment purchase) to ask for repayment of the money. In return, the government promised CellTel the second cellular license. CellTel complied by demanding its money back, and recruited new partners, among them the President's nephew, some ministers, and other prominent people. Around this time, the PTC launched its own cellular phone service in Harare with 2,000 lines, using a US$24 million loan from international financial institutions.

Masiyiwa now turned to an American friend in Johannesburg, who was the Vice President for Africa of Southwestern Bell Corporation (SBC). This friend helped Masiyiwa negotiate a deal whereby Ericsson would repay the US$1 million it had taken for the equipment and convert it into a loan. This friend then approached MTN, the South African telecommunications company in which SBC had a stake, to take up an option for a 40% stake in Econet in return for 8 million South African Rands. The deal, which provided much needed cash at a critical juncture for Econet, also included technical assistance.

Masiyiwa challenged the Presidential Decree in the Supreme Court and personally wrote to President Mugabe. Mugabe directed him to speak with the Justice Minister and Masiyiwa recalled, "The Minister of Justice said he had reviewed our position, and he was of the view that we should be licensed immediately. But there was something he said and, I knew that we had a problem . . . we realized that they were buying time."

Masiyiwa had invested US$5 million of his own funds and was now in danger of running out of money. While many Ministers and officials tried to convince Masiyiwa to end the battle by "accommodating" the interests of powerful constituencies, he stood by his convictions. It turned out to be fruitful—the Supreme Court, in a unanimous judgment, ordered the Minister of Information to grant Econet a license by the end of February 1997. It added that if the government did not grant Econet or any other operators licenses by February 1997, then "Econet shall be deemed to be licensed for a period of three years."[10] The Court stipulated, however, that the license should be granted only if the provisions of the amendment to the Telecommunications Act were met. This meant that in spite of a favorable verdict, Econet had no choice but to participate in the tender process for a license.

The Tender Process for a Second License

Econet applied to the Supreme Court towards the end of January 1997 seeking confirmation that it was duly licensed. It argued that the government had failed to comply with the verdict of the Supreme Court to issue a license. A legal analyst commented, "Masiyiwa's only hope is now the Supreme Court. If he wins the case, this will kill the current tender selection exercise and literally bring him back from the brink. But if he loses, he can kiss goodbye to this long struggle and be content, maybe, with whatever costs the court may impose on the government, if it does so, for the waste of his efforts."[11]

In early 1997, Masiyiwa received an unexpected telephone call from the Zimbabwean Vice President Nkomo, who was over 80 years old. Masiyiwa recalled their conversation:

> "And he (Nkomo) said to me: Every time I hear your name it's to do with this fight, tell me about it. And I told him the whole story. We must have spoken for maybe two hours. And he started crying. He said: This is not what I fought for, this is not the Zimbabwe I fought for. So he went to see the President. He found the President in a Cabinet meeting, and just stood in the middle of the room and said: Why, why, why are you doing this? And then Mugabe turned around and said: Okay, let's talk about it later. In the evening the Vice President called me and said to me Mugabe had agreed to issue a third license, so Zimbabwe would have three operators instead of two. And I said fine. And he said: But do you accept one condition, that the other people should be shareholders in the company? He (Mugabe) simply said that you cannot be alone in the business, you have to have other shareholders and you should accommodate others in the company.[12] I said: I am not going to accommodate anybody. I'll take the company public, anyone who wants to buy a share can buy."

Political Divisions in the Zimbabwean Government

In what was seen as a major rift in the political leadership on the cellular license issue, Nkomo threatened to resign from the government in protest against the government's decision to award the license to CellTel. A compromise was then worked out whereby all four of the contenders would have a share in the second cellular operator, to be called Net Two (PTC's cellular service was called Net One). Masiyiwa, however, made it clear that he would not participate in such a project.

The Information Minister filed an affidavit in the Supreme Court complaining that Econet's "constant barrage of litigation" had delayed the introduction of a cellular phone service. In March 1997 the Acting President Nkomo (Mugabe was away in Europe) had ordered that the Information Minister give a license to Econet. The Information Minister had professed ignorance of such instructions, saying: "I am not aware of any instruction from President Mugabe or Vice President Nkomo to issue a license to Masiyiwa." In an official visit to Paris in March 1997, Mugabe told reporters that there was one person (in apparent reference to Masiyiwa) who thought he had a right to the country's second license just because he was assisted by certain foreign companies.[13]

Protesting CellTel's License

The Information Minister stated, after the awarding of the second license to CellTel, that the government would only award a third license if the first two licensees proved unreliable. The debate split the government in two, with the Vice-President Nkomo on one side and Mugabe and the Information Minister on the other.

Moore recalls that news of the award of the cellular license to CellTel was a very big blow to the morale of the Econet team. She talked about how the team bounced back:

> "Strive came in with a smile on his face, a lot of energy, and said: Right, we're going to inspect the tender, we're off to find out why CellTel won that tender, and we're going to question it if it's not right. . . . And that time with the team was one of the best as well,

because it was hilarious, and everybody had their little section where you had to pick their (CellTel's) tender document to pieces ... And their marketing plan for instance, I think theirs was three pages long, ours was a 56 page document with detailed retail outlets. We had clear ideas about how we were going to market the product."

A lawyer working on Econet's side described the atmosphere during the court battles:

"Well, there was a great sense of feeling amongst the team that this was a principle case, it was a case for justice, it was a case against corruption, and there were excesses at that stage of the Zimbabwean government. The employees (of Econet) weren't paid because they just didn't have the money. And the lawyers weren't being paid either, and that caused some friction within the (law) firm."

Hope vs. Reality: Econet Presses On

An industry executive talked about Masiyiwa's chances of getting a license—"It's not a question of faith or hope in this or that thing. It's really a question of getting things done, and as things stand now, Masiyiwa appears to stand no chance of getting this project off the ground. There are simply too many forces that are too strong ranged against him."[14] In spite of this pessimism, the staff at Econet, which had grown to 51, carried on working normally.

In March 1997, Information Minister ordered Masiyiwa to either sell his equipment to CellTel, or surrender it to the government for no compensation. The Minister said that if he did not comply, the police or state security service might be instructed to arrest him, for having violated the security and defense laws of the country. After Masiyiwa protested to the High Court, the Information Minister finally relented, "I accept that I have no right to direct the applicant as to what it must do with the equipment and I claim no right to seize the equipment or to have it confiscated by the state."[15]

One press article reported that a middleman for three government ministers had stated outright to Masiyiwa—"The price for a license is $400,000 US." He then reportedly consulted with the ministers, who were in an adjoining room, and returned to say—"OK. You can pay in installments."[16]

The Challenge to the Tender Outcome

In its challenge, Econet presented a 100-page letter to the Government Tender Board (GTB), which outlined its objections to the award of the license to CellTel. Upon receiving the letter, the Chairman of the GTB instructed CellTel to stop all action until the complaints of Econet had been addressed. He then asked the Minister of Information not to confirm CellTel as the winner of the tender process, and gave her three weeks to respond to Econet's complaint point by point. This decision by the GTB was received with disbelief in government circles. The Information Minister refused to respond—"There is no point in providing you with a point-by-point response to the appeal. The Tender Board has no power to suspend the license as the Chairman purports to have done."[17] There were also allegations of a conflict of interest against the Information Minister: in addition to her husband being a business associate of a leading member of the CellTel team, it was also reported that she had been listed as a referee in the tender document that CellTel had submitted.[18]

The lawyers representing the government approached companies that Econet owed money to requesting that they cede their debt to the government. Once they had Econet's debt, they could force it into liquidation. In these situations, Chanakira from Kingdom Holdings was asked to step in and pay off Econet's debts.

An Unexpected Intervention

After CellTel had been awarded the second license, an American missionary walked into Masiyiwa's office, and demanded an Econet phone line. Although Masiyiwa informed him that they could not give him one, the missionary insisted on prepaying immediately for a line, offering Zim$10,000. The missionary then drew up a list of candidates who would be given special numbers and become customers. Later, a group of Christian journalists published an article supporting Masiyiwa's effort to secure a license:

> "Masiyiwa has constantly been at the receiving end of government decisions, which seem to have been made to blatantly frustrate the genuine initiative of this indigenous businessman. . . . We therefore see the tender board decision to award a second cellular network to a certain clique with strong political connections as confirmation that there exists an element of partiality. The government is not above the law and must follow the Supreme Court ruling which has underscored Masiyiwa's right to operate a cellular network."[19]

A large number of people wrote letters to the editorial offices of national newspapers expressing support for Masiyiwa, and stating that they would only subscribe to Econet's cellular service. Masiyiwa received encouragement from citizens to continue fighting. The international media also took notice—a Danish television crew made a documentary about Econet. About 4,000 students of the University of Zimbabwe held a demonstration to protest against the rampant corruption in the public tender system.

A pleasant surprise surfaced—the GTB had made a mistake in adding up the marks to arrive at the final total, meaning that a legal opinion from the judge was no longer necessary; the challenge to the CellTel award could be substantiated on factual issues alone.

The Final Victory

The High Court's decision finally came on December 31, 1997, which revoked the license awarded to CellTel, and ruled that the second cellular license be awarded to Econet. By this time, CellTel had already started installing its infrastructure; its Chairman announced that his company would contest the High Court decision. A month later, a third license was issued to CellTel, which accepted the license and withdrew its appeal to the Supreme Court. The decision to grant CellTel a license without any tender was received with outrage by Zimbabweans. An editorial was scathing in its criticism of the government:

> "In one single strike, President Robert Mugabe's government unashamedly overturned repeated and unambiguous rulings of the country's highest courts, the very foundations of the rule of law, just in order to curry favor with its cronies stunned that they cannot have things go their way all the time."[20]

By April, Econet had drafted an interconnection agreement with PTC that they hoped would be signed by the end of May. The agreement was expected to earn PTC Zim$64 million annually in the first year; this would increase to Zim$600 million by the tenth year.

The Challenges Ahead

Econet's staff had increased from 51 at the end of 1997 to more than 100 at the end of May 1998. More than 20,000 subscribers had applied for service. A lawyer who had earlier represented Econet later joined the company. He commented:

> ". . . the engineers, whilst they'd been helping with the court case, they'd spent those years designing the network and planning it to a meticulous level of detail. The marketing people had been preparing brochures and booklets and strategies and branding. [T]here was an enormous level of thought and preparation that had gone into it."

Econet assets were valued on 30 June 1998 at approximately Zim$240 million, which was equivalent to US$13.25 million.[21] Econet planned to raise a further Zim$540 million of proceeds from an initial public offer (IPO) of share capital (290 million) and debentures (250 million) to fund its expansion. Half the share capital was to be placed with institutional investors in London, who had shown great eagerness to participate in Econet's equity capital.

Masiyiwa and his team felt that the IPO was necessary so early in the company's life because they were having great difficulty in raising funds from traditional sources such as banks. FD commented:

> "The challenge we faced at that time was that nobody understood this business. The only other operator who was out there was Government, and therefore the banks, none of the banks had ever financed a mobile cellular company. So there were no reference points, no experience at all, and we challenged—we went to a lot of local merchant banks and said: We need finance for 17 base stations. So they added them up and calculated it and said: My goodness, this is too much. How many customers? Well, we said, we'll probably start with 1,000 and rise. They said: No, no, no, no, no, why don't you start with two base stations and let's see where that goes? We said: No, the cellular business doesn't work that way."

The license for Econet to operate was officially signed by the Ministry in July 1998. Ironically, Econet, as part of a consortium, was awarded a telecommunications license in Botswana (February 17, 1998) before it got one in Zimbabwe. Upon officially opening its doors, Econet had 30,000 subscribers who were eagerly waiting to be connected.

Dilemma

With the license in his hands, Masiyiwa pondered if he had won the battle but lost the war. He knew competing in a highly regulated industry would be tough and he felt that he would be constantly breaking new ground in Zimbabwe. Masiyiwa wondered how he could go about building a successful business.

"No Fuel No Forex Vote No"

In February 2000, those six words rung in Masiyiwa's head. They were being passed around as a text message on Econet's cellular network to oppose President Mugabe's referendum on constitutional reforms. Masiyiwa had immediately ordered an investigation into the origin of the messages to ensure that no one in Econet could be accused of starting this political campaign, and had concluded that the messages had originated with the subscribers

Exhibit 7.1.1 Zimbabwe: a brief history[22]

1890—British settlers named the area (currently called Zimbabwe) Northern and Southern Rhodesia after Cecil John Rhodes. The country was administered by the British South Africa Company.

1923—The Company's charter was abrogated in 1923. White settlers chose to become part of the British Empire.

1934—Legislation was passed that reserved certain areas for the white settlers.

1964—Northern Rhodesia became the independent state of Zambia. The white settlers in Southern Rhodesia showed little interest in granting political representation to the blacks. At the same time, an increasing number of whites wanted independence from the United Kingdom.

1965—The United Kingdom was prepared to grant independence only if Southern Rhodesia took the first steps towards eventual majority rule. The whites, under the leadership of Prime Minister Ian Smith, refused and unilaterally declared independence (UDI) on November 11, 1965. Southern Rhodesia was renamed Rhodesia.

During 1960s—Frequent armed conflicts between the Zimbabwe African People's Union (ZAPU) and the Zimbabwe African National Union (ZANU) debating whether armed confrontation or international intervention should be used to oust white ruling power.

1976—The Patriotic Front was formed jointly headed by Joshua Nkomo and Robert Mugabe. The negotiations in Geneva between the nationalists and the white minority were inconclusive, which led to the nationalists resuming guerilla warfare.

1979—The conflict was finally resolved at the Lancaster House Conference in England with an agreement that free elections would be held.

1980—Mugabe was elected prime minister of the free nation called Zimbabwe.

Zimbabwe—GDP and Inflation 1995–1998

	1995	1996	1997	1998
Real GDP growth rate	0.6	8.7	2.8	3.7
Inflation	25.8	16.4	18.8	31.8

---

themselves. A few days later, the people of Zimbabwe voted "no", signaling the first defeat of the Mugabe government in a public vote.

The President believed that there was a political motive behind the messages, and that Masiyiwa was supporting the Opposition party Movement for Democratic Change (MDC). Masiyiwa was informed that Mugabe had said that he should be eliminated. The government denied any such comment by Mugabe.[23] The government then introduced a bill, giving it sweeping powers to eavesdrop on telephone conversations and to intercept e-mail messages between individuals and companies. Security police sympathetic to Masiyiwa recommended that he should leave the country because his life was under threat.[24]

Econet: July 1998 to February 2000

After securing the license in July 1998, Econet was quick to launch its prepaid cellular service. The combination of this innovative product and the goodwill it had accumulated with Zimbabweans over the five years of court battles took it to a position of market leadership in just three months, even though PTC's cellular service (Net One) had been launched nearly two years earlier in September 1996. Masiyiwa talked about the prepaid strategy:

"... I saw where prepaid was going very quickly, even before your Vodacoms and what

Exhibit 7.1.2 Mugabe's Tenure: 1980–1998

Although Mugabe was successful during the first two years after independence in pursuing a policy of national reconciliation, factional differences between Nkomo and Mugabe continued. In 1983 and 1984, government troops were deployed to quell unrest by pro-Nkomo dissidents, during which the troops were accused of committing atrocities. The situation improved, a unity pact was signed and the parties merged. Mugabe won the presidential elections in 1990 and again a comfortable second six-year term in 1996.

Mugabe's government made impressive progress in education and the provision of healthcare during the 1980s—the adult literacy rate had reached almost 90% by the early nineties.[25] This progress came through an increase in public expenditures, which during most of the 1980s were around 45% of GDP. The government's deficit also grew steadily in this period from 9.7% of GDP in 1980/81 to 13.6% in 1994/95.

In 1991, the Government introduced the Economic and Structural Adjustment Program (ESAP), with support from the World Bank, in the form of a US$125 million loan and a US$50 million credit. The ESAP sought four objectives: 1) reduction of fiscal deficit through downsizing of the civil service and reduction of subsidies to state owned enterprises; 2) liberalization of trade policies and exchange regulations; 3) deregulation of the domestic economy; and 4) establishment of a social safety net for the vulnerable groups. The Government made good progress on objectives 2) and 3), but not on 1) and 4).[26]

In 1998, the Government came under severe pressure from the war veterans who had fought in the 1970s for the liberation of the country from colonial rule. These veterans felt that 18 years after independence, the Government had failed to keep its promises of paying them a decent pension and of giving them land. Mugabe ordered the Treasury to pay the war veterans Zim$5 billion as grants and pensions. This payment had not been budgeted for and therefore the Treasury had no alternative but to print money to make these payments.

With a view to redistributing white owned land to blacks, parliament approved legislation in 1992 allowing the compulsory acquisition of land provided adequate compensation was paid, but a lack of funds slowed down this process. Roughly 30 million acres of land was in the hands of just 4,500 white farmers. While the vast majority of the population was in favor of the redistribution of the land, they were dismayed at the manner in which it was implemented. In 1997, the government announced an accelerated land resettlement program, and published a list of 1,000 properties whose white occupants were ordered to voluntarily leave their land. They were asked to seek compensation from the United Kingdom.

have you, I figured out what prepaid was going to do. I remember going to look for a prepaid platform. We couldn't find one. People were saying: But it's still a conceptional thing. We said: No, no, we must have prepaid. So prepaid was to play a pivotal role in giving us market leadership, because what we recognized was the fact that the African consumer was the perfect consumer for prepaid, because the issues of credit management, credit control, credit cards, all this was not relevant. That doesn't mean that somebody doesn't have money, you know. . . . And so prepaid for me was an incredible strategic tool when it came through, and so we were very quick in spotting it. We had to go to Israel to get prepaid technology, because the Israelis were the ones who were playing with it and had the cutting edge."

The prepaid product was branded Buddie, which soon became the generic term for all prepaid products. The product targeted to the business segment was called Excel, and it allowed customers to have two cellular numbers on one phone. Other products that were new to the Zimbabwean market were introduced quickly, such as voicemail, faxmail, the Short Messaging Service (SMS), and the News on Demand, for which the content was provided by CNN. The company was also the first to offer a 24-hour customer care service.

Exhibit 7.1.3 Zimbabwe's Institutions

The Judiciary:[27] The general common law of Zimbabwe is Roman Dutch Law, mixed with English Common Law. The Court System is divided into a number of tiers: the Supreme Court, the High Court, the Magistrates' Courts, and the Local Court. The judiciary was respected both nationally and internationally as independent and impartial. There were many instances in the 1980s and early 1990s in which the Courts had demonstrated their independence.

Civil Service:[28] The Civil Service increased from 10,570 posts in 1980 (only 31% blacks) to 193,000 in 1994. As part of the Economic Structural Adjustment Program (ESAP), the civil service was drastically reduced in 1995 by 23,500 to 169,500, with a further reduction planned of 26,000 jobs over the following two years. Considering that no reductions were permitted in the Ministry of Health and Child Welfare and the Ministry of Education, which employed 114,816 persons (nearly 60%), the cuts in the remainder of the ministries were quite deep. In addition to these cuts, many other measures such as performance evaluations and decentralization were introduced. There were reports of problems in communications between the government and the civil service about the motives and objectives of the reforms. Senior civil servants were reported to have resisted these changes. Salaries had also not kept pace with the rising cost of living.

The Press:[29] The press was highly politicized, with a very strong pro-government section and a smaller but equally vociferous anti-government (or pro-opposition) section. The pro-government papers were The Herald (the oldest daily in Zimbabwe), The Chronicle (published in Bulawayo), The Sunday Mail (weekly), and the Zimbabwe Mirror (weekly). The pro-opposition papers were The Daily News, The Financial Gazette (weekly), the Zimbabwe Independent (weekly), and The Standard (weekly).

Religion: Roughly 40% of the 11.5 million people of Zimbabwe were considered to belong to some Christian denomination, although the influence of Christianity was far greater. The next biggest religion in Africa was African Traditional Religion, with nearly 30% adherents. Other religions such as Islam, Judaism, Hinduism were also represented.

Econet's IPO and Zimbabwe's Political Moves

The Initial Public Offering (IPO) took place in September 1998 and was hugely successful—it was oversubscribed. However, just the month before, when Econet's IPO campaign was in full swing, Mugabe's government decided to send Zimbabwean troops to the Democratic Republic of Congo (DRC), to support President Kabila against rebels, who were being backed by Rwanda and Uganda. An Econet lawyer talked about the interplay of the events:

> "The IPO went very, very well. It was oversubscribed, and I remember at the beginning of the IPO we were looking at all the things that could go wrong were political, because we were dealing at that stage with what we thought was an irrational President. We didn't realize at that stage how irrational. What he did was he went to war in the Congo, in the middle of the IPO."

The decision to intervene militarily in the DRC only exacerbated the already severe economic problems of the country. The Zim$/US$ exchange rate, which had hovered around 18 in July 1998, fell sharply to 30 by mid-September when the Econet share started trading on the Zimbabwe Stock Exchange, and continued to deteriorate to 38 by the end of September. Considering that Econet was heavily dependent on imports to finance its network development, this fall in the value of the Zim$ reduced the purchasing power of its IPO proceeds by half. Econet's lawyer commented:

> "It affected our roll out very dramatically. Simply, the equipment that we thought we

Exhibit 7.1.4 Mugabe's Regime: 1998 to 2000

In August 1998, the government decided to send Zimbabwean troops to support the leader of the Democratic Republic of Congo, Laurent Kabila. This decision, coupled with an already deteriorating economy, put pressure on the Zimbabwean dollar, which fell almost 100% in value in the space of a couple of months with respect to the US$. In 1999, a parallel exchange rate emerged which reflected the true demand and supply of the US$ in the Zimbabwean economy. By the end of June 2002, the official rate of the US$ was Zim$55, but the parallel market rate was as high as Zim$700.

In February 2000, the government conducted a referendum on constitutional reform that would have allowed it to seize white owned land without any compensation. This referendum was defeated, the first time the ZANU-PF party had lost a public vote since it came to power in 1980. Militia groups, made up of war veterans and unemployed urban youth, forcibly occupied some 500 farms by mid March and in some cases killed the white farmers. Mugabe, while recognizing that these invasions were illegal, expressed its inability to evict the invaders. Mugabe and the ruling party characterized these invasions as spontaneous. However, the Zimbabwe Human Rights and other non-governmental organizations researched these incidents and published several reports indicating that considerable planning had gone into them. These reports also pointed the finger at the ruling party, the army, and the CIO for having supported the violence.

Many white farmers emigrated from Zimbabwe, thus affecting the agricultural production in the country. The country went from being the "grain bowl" of Southern Africa to facing food shortages. The second half of the nineties saw the population increasingly disenchanted with the Mugabe regime, as a result of political oppression, human rights violations, widespread corruption, and economic mismanagement leading to steep increases in the prices of basic commodities. By 2000, the unemployment rate was estimated at 55%. In 1999, the Movement for Democratic Change under Morgan Tsvangirai emerged as an organized opposition.

could buy we could no longer buy, so it affected coverage, not so much in the cities but the rural area coverage it would have been given didn't take place. And then with time and the very rapid uptake of subscribers, we had congestion problems in the cities and, that was also—our capacity was affected by—we just had to buy less equipment."

Business Performance

In spite of this difficult macro-economic environment, Econet had 63,000 subscribers by the end of its financial year June 30, 1999, which was 85% higher than the original forecast of 34,000, giving it a market share of 55%. Agreements had been signed with the 20,000 member Government Workers Association, and the 30,000 member Civil Service Cooperative Society. Revenues stood at Zim$434 million. The company also achieved the very unusual feat in the telecommunications business of reporting a profit in its very first year of trading. The average time to profitability in the capital-intensive cellular business was considered to be three years. The Econet share was quoting at approximately Zim$4.50 by the end of June, giving the company a market capitalization of Zim$3.26 billion (US$86 million).

In November 1999, Masiyiwa was named one of the top 10 outstanding young global leaders by the International Junior Chamber.[30] The Zimbabwe Independent cited telecommunications experts who believed that the competitive spirit unleashed by Masiyiwa in Botswana and Zimbabwe had contributed to the highest cellular penetrations in Africa, with cellular phone numbers exceeding fixed lines.[31]

Due to foreign exchange being unavailable, Econet's management could not expand capacity as projected, and decided during 2000 to concentrate on the more profitable contract users. They consequently curtailed the sales to new prepaid customers.

The Strategic Decision to Internationalize

Given the fast deteriorating economic environment, the Econet management took in February 2000 perhaps its most significant strategic decision: to reduce the exposure to Zimbabwe by developing other markets in Africa and beyond. The vision of the company, which had been "To provide telecommunications to all the peoples of Zimbabwe" (IPO prospectus August, 1998), was now reformulated "To provide telecommunications to all the peoples of Africa."

> "We did a strategic review and we basically concluded that one of the biggest risks we had is single country exposure. There was an absolute howl amongst shareholders, because shareholders, particular market analysts, they can't see beyond this afternoon. They said: How can Strive get up, abandon a company two years into operation? If you guys want to expand, why don't you send a marketing department to be based in South Africa. You don't have to leave Zimbabwe. I said: Listen, the biggest risk this company has is single country exposure."

Masiyiwa saw five reasons for expanding into Johannesburg, South Africa: access to capital; access to international skills; a banking system that was accustomed to supporting international companies; networks of senior managers; and logistics—Johannesburg was the city with the largest number of international airlines in Africa.

The macro-economic environment in Zimbabwe continued to deteriorate with high inflation, shortages of essential commodities such as food and fuel, and a falling currency. In spite of these economic difficulties, the company performed impressively. Less than two years after start-up, Econet was the second largest company on the Zimbabwe Stock Exchange in terms of market capitalization. Since its shares started trading in September 1998, it had outperformed NASDAQ's telecommunications sector. Salomon Smith Barney rated Econet one of the most exciting shares in Africa for international investors. In spite of the economic problems in Zimbabwe, HSBC recommended the Econet stock as a "buy."[32]

Dilemma

Masiyiwa wondered what would happen if he left his home country to continue with Econet from South Africa. While he understood that Econet's strategy could benefit from opening up other African countries, he debated the personal and business risk inherent in making a relocation decision.

Epilogue

> "Strive is personable and has demonstrated extreme resilience under pressure. But he is known for pushing the limits and has done extremely well in building up his group on the smell of an oil rag."[33]
>
> Ross Macdonald, former MTN executive and telecom consultant

Strive Masiyiwa's Decision to Move

In February 2000, Masiyiwa left Zimbabwe and moved to Johannesburg, South Africa. As of February 2004, he had not returned to visit his native country. Aside from the personal risk of staying in Zimbabwe, Masiyiwa felt that Econet was exposed to a single country risk. Being in South Africa also provided access to capital and international skills, networks of senior managers, a more robust banking system and better logistics. Masiyiwa recalled:

"Now you've got to realize that we're coming from a country where there's a foreign currency control regime. So we could not transfer capital. So coming here was a massive challenge. That's why a lot of Zimbabwean business wouldn't do what we did, but we said: Look, we will find a way to build the relationships and access the capital, but we wanted to be in South Africa . . ."

Consumers Reactions in Zimbabwe

All three cellular companies had stopped investing in their network infrastructures because of the exorbitant cost of buying US dollars. This had led to high congestion and a drop in the quality of service. No new subscribers were being accepted, which meant that there was a black market for telephone lines. Econet's goodwill with the public had begun to erode. In spite of this erosion in popularity, Econet still fared better than its two competitors on indicators such as brand awareness, purchase intention, breadth of product and services offered. Net One was considered the best in geographical coverage and CellTel offered the best tariffs.

Zimbabwe Strategy: In a Storm

The macro-economic situation in Zimbabwe deteriorated further in the year 2000–2001. US dollars were not available at the official rate of Zim$55. By April 2001, the Zim$ was being traded in the parallel market at 200 to the US$ with inflation high at 70%. Despite these grave economic conditions, one of the biggest and most dramatic problems was social: roughly 25% of the adult population was HIV positive, and the life expectancy at birth of Zimbabweans had gone down to under 40 years. Masiyiwa explained the strategy in his home country:

"So our whole approach to Zimbabwe is basically, it's like a ship. Take down the sails, put it into a safe harbour, because it's in the middle of a storm. Now, my customer on the ground is saying: You know, I'm suffering from congestion, I want more coverage. . . . The public pay phone generates more revenue than a normal cellphone. Prepaid, although Buddie is extremely popular, does not generate as much air time as a contract, so we deliberately make decisions here to say: limit the delivery of prepaid, so it's not available, so it becomes a black market product. But all those are really strategies to carry the business through the storm."

During 2000–2001, Econet lost roughly 30% of its skilled workforce of technicians and IT specialists. Econet was unable to sufficiently compensate its employees for the inflation in Zimbabwe and new cellular networks in other African countries had recruited well-trained Econet employees, offering them salaries in hard currencies. Masiyiwa commented, "It's a massive problem, because how do you sufficiently remunerate an employee who faces inflation of 250%? How do you remunerate such a guy? It's impossible. So you've got to face the fact that your employee cannot be satisfied with his situation."

To stem the tide of departing skilled workers, the management devised a strategy of deploying its trained Zimbabwean workforce on short and long term contracts in its international operations. By this time, the company was also present in Lesotho and Morocco. These international operations served as attractive postings for employees who were frustrated with their remuneration in Zimbabwe. Masiyiwa elaborated:

". . . because the biggest tragedy of the Zimbabwean situation is that although Mugabe's policies from a public perspective appear to be directed at the white farmers, the white farmers are not leaving the country, they've nowhere to go, it's the black professionals who are hurt by the fall in the currency. So you've got a massive exodus of young black professionals. So for us, our key people are part of Econet Wireless International, and basically we're able to move technicians, engineers, accountants, around inside our global operation."

Internationalization: Nigeria and Beyond

In January 2001, a consortium of which Econet was a member was awarded one of the three cellular licenses in Nigeria, a huge market with a population over 120 million. The license fee was US$285 million. Econet was originally allocated 40% of the equity in the Nigerian company, which was called Econet Wireless Nigeria, but could not put together the resources to pay for this equity share. Consequently, an agreement was reached whereby it was given a 5% share and the responsibility of managing the business: it would provide the CEO and other senior officers, and would receive a management fee in compensation. As of June 30, 2002, less than a year after Econet Wireless Nigeria (EWN) was launched, it had achieved a subscriber base of 415,000 for a market share of 50%, after a marketing campaign that industry experts characterized as outstanding. EWN employed 500 people, and had already provided coverage to 12 Nigerian cities. By the end of 2003, Econet was in competition with South African based MTN for the top spot in the Nigerian marketplace.

Telecom Lesotho (TCL) launched both fixed and mobile services in May 2002, and had achieved a subscriber base of 12,400 for a market share of 20%. Econet Satellite Services (ESS), headquartered in London, had installed a US$1.2 million satellite port outside London, and two earth stations in Nigeria. The Maori tribe had been given a license in New Zealand, and had chosen Econet as its partner. Econet had taken a 63% equity in the company, which was called Econet Wireless New Zealand (EWNZ). In Botswana, Econet was in a consortium with Portugal Telecom called Mascom Wireless, which had a market share of 70%.

Econet's Business Performance

Exhibit 7.1.5 shows Econet's performance in Zimbabwe for the period 1999–2002.

There was a steep fall in the Econet share price on the Zimbabwe Stock Exchange during April 2002, when the stock fell to Zim$4, as a result of the panic selling by foreign investors withdrawing en masse from Zimbabwe. On the whole, it was clear the Econet share had lost its popularity with investors. The economic environment in Zimbabwe did not foster foreign investor confidence. Zimbabwean investors, who could not take their capital out of the country, had lost their appetite for Econet for several reasons: no dividends had been declared for a couple of years; many investors did not really understand why Masiyiwa had left the country; they were not very knowledgeable about the group's international operations; and they saw frequent changes in the top management team in Zimbabwe, as managers were seconded to the newer international operations such as Nigeria and Lesotho. Moore, the CFO commented, ". . . they're an unpopular share at the moment. I think they feel a bit let down mainly because Strive's gone, and also all the senior management that were there are not here any more."

By the end of June 2002, Econet Zimbabwe also had an unpaid US dollar denominated debt with Ericsson that was long overdue and that it was unable to repay because of the high foreign exchange rate. Ericsson had threatened to cut off all support to Econet Zimbabwe

Exhibit 7.1.5 Econet Wireless Zimbabwe Financial Performance Key Indicators 1999–2002

	1999	2000	2001	2002
Zim$				
Revenues (Zim$—millions)	434	1279	2864	6083
Average Revenue Per User (Zim$)	1147	1358	2096	3708
Net Profit (Zim$—millions)	8	77	279	1024
EPS (Zim $)	0.0125	0.0975	0.322	1.2445
USD$				
F/X Rate	0.02639	0.01818	0.01877	0.01862
Revenues (US$—millions)	11.5	23.3	53.8	113.3
Average Revenue Per User (US$)	30.27	24.69	39.34	69.04
Net Profit (USD$—millions)	0.2	1.4	5.2	19.1
EPS (USD$)	0.00	0.00	0.01	0.02
Subscribers	63,000	94,000	133,976	139,402

F/X Rate: December 31 for each year from www.oanda.com

until payments started. Some of Econet's management felt that the company had had several windows of opportunity, especially in 1999 and 2000, for raising capital to repay the debt, but felt that Masiyiwa was hesitant to dilute his shareholding in the company.

By the end of 2002, the group had been restructured, so that Econet Zimbabwe had no foreign currency debt. Its total debt in early June 2003 stood at Zim$1.4 billion. Network development resumed and progress had been made in clearing up the congestion. New lines were being issued on a limited basis to corporate customers. All new equipment was being purchased on a cash basis. Masiyiwa also indicated that the first dividend would be declared in June 2003.

In accordance with the restructuring, all of Econet's activities in all countries, except Zimbabwe, came under the Econet Wireless Group (EWG), which was domiciled in Botswana. The Zimbabwean operations were left out because of the difficulties involved in getting approval from the Zimbabwean government. EWG therefore was the umbrella company for Nigeria, United Kingdom, New Zealand, Lesotho, South Africa, Morocco, and Botswana.

Econet's Battle with Vodacom for Nigeria

Despite the success in Nigeria, Econet's stake in its Nigerian business was vulnerable since it only had 5% ownership. As a result, the largest South African operator, Vodacom (owned by Telekom SA 50%, Vodafone plc 35% and Ven Tin Ltd. 15%), got the agreement from Econet Wireless Nigeria board members to purchase 51% of the company in October 2003.[34] The deal was worth $260 million in equity and $300 million in the form of a loan.[35] This deal contradicted Econet's binding contract, which called for Econet International to increase its stake in Econet Wireless Nigeria (EWN). For this deal, Masiyiwa was reported to offer $150 million to increase its stake in EWN, which was accepted by the board in May 2003.[36] Masiyiwa filed an application to Nigeria's High Court to challenge Vodacom on inducing a breach of contract.[37] Masiyiwa commented in the press:

"We filed papers in the court because there was no proper notice issued for this meeting. It is quite astounding that an EGM can be called without shareholders being properly notified according to the law . . . There is a principle in international law that if a matter is before the courts, parties should not take decisions aimed at frustrating the outcome. Even if one party thinks it has an unassailable case, it must show respect for the courts. It is disturbing that this blatant disrespect for the rule of law in Nigeria is being supported by a major multinational which should know better."[38]

Vodacom received bruising in the press as journalists and observers asked, "Where was Vodacom in 2001 when General System for Mobile (GSM) Communication firms were dueling for licenses to operate in Nigeria?"[39] At that time, the CEO of Vodacom had said that Nigeria was not appropriate due to its corruption and instability.[40] However, Vodacom saw the Nigerian mobile marketplace explode and realized that there were profits to be gained. As well, Vodacom was the largest operator on the African continent and saw that its arch rival MTN could gain the stronghold in Nigeria—the African nation boasting the largest population.

Masiyiwa also received negative press, one article even claiming that he was a fugitive from his home country and that he had been involved in corrupt business dealings.[41] Some observers criticized him and Econet for not coming through with equity payments.[42] The Econet Wireless Nigeria board was also embroiled in allegations of fraud.[43]

Masiyiwa felt that his company's financial position was strong and that EWN was open to prospective investors wishing to purchase equity in the company. In late January 2004, Econet Wireless formed a joint telecoms venture with South African based technology group Altech. Altech was involved in the design, development, manufacturing and distribution of telecommunications equipment, multi-media systems, IT solutions, electronic components, cellular telephony service provision and industrial electronic products. The company had revenues of 4 billion Rand (US$570 million approximately) and operating income of 400 million Rand (US$57 million approximately).[44] Altech invested $70 million while Econet contributed its operations in Nigeria, Botswana, Lesotho, Kenya and its license in New Zealand. The intent was to use the cash injection to increase Econet's stake in each of those countries before moving on to other areas.[45]

One analyst commented about the joint venture:

"Most people are rather perplexed. I don't think Econet is a company of substance. Its operation in Botswana is tiny, its new operation in Kenya will be nothing without a massive amount of money, and New Zealand is still a pipe dream. . . . This also means Altech is getting involved in networking, where it hasn't any experience, and going up against MTN and Vodacom with 10 years of experience."[46]

As of February 2004, Econet was still fighting to prevent the Vodacom purchase through the Nigerian court system with a decision expected in April 2004. A former MTN executive and telecom consultant believed that Nigeria would not be successful for Econet and Masiyiwa in the long run:

"I think Strive may have bitten off more than he can chew this time. By all accounts he has alienated most of his local partners in the Nigerian consortium. He likes a good scrap and may well hang in there for a while. But my sense is that eventually Vodacom will come in and take over."[47]

The Strategy for the Future

In early 2004, Masiyiwa talked about what lay ahead:

"We have two simple strategies going forward. We want to establish control of our existing operations to have a minimum of 51% in all those operations. Then we will continue to develop new opportunities."[48]

Notes

* This case was written by Prof. S. Ramakrishna Velamuri, with editing support from Jordan Mitchell, as a basis for class discussion and not to illustrate either effective or ineffective management.
1 As reported in Time magazine's List of Global Influentials 2002.
2 The Goromonzi Detention Centre had gained notoriety only some months earlier, when a young woman, Rashiwe Guzha had been taken there, and no one had seen her since. She was (and still is) presumed dead. Guzha's case had been widely reported in the press.
3 Strive Masiyiwa—cited in an undated newspaper article, titled "CIO detained Strive Masiyiwa."
4 Approximately US$33 million at the prevailing exchange rates.
5 *The Herald*, January 4, 1996: "PTC enters race to establish cellular telephone network."
6 Name disguised.
7 A Presidential Decree was meant to be used only in situations of national emergency.
8 A grandfather right is "a clause in a statute . . . which permits the operator of a business . . . to be exempt from restrictions on use if the business or property continues to be used as it was when the law was adopted" (*Law.com Dictionary*).
9 *The Vancouver Sun*, June 9, 1996: "Unspeakably useless phone system tells *the* Zimbabwean story."
10 *Financial Gazette*, December 19, 1996: "Masiyiwa wins cellular court battle."
11 *The Financial Gazette*, February 27, 1997: "Dramatic climax to Econet court battle."
12 Another condition was that Masiyiwa's share in the company should not exceed 25%.
13 *The Sunday Mail*, March 9, 1997: "Telecommunications a sensitive area."
14 *Financial Gazette*, April 17, 1997: "Masiyiwa says he's down but not out."
15 *Financial Gazette*, March 27, 1997: "Masiyiwa asks High Court to bar the govt from seizing his equipment."
16 *The Christian Science Monitor*, March 1, 2000: "How one entrepreneur beat corruption."
17 *Financial Gazette*, April 24, 1997: "Govt mulls more cellular licenses."
18 *News Digest*, April 2, 1997: "Favoritism charge takes Zim cellular license saga to new juncture"; *Financial Gazette*, April 3, 1997: "Losing bidders demand cancellation of license."
19 *Zimbabwe Standard*, April 11–17, 1997: "Transparency needed in the award of public tenders."
20 *Financial Gazette*, February 19, 1998: "A travesty of justice."
21 At the prevailing exchange rate of 1US$ = Zim$18.06.
22 This section draws from GlobalEdge's on-line Zimbabwe history, from BBC's online history of Zimbabwe, and from a document titled "Zimbabwe's Struggle for Liberation" authored by Allison Ray (Fall, 1997).
23 *Wall Street Journal Europe*, April 25, 2000: "Zimbabwe falls victim to politics of vengeance."
24 *The Namibian*, May 8, 2000: "Mugabe targets top business."
25 *OECD/AfDB* report on Zimbabwe, 2002.
26 *Operations Evaluations Department (The World Bank Group)*, February 1, 1996: "Structural Adjustment and Zimbabwe's Poor."
27 This section draws from a report of the *International Bar Association* titled "Report on Zimbabwe Mission 2001."
28 This section draws from a document titled "Civil Service Reform in Southern and Eastern Africa— Zimbabwe" by July Moyo, Elia T. Gwarada, and Cuthbert Zhakata.
29 This section draws from "Free and Fair: an ambition for Press Reporting," a report to the Commonwealth Press Union on Press Practices in Zimbabwe, by G. Ahnee, H. Hoyte, J. Mbwambo, and W. Mwangi.
30 Past recipients of the award had been the late US President John Kennedy, slain Filipino leader Benigno Aquino, ice hockey star Wayne Gretzky, and former US Secretary of State Henry Kissinger.

31 *Zimbabwe Independent*, November 5, 1999: "Masiyiwa lands global leadership award."
32 *Wall Street Journal Europe*, April 25, 2000: "Zimbabwe falls victim to politics of vengeance."
33 Bidoli, Marina, "A Tough Nut," *Financial Mail*, 5 December 2003.
34 Ikobasi, Charles, "Vodacom: Predator or Messiah," www.dailytimesofnigeria.com, 23 November 2003, Accessed 4 February 2004.
35 Ajakaye, Tayo, "Vodacom Takes over Econet for $600m," www.thisdayonline.com 7 October 2003, Accessed 4 February 2004.
36 "Vodacom Faces New Obstacle to Nigeria Venture," *Business Day/All Africa*, 23 October 2003.
37 Anderson, Belinda, "Vodacom sued over Nigeria," ml.mny.co.za, 22 October 2003, Accessed 4 February 2004.
38 Ajakaye, Tayo, "Vodacom Takes over Econet for $600m," www.thisdayonline.com 7 October 2003, Accessed 4 February 2004.
39 Ikobasi, Charles, "Vodacom: Predator or Messiah," www.dailytimesofnigeria.com, 23 November 2003, Accessed 4 February 2004.
40 Ibid.
41 Ibid.
42 Bidoli, Marina, "A Tough Nut," *Financial Mail*, 5 December 2003.
43 Ikobasi, Charles, "Vodacom: Predator or Messiah," www.dailytimesofnigeria.com, 23 November 2003, Accessed 4 February 2004.
44 Allied Technologies Limited Website, www.altech.co.za, Accessed 24 February 2004.
45 Stones, Lesley, "Altech, Econet Take Aim At Big Guns," *All Africa*, 22 January 2004.
46 Ibid.
47 Bidoli, Marina, "A Tough Nut," *Financial Mail*, 5 December 2003.
48 Stones, Lesley, "Altech, Econet Take Aim At Big Guns," *All Africa*, 22 January 2004.

7.2 Infosys Technologies
Powered by Intellect, Driven by Values[*]

"A clear conscience is the softest pillow."

Narayana Murthy

Introduction

At of the end of their fiscal year in March 2004, Infosys had just completed another stellar period, posting revenue growth of 31 per cent and operating income growth of 24 per cent over the prior year (see Exhibit 7.2.5 which shows Infosys's financial performance). Based in Bangalore, India, Infosys was the second largest Indian provider of IT services such as software development and consulting to around 400 top tier corporate clients spread throughout the world. The company had just broken the $1 billion mark in sales and had become the media darling of the Indian IT industry. Based on its share price on NASDAQ (INFY) on March 31, 2004, the company's market capitalization was $10.9 billion. Infosys's visionary leader Narayana Murthy and the other founding members of Infosys had worked tirelessly to instill a broad based set of values in all of their business operations—from resisting government corruption through to fostering an environment of high employee loyalty and trust.

In spite of having experienced a compound annual growth rate (CAGR) in revenues and profits of approximately 60 per cent for the last ten years and moving from 573 employees in 1994 to 25,634 employees in 2004, the management of Infosys was aware of the difficult challenges that lay ahead.

First, the company had articulated a strategy of moving up the value chain by offering high end consulting services such as systems integration and technology strategy. However, the competitors in this segment of the IT services market—IBM Global Services, Accenture, and EDS—were large, well established companies with very strong customer relationships. All of them had established themselves in India, and had access to the same high quality, low cost manpower that Indian companies did. They had also announced aggressive plans to scale up their Indian operations. How could Infosys compete with them in the future?

Second, the company had also decided to move into the lower value added business process outsourcing (BPO) services through its wholly owned subsidiary Progeon. In this segment, the company was growing rapidly but was still quite small and had only broken even as of the end of March 2004. It did not figure among the fifteen largest Indian companies in the BPO sector. In April 2004, IBM had announced the acquisition of the third largest Indian BPO company; newspaper reports estimated the price paid to be $155 million. How could Infosys establish itself as a leading Indian provider of BPO services?

Third, the company had added around 10,000 new employees in the fiscal year 2003–04. The number of locations and the diversity of its workforce had also increased dramatically over the recent years. The company wondered whether it could preserve the predominantly middle class Indian values that had been so important to its success to date in such a rapidly growing organization.

Establishing Infosys

Infosys was born in 1981, after Narayana Murthy and six of other IT professionals broke out on their own. The seven founders shared a common vision of creating a world-class company, "of the professional, for the professional, and by the professional."[1] They had a debate about the long term goals of the company, and concluded that they wanted to become the most respected company in India. Dinesh, a co-founder, explained the early days: "[In building the company] the end is important, but the means are as important."

The co-founders pooled together their resources, which amounted to about $250, to start the company. The group believed that there was little opportunity to develop software for the local market and thus set their sights on the US. At the time, Indian firms could not easily import foreign equipment, which hampered Infosys's ability to compete internationally. It took the company one year to get permission to import a computer and a year to get a telephone line. Infosys requested its first customer, Databasics of the US, to pay the travel expenses associated with sending the team from India and to allow the team to work on Databasics's computers. Nandan Nilekani, a co-founder and the current CEO of Infosys commented: "A part of the money was given to us as our stipend in the U.S., [but] whatever profits we made, we either put them as reserves or we gave them as a dividend to the shareholders and they put it back as fresh equity. That is how we bootstrapped the capital."

Murthy reflected back on the early days: "It was a challenge to attract smart people to work with us—we had no name, no money, no brand recognition, and no physical or financial assets. When we recruited in 1982, I managed to borrow some table space from a friend's company. Further, I approached another friend who had access to a large computer center. He allowed us to use the computers during the night at an attractive rate . . . In fact, my wife had to pawn her jewelry to help pay our employees' salaries. The best part was that in all these times of difficulty, we did not have to compromise on our value system."[2]

In 1984, when they imported the first computer to Bangalore, a customs official indirectly asked them for a bribe. When Murthy pretended that he did not understand the request, the official refused to recognize a government certificate that entitled the company to a concessionary import duty of only 100,000 rupees, compared to the regular duty of approximately 1,000,000 rupees. The company ended up paying the higher duty, and had to go through a lengthy claims process lasting six years to recover the excess duty paid.

In 1996, the company refused to pay a bribe of Rs.400,000 in the purchase of land on which its modern offices are located in Bangalore. It ended up paying Rs.4,000,000 extra for the land (40% more than what other companies had paid in the same area).

Murthy defined a value system as, "a protocol or set of protocols that a community uses in every transaction so that it enhances the confidence, the comfort and energy of every member in the community. By definition, being committed to values means a willingness to pay a price for them in the short term. Otherwise, there is no meaning in saying you are values driven." He related this to the foundation of Infosys: "From day one we wanted to run the business legally and ethically to demonstrate that by putting the interest of the corporation above your own personal interest in the long term you will benefit. We were convinced that the softest pillow was a clear conscience. We were convinced about running the business using simple rules because simple rules are easy to communicate, easy to practice, and easy to understand. Most importantly, you cannot cheat anybody with simple rules. Also, not using corporate resources for personal benefit was a dictum that we practiced right from day one." Murthy lived by this rule strictly even in 2004—for example, when traveling with his wife, a non-Infosys employee—he refunded the company the difference between the hotel cost of a single and double room. He commented on why he took this stance: "The best way of communicating any message is walking the talk. You get the best credibility."

Narayana Murthy

Murthy was born in 1946 as the fifth of eight children in Karnataka state in the south of India. Murthy talked about his education: "Those days our role models were our teachers, both in school and university. They taught us to be inquisitive and articulate. My father used to tell us about the importance of putting public good before private good; my mother would talk about sacrifice and truth."[3] Murthy's father also instilled in his children an appreciation for other cultures: "My father always told us that India had a lot to learn from the West. Also, he was a great fan of classical music. One day I asked him: why should I listen to this alien music? He said: What appeals to me is that in a symphony there are over 100 people, each of whom is a maestro, but they come together as a team to play according to a script under this conductor and produce something divine. They prove that one plus one can be more than two. It's a great example of teamwork."[4]

Murthy later pursued his master's degree at IIT (the school he had been admitted to for his undergraduate studies but could not attend due to financial reasons) and basked in the energy: "We had so many young professors who had done their PhDs in the U.S. and had come back to India. We were introduced to computers—that wonder machine—and I was hooked."[5]

After graduating, Murthy worked for a stint in Paris, programming an airline cargo system. Beyond the work experience, Murthy was seeking to unearth the roots of French socialism. He commented, "I observed how in a western country even the socialists understood that wealth has to be first created before it can be distributed . . . You cannot distribute poverty."[6]

Back in India, in 1974, Murthy worked for three years at Systems Research Institute in Pune and then joined Patni Computer Systems (PCS) in 1977. He handed in his resignation in 1980 to start Infosys with other PCS employees. Over twenty years later, one of the Patni's owners, gave vent to his feelings in a newspaper, "The idea [with Infosys] would be to acquire a stake, incubate it and then let them go. But we were not given a choice. We were given an ultimatum. One fine day, all of them came and handed in their resignations."[7] Murthy artfully retorted in the same publication, "I put in my papers at PCS on December 29, 1980. I assured Mr. Patni that I would personally ensure that the ongoing projects do not suffer. Thus, I ended up leaving the company on March 18, 1982—about 14 months and 20 days after I tendered my resignation . . . In my value system, a group of people leaving a company to pursue their dream is not an offence. I have always said it's the responsibility of Infosys to retain its employees by protecting their dignity and by ensuring that they are happy in all ways. At Infosys, we treat our former employees as our goodwill ambassadors."[8]

The Co-Founders

The six other co-founders of Infosys were all considered to offer complementary skills to the company: Nandan Nilekani was known for his networking ability, Gopalakrishnan was heralded for his operational skills, Raghavan was regarded as a man of the people, Shibulal was regarded for his technological ability, and Dinesh was known for his quality, productivity and process focus.[9] The other founder Ashok Arora left Infosys in 1989 to pursue a career in the United States. Each founder had a similar educational background and had gained experience working in engineering or computer programming across a number of different companies. Dinesh explained the match of the seven founders, "we were like-minded people in terms of the kind of values that we shared." Exhibit 7.2.1 shows profiles of five of the seven co-founders still with the company in 2004.

Exhibit 7.2.1 Selected Founders Profiles

Nandan M. Nilekani—CEO, President and Managing Director   Mr. Nilekani graduated from the Indian Institute of Technology (IIT), Bombay in 1978. He was named among the "World's most respected business leaders" in 2002 and 2003, according to a global survey by Financial Times and PricewaterhouseCoopers. He has been elected one of "Asia's Power 25"—the most powerful people in business in Asia by Fortune, 2004. Mr. Nilekani, along with Infosys Chairman Mr. N. R. Narayana Murthy, received the Fortune magazine's "Asia's Businessmen of the Year 2003" award. Mr. Nilekani has been awarded the Corporate Citizen of the Year Award, at the Asia Business Leader Awards (2004), organized by CNBC. Mr. Nilekani has also received the Indian Institute of Technology (IIT), Bombay's "Distinguished Alumnus" award in 1999. Mr. Nilekani serves on the London Business School's Asia Pacific Regional Advisory Board, and also on the Board of Trustees of The Conference Board, Inc.—an international research and business membership organization. Mr Nilekani is a Co-founder of India's National Association of Software and Service Companies (NASSCOM).

S. Gopalakrishnan—Deputy Managing Director and COO   Gopalakrishnan (Kris) is a co-founder of Infosys and has served as a Director since 1981. From 1996 to 1998 Kris was the Head of Client Delivery and Technology and from 1994 the head of Technical Support Services for Infosys. From 1987 to 1994, he was Technical Vice President and managed all projects at the U.S.-based KSA/Infosys, a former joint venture between the company and Kurt Salmon Associates. Prior to that, Kris was Technical Director of Infosys, responsible for the technical direction of the company. Kris received a M.Sc. in Physics and an M. Tech. in Computer Science from IIT, Madras.

K. Dinesh—Director and Head of E&R, IS, Quality & Productivity, and CDG   K. Dinesh is a co-founder of Infosys and has served as Director since 1985. He has served as Head—Quality and Productivity and Information Systems (IS) since 1996. From 1991 to 1996, Dinesh served in various project management capacities and was responsible for worldwide software development efforts for Infosys. From 1981 to 1990, he managed projects for Infosys in the United States. Dinesh received a Masters degree in Mathematics from the Bangalore University.

S.D. Shibulal—Director, Head—World-wide Customer Delivery   Shibulal is a co-founder of Infosys and has served as a Director from 1984 to 1991 and since 1997. He has served as Head—Manufacturing, Distribution and Year 2000 Business Unit and Head—Internet and Intranet Business Unit of Infosys since 1997. From 1991 to 1996, Shibu was on sabbatical from Infosys and served as Senior Information Resource Manager at Sun Microsystems, Inc. From 1981 to 1991, he worked for Infosys in the United States on projects in the retail and manufacturing industries. Shibu received a Masters in Physics from the University of Kerala and a Masters in Computer Science from the Boston University.

N. R. Narayana Murthy—Chairman of the Board and Chief Mentor   N. R. Narayana Murthy (B.E. Electrical '67. Univ. of Mysore, M. Tech. '69, Indian Institute of Technology, Kanpur) is the Chairman and Chief Mentor of Infosys Technologies Limited. In 1999, Infosys was listed on NASDAQ (INFY). Mr. Murthy is the chairman of the governing body of both the Indian Institute of Information Technology, Bangalore, and the Indian Institute of Management, Ahmedabad. In addition, he is a member of the Board of Overseers of the University of Pennsylvania's Wharton School, Cornell University Board of Trustees, Singapore Management University Board of Trustees and the Board of Advisors for the William F. Achtmeyer Center for Global Leadership at the Tuck School of Business. Mr. Murthy serves as an independent director on the board of the DBS Bank, Singapore, the largest government-owned bank in Singapore. He also serves as a director on the Central Board of the Reserve Bank of India, as the co-chairman of the Indo-British Partnership, as a member of the Prime Minister's Council on Trade and Industry, as a member of the Asia Advisory Board of British Telecommunications plc., and as a member of the Board of NDTV.

Mr. Murthy's Awards:
Updated April 2009: Mr. Murthy is the recipient of numerous awards and honors. The Economist ranked him 8th in the list of the 15 most-admired global leaders in 2005. He was ranked 28th among the world's most-respected business leaders by the Financial Times in 2005. In 2004, the TIME magazine identified him as one of the 10 global leaders who are helping shape the future of technology. In 2006, the TIME magazine voted him as one of the Asian heroes who have brought about revolutionary changes in Asia in the last 60 years. He was featured in BusinessWeek's "The Stars of Asia" for three consecutive years—1998, 1999 and 2000. He was voted the "World Entrepreneur of the Year" by Ernst and Young in 2003. He was voted India's most powerful CEO for three consecutive years—2004, 2005 and 2006—by Economic Times. He was chosen as the "Business Process Innovator" by The Economist in 2007. He received the Ernst Weber Engineering Leadership medal from The Institute of Electrical and Electronics Engineers in 2007 for his pioneering role in the globalization of IT services. He was awarded the "Padma Vibhushan," the second highest civilian award by the Government of India in 2008. The Government of France conferred on him the Office of the Legion of Honor in 2008.

Source: Infosys Corporate Website, www.infy.com, Accessed 15 December 2004.

The Road to Becoming a World Class Organization

Infosys added its second customer in 1984, an Indian company called Mico, and by the end of the 1980s, the group had secured four clients. 1989 was a watershed year for the company. Late that year the founders all gathered to evaluate whether their efforts were going in the right direction. "The company was eight years old and we felt it was time to see if the company we had created was aligned to our long term objectives," says Murthy. N. S. Raghavan, one of the co-founders recalls, "Murthy spoke to all of us and asked us if we felt comfortable with the company we had built and whether we were committed to the strategic vision of our company." Revenues had continued to grow at a steady pace but the co-founders felt that they were spending too much time working in locations far from home. The company employed less than 50 people and Murthy felt it was a good time to come together and decide if their business model was adequate to making the company a major power in the software industry or whether they should disband the operation. "There were many constraints to allowing us to grow in the manner we wanted to and prime among these was severe restrictions imposed by the government on foreign trade and acquisition of leading edge technology! It took nine months to get a simple import license," says Murthy. All of the partners debated and finally came to a conclusion that they should dissolve the company. "Murthy allowed us to express our opinions and frustrations and stayed silent throughout the debate," recalls Nilekani. "When we had finished and decided, he spoke for the first time." Murthy offered to buy out each of his partners and reaffirmed that he had absolute confidence in overcoming the hurdles while going forward and promised to take the company public within five years if they all stuck it out with him. All of them agreed and Infosys Technologies survived its first and only major organizational shakeout. He admitted later that if his partners had accepted his offer to buy them out, he did not know where he would have found the money to pay them.

While working for a client in late 1985, Infosys had come in contact with Kurt Salmon and Associates (KSA), a management-consulting firm located in Atlanta, Georgia. Infosys explored partnership possibilities with KSA to expand their marketing effort in the United States. KSA suggested a joint venture, as it would allow them to manage quality control and continuity. In the beginning, KSA and Infosys were 60/40 partners but in 1993, Infosys increased its share to a 50% stake. The name of the new company was changed to Software Sourcing Corporation to better reflect its charter. KSA was responsible for sourcing projects for the joint venture and Infosys provided the software expertise and technical knowledge. KSA/Infosys was formed in 1987 with offices in Atlanta, which were responsible for soliciting software projects while the Infosys offices in India provided the personnel. In 1990, the company achieved sales of $3.24 million with a profit of $553,000. "At that time, this joint venture allowed us to build credibility in a market where we were relative newcomers and gave us access to a number of opportunities we would not have otherwise had," recalls S. Gopalakrishnan who was responsible for managing the relationship. The joint venture with KSA was terminated in 1995 as Infosys formed a marketing office in the States and sought to market its products based on its own brand recognition. Infosys also won a large project with Reebok of France after making a significant investment to prepare for the bid. The 20-person year project was to design and build an ordering and distribution automation system that would track and maintain Reebok orders worldwide. The project team overcame many hurdles, including the language barrier (many of the project specifications were provided in French) and completed the project ahead of time, which won them accolades and a new customer for life. Gradually Infosys gained acceptance and came to be recognized as a quality provider of application services and, by 1993, they were working on projects for a number of customers that included GE and Nestlé among others.

Economic Liberalization in India

The company regrouped and in 1991 the Indian government took a series of measures to liberalize the economy. These changes made it easier for private firms to issue equity on stock markets, open offices in other countries, send workers abroad and take advantage of improvements in telecommunications through satellite earth stations. Balakrishnan, Infosys's vice president of finance commented: "We felt that 1993 was the opportune time [for an initial public offering] because all the controls were removed and we were in a global market. We felt that accessing the capital market was very important, and not only for the money, but it brings a lot of discipline within the organization when you bring in external stakeholders. It also increases your profile because a lot of people talk about you, write about you and if you are a closed company, you miss out on all of that."

Around the time of the IPO, about 40 per cent of Infosys's revenues were derived from one sole customer—General Electric (GE). When GE tried to whittle down the price of Infosys's services, Infosys resisted and eventually terminated the relationship. This fostered management's belief that one customer should not account for more than 10 per cent of Infosys's revenues. In spite of losing its biggest customer, Infosys did not compromise on its professional obligations. Although the handover of the GE project to an Indian competitor took more than a year, it was done meticulously by the Infosys team, so much so that both GE and the Indian competitor expressed their admiration.

Murthy explained the doctrine, "I work with four business principles. First is predictability of revenues. Second is the sustainability of those predictions. Third is the profitability of those revenues. Fourth, it's not sufficient to have just predictability, sustainability and profitability—you need to have a 'de-risking model'."[10] By "de-risking," Murthy meant that Infosys should not be too reliant on any one customer or market.

Organizational Processes

During the early 1990s, Infosys perfected its model of offshore software development centers (OSDCs). Infosys sales people sought software development contracts in other countries and then shipped the work to be done in India by Indian programmers at OSDCs. This differed from previous model of "bodyshopping" where Indian nationals were sent abroad to work on software programming at clients' sites. OSDCs were seen to offer two main benefits over "bodyshopping": 80 per cent lower costs because the Indian programmers worked in India instead of the United States; and the advantage of time zones, where Indian programmers could work on projects throughout the U.S. night.[11]

In expanding its customer base, Infosys focused on delivery quality and consistency by utilizing cutting-edge process measurement systems such as Six Sigma and the Carnegie Mellon Software Engineering Institute's level four and five certification of the Capability Maturity Model (CMM)—the fifth level being a certification that very few firms in the world had been able to achieve. Dinesh reflected about the environment that led to a focus on processes: "One is the human related skill and another is the technology which enables that and the third is the process. So, when you look at ethical practices and corporate governance, ultimately you have to combine all these to get the results you want. It is very important to have the people geared towards the intentions of what is to be done. That is where the values come. If the people don't believe in the values any amount of processes and systems won't help. You can't have monitoring for every person."

A co-founder, Raghavan explained Infosys's values, "we have middle class values. It is dignity of and respect for all people irrespective of their background. Don't do anything, which is [harmful] to the fairness in all our transactions. It's an ethical and moral means of making money, so creating money is not the essential thing. Money will automatically come."

Balakrishnan, who joined the company in 1991, shared his view of the founders' value set: "They have all come up very hard in life. In India middle class always struggles, so the ethics are very high . . . I think [the founders] continued with their values, and in fact, when we were small there was a lot of pressure from the government in terms of corrupt practices, but we never compromised. For example in one of the foreign exchange cases, [a government official] conducted an inquiry and said, 'I want a PC for my wife, she is running a clinic.' We said we couldn't give him one. He said, 'I will see to it that maximum damage is done to you. We said, 'sure, do it.' It went on and on and we wrote to the finance minister and he was transferred."

A senior executive talked about the difficulty of resisting corruption in one's individual transactions with respect to professional transactions: "I was taking a flight back from Nigeria. They just said 400 Nairas ($3 USD) for a yellow fever card, [which we didn't need]. What can you do in such cases? Most people don't even think of it as corruption. In fact when I told my colleagues what we did was not exactly in keeping with Infosys' philosophy, all of them were shocked, they asked, 'what have you done wrong?' These are very difficult moral choices."

Murthy summarized Infosys's value system, "Our value system was like the British Constitution—it was all unwritten but extremely well practiced. How do we stay together? We have unwritten rules. Everybody knows that if we want to work as a team we have to be transaction based, which means treating every transaction solely on its merits and being as fact based as possible. We start every transaction on a zero base. People are free to express their views, and disagree with their superiors. We have two adages that summarize this: 1) You can disagree without being disagreeable, and 2) In God we trust; everybody else brings data to the table. Only an argument that has merit wins; it has nothing to do with hierarchy."[12] Dinesh explained Infosys's approach to balancing the need for debate on the one hand and for being action oriented on the other—"If two people always agree, then one of them is not needed. If they always disagree, then both are not needed."

Explosive Growth

From 1994 to 2004, the company experienced 10 years of unprecedented growth moving from $9.5 million in revenues to $1,063 million, and from 573 employees to 25,634 employees. Nandan Nilekani contrasted the 1990s with the 1980s:

"Customers started to appreciate Indian capabilities only in the 1990s. So if you see our growth pattern from the beginning, it took us about 10 years to go from 0 to $5 million and it took us just 10 more years to go from $5 million to $700 million. Clearly the growth rate in the next 10 years was dramatically different. That is because two things happened: one the environment changed and second, our aspirations also changed. We said we must become world class, we must become a big company. It was to be international, to be global, to have a high value system, to have high ethics—all those things were there from day one, but it was in the early 1990s that we said we really need to get hold of ourselves and put in place the systems and processes and the technology, infrastructure and all that to achieve growth. That is where our mindset changed."

India's economic liberalization permitted 100 per cent foreign ownership in high-tech companies, causing Microsoft, Sun, Oracle, Citibank, IBM and General Electric to open up offices in India. Rather than lobby the government to keep competitors out, Infosys chose to respond to foreign competition by creating a world-class environment, such that employees would not want to leave to work for a multinational. This included investing heavily in a stunning campus and offering competitive salaries and wealth-sharing mechanisms such as stock options. Murthy commented: "[First, multinationals] provided the latest technology to Indian companies. Second, their entry also created tremendous competition for a very important resource, which is human resources, and we realized that unless we compete with these multinationals in attracting and retaining those resources, we will disappear like dew on a sunny morning. Because if we can't compete with multinationals in India, what is the hope of us competing with them in the UK, or in the U.S.?"[13]

Another positive factor for Infosys was that the IT industry in India did not have heavy restrictions such as those faced by the construction or manufacturing sectors. Nandan explained, "We are largely in an area that is completely free of government regulations. We are not really in the Indian tax system. In India there are a lot of local taxes like sales tax, excise duty, etc., which are not there on software and on exports. And our revenues come mostly from exports. And being in the software industry and not a factory we don't come under things like the Factory Act. As an industry I would say that we are considerably less constrained by the environment."

The lead-up to the year 2000 provided Infosys with a surge of new work to make systems Y2K compliant. In 2000 alone, the company's revenues grew by 80 per cent with profits climbing 115 per cent. Just before in 1999, Murthy passed his presidency title to the youngest of the founders—Nandan Nilekani. In the 1999 Infosys annual report, Murthy explained the transition, "As the company takes on new challenges of growth and globalization, I felt the need to share my responsibility with another person. [The board appointed Nandan] so that I could concentrate on strategic issues as we move to the next millennium."[14] By the end of Infosys's 2002 fiscal year, Nandan had taken over as the CEO, while maintaining his Managing Director and President titles. Golapkrishnan became the COO and Murthy remained the Chairman and took on a new role as Chief Mentor.

Strategy and Business Model

Infosys was split between the following operations: software services, consulting, testing, engineering, other services and products. Exhibit 7.2.2 shows the breakdown of revenues by service offering.

Nandan, the CEO and Gopalakrishnan, COO wrote to shareholders in the 2004 annual report, "Today, our model has become mainstream. Additionally, we have achieved the size,

Exhibit 7.2.2 Infosys Service Offerings

Service Offerings	2002	2003	2004
Development	32.0%	32.1%	25.7%
Maintenance	29.0%	28.2%	30.1%
Re-engineering	10.1%	5.5%	6.0%
Package implementation	9.8%	11.0%	14.5%
Consulting	4.2%	4.3%	3.7%
Testing	2.9%	3.4%	5.3%
Engineering Services	2.6%	2.6%	2.2%
Other services	5.4%	8.3%	9.7%
Products	4.0%	4.6%	2.8%
TOTAL	100.0%	100.0%	100.0%

scalability, brand, and ambition necessary to create the next generation consulting and software services company . . . We completely redesigned our planning and implementation process, and evolved a clear strategy to aim for global leadership on the theme of rapid growth and rapid differentiation. We recently launched Infosys Consulting (with a planned investment of US$20 million), thereby taking the battle into the competitors' camp. Through this initiative, we combine world-class consulting with the excellence and cost competitiveness of global delivery."[15]

In launching Infosys Consulting, the company was pinning its hope on moving up the value chain to compete head to head in the world information technology market against well-established giants such as EDS, IBM Global Services and Accenture. As Murthy explained, "we are going to put the power of the GDM (global delivery model) inside the consulting business."[16] This meant that for consulting services such as package implementation, Infosys could apportion some work to India taking its blended rate to $75 to $80 an hour where multinationals were charging $125 to $130 (Infosys's hourly rate in India for its current mix of services was about $37 to $38).[17]

On the opposite end of the scale, Infosys was trying to ride the wave of business process outsourcing (BPO) through its division Progeon, by offering tasks requiring less training than software development. Business processing included activities such as call centers or payment processing. While Progeon had expanded by adding over 350 employees to a total of 1,500 employees, the company had only 12 customers, of which nine had been added in the last year. Only 17 per cent of Progeon's services were voice-based services. Progeon had just broken even in 2004 after two years of operations and was planning on expanding through an integrated BPO and IT offering—something which Infosys and Progeon were working on perfecting.[18]

The concept of offshore outsourcing had also brought about great debate in other countries, especially the U.S., where it had become a focal point in the 2004 election. As Nandan and Gopalakrishnan wrote in the annual report, "the clamor against outsourcing, while abating to some extent, has the potential to create an unpredictable regulatory response."[19]

Marketing and Sales

The proximity centers were responsible for managing customers, or ensuring "customer delight." The company's approach to managing customer relationships was summarized in the adage: underpromise and overdeliver. The central sales effort was based in Fremont,

Exhibit 7.2.3 List of Infosys Locations (As of 2004)

Sales Offices		Global Development Centers	
1	Fremont, California	Bangalore	6
2	Atlanta, USA	Bhubaneswar	2
3	Boston, USA	Chennai	2
4	Chicago, USA	Mangalore	2
5	Dallas, USA	Pune	2
6	Detroit, USA	Hyderabad	1
7	Los Angeles, USA	Mohah	1
8	New York, USA	Thirvananthapuram	1
9	Seattle, USA	Mysore	1
10	New Jersey, USA	Toronto, Canada	1
11	Charlotte, USA	Fremont	1
12	Reston, USA	Boston	1
13	Bangalore, India	Chicago	1
14	Chennai, India	New Jersey	1
15	Mumbai, India	Phoenix	1
16	New Delhi, India	Charlotte	1
17	Frankfurt, Germany	London	1
18	London, UK	Croydon	1
19	Tokyo, Japan	Tokyo	1
20	Toronto, Canada	Melbourne	3
21	Amsterdam, Holland		
22	Belgium		
23	Paris, France		31
24	Sweden		
25	Switzerland		
26	Beijing, China		
27	Shanghai, China		
28	Hong Kong		
29	Sharjah, UAE		
30	Italy		
31	Australia		

Source: Infosys AR04. Page 112.

California. The company did not actively advertise to its end customer, but relied on face-to-face presentations and building a reputation with its clients—this proved successful as the retention rate of its client base had been between 85 and 95 per cent. However, the growing Indian IT industry coupled with Infosys's advertisements for recruiting worked to enhance the image of the company. While the mandate of the company was not to be too reliant on one customer, 72.4 per cent of the company's revenues were derived from the U.S.[20] By comparison, only 2 per cent of the company's revenues came from India. By 2004, the company had 379 customers and 31 global development centers (18 of which were in India) and 31 sales and marketing offices.[21] Exhibit 7.2.3 shows a list of Infosys's worldwide locations and Exhibit 7.2.4 shows quotes from some of Infosys's customers.

Basab Pradhan, the head of worldwide sales, commented on the challenge of matching Infosys's new sales pitch to its shift in strategy, "Our selling pitch so far was 'we have a 100 Java engineers, and we can deliver for you from offshore, now tell us what you want us to do.' Today that is being replaced with 'we can give you a technical solution which can cut your inventory expenses by $100 million.' "[22]

A large part of the company's sales growth had been attributed to the former head of worldwide sales, Phaneesh Murthy (no relation to Narayana Murthy). However, in 2002,

Exhibit 7.2.4 Customer Quotes

Donn Liles, Infosys's first customer in 1981, speaking in 2004: "What I thought then and what I think today is really not very much changed. These gentlemen embody intelligence, integrity, and commitment. That is what I think."

AMR Research, April 8, 2004. "Infosys is building the right expertise to dominate the next generation of consulting and IT."

Forbes: "Infosys is a model of transparency not just for the rest of corporate India but for companies everywhere."

Bill Homa, CIO, Hannaford Brothers (part of the Delhaize Group): "Our relationship with Infosys has exceeded our expectations. It has actually allowed us to do things we couldn't have done before."

Phil Zweig, VP, Northwestern Mutual Life – "Infosys is very deliberate in the way they do things, very organized, very methodical, they have solid processes, and will deliver on time."

Sajiro Suzuki, CIO, Toshiba Corporation – "Quality is very high, so I think we can rely on Infosys people's level of quality."

Phaneesh's executive assistant in the U.S. filed a sexual harassment suit against him and the company asking for $3 million in damages. Phaneesh resigned and later moved on to become the CEO of iGate, another IT services company.[23] Several months later, the company and Phaneesh settled the lawsuit—Infosys paid half and the insurers under the Directors and Officers Liability insurance paid the other half.[24] Immediately upon the announcement of the sexual harassment charge, Infosys's management addressed the press with a release and a definitive stand on the issue. Tina George, in media relations at Infosys, talked about the communication from the company's standpoint: "as always Infosys took a pro-active step to openly tell everybody . . . What was most important was to quickly communicate that another person has been appointed and the transition has been made. Business will go on and there is no change in our (earnings) guidance, and there is no change in the forecasts that we've made."

A journalist from the Financial Express, Kavitha Vivek, complimented the management on their handling of this very delicate issue and commented: "So [the lawsuit] came at the wrong time, and to have such a top-level guy, it's something quite serious. Personally, I think the company has built itself quite a good track record. I don't believe that they completely have a squeaky clean image but I think along the line they are quite sharp and they chalk their path very, very well before they make an announcement."

Financials

Infosys had taken the coveted position in the Indian IT sector for its explosive growth. Since 1994, the company's revenues had grown at a compound annual rate of 60.2 per cent, with profits climbing at 58.7 per cent. Exhibit 7.2.5 shows financial highlights.

In financing, Infosys followed a financing policy that required a liquidity level of 25 per cent in cash or liquid assets (based on paying eight months of expenses), a maximum dividend of 20 per cent paid from cash surpluses only, and all working capital and capital expenditures were to come from cash flow. The company wrote off its buildings in 15 years (half of the average) and computer equipment in 2 years and did not offer any of its employees company cars.[25] The company's CFO Mohandas Pai explained, "The financing history of Infosys is partially the history of the business and partially the culture instilled by Murthy. Service businesses generally have positive cash flow and this helped shape our financial policy. But

Exhibit 7.2.5 Financial Highlights

A. As per US GAAP

Fiscal year ended March 31	Employees	Growth %	Revenues in $ million	Growth %	Net income in $ million	Growth %
1994	573		9.53	82	2.67	106
1995	903	58	18.11	90	3.96	48
1996	1172	30	26.61	47	6.82	72
1997	1705	45	39.59	49	8.64	27
1998	2605	53	68.33	73	13.86	60
1999	3766	45	120.96	77	30.35	119
2000	5389	43	203.44	68	61.34	102
2001	9831	82	413.85	103	131.95	115
2002	10738	9	545.05	32	164.47	25
2003	15876	48	753.81	38	194.87	18
2004	25634	61	1062.58	41	270.29	39

1996–2004 from Annual Report 2004, Page 114, 1994–1995 from Annual Report 1999, Page 191

(Continued)

Exhibit 7.2.5 Financial Highlights Continued

B. Infosys Historical Financials (in Rs. Millions)

in Rs. Millions	1982	1996	1997	1998	1999	2000	2001	2002
For the year								
Income	1.2	885.6	1392.1	2576.6	5088.9	8823.2	19005.6	26035.9
Operating profit (PBIDTA)	0.4	313.7	467.9	859	2016.3	3465.7	7648.4	10376.3
Interest	0	0	6.1	0	0	0	0	0
Depreciation and amortization	0	86.3	105.2	227.5	358.9	532.3	1128.9	1606.5
Provision for taxation	0	43.1	52.5	55	229.4	397	727.1	1354.3
Profit after tax from ordinary activities	0.4	210.1	336.8	603.6	1329.2	2859.5	6233.2	8079.6
Dividend	0	36.3	39.9	70.3	121.1	297.6	661.5	1323.6
One-time special dividend	0	0	0	0	0	0	0	0
Capital expenditure	0	155.5	273.1	344.1	716.8	1598.7	4633.5	3227.4
Return on average networth (%)	96.88%	29.53%	34.96%	42.24%	54.16%	40.63%	56.08%	46.57%
Return on average capital employed (PBIT/average capital employed) %	96.88%	33.12%	40.16%	46.09%	63.51%	46.27%	62.62%	54.37%
As at the end of the year								
Share capital	0	72.6	72.6	160.2	330.7	330.8	330.8	330.9
Reserves and surplus	0.4	725.8	1055.8	1569.4	5413.6	8002.3	13565.6	20472.2
Loan funds	0	42.6	0	0	0	0	0	0
Gross block	0	468.6	712.9	1051.4	1689.2	2840.3	6311.4	9606
Cash and cash equivalents	0.2	297.8	287.8	511.4	4166.6	5083.7	5777.4	10269.6
Investment in money market funds	0	0	0	0	0	0	0	0
Net current assets	0.6	411.7	542	972.3	4729.6	6121.3	7978.6	12934.1
Debt-equity ration	0	0.5	0	0	0	0	0	0
Market capitalization	0	3556.7	7310.4	29634.2	96728	593381.7	269263.5	246543.3
Per share data								
Basic earnings from ordinary activities (Rs.)	0.00	3.18	5.09	9.13	20.71	43.23	94.23	122.12
Dividend (Rs.)	0.00	2.50	2.75	3.00	3.75	4.50	10.00	20.00
One-time special dividend (Rs.)	0.00	0.00	0.00	0.00	0.00	0.00	0.00	0.00
Book value (Rs.)	0.00	12.07	17.06	26.15	86.84	125.97	210.05	314.31
Other information								
Number of shareholders	7	6,909	6,414	6,622	9,527	46.314	89.643	88.650
Credit rating from CRISIL								
Commercial paper	"PI+"	"PI+"	"PI+"	"PI+"	"PI+"	"PI+"	"PI+"	"PI+"
Non-convertible debentures	"AA"	"AA"	"AA"	"AA"	"AA"	"AA"	"AAA"	"AAA"

Source: Infosys AR04. Page 28.

equally important is the company's reluctance to use debt financing. The conservative, middle class background of Murthy and the other founders has directly contributed to that reluctance."[26]

Infosys's management believed that it should make all financial results extremely visible to all stakeholders. Each year the company produced an annual report often exceeding 200 pages complete with inspirational quotes and explanations of strategies, divisional perform-ance and detailed financials, prepared in substantial compliance of the generally accepted accounting principles (GAAP) of the eight countries in which it had operations. Infosys had received the award for the best annual report from the Institute of Chartered Accountants of India six years in a row. Balakrishnan talked about Infosys's high level of transparency and debates that emerge when putting everything in public view:

> "People in India never knew about US GAAP until we did it in 1994. We have improved the transparency and improved the disclosure practices. Being a cash surplus company, to manage the cash and manage the expectations of the investors is too big a thing. In 1994 like all the companies we also invested in the capital markets, and we lost money. At that time all our shareholders wrote to us and said why the heck did you guys do it, because your job is software, not to manage cash. The CFO of the company went before the shareholders and apologized and he said that we will never do it again."

Murthy explained the company's approach to disclosure to stakeholders such as investors and the community in general through two adages: 1) Let the good news take the stairs and the bad news the elevator; and 2) When in doubt, disclose.

The company prided itself on its internal processes and planning, not only in delivering software services, but also in its ability to predict sales and profits. The company's prediction dovetailed into Murthy's principle of de-risking and gave Infosys the ability to plan with greater certainty. Infosys employed a variety of measurement tools on its financials such as the balanced scorecard with the intention of sharing a combination of financial and non-financial measurements evaluating the effectiveness of the firm's strategy. Murthy tied the idea of financial transparency to the workforce: "The key to employee involvement in organizations is the sharing of information about business performance, plans, goals and strategies. What happens by a shout across the corridor in a smaller organization, calls for a more systematic process in a large organization like ours."[27]

Human Resources

By 2004, Infosys had won a number of awards for the company's HR practices highlighting the company's learning organization and its training program. It was ranked as the number one place to work in India by Hewitt Associates and Business Today and one of the 100 best places to work in North America by the magazine Computer World.[28] In the last couple of years, the company had also transitioned from a structure with 15 grade levels to a flatter role-based structure with six broad bands.[29] The company had made a major change in its structure from geographically organized practice units to vertical structure at the end of 2003, which resulted in the departure of several key second-line managers.[30]

Recruiting

Infosys had been renowned for its recruiting practices. From the company's inception, none of the founders gave special treatment to family members who wanted to work for Infosys.

Exhibit 7.2.6 Employee Information and Infosys's Facilities

		1998	1999	2000	2001	2002	2003	2004
Gender								
	Male	2228	3212	4558	8140	8928	12732	19833
	Female	377	554	831	1691	1810	3144	5801
		2605	3766	5389	9831	10738	15876	25634
Age								
	20–25 years	1040	1955	3057	6030	5351	7874	14631
	26–30 years	1200	1286	1659	2794	3981	5825	7894
	31–40 years	308	448	579	870	1210	1911	2737
	41–50 years	50	68	83	120	171	235	334
	51–60	7	9	11	17	25	29	37
	60+ years						2	1
		2605	3766	5389	9831	10738	15876	25634

The one quality that Infosys looked for in job candidates was learnability. Nilekani defined learnability as "the abiliity to derive generic knowledge from specific experiences and apply it in new situations." Infosys was not concerned with whether the candidate had specific software skills, because the company had the training programs to impart them. As one article described the hiring policy, "even if you have topped your class in IIT (Indian Institute of Technology) this year, Hema Ravichandar [senior vice president of Human Resource Development] might well decide not to hire you. In 2003–2004, her department sifted through nearly 1,000,000 job applications for 10,000 openings. She is clear that Infosys doesn't want erratic geniuses. Ravichandar's entire approach is aimed at ensuring one thing—good performance, again and again and again. Dependability, predictability, sustainability, consistency, reliability, uniformity, conformity . . . call it what you will, but that is what Infosys wants."[31] Vijaykumar Bhakta, regional manager for Infosys in Delhi at one point, commented on the type of employees Infosys wanted: "We want them to have these three traits: honesty, sincerity and dedication."

Joseph Alenchery, a recent MBA graduate who joined Infosys's corporate planning department, talked about his final interview before getting hired: "For corporate planning sometimes Nandan takes the final interview, sometimes Murthy. First Murthy started off by asking me about electronics, my specialization for engineering school. He then enquired on my background, my family, what do they do and where they are now. He asked me my expectations from Infosys. He said he likes people who are hardworking. Of course, he could not judge whether I am hardworking or not. But he said he could judge other things like openness. He told me, 'if you make a mistake it is okay, I will tell you that it is a mistake. I will give a few chances with mistakes made, but if you made a mistake because you did not work hard enough, that is not a good indicator.' "

Training and Becoming an "Infoscion"

Infosys trained its new software developers through a 14-week training program. After the training, the company put new recruits in teams of 20 people. The challenge had changed from recruiting merely good programmers to programmers with the ability to interface with customers. Infosys systematically asked new employees or employees sent on a foreign assignment to sign a bond agreeing to stay with Infosys for a set period of time (one year for new recruits).[32]

The company offered "Infoscions" (the name given to Infosys employees) several perks, which included state-of-the-art campuses, high quality food courts, a fitness centre, and a dormitory for on-site resting, bank branches and ATMs, a medical center, a grocery store, a clothing store etc. Infosys sought to provide the same benefits to all levels of the organization. Some observers felt that Infosys's facilities were some of the most beautiful in the world. Binod, a senior executive, said: "In some organizations the top floor for the management level may be paved with Italian marble and fantastic furniture and you go one floor below to find low quality furniture. [Here] if I had a table, Mr. Murthy would also be using a similar table. All of us Infoscions use the same furniture and facilities as used by anyone, including the Chairman. Simple living and high thinking—that is one core value of this company and so generally you will find people very simple and not carrying too much of an aura about themselves. Feet always on the ground wherever you are."

Suma Subramanian of employee relations talked about orienting new employees: "[After a workshop involving several levels from the company], we landed up with five basic values: [CLIFE which stands for] Customer delight, Leadership by example, Integrity and transparency, Fairness, and pursuit of Excellence [see Exhibit 7.2.7 for definitions]."

With expansion into new countries such as the recent acquisition of an Australian company, Infosys had to cater to 37 different nationalities. The company had to adapt some of its methods of communication to appeal to different cultures. As Hema openly asked, "[When operating around the world], how do you reconcile being an Indian company?"

Exhibit 7.2.7 CLIFE—Values

Our Values

The Values and Business Conduct of the organization are the means of achieving the Vision. Values are enduring concepts or core beliefs or desires that guide or motivate attitudes and actions.

These principles provide:

- A framework for day-to-day decision-making,
- Direction in ambiguous situations, and
- A rationale for decisions and actions.

The "Values" of the organization set acceptable or expected norms or boundaries of behaviour for the individual members of the organization.

Customer Delight—A commitment to surpassing our customers' expectations.

Leadership by Example—A commitment to set standards in our business and transactions and be an exemplar for the industry and our own teams.

Integrity and Transparency—A commitment to be ethical, sincere, and open in our dealings.

Fairness—A commitment to be objective and transaction-oriented, thereby earning trust and respect.

Pursuit of Excellence—A commitment to strive relentlessly, to constantly improve ourselves, our teams, our services and products so as to become the best.

Conclusion

In order to navigate in an environment that demands leveraging change and uncertainty, the business strategy of the organization rests on four pillars: Predictability, Sustainability. Profitability and De-risking.

As an Infoscion who operates within this reality, this is a challenging journey. We hope that the seed that has been sown today will give you the impetus to succeed and you will, in turn, enthuse other Infoscions.

Source: http://sparsh/EmployeeCommunication/Valuesmanual. Accessed 26 July 2002.

To develop new leaders, Infosys had instituted the Leadership Institute, which involved the selection and training of high potential employees across the entire organization. Dinesh commented, "we believe that very few leaders are born and many leaders are bred. So when you ask about how do you make sure your [25,000] people subscribe to this it's very important how you bring up that leadership. The Leadership Institute looks at all the components of the overall development and traits of an individual required to be a leader and then we groom them to become leaders."

Compensation and Retention

As of 2004, Infosys had an attrition rate of 10.5 per cent (up from 6.9 per cent in 2003) against an industry average of 17 per cent[33] with the average age of employees being 26 years and promotion time being two years for good performers. Compensation had become a hot topic amongst "Infoscions" especially with the continued debate in the United States on the loss of IT jobs to India. The average compensation of a software engineer was approximately $7,000 per year. By 2003, the company faced a minor human resource crisis, with employees expressing dissatisfaction with their salaries. One Infoscion at a gathering drilled Murthy, "When we still make gross margins of 47%, why aren't our salaries higher?"[34] The company introduced a variable compensation structure in 2003 as it expected pressure on wages to increase and Rupee appreciation (each percentage increase in the Rupee vis-à-vis the US$ translated to a decrease in 30–35 bps from Infosys's margins)[35]. For example, the company expected an average salary increase of 17 per cent in 2005, whereas expected inflation during the year was under 5 per cent.[36]

The company had first offered a stock options program in 1994 and then again in 1998 and 1999 to share its success with its employees. It was reported that through these stock option programs, the company had created over 400 millionaires. When asked if this amount of money decreased the motivation of employees, Dinesh shared his view: "Money is required but money alone won't [be the motivator]. The majority of the [millionaires] are still here. Even the guy who serves the tea and my driver [are millionaires]."

Murthy himself shunned the ostentatious lifestyle by continuing to live in a three-bedroom house in a middle-class neighborhood and driving in a modest Opel. Murthy explained his simple living credo, "beyond a certain level of comfort I think one's wealth should be seen as an opportunity to make a difference to society. The power of money is the power to give."[37]

One example of integrity arose with an Infosys employee named Sudheer who was awarded with the title of "value champion" for identifying a miscoding in his pay scale, which meant that he would have been paid at a higher salary: ". . . it was a substantial reduction in my pay [for identifying the problem], so [my boss] was very happy that I still brought it to his attention."

Deeshjith, the Head of the Asia Pacific business unit, talked about the challenge of extending Infosys's stock options across countries with different legal guidelines: "Even today we face many difficulties offering stock options in certain countries."

Industry and Competition

Indian IT and BPO exports were logged at $12.5 billion[38] in the fiscal 2003/04 year with a compound annual growth rate of approximately 25 per cent over the past two years.[39] While ranges for the growth of India's IT sector varied, some industry observers felt that total exports would reach $50 billion by 2008.[40] India had become a premier destination for quality software development and was considered to be the second largest developed market

Exhibit 7.2.8 Competitors' Profiles

in USD 000's	EDS		IBM		Accenture		Wipro		Infosys	
	Dec'03	Dec'02	Dec'03	Dec'02	Aug'03	Aug'02	Mar'04	Mar'03	Mar'04	Mar'03
Revenue	21,476.0	21,502.0	89,131.0	81,186.0	13,397.2	13,105.0	1,349.8	904.1	1,062.6	753.8
Gross Profit Margin	21.0%	24.2%	42.3%	42.7%	33.9%	37.9%	36.7%	40.3%	47.7%	49.9%
Operating Income	72.0	1,869.0	10,089.0	6,796.0	1,551.2	1,495.9	241.2	191.0	293.2	218.6
Total Net Income	(1,698.0)	1,116.0	7,583.0	3,579.0	498.2	244.9	230.8	170.9	270.3	194.9
Net Profit Margin	–	5.2%	8.5%	4.4%	3.7%	1.9%	17.1%	18.9%	25.4%	25.9%
Diluted EPS from Total Net Income ($)	(3.55)	2.28	4.32	2.06	1.05	0.56	0.33	0.25	1.01	0.73
Balance Sheet	Dec'03	Dec'02	Dec'03	Dec'02	Aug'03	Aug'02	Mar'04	Mar'03	Mar'04	Mar'03
Assets										
Cash	2,197.0	1,642.0	7,290.0	5,382.0	2,332.2	1,317.0	76.2	297.4	444.6	354.4
Total Current Assets	6,823.0	9,385.0	44,998.0	41,652.0	5,037.2	4,061.1	954.9	593.9	871.9	507.9
Total Assets	18,280.0	18,880.0	104,457.0	96,484.0	6,459.2	5,478.9	1,333.8	902.7	1,132.2	704.3
Liabilities and Shareholders' Equity	Dec'03	Dec'02	Dec'03	Dec'02	Aug'03	Aug'02	Mar'04	Mar'03	Mar'04	Mar'03
Total Current Liabilities	7,473.0	6,129.0	37,900.0	34,550.0	3,351.1	3,327.1	246.9	151.0	152.0	63.1
Total Liabilities	12,566.0	11,858.0	76,593.0	73,702.0	5,665.1	5,040.3	262.8	155.1	178.6	78.2
Total Equity Shares	5,714.0	7,022.0	27,864.0	22,782.0	794.2	438.6	1,071.0	747.6	953.6	626.0
Outstanding (mil.)	480.6	476.9	1,694.5	1,722.4	961.1	944.1	699.0	698.4	133.3	132.5
Cash Flow Statement	Dec'03	Dec'02	Dec'03	Dec'02	Aug'03	Aug'02	Mar'04	Mar'03	Mar'04	Mar'03
Net Operating Cash Flow	1,386.0	2,246.0	14,407.0	13,066.0	1,513.1	1,063.4	249.8	161.7	373.5	211.2
Net Investing Cash Flow	(700.0)	(997.0)	(5,122.0)	(6,897.0)	(108.8)	(248.0)	(331.4)	(23.9)	(304.7)	(53.9)
Net Financing Cash Flow	(71.0)	(166.0)	(7,798.0)	(7,265.0)	(491.6)	(1,414.8)	12.8	3.9	(9.8)	(21.1)
Net Change in Cash	555.0	1,121.0	1,908.0	(948.0)	1,015.2	(563.1)	(69.0)	141.8	90.2	143.9
Depreciation & Amortization	2,529.0	1,443.0	4,701.0	4,379.0	237.2	285.4	53.7	36.9	55.1	44.2
Capital Expenditures	(1,186.0)	(1,080.0)	(6,229.0)	(7,911.0)	(231.4)	(332.5)	(106.1)	(168.2)	(103.6)	(43.2)
Cash Dividends Paid	(287.0)	(287.0)	(1,085.0)	(1,005.0)	0.0	0.0	(6.1)	(4.9)	(47.2)	(33.9)

Source: Hoovers Company Profiles, www.hoovers.com, Accessed 21 October 2004.

Note: TCS numbers were not available as it was a private company as of April 2004.

MNC Competition	Current Strength in India	Future Plans
IBM	5,500	Plans to double manpower in a couple of years
Accenture	6,000	10,000 by year-end
EDS	1,200	Plans to double manpower

Source: Infosys Technologies Analyst Report, SSKI, 11 May 2004.

Exhibit 7.2.8 (*Continued*) Tata Consultancy Services Performance

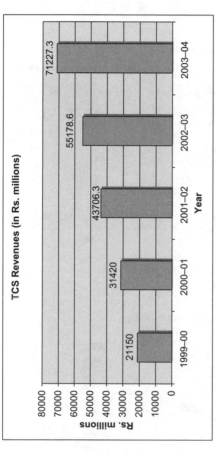

Source: TCS from Consolidated Financial Statements, 31 March 2004, www.tcs.com. Accessed 15 May 2005. Years 00–01 from "TCS profits grew . . .", TCS Press Release, 30 July 2001. www.tcs.com, Accessed 15 May 2005.

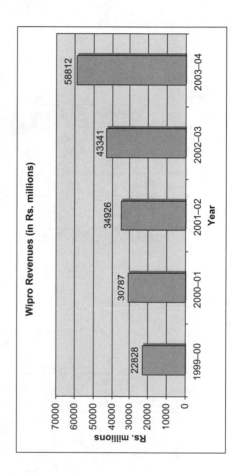

Source: Wipro from Annual Report 2004, 31 March 2004, Years 02–04, Page 3, Years 00–01 from Annual Report 2002, 31 March 2002, Page 131.

Exhibit 7.2.9 Indian IT Industry Growth

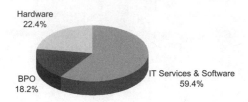

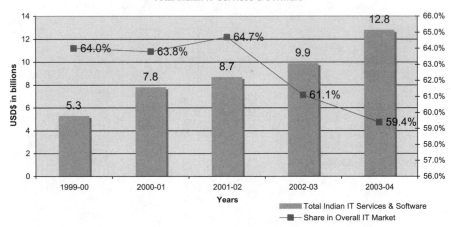

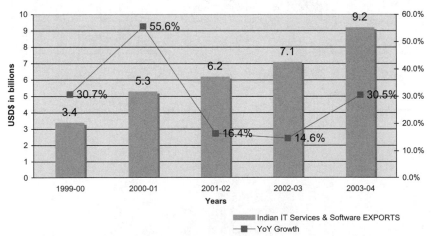

Source: Nasscom Website, Resource Center, www.nasscom.org, Accessed 15 May 2005.

next to the United States. Some observers even predicted that Bangalore, where many IT firms were located, would overtake Silicon Valley in number of employees.[41] A senior executive for Wipro painted a picture of the Indian IT environment as of early 2004: "It's like a gold rush town here. You can't get a hotel room. There are headhunters outside the office complexes, waiting to jump designers when they leave work. It looks like nothing so much as Silicon Valley in 1999. I give it two to three years (before the bubble bursts) . . . You can see the trend already. Salaries are going up; rents are rising. Design costs are moving toward parity with the U.S."[42]

Over 25 per cent of Indian IT exports were generated from the country's three dominant firms: Tata Consultancy Services (TCS), Wipro and Infosys. Each company had experienced rapid growth due to the Indian IT boom and actively competed for young recruits. TCS, founded in 1968, was the oldest Indian IT firm and was backed by the huge conglomerate Tata Group. It was expected that TCS would attempt an initial public offering (IPO) of approximately $2 billion in mid-2004, which would be the largest of any Indian software company. With revenues of approximately $1.56 billion[43] in 2003/04, TCS was India's largest IT firm. Infosys's Nandan had high praise—"TCS pioneered the Indian software industry and has played a seminal role in the global acceptance of Indian software capabilities."[44]

Wipro had sales of $1.3 billion in 2003/04 that were divided amongst products and services, making it the third largest in IT exports behind TCS and Infosys. Wipro's acquisition of the BPO company Spectramind in 2002 was seen to be highly successful as Spectramind was the number one BPO company in India with a dozen Fortune 500 customers contributing 11 per cent to Wipro's overall revenues.[45] Indian press often compared Infosys with Wipro as competitive siblings. Wipro's vice-chairman quipped, "Siblings don't hate each other, they have a lot of mutual respect and even affection, but they like to compete."[46] Infosys was seen to be different than Wipro in a few key areas with Infosys maintaining a higher willingness to experiment, greater openness towards the press, and sharing wealth across a larger employee base.

Murthy talked about Wipro, "I do believe it's possible to be fiercely competitive yet friendly with your competitors, as long as both parties are professional and ethical. Azim [chairman of Wipro] and I maintain a very healthy relationship . . . We believe we can learn a lot from each other."[47]

There were two main shifts that Indian IT service firms were experiencing—the development of IT-enabled business process outsourcing (BPO) and moving up the value chain to compete against global IT service firms such as IBM, EDS and Accenture. In BPO, India was being challenged by countries such as China, the Czech Republic, Hungary and Romania where transaction-based processing could be performed at a cheaper rate, as the tasks did not typically involve specialty programming knowledge. On the other end of the scale, Indian IT companies were trying to develop their consulting arms to be on par with the likes of established global brands such as IBM, EDS and Accenture. Exhibit 7.2.8 shows the competitors' profiles and Exhibit 7.2.9 shows some key facts about the Indian IT industry.

The Future

Four words, "New Game. New Rules," graced the cover of Infosys's 2004 annual report. Alongside, their slogan, "Infosys: powered by intellect, driven by values," proudly stood. With 10,000 new employees and an attempt to secure more business in the BPO sector while moving up the value chain, the six founders of Infosys all wondered about what the "new game" would entail. Infosys was well aware of the challenges of instilling its much celebrated culture and values to its new employee base. In true Infosys fashion they had disclosed this in their annual report stating, "rapid growth brings with it the risk of being unable to ensure consistency in culture and core values. This is important considering that [Infosys] freshly inducted a major portion of its employee base in over just one year."[48] Infosys had undoubtedly become a world class company. Nandan, Murthy and the rest of the senior management team wondered what it would take to make the company a truly global force in the IT market.

Notes

* This case was written by Prof. S. Ramakrishna Velamuri, with editing support from Jordan Mitchell, as a basis for class discussion and not to illustrate either effective or ineffective management. Copyright IESE Publishing. Used with Permission.

1 Povaiah, Roshun, "Playing the Future," Advertising Marketing, 30 June 1999.
2 Interview with N.R. Narayana Murthy, www.india-seminar.com, 2000.
3 Interview with N.R. Narayana Murthy, www.india-seminar.com, 2000.
4 Interview with N.R. Narayana Murthy, www.india-seminar.com, 2000.
5 Interview with N.R. Narayana Murthy, www.india-seminar.com, 2000.
6 Interview with N.R. Narayana Murthy, www.india-seminar.com, 2000.
7 "Murthy, Panti Aur Woe," Corporate Dossier, The Economic Times, 4 October 2002.
8 "Murthy strikes back," Corporate Dossier, The Economic Times, 18 October 2002.
9 "The Men behind Infosys," Business World, 7 November 1998.
10 Nanda, Ashish, and Delong, Thomas, "Infosys Technologies," Harvard Business School, 9–801–445, 11 April 2002.
11 Nanda, Ashish, and Delong, Thomas, "Infosys Technologies," Harvard Business School, 9–801–445, 11 April 2002.
12 Interview with N.R. Narayana Murthy, www.india-seminar.com, 2000.
13 Interview with Narayana Murthy for PBS, 5 February 2001.
14 Infosys Annual Report 1999, Page 7, 31 March 1999.
15 Infosys Annual Report 2004, Page 15, 31 March 2004.
16 Jayashankar, Mitu and Prasad, Shishir, "Remaking INFY," Businessworld, 22 September 2003.
17 Jayashankar, Mitu and Prasad, Shishir, "Remaking INFY," Businessworld, 22 September 2003.
18 Infosys Annual Report 2004, Page 16, 31 March 2004.
19 Infosys Annual Report 2004, Page 15, 31 March 2004.
20 Infosys Annual Report 2004, Page 19, 31 March 2004.
21 Infosys Annual Report 2004, Page 112, 31 March 2004.
22 Jayashankar, Mitu and Prasad, Shishir, "Remaking INFY," Businessworld, 22 September 2003.
23 Prasad, Shishir, "It's hard to keep Phaneesh Murthy down," Businessworld, 22 September 2003.
24 Infosys Annual Report 2004, Page 20, 31 March 2004.
25 T.V. Mohandas Pai, "The Infosys Financial Model", INFY Analyst Day, August 2001.
26 Kueemerle, Walter and Coughlin, William, "Infosys: Financing an Indian Software Start-up," Harvard Business School, 9–800–103, 10 December 2001.
27 Dharchaudhuri, Indira, "The Murthy Factor," Hindustan Times, 24 October 2002.
28 Ravichandar, Hema. Speech: "Architechting a high performance Infosys," 11 August 2003.
29 Ravichandar, Hema. Speech: "Architechting a high performance Infosys," 11 August 2003.
30 Infosys Technologies, Credit Suisse First Boston Analyst Report, Page 4, 14 July 2004.
31 Viswanathan, Vidya, "Magnificient: Infosys," Business World, 17 June 2002.
32 MacDonald, Claire and Rattanani, Jagdish, "Programming for Profits," Asiaweek, June 1999, p. 59.
33 "Infosys to add 10,000; hike capex," www.thehindubusinessline.com, 13 April 2004.
34 Jayashankar, Mitu and Prasad, Shishir, "Remaking INFY," Businessworld, 22 September 2003.
35 Infosys Technologies, SSKI Analyst Report, Page 9, 11 May 2004.
36 Infosys Technologies, Citigroup Smith Barney Analyst Report, Page 3, 14 April 2004.
37 Karmali, Naazneen, "N.R. Narayana Murthy," Business India, 13 to 26 December 1999.
38 "Indian software exports booming, industry head says," Reuters, www.computerworld.com, 13 September 2004, Accessed 27 October 2004.
39 Glick, Brian, "All outsourcing roads lead to India," Computing, 5 December 2003.
40 Glick, Brian, "All outsourcing roads lead to India," Computing, 5 December 2003.

41 McCue, Andy and Frauenheim, Ed, "Is Bangalore bigger than Silicon Valley?," CNET News.com, 28 July 2004.
42 Wilson, Ron, "Gold Rush Days for Global Design?", Electronic Engineering Times, 29 March 2004.
43 Kanavi, Shivanand, "Megasoft," Business India, Pages 46–54, 7–20 June 2004.
44 Kanavi, Shivanand, "Megasoft," Business India, Pages 46–54, 7–20 June 2004.
45 Yahoo! India Business, http://in.biz.yahoo.com/041015/21/2hcg4.html, Accessed 19 November 2004.
46 Rai, Asha, "Infosys vs Wipro," The Economic Times, 21 December 2001.
47 Rai, Asha, "Infosys vs Wipro," The Economic Times, 21 December 2001.
48 Infosys Annual Report 2004, Page 91, 31 March 2004.

7.3 Resisting Bureaucratic Corruption
Alacrity Housing Chennai[*]

Introduction

By March 2003, Alacrity was in deep financial difficulties, and fighting a grim battle for its survival. At the end of this period the company's revenues had declined nearly 40% with respect to 1997. Rumors had started to circulate in the industry that Alacrity was going out of business, and that the founders were planning to emigrate to Australia.

From 1994 to 1996, Alacrity had gained strong revenue and income growth. However, the company experienced a consistent decline in business results from 1997 to 2003. As a result, Alacrity had severe cash flow problems. The one area that was still very unpredictable was governmental relations, and especially relations with the Chennai Metropolitan Development Authority (CMDA). An online equity analyst report dated April 10, 2003 had this to say:

> "Alacrity Housing Ltd has been facing a cash crunch as the sanction of cash credit limits to replace the company's term loans with ICICI and Union Bank of India has been taking longer than expected, according to the company's annual report. As a result of this progress in construction and delivery times have remained unpredictable and even customers who had displayed great faith to stay in delayed projects, justifiably, were cautious in paying their installments. The main contributions to sales came from new booking for a project at Saligramam.
>
> The operations have slowed down because of the liquidity constraints, only two projects with 58,000 sq ft of built up area worth of Rs 82.6 million could be completed. Another two projects with 29,000 sq ft valued at Rs 58.4 million are close to completion. These projects apart, the effective business on hand is worth Rs 1.8 billion, the report said. The report said that while large housing businesses have taken the delayed permit phenomenon in their strides, the liquidity crunch has constrained the company in its efforts to make up for the lost time. The consortium of banks in the State Bank group is in the process of providing the company with the required additional working capital in the form of cash credit. The company also proposes to explore more opportunities for taking up construction other than housing following the completion of the housing project."

Apart from Alacrity's cash dilemma and building projects, Amol had introduced some new programs bringing about changes in the organization and emphasizing the company's values. With a struggling business, cash flow problems and a number of new initiatives underway, observers wondered whether Alacrity was on the right path.

Business Performance

During 1995 there was a rumor in the market that the Chennai Metropolitan Development Authority (CMDA) would increase the amount of permissible construction per square foot of land (known as the Floor Space Index, or FSI) by 67%, from 1.5 times to 2.5 times.[1] Construction companies, seeing huge profits, started buying land in the city. The landowners, who had no intention of being left out of the property boom, started raising their prices. The speculation on land prices was such that a leading international bank lent Rs. 1.5 billion for the construction of a huge multi-storied complex to one individual who owned a large piece of land in a prime commercial area. This individual had no experience in construction whatsoever. As a comparison, in 1996, Alacrity was managing 85 projects, and had total loans of only Rs. 80 million.

At the beginning of 1997, Alacrity's management saw the escalation of land prices in the city, and accordingly changed its strategy and decided to invest in the suburbs. The company invested Rs. 136.69 million in payments to land owners. The CMDA did not increase the FSI, and the construction companies that had purchased large parcels of land in the city started to offer flats at "distress prices." Many started going out of business and defaulted on their loans to banks and other financial institutions. The banks then withdrew funding to all constructors, including Alacrity, sending the industry into a recession. Ashok (Amol's brother) explained:

> "What also happened is in 1996 the crash, but for a full year it did not touch us, but by 1997 media reports, which were not very well done in the sense they were not too accurate; the media has the habit of sensationalizing things. So in Bombay the market crashed. Bombay, I have always believed has been a very speculative market. . . . We believed Chennai market was less speculative or there was very little speculation because we had the largest market share, on day one we would advertise the prices, no black money, and it has a sobering influence on the industry. In this phase everybody came in. Bombay builders came in a big way, the bank speculated with them in their own way, and when the market crash came, the media reports said the prices have fallen 50% and the reports were common, but that was not the case in Chennai. Chennai had dropped maybe 15% to 20%, but they made those reports common (this was in 1997). In one year, 125 people withdrew from our projects. See, we keep agreements as simple as possible. There is no deterrent or there is no forfeiture fee on their part for withdrawing from our projects. We never kept that, believing people are always responsible and they won't withdraw unless they have good reason to. . . . No financial planning can be done in these circumstances and on the other hand, the banks had got jittery and withdrawn support."

From 1998 to 2002, the company was fighting the effects of the unfavorable events of 1997. Payments to suppliers started getting delayed. Suppliers were increasingly being asked to set off their outstanding balances by purchasing Alacrity flats. Delivery of flats to customers was systematically delayed, due to two reasons: longer processing times for documents at CMDA, and the company's severe cash flow problems. One customer, whose flat was originally scheduled to be delivered in December 1995, was able to move into his new home only in October 1999—a nearly four-year delay. This customer was very happy with the quality of the construction and the honesty and integrity of the Alacrity managers. However, he accused them of creating false expectations, especially about the completion times of the projects. While acknowledging that Alacrity was a company that followed principles, he added—"You can't compromise efficiency for principles alone." In his extensive interaction with the company's officers over a five-year period, he had reason to suspect that its internal efficiencies were low. As an example, he cited the inordinate delay by the company in collecting monies from him for work that had been done after he moved in.

The competitors were faring even worse. Several companies went out of business. A few, including the construction divisions of large diversified corporations, became inactive, hoping to reinitiate business once the economic scenario improved. As a former manager pointed out, Alacrity's survival in a very difficult economic environment was a major achievement, especially in light of the closure of many of its rival companies.

The shareholders had received dividends for only one year in the 1998–2003 period. The share price of the company was also performing very poorly—it was trading below its par value of Rs. 10 per share. An investment weekly had the following to say about Alacrity's financial performance:

> "In the process of setting high moral and ethical standards for business practices it created a sense of confidence in individual buyers of its residential outlets that most of its competitors could not. Yet, for all this path-breaking positioning and pioneering culture in a corruption-ridden industry, Alacrity has perhaps not encashed its brand equity as much as it should have done. Consequently while the buyers of Alacrity's flats might not have any major complaints against the company, it is a pity that the same cannot be said about its shareholders."[2]

Alacrity responded to this assessment with the following statement in its Annual Report for 1999:

> "Alacrity knows that any exclusive attempt to 'encash brand equity' particularly in a recession exposes the very source of that equity—product quality, customer satisfaction and market goodwill—to the risk of dilution. In fact Alacrity believes that it is such shortsighted and non-institutional attempts to gratify shareholders that create market recessions in the first place and they are best avoided."[3]

One former manager summed up Alacrity's attitude towards profit—"There was no profit goal. Today they are struggling because there was no profit goal, there were only other goals."

See the company's financial statements in Exhibits 7.3.1A and 7.3.1B.

Alacrity's Organization: 1995 to 2003

Leadership Program

Amol had set in motion a third leadership selection process in 1995. Eight individuals, of which three were outsiders, were chosen to be groomed into future leaders. They were placed in two grades that reflected individuals with two different temperaments, one radical and the other more disciplined. The first grade, Grade T was made up of specialists—an architect; a journalist and activist; and a medical doctor. The second grade, Grade P, was meant for individuals who were disciplined in the implementation of standards. Although both grades had the potential to become members of the top management team, Grade T individuals were on the faster track.

Amol commented on the social resistance to Alacrity's many unconventional initiatives:

> "I became convinced that similar leadership initiative and risk taking were now called for

if the experience of organized business, the most active and pervasive institution of our times, was to be taken advantage of for influencing a qualitative change in social living; there was clearly an irresistible case for making human change a central part of the very purpose of business."

Amol gave up operational responsibilities by appointing his brother Ashok to the position of Managing Director during 1997, but retained the Chairmanship of the Board.

During the same year, a new group of youngsters joined the leadership development process, which was referred to as the Research Program. This group, with one exception, was made up of sons of Alacrity managers. Amol felt that these youngsters, having grown up in the Alacrity community, would find it easier to imbibe the company's values. Around the same time, the Alacrity managers started participating in the process of individuation (a concept first articulated by Carl Jung). This process was initiated after considerable discussion and internal debate.

The core group of young managers who had been through the leadership development process (Grade T) left the company in 1999 and 2000. Amol reflected on the departure of these four managers and of another senior manager, and concluded that they were specialists—architect, journalist/activist, doctor, psychiatrist—who had all chosen to return to their respective fields of specialization. He felt that perhaps they believed that their aspirations could not be fulfilled within an organizational context.

The first three leadership selections had not been very successful—17 of the 26 individuals who had been selected to participate in them had left the organization, although some had left for personal reasons (such as relocation due to marriage).

Employee Morale

The employees were also suffering the effects of Alacrity's precarious financial situation—as of 2003, the managerial cadre had not been paid salaries for more than a year, and the junior staff had not been paid for several months. A large number of employees resigned and took up jobs elsewhere. Almost all the senior managers had pledged their flats as collateral for the company's loans. Some had contributed cash by way of loans. For most of these senior managers, the assets pledged represented a significant percentage, and in some cases the entirety, of their life savings. Many had even convinced their relatives to give loans to Alacrity.

Alacrity's Home Schooling Program

Another of Amol's initiatives that created considerable controversy was the concept of home-schooling. Unlike North America and Europe, where home schooling had been recognized as an alternative route for education, India did not have any recognized home schooling system.[4] At the time the initiative was adopted in Alacrity, it was unclear how, or whether, the children who had been home-schooled would be able to go back to the formal educational system. When the question was raised whether there was a future for the youngsters outside Alacrity, one of the youngsters stated, "After all, 'Alacrity,' as we view it, is a process of human development before being either a business enterprise or a community."

As of 2002, there were eight children in the Alacrity home-schooling system, with ages ranging from 6 years to 15 years. Not all the children of school-going age of the managers were participating in the system; several continued to attend conventional schools. These home-schoolers interacted closely with five "young home-makers" (all females) aged 16 to 20

Exhibit 7.3.1A Alacrity's Financial Balance Sheet

In Rupees	1995	1996	1997	1998	1999	2000	2001	2002
Share Capital	80,000	80,000	80,000	80,000	80,000	80,000	80,000	80,000
Reserves and Surplus	34,888	56,786	60,809	63,320	67,954	71,793	75,876	73,656
Shareholders Equity	114,888	136,786	140,809	143,320	147,954	151,793	155,876	153,656
Deferred tax	—	—	—	—	—	—	—	9,942
Secured loans	30,637	70,417	101,536	87,519	52,981	200,000	232,541	247,308
Unsecured loans	1,581	9,000	37,500	119,555	91,309	5,671	3,949	2,655
Total long term debt	32,218	79,417	139,036	207,074	144,290	205,671	236,490	249,963
Current liabilities and provisions	97,053	130,038	207,536	192,545	159,303	130,366	125,378	111,999
Total liabilities	244,159	346,241	487,381	542,939	451,547	487,830	517,744	525,560
Gross fixed assets	3,401	7,320	14,612	15,761	15,783	16,186	16,346	16,479
Depreciation	845	2,051	4,612	7,631	9,513	10,899	11,908	12,653
Net fixed assets	2,556	5,269	10,000	8,130	6,270	5,287	4,438	3,826
Investments	519	164	63	45	38	25	20	47
Inventories	16,646	29,081	34,960	18,377	12,200	8,935	6,856	8,273
Work-in-progress	206,085	379,021	567,013	738,495	844,249	922,066	878,839	786,260
Less: Progressive payments from customers	259,182	447,917	624,321	728,949	820,203	892,155	845,202	747,148
Net Work-in-progress	(53,097)	(68,896)	(57,308)	9,546	24,046	29,911	33,637	39,112
Sundry debtors	125,777	154,257	127,964	212,112	155,734	180,982	211,856	222,883
Cash and bank balances	11,643	31,767	13,732	10,680	4,695	7,130	2,116	1,764
Loans and advances	113,018	172,456	342,086	272,873	243,470	249,765	253,977	246,235
Total current assets	213,987	318,665	461,434	523,588	440,145	476,723	508,442	518,267
Miscellaneous expenditure	27,097	22,143	15,884	11,176	5,094	5,795	4,844	3,420
Total assets	244,159	346,241	487,381	542,939	451,547	487,830	517,744	525,560

Exhibit 7.3.1B Profit and Loss Statement

In Rupees except number of employees	1995	1996	1997	1998	1999	2000	2001	2002
Sales in thousands of square feet	562	470	301	190	269	288	369	390
Sales turnover (including land)	721,100	815,800	575,600	443,200	522,600	588,400	704,700	799,500
Income from Operations (excluding land)	240,157	340,602	429,116	411,016	280,216	245,501	251,419	260,908
Other income	2,659	10,267	8,469	8,376	8,023	5,871	6,493	2,400
Total income	242,816	350,869	437,585	419,392	288,239	251,372	257,912	263,308
Construction Expenses	148,443	222,460	319,230	300,998	174,221	149,271	138,518	142,732
Employee Costs (excluding contract laborers)	9,073	16,835	18,751	19,391	23,455	23,304	22,020	21,821
Marketing Expenses	10,531	21,037	30,314	23,781	17,880	17,459	24,159	19,417
Administration Expenses	14,407	22,817	33,458	28,070	25,018	22,568	19,655	23,792
Financial Overheads	4,556	5,990	8,063	34,066	33,091	29,629	40,225	40,877
Deferred Revenue Expenditure written off	6,399	6,618	7,225	6,528	7,371	2,841	2,692	2,893
Preliminary Expenses written off	35	35	35	35	35	35	35	35
Depreciation	655	1,206	2,561	3,019	1,882	1,386	1,120	1,002
Total expenditure	194,099	296,998	419,637	415,888	282,953	246,493	248,424	252,569
Profit before tax	48,717	53,871	17,948	3,504	5,286	4,879	9,488	10,739
Provision for Income Tax	17,266	18,373	5,125	368	560	1,000	1,000	3,000
Provision for Income Tax – Deferred	–	–	–	–	–	–	–	3,762
Profit after tax	31,451	35,498	12,823	3,136	4,726	3,879	8,488	3,977
Number of employees as of March 31	190	222	255	267	254	229	209	197
Per capita employee costs (in thousands)	47.75	75.83	73.53	72.63	92.34	101.76	105.36	110.77
Employee costs per square foot sold (in Rs)	16.14	35.82	62.30	102.06	87.19	80.92	59.67	55.95
Income from operations per square foot (in Rs)	427.33	724.69	1,425.63	2,163.24	1,041.70	852.43	681.35	668.99
Liquidated damages (in thousands)	2,049	3,933	3,649	4,424	4,965	4,131	11,483	3,644

years, and six male trainees (Grade T) aged 16–25 on the fast track management development program. A company document drafted by sons and daughters of Top and Senior Managers in the 16–25 age group wrote, "Every pioneer goes through turmoil while balancing on the one hand, the benefits accruing from the evolving system and on the other, the constant criticism that is received from the conservative sections of society."

A reporter from a national newspaper was on the verge of publishing a story that was very critical of the company and particularly of Amol. Before publishing the story, the Editor asked Amol to present his side of the story. The Editor opened the meeting with an aggressive remark—he said that if Amol continued to pull children out of school, people would call him a madman. Amol replied that it would not be the first time, as people had done so even twenty years earlier, when he had declared his intention of setting up a construction business without any bribery.

One former manager criticized the progressive loss of focus of the business—"It can never be. You can't be confused. See, you want to run a university, you have the facilities of a university. You want to run a building company, run a building company. You want to run a research center, run a research center. But you can't do a *kitchdi*[5] of the whole stuff and say here I am all right . . ."

Future Prospects

Yet, in spite of all the difficulties the company was facing, and the suspicions it was arousing in some quarters, there was consensus that its product quality was excellent. Even a former manager, who was critical of Alacrity in other respects, stated that he would unhesitatingly purchase another flat from the company.

The Alacrity managers, especially the youngsters, would not entertain the notion that the business could close down. They were convinced that it was only a question of time before Alacrity recovered its strong position in the construction business.

Notes

*   This case was written by Prof. S. Ramakrishna Velamuri, with editing support from Jordan Mitchell, as a basis for class discussion and not to illustrate either effective or ineffective management. Copyright IESE Publishing. Used with Permission.

1   An FSI of 1.5 meant that a construction company could construct a built up area 1.5 times the area of the land. If the land area was 4,000 square feet, then it could construct 6,000 square feet of flats. If the FSI were to go up to 2.5, then on the same land, 10,000 square feet of flats could be constructed.

2   *Express Investment Week*, January 18–24, 1999.

3   *Alacrity Housing Ltd, Annual Report 1999.*

4   Even in the US and Europe, home-schooling was not universally accepted. For example, it was not allowed in some US states.

5   An Indian dish, mixture of several ingredients.

Chapter 8

Sustaining the Environment

8.1 Unilever

Corporate Venturing and Environmental Sustainability[*]

In 1994 Dr. Jan-Kees Vis was attending a social function for his new job with the Unilever Foods Executive Quality Assurance Group (FEQAG). At the reception, Vis was approached by his new boss, Jan Peelen, the Chairman of the Foods Executive, who had operational and strategic responsibility for Unilever's food product businesses in Europe and North America. In the ensuing discussion, Peelen asked him about his plans for his new position.[1]

Vis had joined FEQAG to work on establishing an environmental audit program and to create training courses for environmental managers at the various Unilever operating facilities. He had discussed this role with senior-level managers within Unilever Foods prior to his taking the job, and they supported this role.

Vis, who had a PhD in chemistry, previously worked in a Unilever margarine factory. At that post, he examined the effect Unilever products were having on the environment at all stages of their life cycles. He studied various margarine products to quantify their environmental impacts and to make environmental efficiency improvements. He left this job for a position at FEQAG where he would be involved in designing the tools to help Unilever operating companies comply with environmental policy.

Vis recognized this encounter with Peelen as a rare opportunity. Vis's work had always been steeped in operational improvements at Unilever, not in influencing company strategy. Peelen reported directly to the Unilever board. He determined the overall performance targets, such as sales targets, brand positioning, and environmental performance goals. He developed the strategic directions for Unilever Foods in the United States and Europe.

Vis suggested to Peelen that Unilever was not doing enough work with sustainable development. Vis mentioned that Unilever had an obligation to more carefully examine its environmental impacts and that fulfilling environmental obligations was consistent with sound business practice. He was convinced that businesses needed to pay attention to the public's cues in order to keep its license to do business.

"What do you mean *we* aren't doing enough?" Peelen responded. "You are Unilever and I am Unilever. If you think more should be done, then do something about it."

Based jointly in the Netherlands and the United Kingdom, Unilever made and marketed more than 1,000 brands of consumer goods in the industrial categories of foods, beverages, detergents, and personal products. At the time, Unilever employed about 300,000 people in companies operating in more than 90 countries around the world; their products were sold through third parties in 70 additional countries. In the United States, some of Unilever's most recognizable brands were Lipton, Five Brothers pasta sauces, Chicken Tonight, "All" detergent, Calvin Klein perfume, Dove, Helene Curtis, Vaseline, and Q-tips. Unilever's products were bought by more than half the families in the world.

Strategy Through Policy Changes

Vis had Peelen's attention, but he realized getting his ideas accepted in the Foods portion of Unilever required tremendous effort for two reasons. First, there was the overwhelming size of the Foods portion of Unilever's organization. Unilever Foods supplied nearly half of Unilever's 1995 turnover of $50 billion. It sold more than 10 million metric tons of food products. It was the third-largest foods business in the world, consisting of more than 150 individual operating companies, with 250 factories in 80 countries. Some of their recognizable brands included: Lipton, Five Brothers pasta sauces, Chicken Tonight, Gorton's frozen foods, Popsicle, Birds Eye frozen foods, Country Crock, Breyer's Ice Cream, and Klondike.

Second, there was the matter of where Vis was located within the organization. Vis worked in FEQAG in a support position within the Foods Executive (Appendix A). His role was to enable the Foods operating companies to implement environmental management policies, such as BS7750 and other precursors to ISO 14000-type environmental management systems. The official FEQAG organizational objectives were to prepare and determine policies on the environment, to develop systems and procedures to implement the policies and to ensure the implementation of the policies through audits.

In general, however, FEQAG personnel were not involved in setting environmental strategic goals. That was the responsibility of the Unilever Environmental Group (UEG). The UEG, an independent, internal consulting group (Appendix A), communicated environmental strategic goals to the Foods Executive to make sure the Foods environmental policies were consistent with Unilever's environmental policy.

Vis saw an opportunity that related directly to the normal tasks of his new job. When he started, he found that the Foods environmental policy needed updating. The current policy had been adopted in May 1990. It focused on reacting to future environmental issues and consumer pressures, like a demand for cleaner products from a growing "green consumer" segment, calls from governments and other consumers to address environmental issues, and potential cost increases due to new regulations. The policy called for acceptance of environmental protection measures and reductions in environmental impacts.

What was missing, in Vis's opinion, was specific management guidance on how to deploy programs to meet those goals. From his previous experience at the margarine factory, he realized that "from the top" policy statements do not work without the tools to implement them. Specific, concrete steps were needed in order to make the policies implementable across a wide and complicated organization. He wanted to include three action-oriented provisions in the new Foods policy in the spirit of ISO 9000 quality management systems: (1) train people to implement environmental management systems; (2) develop and implement environmental auditing programs; and (3) work to improve eco-efficiency.

More alarmingly, however, Vis recognized that the goals of the Unilever Foods Environmental Policy were rather difficult to grasp. In his opinion, the actions would fail unless he could articulate a clearer vision for the policy.[2] In the spirit of his conversation with Peelen at the reception, Vis saw an opportunity to build the policy around the theme of sustainable development.

There were factors that complicated his initiative. First, UEG provisions involving sustainability already existed as part of the companywide 1994 Unilever Environmental Policy. The UEG included the following statement in this policy, "Unilever wishes to be part of a sustainable future, in which economic growth combines with sound environmental management to meet the needs and aspirations of people throughout the world."[3]

On one hand, Vis recognized that this statement reflected the UEG's, the Board's, and Special Committee's growing concerns about the environment. The statement followed after the Special Committee signed the International Chamber of Commerce (ICC) Charter for Sustainable Development in 1993. That charter was designed to capture the spirit of both corporate self-regulation and environmental sustainability in response to *Agenda 21*, the declaration made in 1992 at the Conference on Environment and Development in Rio de Janeiro.

On the other hand, Vis understood that the statement provided no guidance or plan of action for achieving sustainability. Vis observed that people within the company had been referring to "sustainability" in 1994–95 without knowing what the term meant in terms of corporate activities. Vis cited that lack of clarity as the reason that sustainable development remained a low-key priority in Unilever. He realized his goal of clarifying the Unilever Foods Environmental Policy around the theme of sustainable development with specific action steps had the possibility of helping to clarify the company-wide initiative. He recognized that he would need the support of UEG members to do this; however, his position in FEQAG limited his access to UEG members.

The second, and more immediate, concern was that he needed to gather support from Ben de Vet, Vis's immediate superior in FEQAG. De Vet had direct responsibility to Peelen for the Foods Environmental Policy. Fortunately, Vis and de Vet hit it off right away. Vis recognized de Vet as someone who knew how to get things done. Mirroring the situation that existed as a result of the UEG's directions involving sustainability, de Vet had an interest in the idea, but he had kept the idea in the background because of its lack of specificity. Vis rekindled de Vet's interest in the subject, and they considered possible ways to address sustainable development for Unilever Foods. De Vet supported Vis's initiative to clarify Foods's environmental policy around sustainable development.

Vis had the green light to proceed. He drafted a new version of the Unilever Foods Environmental Policy in early 1995 (Appendix B). Vis's vision for sustainable development found its place in the opening sentence of the policy, "We will aim for sustainable development. In the years to come, we will work towards a definition of sustainability that is meaningful to our business and acceptable to relevant stakeholders."

Both de Vet and Peelen approved the vision, and the policy was adopted by the Foods Executive Committee and issued as part of the formal Foods Environmental Policy in May 1995. Vis saw that as a significant endorsement of his vision; however, he still had the problem of defining what sustainability meant in specific business terms and how the vision could be implemented in Foods. Furthermore, the policy would remain a local, Foods initiative unless he could get the UEG involved.

Vis's attention, however, remained with his responsibilities at FEQAG. De Vet asked for Vis's help to implement the policy. De Vet recommended to Peelen that a working group be formed to implement the new policy. Peelen approved that idea, and he arranged for the formation of the Foods Environmental Implementation Group (FEIG). Peelen and the Foods Executive required that FEIG work to relate sustainable development to Unilever's activities in business terms. The FEIG was also expected to develop a set of sustainability indicators suitable for determining how sustainable Unilever Foods operations were.[4]

The FEIG was comprised of senior managers from the Foods Executive, other members from the various Foods operating companies, De Vet, and Vis, who was appointed secretary. The members possessed various perspectives on implementing policies in the operating companies. Only some members of the group had experience with environmental management, and that did not include the chair of FEIG.

The result was that several members of FEIG became uncomfortable with the sustainable development vision. They could only hold general conversations about what it meant, and they found it difficult to link to business operations. Conversations fell apart when they would start to talk about any specific operational changes that they thought sustainable development implied.

Vis proposed that the FEIG begin by projecting scenarios of what the state of affairs in the world might look like in 20 to 25 years. From this perspective he proposed the FEIG construct scenarios of what their business might look like for the various operating companies in Foods. Projecting backwards, they could get an idea of what decisions could be made at the current time. The FEIG rejected that idea because of the group's operational orientation—they thought the group lacked the type of strategic thinkers necessary to conduct the exercise.

Vis then recalled an idea that he got from when he worked at the margarine factory: Bring in external consultants to bring in outside perspectives. What did outside stakeholders think about sustainable development in business terms? De Vet and Peelen approved the idea, so they went with the external study plan.

Vis arranged for two external studies by two separate consultants. The goals of the studies were: (1) to perform a review of external perspectives, focusing on the views and the needs of key stakeholder groups in Unilever's Foods business; and (2) to perform a review of existing theories, concepts, and definitions of sustainable agriculture and food production and processing; sustainability indicators; and associated metrics in economic terms.

The first task was contracted to SustainAbility, an environmental consulting company based in the United Kingdom. SustainAbility sought the opinions of different stakeholders around the world to construct a definition of sustainable development that was appropriate for Unilever's Foods businesses. They obtained opinions from leading players and opinion-formers from the perspectives of consumers, farmers, agribusinesses, retailers and non-government organizations allied with environmental and sustainable development communities. They aimed to review stakeholders' perceptions and to make practical recommendations for Unilever's Foods business to start implementing sustainability.[5]

The Institute for Applied Environmental Economics (TME) in the Netherlands performed the second study to determine a set of indicators for measuring sustainable development in Unilever Foods operations. The "project aimed to translate the concept of sustainability into a set of operational indicators for use in Unilever practice. The outcome of the project was to be such that it [could] be used by Unilever to assess 'fitness for sustainability' of its products."[6] Vis, FEIG members, and the Foods Executive waited while TME looked for a way to quantify the level of sustainability in Unilever's Foods operations.

September 1996: Unilever Reorganizes, Vis Gets Moved

While Vis and the FEIG were involved with the two studies, Unilever was undergoing a major reorganization of its senior management in an effort to separate strategic and operational responsibility. As a result of the reorganization, Unilever's worldwide operations were consolidated into two categories. The first was Foods. The second was Home and Personal Care (HPC). Additionally, a new seven-member Executive Committee was formed (Appendix C). Sitting on that committee were two Unilever chairmen, two category directors (one for Foods, one for HPC), a science and technology director, a finance director, and a personnel director. The Executive Committee became responsible for setting strategic goals for the regional and category operating companies.

The Foods Executive was dissolved in the reorganization. It was replaced by the Foods Category, a new management body with strategic responsibility for Unilever's Foods business worldwide. Jan Peelen, the former chairman of the Foods Executive, was moved to the position of personnel director on the Unilever Executive Committee. Lex Kemner became the Foods Category director, responsible for all of Unilever Foods business worldwide.

The reorganization directly affected Vis. First, his working relationships were disrupted. Vis no longer worked directly for Peelen, or for de Vet. Nevertheless, he still maintained contact with both in order to carry out the vision they had crafted. Second, his job requirements changed. The newly created Foods Category did not want to make the money available to maintain the environmental and quality assurance function performed by FEQAG. Therefore, Vis and other members of FEQAG were moved to the Safety and Environmental Assurance Center (SEAC).

As part of SEAC (Appendix C), Vis became an internal Unilever consultant, making sure Unilever management, employees, and operating companies could cope with health, safety, and environmental quality matters within the company. His main tasks became providing scientific support for the implementation of new environmental initiatives and policies in the areas of toxicology and human safety, life cycle assessments (LCAs), environmental management systems, and raw material and product quality.[7] His function as a member of SEAC was to provide support to the two categories (Foods and HPC) and the business groups (Appendix C). Again, he found himself in a situation where his job involved operational support work, not setting corporate strategy.

Fortunately for Vis, reorganization did not result in the termination of his sustainability work with FEIG, which merely changed names and became the Foods Environment Group Europe (FEGE) (Appendix C). The function remained unchanged: dealing with the implementation of the Foods Environmental Policy and looking after long-term implications of the Unilever Environmental Policy for the Foods part of the business. Vis remained secretary of this group. The FEGE now reported to Lex Kemner, the Foods Category director, who sat on the seven-member Executive Committee. Vis then had direct access to two Executive Committee members. He gained access to Kemner because of the reorganization, and he maintained his contact with Peelen, who still harbored interest in sustainable development.

Vis found yet another ally shortly after the reorganization—Hans Broekhoff, who joined SEAC as its deputy head of the Environment.[8] Broekhoff shared many of Vis's opinions about the potential role for sustainable development in Unilever and was also very passionate about the environmental responsibilities the company faced. Broekhoff left his previous position involving detergents research with HPC (the non-Foods half of Unilever). HPC did not have a focused sustainable development effort. Broekhoff looked to SEAC as a chance to explore sustainable development ideas and relate them to the HPC part of the business through his consulting.

As deputy head of the environment, Broekhoff was considered a senior manager within SEAC. His primary responsibility was environmental research and technology. Broekhoff also had a seat on the UEG, Unilever's leading group on the environment, which was preserved intact through the reorganization. Vis had finally made contact with someone on the UEG who was responsible for setting environmental strategy for all of Unilever through its recommendations to the Executive Committee.

Because of their overlapping interests, Broekhoff and Vis decided to work together on the investigation of sustainable development for Unilever. Broekhoff joined the FEGE (formerly FEIG) project on behalf of HPC. He worked closely with TME on expanding the scope of the sustainability indicators project beyond the original Unilever Foods boundaries so that it encompassed Unilever HPC operations as well. What began as an investigation of sustainable development for Unilever Foods had grown to a study of Unilever's worldwide operations.[9]

Although pleased by the potential magnitude of the impact of their project, Vis and Broekhoff recognized that their efforts in sustainable development work through the FEGE would ultimately have to support the new mission statement generated during reorganization. The mission statement, called "Unilever's Corporate Purpose," defined the company's highest-level strategy and objectives. The Executive Committee's main responsibility was to fulfill the obligations set forth in this statement. Unilever operations and initiatives at all levels of the company needed to reflect its ideology:

> Our purpose in Unilever is to meet the everyday needs of people everywhere—to anticipate the aspirations of our consumers and customers and to respond creatively and competitively with branded products and services which raise the quality of life.
>
> Our deep roots in local cultures and markets around the world are our unparalleled inheritance and the foundation for our future growth. We will bring our wealth of knowledge and international expertise to the service of local consumers—a truly multi-local multinational.
>
> Our long-term success requires a total commitment to exceptional standards of performance and productivity, to working together effectively and to a willingness to embrace new ideas and learn continuously. We believe that to succeed requires the highest standards of corporate behavior towards our employees, consumers, and the societies and world in which we live.
>
> This is Unilever's road to sustainable, profitable growth for our business and long-term value creation for our shareholders and employees.[10]

Vis and Broekhoff considered the significance of the new company vision. Although it was not immediately clear how sustainable development would help Unilever fulfill those obligations, Vis and Broekhoff believed there was a potential connection, and they began to discuss the possibilities. Vis and Broekhoff were convinced that sustainable development had a place in Unilever's operations and company strategy. However, they could not develop the necessary concrete challenges for Unilever until the two reports were concluded. Vis and Broekhoff remained convinced that Unilever would require a definition of sustainable development that was meaningful to its everyday business and that specific metrics existed for evaluating the implementation of the vision.

February 1997: Studies Completed

In February 1997, the reports were submitted to the FEGE. SustainAbility interviewed stakeholders, mainly in Europe and North America, and reported the perceived potential role for sustainable development in Unilever's Foods business. TME developed a set of sustainability indicators for both Unilever Foods and HPC operations around the world.

Vis and Broekhoff reviewed the reports. At their previous meeting in late 1996, they had decided to aim to have sustainable development adopted as a corporate-wide strategic goal. They were hoping to develop an argument that could be presented to the UEG and from there to the Executive Committee, the decision-makers who ultimately needed to be convinced to adopt such a strategy. They focused on the connection between sustainable development and the issues the UEG and the Executive Committee considered relevant to Unilever's business in the corporate purpose and environmental strategies. They looked for evidence in the two reports that suggested sustainable development could be aligned with Unilever's strategy and could be integrated into its business operations.

Stakeholders' Perspectives Report

Although there was considerable variation in Unilever's global stakeholders' opinions about whether or not sustainable development was a viable option for Unilever, there was consensus among the stakeholders about what sustainable development meant. The generally agreed-upon perception was that sustainable development at Unilever required concern for the physical, human, and financial aspects of its business, paralleling environmental, social, and economic responsibilities.

Of those three central issues, the discussion in the report tended to concentrate on the physical and social aspects of the debate. Stakeholders clearly identified the need for Unilever Foods to address the environmental impacts of its operations. In the case of Unilever's Foods agricultural businesses, there was a consensus that intensive, chemical-based farming was environmentally harmful. Furthermore, the social dimensions of Unilever's Foods business were a top concern. The consensus was that preserving the communities in which Unilever operated was key to sustainable development. The preservation of farming and rural communities was considered a dominant issue.[11]

Vis and Broekhoff were concerned that that was too vague a concept to be useful to Unilever's decision-makers. The report did not include a discussion of how Unilever Foods should address the economic aspects of sustainable development or sustainable agriculture. The report indicated that sustainability in Unilever Foods needed to account for economic issues; however, there was no indication of the relationship between sustainability and Unilever Foods's economic or business obligations.

Fitness for Sustainability

From a literature review, TME generated a list of over 200 sustainability indicators. In the final report the list was reduced to contain only 15 measurable sustainability indicators. The 15 indicators were allocated among three dimensions of sustainability: social, economic and environmental. Two indicators related to economic issues, six related to social aspects, and seven related to environmental dimensions. TME hoped their work helped "translate the concept of sustainability into a set of operational indicators for use in Unilever practice."[12]

Translating Sustainability into Business Terms

Vis and Broekhoff recognized in early 1997 that both reports lacked clear translations of sustainable development into business terms. The major challenge remained. They needed to describe how sustainable development could contribute to Unilever's business performance.

They chose to write a paper for the UEG. In the paper, they decided to argue that sustainable development was an opportunity for Unilever to actively pursue the Corporate Purpose. The goal for the paper was to preempt any concerns the UEG and the Executive Committee might have regarding sustainable development.

The commissioned reports made Vis and Broekhoff realize that any definitive implementation of sustainable development would require Unilever to address the stakeholders' consensus involving social, environmental, and financial concerns. They also received indications through discussions at FEGE that the UEG and Executive Committee potentially viewed initiatives that focused on these issues as threatening to the financial wellbeing of the company.

Their strategy was to show that Unilever was already involved in managing issues in all three areas of sustainable development—social, environmental and financial. By doing so, they could show that sustainable development was merely an extension of the current business operations.

In their September 1997 paper, "Sustainable Development in Unilever: Putting the Corporate Purpose into Practice," they introduced a concept they called "the triple bottom line," to capture the idea that Unilever was already involved in the three issues of sustainability. That principle suggested that the true value Unilever realized from its operations was not simply dependent on the sustainable growth of financial assets. Vis and Broekhoff argued that Unilever already valued social, ecological, and financial assets. They summarized the dependence and value of the triple bottom line principle:

> A company needs access to various types of assets to succeed: financial capital to establish and maintain high-performance production facilities. It needs a variety of mostly external physical and ecological assets, in the form of raw materials and resources for production (fossil fuel reserves, mined raw materials, the harvest from seas and oceans, fertile lands, pastures and woods). It is also totally dependent on natural resources in order to deal with the wastes generated in the production or the consumption phases of the life cycle of the products produced. It needs motivated employees who bring their commitment, their talents, and their energy. It needs stable, expanding markets and healthy, affluent consumers who can afford its products.[13]

In the paper, Vis and Broekhoff argued that financial assets were already managed with the highest degree of professionalism. Unilever leaders monitored financial yields and ensured strong financial development was safeguarded over time. Furthermore, Unilever had a strong track record with employee career development and employee training. Unilever also made positive contributions to society through generating employment and providing goods and services that raise consumers' quality of life. Those were examples of Unilever's commitment to some of the social aspects of the triple bottom line, but unlike financial assets, there was no formal mechanism for measuring the value of Unilever's social assets.

Unilever was also beginning to realize its dependence on environmental assets. The company created a group of external environmental advisors in 1995 who met with the UEG and individual Unilever leaders a couple of times yearly. That group had helped Unilever understand how it depended on natural resources in its business. In 1996, with the help of the external advisors, Unilever declared that fish, agricultural produce, and water were its major resource dependencies. Vis and Broekhoff saw that as evidence that Unilever understood the importance of ecological assets to its business success.

Broekhoff and Vis proposed that Unilever attempt to begin monitoring the value of those assets. The indicators developed by TME provided a useful starting point; Broekhoff and Vis recommended they be tested in practical situations to help Unilever develop its strategy with regard to sustainable development. They provided this proposal on how Unilever should proceed:

> Overall, our strategies for sustainable development should address each issue from three different perspectives, where each perspective operates on a different time scale. We must also be prepared to address these questions from a position of openness, realism, and pragmatism, while avoiding the trap of problem denial:
>
> 1   Clean up product and process emissions, introduce management systems:
>   *current status*—in progress
>   *time-scale*—ongoing
> 2   Design and implement clean processes and much cleaner and less resource-intensive products, on the basis of rational environmental product strategies:
>   *current status*—partly in place
>   *time-scale*—to be emphasized over the next five years

3   Radical redesign of systems and services, so as deliver outstanding consumer benefits within the limits of global carrying capacity; development of the necessary business restructuring scenarios.

current status: — strategic investments in intellectual capital are underway.

time-scale: — 25 years, but starting now: exploration of opportunities and prospects for business adaptations.[14]

Unilever was already aware of the value of these assets, they argued, but lacked a formal framework to conceptualize the value they added to the company. The triple bottom line principle allowed Unilever to "tap the large reservoir of value locked up in sustainable development and translate it into shareholder value."

Vis's and Broekhoff's efforts had reached a critical juncture. They believed they had made the best argument they could to demonstrate that environmental sustainability belonged at the highest level of strategy for Unilever. Although the argument still lacked specifics on operational details, their argument specifically called for organizing workshops and pilot projects in 1998 to investigate the feasibility of measuring environmentally sustainable initiatives. They decided to submit their proposal to the UEG.

Broekhoff was an influential member of the UEG; however, Broekhoff knew that the UEG would only pass the strategic recommendations on to the Executive Committee if the members agreed that the strategic initiative possessed sufficient merit and was reasonably well specified. Vis and Broekhoff were confident that the UEG would endorse their arguments at least to some degree. It was a question of whether the measures were passed on as specified or if the measures were softened or slowed for further refinement.

Vis and Broekhoff also counted on their supporters who sat on the Executive Committee once the UEG passed the strategic recommendations on to them. Vis kept Peelen, who held the personnel director seat, updated on the details of their plans. Peelen remained a strong supporter. Vis and Broekhoff also reported to Kemner, who held the Foods Category seat and supervised the FEGE. Kemner was leaning towards supporting the measure, but was waiting to see how strongly Vis and Broekhoff's arguments resonated with the other members. Vis and Broekhoff had few indications from the other five Executive Committee members. They depended upon the merits of their argument to sway their opinions.

What started as a general investigation of sustainable development for Unilever Foods had turned more towards a debate over sustainable agriculture. According to the study performed by SustainAbility, stakeholders held the opinion that agriculture posed the largest challenge to sustainable development for Unilever Foods. Also evidence from Unilever's life cycle analysis (LCA) work indicated agriculture was a major source of dependency and environmental impact for Unilever Foods.

Vis decided to write a paper specific to sustainable agriculture. His goal was to use the report by SustainAbility as a basis for suggesting initiatives Unilever Foods could implement in its agricultural operations. There was considerable debate over the future of agriculture, the definition of sustainable agriculture, and how Unilever should prepare for an uncertain future in the agriculture business. As the study revealed, there were a variety of differing opinions of the role of technology, the use of biotechnology and the importance of social factors in farming.

Vis began to shape a definition of sustainable agriculture that he felt would best benefit Unilever in the years to come. He aimed to propose specific initiatives to implement a new form of agriculture in the coming year.

Stakeholders' Opinions on the Future of Agriculture

Stakeholders around the world have very different opinions about the future of agriculture. As a result, there are different perceptions about how Unilever Foods should meet the future challenges it will face in agriculture. The range of viewpoints was reflected in the Sustain-Ability study performed for Unilever Foods. Jules Pretty,[15] an author of several books on sustainable agriculture, provided input to the SustainAbility study. He provided useful descriptions of the popular opinions on the future of agriculture, which were included in the report submitted to Vis:

Environmental Pessimists

The *environmental pessimists* believe that there are limits to the growth the earth can sustain. Furthermore, they contend that these limits are being approached and have already been met in some areas.[16] As populations grow rapidly, the world will be met with falling agricultural yields. The growth of ecological output, they argue, is constrained by factors such as deforestation, loss of topsoil, overuse of pesticides and fertilizers, and increased consumption of livestock products. Technology will not be capable of meeting the ecological demands of a growing world population. Therefore, population control is the major priority of environmental pessimists. Lester Brown of the Worldwatch Institute in Washington represents this point of view: "I don't see any prospect of the world's fishermen and farmers being able to keep up with the growth in world population."[17]

Business-as-usual Optimists

This is a mainly market-driven viewpoint. The *business-as-usual optimists* believe that supply will always meet increasing demand. Thus, they expect a growth in world food production.[18] The fact that food prices are falling is an indication that there is no lack in supply. For example, the price of most commodities has fallen by over 50% in the last decade. Additionally, research in biotechnology and plant technology will continue to boost food production in industrialized countries. They foresee a growth in exports of foods from industrialized countries to underdeveloped parts of the world. If food production is left to respond to market conditions, they argue, world food demand will be met. There is limited use in implementing lower yield technologies. Referring to arable farming in East Anglia, Sir Derek Barber famously put it this way in the 1991 Royal Agricultural Society of England study on agriculture and the environment: "Why clutter up such landscapes with thin green threads of new hedges? Why not let this type of highly efficient grain country get on with its job of producing a tonne of wheat at the very lowest cost?"[19]

Industrialized-world-to-the-rescue

The *industrialized world to the rescue* viewpoint is that the poorer countries will never be able to meet their own food production demands. These demands will be met by increased production in industrialized countries.[20] Proponents of this viewpoint believe that the key to saving wildlife and ecosystems is through the implementation of highly mechanized and technological agricultural techniques that require less land than low-input farming. Smaller farmers will go out of business as larger, high-output operations become very efficient. This, they argue, will relieve pressures on the environment by allowing massive food production on less land. The threats of using large amounts of pesticides, fertilizers, and chemicals are minor when compared to the danger of committing large amounts of land to low-output agriculture. One of the best known advocates of these techniques is Dennis Avery of The Hudson Institute, and author of *Saving the Planet with Pesticides and Plastic*. In an edition of *Farmer's Weekly* the view was summarized: "The biggest threat to bio-diversity is the ploughing down of much of the world's remaining forests to produce low yielding crops and livestock."[21]

The New Modernists

The *new modernist* view is a combination of those already presented. They believe that through the use of modern technology, yield increases are possible on existing farmland in poorer nations.[22] Their argument is that farmers in the underdeveloped parts of the world are not using enough pesticides and fertilizers. By implementing more scientific approaches to agriculture, pressure will be kept off natural habitats. They fully support the high-input approach. This is exemplified by Norman Borlaug, Nobel laureate for his contribution to international agricultural development. In 1992, he said that agriculturalists "must not be duped into believing that future food requirements can be met through continuing reliance on . . . the new complicated and sophisticated 'low-input, low-output' technologies that are impractical for the farmers to adopt." In 1995, he then said, "Over the last decade, extremists in the environmentalist movement in the affluent nations have created consumer anxiety about the safety of food produced using agricultural chemicals."

Sustainable Intensifiers

The *sustainable intensifiers* contend that high productivity is possible with low-input techniques. This group does not support no-input farming; rather they feel that higher reliance on human ingenuity, and a lower reliance on chemical inputs, will increase yields and decrease damage to the environment.[23] This form of agriculture seeks to develop better pest, nutrient, soil, and water management technologies. Specific aims are waste reduction and an increase in the use of natural processes on farms to replace high levels of external inputs. They argue that this can result in high-yield farming that is less environmentally damaging and even restorative.

> The debate over agriculture was characterized by these viewpoints. Stakeholders held very different opinions of the future of agriculture, depending on their affiliations. The opinions of large, chemical-based agribusinesses were different from those of non-governmental organizations (NGOs). Viewpoints also differed regionally.

Stakeholders Identify Issues and Define "Sustainable Agriculture"

A wide range of issues was raised in the report. The two major issues were:

1   Intensive, chemical-based farming
2   Preservation of farming and rural communities.

These issues were represented through the viewpoints discussed previously. At one extreme, the predominant view was that the future of agriculture would be one of high-technology; at the other extreme was support for the organic movement. These polar opinions were generally held by industrialists and NGOs, respectively.

Table 8.1.1 Goals for Sustainable Agriculture[24, 25]

1	Maximize the incorporation of natural processes such as nutrient recycling, nitrogen fixing, and pest-predator relationships
2	Minimize the use of external and nonrenewable inputs that damage the environment or harm the health of farmers or consumers
3	The full participation of farmers and rural communities in all processes of problem analysis, and technology development, adaptation, and extension
4	A more equitable access to productive resources and opportunities
5	The greater productive use of local knowledge, practices and resources
6	An increase in self-reliance among farmers and rural communities
7	An emphasis on building strong rural social organizations and dynamic rural economies

Nearly all stakeholders agreed that meeting the food needs of between eight and ten billion people in the next century would be a central challenge. There was much less agreement on the methods of meeting this need. Again, the two ends of the debate were characterized by high-input technology-intense agriculture and organic approaches.

Despite the extreme differences in opinion regarding how Unilever should proceed with agriculture, stakeholders generally agreed that sustainable agriculture should aim for the goals listed in Table 8.1.1.

Sustainable agriculture is a subset of sustainable development, and therefore it must account for not only environmental issues, but also social and economic considerations. Most stakeholders agreed that social issues, although the most difficult to address, were central to the debate.

Further complicating the discussion of sustainable agriculture was the fact that viewpoints differed regionally; Unilever operates in over 90 countries around the world. The agricultural and food production issues of most concern varied by region. Some of the major issues and viewpoints as identified by regional stakeholders were:

North America (United States mainly)

- Preservation of wilderness and the physical environment.
- Soil erosion.
- Maintaining the number of farms (not losing farms).
- Support of biotechnology as a useful component of sustainable agriculture. Stakeholders believe that the benefits are greater than the risks. Support at the consumer and government level.
- Support for the labeling of foodstuffs containing genetically modified organisms (GMOs).

Europe

- Maintaining biodiversity.
- Distribution of government food subsidies.
- Producing high-quality and enjoyable food products.
- Transportation issues.
- Fear of contaminated food (partially a result of "mad cow" disease).
- Labeling all foodstuffs containing GMOs to give consumers a choice.
- Skepticism over the consumer benefit of foodstuffs using GMOs.
- Food industry should be held responsible for problems with new technologies.

The Developing World

- Land tenure.
- Farmers' rights.
- Women's rights.
- Ownership of genetic resources and equitable distribution of profit derived from the commercial use of genes from these countries.
- Introduction of fat- and meat-rich diets.

The report by TME aimed to "translate the concept of sustainability into a set of operational indicators for use in Unilever practice."[26] The objective was to develop a set of indicators for use in Unilever's Foods and HPC Categories. The indicators were intended to cover a range of Unilever products and to be relevant to a variety of definitions of sustainable development. The delivered report covered Unilever's worldwide operations.

Similar to the report on stakeholders' perspectives, TME identified three dimensions of sustainability: social, economic, and environmental. Provided in the report were indicators that could be used to measure Unilever's level of sustainability. The list of fifteen indicators consisted of two relating to economics, six relating to social aspects, and seven with environmental relevance. Table 8.2.2 contains the fifteen indicators developed by TME.

Internal and External Issues Affecting Agriculture

The discussion of sustainable agriculture for Unilever Foods was influenced by a range of issues internal and external to the company. As Vis shaped his proposal for new agricultural initiatives, he had to consider the relevance of issues such as biotechnology, consumer confidence, and supply chain management. Embedded in each issue were arguments for and against introduction of new agricultural policies. Addressing these issues was necessary to fully

Table 8.2.2 Sustainability Indicators

Indicators
Economic
1   Total life cycle value to total life cycle cost
2   Ratio of local investments to local profit
Social
3   Compliance with legislation or internal guidelines
4   Number of consultations with stakeholders
5   Hours vocational training to working hours
6   Frequency of product safety incidents
7   Working hours lost due to incidents
Working hours lost due to occupation-related illnesses
8   Periodic assessment of product functionality in a regional setting
Environmental
9   Material use per functional unit of product
10   Product miles
11   Energy use per functional unit of product
12   Water use per functional unit of product
13   Percentage supplies from preferred suppliers
14   Foods: amount of (H)CFC consumption per unit of product
15   HPC: amount of volatile organics per functional unit of product

understanding the implications of sustainable agriculture for Unilever. Following are three sections describing events that directly affected agriculture at Unilever.

Unilever Sells Out of the Biotech Business

In the 1990s Unilever began to sell companies that did not contribute to its core strengths. This was part of an effort within the company to concentrate on its core strengths. These core strengths, or core concentrations, were determined to be in product areas such as margarine, tea, ice cream, frozen foods, culinary products, yellow fats and a range of areas in the non-foods portion of the business. As part of this sell-off strategy, Unilever disposed of its specialty chemicals business in 1997. Other businesses that were not contributing to these core areas were candidates for disposal.

During the same time Vis was doing work with sustainable agriculture, Unilever executives were making strategic decisions relating to the company's biotechnology interests. Unilever owned Plant Breeding International (PBI), a British-based company that was a leader in the development of genetically modified strains of wheat and other cereal crops. PBI represented the large majority of Unilever's scientific plant knowledge, and their only commercial interest in biotechnology.

Unilever disposed of PBI in a sale to Monsanto, the US-based biotechnology giant. Unilever officials stated that the sale was based on an effort to further concentrate all Unilever operations around their core strengths (see above). Biotechnology and plant science, they stated, were not areas where Unilever intended to develop strong business interests.

It remained unclear to some within Unilever how sustainable agriculture would support Unilever's core strengths any more than biotechnology did. Given the debate over the future of agricultural production, it seemed possible that Unilever management would not support sustainable agriculture on the grounds that it was not in line with their commitment to build around their core concentrations.

Issues of Supply Chain Management

Adopting new agricultural practices would require Unilever to influence the operations involved in agriculture. This raises the issue of ownership of supply chains. Unilever does not own all of the operations that grow (agricultural produce), raise (livestock and poultry), or catch (fish) its raw materials. In fact, Unilever owns only a small percentage of its supply chain—roughly 25 percent in the case of agriculture. The remaining quantities are bought from farmers under contract to Unilever or as commodities on the open market.

In the case of fish, Unilever does not own a single fishing business, and therefore purchases 100 percent of its fish from independent fisheries. Since Unilever does not actually own any fishing businesses, it cannot directly influence the operations of its suppliers. However, Unilever is one of the world's largest purchasers of fish. Therefore, many of its suppliers depend heavily on Unilever's business. In 1996 Unilever decided to use its economic clout to encourage changes in the supply chain of its fish products. Unilever was concerned that declining fish stocks would threaten its business and decided to take measures to address this issue.

The Marine Stewardship Council (MSC) was established by Unilever and the World Wide Fund for Nature (WWF) to develop a method to certify fisheries that were being sustainably operated. Unilever pledged that by 2005 it would purchase its fish exclusively from fisheries that complied with MSC certification criteria. The hope was that this would provide an economic incentive for fisheries to adopt sustainable practices and attain MSC-certification.

Fisheries that complied with MSC standards would be allowed to carry an MSC logo on their products.

The supply of Unilever's agricultural raw materials was much more complicated. Agricultural raw materials generally came from three sources: from operations that Unilever owned, from farmers under contract with Unilever, or through commodity trading on the open market. Unilever-owned operations accounted for only a small percentage of the yearly agricultural raw material requirements (less than 25 percent in most cases). The majority of Unilever's agricultural raw materials were grown by contract farmers or bought on the open market. Therefore, the level of control Unilever could exert over operations it did not own was limited.

Unilever made efforts to build relationships with the farmers under contract with them. They would work to establish guidelines and regulations for "agricultural best practice." Unilever would dictate the types and amounts of fertilizers, pesticides and herbicides the farmers could use. Furthermore, Unilever agricultural officers would make the decisions about when and how to irrigate, and ultimately when to harvest the crops. The farmers were obligated to follow these practices after signing a contract; however, they were not obligated to sign contracts with Unilever.

Introduction of sustainable agriculture guidelines would represent a significant change from the practices used by most of Unilever's suppliers. Considering its limited influence over its supply chain, an area of major concern for Vis was how Unilever could expect to implement any practices that were consistent with the definition of sustainable agriculture in the study.

Issues of Consumer Confidence

Unilever's Foods business was fundamentally dependent on consumers' confidence in their branded goods. Vis, in an interview, summed up the importance by stating that "maintaining consumer confidence in the quality and safety of our goods is absolutely necessary. What do you think would happen if tomorrow people lost confidence in our product? It would be disastrous."

There were several incidents, relating to agriculture, that eroded consumers' confidence in Unilever's Foods products. Two that were particularly damaging were the bovine spongiform encephalopathy (BSE or "mad cow disease") contamination, and the introduction of GMOs into Unilever products. These two incidents were highly publicized and somewhat damaging to Unilever's business, especially in Europe.

In March of 1996, Britain released a report suggesting that mad cow disease could be passed on to humans. As a result, demand for beef throughout Europe slumped dramatically as consumers reacted to the news. For Unilever, who sells beef products, this was a major problem. Unilever was forced to report losses of over £21 million (around $34 million) to remove beef from its stocks. A Unilever spokesman commented that "consumer confidence is still being unnerved by the continuing debate over the BSE issue. We have seen some recovery in meats in the UK but not back up to pre-BSE levels."[27]

A result of BSE was that the demand for organic beef increased. The two potential causes of BSE, feeding bonemeal to cattle and the use of organophosphorus compounds for parasite control, were not allowed in organic farming.[28] Therefore, there was more consumer confidence in organic beef. Suppliers of organic beef were seeing drastic increases in demand. Butchers in Ireland experiencing bad sales began to react to consumers' desires and offer organic beef.[29] In 1996, sales of organic food in England rose by 40 percent, driven in part by consumers' concerns over BSE.[30]

One product that is widely used in Unilever's food goods is soya. As with most of its fats and oils, Unilever purchases a vast majority of its soya as a commodity on the open market. The soya that Unilever purchases is grown around the world by thousands of farmers. By the time Unilever receives the goods it is very difficult, or impossible, to determine their original source. The nature of the commodities market is such that tracing products to the original producer is impossible.

In 1996 and 1997, Unilever faced a problem with the supply of soya. Monsanto, a life sciences company based in the US, had developed soya containing genetically modified organisms (GMOs). The strain was "designed" to resist damage to an herbicide that they also sold. The genetically modified seeds and the herbicide had been sold throughout the US, and in 1996 an estimated 2 percent of the US output of soya was genetically modified. There were no efforts made to segregate genetically modified and non-genetically modified soya. On the commodities market, where the majority of soya is purchased, there was no means of determining the origin of the product, and consequently no way for Unilever to segregate the supply.[31]

The end result was that Unilever could not guarantee its consumers that its products were GMO-free. The introduction of GMO soya in Europe was met by consumer protests. Greenpeace protested at Unilever headquarters in London,[32] and other activists held demonstrations at the homes of Unilever management elsewhere in Britain.[33] Customers were demanding that Unilever label its products that contained GMOs. Unilever claimed it could not separate the soya and was therefore unable to guarantee GMO-free products containing soya. The London *Financial Times* reported that a spokesman said that Unilever had found it was "just not practicable" to buy GMO-free soya "because of the quantities of soya required for its products."[34] However, some companies were able to offer GMO-free goods to consumers. Sainsbury, a giant supermarket chain in Europe, was the first to offer GMO-free goods.

According to Vis, these two incidents related to the discussion of agriculture at Unilever. In both cases, Unilever had suffered from practices used in its supply chain. Consumer confidence had been eroded by BSE, yet Unilever was not in direct control of the farmers raising the beef they sold. Additionally, consumers were protesting the use of GMOs and the lack of alternative, GMO-free products. According to Vis, Unilever was very concerned over the "mixing" of GMO soya with non-GMO soya. However, Monsanto was refusing to make efforts to segregate the supply.

Vis's Proposal

In 1997, Jeroen Bordewijk became the Senior Vice President of Unilever's Manufacturing and Supply Chain Technology division (SVP MAST). The MAST division is responsible for generating competitive advantage in the Foods supply chain. This is done by developing and capitalizing on supply-chain opportunities in the areas of manufacturing, sourcing, and delivery. As the SVP MAST, Bordewijk assumed direct responsibility for generating advantage in all supply chains in Unilever's Foods business.

Shortly after he assumed his new position, Bordewijk was offered a seat on the UEG. At one of his first meetings with the UEG, it was decided that he would be placed in charge of the work Vis had done with the FEIG, and with sustainable agriculture.[35] Bordewijk reported directly to the Foods Category Director, Lex Kemner, and had regular interaction with the UEG. In September of 1997, Bordewijk presented Vis's work to Kemner, who would decide whether or not Foods would support implementation of sustainable agriculture.

In his proposal, Vis drew on work he had done with Broekhoff to make the argument that sustainable agriculture was beneficial to Unilever's business.

> It is conceptually simple to define sustainable agriculture in terms of shareholder value. In our definition of sustainable agriculture, the land is managed so as to guarantee ongoing high yields of organic produce over time, while minimizing inputs and costs in terms of fossil energy, fertilizers, pesticides, herbicides, or other auxiliaries. It is in our definition not sustainable to keep yields high by continuously increasing inputs into the process, while eroding the intrinsic productivity of the soil.[36]

Vis outlined an approach Unilever Foods could take to implement sustainable agriculture. The plan included setting up a number of pilot projects around strategic crops, using internal and external agronomic knowledge to provide the required expertise, and working with local NGOs and other groups to create the network necessary to facilitate sustainable agriculture.[37]

In order for sustainable agriculture to be successful, Vis proposed setting up projects that would work towards achieving the goals identified by stakeholders (see Table 8.1.1). He argued for projects that would address the environmental, social, and economic challenges of sustainable agriculture. To achieve this, Vis proposed that the pilot projects ensure that:

- Output was high enough
- Negative environmental impacts were reduced
- Product quality and safety were guaranteed
- Changing consumer demands were met
- Profitability remained competitive with other industry sectors
- Agriculture offered an attractive livelihood to workers.[38]

Vis proposed formation of a Sustainable Agriculture Steering Group to design and implement pilot projects. One of the priorities of the pilot projects would be to set up the systems required to measure Unilever's level of sustainability. Implementing the list of indicators developed by TME (see Table 8.1.2) served as a good starting point. Regarding the indicators, Vis noted,

> The indicators now need to be tested in practical situations. They have been chosen on the grounds that they can be measured at site level or product level as well as at category or market level. While this represents a useful starting point, it is the product of an external review of Unilever, and is not yet driven by a clear Unilever strategy on how to pursue Sustainable Development. The indicators will therefore need further pruning and selection as our strategy develops.
>
> Sustainable agriculture poses the greatest challenge to Unilever. The company currently lacks a broad strategic initiative [in sustainable agriculture]. There is now an urgent need to initiate [a] strategic investigation covering Unilever Foods world-wide and any other Unilever raw materials sourced from agriculture.[39]

Vis's proposal called for immediate action. He was arguing for a world-wide investigation of sustainable agriculture in all of Unilever Foods operations. If his proposal were accepted, funds would be allocated to create the Sustainable Agriculture Steering Group and to coordinate the creation of pilot projects as part of the 1998 work schedule.

Appendix A: Unilever Organizational Diagram (1995)

This diagram shows the general management chain existing for Unilever Foods prior to the 1996 reorganization. Similar structures existed for Unilever Personal Products, Detergents, and Specialty Chemicals Product Groups.

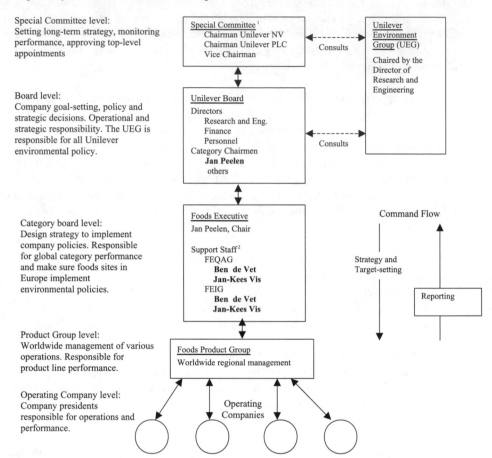

Notes:
1   The Special Committee is Unilever's highest level of management. The Unilever Board consists of the Special Committee, the directors, and the Category chairmen.
2   Within the Foods Executive are various support functions, such as the Foods Executive Quality Assurance Group and the Foods Environmental Implementation Group (FEIG). These groups assist in the implementation of Unilever policy and strategy at the Foods category level.

Appendix B: Unilever Foods Environmental Policy
(drafted by Jan-Kees Vis)

We will aim for sustainable development. In the years to come, we will work towards a definition of sustainability that is meaningful to our business and acceptable to relevant stakeholders.

In the short term, we will ensure full introduction of comprehensive environmental management systems in all our companies throughout the world, thus making environmental management part of day-to-day business. In order to do this, we will provide appropriate training and we will monitor this process through auditing.

We will continuously improve the environmental performance of our operations, processes, products and packaging, looking for cradle-to-grave wherever practicable. We strongly believe a cradle-to-grave approach to environmental performance is essential to achieve sustainability. We will also use waste minimization programmes to achieve this aim.

We will actively promote environmental awareness throughout the organization, at all levels. We believe that people are best motivated by providing them with the opportunity to contribute through their work, to the best of their ability, to the fulfillment of their own objectives.

We will responsibly communicate about our aims and achievements. We will work with industry bodies, government agencies and local authorities, business partners and other concerned organizations and relevant stakeholders, to promote environmental care, increase knowledge and disseminate best practice. We will remain alert and responsive to developing issues, knowledge and public concern.

Agricultural products form the bulk of our raw materials. Therefore we take an active interest where possible in the development of sustainable agricultural practices.

We will develop appropriate action plans and targets, based on identified parameters that can serve to monitor the transition to sustainable business. We will activate bodies within the Foods Executive and individual companies to develop their own specific policies and action plans. We will set up reporting structures, preferably within the existing management structures, to monitor progress towards targets. Action plans and targets will be reviewed annually.

This policy will be reviewed at least every four years.

Appendix C: Unilever Organizational Structure After Company Reorganization (1996)

This diagram shows the general management chain existing for Unilever Foods after the 1996 reorganization.

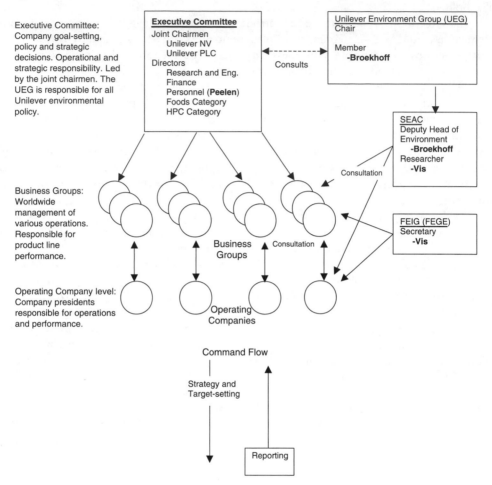

Notes

*   This case was written by Myles Standish, graduate student, Systems Engineering and Division of Technology, Culture and Communication at the University of Virginia, under the direction of Michael E. Gorman, Division of Technology, Culture and Communication, and Patricia H. Werhane, Ruffin Professor of Ethics, Darden School of Business Administration, University of Virginia. Partial support for this project was supplied by grants from the Ethics and Values in Science program of the National Science Foundation (SBR-9319983), the Batten Center for Entrepreneurial Leadership at the Darden School, University of Virginia, and the Geraldine R. Dodge Foundation. The conclusions are the responsibilities of the authors, and do not reflect the views of the foundations. This case was written as a basis for class discussion rather than to illustrate effective or ineffective handling of an administrative situation. Copyright © 1998 by the University of Virginia Darden School Foundation, Charlottesville, VA. All rights reserved.

1 Unless otherwise stated, the information in this case was taken from interviews and correspondence between the authors and Unilever employees between January and December, 1998.

2 Foods Executive Environmental Policy, May 11, 1990.

3 Information in this section was taken from correspondence between the authors and Vis, dated March 4, 1998.

4 Information in this section was taken from a discussion with Jan-Kees Vis at Unilever Head Office, Rotterdam, the Netherlands, July 20, 1998.

5 Vernon Jennings, "Sustainable Agriculture and Food: A Summary of Stakeholder Perspectives," SustainAbility, February 12, 1997 (confidential).

6 J. Krozer and K.E.H. Maa, *Fitness for Sustainability*, Institute for Applied Environmental Economics (TME), February 1997.

7 Unilever Environment Group, "Unilever Environmental Report 1996: Our worldwide approach," Unilever Corporate Relations Office, April 1996.

8 Information in this section is from correspondence between the authors and Vis, dated June 11, 1998.

9 Hans Broekhoff, and Jan-Kees Vis, "Sustainable Development and Unilever: Putting the Corporate Purpose into Action" (unpublished).

10 Unilever Environment Group, "Environmental Report 1998: Making progress," Unilever corporate relations department, April 1998.

11 Jennings.

12 Krozer and Maa.

13 Broekhoff and Vis.

14 Broekhoff and Vis.

15 Information in this section on the viewpoints of the future of agriculture were provided by Jules N. Pretty, director, Centre for Environment and Society, John Tabor Labs, University of Essex, Wivenhoe Park, Colchester CO4 3SQ, email: Jpretty@esses.ac.uk. More information is available in Jules N. Pretty, *The Living Land: Agriculture, Food, and Community Regeneration in Rural Europe* (London: Earthscan Publications, 1998) 128–132; and Pretty, *Regeneration in Agriculture: Policies and Practices for Sustainability and Self Reliance* (Washington, D.C.: Joseph Henry Press, 1995).

16 L.R. Brown, "The World Food Prospect: Entering a New Era," in *Assisting Sustainable Food Production: Apathy or Action?* (Arlington, VA, Winrock International, 1994); L.R Brown, and H.Kane, *Full House: Reassessing the Earth's Population Carrying Capacity* (New York: W.W. Norton and Co., 1994); P. Ehrlich, *The Population Bomb* (New York: Ballantine Books, 1968).

17 L.R. Brown, "The World Food Prospect."

18 See M. W. Rosegrant and M. Agcaolli, *Global and Regional Food Demand, Supply and Trade Prospects to 2010* (Washington, D.C.: IFPRI, 1994), D.O. Mitchell and M.D. Ingco, *The World Food Outlook* (Washington, D.C.: International Economics Department, World Bank, 1993); FAO, *Strategies for Sustainable Agriculture and Rural Development (SARD): The Role of Agriculture, Forestry and Fisheries* (Rome: UN, FAO, 1993).

19 D. Barber, "State of Agriculture in the UK," Report to RASE prepared by a study group under the chairmanship of Sir Derek Barber, RASE, Stoneleigh, 1991.

20 D. Avery, *Saving the Planet with Pesticides and Plastic* (Indianapolis: The Hudson Institute, 1995); I. Carruthers, "Going, Going, Gone! Tropical Agriculture as We Knew It," *Tropical Agriculture Association Newsletter* Vol.13, No. 3 (1993): 1–5; R.D. Knutson, J.B. Taylor, J.B. Penson, and E.G. Smith, *Economic Impacts of Reduced Chemical Use* (College Station: Texas A&M University, 1990).

21 C. Abel, "Big Threat from Low Input Farms," *Farmers Weekly* (November 21, 1997): 8.

22 N. Borlaug, "Small-scale Agriculture in Africa: the Myths and Realities," *Feeding the Future* (Newsletter of the Sasakawa Africa Association, Tokyo, 1992): 42; N. Borlaug, "Agricultural Research for Sustainable Development," Testimony before U.S. House of Representatives Committee on Agriculture, March 1, 1994; N. Borlaug, "Chemical Fertilizer 'Essential,' " in letter to International Agricultural Development (Nov-Dec, 1994) 23; Sasakawa Global 2000, Annual Reports, 1993–1995 (Tokyo: Sasakawa Africa Association); World Bank, *Agricultural Sector Review* (Washington, D.C.: Agriculture and Natural Resources Department, 1993).

23 Pretty; A. McCalla, "Agriculture and Food Needs to 2025: Why We Should Be Concerned," Sir John Crawford Memorial Lecture, CGIAR Secretariat, The World Bank, Washington, D.C., October 27, 1994; NAF, *A Better Row to Hoe, The Economic, Environmental and Social Impact of Sustainable Agriculture* (Minnesota: Northwest Area Foundation, 1994); T.I. Hewitt and K.R. Smith, *Intensive Agriculture and Environmental Quality: Examining the Newest Agricultural Myth* (Greenbelt, MD: Henry Wallace Institute for Alternative Agriculture, 1995).

24 Pretty, *Regenerating Agriculture*.

25 Vernon Jennings, "Sustainable Agriculture and Food: A Summary of Stakeholder Perspectives," SustainAbility, February 12, 1997 (confidential).
26 J. Krozer and K.E.H. Maa, "Fitness for Sustainability," Institute for Applied Environmental Economics (TME), February 1997.
27 Christopher Sims, "Birds Eye Hamburgers Suffer Losses as Consumer Confidence is Dented by Mad Cow Disease: Unilever Counts Cost of BSE," *The Herald*, Glasgow, August 10, 1996, 17.
28 Josef Finke, "Organic Beef," in Letters to the Editor, *The Irish Times*, December 8, 1996.
29 Audrey Magee, "BSE Threat Shows the Consumer is Boss," *The Irish Times*, April 13, 1996, 7.
30 "Organic Sector Reaps Benefits of Food Awareness," *London Financial Times*, November 7, 1998, 5.
31 Joe Rogaly, "Beans and Genes: Genetically Altered Soyabeans Are in Our Food—Like It or Not," *London Financial Times*, December 7, 1996, 1.
32 *The London Independent*, October 17, 1996, 2.
33 Peter Beaumont, "Greens Target Crop Designers' Homes and Research Stations," *The Observer*, December 15, 1996, 14.
34 Peggy Hollinger and Maggie Urry, "Sainsbury Claims Modified Soya 'First,' " *London Financial Times*, May 2, 1998.
35 From an interview with Jeroen Bordewijk, at Unilever Head Office, Rotterdam, the Netherlands, July 22, 1998.
36 Information in this section was taken from: Hans Broekhoff and Jan-Kees Vis, "Sustainable Development and Unilever: Putting the Corporate Purpose into Action" (unpublished).
37 Information in this section was taken from correspondence between the authors and Jan-Kees Vis, dated November 5, 1997.
38 Jan-Kees Vis, Unilever and Sustainable Agriculture: discussion paper and preliminary project proposal (unpublished).
39 Broekhoff and Vis.

8.2 DesignTex, Incorporated[*]

> The contract textile business is about offering choice, not volume.
>
> Susan Lyons

Susan Lyons, vice president of Design at DesignTex, a firm specializing in the design and manufacture of textiles for commercial interiors, knew the importance of looking ahead to the next design breakthrough. In February 1991, she had helped launch a new line of fabrics called the Portfolio Collection™, a design that evolved out of collaboration with very famous architects, Aldo Rossi, Robert Venturi, Denise Scott Brown, and Richard Meier. This collection was provocative in its aesthetic sense, and it also demonstrated that well-designed fabrics could be marketed at reasonable prices.

Although Lyons was proud of the latest collection, she wanted the next design to focus on an issue, not be just a change in aesthetics. The issue of environmental responsibility seemed perfect. "Green" was popular in the trade literature and in the general media, and she had been receiving inquiries from DesignTex's customers about how environmentally responsible DesignTex's products were. Her desire to pursue an environmental agenda was not, however, simply the result of customer demand. It sprang from deep personal beliefs about environmentalism that reflected her mother's influence. Lyons' mother had been "way ahead of her time": she had been recycling trash and other items and had been conservation minded back in the 1960s when Lyons was growing up. These childhood experiences had made Lyons sensitive to environmental concerns, and she had a strong impulse to act upon them.

Such a breakthrough, thought Lyons, would maintain DesignTex's leadership in the commercial-fabrics design market. DesignTex was vying to be the largest member of the Association of Contract Textiles (ACT), the industry trade organization. Located in New York, DesignTex worked with over 40 mills around the world, many of which manufactured the designs created by DesignTex.

DesignTex was also a member of the Steelcase Design Partnership, a collection of design industries purchased in 1989 by Steelcase, a giant corporation located in Grand Rapids, Michigan, that manufactured office furniture and supplies. Steelcase formed this partnership to capture a market that otherwise eluded the firm. Although the company was able to turn out huge amounts of products very profitably, it was not responsive to customers such as architects, who demanded specialty or custom designs. Small, nimble, and entrepreneurial companies were able to meet the demands of this growing market better than Steelcase, and DesignTex was such a company.

In order to maintain DesignTex's ability to respond to the rapidly changing, custom-design market, Steelcase permitted DesignTex's management to operate autonomously. In fact, as a fabric supplier, DesignTex sometimes competed against Steelcase for contracts. Steelcase typically brought in DesignTex as a consultant, however, in matters involving specialty-fabrics design. Susan Lyons summarized the relationship, "DesignTex is very profitable, and Steelcase receives a large amount of money from DesignTex's operation with no oversight, so Steelcase is happy to let DesignTex do its own thing. However, this situation could change if DesignTex's profitability began to decline." By taking the lead in the still volatile environmental market, Lyons hoped DesignTex would maintain its autonomy.

To launch her project, she began surveying the trade literature, contacted yarn spinners who claimed to be environmentally "correct," and paid attention to competitors who were also attempting to enter this market. The work was difficult because (1) she was also looking at approximately 40 other new designs and design improvements, (2) she wanted the design to look like others in the DesignTex line and (3) she wanted the design to be durable as well as environmentally viable.

Lyons continued her "research" for about two years, from 1991 through 1993. What she found was a jumble of information. As she pointed out, there were "conflicting claims about environmentally safe materials." Cottons were often heavily bleached, and most manufacturers were reluctant to talk about what was in their dyes. She considered using foxfiber with vegetable dyes, but the combination was available in only two colors. She considered using a yarn that was made from PET-recycled soda bottles. In fact, this appeared to be the most promising option, but the vendors were unreliable. These problems seemed difficult to reconcile with her belief that the "contract-textile business is about offering choice, not volume."[1]

The Climatex Option[2]

Because DesignTex also worked with over 40 contract mills around the world, Lyons contacted some of them to investigate their environmental efforts. In December 1992 she became interested in a sample of a fabric product line called Climatex. Albin Kaelin, managing director of Rohner Textil, a mill located in Switzerland, sent Lyons a sample. He and Rohner Textil had been pursuing an environmental agenda of their own, and he was willing to team up with Lyons and DesignTex in developing a new product based on Climatex.

The fabric, a patented combination of wool, ramie, and polyester, was unique because it wicked away moisture from a person who was in contact with the material over long periods. It was intended to improve comfort in wheelchairs and trucks, since those applications involved extended periods of contact between people and fabrics. Exhibit 8.2.1 contains additional information on Climatex.

Lyons also inquired about the possibility of recycling Climatex. Kaelin informed her that recycling fabrics was possible only if the material was pure (e.g., 100 percent wool or cotton), but not if it was a combination of materials. Because Climatex was a blend of wool, ramie, and polyester, no recycling was possible. In addition, Kaelin mentioned that recycling any commercial fabrics was questionable, because they were typically glued as upholstery, and the glue itself made recycling difficult. Nevertheless, he went on to add, "there is a far more important argument on the aspect of ecology to Climatex." Since the fabric was created without any chemical treatments, "the yarn in the fabric can be burnt [sic] without any damaging chemical reaction and are consisting [sic] of a good heating factor." By "good heating factor," Kaelin meant that the fabric released a large amount of energy when burned, and he proposed using this energy in the operation of the mill. He also mentioned that Climatex was being tested in Germany by an independent institute, the International Association for Research and Testing in the Field of Textile Ecology (OEKO-Tex).[3]

Exhibit 8.2.1 Information on Climatex[R]

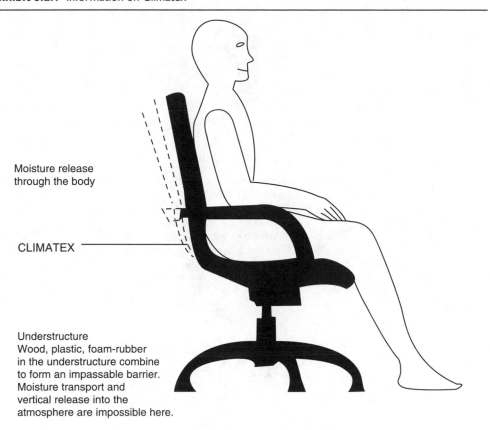

Moisture release
through the body

CLIMATEX

Understructure
Wood, plastic, foam-rubber
in the understructure combine
to form an impassable barrier.
Moisture transport and
vertical release into the
atmosphere are impossible here.

CLIMATEX assures an optimal environment
through vertical and horizontal
moisture transport.

Exhibit 8.2.1 *Continued*

Two patents assure double security for the
discovery of CLIMATEX:
CLIMATEX ® as final product with
excellent seating comfort and
excellent hard-wearing properties.
FIRON ® for the unique combination
of pure wool and ramie.
Securing the definite and long-term lead position.

The unique selling proposition (USP)
for brand consistency.
Word-picture-symbol for increased awareness.
Slogan as the key claim to the product's properties.
Could become a focal point of argument
for the office-chair manufacturer.

New: CLIMATEX.
The secret formula of pure wool, polyester
and ramie.
Ramie. Long-fibred plant, native to
tropical and subtropical areas.

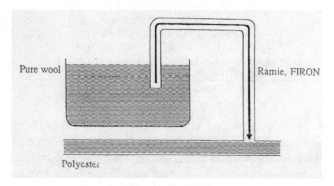

To clarify:
Pure wool collects up to 1/3 of its own weight
in moisture. Then 'overflows'.
Polyester is incapable of taking up
this moisture and transporting it.
Now ramie comes into play. The secret of the formula.
Ramie absorbs moisture from pure wool
and releases it to polyester for transport.
The result: CLIMATEX.

Exhibit 8.2.1 *Continued*

CLIMATEX:
The best attributes from three different fibres,
optimally combined.
Polyester with its high resistance to chafing,
minimal creasing, good absorption transport.
Pure wool with its high elasticity,
good heat conservation,
great moisture absorption.
Ramie with its great absorbency,
cooling effect, strong moisture transport
acts as a middleman between pure wool and polyester.

Both Kaelin and Lyons were pleased when Climatex passed the OEKO-Tex inspections in May 1993. The institute, concerned with human-ecology issues, tested for pH value, content of free and partially releasable formaldehyde, residues of heavy metals, residues of pesticides, pentachorophenole content, carcinogenic compounds, and color fastness. Having passed these tests, Climatex could bear the OEKO-Tex trademark and was certified to be allergy-free. Exhibit 8.2.2 contains the English translation of the OEKO-Tex Standard 110, which outlines in greater detail the criteria used in the certification process.[4]

By the middle of 1993, Lyons had several options to consider for an environmental design. The most promising one seemed to be the Climatex fabric from Rohner, which was certified to be manufactured within the OEKO-Tex specifications. But she was worried that because the fabric was not recyclable, and because it was difficult to make a grand environmental statement using the OEKO-Tex label, that option might not be as good as it seemed. In addition, the product was not cheap. It was priced competitively within the worsted-wool market niche, but that particular niche was on the expensive end of the overall market. She considered using yarn made from PET-recycled soda bottles, but she was not confident that the vendors could deliver reliably. Her research uncovered promising options, but each had difficulties and risks.

In July 1993, DesignTex owner Ralph Saltzman, President Tom Hamilton, Consultant Steve Kroeter, and Lyons met to consider what the next generation of the Portfolio™ Collection would be. Launched in 1991, Portfolio™ had been a highly successful major product line. By mid-1993, however, the product's demand had peaked. At this meeting, the team agreed that the next Portfolio™ collection would have a major impact on the market if its design focused on the green issue.

Exhibit 8.2.2 English Translation of OEKO-Tex Standard 110

DESIGNTEX, INCORPORATED (A)

English Translation of OEKO-Tex
Standard 110

International Association for Research and Testing in the Field of Textile Ecology (Öko-Tex)

OEKO-Tex STANDARD 110
English Translation of ÖKO-TEX Standard 110
Edition 5/1993

Special conditions for the authorization to use
the Oeko-Tex mark for
textile upholstery fabrics

Contents

1. Purpose
2. Applicability
3. Terms and definitions
4. Conditions
5. Criteria for granting of authorization

Exhibit 8.2.2 *Continued*

1. PURPOSE

The Oeko-Tex Standard 100 specifies the general conditions for granting authorization to mark textiles with "Confidence in Textiles – Passed for harmful substances according Oeko-Tex Standard 100".
This Oeko-Tex Standard 110 adds to Oeko-Tex Standard 100 laying down the special conditions for granting authorization for marking textile upholstery fabrics.

2. APPLICABILITY

This standard is to be applied to textile upholstery fabrics.

3. TERMS AND DEFINITIONS

The following terms add to those defined in Oeko-Tex Standard 100:

Textile upholstery fabrics are those qualified for the purpose by the producer.

Producer of textile upholstery fabrics refers to the company producing the ready-made product or having ordered the production of the ready-made product.

Retailer of textile upholstery fabrics refers to the company selling the ready-made product as wholesale dealer or retailer (warehouses, mail order houses, etc.).

4. CONDITIONS

The following conditions are added to those laid down in Oeko-Tex Standard 100:

4.1 Application

4.1.1 Applicant

The applicant may be either the producer or the retailer of the product.

4.1.2 Designation of the product

The designation of the product used by the producer or retailer is to be indicated.

4.1.3 Technical details

The following technical details are to be indicated as far as they are known or may be reliably ascertained from the deliverer or the pre-deliverer.

4.1.3.1   Qualitative denomination of all types of fibres included in the textile upholstery fabrics:

The fibre types are to be denominated according to DIN 60 001, part 1, and part 3. In case of fibres containing incorporated agents, e.g., delustrants, colour pigments (spun dyed fibres), antistatic agents, flame retardants, etc., the agents are to be indicated.

4.1.3.2   *Qualitative denomination of fibre and yarn preparations*

All preparations, e.g., spinning avivages, softeners, sizing agents, etc., with which fibres or yarns have been treated during production and processings are to be indicated. The trade names of the products are to be given; product and safety data sheets are to be added.

4.1.3.3   *Denomination of finishing agents and dyestuffs:*

Dyestuffs are to be classified according to dyestuff classes. Their product denominations and trade names are to be indicated. The trade names of finishing agents are to be indicated. Product and safety data sheets are to be added.

4.1.3.4   *Denomination of special finishings:*

If special finishing procedures have been used (e.g., to obtain an improvement of handle, anti-static, anti-soil, antimicrobial, mothproof, and other effects), the finishing agents and procedures used, are to be indicated. Either the trade name and the producer or the chemical compositions of the finishing agents are to be denominated. Product and safety data sheets are to be added.

4.2 Sample material

For test purposes and for evidence samples the applicant shall provide at least 2 running meters per article.
The regulations of the packing instruction have to be met.

4.3 Issuing a commitment undertaking and a conformity declaration

4.3.1 Commitment undertaking

The commitment undertaking shall be given according to Oeko-Tex Standard 100.

4.3.2 Conformity declaration

The conformity declaration shall be issued according to Oeko-Tex Standard 100.

4.4 Testing

Test specimens having an odour extraneous to the product or an odour indicating an improper production technology will be rejected from testing.

Type and scope of testing depends on the type of the product and on the information about the product the applicant has given. They are determined by the respective institute of the International Association for Research and Testing in the Field of Textile Ecology (Öko-Tex).

Examples for tests are listed below. The respective testing procedures are laid down in Oeko-Tex Standard 200.

- Determination of the pH value.
- Determination of the content of free and released formaldehyde.
- Extraction with artificial acid sweat solution, testing of the extract for heavy metals.
- Testing for pesticides residues (only at textile fabrics containing natural fibres).
- Testing for pentachlorophenole (PCP) (only for textile fabrics containing natural fibres).
- Testing for dyestuffs unquestionably having or being suspected of having a cancerogeneous potential either for themselves or after a reductive cracking to aryl-amines.
- Testing of colour fastnesses.

Exhibit 8.2.2 *Continued*

5. CRITERIA FOR GRANTING THE AUTHORIZATION FOR MARKING

5.1 pH value

Testing procedure according to Oeko-Tex Standard 200 point 1.

Textile upholstery fabrics shall exhibit a pH value of the aqueous extract between pH 4.8 and pH 7.5. Only for articles made from wool a value of pH 4.0 may be accepted as the lower limit.

5.2 Content of free and partially releasable formaldehyde, referenced to the textile

Testing procedure according to Oeko-Tex Standard 200, points 2.1 and 2.2, respectively.

less than 75 ppm

5.3 Residues of heavy metals, referenced to the textile

Testing procedure according to Oeko-Tex Standard 200, point 3.

Page 5 Oeko-Tex Standard 110

● Mercury (Cotton only)	less than 0.1 ppm
● Copper	less than 50 ppm
● Chromium	less than 20 ppm
● Chromium (VI)	not detectable
● Cobalt	less than 20 ppm
● Nickel	less than 10 ppm

5.4 Residues of pesticides, referenced to the textile

Testing procedure according to Oeko-Tex Standard 200, point 4.

Total pesticide content   less than 1 ppm

5.5 Pentachlorophenole (PCP) content, referenced to the textile

Testing procedure according to Oeko-Tex Standard 200, point 5.

PCP content   less than 0.5 ppm

5.6 Dyestuffs, that may reductively be cracked to aryl-amines of MAK group III A 1 (cancerogeneous) and III A 2 (probably cancerogeneous):

Testing procedure according to Oeko-Text Standard 200, point 6.

- Benzidine
- 4-Chloro-o-toluidine
- 2-Naphtylamine
- 4-Aminodiphenyl
- o-Tolidine
- o-Dianisidine

- 4-Chloroaniline
- o-Toluidine
- 3,3'-Dichlorotenzidine
- o-Aminoazotoluene
- 2-Amino-4 nitrotoluene
- 2,4-Toluylendiamine

The substances of the above list must not be detectable.

5.7 Colour fastness

Testing procedure according to Oeko-Tex Standard 280, point 7.

Minimum colour fastness grade for staining:

• Colour fastness to water (heavy stress)	3
• Colour fastness to laundering (according to clearing symbol)	3–4
• Colour fastness to perspiration, acid	3–4
• Colour fastness to perspiration, alkalic	3–4
• Colour fastness to rubbing, dry	4
• Colour fastness to rubbing, wet	2–3

If in the case of pigment or vat dyestuffs the above minimum grade is not achieved a minimum colour fastness to rubbing grade of 3 (dry) and 2 (wet) may be accepted.

During the meeting, Lyons brought up another factor that could not be neglected: aesthetics. In addition to being environmentally friendly the next Portfolio collection had to be as beautiful as the last. Lyons hoped to collaborate with a prestigious designer in producing beautiful fabrics for the new line, just as she had for the original Portfolio Collection™. At the meeting, Kroeter suggested that they contact Suzy Tompkins of the Esprit Clothing Company, which had just released a unique line of clothing based on organic cotton. Lyons suggested an architect who was well known for his environmental philosophy and his architectural-design accomplishments, William McDonough. The group agreed that they would contact both designers and invite them to participate in the next generation of Portfolio™. Tompkins declined to participate because as a clothing manufacturer, she rarely worked with commercial-fabric designers. Lyons did, however, receive a more enthusiastic response when she contacted McDonough.

William McDonough

During her environmental-literature search, Lyons had come across the name of William McDonough in two places. She had read the March 1993 issue of *Interiors* magazine, which was dedicated entirely to McDonough and his projects. She had also seen an article about him in the *Wall Street Journal*.[5] McDonough had just accepted a job as the dean of Architecture at the University of Virginia. After reading about him, Lyons viewed him as the most high-profile person working with environmental concerns in the design industry.

McDonough had no immediate plans to develop sustainable fabrics, but he responded quite enthusiastically when she made the suggestion to him. He was looking for opportunities to apply his design philosophy. The fabric-design project fit into his plans perfectly.

McDonough came to visit DesignTex in early October 1993. During their meeting, Lyons described the options she had turned up in her literature and marketplace searches and suggested the idea of the PET soda bottle fabric to him. In turn, McDonough presented his design philosophy (the elements of this philosophy are outlined in Exhibit 8.2.3).

"Two key principles hit home really hard," Lyons said, "the idea that waste equals food and the idea of a cradle-to-cradle design, not a cradle-to-grave design." McDonough stated that in order to meet the waste-equals-food and cradle-to-cradle design criteria, the product had to be able either (1) to compost completely with no negative environmental impact, thereby becoming food for other organisms (organic nutrients) or (2) to become raw material for another industrial product (technical nutrients). Furthermore, one should not mix the organic and the technical, or one would end up with a product that could be used neither as food for organisms nor as raw materials for technology. "The product should be manufactured without the release of carcinogens, bioacumulatives, persistent toxic chemicals, mutagens, heavy metals, or endocrine disruptors." McDonough discouraged the use of the term "environmentally friendly" and instead proposed "environmentally intelligent" to describe this method of design, because it involved having the foresight to know that poisoning the earth is not merely unfriendly, but unintelligent.[6]

"The key to the project," McDonough stated, would be "getting the fabric mills to open up their manufacturing processes to inspection to see where problems arise." In addition, the mills would have to examine the processes of the mill partners—the farmers, yarn spinners, twisters, dyers, and finishers—so that they could also meet the design protocol. McDonough suggested that his close colleague, Dr. Michael Braungart of the Environmental Protection Encouragement Agency (EPEA) in Germany, could help with this project. Braungart's profession was chemistry and he had led the chemistry department of Greenpeace. He had collaborated before with McDonough in implementing McDonough's design protocols.

In addition to the environmental criteria, McDonough's proposal addressed the aesthetic component of the fabrics. "The fabrics needed to be incredibly beautiful as well." He suggested that they use the mathematics of fractals to generate the patterns. Fractals were appealing to McDonough because "they are like natural systems . . . the smallest component is the same as the whole." He was interested in harmonic proportions throughout nature, and he felt that the new designs should reflect natural harmonies in the protocols and in the esthetics.[7]

Forming the Network

The day following the McDonough meeting, Lyons contacted Rohner Textil to see if Kaelin would be willing to participate in this project. He was encouraged by Lyons' report and looked forward to meeting McDonough, who traveled to Rohner a fortnight later. McDonough was encouraged by the Climatex project. Nevertheless the Climatex fabric was far from compostable, because the OEKO-Tex standards did not exclude all harmful chemicals that would be released during composting. In addition, McDonough was concerned about the use of polyester because it came from a fossil fuel. He explained to Kaelin his design protocols, which, according to Lyons, was like asking Kaelin to "reinvent his mill." Kaelin responded enthusiastically to McDonough's ideas and eagerly awaited Braungart, who would help begin the assessment of the manufacturing processes.

Exhibit 8.2.3

DESIGNTEX, INCORPORATED

A CENTENNIAL SERMON

DESIGN, ECOLOGY, ETHICS AND THE MAKING OF THINGS

BY
WILLIAM McDONOUGH

THE CATHEDRAL OF ST. JOHN THE DIVINE
NEW YORK, NEW YORK

FEBRUARY 7, 1993

ADAPTED BY
WILLIAM McDONOUGH
AND
PAUL HAWKEN

Exhibit 8.2.3 *Continued*

It is humbling to be an architect in a cathedral because it is a magnificent representation of humankind's highest aspirations. Its dimension is illustrated by the small Christ figure in the western rose window, which is, in fact, human scale. A cathedral is a representation of both our longings and intentions. This morning, here at this important crossing in this great building, I am going to speak about the concept of design itself as the first signal of human intention and will focus on ecology, ethics, and the making of things. I would like to reconsider both our design and our intentions.

When Vincent Scully gave a eulogy for the great architect Louis Kahn, he described a day when both were crossing Red Square, whereupon Scully excitedly turned to Kahn and said, "Isn't it wonderful the way the domes of St. Basil's Cathedral reach up into the sky?" Kahn looked up and down thoughtfully for a moment and said, "Isn't it beautiful the way they come down to the ground?"

If we understand that design leads to the manifestation of human intention, and if what we make with our hands is to be sacred and honor the earth that gives us life, then the things we make must not only rise from the ground but return to it, soil to soil, water to water, so everything that is received from the earth can be freely given back without causing harm to any living system. This is ecology. This is good design. It is of this we must now speak.

If we use the study of architecture to inform this discourse, and we go back in history, we will see that architects are always working with two elements, mass and membrane. We have the walls of Jericho, mass, and we have tents, membranes. Ancient peoples practiced the art and wisdom of building with mass, such as an adobe-walled hut, to anticipate the scope and direction of sunshine. They knew how thick a wall needed to be to transfer the heat of the day into the winter night, and how thick it had to be to transfer the coolness into the interior in the summer. They worked well with what we call "capacity" in the walls in terms of storage and thermal logs. They worked with resistance, straw, in the roof to protect from heat loss in the winter and to shield the heat gain in summer from the high sun. These were very sensible buildings within the climate in which they are located.

With respect to membrane, we only have to look at the Bedouin tent to find a design that accomplishes five things at once. In the desert, temperatures often exceed 120 degrees. There is no shade, no air movement. The black Bedouin tent, when pitched, creates a deep shade that brings one's sensible temperature down to 95 degrees. The tent has a very coarse weave, which creates a beautifully illuminated interior, having a million light fixtures. Because of the coarse weave and the black surface, the air inside rises and is drawn through the membrane. So now you have a breeze coming in from outside, and that drops the sensible temperature even lower, down to 90 degrees. You may wonder what happens when it rains, with those holes in the tent. The fibers swell up and the tent gets tight as a drum when wet. And of course, you can roll it up and take it with you. The modern tent pales by comparison to this astonishingly elegant construct.

Throughout history, you find constant experimentation between mass and membrane. This cathedral is a Gothic experiment integrating great light into massive membrane. The challenge has always been, on a certain level, how to combine light with mass and air. This experiment displayed itself powerfully in modern architecture, which arrived with the advent of inexpensive glass. It was unfortunate that at the same time the large sheet of glass showed up, the era of cheap energy was ushered in, too. And because of that, architects no longer rely upon the sun for heat or illumination. I have spoken to thousands of architects, and when I ask the question. "How many of you know how to find true South?", I rarely get a raised hand.

Our culture has adopted a design stratagem that essentially says that if brute force or massive amounts of energy don't work, you're not using enough of it. We made glass buildings that are more about buildings than they are about people. We've used the glass ironically. The hope that glass would connect us to the outdoors was completely stultified by making the buildings sealed. We have created stress in people because we are meant to be connected with the outdoors, but instead we are trapped. Indoor air quality issues are now becoming very serious. People are sensing how horrifying it can be to be trapped indoors, especially with the thousands upon thousands of chemicals that are being used to make things today.

Le Corbusier said in the early part of this century that a house is a machine for living in. He glorified the steamship, the airplane, the grain elevator. Think about it: a house is a machine for living in. An office is a machine for working in. A cathedral is a machine for praying in. This has become a terrifying prospect, because what has happened is that designers are now designing for the machine and not for people. People talk about solar heating a building, even about solar heating a cathedral. But it isn't the cathedral that is asking to be heated, it is the people. To solar-heat a cathedral, one should heat people's feet, not the air 120 feet above them. We need to listen to biologist John Todd's idea that we need to work with living machines, not machines for living in. The focus should be on people's needs, and we need clean water, safe materials, and durability. And we need to work from current solar income.

There are certain fundamental laws that are inherent to the natural world that we can use as models and mentors for human designs. Ecology comes from the Greek roots Oikos and Logos, "household" and "logical discourse." Thus, it is appropriate, if not imperative, for architects to discourse about the logic of our earth household. To do so, we must first look at our planet and the very processes by which it manifests life, because therein lie the logical principles with which we must work. And we must also consider economy in the true sense of the word. Using the Greek words Oikos and Nomos, we speak of natural law and how we measure and manage the relationships within this household, working with the principles our discourse has revealed to us.

And how do we measure our work under those laws? Does it make sense to measure it by the paper currency that you have in your wallet? Does it make sense to measure it by a grand summation called GNP? For if we do, we find that the foundering and rupture of the Exxon Valdez tanker was a prosperous event because so much money was spent in Prince William Sound during the clean-up. What then are we really measuring? If we have not put natural resources on the asset side of the ledger, then where are they? Does a forest really become more valuable when it is cut down? Do we really prosper when wild salmon are completely removed from a river?

There are three defining characteristics that we can learn from natural design. The first characteristic is that everything we have to work with is already here—the stones, the clay, the wood, the water, the air. All materials given to us by nature are constantly returned to the earth without even the concept of waste as we understand it. Everything is cycled constantly with all waste equaling food for other living systems.

The second characteristic is that the one thing allowing nature to continually cycle itself through life is energy, and this energy comes from outside the system in the form of perpetual solar income. Not only does nature operate on "current income," it does not mine or extract energy from the past, it does not use its capital reserves, and it does not borrow from the future. It is an extraordinarily complex and efficient system for creating and cycling nutrients, so economical that modern methods of manufacturing pale in comparison to the elegance of natural systems of production.

Finally, the characteristic that sustains this complex and efficient system of metabolism and creation is biodiversity. What prevents living systems from running down and veering into chaos is a miraculously intricate and symbiotic relationship between millions of organisms, no two of which are alike.

As a designer of buildings, things, and systems, I ask myself how to apply these three characteristics of living systems to my work. How do I employ the concept of waste equals food, of current solar income, of protecting biodiversity in design? Before I can even apply these principles, though, we must understand the role of the designer in human affairs.

In thinking about this, I reflect upon a commentary of Emerson's. In the 1830's, when his wife died, he went to Europe on a sailboat and returned in a steamship. He remarked on the return voyage that he missed the "Aeolian connection." If we abstract this, he went over on a solar-powered recyclable vehicle operated by craftspersons, working in the open air, practicing ancient arts. He returned in a steel rust bucket, spilling oil on the water and smoke into the sky, operated by people in a black dungeon shoveling coal into the mouth of a boiler. Both ships are objects of design. Both are manifestations of our human intention.

Peter Senge, a professor at M.I.T.'s Sloan School of Management, works with a program called the Learning Laboratory where he studies and discusses how organizations learn. Within that he has a leadership laboratory, and one of the first questions he asks CEOs of companies that attend is, "Who is the leader on a ship crossing the ocean?" He gets obvious answers, such as the captain, the navigator, or the helmsman. But the answer is none of the above. The leader is the designer of the ship because operations on a ship are a consequence of design, which is the result of human intention. Today, we are still designing steamships, machines powered by fossil fuels that have deleterious effects. We need a new design.

I grew up in the Far East, and when I came to this country, I was taken aback when I realized that we were not people with lives in America, but consumers with lifestyles. I wanted to ask someone: when did America stop having people with lives? On television, we are referred to as consumers, not people. But we are people, with lives, and we must make and design things for people. And if I am a consumer, what can I consume? Shoe polish, food, juice, some toothpaste. But actually, very little that is sold to me can actually be consumed. Sooner or later, almost all of it has to be thrown away. I cannot consume a television set. Or a VCR. Or a car. If I presented you with a television set and covered it up and said, "I have this amazing item. What it will do as a service will astonish you. But before I tell you what it does, let me tell you what it is made of and you can tell me if you want it in your house. It contains 4,060 chemicals, many of which are toxic, two hundred of which off-gas into the room when it is turned on. It also contains 18 grams of toxic methyl mercury, has an explosive glass tube, and I urge you to put it at eye-level with your children and encourage them to play with it." Would you want this in your home?

Michael Braungart, an ecological chemist from Hamburg, Germany, has pointed out that we should remove

Exhibit 8.2.3 *Continued*

the word "waste" from our vocabulary and start using the word "product" instead, because if waste is going to equal food, it must also be a product. Braungart suggests we think about three distinct product types:

First, there are consumables, and actually we should be producing more of them. These are products that when eaten, used, or thrown away, literally turn back into dirt, and therefore are food for other living organisms. Consumables should not be placed in landfills, but put on the ground so that they restore the life, health, and fertility of the soil. This means that shampoos should be in bottles made of beets that are biode-gradable in your compost pile. It means carpets that break down into carbon dioxide and water. It means furniture made of lignin, potato peels and technical enzymes that looks just like your manufactured furniture of today except it can be safely returned to the earth. It means that all "consumable" goods should be capable of returning to the soil from whence they came.

Second are products of service, also known as durables, such as cars and television sets. They are called products of service because what we want as customers is the service the product provides—food, entertainment, or transportation. To eliminate the concept of waste, products of service would not be sold, but licensed to the end-user. Customers may use them as long as they wish, even sell the license to someone else, but when the end-user is finished with, say, a television, it goes back to Sony, Zenith, or Philips. It is "food" for their system, but not for natural systems. Right now, you can go down the street, dump a TV into the garbage can, and walk away. In the process, we deposit persistent toxins throughout the planet. Why do we give people that responsibility and stress? Products of service must continue beyond their initial product life, be owned by their manufacturers, and be designed for disassembly, re-manufacture, and continuous re-use.

The third type of product is called "unmarketables." The question is, why would anyone produce a product that no one would buy? Welcome to the world of nuclear waste, dioxins, and chromium-tanned leather. We are essentially making products or subcomponents of products that no one should buy, or, in many cases, do not realize they are buying. These products must not only cease to be sold, but those already sold should be stored in warehouses when they are finished until we can figure out a safe and non-toxic way to dispose of them.

I will describe a few projects and how these issues are implicit in design directions. I remember when we were hired to design the office for an environmental group. The director said at the end of contract negotiations, "By the way, if anybody in our office gets sick from indoor air quality, we're going to sue you." After wondering if we should even take the job, we decided to go ahead, that it was our job to find the materials that wouldn't make people sick when placed inside a building. And what we found is that those materials weren't there. We had to work with manufacturers to find out what was in their products, and we discovered that the entire system of building construction is essentially toxic. We are still working on the materials side.

For a New York men's clothing store, we arranged for the planting of 1,000 oak trees to replace the two English oaks used to panel the store. We were inspired by a famous story told by Gregory Bateson about New College in Oxford, England. It went something like this. They had a main hall built in the early 1600s with beams forty feet long and two feet thick. A committee was formed to try to find replacement trees because the beams were suffering from dry rot. If you keep in mind that a veneer from an English oak can be worth seven dollars a square foot, the total replacement cost for the oaks was prohibitively expensive. And they didn't have straight forty foot English oaks from mature forests with which to replace the beams. A young faculty member joined the committee and said, "Why don't we ask the College Forester if some of the lands that have been given to Oxford might have enough trees to call upon?" And when they brought in the forester he said, "We've been wondering when you would ask this question. When the present building was constructed 350 years ago, the architects specified that a grove of trees be planted and maintained to replace the beams in the ceiling when they would suffer from dry rot." Bateson's remark was. "That's the way to run a culture." Our question and hope is, "Did they replant them?"

For Warsaw, Poland, we responded to a design competition for a high-rise building. When the client chose our design as the winner after seeing the model, we said, "We're not finished yet. We have to tell you all about the building. The base is made from concrete and includes tiny bits of rubble from World War II. It looks like limestone, but the rubble's there for visceral reasons." And he said, "I understand, a phoenix rising." And we said the skin is recycled aluminum, and he said, "That's O.K., that's fine." And we said, "The floor heights are thirteen feet clear so that we can convert the building into housing in the future, when its utility as an office building is no longer. In this way, the building is given a chance to have a long, useful life." And he said, "That's O.K." And we told him that we would have opening windows and that no one would be further than twenty-five feet from a window, and he said that was O.K., too. And finally, we said, "By the way, you have to plant ten square miles of forest to offset the building's effect on climate change." We had calculated the energy costs to build the structure, and the energy cost to run and maintain it, and it worked out that 6,400 *acres of new forest would be needed to offset the effects on climate change from the energy requirements. And he said he would get back to us. He called back two days later and said, "You still win. I checked out what it would cost to plant ten square miles of trees in Poland and it turns out it's equivalent to a small part of the advertising budget."*

The architects representing a major retail chain called us a year ago and said, "Will you help us build a store in Lawrence, Kansas?" I said that I didn't know if we could work with them. I explained my thoughts on consumers with lifestyles, and we needed to be in the position to discuss their stores' impact on small towns. Click. Three days later we were called back and were told, "We have a question for you that is coming from the top. Are you willing to discuss the fact that people with lives have the right to buy the finest-quality products, even under your own terms, at the lowest possible price?" We said, "Yes." "Then we can talk about the impact on small towns."

We worked with them on the store in Kansas. We converted the building from steel construction, which uses 300,000 BTUs per square foot, to wood construction, which uses 40,000 BTUs, thereby saving thousands of gallons of oil just in the fabrication of the building. We used only wood that came from resources that were protecting biodiversity. In our research we found that the forests of James Madison and Zachary Taylor in Virginia had been put into sustainable forestry and the wood for the beams came from their and other forests managed this way. We also arranged for no CFC's to be used in the store's construction and systems, and initiated significant research and a major new industry in daylighting. We have yet to fulfill our concerns about the bigger questions of products, their distribution and the chain's impact on small towns, with the exception that this store is designed to be converted into housing when its utility as a retail outlet has expired.

For the City of Frankfurt, we are designing a day-care center that can be operated by the children. It contains a greenhouse roof that has multiple functions: it illuminates, heats both air and water, cools, ventilates, and shelters from the rain, just like a Bedouin tent. One problem we were having during the design process was the engineers wanted to completely outomate the building, like a machine. The engineers asked, "What happens if the children forget to close the shades and they get too hot?" We told them the children would open a window. "What if they don't open a window?" the engineers wanted to know. And we told them that in that case, the children would probably close the shade. And then they wanted to know what would happen if the children didn't close the shade. And finally we told them the children would open windows and close shades when they were hot because children are not dead but alive. Recognizing the importance for children to look at the day in the morning and see what the sun is going to do that day and interact with it, we enlisted the help of teachers of Frankfurt to get this one across because the teachers had told us the most important thing was to find something for the children to do. Now the children have ten minutes of activity in the morning and ten minutes of activity when they leave the building, opening and closing the system, and both the children and teachers love the idea. Because of the solar hot-water collectors, we asked that a public laundry be added to the program so that parents could wash clothes while awaiting their children in school. Because of advances in glazing, we are able to create a day-care center that requires no fossil fuels for operating the heating or cooling. Fifty years from now, when fossil fuels will be scarce, there will be hot water for the community, a social center, and the building will have paid back the energy "borrowed" for its construction.

As we become aware of the ethical implications of design, not only with respect to buildings, but in every aspect of human endeavor, they reflect changes in the historical concept of who or what has rights. When you study the history of rights, you begin with the Magna Carta, which was about the rights of white, English, noble males. With the Declaration of Independence, rights were expanded to all landowning white males. Nearly a century later, we moved to the emancipation of slaves, and during the beginnings of this century, to suffrage, giving the right to women to vote. Then the pace picks up with the Civil Rights Act in 1964, and then in 1973, the Endangered Species Act. For the first time, the right of other species and organisms to exist was recognized. We have essentially "declared" that Homo Sapiens are part of the web of life. Thus, if Thomas Jefferson were with us today, he would be calling for a Declaration of Interdependence which recognizes that our ability to pursue wealth, health, and happiness is dependent on other forms of life, that the rights of one species are linked to the rights of others and none should suffer remote tyranny.

This Declaration of Interdependence comes hard on the heels of realizing that the world has become vastly complex, both in its workings and in our ability to perceive and comprehend those complexities. In this complicated world, prior modes of domination have essentially lost their ability to maintain control. The sovereign, whether in the form of a king or nation, no longer seems to reign. Nations have lost control of money to global, computerized trading systems. The sovereign is also losing the ability to deceive and manipulate, as in the case of Chernobyl. While the erstwhile Soviet Republic told the world that Chernobyl was nothing to be concerned about, satellites with ten-meter resolution showed the world that it was something to worry about. And what we saw at the Earth Summit was that the sovereign has lost the ability to lead even on

Exhibit 8.2.3 *Continued*

the most elementary level. When Maurice Strong, the chair of the United Nations Conference on the Environment and Development, was asked how many leaders were at the Earth Summit, he said there were over 100 heads of state. Unfortunately, we didn't have any leaders.

When Emerson came back from Europe, he wrote essays for Harvard on Nature. He was trying to understand that if human beings make things and human beings are natural, then are all the things human beings make natural? He determined that Nature was all those things which were immutable. The oceans, the mountains, the sky. Well, we now know that they are mutable. We were operating as if Nature is the Great Mother who never has any problems, is always there for her children, and requires no love in return. When you think about Genesis and the concept of dominion over natural things, we realize that even if we want to get into a discussion of stewardship versus dominion, in the end, the question is, if you have dominion, and perhaps we do have dominion, isn't it implicit that we have stewardship too, because how can you have dominion over something you've killed?

We must face the fact that what we are seeing across the world today is war, a war against life itself. Our present systems of design have created a world that grows far beyond the capacity of the environment to sustain life into the future. The industrial idiom of design, failing to honor the principles of nature, can only violate them producing waste and harm, regardless of purported intention. If we destroy more forests, burn more garbage, drift-net more fish, burn more coal, bleach more paper, destroy more topsoil, poison more insects, build over more habitats, dam more rivers, produce more toxic and radioactive waste, we are creating a vast industrial machine, not for living in, but for dying in. It is a war, to be sure, a war that only a few more generations can surely survive.

When I was in Jordan, I worked for King Hussein on the master plan for the Jordan Valley. I was walking through a village that had been flattened by tanks and I saw a child's skeleton squashed into the adobe block and was horrified. My Arab host turned to me and said, "Don't you know what war is?" And I said, "I guess I don't." And he said, "War is when they kill your children." So I believe we're at war. But we must stop. To do this, we have to stop designing everyday things for killing, and we have to stop designing killing machines.

We have to recognize that every event and manifestation of nature is "design," that to live within the laws of nature means to express our human intention as an interdependent species, aware and grateful that we are at the mercy of sacred forces larger than ourselves, and that we obey these laws in order to honor the sacred in each other and in all things. We must come to peace with and accept our place in the natural world.

William McDonough

Braungart traveled to the mill in December 1993. He examined it closely to determine the changes needed to meet McDonough's design protocol. Braungart was "pleasantly surprised" by Climatex and its OEKO-Tex approval. He was also impressed with the mill, which, he thought, had dealt with ecology issues in a manner far ahead of everything he had seen up to that point. Braungart's early suggestions were, as expected, in agreement with McDonough's: produce the Climatex product without using polyester so that all-natural materials would be used, which would make the fabric compostable. The problem with Climatex, from McDonough's perspective, was that it mixed organic and technical nutrients, so the fabric could not be composted, yet the technical nutrients could not be recovered.

Braungart's evaluation required him to examine all stages of the fabric-construction process. Because the mill was involved with the fabric weaving, he also inspected the mill's suppliers: farmers, yarn spinners, yarn twisters, dyers, and finishers. Yarn spinners created a cord of yarn/thread from the pieces of individual material fibers, such as wool. Yarn twisters took two or more cords of thread/yarn and twisted them together, producing a much thicker, stronger piece of yarn. Dyers added the colors to the yarn. Finishers added chemicals to the finished weave to make it more durable, flame resistant, static resistant, and stain resistant, if these qualities were required.

Lyons was the main project coordinator and was responsible for creating the "construction," or generalized set of weaving patterns and color palette based on McDonough's designs. "Everyone on the project," she said, "knew that getting the mill contractors to open their books for Braungart's inspection would be difficult, and keeping track of the fabric's production would involve complex management well beyond the normal levels of supervision." Consequently, the team had concluded that the more they could do themselves, the easier it would be to produce the new fabrics. Acting on this philosophy, they intended to have the mill perform the role of dyer as well as of weaver. Kaelin agreed: "We need as few members in the pool as possible."[8]

The Project Underway?

By the end of January 1994, Kaelin had eliminated polyester from Climatex, producing a new blend of ramie and wool that preserved the fabric's moisture-wicking properties. He called this new fabric Climatex Lifecycle™. Using this fabric seemed easier than using material that reclaimed and reused polyester and other technical nutrients.

By the end of January, Kaelin had sent Braungart all of the security data sheets and production details pertaining to the chemicals and dye substances used in the manufacturing of Climatex Lifecycle™. The team hoped that this information would be enough for Braungart to make recommendations on how to proceed by the end of February 1994. They wanted Braungart's examination to be totally complete by the end of March 1994.

At the beginning of March 1994, Braungart had some bad news. The chemicals used in the dye materials did not meet the design protocol. Furthermore, questions about the manufacture of the dye chemicals could not be answered by examining the security data sheets, even though they had passed the OEKO-Tex standards. DesignTex's next Portfolio Collection, McDonough's fractal patterns and design protocols, and Rohner's next generation of Climatex, depended on Braungart's ability to gain access to the manufacturing processes of the dye suppliers, which meant the dye suppliers had to open their books to Braungart. Kaelin contacted Rohner's dye suppliers and asked them to cooperate with Braungart's inspection and answer his questions. By the end of March, however, it was clear that cooperation was not forthcoming. Braungart had contacted over 60 chemical companies worldwide, none of which had agreed open their books for his inspection.

Another concern was the project's cost. Someone needed to pay Braungart and the EPEA as he studied the manufacturing processes. Kaelin agreed to hire Braungart and the EPEA, because Rohner expected to acquire the patent rights for the next generation of Climatex. By the end of April, however, Braungart had already spent the funds Rohner had provided and needed an extension. Rohner was willing to consider an additional payment, but only after the product had been introduced into the marketplace. None of the team were sure how much more money Braungart would require.

Lyons reflected on the situation. DesignTex had made a large commitment to this project, hoping it would propel the firm into the lead of the commercial-fabric market. It had already been three years since DesignTex had launched the first Portfolio Collection™, and she was aware of the pressure to get a product out the door. Waiting for Braungart to gain access to the dye process risked the whole project and would dramatically increase its cost, even if he succeeded. On the one hand, perhaps it would be better to relax McDonough's and Braungart's standards a little and test the results of the manufacturing process without inspecting the dye suppliers' dye-production processes. After all, Climatex Lifecycle was already a major improvement over currently available environmental designs. On the other hand, the whole project was about making a breakthrough in environmental design, and it was not clear that anything short of the McDonough/Braungart approach would represent a sufficient leap forward.

As a result, chemical-dye suppliers reacted to these principles by stonewalling her company. In hopes of achieving a large gain in terms of environmental design, should Lyons uphold the principles, or should she back down and settle for a more incremental, "reasonable" improvement?

The chemical companies continued to resist Dr. Michael Braungart's requests to review their procedures throughout March and into the first three weeks of April 1994. At that time, Braungart was able to convince Ciba Geigy Corporation that it was actually in their best interest to adopt the protocol. Braungart's convincing argument was that if there was nothing toxic coming out of Ciba Geigy's factory, there was nothing to be regulated, and Ciba Geigy would not have to worry about unforeseen litigation due to long-term toxicity.

Gaining access to the dye process, however, hardly alleviated the difficulties associated with the project. Braungart still needed to inspect over 1,800 dye chemicals to see if they passed the protocol. This inspection would take some time, but good estimates of the cost and time were not available. The question remained: Was it really worth all this trouble to implement McDonough's stringent design protocol?

Lyons and Kaelin thought the effort was worthwhile, and they decided to give Braungart the resources and freedom to perform all necessary testing. Braungart conducted tests throughout April and May 1994, and was able to find 16 out of 1,800 available dyes that passed the protocol. From these 16 dyes, they could produce any color except black. The problem was that when they attempted to mix dyes to make black, the resulting chemical reaction produced a chemical that would not pass the protocol.

After dye validation, Braungart inspected the finishing chemicals and designed tests to measure how well these products performed and composted. In all, he evaluated over 8,000 chemicals in terms of the protocol, and the final product contained about 43 of them.

When Swiss inspectors came to test the water leaving the Rohner plant, they were impressed by the results, which were far below the legal limits.

The fabric was released to the public in a grand display at the Guggenheim Museum in New York City in June 1995. It won the "Best of the Show" award in Chicago in June 1995, at the NEOCON convention, the largest annual gathering of textile-design companies. The fabric became available to the DesignTex sales offices in late August 1995. The sales force learned about the fabric by watching a video of McDonough and listening to an audio tape conversation of Susan Lyons. Both presentations underscored the importance of the design protocol in creating "environmentally intelligent" products.

McDonough, Braungart, Lyons, and Kaelin believed that the product would not be truly appreciated (or desired) unless they provided an explanation of the protocol. Consequently, DesignTex decided to send with each fabric purchase a substantial brochure discussing why the design of the fabric was important.

Initial sales reports from DesignTex and Rohner were very positive. Swiss TV dedicated two reports, one seven minutes, the other three minutes, to highlight the operations of the Rohner mill in October 1995 and again in April 1996. The product was introduced to the European market in January 1996.

Notes

* This case was prepared by Matthew M. Mehalik under the supervision of Michael E. Gorman, School of Engineering and Applied Science at the University of Virginia, Andrea Larson, Assistant Professor of Business Administration at the Darden Graduate Business School, University of Virginia, and Patricia H. Werhane, Ruffin Professor of Business Ethics at the Darden Business School, University of Virginia. Partial support for this project was supplied by grants from the Ethics and Values in Science program of the National Science Foundation and the Geraldine R. Dodge Foundation. The conclusions are the responsibilities of the authors, and do not reflect the views of the foundations. Copyright © 1996 by the University of Virginia Darden School Foundation, Charlottesville, VA. All rights reserved.

1 The information in this section was obtained during an interview with Susan Lyons on 31 July 1995.

2 Climatex is a registered trademark of Rohner Textil, AG.

3 Kaelin quotes from correspondence from Kaelin to Lyons, 3 December 1992, supplemented by the Lyons interview of 31 July 1995.

4 Correspondence, Kaelin to Lyons, 28 May 1993.

5 *Wall Street Journal*, October 23, 1989.

6 The concepts "cradle-to-cradle," "waste equals food," "current solar income," "environmentally intelligent," and the design protocol discussed above are proprietary to William McDonough and are included in this document with his permission.

7 The material in this section was developed from interviews conducted with William McDonough on 29 June 1995, 16 August 1995, and 21 September 1995, and with Susan Lyons on 31 July 1995.

8 Interviews with Lyons on 21 July 1995.

8.3 Rohner Textil AG *

> It exists; therefore, it is possible.
>
> William McDonough

> If you compare, you start to compromise.
>
> Albin Kälin

Albin Kälin[1] recalled making a special drive from Zürich airport, where he had just picked up the American architect William McDonough, to his workplace, Rohner Textil AG in Heerbrugg, Switzerland in October 1993. During their conversation on that hour-long trip McDonough said three words that Kälin had never forgotten: "Waste equals food."[2]

Kälin, managing director of Rohner Textil AG, had been systematically pursuing ecological issues in manufacturing since 1987 and had managed to position the company as a leader in industrial ecology. Until that moment with McDonough, however, he had never been able to clarify his product design and manufacturing choices concerning the environmental profile of his weaving and dyeing mill to achieve perfection in eliminating waste emissions.

McDonough was a prominent designer of buildings and products using environmental criteria. Articles in the *Wall Street Journal* and *Interiors* magazine highlighted his accomplishments, such as the design of the Environmental Defense Fund's headquarters.[3] McDonough was bringing his expertise to Kälin to develop a fabric for commercial interiors that had minimum environmental impact.

This meeting came after one of Kälin's customers asked him to push the envelope in textile ecology. That customer was Susan Lyons, vice president of design at the New York company DesignTex, Inc., the second-largest textile design company in the United States. Lyons was aware of McDonough's accomplishments and had worked with Kälin in the past. Since 1991, she had been researching ways to define a new market in environmental textiles. By integrating her knowledge and skills with McDonough's and Kälin's, she hoped she would be able to sell a bold new product. She saw the meeting between Kälin and McDonough as a first step in achieving their mutual goal.

McDonough said that in order to meet the "waste equals food" criterion, the product either had to be able (1) to compost completely with no negative environmental impact, thereby becoming food for other organisms (organic nutrients), or (2) to become raw material for another industrial product without any reduction in material quality (technical nutrients). Furthermore, "The product should be manufactured without the release of carcinogens, bioaccumulatives, persistent toxic chemicals, mutagens, heavy metals, or endocrine disruptors."[4] One should not mix the organic and the technical, or one would end up with a product that could neither be used as food for organisms nor as raw materials for technology.

McDonough's statement "waste equals food" was exactly the inspiration Kälin hoped to get from the collaboration. The vision guided him and his network to create a fully compostable fabric. Kälin named the potential fabric Climatex Lifecycle.[5]

Eight months later, in late May 1994, the bold new product was in jeopardy. Kälin needed to find a twisting mill subsupplier who was able to experiment with his or her yarn-twisting procedures and who was willing to submit them for review so that they would pass the McDonough protocols, especially the "waste equals food" criterion.

Rohner Textil[6]

Kälin's previous efforts at ecological design and manufacturing began in 1987 with Kälin's decision that Rohner Textil remain a leader in the segment of high-quality upholstery fabrics. The mill was the smallest component of a much larger enterprise: Forster-Rohner, a company that employed more than 700 employees in five European textile mills with specialties that ranged from socks to jerseys to embroidery. Embroidery was the largest segment, comprising over fifty percent of Forster-Rohner's manufactures. In addition, the embroidery output was the largest in Europe.

Rohner Textil had 30 employees. In order for such a small company to remain useful to the larger enterprise and be competitive in general, it needed to remain at the cutting edge of providing the most creative and high-quality upholstery fabrics. Thus, the mill needed to be able to customize quickly to the demands of customers who wanted small lots of unique upholstery designs. It also needed to remain price competitive and profitable, and wanted to increase production.

One of the first challenges in 1987 was to improve their looms to high-speed Jacquard looms. These new looms would have produced more noise and vibrations than the old looms. This was a major problem since the mill long had been part of a residential neighborhood in Heerbrugg. The building had been constructed in 1912, and the former parent company of Rohner Textil, Jacob Rohner AG, had occupied it since 1947. A kindergarten stood across the street to the east and houses surrounded the mill less than ten yards away on the other three sides. The vibrations from the new looms would disrupt the neighborhood and force regulators to eliminate the evening shift.

Moving the mill was immediately dismissed. The mill was already located in the "country." It was situated in the Rhine Valley and surrounded by mountains, just across the borders from both Germany and Austria. Land in the region was prohibitively expensive, and attempting to move the mill in that area or to another location would negate any benefit to the parent company for the mill's existence.

Kälin thus proposed to construct a special, independently suspended floor on which all of the weaving equipment would be mounted. The floor would be designed to dampen the noise and vibrations. This proposal was implemented reluctantly because it was expensive, but it achieved the desired result. The mill was quieter than before the new equipment was installed (one could barely hear the operation of the looms outside the mill), and the flexibility and quality of products increased dramatically, as well as the speed of production. There was no net reduction in profit from this ethical decision. With this new equipment, Rohner Textil was the first upholstery fabric weaver in the world to be able to produce fabrics with sixteen different colors in the weft, or crosswise, yarn. This ability permitted Rohner's designers to create fabrics with richer, more complex, and more beautiful color patterns.

This experience gave Kälin an important insight: Rohner Textil needed to consider a larger context when implementing design changes to improve quality. This larger context included a responsibility to people in the neighborhood and an environment that they shared in common. He also realized that policies were needed for handling such issues, so that future experiences could be handled more efficiently.

Kälin realized that merely updating his machinery was not sufficient to guarantee that his products' quality would improve over time. What was necessary was a system that committed every employee of Rohner Textil to look for ways to improve its products so that it remained on the cutting edge of its high-end product niche. Such a system co-evolved from 1987 to 1994 with the management system that was leading toward ISO 9001 certification. This process was part of the International Standards Organization (ISO) 9000 series management system. ISO 9001 required the development of a management plan that specified responsibility, authority, and operational procedures for employees so that an entire organization would be committed to improving the quality of its products and services. The certification process was taking place while Climatex Lifecycle was in progress, over 1993 and 1994. The ISO 9001 process was an important part of Rohner's commitment to quality.

An additional factor made Kälin sensitive to environmental issues: it was expensive to dispose of his waste selvages. The selvages consisted of the end-trimmings of the fabric. As the fabric came off of the loom, the edges were cut to a uniform length and were sewn to secure the edge. Additionally, some fabric at the beginning and end of the fabric needed trimming to the proper length. The selvages typically needed proper disposal, and this disposal cost was expensive. Some of the selvages were burned in the regional incinerator to generate electricity. The air pollutants were scrubbed before being released into the environment. Overall, the waste selvages consisted of about thirty percent of the total environmental costs at Rohner Textil.

This cost was an extra burden for a company such as Rohner Textil that processed smaller lots of fabrics. For instance, Rohner might process a sixty-meter order for a fabric from which one meter of waste and selvages was generated. A company which processed larger orders might generate 2.5 meters of waste selvage for a 240-meter order. Because of this disproportionality, it was easier to distribute the disposal cost of the selvages to customers who ordered a larger lot size than those who ordered the smaller size.

Rohner Textil was also conducting much of the fabric dyeing in its own dye house. This meant that it had to treat and dispose of its waste water. The cost of meeting strict Swiss regulatory requirements was high. If not properly treated, the waste water posed a potential threat to the largest drinking water reservoir in Europe: the Rhine River, just yards away, and the Lake of Constance, a few miles downstream.

Kälin realized in 1989 that the only way to decrease these disposal costs was to pursue a more environmentally sustainable agenda, since changing the process by which the fabrics were woven was not possible. In 1992, Kälin and the Rohner Textil crew debated an environmental policy while on a retreat in a cabin at the top of a small mountain in the Swiss countryside. The policy, entitled "Eco-Eco Conzept, 1993–2000," consisted of a plan of ecological and socially responsible goals as guiding principles for their entire product line. Kälin had also developed an environmental costing system in 1992. This system helped him identify ways of reducing the environmental costs of his products.

By late 1992 the mill had received certification by the German-based association, Eco-Tex, which tested and approved as ecologically safe for humans all of Rohner Textil's main products, such as Climatex.[7] According to Eco-Tex's standards, Climatex contained no chemicals that were found harmful to human beings. The process by which the material was manufactured was also free from harmful chemicals. Such an approval constituted one of the most stringent environmental tests that could be performed on textiles at the time. This approval was an important step for Kälin and Rohner Textil; however, they had only slightly reduced their disposal costs. The tests did not certify that the products were *completely* ecologically safe outside the human sphere. Plants, domestic animals, wildlife, and ecosystems could be harmed potentially by the chemicals used in Climatex.

It was at that same time that Susan Lyons of DesignTex asked him to push the envelope in textile ecology. Lyons first proposed the idea of going beyond the Eco-Tex ecologically-safe-for-humans fabric by creating an environmentally sustainable fabric. Rohner would supply the woven product to DesignTex, and DesignTex would then market the product to its commercial interior customers, such as Steelcase, a giant office furniture manufacturing company. Lyons wanted to work with Kälin because he had produced a high-quality product for her and DesignTex in the recent past, and because Rohner Textil had committed to an environmentally sustainable agenda.

Lyons' background research and networking brought together McDonough and Kälin in October 1993 to get the project underway. She wanted to work with McDonough because of his revolutionary design principles. As she had hoped, Kälin was stunned by McDonough's principle, "waste equals food." At that moment during the drive from Zürich, Kälin realized that his disposal problem could be eliminated if he pursued McDonough's philosophy of zero emissions. If what was coming out of his factory was suitable to be food for biological cycles, he would have no disposal costs. Climatex Lifecycle would thus be a compostable product.

Initial Success[8]

In order for Climatex Lifecycle to be a successful "environmentally intelligent" product, McDonough insisted that Climatex Lifecycle be designed according to his other ecology design principles in addition to "waste equals food." These were "work from current solar income and respect diversity," as well as his five design criteria, "cost, performance, aesthetics, environmental intelligence, and social justice." Every aspect of the fabric's development would be evaluated according to that framework.[9]

It was therefore necessary to inspect every chemical in every process of the fabric's design. McDonough's close friend and business associate, Dr. Michael Braungart, whose profession was chemistry, would handle the inspections. Braungart was the former head of the chemistry division of Greenpeace. At the time of the project, he directed the Environmental Protection Encouragement Agency (EPEA), an organization based in Hamburg, Germany. Braungart and the EPEA would evaluate the raw materials and all production processes.

Kälin and his Rohner staff committed completely to examining every aspect of Climatex Lifecycle's design. The review eventually led to a standoff with dye manufacturers. By the beginning of March 1994, Kälin contacted Rohner's dye suppliers and asked them to cooperate with Braungart's inspection and answer his questions. By the end of March, however, such cooperation was not forthcoming. Braungart contacted over 60 chemical companies worldwide, none of which had agreed to open their books for his inspection.

To the delight of everyone working on the project, however, by the end of April 1994 Braungart was able to convince Ciba Geigy that it was in their best interest to permit the inspections of their proprietary dye formulas. Among other reasons, Braungart argued that if the products coming out of their factories were nontoxic, there would be no need to worry about regulations or unforeseen litigation due to long-term toxicity.

By the end of May 1994, success with McDonough's protocols continued. Out of 1,600 dyestuff chemicals that Braungart and the EPEA screened from Ciba Geigy, they found sixteen that were safe for disposal in the environment, with a minimum of risk. Out of these sixteen they could make any color for their textiles except black.[10]

All members of the network—Kälin, McDonough, Braungart, and Lyons—were quite pleased that two major hurdles had been cleared. Kälin realized that this situation was highly unusual: a project at his small, 30-person textile mill in the Swiss countryside had resulted in one of the world's largest chemical companies, Ciba Geigy, agreeing to submit to highly unorthodox scrutiny for the sake of the environment. Such a breakthrough gave Kälin a sense that, with diligence, any remaining obstacles could be cleared. William McDonough had repeatedly stated that redesign for the environment constituted the "Second Industrial Revolution." The change at Ciba Geigy made Kälin realize that such a bold statement might indeed be accurate.

Managing the Second Industrial Revolution: Getting to Food[11]

Because of their commitment to constantly improve the process by which the fabric would be made, celebrations did not last long. Kälin and the EPEA's Dr. Alain Rivière, who worked under Dr. Braungart, had many other aspects of the fabric's manufacture to investigate.

One such component of the manufacturing process was the twisting of the yarn. After the wool and ramie had been harvested, combed, blended, and spun into a single yarn onto cones, the two or more single yarns needed to be twisted about one another in order to make the yarns strong enough to be fed through the loom. If the yarns were not strong enough or nonuniform, they would break, forcing the weaver at Rohner Textil to stop and repair them. This process kept the loom down for some time, obviously reducing productivity and quality of the product.

The problem that Kälin faced was eliminating a coating chemical from the twisting process. It was a normal procedure to apply a chemical to the yarns as they were twisted. This process improved the strength of the twisted yarn. Rivière and the EPEA, however, rejected the chemical since it did not meet the design criteria. Thus, Kälin had to come up with a way to increase the strength of the twisted yarns without it.

This posed an additional problem: finding someone who was willing to experiment with their twisting procedures and submit them for review by Rivière at the EPEA. Kälin reconnoitered the local region in Switzerland, Germany, and Austria for such cooperation.[12] He evaluated companies based on the following criteria:

- Does the supplier possess the technology or machinery to handle the project?
- Is the company willing to open their books to reveal their manufacturing processes to Rohner Textil and the EPEA at any time?
- Will the company be willing to sign nondisclosure agreements in order to protect their joint project with Rohner Textil?
- Is the company open to change?
- Does the company have a past history of integrity and an image of credibility?
- Is the company aware of its own environmental issues? If so, is there some system in place to handle such issues?

Based on these criteria, Kälin and his team narrowed the field to two potential yarn-twisting companies, both of which offered possible solutions.

One option consisted of using the same German company that was doing the spinning of the yarn for this project. They had already agreed to submit to the EPEA all information on the spinning of the yarns, and they were willing to cooperate for the twisting as well. This company was medium sized, consisting of about 270 full-time employees. It had a good past history of reliability and technological capability. It was putting out its own line of environmental textiles; they were of the undyed variety, however, which made them limited in color range.

The EPEA had approved a procedure that could be implemented at this company. Instead of the original chemical used for twisting, this company could use a natural, oil-based chemical. The technological capability of this company was such that the process could be completed at a rapid pace. Having both the spinning and twisting done at the same place was an attractive situation since this agreed with Albin Kälin's philosophy of "keeping the number of players in the pool as small as possible."[13]

Another option consisted of a small, four-person operation in Switzerland, located halfway between Rohner Textil and the spinning factory. This factory also had worked previously with Kälin and Rohner. Its entire business consisted of twisting yarn. This mill used older machinery that operated at lower speeds than newer machines, such as those located at the spinning mill. Because the machinery was slower, the price of twisting here was higher than at the spinning mill; however, this slower speed afforded two advantages. First, the yarn could be twisted in such a way that it was strong enough for the loom without added chemicals that had to be washed out after weaving. Second, the slower winding on the cones made the yarn rest more uniformly on the cones. Since the cones were dipped at Rohner in the EPEA-approved dyes purchased from Ciba Geigy before proceeding to the looms, this uniformity could produce a dyed product with less waste than by the method at the spinning mill. The small company worked with natural yarns and used no chemicals in any of its twisting operations, except for lubricants for the machinery. The EPEA approved the twisting procedure of this company.

Both companies satisfied all of Kälin's screening criteria. They also satisfied McDonough's criteria that waste equals food, and the EPEA gave its approval to both processes. Even though the project could continue with either twisting methodology, one was the clear choice for Kälin.

Even though you have the product, the project is not finished

Albin Kälin

When you come to a fork in the road, take it.

William McDonough

The McDonough design protocol was paying off for Albin Kälin. Back in March 1994, even before Ciba Geigy agreed to grant access to their dye formulas, an agreement between Susan Lyons of DesignTex, William McDonough, and Kälin gave Rohner Textil the patent rights for the manufacture of Climatex Lifecycle.[14] In exchange, Kälin agreed to pay the cost of having the Environmental Protection Encouragement Agency (EPEA) continue its inspections of other stages of the manufacturing process. Kälin also agreed to grant DesignTex exclusive use of the fabric in the United States until the end of 1996, after its planned release in July 1995 under the trade name "The William McDonough Collection."[15] The product was not set for release in Europe until December 1995, so this arrangement gave DesignTex and McDonough a head start in the market. Possessing the patent and trademark, however, gave Rohner Textil a great deal of flexibility over the projected long-term product life of Climatex Lifecycle.[16]

Granting exclusive use to DesignTex also had potential additional benefits for Rohner: access to a very large customer. DesignTex existed in a partnership with Steelcase, at that time the world's largest manufacturer of office furniture. In 1994, Steelcase was a $2.3 billion company, employing 17,700 people worldwide.[17] Between 1986 and 1990, Steelcase averaged a dominant 21 percent of the U.S. office furniture industry, and in 1989 it purchased a series of design-oriented companies to bolster this level, which they feared was stagnating. DesignTex was one of the companies it purchased to create the Steelcase Design Partnership, and the office furniture giant desired creative products from the partnership members.[18] The William McDonough Collection could deliver what Steelcase wanted.

In the fall of 1994, Susan Lyons made arrangements to use the McDonough Collection fabric on Steelcase's award-winning Sensor chair. The chair was designed in 1986 using two radical ideas for furniture design at the time—ergonomics and simultaneous engineering. Steelcase's Business Management Group, a multidisciplinary team, put the Sensor through design, engineering, and marketing at the same time, resulting in a better quality product. They also made the chair adjustable to make it adaptable to the user. Proof of the success of these methodologies came when the Industrial Designers Society of America gave the Sensor chair its highest honors. Steelcase sold over one million chairs from 1986 to 1990.[19] The Sensor chair had become a benchmark for the industry by 1994, and it presented an opportunity for the McDonough Collection to reach a large customer base quickly.

In addition, Steelcase pursued environmental conservation. In 1993 the company implemented two different task forces that met every two weeks to evaluate products and processes in environmental terms. The company joined the Environmental Protection Agency's Green Lights program in 1992. This meant that they began converting their lighting to more energy-efficient technology. They also pursued a massive recycling and waste-reduction initiative. This initiative produced many instances of waste reduction, including the following achievements:

- selling 15,000 tons of scrap steel to mills for recycling
- selling 335 tons of scrap fabric to be used in automotive sound-damping material
- selling 96 tons of foam scrap for carpet backing
- recycling over 1,300 tons of corrugated cardboard
- recycling 6,750 gallons of used oil
- reclaiming 400,000 gallons of paint solvents.[20]

The William McDonough Collection would be a benefit to Steelcase's efforts, and Kälin, Lyons, and McDonough may have been encouraged by the initiative. By mid-October 1994, Kälin had samples of the William McDonough Collection ready for the Sensor chair, and Susan Lyons passed them along to Steelcase in early November.[21]

Meeting Standards

Before the fabric could be used, it needed to undergo rigorous testing to meet a number of different performance standards. Kälin desired that the fabric meet all International Standards Organization (ISO) and Swiss textile standards since he eventually wanted to sell Climatex Lifecycle in the European market after December 1995. Testing the fabric was the responsibility of Rohner's assistant production manager and quality and environmental manager, Alexandra Rumpf. Rumpf, a chemical engineer specializing in textile chemistry, ran several tests to check fabric peeling, colorfastness to perspiration, flame resistance, and abrasion resistance.[22] She strove to make Rohner's internal performance and environmental standards exceed those set by the outside organizations, a requirement that led to several incremental improvements in the fabric's design. By controlling the yarn's thickness, twisting process, mixture of fibers, and finishing procedure, she could control the quality of the fabric.[23]

More immediately, to sell the William McDonough Collection in the United States, Climatex Lifecycle had to pass the standards set by the Association of Contract Textiles (ACT), to which DesignTex belonged. In 1994, ACT consisted of over 36 members with a combined annual fabric sales volume of over 450 million yards, with woven upholstery consisting of about half the total volume.[24]

ACT standards were important because Steelcase was an associate member of the organization. Before the William McDonough Collection could be used on the Sensor chair, it needed to pass the ACT standards. As Susan Lyons wrote, "Needless to say that it is critical that we have a product that meets the ACT standards—otherwise it won't be taken seriously."[25] Testing to meet ACT standards continued through November 1994, again resulting in incremental changes and improvements to the fabric.

Moving Target

By the middle of November, the efforts of Kälin, Rumpf, and Lyons were paying off. Each iteration of testing resulted in an improvement of the fabric, and it appeared that the performance goals were within reach. At that time, however, Steelcase introduced a new test required of all fabrics to be used on its furniture. The test was not the result of a new standard set by ACT, but in response to Steelcase's updating its manufacturing processes. As Kälin later reflected, "As this test was new at the time, we were not able to get sophisticated details. The only parameters we knew were that it was a test to ensure that the newly introduced robots could upholster the chairs easily, so that the fabric did not slip out of the grips of the robot."[26] During the upholstering process for molded seating, the robotic machinery gripped the fabric tightly and wrapped the fabric around the shells of chairs. The test ensured that the fabric would not slip out of the robotic machinery.

The new test was a disaster for the fabric project. The ramie content made the fabric unable to be stretched in order to pass the new test; the fabric was ripping instead of stretching. Lyons wrote to Kälin, "Well, this is an adventure—everything failed on Steelcase. . . . The reason for failure was cited as a lack of stretch in the filling direction. I am thinking that the ramie may be too rigid . . . I think it is . . . urgent to get the molded seating pass."

At Rohner, Kälin, Rumpf, and the other textile technicians proceeded to make the fabric less rigid so that it could pass the new test.[27] They tried a number of approaches, but the only ones that were successful involved adding chemicals to the fabric. The chemicals were applied during the finishing process, after the fabric had been dyed and woven. The chemicals made the fabric more stretchable. The team came up with four different finishing chemicals that permitted the fabric to pass the Steelcase robot test.

All four chemicals were from Ciba Geigy and were open to inspection by the EPEA. The EPEA approved only one of the four chemicals, and expressed its dissatisfaction with the addition of any chemicals to the fabric at all. It could pass the EPEA protocols, but only with the caveat that Rohner would have to commit to eliminating it. Moreover, the fabric would now have to be retested according to all of the ISO and ACT standards because of the new finishing chemical.[28]

Kälin needed to make a decision. Along with McDonough, Braungart, and Lyons, he had fought an uphill battle to make the product as environmentally intelligent as possible, and they had overcome overwhelming odds in the past. Now he was faced with having to compromise the "waste equals food" standard in order to please one major customer.

The Dye-Auxiliary Switch[29]

Paul Flückiger, dyemaster at Rohner Textil AG, had just finished speaking with a fabric-dye salesperson. Without hesitation, he decided to substitute one of the dye-auxiliary chemicals this salesperson offered for one that Rohner was currently using in its compostable fabric line, Climatex Lifecycle.[30] To him, the choice seemed clear. The salesperson argued that his dye auxiliary was much less expensive than the one they were currently using, was of equal quality, and contained no chemicals harmful to the environment. The fabric would still be compostable, and it would now be a little cheaper to make. He did not realize that his decision would alarm his supervisor, Albin Kälin, managing director of Rohner Textil.

Flückiger strongly believed that he acted within his authority to decide to substitute the dye-auxiliary chemical. Having this authority and flexibility was the reason Flückiger decided 10 years ago to work for Rohner as its dyemaster. He was happy to be in a small company so that he could be responsible for everything in the dye department.

Flückiger had over 35 years of experience in several different textile mills, with expertise ranging from laboratories to the dyeing of stockings, from piecedyes to hanksdyes and yarn dyes. Flückiger was awarded his master's certificate in textile dyeing and had worked in both large and small plants long before coming to Rohner. Kälin had great confidence in Flückiger's abilities, and gladly let him run the dyehouse.[31]

Flückiger's autonomy had been reinforced under Kälin's tenure since 1988. Kälin was a strong believer in continually increasing the quality of textile products that he and his team dyed and wove at Rohner.[32] At the heart of his beliefs was the recognition that employees with experience should be given responsibility, authority, and autonomy to take measures to improve quality in every process and product.[33] Kälin's management style was to act as a collaborator with his team of leaders. Kälin was ultimately responsible for all operations at Rohner, but he felt the best way to accomplish this was to work together with his team.

Quality Management

Kälin's emphasis on product and plant environmental quality was not merely ideology, but a serious, systematic approach to management: "You cannot produce environmental products without quality, and there must be a control system in place to direct it."[34] By control system, Kälin was referring to the International Standards Organization (ISO) 9000 series management system. Through Kälin's and his team's commitment, Rohner successfully passed its quality system audit in 1994 and received its certificate for quality management according to ISO 9001, the applicable standard for suppliers during "design, development, production, installation, and servicing."[35] The ISO 9001 standard included specifications for the purchasing of materials from subsuppliers: "[Rohner] shall establish and maintain documented procedures to ensure that [a] purchased product conforms to specified requirements."[36] In addition,

> [Rohner] shall . . . evaluate and select subcontractors on the basis of their ability to meet subcontract requirements including the quality system and any specific quality-assurance requirements . . . This shall be dependent upon the type of product, the impact of subproduct on the quality of final product, and, where applicable, on the quality audit reports and/or quality records of the previously demonstrated capability of performance of subcontractors.[37]

The ISO 9001 certification process also required the development of a management plan, which specified responsibility, authority, and operational procedures for employees. "Mr. Flückiger is responsible for the dyehouse, with all co-workers in the dyehouse responsible to him,"[38] read Rohner's management plan, "Eco-Eco Conzept, 1993–2000," which documented a process that had been in place nearly a decade before the ISO 9001 certification.

The management plan also contained a strong emphasis on improving the ecological aspects of Rohner's products as a natural extension of product quality. In early 1995 there was no approved "standard" of environmental quality. The International Standards Organization had been moving towards creating such a standard, but there was still much debate over what such a standard should contain. A draft of ISO 14001, "Environmental Management Systems" existed, but nothing had been officially approved at the time. It was possible, however, to be certified against the draft of ISO 14001, and Kälin was already taking the steps to obtain that certification.

"But," Kälin stated, "these management systems do not work by themselves. With them, we still must maintain the commitment to McDonough's protocols and the EPEA approval process."[39] In other words, only all four things together—the ISO 9001 certification, Rohner's management plan, the McDonough protocols, and the EPEA approval process—would make Climatex Lifecycle a successful product and Rohner a competitive company over the long term. If you took away any one of these items, Kälin believed, Climatex Lifecycle and Rohner faced jeopardy.

Jeopardy?

"What is this?" Kälin asked Paul Flückiger about a week after Flückiger's meeting with the salesman. Kälin noticed on the shelf a dye-auxiliary container bearing a label not from Ciba Geigy, the company whose chemicals had been approved by the EPEA for Climatex Lifecycle yarn. Flückiger explained his meeting with the salesperson and his subsequent decision to substitute the dye auxiliary.

Kälin thought that Flückiger's judgment was probably correct; however, if he was not, Rohner had just produced a week's worth of yarn that Kälin could not weave into his products and sell. He had to decide what steps he could take to resolve this potential immediate crisis. Kälin was most concerned about his decision to give his employees such freedom, especially when one of his major team players had fallen back into the "old" way of thinking, not taking into account McDonough's design criteria and the EPEA's inspections.

> This process never ends. If you never get this point, you never get to food.
>
> Albin Kälin

Tough Times[40]

Given the terrible state of the Swiss textile industry, Albin Kälin was not surprised when the ramie spinning mill closed its doors in early 1996. The textile industry worldwide was changing with the opening of markets in Eastern Europe and the continued expansion of production in Asia. The Swiss textile industry, with its tradition of stability and high standards for wages, was suffering from these structural changes. A recession in European and North American textiles since 1993 was not helping matters. Overall, Swiss textile industry sales were down 9.5 percent between 1994 and 1995, and the trend was continuing. See Exhibit 8.3.1 for more statistics on the Swiss textile industry.

The spinning mill's closing could not have occurred at a worse time for Kälin and his team of 30 at Rohner. They could not afford to be cut off from their supply of ramie yarn when

Exhibit 8.3.1 Swiss Textile Industry Statistics

A. Swiss Textile Industry Sales (in millions of Swiss Francs unless noted)

(1 sFr ≈ $0.83 U.S)	1994	1995	% Change
Chemical fibers	501.9	425.4	−15.3
Spinning	340.5	298.2	−12.5
Twisting	21.2	18.2	−14.2
Weaving	**538.7**	**486.5**	−9.6
Fabric and embroidery exports	333.2	341.7	+2.6
Carpeting	128.1	116.0	−9.4
Total	**1,863.6**	**1,686.0**	−9.5

B. Swiss Textile Production

	1975	1980	1990	1995
Synthetic fibers (in metric tons)	80,100	82,650	121,486	124,000
Spinning (in metric tons)	47,012	64,330	57,181	38,926
Weaving (in million linear meters)	**149**	**155**	**101**	**64.8**
Embroidery (in metric tons)	1,471	1,602	1,035	1,262

C. Swiss Spinning Materials Imports (in metric tons)

	1980	1990	1993	1995
Silk	473	406	291	238
Wool/fur	**15,066**	**14,504**	**10,737**	**7,560**
Cotton	64,735	74,412	58,023	3 6,220
Other natural fibers	**1,545**	**274**	**412**	**399**
Synthetic fibers	24,891	19,883	18,146	19,392
Total	**106,710**	**109,480**	**87,609**	**63,809**

D. Gainfully-Employed Swiss Citizens

Sector	3rd. Qtr. 1985	3rd. Qtr. 90	3rd. Qtr. 95
Agricultural	221,500	197,200	161,000
Industrial	1,228,400	1,225,600	1,109,000
Service	1,968,100	2,120,300	3,801,000
Total	3,418,000	3,563,200	5,071,000
Textile Industry	**34,600**	**32,100**	**22,000**

E. Wool Industry Spinning and Weaving Installations (in thousands)

	1980 Spinning	1980 Weaving	1993 Spinning	1993 Weaving
Africa	213	2.6	180	1.9
North America	1,262	6.1	836	3.4
South America	685	6.7	590	21.2
Asia	3,840	37.5	7,034	64.2
European Union	7,504	49.7	5,978	35.6
Other European	1,566	14.0	1,668	30.3
World total	15,070	116.6	16,286	156.6
Swiss	**131**	**0.7**	**47**	**0.2**

F. World Production of Textile Raw Materials (in thousands of metric tons)

	1970	1980	1990	*1994*
Cotton	11,784	13,844	18,997	18,982
Wool (washed)	**1,659**	**1,599**	**1,927**	**1,544**
Silk	41	55	67	100
Rayon/cellwool	3,579	3,557	3,145	2,863
Synthetics	4,818	10,625	16,006	18,239
Total	21,881	29,680	40,142	41,728

All tables translated and quoted from *Textilwirtschaft In Zahlen* (Zürich: Textilverbrand Schweiz, Ausgabe 1996).

Climatex Lifecycle, which consisted of a blend of wool and ramie, was new to the market-place.[41] Rohner Textil was weathering the recession rather well because Climatex Lifecycle had been well received in the United States through Rohner's large, important customer, DesignTex, Inc. DesignTex released the fabric to the public in a grand display at the Guggenheim Museum in New York City in late May 1995 under the design trade name the William McDonough Collection.[42] It won the Best of the Show award at the NEOCON convention in Chicago in June 1995, the largest annual gathering of textile design companies. The fabric became available to the DesignTex sales offices in late August 1995. The sales force was educated by watching a video presentation of William McDonough at the museum and by listening to an audio tape conversation with Susan Lyons, DesignTex's vice-president for design. Both presentations delineated the necessity of the design protocol to create "environmentally intelligent" products. DesignTex shipped a brochure with the fabric that discussed why the environmental design of the fabric was important. Customers were responding to the information.

Initial sales reports from DesignTex and Rohner were very positive. Swiss television dedicated seven minutes of the business news to the operations of the Rohner mill. The product was introduced to the European market in January of 1996, and because of all of the good publicity about the product, Kälin had little trouble attracting customers.

Kälin needed to act quickly since his team did not have a significant stockpile of ramie yarn. He needed to find another spinning mill capable of handling ramie fibers before he could drastically increase his customer base, or even fulfill the contracts he already had.

Unfortunately, the mill that was spinning the wool fibers for Climatex Lifecycle did not have the machinery for preparing the ramie for spinning. Not every spinning mill was capable of processing ramie fibers because it was a particularly difficult process. The fragile fibers were harvested from the ramie plant. When the raw ramie arrived at the spinning mill, the fibers were bunched together with an inconsistent texture. The raw ramie was then combed and stretched in a process called "worsting." Worsting and spinning ramie was identical to processing wool, except that wool fibers were only 10–15 cm (3–6 inches) long, whereas ramie fibers were up to 60 cm (24 inches) long. The length of the fibers was the source of the difficulty.

The stretching part of the worsting process used a series of rollers that pulled on the ramie in order to create the desired consistency of the ramie before spinning (see Figure 8.3.1). On typical stretching machinery, wool fibers were much shorter than the distance between the stretching rollers. As the material passed through the successive sets of rollers, which rotated at increasing speeds, the wool fibers were pulled apart from one another and the material was stretched. Ramie fibers, however, were longer than the distance between rollers. If ramie

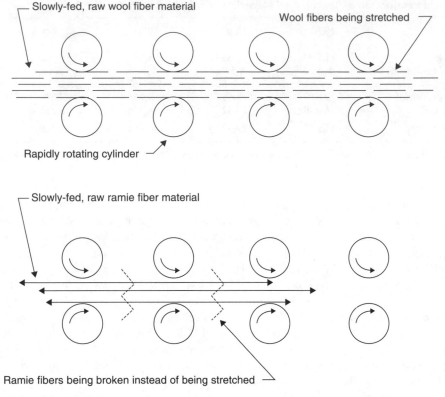

Figure 8.3.1 Stretching of Wool and Ramie Fibers

fibers were fed through the series of rollers, the fibers would be snapped or broken as the rollers pulled on them. Instead of stretching the raw ramie material, the process would break and shred it.

What was needed was machinery that had the stretching rollers set farther apart than the length of ramie fibers. Kälin was aware of manufacturers worldwide that made all types of textile machines, such as looms, twisting machines, spinning machines, and stretching machines. Because very few firms processed ramie fibers, not one manufacturer made machines suitable for stretching ramie. Kälin explained, "For most cases manufacturers can use linen and cotton as substitute materials for ramie, so ramie is not a popular fiber."[43] This was not an option for Kälin, since ramie and wool were the materials the EPEA approved for Climatex Lifecycle.

The spinning mill that had just closed overcame this problem when one of its machine operators was able to modify a wool worsting machine to handle ramie fibers. The operator moved the rollers farther apart and knew how to modify the speed of the machinery so that the ramie fibers would not break. The process was highly dependent on his skill at operating and maintaining the modified machinery, in contrast with wool spinning, which was highly automated.

Kälin and designer Lothar Pfister, also responsible for product development, canvassed Europe to see if there were other mills that might have modified their equipment accordingly. They found none, but they did find four spinning mills that were willing to purchase the equipment from the recently closed spinning mill and transfer the equipment to their location. Each mill said it would be willing to finance the cost of purchasing and transporting the machinery.

Knowing the state of the industry, Kälin and Pfister were not sure if the mills could afford to finance the machinery. They wanted to avoid repeating this process by choosing a spinning mill in danger of bankruptcy. They were not even sure if the machinery, once transported, could be reassembled to deliver high-quality ramie fibers. They gathered as much information about each alternative as they could.

The first mill that they considered was located less than 100 km (about 60 miles) from Rohner. It was a large company and possessed several other spinning mills in Europe. This company had the technological know-how and financing available to acquire the ramie equipment from the closed spinning mill. The management of this company seemed very committed and ethical, although it was difficult for Kälin and Pfister to judge because the company was large. The financial condition of the company seemed stable, and the risk of failure unlikely. The company had a clear and feasible market strategy: spin and sell a large volume of materials. They were willing to take risks to develop new products if the sales volume justified it. At the time, they had little experience with producing ecological projects, but the company met all environmental legal limits and indicated that it might be willing to cooperate with the EPEA for process evaluations. Since the company was large, it was unlikely that they would modify their processes to adopt Rohner's quality standards; however, Rohner had worked with them in the past without notable problems.

The second firm owned its yarn dyeing and spinning mills in Northern Europe, about 1,000 km (600 miles) from Rohner. This was a medium-sized company that was willing to purchase the equipment from the bankrupt spinning mill. Rohner had worked with this company in the past by using a few samples of their work in Rohner's products. The company had proven to be highly flexible at meeting Rohner's demands for producing these sample lots, showing that they valued Rohner's business. Because this company was located in Northern Europe, Kälin and Pfister were not sure if this company was meeting all environmental legal limits because they were not sure of the regulatory requirements in place there; however, the company indicated that it would likely cooperate with the EPEA inspections.

The third company under consideration possessed yarn dyeing and spinning facilities about 100 km (60 miles) from Rohner. Rohner had ten years of experience working with this small company, which was bought out by its managers two years earlier in an effort to save its probable closure. The company was producing one ecological line of products and was in compliance with local environmental legal limits. It was likely that the company would cooperate with the EPEA inspections and would be flexible about Rohner's quality demands. The firm had the technological expertise to operate the ramie spinning equipment, but purchasing the equipment seemed a sticking point. Money was not previously an issue for this mill, when it had been owned by a large European department-store conglomerate. After the buyout, however, the company's future was uncertain and depended on innovation to secure its long-term stability. Although the company was willing to purchase the equipment, Kälin and Pfister wondered whether the investment would be too great for this struggling mill.

The last mill under consideration was located 300 km (190 miles) from Rohner. It was a medium-sized company with experience in spinning for the fashion industry. This was a very old, family-owned company with highly committed family members managing the operations. Since the company worked for the fashion industry it was very flexible and adaptable to rapid changes in customer demands. Management was also willing to take risks in developing new products, a necessary condition for survival in the fashion industry. Rohner had worked with this company in the past, successfully producing a few sample trials. The mill did not have an ecological line of products, but it indicated possible cooperation with EPEA inspections.

The company was willing to purchase the ramie spinning equipment from the closed mill, but because this was a family-owned company, Kälin and Pfister could not glean information about the financial condition, the environmental legal compliance, nor the technical expertise of the company.

After gathering this information over several months of research, Kälin and Pfister were hoping that one of their alternatives would outperform its rivals. The men needed to choose a course of action since moving and assembling the machinery and fine tuning the equipment to produce good quality would take several months. Their stockpile of ramie yarn was being depleted daily. The task of choosing a spinning mill would require detailed analysis, but that did not discourage them.

Notes

* Written by Matthew M. Mehalik and Michael E. Gorman, Division of Technology, Culture and Communication at the University of Virginia, under the direction of Patricia H. Werhane, Ruffin Professor of Ethics, Darden School of Business Administration, University of Virginia. Partial support for this project was supplied by grants from the Ethics and Values in Science program of the National Science Foundation (SBR-9319983), the Batten Center for Entrepreneurial Leadership at the Darden School, University of Virginia, and the Geraldine R. Dodge Foundation. The conclusions are the responsibilities of the authors, and do not reflect the views of the foundations. Copyright © 1997 by the University of Virginia Darden School Foundation, Charlottesville, VA. All rights reserved.

1 Information in this section was obtained through interviews with Albin Kälin May 28 to June 1, 1996.

2 The concept "waste equals food" quoted in this paragraph and case is proprietary to William McDonough and is used here with his permission.

3 See *Interiors*, March 1993, and *Wall Street Journal*, Monday, October 23, 1989.

4 As quoted in Darden case "DesignTex, Inc." (UVA-E-0099). The maxims quoted in this paragraph are proprietary to William McDonough and are used here with his permission.

5 Climatex Lifecycle is a registered trademark of Rohner Textil AG.

6 Information in this section was obtained through interviews with Albin Kälin May 28 to June 1,1996.

7 Climatex is a registered trademark of Rohner Textil AG.

8 Information on this section was obtained from interviews and correspondence with Susan Lyons, William McDonough, and Albin Kälin.

9 The maxims quoted in this paragraph are proprietary to William McDonough and are used here with his permission. See Darden cases DesignTex, Inc. (UVA-E-0099) and DesignTex, Inc. (UVA-E-1000) for more information about McDonough.

10 See "DesignTex, Inc." for a complete portrayal of the issues of this dye chemical dilemma. The current case, "Rohner Textil AG" is designed to be used independent of or in a sequence immediately following "DesignTex, Inc."

11 Kälin interviews.

12 With assistance from his designers, Lothar Pfister and Fabiola Fornasier, and his production manager, Walter Fehle.

13 Kälin interview.

14 Climatex Lifecycle is a registered trademark of Rohner Textil AG.

15 The William McDonough Collection is a registered trademark of DesignTex, Inc.

16 Correspondence, Kälin to Lyons, April 7, 1994.

17 Robin Yale Bergstrom, "Probing the Softer," *Production* (November 1994): 52.

18 Margery B. Stein, "Teaching Steelcase to Dance," *The New York Times Magazine*, April 1, 1990.

19 Ibid., 52.

20 Patricia M. Fernberg, "No More Wasting Away: The New Face of Environmental Stewardship," *Managing Office Technology* (August 1993): 16, 19.

21 Correspondence, Kälin to Siblano, September 14, 1994, and Lyons to Kälin, November 7, 1994.

22 For example, *ISO/DIS 12947–1 Textiles*: "Determination of abrasion resistance of fabrics by the Martindale Method." *ISO/DIS 13934–1 Textiles*: "Tensile properties of fabrics—Part 1:

Determination of maximum force and elongation at maximum force—strip method." *ISO/DIS 13934–2 Textiles*. "Tensile properties of fabrics—Part 2: Determination of maximum force—grab method" (Revision of ISO 5082:1982).

23 Interview with Alexandra Rumpf, May 30, 1996.

24 ACT financial survey, 1994.

25 Lyons to Kälin, November 7, 1994.

26 Facsimile correspondence with Albin Kälin, August 3, 1996.

27 Correspondence, Lyons to Kälin, November 30, 1994.

28 Interviews with Albin Kälin, May 28 to June 1, 1996, and correspondence, Kälin to Lyons, December 6, 1994.

29 Information in this section was obtained through interviews with Albin Kälin May 28 to June 1, 1996, at Rohner Textil.

30 Climatex Lifecycle is a registered trademark of Rohner Textil AG.

31 Facsimile communication with Kälin, August 6, 1996.

32 Recall from earlier that, "In order for such a small company to remain useful to the larger enterprise and be competitive in general, it needed to remain at the cutting edge of providing the most creative and high-quality upholstery fabrics. Thus, the mill needed to be able to customize quickly to the demands of customers who wanted small lots of unique upholstery designs. It also needed to remain price competitive and profitable, and wanted to increase production."

33 Lothar Pfister, designer and research and development director; Fabiola Fornasier, designer; Walter Fehle, production manager; Markus Diethelm, weaving master; Alexandra Rumpf, assistant production manager and quality and environmental manager; and, of course, Paul Flückiger.

34 Kälin interviews May 28 to June 1, 1996.

35 ANSI/ISO/ASQC 9001–1994, vii.

36 ANSI/ISO/ASQC 9001–1994, 4.

37 ANSI/ISQC 9001–1994, 4–5.

38 "Eco-Eco Conzept, 1993–2000," Rohner Textil AG, section 6.1.2.

39 Kälin interviews.

40 Information in this section was obtained through interviews with Albin Kälin, May 28 to June 1, 1996, at Rohner Textil.

41 Climatex Lifecycle is a registered trademark of Rohner Textil AG.

42 The William McDonough Collection is a registered trademark of DesignTex, Inc.

43 Kälin interview, November 23, 1996.

Chapter 9

Leadership

9.1 Developing Responsible Leaders as Agents of World Benefit

Learnings from Project Ulysses [1]

The Quest for Responsible Leaders as "Agents of World Benefit"

Among the key lessons from Enron and other corporate scandals in recent years is arguably the point that it takes *responsible leadership*—and responsible leaders—to build and sustain a business that is of benefit to multiple stakeholders and not just to a few risk-seeking individuals. The corporate scandals have triggered a broad discussion on the role of business *in* society—its legitimacy, its obligations and its responsibilities. As a result, businesses and their leaders are increasingly held accountable for their actions—and non-actions—by a multitude of stakeholders and society at large. These stakeholder expectations extend beyond mere compliance with rules and regulations and adherence to ethical standards; they go beyond sustaining the economic bottom line, acting as good citizens and ensuring safe, fair, equal and respectful treatment of all employees. Instead, given the power of large corporations in particular, stakeholders expect that business leaders take a more active role and thus acknowledge their co-responsibility vis-à-vis the pressing problems in the world: protecting and promoting human rights, ensuring sustainability, contributing to poverty alleviation and the fight against diseases such as HIV/AIDS. There is agreement in both business and society that multinational corporations and their leaders have an enormous potential for contributing to the betterment of the world (WBCSD, 2006). Moreover, active engagement of corporations and their leaders in initiatives such as the Business Leader's Initiative on Human Rights (BLIHR), the World Business Council for Sustainable Development's (WBCSD) "Tomorrow's Leaders Group", or the Global Business Coalition on HIV/AIDS may be seen as an indicator for a growing willingness among business leaders to spend time, expertise and resources to help solve some of the world's most pressing problems by engaging in problem alleviation at the local level, especially in developing countries where the problem impact is most severe.

Yet, while business engagement of MNCs in developing countries has a long tradition it has not always or necessarily been for the benefit of local people as we know, e.g., from well documented cases, such as the Nestlé milk powder scandal and Shell's operations in Nigeria. While the commitment to contribute to solving social and environmental problems is arguably a positive change in business attitude and behavior, a cautious and critical position vis-à-vis this new development remains important from an ethical point of view. There are at least three fundamental questions that come to mind. Firstly, why do MNCs and their leaders all of a sudden engage in the fight against some of the world's most pressing problems? Secondly, is it legitimate and thus justifiable that business leaders act as "agents of social justice"? And thirdly, if one concludes that business leaders should in fact engage themselves and their organizations as "agents of world benefit", what is a meaningful approach to contribute to problem alleviation and thus the betterment of the world? We discuss each of these questions consecutively.

Should Business Leaders Act as "Agents of World Benefit"?

The first question addresses the discussion around the underlying *motives* of this engagement: Is it driven by business reasons such as the desire to satisfy stakeholder expectations, to improve reputation, to increase profits through engagement in new markets? Or, is it driven by concern for social issues and affected people at the local level? While in few cases the business driven engagement for social issues (*doing good*) might in fact be beneficial for both companies (*doing well*) and people at the local level, we assume that the two approaches—namely the *business driven* and the *social issue driven* approach—may lead to different solutions. In other words, the motives of "doing good" and thus *the way* business leaders think about their responsibilities (Basu & Palazzo, 2008) in a connected world will have an impact on the quality of the outcome and ultimately also the sustainability of the problem solution.

Take, for instance, the problem of access to clean drinking water. An example of a primarily business driven solution to the problem is Procter & Gamble's PUR, a water purifiying powder. PUR is arguably an excellent product which can help people in disaster areas, e.g. following a tsunami. Yet, it remains an unsatisfactory solution on a regular, long-term basis because it does not solve the core problem, that is, access to clean drinking water. Moreover, it may keep local people dependent on (more or less) expensive "Western" products. Watzlawick et al. (1988) calls this a first order solution, in contrast to a second order solution which would aim at helping people to get access to clean drinking water, e.g. by installing wells, and thus be sustainable. A business leader, acting as an "agent of world benefit", would certainly try to find sustainable, impactful solutions that benefit both business and society alike. Yet, if no win-win solution can be realized the leader would give priority to developing solutions for the benefit of people in need.

The second question concerns the *legitimacy* of business leaders acting as "agents of social justice". Let us assume, for the sake of the argument, that there is in fact widespread agreement among stakeholders that corporations and their leaders ought to act more responsibly and engage in more active ways in tackling the above mentioned problems. Is it legitimate that business leaders and corporations act as active proponents of human rights and agents of social justice? The scepticism inherent to this question is caused by the common perception that states are in fact the "primary agents of justice" (O'Neill, 2004) and thus are "ontologically privileged" (Held, 2005: 10) in the delivery of equal liberty, social and humanitarian justice. Yet, O'Neill (2004) gives at least three reasons why states should *not* be considered the primary or sole agents of justice: firstly, many states in developing regions are simply unjust; secondly, there are "weak states and failing states" that fail to secure the rights of their inhabitants; and thirdly, globalization has arguably led to more porous borders and weaker power of nation states, "allowing powerful agents and agencies of other sorts to become more active within their borders" (246 et seq.). O'Neill posits therefore that in instances such as weak states or oppressive governments multinational corporations cannot simply see themselves as secondary agents of justice; on the contrary: they need to shoulder *active* duties in carrying *some* of the obligations of international justice, e.g. by actively promoting human rights in and beyond their own business; by instituting social and economic policies that "bear on human rights, on environmental standards or on labour practices, and even on wider areas of life" (O'Neill, 2004: 253); by ensuring transparency and accountability, fighting nepotism and corruption; and by implementing globally respectable social and environmental standards. Moreover, since corporations and their leaders are able to exercise active agency *and* have the capabilities to act as agents and thus proponents of (social) justice in the countries in which they operate, we argue in line with O'Neill that it is not only legitimate for them to do so; but that they in fact bear a *co-responsibility* in promoting human and social rights and social well-being.

Having addressed two main areas of concern—motivation and legitimacy of "doing good" —the third question leads us more closely to the focus of this article which is to derive lessons for business leaders from "Project Ulysses" regarding the question of *how* to act as agents of world benefit and engage successfully and responsibly in the fight against problems at the local level. This question is based on the assumption that desirable social change requires *responsible global leaders*—leaders who lead with head, hand and heart; who have a responsible mindset, care for the needs of others and act as global and responsible citizens. Maak and Pless (2006a,b) understand responsible leadership as a relational and ethical phenomenon that "occurs in interaction with those who affect or are affected by leadership" (2006b: 103). Pless (2007) defines a responsible leader as a person who reconciles "the idea of effectiveness with the idea of corporate responsibility by being an active citizen and promoting active citizenship inside and outside the organization" (450). They build and cultivate "sustainable relationships with stakeholders inside and outside the organization to achieve mutually shared objectives based on a vision of business as a force of good for the many, and not just a few (shareholders, managers)" (Maak, 2007: 331). This can imply the creation of social value and the support of desirable social change (e.g. poverty alleviation, equal opportunity etc.) at the local level.

In what follows we introduce "Project Ulysses", a global in-company leadership development and service learning program run by PricewaterhouseCoopers, which takes place in partnership with organizations from other sectors in developing countries. We then introduce the research methodology which follows an interpretive narrative approach and present four Ulysses narratives which tell about learnings in the light of fundamental human challenges such as poverty, disease and misery. Each story is then analyzed with regard to the above question. We conclude the paper by summarizing key lessons learned and recommendations for business leaders who want to contribute to the betterment of the world by improving living conditions and livelihoods in developing countries.

"Project Ulysses"

"Project Ulysses" is a global firm-wide citizenship and leadership development program run by PricewaterhouseCoopers (PwC) to develop the next generation of global and responsible leaders within the firm and to foster business in civil society partnerships by strengthening the personal involvement of PwC in local communities and by building effective global networks with external stakeholders. The key feature of the program is that participants are sent in multicultural teams of three to four people to developing countries to work on social and environmental projects with NGOs, social entrepreneurs or international organizations supporting them in their fight against some of the world's most pressing problems such as diseases, poverty and environmental degradation at the local level (Pless and Schneider 2006).

Program Design

The program consists of five phases: a nomination phase, a preparation phase, an assignment phase, a debriefing phase and a networking phase. Around 20 participants are nominated each year by their territories to participate in Project Ulysses *(nomination phase)*. Participants meet for the first time in a seven-day foundation week during which they get input on the program dimensions (diversity, sustainability and leadership), form multicultural project teams and meet with representatives of the partner organizations with whom they are going to work in the field *(preparation phase)*. Immediately after this week they embark on an eight to ten-week field trip in developing countries where they work with partner organizations from other sectors (social entrepreneurs, NGOs, international agencies) on service projects *(assignment phase)*. Content and objectives of each project are defined in collaboration with the partner organization. Immediately after the field assignment project results are celebrated and learning experiences are debriefed in a review week *(debriefing phase)*. The debriefing process aims at helping participants to make sense of their experience and results in presentations of their refined team stories to members of the firm's global leadership team. After this week participants become members of the larger Ulysses network which meets personally every one to two years and consists of more than 100 alumni from all continents.

Contributing to Social Change by Working in Cross-sector Partnerships

The Ulysses projects are carefully selected by the program office on the basis of criteria such as geographic location, the impact of the project on local communities, the long-term sustainability of the project, the support of the partner organisation, the match of required project skills and participants' expertise and the breadth of interaction opportunities for participants with a diversity of stakeholders from different sectors and local society, including local and national governments. This cross-sector collaboration is intended to be mutually beneficial with project partners receiving pro-bono access to the knowledge and expertise of highly skilled professionals and the program participants getting access to a work and learning environment that forces them out of their comfort zone (Pless and Schneider, 2006) by confronting them with fundamentally different realities of human existence which are often shaped by the world's most pressing problems such as poverty, hunger, HIV/AIDS and malaria, lack of clean water and sanitation, among others. Participants *experience* first hand what these problems are, they *reflect* on what can be done about them while they provide partner organizations and/or communities with professional services. For many of the partners Ulysses is a "once in a lifetime opportunity to broaden the perspective on the global challenges of responsible leadership" as one of the participants put it. In fact, Ulysses participants receive the opportunity to support their partner organizations in creating social value and realizing desirable social change by providing their business knowledge and professional expertise. In these projects they develop for instance solutions for strengthening coordination of local groups and NGOs in the fight against HIV/AIDS (e.g. AMICAALL in Uganda), build strategic business plans for NGOs (e.g. Basic Needs in Ghana) and social entrepreneurs (e.g. Hagar in Cambodia), provide frameworks for income generation (e.g. for the NGO Save the Children in China) and support organizations in expanding their successful operations to other regions and countries (e.g. Ciudad Saludable in Peru or GRAM VIKAS, a developmental agency in Orissa, India).

Moreover, by working in cross-sector partnerships PwC Ulysses participants in collaboration with their partner organizations contribute to the realization of some of the UN Millennium Development Goals, such as alleviating poverty, achieving universal primary education, promoting gender equality and empowering women, combating HIV/AIDS and other maladies and ensuring environmental sustainability (UN, 2006).

Before we examine in more detail some learning narratives of program participants and discuss how their learnings can inform responsible leadership practice for world benefit we will provide in the following some information on our research approach.

Methodological Approach

In this article we apply a narrative approach to derive learnings from Ulysses participants' experiences. This narrative method is rooted in an interpretive paradigm (Burrell and Morgan, 1979), representing a subjectivist technique (and thereby the left side) on Morgan and Smircich's (1980) continuum of approaches to social science.

There are different understandings of the notions of "narratives" and "stories". Boje (2001), for instance, understands narratives as meaningful wholes with a plot and stories as fragmented, incomplete and incoherent. Gabriel, on the other hand, contrasts narratives—as a more general linguistic form which require words, characters and sequencing—with stories, which are characterized by two additional qualities: having a plot and at the same time representing reality (2004: 64). We understand stories as a specific form of a narrative, which has a plot. While our main focus of analysis is on stories, we also include other forms of narratives like fragments of stories and reflections on situations and/or characters.

According to Kohler Riesman (1993) there are different foci for analyzing narratives: e.g., sociolinguistic analysis to determine the features of a narrative (e.g., Labov, 1982; Harvey, 2006); discourse analysis to unravel the rhetorical construction of speeches (Potter and Wetherell, 1987; Den Hartog and Verburg, 1997); psychoanalysis to interpret dreams (Freud, 1900) or content analysis (Krippendorff, 1980). For our purpose we took an issue-focused view to analyze the narratives and thereby followed Weiss's procedure (1995) of data analysis.

All forms of narratives that we analyzed in this study were based on personal experiences of the participants. We conducted and transcribed qualitative interviews with 70 Ulysses participants of the programs in 2003, 2004, 2005 and 2006, which represents the entire participant population. We interviewed participants before the field assignment in the foundation week and after the assignment in the review week. The interviews in the foundation week served a dual purpose: firstly, to collect some data on the living and working context of the participants in their home countries and, secondly, to build a relationship of trust with each participant. In the interviews in the review week we applied appreciative inquiry (Heron and Reason, 2001) to invite participants to share the experiences they made within the team, with the partner organization and in the larger communities using the critical incident technique (Flanagan, 1954).

The basis of the data analysis was provided by twenty one videotaped team stories and seventy individual interviews conducted in the review weeks of the program. The first step was to search the interviews for narratives and stories that told about situations at the local level that were the object of developmental initiatives, that called for change or provoked thoughts about the necessity of change implying lessons for responsible leaders as agents of world benefit. The selected narratives were then coded by two separate coders (who are familiar with the content of research on responsible leadership) who then discussed their results in order to reach a consensus on what constitutes a responsible learning narrative. The narratives where edited following Weiss's (1995) guidelines (e.g. dropping out conversational spacers and repetitions) with the exception of two rules. Firstly, due to the best-practice character of this executive program we did not disguise the name of the company. Yet, we disguised the names of the participants and the names of the partner organizations. Secondly, in order to preserve the character of the original speech we refrained from condensation of speech and tried to preserve the personal dialect (e.g. "she is *gonna* bring").

Learning in the Field: Stories Told

The following analysis of selected learning narratives is guided by the question "What can business leaders learn from the Ulysses narratives for acting responsibly as agents of world benefit and tackling some of world's problems?" The analysis is based on four stories from four different projects. After having briefly introduced the narrator and the focus of the narrative we present the narrative itself. We then briefly examine the structure of the narrative, discuss aspects of its content with regard to the research question and derive lessons for responsible leadership practice.

Respecting the Way of Life of Indigenous People: A Narrative of Undesired Conversion

The following story told by a member of "Team Ecuador" reflects the team's experience with the developmental practice of their project partner, an international organization that lacks a license to operate in the local community.

> A good example in connection with our project (poverty reduction in Ecuador through the development of small businesses) relates to how the project sponsor was attempting to provide a "one size fits all" solution. There were different regional areas and different peoples to consider in the equation. The indigenous people of Ecuador had a way of life that involved communal village contributions for the good of all in the village. No individual wealth. If one prospered in a year, all prospered. If one suffered, all suffered. Historically, in prosperous times (bountiful harvests), great celebrations took place but the concept of attempting to save for less prosperous times was foreign. In less prosperous times of poor harvests, if left without interference, more sickness occurred and, in the extreme, natural selection kept the villages and peoples in check and in balance with the environment.
>
> Our sponsor was intent on assisting the indigenous peoples, along with others, to develop businesses and "prosper" in the classic Western cultural sense. In our interviews with representatives of the indigenous peoples, it was clear the question was "Why?". The people understood what they were doing, how they kept in balance with the environment—to change was not in their culture. The celebrations in good times were an important part of life—the highs and the lows of the chosen life were reflected in the culture. They did not need or want the value judgment that this chosen way of life could be "improved" if they learned to celebrate less in the good times and save for the bad times.
>
> It was very clear that we all need to listen to the perspective of others and suspend our judgment. It was not clear that this message got through to our sponsor or other organizations determined to convert others to their way of thinking.

The story consists of four parts: first, an introduction specifying what the story is about—the questionable "one size fits all" solution approach of the project sponsor; second, a descriptive part containing information about the situation of indigenous people of Ecuador; third, a critical reflection on the sponsor's approach which implied imposing their problem perception and solutions approaches on others, reflecting that this contradicts the needs and wants of the local people; and fourth, a conclusion regarding lessons learned, namely that one should not convert others to one's own way of thinking.

This story raises the question of the legitimacy of being an agent of social change: Who determines if, and in which direction, a local community should develop? In the case at hand the developmental agency acts without a license to operate from the local people. Thus, if developmental activities result from external pressure with no mandate or legitimacy from local or indigenous people, then social change, inflicted on a community, e.g. by external change agents (i.e. the developmental agency), may be perceived as neocolonialistic behavior. Put differently, helping indigenous people to develop in a certain direction is not a good enough reason to impose one's own ideas on others, or even to convert them to a certain way of thinking.

Therefore, the desire to support development at the local level requires the identification of a real need for help and a desire to change; good intentions are not good enough. Imposing solutions on others without buy-in and/or mandate may equal despotism and patronage and ultimately undermines the sovereignty of local people and communities. Thus, the moral of this particular narrative is to respect and tolerate the way of life of indigenous people in its own right and to develop collaborative, "indigenous" solutions.

A respectful approach would imply considering the impact of a developmental intervention and asking if the intervention is really going to change the life of people on the ground for the better; as the following critical reflection of a participant demonstrates:

> I had a similar "evolving perspective" during my experience—our work was to conduct a micro-business study of rural villages to provide data and guidance in determining which villages should receive electricity when a hydro-power dam was constructed. We had initially thought that bringing electricity would of course be good for these villages and allow for them to be happier and more developed. After some time observing the simple life that they led without electricity and without being connected to the outside world— we began to feel that perhaps providing electricity and connectivity would not be that good an idea since it would likely change and perhaps corrupt this wonderfully simple life that these people enjoyed.

Ultimately, the question raised is: Who determines what a *good* life is? Is it defined in materialistic, quantitative, economic terms and measured in numbers, such as the gross national product (GNP), or in qualitative terms, such as: clean water and an unspoiled environment; life with, and from, nature; intact social and cultural communities; material independence and self-sufficiency; or even happiness? Helena Norberg-Hodge demonstrated in her research on Ladakh how a prospering culture, characterized by happiness and humanity, was profoundly and ultimately negatively changed by Western influences and developmental projects: "In Ladakh I experienced how 'progress' has alienated people from their environment, from each other and ultimately from themselves." (1993: 17); and how it led to environmental pollution and isolation, inflation and unemployment, intolerance and envy.

Obviously then, the question "What is a good life?" can only be answered properly by the affected people themselves. Yet, since in many cases they do not have the experience to assess the impact of "modernity" on their lives it becomes the role of a responsible change agent to make people at the local level aware of the consequences and thus the pros and cons of "development". Therefore, business leaders, too, who intend to act as agents of world benefit should be cautious about imposing their own ideas and "expert" imagination on others, not only because this might be criticized as paternalisitic and neocolonialistic behavior by stakeholders, but more importantly because they ought to respect indigenous cultures and protect cultural diversity.

Knowing When Different is Different and When it is Wrong: A Narrative of Incest

The following narrative was told by a member of "Team Madagascar" who struggled with accepting the following local practice.

> We saw many girls starting from ages of 11 already having children of their own, sometimes their very own fathers have fathered these children's children. Is this due to poverty or lack of education or many other factors? As a woman I struggled to accept this condition when I saw many thirteen year olds having a child in the womb and one other being carried on the hip or back. Quite honestly, I was powerless in that situation at that moment—but was very angry.

The narrator starts the narrative by reporting about the local practice of incest with teenage girls. The brief question she asks not only reveals her difficulty but also an unwillingness in finding reasons to explain such an inhuman and degrading treatment of young women depriving them of all chances in life. She concludes the story by expressing her sheer helplessness in the face of such inhuman practices and sharing her emotional feelings of anger that disclose her deep disapproval and mark an overstepping of the limits of tolerance.

This narrative raises the ethical question of how to approach different practices and how to navigate between cultural relativism ("this is how people behave in this part of the world . . .") and ethical imperialism ("everyone should follow our norms . . ."). Donaldson (1996) states that the challenge is to find a balanced way between these extremes. In order to approach moral differences across cultures and to distinguish between when different is different and when different is wrong he proposes three guiding principles: firstly, to respect local traditions, secondly to consider the context in which the situation occurs, and thirdly to respect core human values and consult internationally accepted and globally binding lists of moral principles such as the United Nations' Universal Declaration of Human Rights. The narrative above is an example of an abusive local practice that clearly violates norms of the UN Convention on the Rights of the Child, namely children's rights to physical and personal integrity and protection "from all forms of physical or mental violence, including sexual and other forms of exploitation . . ." (United Nations, 2008). Therefore, "different" in the case at hand is simply wrong.

In conclusion, while tolerance of local practices is an important virtue, especially with respect to the socially desirable change to be accepted, and thus for implementing sustainable meaningful change in order to improve the lives of people and their living conditions, it finds its limits where human dignity and internationally accepted core human values are violated.

Stop-Look-Listen and Don't Prejudge: A Narrative of a Failed Developmental Project

The following story, told by a member of "Team Namibia", describes a situation in which the team learns about a developmental solution provided by an international political body which was not accepted by the local community and led to project failure and a waste of financial resources in the fight against poverty.

> It was a political body who had donated toilets to the village. These toilets don't require running water. They work on a filtration system. Essentially they require wind that decomposes the human faeces. And the shantytowns are part of the village that is

required to dig some holes in the ground for these toilets to be erected. Holes of prob-ably three feet by three feet or about two yards by two yards. And the toilets were sitting in the council compound because the community had refused to dig the holes. So that's what we heard in the meetings. And you say: "Well how hard is it to dig a hole in the ground when you have probably 60% unemployment in the village? Why can't you encourage somebody to dig some hole, because that does improve the lifestyle of lots of people who live in that community?"

The thing I learned, and the thing that I probably learned afterwards when we were into the second village visit, was something that you get told when you are very young and when you cross the street: and it was the *stop-look-listen routine*. And I remember telling my team mates that if there is one thing that has been changing in me from the first to the second to the third week, it's that I am realizing: I am stopping more, I am looking more, and I am listening more. And this was the one place I had to constantly do it, I really constantly stopped, looked, listened as to what was going on in this com-munity. It was probably a day or two after that initial meeting, when we met some of the people in the community that should have dug the holes to put these toilets in. And I remember asking the question: "Why did you not dig the holes for these toilets? You have to explain this to me, because I am really struggling with why you don't do this for your community." And the individual we were speaking to said: "You know there are some good reasons we didn't dig the holes. One of them is that they were in an area where many of the unemployed children go and play in, and they use it as a sports area. And they wanted us to dig holes right in the middle of that area. And we said no, not there, somewhere else, but the council wanted them there." The second thing he said was that putting the toilets in place is going to bring more people into the village, who believe they are going to improve their habit of living—and it's going to be actually worse. So, now you start to hear a different side, a different story. And not one that you'd ever turned your mind to, when you were hearing the first story, a day and a half ago. So that was part of the *stop-look-listen and don't prejudge* routine because you don't really know all the facts.

The narrator uses the story of an unsuccessful development project to tell us about his learn-ing how to broaden his own perspective and to understand issues from a different perspective. The narrative consists of three parts: In the first part the narrator introduces the story of the unsuccessful toilet project. In the second part he describes his struggle to understand why the local people did not install the toilet system. And in the third part he talks about his learning and reveals the process that enabled him to understand the indigenous perspective. He calls this approach: "Stop-look-listen". The approach implies not prejudging others and forming an opinion too quickly, but talking to different constituencies (also in the local communities), and observing and actively listening to different voices. This practice allowed him to see and understand the toilet project from a different perspective and to get new insights into the causes of the project failure.

Responsible business leaders who are not only committed to business success but also to the common good and well-being of local communities and global societies can learn from this story that firstly, ready-made "Western" solution approaches do not necessarily help affected people (see also Easterly, 2006) and solve the problem at hand. While the intention to engage in finding solutions for a problem is laudable, the toilet story exemplifies that helping people requires more than "downloading" a "Western" solution on them. In fact, it requires, as a starting point, a comprehensive understanding of the cultural, political and economic context and a desire and ability to understand the mindset of the affected people at the local level so as to develop sustainable solutions *with* them, not for them. Secondly, observing and actively listening to different stakeholders is helpful for developing a broader and deeper understanding of the issues at hand and for learning to see and understand different mindsets.

Reconciling Old and New—A Narrative of Traditional Healing

In Subsaharan Africa (e.g. Kenya, Ghana) traditional healers play an important role in the local health care system. They are respected in their societies as eminent authorities in the treatment of maladies and their advice is usually followed. However, this medical advice is not necessarily in line with Western medical knowledge and international standards of human practices and can even be part of the problem as the following example demonstrates. A team working in Kenya reported about an appalling and obviously intolerable local practice called "virgin cleansing" that is recommended by local healers and means that "if you have AIDS, the way you can cure the virus is by passing it on to a virgin!". The social consequence is that "the average age of rape victims in that area was between the ages of 4 and 12." So instead of curing a malady healers contribute knowingly or not to the spread of the disease. This has profound consequences for the fight against maladies such as HIV/AIDS.

Similar inhumane practices can be found in other medical areas such as, e.g., mental health. The following narrative, told by a member of the Ghanaian team, describes the local practice of chaining mentally ill people—and the role of the PwC team in kicking off a discussion on treatment methods among local healers.

> How do you deal with a psychotic who goes wandering in front of cars? That is the question facing the parents of Abu, a 25 year old psychotic who started wandering in front of traffic completely oblivious to where he was. Along with 95% of Ghanaians they turned to a traditional healer who prescribed a treatment of herbs and restraint. The restraint involved Abu being confined to a dark room and having his leg attached to a tree trunk. When we met him on Thursday he had been there for over a month. . .
>
> Restraining patients by chaining them up or attaching them to tree trunks is not unusual. In the case of Abu, his leg was inserted in a hole in the trunk, and then an iron nail inserted to prevent him removing his foot. He had to eat, sleep and spend the day in the room, with the constant weight of his foot underneath a tree trunk. The scene was almost medieval and one that I will not forget easily.
>
> We heard about this case through Walter, a psychiatric nurse based in Wa, where we were staying. Walter administered some tranquilizers which would last six weeks, and this would control Abu's tendencies to go wandering. However in order to secure Abu's release, the traditional healer would need to make a sacrifice of a chicken or fowl, so the next day his parents would pay some money for the animal and call the healer. Only then could he be released. In some circumstances where the family is too poor, Basic Needs have had to pay for the animal to be sacrificed in order to release a mentally ill person from their restraint. We met an association of traditional healers then next day at their monthly meeting, and we raised the sensitive issue of chaining and restraining patients. Before the meeting we had met the chairman of the association at one of our training sessions for Basic Needs' partners, and at the meeting the chairman stood up and talked to the other healers about the benefits of "white man medicine's" tranquilizers which can stabilize patients without the need for restraints, before they go on to administer herbal remedies. This was the catalyst for a number of other healers to stand up and talk about their experiences combining the "new medicines" with the "traditional" approaches, and

this avoided having to chain people up for months on end. Some healers, however, stated they never used the "new" medicines—implying that they did indeed use some pretty rudimentary and backward approaches.

It has become clear from our conversations with many people that there is a real gulf of distrust between the traditional healers and the modern medical community, yet the traditional healers are at the front line of care for most of the population.

The story consists of four parts. The narrator starts with an engaging question related to a specific case of a mentally ill person. After having outlined the context of the narrative and the role of traditional healers the narrator describes the traditional treatment in more detail, unveiling the inhumane character of chaining and restraining patients. In the second part he introduces an alternative Western approach (tranquilizers), the conditions for its application being to sacrifice poultry in order to release the patient. He then discusses the role of the local partner organization which is to pay for the animal. In part three he describes a meeting of the team with an association of traditional healers at which they addressed the sensitive issue of treatment and started a discussion on possibilities and experiences in combining "new medicines" with the "traditional approaches", with the chairman of the association acting as a catalyst in the discussion. The narrator finishes his narrative by underscoring the divide between traditional healers and the modern medical community, stressing the influential role of traditional medicine.

While the narrator does not draw a particular conclusion one can derive the following lessons to be learned from this narrative: firstly, even if Western medicine provides solutions that may alleviate certain cases of mental illness, providing a more humane treatment to patients, we cannot expect that these solutions will be readily accepted by indigenous people. Secondly, if one intends to initiate desirable social change it is necessary to identify local health care authorities. These authorities may not be the "official" ones, at least not on the local level. Thirdly, even if one cannot tolerate the customs and practices of these local authorities, in particular for ethical reasons, it is indispensable to respectfully engage with them and make them allies in search of new ways to change practices for the better. Thus, despite the urgency of many health-related problems, collaborative and sustainable solutions will be long-term, not short-term. And thirdly, the narrative also illustrates that external change agents can play a mediating and facilitating role in supporting the process of developing solutions by forging links between traditional and "Western" approaches.

The Moral of the Tales . . .

To answer the question "What can business leaders learn from the Ulysses narratives for acting as agents of world benefit and for engaging responsibly in the fight against problems at the local level?" we summarize in the following some key lessons learned and derive recommendations:

One, if business leaders want to engage in the fight against some of the world's most pressing problems on the ground at the local level and contribute to the betterment of living conditions and livelihoods, they should refrain from assuming that all people in developing countries appreciate external help and in fact want to change their chosen life style. Good intentions are not enough—"doing good" requires more. Most notably, it requires from a responsible business leader to respect and tolerate the way of life of indigenous people and to aim at finding out if there is a need for help and a desire to change in the first place. Ultimately, such practice is also in the interest of time and resource investment and thus efficiency.

Two, ready-made "Western" solutions do not necessarily meet the needs of affected people and solve problems at the local level. To be accepted, such solutions need to be developed *with* local people, not *for* them. This requires an understanding of the context (economic, cultural, political) and the mindset of the affected people and a willingness to engage with different stakeholders. Observing and active listening are qualities that can help responsible leaders to get a broader and deeper understanding of the issues at hand and to understand local people, their practices and mindsets.

Three, while tolerance of local mindsets and practices is an important virtue for changing lives and living conditions for the better it finds its limits where human dignity and internationally accepted ethical standards and core human values are violated. Therefore, knowing when different is different and when different is wrong is key and can in fact be learned in real-life experiences like "Project Ulysses".

Lastly, while it is important to know the limits of tolerance it is important not to condemn people but still to be willing to engage *with* them to find ways to change practices for the better. A useful role of external agents can be that of facilitating and mediating the process of developing solutions by forging links between traditional and "Western" approaches.

Conclusion: Developing Responsible Leaders as Agents of World Benefit

In this article we derived lessons learned from selected Ulysses narratives to inform business leaders with an aspiration to become "agents of world benefit" about a responsible approach to contributing to the public good. The analysis demonstrated that the role of agent of world benefit is a demanding one requiring an understanding of the complexity of social issues, a reflective and responsible mindset and interpersonal qualities for interacting with different stakeholders and generating solution approaches. Due to the enormous responsibility that comes with this role and the fact that interventions at the local level often have an irreversible effect on the life of indigenous people, as Norberg-Hodge's research demonstrated, a systematic preparation of leaders to take over such roles is imperative. "Project Ulysses" offers a learning context in which program participants can personally experience what it means to work with diverse stakeholders at the local level and to get engaged with those people who are directly affected by some of the world's most demanding problems; and what it takes to contribute to tackling social, humanitarian and environmental problems and to searching for sustainable solutions. It is also stressed in the service learning literature that such assignments bear the potential for moral development (Markus, Howard & King, 1993; Boss, 1994), for developing a greater tolerance for diversity (Dumas, 2002), for raising awareness of social issues (Kolenko et al., 1996) and for encouraging civic and social responsibility (Fleckenstein, 1997; Gabelnick, 1997; Eyler & Giles, 1999; Morgan & Streb, 1999; Godfrey et al., 2005; Lester et al., 2005).

Yet, as our experience as researchers and facilitators in the Ulysses program shows, no learning experience is without limitations. In order to fully and systematically leverage the program's potential for developing responsible business leaders (as agents of world benefit) the development of a reflective moral and responsible mindset needs to be defined explicitly as a key learning objective. Moreover, for developing a responsible mindset it is not enough to send participants on experiential projects in developing countries and debrief their experience along general dimensions such as leadership, diversity and sustainability. It is also important to provide a systematic *moral learning approach* throughout the experiential learning cycle (Kolb, 1984) and to coordinate the interaction between concrete experience, reflective observation, abstract conceptualization and active experimentation accordingly in order to support the process of transformation of experience into learning.

Thus, with respect to developing business leaders as agents of world benefit through a service and experiential learning methodology—as in "Project Ulysses"—the following actions ought to be taken (none of which is employed, as yet, in the program): providing ethical input in the foundation week (program foundation), for instance on moral thinking, responsible leadership frameworks and models on ethical decision making; debriefing in systematic ways participants' experiences with a focus on moral encounters and situations from which moral learning can be derived; in our case in particular lessons learned with respect to acting as "agents of world benefit". This requires coaches and facilitators with an educational background in philosophy or business ethics who can facilitate ethical discussions around participants' narratives and help them to derive lessons learned as demonstrated in this paper. To close the learning cycle it is helpful to foster and support further experimentation and action of participants in their home territories. This stage can also be accompanied by coaches and facilitators who foster ongoing learning with regard to responsible thinking and acting.

Learning experiences like "Project Ulysses" have the potential to further responsible leadership capabilities and capacities around the world. Participants experience outside their comfort zones how some of the world's most pressing public problems impact people on the local level, that the "right thing" might not always be the right thing to do, and that ethical behavior, or leading responsibly for that matter, "is not so much a matter of having exact rules about how we ought to behave, as of recognizing the relevance of our shared humanity in making the choices we face" (Sen, 1999: 283). As such, these experiences are just the beginning, and not the end, of developing responsible global leadership.

Note

1   Written by Nicola M. Pless and Thomas Maak. ©2008 Thomas Maak and Nicola Pless. Reprinted by permission of the authors. All rights reserved. "Business as An Agent of World Benefit" was the title of a conference which was hosted by Case Western Reserve University in collaboration with the Academy of Management and the UN Global Compact in Cleveland, OH (October 24–26, 2006).

References

Basu, K. and G. Palazzo: 2008, "Corporate Social Responsibility: A Process Model of Sensemaking", *Academy of Management Review* **33**(1).

Boje, D.M.: 2001, *Narrative methods for organizational and communication research* (Sage, London).

Boss, J.A.: 1994: "The effect of community service work on the moral development of college ethics students", *Journal of Moral Education* **23**, 183–198.

Burrell, G. and Morgan, G.: 1979, *Sociological paradigms and organizational analysis* (Heinemann, London).

Den Hartog, D.N. and Verburg, R.M.: 1997, "Charisma and rhetoric: Communication techniques of international business leaders", *Leadership Quarterly* **8**, 355–391.

Donaldson, T.: 1996, "Values in tension: Ethics away from home", *Harvard Business Review* **74**, 48–62.

Dumas, C.: 2002, "Community-based service-learning: Does it have a role in management education?" *International Journal of value-based management* **15**, 249–264.

Easterly, W.: 2006, *The white man's burden: Why the west's efforts to aid the rest have done so much ill and so little good* (The Penguin Press, New York).

Eyler, J. and Giles, D.E.: 1999, *Where's the learning in service-learning?* (Jossey-Bass, San Francisco, CA),

Flanagan, J. C.: 1954, "The critical incident technique", *Psychological Bulletin* **51**, 327–358.

Fleckenstein, M.P.: 1997, "Service learning in business ethics", *Journal of Business Ethics* **16**, 1347–1351.

Freud, S.: 1900, *The interpretation of dreams*, Vol. 4 (Penguin, Harmondsworth).

Gabelnick, F.: 1997, "Educating a committed citizenry", *Change* **29**, 30–35.

Gabriel, Y.: 2004, "Narratives, stories and texts", in D. Grant, C. Hardy, C. Oswick and L. Utnam (eds.), *Organizational discourse* (Sage, London), pp. 61–77.

Godfrey, P.C., Illes, L.M. and Berry, G.R.: 2005, "Creating breadth in business education through service learning", *Academy of Management Learning & Education* **4**: 309–323.

Harvey, A.: 2006, "Autobiography as a rhetoric: A tale of three leaders", paper presented at the sixty-sixth *Annual Meeting of the Academy of Management*, Atlanta, Georgia, 11–16 Aug., 2006.

Held, D.: 2005, "Principles of Cosmopolitan Order", in G. Brock and H. Brighouse (eds.), 2005, *The Political Philosophy of Cosmopolitanism* (Cambridge University Press, Cambridge), 10–27.

Heron, J. and Reason, P.: 2001, "The practice of co-operative inquiry: Research 'with' rather than 'on' people", in P. Reason and H. Bradbury (eds.), *Handbook of action research* (Sage, London), pp. 179–188.

Kohler Riesman, C.: 1993, *Narrative analysis* (Sage, Newbury Park, CA).

Kolb, D.A.: 1984, *Experiential learning: Experience as the source of learning and development* (Prentice Hall, Upper Saddle River, NJ).

Kolenko, T.A., Porter, G., Wheatley, W. and Colby, M.: 1996: "A critique of service learning projects in management education: pedagogical foundations, barriers, and guidelines", *Journal of Business Ethics* **15**, 133–142.

Krippendorff, K.: 1980, *Content analysis: An introduction to its methodology* (Sage, Newbury Park, CA).

Labov, W.: 1982, "Speech actions and reactions in personal narrative", in D. Tannen (ed.), *Analyzing discourse: Text and talk* (Georgetown University Press, Washington, DC), pp. 219–247.

Lester, S.W., Tomkovick, C., Wells, T., Flunker, L. and Kickul, J.: 2005, "Does service-learning add value? Examining the perspectives of multiple stakeholders", *Academy of Management Learning & Education* **4**, 278–294.

Maak, T. and Pless, N.M.: 2006a, "Responsible Leadership: A Relational Approach", in T. Maak and N.M. Pless (eds.), *Responsible Leadership* (Routledge, London, New York), pp. 33–53.

Maak, T. and Pless, N.M.: 2006b, "Responsible Leadership in a Stakeholder Society. A Relational Perspective", *Journal of Business Ethics* **66**, 99–115.

Maak, T.: 2007, "Responsible leadership, stakeholder engagement, and the emergence of social capital", *Journal of Business Ethics* **74**, 329–343.

Markus, G.B., Howard, J. and King, D.: 1993, "Integrating community service and classroom instruction enhances learning: Results from an experiment", *Educational Evaluation and Policy Analysis* **15**, 410–419.

Morgan, G. and Smircich, L.: 1980, "The case for qualitative research", *Academy of Management Review* **5**, 491–500.

Morgan, W. and Streb, M.: 1999, *How quality service-learning develops civic values* (Indiana University, Bloomington, IN).

Norberg-Hodge, H.: 1993, *Leben in Ladakh* (Herder, Freiburg).

O'Neill, O.: 2004, "Global Justice: Whose Obligations?", in D.K. Chatterjee (ed.), *The Ethics of Assistance: Morality and the Distant Needy* (Cambridge University Press, Cambridge), 242–259.

Pless, N.M.: 2007, "Understanding responsible leadership: Role identity and motivational drivers", *Journal of Business Ethics* **74**, 437–456.

Pless, N.M. and Schneider, R.: 2006, "Towards developing responsible global leaders: The PwC Ulysses experience", in T. Maak and N.M. Pless (eds.), *Responsible Leadership* (Routledge, London, New York), pp. 213–226.

Potter, J. and Wetherell, M.: 1987, *Discourse and social psychology* (Sage, Newbury Park, CA).

Sen, A.: 1999, *Development as Freedom* (Oxford University Press, Oxford/New York).

United Nations: 2006, *UN Millennium Development Goals*. Available: http:www.un.org/millenniumgoals/ (accessed 27 June 2006).

United Nations: 2008, *The United Nations study on violence against children*. Available: http://www2.ohchr.org/english/bodies/crc/study.htm (accessed 3 January 2008).

Watzlawick, P., Weakland, J.H. and Fisch, R.: 1988, *Lösungen: Zur Theorie und Praxis menschlichen Wandels* (Huber, Bern).

WBCSD: 2006, *From challenge to opportunity. A paper from the Tomorrow's Leaders group of the World Business Council for Sustainable Development*, edited by Lloyd Timberlake.

Weiss, R.S.: 1995. *Learning from strangers: The art and method of qualitative interview studies* (The Free Press, New York, NY).

9.2 The Female Health Company*

As a biochemist, activist, and entrepreneur, Mary Ann Leeper wanted nothing more than to slow, if not halt the spread of HIV/AIDS. Though massive public health efforts targeted toward gay men had begun to slow the disease among that population, statistics indicated that between 1992 and 1995 the number of women with the disease had begun to rise. A female-controlled method for HIV/AIDS prevention had been discussed at the 1987 World AIDS Conference. Since then Leeper had found an inventor who had designed one—a female condom. She persuaded him to work with her to perfect the design, and she ushered the product through a tortuous FDA approval process. As the President of the Chicago-based Female Health Company (FHC), she had surmounted many business challenges, including most recently a major restructuring of the company, but none prepared her for what she now faced.

Knowing that a female condom would be a tough sell, Leeper had sought the best advertising and public relations help for the product launch in the U.S. private and public sectors. It was obvious to Leeper and the big-name firms that a novel product such as a female condom would take time to catch on. But the consumer and public response to the new product was not at all what they expected. It was 1996 and after spending years and millions of dollars on the female condom's product development and launch, the company was operating on seriously depleted resources. Leeper spent a lonely winter weekend in her office on Michigan Avenue in Chicago. She kept thinking, "Here we are with a revolutionary life-saving and important product, not moving off the shelves and costing big dollars to promote." On the verge of giving up, the question for Leeper now was how to respond to what she was hearing.

The Spread of HIV/AIDS in the United States

AIDS (acquired immunodeficiency syndrome) was first recognized in the early 1980s. Later, the virus that causes AIDS, HIV (human immunodeficiency virus) was found by the early 1990s all over the world. The nature of HIV/AIDS and cultural norms accounted for the higher incidence in women. Women's anatomy and traditional sexual roles made them more vulnerable to contracting the disease. HIV/AIDS could also be spread to the children of HIV-infected women, either through childbirth or breast milk. Therefore, preventing HIV/AIDS in women meant preventing the disease in their children too.

The Center for Disease Control and Prevention (CDC) revealed alarming statistics on HIV/AIDS in the United States:

- Between January 1985 and December 1996, 581,429 persons with AIDS had been reported to the CDC.[1] This figure almost doubled from the 1993 cumulative total (361,164).

- Children made up 7,629 or one percent of that number and women 85,500—15 percent. In 1996 women represented 20 percent of adults/adolescents reported to be living with AIDS.[2] This figure is greater than the proportion in any previous year.
- In the United States, HIV-related death had the greatest impact on young and middle-aged adults, particularly racial and ethnic minorities. In 1996, African American adults and adolescents exceeded the percentage of whites for the first time. Many of these young adults likely were infected in their teens and twenties.

From Concept to Market

The male condom had been shown to be effective at reducing the risk of spreading HIV/AIDS, yet it had a major drawback—use of a male condom required the man's compliance, if not consent. Like health and human rights activists who for years urged scientists to develop safe, reversible, female-controlled contraceptives, Leeper thought there ought to be a similar device that protected against HIV/AIDS and other sexually-transmitted diseases.[3]

When Leeper began her quest, she worked for FHC's progenitor, Wisconsin Pharmacal, a company that manufactured and marketed a wide variety of specialty chemicals and branded consumer products. Originally trained as a biochemist, Leeper had years of experience bringing products to market in the U.S. Leeper saw her opportunity to do something about the spread of HIV/AIDS when she heard about a female condom, invented by Lasse Hessel, a Danish physician. The product was already available in a few European countries, but Leeper convinced Hessel to let her firm develop his device for the North American market.

The hope was that if the U.S. Food and Drug Administration (FDA) approved the female condom, most countries around the world would ultimately approve it. An agreement was signed in October 1987 for Leeper to develop the product to meet FDA criteria. Hessel, through his company later called Chartex International, developed the manufacturing processes and ironed out the bureaucratic detail necessary to allow multi-country distribution of the female condom. A U.S. patent was obtained on April 5, 1988.

Under Leeper's watchful eye the company pursued the pre-clinical and clinical studies necessary to develop the female condom for worldwide use. Near the end of 1988, Leeper was convinced the product met FDA requirements and scheduled a final approval, without knowing that a major, and somewhat ironic, wrinkle lay ahead. Unbeknownst to Wisconsin Pharmacal, the National Women's Health Network (NWHN) had at the same time filed a petition with the FDA. NWHN persuaded FDA regulators to use stricter criteria to evaluate all new condoms, male and female. As Leeper recalled:

> The petition was aimed at the new models of male condoms that only covered the glans not just female-controlled condoms. The result of the NWHN action was that the FDA held an advisory committee meeting at which they decided the female condom was so different and addressed such a critical disease that it should be classified as a Class III medical device and therefore undergo even greater scrutiny. This category placed the female condom amongst products such as heart valves and other implants that addressed other life-threatening diseases, in contrast to previously-developed male condoms that were Class II. Approval of our product now looked as remote as the moons of Jupiter.
>
> Being placed in Class III meant we had to file a Pre-Market Application (PMA) for medical devices. This is similar to New Drug Applications (NDA). PMAs require extensive safety and efficacy studies—very different from what a new male condom manufacturer, at the Class II level, would have to do. They would file a simpler form called a 510k. PMA studies cost millions of more dollars and many more years of work to

complete. Class II male condoms had never been tested to the extent that we had to test the female condom.

The new classification criteria resulted in costly, extensive, and time-consuming research projects at Wisconsin Pharmacal. But five years later, Leeper's persistence was rewarded when the FDA finally approved marketing and distribution of the female condom as a Class III medical device. Wisconsin Pharmacal began making plans to begin limited distribution in the summer of 1993.

The Product and its Launch

Having passed the FDA approval process, the female condom was now ready to be introduced to the U.S. market. The product itself was made of a sheer, non-latex, polyurethane material and shaped as a sheath with flexible O rings on each end (see Exhibit 9.2.1). While the female condom transferred heat, the plastic used was extremely strong and impermeable to temperature changes, humidity, and oil or water-based lubricants. More importantly the sheath was impenetrable to various viruses and bacteria that cause sexually transmitted diseases (STDs) like trichomoniasis, cytomegalovirus, herpes virus, hepatitis B virus, OX174 and HIV. The condom's uniqueness lay in the control it gave women to protect themselves against STDs, as well as unintended pregnancies.

The results of market research were mixed. As Leeper said, "For every complaint we got, there was an equal amount of positive feedback. No one really knew how the consumer was

Exhibit 9.2.1 Female Condom

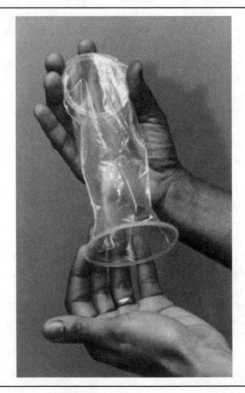

going to judge the product." The product had many perceived benefits when compared to other prophylactics and contraceptives. The device did not require health care services to fit, prescribe, refill, insert, or remove; it had no systemic (hormonal) side effects for the user; it did not require partner consent because it could be inserted well in advance of sexual activity and therefore was less disruptive to intercourse; it was not necessarily obvious to the male partner, and was odor and taste free. There were, however, some obstacles noted that included: being aesthetically unusual; difficult for some to insert; for others it produced discomfort or reduced sensation; occasionally became dislodged; and some partners objected.

Wisconsin Pharmacal prepared to distribute the female condom in both the public sector and on the commercial market. By the end of 1993, the female condom was available in the public sector, where physicians and public health care providers were the customers who would be responsible for recommending the product to end users. Broad-scale commercial distribution was initiated nine months later.

Product branding and marketing targeted women's empowerment and positioned the product as an alternative to the male condom. The female condom sold under the trademark "Reality." Ads for Reality used the tagline "Count on Yourself," with the intention of encouraging women to feel empowered to protect themselves (see Exhibit 9.2.2). In supermarkets and drug stores, Reality was shelved with other personal care products. The packaging included directions and a 1–800 customer information number. The female condoms came in boxes of three or six, priced at about $7.50 and $15.00, respectively. Leeper recalled those early days:

> We had hired a high-profile publicity firm to handle public relations and a New York ad agency to design the overall campaign. The initial mailing promotion to physicians cost well over $250,000, with a sales rep promotion that averaged $1 million per month. Advertising to the consumer was in the multi-million dollar range. Plus, of course there were big retainer fees to keep the advertising and PR firms on board.
>
> The product launch to the public sector progressed slowly but on track. A lot of education for public health workers and end users was needed. It was a new method so the way it was offered was important. Presentation had to be favorable for the product to be accepted both by providers and potential users.
>
> As for the commercial introduction, directly to consumers—that was a different story. Even the market research did not foretell what would happen.
>
> Despite the hefty costs, the whole campaign flopped. Within six weeks of the national launch that fall I knew we were in for a struggle. Most of the typically white, affluent, young women we were trying to reach simply did not hear the message. Intellectually they thought it was a good idea to be able to protect themselves, but emotionally, in the heat of the moment, forget it—safe sex stayed outside the bedroom! These young women really did not recognize they were at risk of getting an STD, let alone the possibility of being infected with HIV and dying from sex.
>
> As an added bonus to our dilemma, the media jeered at the female condom. Numerous jokes and embarrassed laughter littered the pages of women's magazines. Something had to be done.

What Now?

Leeper didn't yet fully understand why the commercial target market wasn't using Reality. So to understand what was happening, Leeper went to the sources that she knew mattered the most—the people who were interested in and using the product. Through conversations with

Exhibit 9.2.2 Count on Yourself Campaign

employees who answered the consumer information line and listening into calls, Leeper's picture of Reality's target market began to change. Inquiries and calls were coming from all kinds of women—and men!—not just young, white, affluent women. Many mentioned that they had heard about the product from a friend. A larger than expected portion of the responses came from women of color. Some of the women and men were in long-standing relationships or married. Often the questions this diverse group of people asked were not about the product, so much as how to suggest using the female condom to a person's partner. The overwhelming commonality was that these people already believed that they were at risk.

Next Leeper investigated what might be happening in public clinics. After several conversations, Leeper realized how dependent the female condom's acceptance was on an important gate keeping audience.

> During my initial contact with public health counselors, I discovered that they were mostly young white female adults who, for the most part, could not image themselves using the female condom. I heard comments like it was too odd looking, and it seemed to be more of a gimmick than a life saver. I was concerned that their attitude may translate into reluctance to recommending their clients use the female condom.

Weighing what she heard, Leeper began to wonder how she could take a different approach. Something was needed; after all, using a female condom was a little more personal and sensitive than buying a new brand of soap.

On an early fall day in 1996 Mary Ann Leeper listened intently while Daisy Nyamukapa, Manager of the HIV/AIDS Coordination Programme for Zimbabwe's Ministry of Health and Child Welfare, explained why she had called. Over 30,000 Zimbabwean women had signed a petition demanding that the government bring Leeper and her company's product, the female condom, into their country. As the President of the Chicago-based Female Health Company, Leeper was stunned by Nyamukapa's extraordinary request. Then again, Leeper had developed a talent for listening to her supply chain customers and end users. This request was bound to be another trial by fire, testing yet again Leeper's and FHC's abilities to adapt to a complex set of new audiences. Based on her recent experience in developing an entirely new approach to marketing the female condom, Leeper had a newfound appreciation for the cultural and communication intensive nature of her company's product. But the challenge would be worthwhile if they could reach a population that desperately needed this product.

Perception Meets Reality

After a very long process leading up to the product launch, Leeper was disappointed that the first attempt to promote the female condom in the U.S.'s commercial and public sectors missed the mark. But there were even more immediate concerns. In 1995, after spending years and millions of dollars on the female condom's product development and launch, Wisconsin Pharmacal's board of directors approved a plan to restructure the company. All of the assets and liabilities of the firm, except those related primarily to the female condom, were transferred to a newly formed subsidiary,[4] which later that year was sold to an unrelated third party. Next Wisconsin Pharmacal renamed itself the Female Health Company (FHC) and in February 1996 acquired Chartex, the inventor's firm which included the female condom's London-based manufacturing facility. (See financial data in Exhibit 9.2.3). In the end, the

Exhibit 9.2.3 FHC Financial Data

Income Statement

Period Ending:	**30-Sep-96**
Total Revenue	**$2,064,258**
Cost of Products Sold	$3,684,698
Gross Profit	($1,620,440)
Operating Expenses	
Research and Development	$361,094
General and Administrative	$2,987,839
Sales and Marketing	$2,980,000
Royalty and Exclusivity Fees	N/A
(Loss) From Operating	($7,949,913)
Nonoperating Income (Expense)	
Interest Expense	($560,030)
Interest Income	$106,708
Other, net	($252,607)
	($705,929)
	$3,357,316
(Loss) From Continuing Operations	($8,655,842)

Exhibit 9.2.3 *Continued*

Income Statement

Discontinued Operations	
Income (loss) From Operations and Gain on Sale	($4,461)
Net (Loss)	**($8,660,303)**
Net Income (Loss) Per Weighted Average Number Common Shares Outstanding	
Continuing Operations	($1.31)
Discontinued Operations	N/A
	($1.31)
Weighted Average Number of Common Shares Outstanding	**$6,611,796**

Balance Sheet

Period Ending	**30-Sep-96**
Current Assets	
Cash and Cash Equivalents	$2,914,080
Trade Accounts Receivable	$457,226
Inventory	$967,398
Prepaid Expense and Other Current Assets	$370,555
Total Current Assets	**$4,709,259**
Other Assets	
Prepaid Royalties	N/A
Note Receivable Net of Unamortized Discount of $189,003	$810,997
Intellectual Property Rights	$1,089,578
Other Assets	$194,032
	$2,094,547
Property, Plant and Equipment	
Land and Building	$1,222,511
Equipment, Furniture, and Fixtures	$3,710,683
	$4,933,194
Less: Accumulated Depreciation	($471,377)
	$4,461,817
Total Assets	**$11,265,623**
Current Liabilities	
Notes Payable to Stockholders	$1,956,670
Notes Payable to Bank	N/A
Current Maturities Long Term Debt	$1,736,706
Trade Accounts Payable	$721,015
Accrued Product Returns and Trade Promotions	$635,000
Accrued Royalty and Exclusivity Fees	N/A
Accrued Expenses and Other Current Liabilities	$533,668
Total Current Liabilities	**$5,612,959**
Long Term Liabilities	
Long Term Debt and Capital Lease Less Maturities	$477,296
Convertible Debentures	$1,910,000
Other Long Term Liabilities	N/A
	$2,708,392

Stockholders' Equity

Convertible Preferred Stock	N/A
Common Stock	$72,117
Additional Paid-In Capital	$32,864,572
Additional Paid-In Capital Warrants	$508,500
Foreign Currency Translation Gain	$83,850
Accumulated Deficit	($30,584,775)
	$2,944,272
	$11,265,623

Cash Flow

Period Ending:	**30-Sep-96**
Net (Loss)	**($8,660,303)**
Adjustments to Reconcile Net (Loss) to Net Cash (Used In) Operating Activities	
Depreciation	$425,084
Amortization of Debenture Issuance Costs	$4,278
Provision for Doubtful Accounts, Returns, and Discounts	$120,126
Provision for Inventory Obsolescence	$950,000
Gain on Sale of Holdings	($224,538)
Loss on Disposal of Equipment	$37,576
Issuance of Stock, Warrants and Options for Services	$706,268
Amortization of Discount on Note Received and Interest Earned on Lease Deposit	($29,703)
Amortization of Discount on Notes Payable and Convertible Debentures	$166,570
Amortization of Other Assets	$250,000
Changes in Operating Assets and Liabilities of Continuing Operations	
Receivables	$47,269
Inventories	$1,935,923
Prepaid Expenses and Other	$177
Accounts Payable	($914,876)
Accrued Exclusivity and Royalty Fees	N/A
Accrued Product Returns and Trade Promotions Allowance	$635,000
Due to Stockholder	($19,795)
Other Current Liabilities	$498,407
Discontinued Operations	N/A
Net Cash (Used In) Operating Activities	**($4,072,537)**

Source: 1996 Female Health Company Annual Report

newly named FHC's sole business now consisted of the exclusive manufacture, marketing, and sale of the female condom.

With the reorganization behind her, Leeper was determined to turn the business around and get acceptance of its important product. The manufacturing facility had an annual capacity of 60 million units, and Leeper estimated that she needed to sell 14 million units a year just to break even. To accelerate U.S. commercial sales, Leeper redefined the promotional strategy and advertising message based on what she had learned about the diversity of people interested in the female condom and the qualities of the relationships that enabled its use. Leeper acted decisively: "I got rid of the big name firm, brought the campaign in-house, hired a designer down the street whose work I admired, and set up a telephone database to do my own research."

Listening to users' feedback, FHC redeveloped its product advertising message and repositioned the female condom. Leeper explained:

> The advertising focus changed to center on communication between partners, shifting the emphasis from women to both sexes. We used slogans such as: "Safer Sex Just Got Better" and "Feeling Is Believing." We showed a loving couple, lovers who cared about each other, not a casual relationship (Exhibit 9.2.4). We drew upon some of the questions people were asking on the phone and answered them in the ad campaign. Most of the ads were print but in some rare markets, such as Austin Texas, local television affiliates allowed us to run television ads.
>
> The new campaign was a great success; the database phone calls increased ten fold. We had four telephone lines installed to try and handle the nearly 1200 calls a day we were getting. Interestingly we noted a pattern. The majority of the calls were from people who were already concerned they were at risk, mostly people of color, particularly females. The rest of the calls were from men, between 40 and 45 percent, which was a surprise.
>
> This information hit me like a lightning bolt. I realized there were people out there who really understood they were at risk. I needed to shift more emphasis to the public sector where women cared about the issue and their own personal health. They would recognize the product's benefit.

The Public and Commercial Sectors

Based on what she was hearing, Leeper drew FHC's attention to the public sector. Key customers in the public sector included public health agencies, city and state health departments, university health centers, as well as non-profit health care advocacy groups like Planned Parenthood. The company also shifted focus from mass advertising in the commercial market to directly addressing the public health communities in several major metropolitan areas. Leeper described the new approach:

> We picked nine major U.S. cities: Atlanta, Baltimore, Boston, Chicago, Philadelphia, Los Angeles, New York City, San Francisco, and Washington. We launched in each city where we met with key health officials for a press conference announcing the availability in the public and not-for-profit clinics.
>
> While this time period should have been exciting, I was still uneasy with the reaction. Some women on the street seemed interested in the product but counselors at the outreach clinics were just not receptive. It was almost like they did not want to be bothered. So I finally realized that in the public sector I had to sell not just the product but also sell clinic workers on why and how they should introduce the female condom to potential users. I found that clinic workers needed help on reaching out to potential users, and both groups needed to be educated about the product.

Executives at the FHC decided that teaching counselors and health care providers how to talk about the female condom was going to be their responsibility. Leeper understood that if health care providers didn't think they would use the female condom their clients would never learn to accept the product. So they got busy working on material to present to the public sector. Leeper tried to anticipate questions and situations that clients and customers may have

Exhibit 9.2.4 Feeling is Believing Campaign

Exhibit 9.2.4 *Continued*

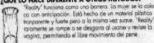

THE **REALITY** FEMALE CONDOM.

FEELS SO GOOD,

YOU WON'T BELIEVE

IT'S SAFER SEX.

FEELING IS BELIEVING.

Imagine practicing safer sex that's sensitive, un-inhibited and totally satisfying for both of you. Better yet, stop imagining and start experiencing the "Reality" female condom. You will discover that you can reduce the risk of pregnancy and sexually transmitted diseases (STD) including AIDS, without reducing the intimacy or the ecstacy.

WHAT ARE THE STATISTICS?*
- 12 million new STD cases/year–86% occur in persons 15-29 yrs
- 1 in 3 college students has an STD
- women's risk to STDs more than 2x's higher than men's
- more than half of the pregnancies each year are unintended *reference on request

WHAT MAKES IT DIFFERENT FROM OTHER METHODS?

"Reality" acts like a barrier. The woman inserts it ahead of time. It's made of clear, strong but soft plastic. "Reality" rarely rips or tears during use and lines the vagina allowing free movement for the penis.

"Reality" can be put in place long before intimacy. To insert "Reality" squeeze the inner ring and push into the vagina as far as possible. This ring helps to hold the female condom in place inside while the outer rim stays outside the body and helps to protect. When both partners are ready, the penis is simply guided into the female condom. Extra lubricant is added for extra pleasure and ease of movement.

DOES IT PROTECT?

Failure Rates, 1 Year	Typical Use	Perfect Use
Reality Female Condom	21%	5%
Male Latex Condom	12%	3%
Cervical Cap	18%	18%
Diaphragm	18%	6%
Spermicide	21%	6%
Implanted	0.09%	

WHY IS IT EASY TO USE...AND KEEP USING?

Most women report that insertion is easy, especially after using "Reality" two or three times. Both men and women report that "Reality" **feels good.** There's no restricting the penis and the soft feel of the thin but strong plastic together with the lubricant is pleasurable. **Men like it! Women like it!** It's available at your pharmacy!

SHOULD YOU TRY REALITY?
Yes, if you:
- can't or won't use male latex condoms
- seek a new nonhormonal method of contraception and sexually transmitted disease (STD) prevention
- use the pill but want an additional method to reduce the risks of STD's
- are allergic to latex

- If used properly, male latex condoms are highly effective at preventing sexually transmitted diseases, including AIDS (HIV infection). • If you are not going to use a male latex condom, you can use "Reality" to help protect yourself and your partner. • "Reality" only works when you use it. Use it every time you have sex. • Before using "Reality", read the directions and learn how to use it properly.

Call **1-800-274-6601** for: Free samples. Questions. Product Information.

Exhibit 9.2.4 *Continued*

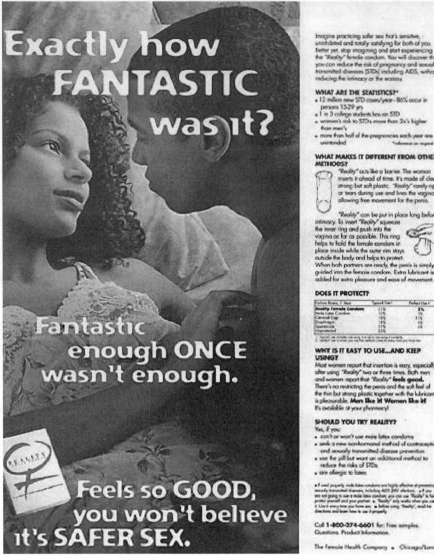

encountered and then addressed each one. The FHC team designed brochures that were specifically targeted to different audiences. For example:

- *How To Use* was a visual only brochure for non-literate or non English reading groups.
- *Inserting the female condom . . . easier than you think* was a pamphlet designed for audiences that were unfamiliar with basic anatomy.
- *Reality Female Condom* in Spanish was for Spanish speaking customers.
- *The Female Condom: A contraceptive choice* appealed to customers looking for a contraceptive option with the added benefit of STD prevention.
- *The Female Condom: Safer sex just got better* was meant for those that understood the need for contraception but not the safer sex issue. This handout encouraged clients and their partners to think about dual protection.
- *What Is Reality* was intended for the commercial audience to build the brand while showing the product's benefits.

The plan was to have master copies of each pamphlet available for health care providers. FHC brochures were purposefully not covered by copyright laws so agencies could make and distribute as many copies to their patients or clients as they wanted to print. As Leeper recalled:

> I had to develop a whole new communication program—a step-by-step program. The public sector campaign amounted to a "train the trainers" program designed to teach the counselors so they, in turn, could help their clients. This approach seemed to generate acceptance and satisfied users.

The training model included a section on how to talk to men about this product. It also addressed the reluctance some females had approaching their partner about using the female condom. Women needed to have the ability to convince their partners that it was in their mutual interest to have safer sex without changing the basis of the relationship or the intimacy of the moment.[5] Negotiating for safer sex was not always an easy task. The FHC material suggested including men in counseling or introducing the condom in group sessions—this offered a friendly setting where women could share information, ideas or apprehensions with their partners and each other. The company also recommended role plays and real-life testimonials be worked into counseling.

At the same time Leeper had not given up on the commercial sector, and she realized that commercial advertising could help demand in the public sector as well. FHC focused its efforts by doing intensive test marketing in a single city. Leeper remembered:

> We chose Austin, Texas as a test market and decided to do everything that we could in that particular city. In Austin we did regional advertising in a cross section of magazines: women's, men's, and unisex. We did bill boards, radio, and television advertising. There were posters on the outside of buses, inside bus depots, and subway stations. We did a three-month blitz in Austin that cost us $350,000. And we could not keep the product on the shelf. The whole experience indicated that we could get the safer sex message across, but we just could not afford to do it on a national basis!

Given its financial constraints, FHC targeted a narrower audience elsewhere, focusing on college and university campuses. Actress Drew Barrymore also agreed to act as a spokesperson and gave her time gratis to get the message of safer sex to young people.

Going International

Daisy Nyamukapa's call gave Leeper the last nudge to forge ahead into international markets. She remembered:

> Our plan was to move our U.S. public sector approach into the global market. I toyed with the idea of a global strategy several years before when discussion of a female condom first came up at the 1987 World AIDS Conference. When we became an international company with the purchase of Chartex, I began negotiations with the joint United Nations Programme on HIV/AIDS (UNAIDS) and the World Health Organization (WHO). On World AIDS day, December 1996, FHC signed an agreement with UNAIDS and WHO to make the female condom available in developing countries at a special rate of 38 British pence (about 68 U.S. cents) a piece, and they in turn would help with the announcement and overall advocacy of the product. At that time, we sold a female condom for $2.50 in U.S. drugstores and 90 cents to the U.S. public sector, so at 68 cents a piece in developing nations volume would be critical.
>
> Here began a communications strategy beyond imagination. I had at least 25 countries identified as targets to get the message out. Their women needed to learn about the female condom and what it could do to help them protect themselves. Somebody (who and how many I did not yet know) within each country had to learn that such a device as the female condom was available. We had to make sure they understood why it was important to them to have it available. Then we needed to train counselors, distribute the product within their systems, and reach out to those who needed it the most. We discovered the most need was in the villages and rural areas of sub-Saharan Africa.

The telephone call from Zimbabwe presented the opportunity Leeper needed. She had learned many lessons in the U.S. by trial and error. The epidemic plaguing Africa made Leeper more determined than ever that the female condom was part of the solution. She just had to make this work.

Zimbabwe's History, Economy, and Geography

To be effective in a new environment and market, Leeper had to investigate Zimbabwe's cultural context, starting with its history, economy, and geography. For the period prior to contact with Europeans in the 1800s, little written history of Zimbabwe survived.[6] Archaeologists and historians pieced together the existence in the region of an advanced civilization and military organization with complex tribal movements. In 1890 Cecil Rhodes and his British South Africa Company used a military force to conquer the Shona territory and the Ndebele kingdom. The former kingdoms were established as a British territory under the name of Rhodesia. By 1923, the colony had full self-governance under an administration controlled by European settlers. African voting rights were restricted and from the start white settlers made every effort to institutionalize their supremacy.[7] In the years that followed, Shona and Ndebele peoples were unhappy with British occupation. They resented the loss of their land and cattle, their role as forced labor, and other abuses that followed European dominance.[8]

Over the years, several organized groups challenged colonial rule and some members attempted to work within political coalitions to institute change. But it was not until 1980 that the people of Rhodesia gained complete independence from British rule—accomplished through a grisly war among various factions. Under the leadership of Robert Mugabe a new government was formed and recognized internationally as Zimbabwe on April 18, 1980. Since this country became an independent republic, the ZANU (PF) political party has most often ruled.

The economy experienced a period of stagnation during the five years before independence and during the war. With a brief recovery in 1980 and 1981, mostly due to international recognition and the lifting of international sanctions, the new country was struck with a severe drought and recession from 1982 to 1984.[9] A four-percent average growth rate was maintained until 1989 when the government introduced a five-year Economic Structural Adjustment Programme (ESAP). Trade liberalization was introduced but the country once more suffered from a severe drought in 1992 that devastated the economy and the ESAP.[10] The economy slowly recovered and the GDP grew in real terms by almost four percent by 1996. Zimbabwe's economy was mixed and very dependent on a symbiotic relationship between a strong and viable private sector and a welfare-orientated government.[11]

Geographically, Zimbabwe was landlocked, but well known for its rich supply of mineral and energy resources. Some of the world's finest deposits of chromate, asbestos, lithium ores, gold, nickel, copper, coal, tin, iron ore, limestone, platinum, pyrites, diamonds, and precious stones were found in Zimbabwe. Zimbabwe was about the same size as California (see Exhibit 9.2.5) and had a population of almost 12 million. The official language for governmental and business purposes was English. Approximately 19 percent of the population spoke Ndebele and 77 percent spoke Shona. The urban population (3.6 million) was vastly smaller than the rural population (8.2 million).[12] The urban population was employed in the developed sectors of the economy with varying levels of education and skills, while a large portion of the rural population was engaged in subsistence agriculture.[13]

HIV/AIDS in Zimbabwe

Leeper soon learned that the global HIV/AIDS epidemic hit Zimbabwe especially hard, and the statistics were staggering. For example:

- In 1994, the average age of life expectancy at birth for females was 62 years and only 58 years for males.[14]
- During 1997, Zimbabwe had the highest percentage (25.8 percent) in the world of people between the ages of 15 and 49 infected with HIV or suffering from AIDS.[15]
- Teenage girls suffered five to six times the infection rate of boys.[16]
- Women and children overwhelmingly represented most of the nearly three million HIV/AIDS infected Zimbabweans.
- In Harare, the capital of Zimbabwe, 32 percent of pregnant women during 1995 were infected.[17]
- In another town that lies between Zimbabwe and the South African border 70 percent of women attending prenatal clinics in 1995 were found infected.[18]

Zimbabwean women were especially susceptible to risk due to their economic and social dependence on men. Most Zimbabwean women were completely financially dependent upon men, and often sex figured into that dependence.[19] For example, Leeper recalled, "In Zimbabwe, women are totally dependent on men for their well being. Most women do not earn money. The men bring in the money and help keep shelter over women's heads. It is an extremely traditional society."

In many African cultures talking about sex was taboo.[20] Culturally, women were not expected to discuss or make decisions about sexuality.[21] Leeper knew that:

Many men do not want to wear male condoms. They want free sex not something that is physically binding. Other differences exist geographically, for example in Zimbabwe, men prefer dry sex. So they want sex to be condom free.

Normally, women could not request or insist on using a condom or any form of safer sex or prophylactic protection. If a woman refused sex or asked for condom use, she often risked abuse, because such a request was interpreted as an admission that she had been unfaithful.

Exhibit 9.2.5 Africa

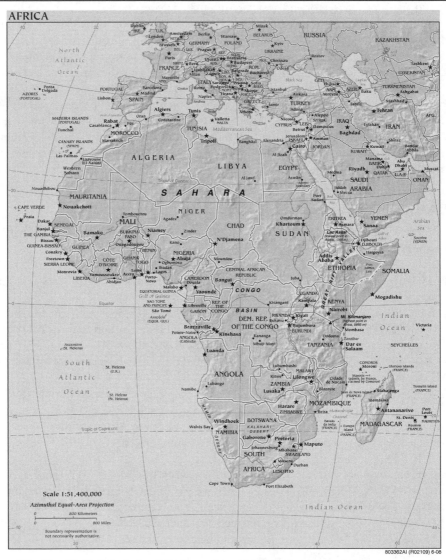

Source: CIA, *The World Fact Book*, <http://www.cia.gov/cia/publications/factbook/reference_maps/africa.html> (accessed on 6 April 2006)

Not using condoms, even in committed relationships, was especially dangerous because it was culturally acceptable for married and unmarried Zimbabwean men to have multiple partners, including sex workers, which increased the opportunity for the virus to spread (especially among young virgin females). At the same time, for daily survival, many women exchanged sex for material favors. These women were not necessarily formal sex workers; rather, by necessity they used informal sex exchange, particularly in poor settings, as a way of providing for themselves and their children.

Conclusion

Leeper wondered how much of what she had learned so far would apply in a new setting like Zimbabwe. Given her experience, she knew that cultural differences would matter, but how? What could she anticipate now? Could she rely on the communication competency she had developed thus far? How could organizations like UNAIDS and WHO help?

Notes

* This case was prepared by Gerry Yemen under the supervision of Elizabeth Powell, Assistant Professor of Business Administration. This case was written as a basis for class discussion rather than to illustrate effective or ineffective handling of an administrative situation. Copyright © 2003 by the University of Virginia Darden School Foundation, Charlottesville, VA. All rights reserved.

1 These statistics should be interpreted with caution because collection of demographic and risk information varies among states.

2 "HIV Surveillance Report." Vol 6, no 2. <http://www.cdc.gov/hiv/stats/hivsur82.pdf> (accessed on 17 March 2002).

3 Lisa Gilbert. *The Female Condom™ (FC) in the U.S.: Lessons Learned*. University of Idaho: Female Health Foundation.

4 The subsidiary was named WPC Holdings.

5 "The Female Condom." The Female Health Company Guide: 71.

6 *Doing Business in Zimbabwe* (PriceWaterhouse: 1995): 3.

7 Kaleidoscope. *Country: Zimbabwe, History*. 2001 <http://web.lexis-nexis.com/universe (accessed on 2 April 2001).

8 Ibid.

9 *Doing Business in Zimbabwe* (PriceWaterhouse: 1995): 8.

10 Ibid: 9.

11 *Doing Business in Zimbabwe* (PriceWaterhouse: 1995): 9.

12 *National Health Profile* (1996) <http://209.88.90.4> (accessed on 17 November 2000).

13 *Doing Business in Zimbabwe* (PriceWaterhouse: 1995): 7.

14 Compare this with the U.S. life expectancy at birth for females being 79 years and 72 years for males in 1994.

15 Lawrence Altman. "Parts of Africa Showing H.I.V. in 1 in 4 Adults," *New York Times* 24 June 1998: A-1.

16 Jeffery Cowley. "Fighting the Disease: What Can Be Done," *Newsweek* 17 January 2000: 38.

17 Altman, A-5.

18 Ibid.

19 *Women and HIV/AIDS* Fact Sheet No. 242 World Health Organization, <http://www.who.int/inf-fs/en/fact242.html> (accessed on. June 2000).

20 "Leaders: The Battle With AIDS," *The Economist* 15 July 2000: 17.

21 *Women And HIV/AIDS* Fact Sheet No. 242 World Health Organization. <http://www.who.int/inf-fs/en/fact242.html> (accessed on June 2000).

Chapter 10

Conclusion

Framing the Narratives

Future Directions for Ethics and Corporate Responsibility

Our purpose in showcasing and in exploring the selected cases in this volume has been to present models of effective practices. We have included those practices that, if replicated by others in their industry or elsewhere, would most likely create value-added for many of a company's primary stakeholders, those most affected by the organization, including shareholders. Prior to publication, the editors discussed the title, bantering about the now well-accepted expression, "best practices" to describe these activities, knowing that this term would be easily accepted and recognized by the cross-disciplinary readers whom we sought to inspire. However, in this volume, we do not contend that the companies whose practices we describe are perfect companies. There are no perfect companies; and some of these firms have made egregious errors of judgment. Moreover, we claim neither to have observed the practices of *all* firms such that we could conclude, even by mere exaggeration, that these practices are anywhere close to "The Best" nor do we in any sense contend in the cases chosen the superlative that the term implies. To the contrary, there are myriad means by which to respond systemically and with moral imagination to both the extraordinary and the ordinary ethical challenges facing global corporations in today's complicated environment.

But systems thinking and moral imagination need not evolve in a vacuum. They can be nurtured by stimulation such as models and examples. Since moral imagination is defined as ". . . the ability to discover, evaluate and act upon possibilities not merely determined by a particular circumstance, or limited by a set of operating mental models, or merely framed by a set of rules" (Werhane, 1999, p. 93), cases and models serve to expand our mental models beyond habit, allowing the decision-maker to then see new possibilities. As was demonstrated by the early cases of J&J and Merck, moral imagination, coupled with a systems approach and driven by a visionary corporate mission, can enable companies to think broadly about a wide range of stakeholders affected by corporate decisions, about economic issues, externalities and social impacts (both positive and negative) . . ." This sort of thinking is critical in a global environment and with the unpredictability of outcomes in diverse cultures. Accepting that the cases presented are not claimed to be "best" (though also not denied), they are instead *exceptional*.

Consider the inclusion of Royal Dutch Shell as number six on a 2007 ranking of the world's 100 largest firms by "the quality of their commitment to social and environmental goals" by *Fortune* magazine, Account Ability and CSRNetwork. Shell is certainly not without its current critics nor its challenges in its past; however, it earned its top ten ranking, apparently, by virtue of its commitment to a reduction of its carbon footprint, stakeholder engagement, and triple bottom line reporting strategy.

While this mention of Shell may seem inconsequential, it is certainly not. Though we deny corporations many elements of individual decision-making reserved for actual individuals, we also tend to hold them to a "holier than ourselves" standard, though these organizations are comprised of nothing more than mere individuals. We scandalize corporations for ethical violations based on theories of moral agency; but we take no notice of the millions of genuine acts of decency that occur daily and that deserve not only honor but also replication. Of course, neither individuals nor corporations are impeccable; but most devote an enormous amount of effort into trying to be ethical, into making appropriate decisions and, when they do not, into making it right.

Interestingly, it is the unethical behavior that captures our emotions, garners attention and therefore also generates the highest cost. Once a corporation engages in wrongdoing, that becomes its distinction, its mark—a Scarlet Letter. The public now will focus on the wrong and it is astoundingly challenging for the firm subsequently to regain the public trust. Traditionally, some communities have tolerated wrongdoing as long as shareholders and at least some other stakeholders benefited. However, that environment represents the old regime, based on a myth of non-compassion. We have now experienced the costs of this failure to observe the precautionary principle and they can be bankrupting. Once a company's wrongdoing is made public, the public is not often forgiving and, in truth, not tremendously interested in learning about the good in which a firm later engages, save in connection with a few extremely large—and effective—multinationals.

As with individuals, no single corporation is without flaws. Thus, we have chosen cases of corporate *practices* to represent in this volume, rather than corporations themselves. An example of an extraordinary response, a firm that through its on-the ground-practices earned the trust of its diverse stakeholders after losing it seemingly completely, is Nike. Nike is one of those organizations that seems perhaps to have beaten the odds mentioned above and instead to have emerged meritoriously from a period in which it received enormous negative publicity for the conditions of its suppliers' workplaces. As you read, Nike originally underestimated the strength of the public and media trust and underestimated the impact of its decisions. However, by reframing its own internal and external scripts and creating solutions that were viable, both within its organization as well as throughout the systems in which it operates, Nike has not only gained the trust of its customers and the public, but also has contributed to a shift in expectations throughout the entire apparel and footwear contract system on a global level.

Nike did not accomplish this task through simply appeasing the myriad wishes of its stakeholders. To the contrary, it undertook an effort to shift the mental models of its stakeholders surrounding deep and long held beliefs, a formidable undertaking. The developed world discourages child labor and at-home work as a standard labor condition. However, when soccer balls were commissioned from Pakistan for the World Cup in 1998, an estimated 20,000 women and children in the Punjab region lost significant family income because of labor standards that did not permit them to work in this manner to which they were previously accustomed. When Nike decided to re-enter the region for soccer ball production in 2007 after pulling out earlier due to supplier noncompliance, it did so only *after* establishing an agreement regarding working conditions with a single factory, which would then serve as a model for other successful contracts (Webb, 2007).

The good news is that you can open the newspaper each day and not lack for examples of innovations and of the ongoing learning curve stimulated by moral imagination and creative responses to the challenges otherwise perceived as barriers to entry. For instance, consider the One Laptop Per Child Project (OLPC), which began shipments in December, 2007. It is OLPC's mission "to provide children around the world with new opportunities to explore, experiment and express themselves." In order to achieve this mission, OLPC has created the means by which to produce laptops at far lower prices than we are used to paying in the West, which enables us to then support the provision of a paired laptop for a child in a developing economy when they are purchased. As a result, for every $400 laptop purchased, one will be delivered to the purchaser and one will be delivered to a child in the developing country. The OLPC Project evidences the continued evolution of enterprises showcased in this volume by contributing to new markets where need for a commodity is greatest—the need for access to information technology at the base of the pyramid—while simultaneously contributing value both to communities globally and to the Project itself. This Project should be reminiscent therefore of several of the case studies discussed earlier, including Manila Water, P&G and Cemex.

Another recent innovation that demonstrates the progression of these critical initiatives is exhibited by clothing company, Nau. Not only does it maintain its sustainable fabric development using open-source technology to encourage their further development, but they actively "challeng[e] the nature of capitalism" through "webfronts," self-serve kiosks in their stores that prompt customers to send purchases home, offering them a 10% discount and free shipping if they opt to do so (LaBarre, 2007). As in the case of DesignTex, companies with moral imagination face questions of environmental sustainability with creativity rather than narrow-minded myopia and hopelessness. Nau's webfronts allow it to save on its geographical footprint with lower in-store inventories and operating costs through energy and material reductions. Further, Nau puts its money where its mouth is as a model for its stakeholders through its commitment of 5% of sales to environmental, social or humanitarian organizations identified by its stakeholders. Through its efforts as an agent for positive change, Nau's CEO explains that it strives to represent "a new form of activism: business activism." These challenges are not without their capitalistic rewards. Nau's projections included $11 million in revenue in 2007, and amounts as high as $260 million and 150 stores by 2010. The moral imagination involved in profitable corporate sustainability is apparent; CEO Van Dyke iterates, "Our challenge is how to design from the ground up to try to do better in every area we can think of—and then making sure we're utterly transparent about how we're doing and where we fall short" (LaBarre, 2007).

It is through our critical analysis of the seminal cases in this text that we learn how to participate in this evolutionary process, how we can expand our mental models to now include the wisdom gained by prior experience. The role of the reader is then active engagement, rather than simple observation. The decisions made by the case protagonists must not be merely accepted for their propriety but instead must be evaluated using moral reasoning skills, based on the circumstances of the case, including the social, institutional, political and other relevant environmental factors. It is vital to identify the mental models under which the original decision-maker is operating and determine to which, if any, she or he also is subject. Alternate perspectives should be embraced as if they were truth, and investigated as if they served as the sole possible solution until, all plausible trails exhausted, the decision-maker abandons them for other possibilities.

The Female Health Company exemplifies this investigation-reframing cycle; and our examination of the case allows an expansion of our understanding of the role that an organization can play in the social fabric of a culture. By recognizing the strength in the expanded stakeholder model, FHC was able to achieve objectives otherwise considered insoluble. Similarly, ExxonMobil's Chad and Cameroon projects illustrate the vast possibilities that emerge from abandoning traditional mental models in favor of the morally imaginative alliance model. The alliance model by necessity considers the system within which the decisions take place, including cultural, economic, social, institutional, political and environmental factors.

With these demonstrations of the evolutionary process of visionary and imaginative leadership, of course there remain examples of less successful choices, representing the continued constraint of those incarcerating mental models. These cases should receive attention, not for their role as positive archetypes but instead as deterrent effigies. British Petroleum recently disappointed advocates who had high hopes for its "*beyond petroleum*" campaign when significant challenges in the area of safety were brought to light, stemming from the damning Baker Report. The Report found material deficiencies in process safety performance, well below acceptable levels (British Petroleum, 2007). In other arenas, consumers had a sense of déjà vu dating back to the days of tobacco litigation surrounding Purdue Pharma's insistence that its medication OxyContin was not subject to the abuse experienced in connection with other drugs. The firm later admitted that it had actually misled doctors and patients through these false claims, and agreed to pay more than $600 million in fines and other payments. (Meier, 2007). Consider lessons learned from the dilemma that Chiquita claimed it faced in Colombia when it opted to pay paramilitary professionals in the form of "protection money" so that its export business could continue to run effectively, but arguably also in order to protect its workers from abuse. Ultimately, Chiquita paid $25 million in fines to the U.S. Department of Justice.

In other work, we have referred to the concept of a "good" that exists within a delimited space, within boundaries that are not prescriptive in terms of what that space may contain but only by reference to what lies outside of the space (Kelley, Hartman & Werhane, 2008). Throughout this text, we have explored the concept of effective and ethical decision-making by virtue of not only the decisions, themselves, but also the social and/or cultural shifts that impact or are impacted by these decisions. In this continued discussion, we suggest that the *space* or those boundaries be further delimited by adding the awareness of those decision qualities that are *not* contained therein (i.e. the "bad," in contradiction to the concept of the "good," effective or ethical). By failing to break free of the traditional mental models, decision-makers are likely to remain in one theoretical space and not have the opportunity to evolve into another.

While no single case study can purport to serve as *the* "best" practice since other practices certainly demonstrate alternate and similarly imaginative means by which to respond to analogous dilemmas, further defining and evolving the space described above, neither can a single volume of cases encompass the complete response to ethical challenges facing global business leaders. Our aim is to be extensive rather than to be complete, since the latter would be an infinite effort. Each day, we learn of new methods, new ideas, new innovations by which global decision-makers have created solutions by which to alleviate barriers, to reduce suffering, to eliminate challenges, and to increase the overall well-being of humans on earth. By illuminating those ideas through the case model, we can best examine, explore and learn from them, thus bringing light to the concept of a *good*, effective and ethical leadership decisions. It then becomes the responsibility of each of us to serve as active participants in the global marketplace by putting that learning into practice through systems thinking, a developed mental model of the nature of stakeholder alliances, and by evolutionary moral imagination.

References

British Petroleum. 2007. BP will implement recommendations of independent safety review panel. January 16. http://www.bp.com/genericarticle.do?categoryId=2012968&contentId=7027577.

Gorman, M., Mehalik, M. & Werhane, P. (2000). *Ethical and Environmental Challenges to Engineering*. Englewood Cliffs, NJ: Prentice Hall.

Kelley, Scott, Hartman, Laura P. and Werhane, Patricia H. 2008 forthcoming. Profit, Partnerships, and the Common Good. In *Frontiers of Business Ethics*. Oxford: Peter Lang.

LaBarre, P. (2007). Leap of Faith. *Fast Company*, 116: 96 (June).

Meier, Barry. 2007. In Guilty Plea, OxyContin Maker to Pay $600 Million. *New York Times*. May 10. http://www.nytimes.com/2007/05/10/business/11drug-web.html?_r=1&hp&oref=slogin.

Webb, Tobias. (2007). Ethical sourcing: Nike shows admirable commitment in going back to Pakistan. *Ethical Corporation*. May 28. http://www.ethicalcorp.com/content.asp?ContentID=5108.

Werhane, P. H. (1999). *Moral Imagination and Managerial Decision Making*. New York: Oxford University Press.

Index